Accounts

25 Years 2025-2001

ISC

CHAPTERWISE QUESTION BANK

Accounts

Class 12

Author
Anshul Sharma

arihant
SUCCESS AND NOTHING LESS

arihant

SUCCESS AND NOTHING LESS

ARIHANT PRAKASHAN

(School Division Series)

卐 ADMINISTRATIVE & PRODUCTION OFFICES

Regd. Office

'Ramchhaya' 4577/15, Agarwal Road, Darya Ganj, New Delhi -110002

Tele: 011- 47630600, 43518550

Head Office

Kalindi, TP Nagar, Meerut (UP) - 250002, Tel: 0121-7156203, 7156204

卐 SALES & SUPPORT OFFICES

Agra, Ahmedabad, Bengaluru, Bareilly, Chennai, Delhi, Guwahati, Hyderabad, Jaipur, Jhansi, Kolkata, Lucknow, Nagpur & Pune.

卐 **PO No :** TXT-XX-XXXXXXX-X-XX

Published By Arihant Publications (India) Ltd.

For further information about the books published by Arihant, log on to www.arihantbooks.com or e-mail at info@arihantbooks.com

卐 **PRICE** ₹395.00

Achieving 99+
Marks in Board Exams

Achieving 99+ marks in board exams is definitely an ambitious goal, but with the right approach and these 7 tips from toppers, you can definitely increase your chances of success!

Here are the 7 Topper Tips to ace your board exams:

1. Master the art of consistency

Consistency builds understanding and confidence, both crucial for excelling in exams.

2. Build a winning study strategy

Create a personalised timetable that prioritises subjects based on your strengths and weaknesses.

3. Befriend the syllabus

Focus on high-weightage topics and prioritise mastering core concepts before moving on to advanced ones.

4. Embrace active learning

Explain concepts to yourself or in study groups to solidify understanding.

5. Conquer the past

Solve Past Years' Papers and Sample Papers under timed conditions to practice time management and understand paper pattern.

6. Seek help, when needed!

Don't hesitate to clarify doubts with teachers, tutors, or study groups. Asking questions strengthens your understanding and prevents confusion.

7. Prioritise well-being

Eat nutritious meals, get enough sleep, regular exercise and practice stress management techniques like meditation to stay calm and focused during exams.

These tips are just a starting point, and you can personalise them to fit your learning style and preferences.

Description of

Newly Added Features

01

Accounting for Partnership Firms

TREND ANALYSIS 5 YEARS

Average No. of Questions Across all Sets

	Types of Questions	2023	2020	2019	2018	2017
01 Basics of Partnership, Capital Accounts and Profit and Loss Appropriation Account	1/2 Marks	—	1	1	1	1
	3 Marks	—	—	—	—	—
	6 Marks	—	—	—	1	—
	10 Marks	1	1	1	—	—

Trend Analysis

At the start of each chapter, trend Analysis is given to indicate the types of Questions asked from different topics of the chapter. This feature helps students to know the importance of different topics of the given chapter from exam point of view and helps them to prepare accordingly.

4. Arav, Rahil and Himmat are partners in a firm sharing profits and losses in the ratio of 5 : 3 : 2. Arav guaranteed a minimum profit of ₹ 30,000 to Himmat.

ISC Sem I 2021

(a) debited by ₹ 30,000 (b) credited by ₹ 54,000
(c) debited by ₹ 54,000 (d) debited by ₹ 6,000

KEY IDEA

Since the firm is in loss, Arav will not only bear the losses of Himmat, but also pay for the guarantee provided by him.

Key Idea

'Key Idea' is given with selected questions with the purpose to help students to get the approach 'to solve the question'. This feature help students to develop the systematic approach to solve difficult/ complex questions.

3. Calculation of interest on drawings

$$\text{Total Drawings} \times \frac{\text{Rate}}{100} \times \frac{\text{Average Period}}{12}$$

$$= 5{,}000 \times 12 \times \frac{4}{100} \times \frac{6.5}{12} = ₹\ 1{,}300 \text{ each}$$

Common Mistake Students usually ignore the information that the capitals are fixed and record everything in the partners' capital account. Since the capitals are fixed, all the transactions be recorded in the current accounts of the partners.

Common Mistakes

It focuses on some of the general but critical mistakes that students commit while solving the questions. This feature helps students to develop the habit of avoiding mistakes while solving questions.

2. One of the important features of non-purchased goodwill, is that it is generated internally and over the years.

3. (c) Debit Partner's Capital A/c; Credit Interest on Loan A/c

4. (c) Deficiency $= \left(1{,}20{,}000 \times \frac{2}{10}\right) + 30{,}000$

$$= 24{,}000 + 30{,}000 = ₹\ 54{,}000$$

5. (b) Super Profit × Number of Years' Purchase

6. (c) Undervalued closing stock of ₹ 3,000

Concept Enhancer In order to calculate normal profit, any abnormal gain included in the profits will be subtracted and any abnormal loss included in the profits will be added to the profit.

Concept Enhancer

Concept Enhancer gives the brief description of the concept, which has been used to solve the question. This feature provides revision of important concept along with practice of question solving.

Most Important Topics

from each Chapter

On the basis of analysis of last 5 Years' Board Examination Papers, we have identified Important Topics from each chapter.

Chapter Name	Important Topics	Weightage in Last 5 Years' Boards				
		2025	2024	2023	2020	2019
Accounting for Partnership Firms : Fundamentals	Basics of Partnership, Capital Accounts and Profit and Loss Appropriation Account	1M, 1M, 10M	10M	10M	2M,10M	2M,10M
	Past Adjustment	10M		10M	3M	
	Guarantee of Profits					3M
Reconstitution of a Partnership Firm : Admission of Partner	Goodwill			1M	2M	
	Treatment for Goodwill, Reserves, Accumulated Profits and Losses	1M, 1M, 3M	1M	6M	3M	6M
	Revaluation of Assets and Reassessment of Liabilities	3M		2M		
	Adjustment of Capital		1M,3M,6M		10M	
Reconstitution of a Partnership Firm : Retirement/Death of a Partner	Revaluation of Assets and Liabilities on Retirement	3M	3M	1M	6M	1M,10M
	Adjustment of Capital	6M		3M		
	Death of a Partner	6M	3M	3M,3M		
Dissolution of a Partnership Firm	Introduction		1M		2M	
	Accounting Treatment on Dissolution	1M,1M, 6M	1M,1M, 6M	1M,1M, 6M	10M	10M
Issue of Shares	Introduction			6M		
	Issue of Shares	1M		1M	2M	6M
	Forfeiture and Reissue of Shares	10M	1M,10M	10M,10M	10M	1M
Issue and Redemption of Debentures	Issue of Debentures and Interest	3M	1M,3M	1M,1M	3M	2M
	Cases from Point of View of Redemption	3M		3M		10M
	Redemption of Debentures	1M,1M,3M	1M,1M,3M	1M,3M,3M	6M	2M
Final Accounts of Companies	Balance Sheet	1M,6M	1M,6M	1M	2M,3M,10M	10M
Financial Statement Analysis	Introduction to Financial Statement Analysis			1M		2M
	Comparative Statements	3M	3M	3M	6M	
	Common Size Statements					6M
Cash Flow Statement	Operating Activity	1M, 1M		1M		
	Investing Activity	1M	1M		2M	10M
	Financing Activity		1M	1M		2M
	Cash Flow Statement	6M, 6M	6M	6M,6M	10M	2M
Ratio Analysis	Liquidity and Solvency Ratios	1M, 1M,2M	1M,1M, 1M,2M	1M,1M	2M,2M	
	Activity Ratios	2M	2M	6M	6M	
	Profitability Ratios	2M, 2M	2M		2M	2M,10M

Dream, Believe, Achieve Insights from ISC Toppers

Follow all the 5P's

• Persistence • Passion • Perseverance • Purpose • Practice

MANYA GUPTA
ISC Topper (99.75%)

Aim for high marks, that's what I was doing. I convinced myself that if I aim for 100 I will at least get a 95. That was my logic, but I ended up getting a 100.

I studied with the help of my school and tuition classes. I didn't study daily much, but before the exams, I used to pull all-nighters and study.

ARYAAN
ISC Topper (99.75%)

Studying for 3-4 hours every day along with six hours of school helped me secure 399 out of 400 marks, scoring 99.75%.

I'm very active on all social media platforms but it has never hindered my studies. I strike a balance between hard work and fun.

The degree of toughness of any subject is merely a subjective outlook. I made sure that I incentivised myself at times when I didn't feel like sitting at my study table, especially for theoretical subjects.

I simply believe in revising the concepts which were taught at school or tuitions that very day and minimise backlogs as much as I could.

POOJA KEJRIWAL
ISC Topper (97.5%)

I believe there is no substitute to hard work. There was no fixed hours of preparation. I read a topic till the time I completely understood it. I had to be satisfied with the topic covered.

See it is important to take breaks and everyone has their own way of entertainment. I do chat with friends on social media. I think it is fine until it becomes addiction.

There is no secret formula as such, but one should not panic and have faith in his/her preparation.

DEVANG KUMAR
ISC Topper

DIMPLE KOTHARI
ISC Topper (97.5%)

- Don't run behind marks, crave for knowledge, experience because ultimately that's gonna help you.
- Don't let peer pressure dominate you.
- If you want to obtain good marks, leave all social media-This is a myth. I was active on Instagram & WhatsApp before my examinations, and even during my examinations. It's just that you need to remember that everyone has the same 24 hours, it's how you utilize it as well as enjoy it better than others.
- Both early morning and late night studies are best ~ you need to choose what's better for you.
- Don't hesitate to ask questions. If you have any doubts, please clarify. Everyone has different learning styles and speed, so it's nothing to be ashamed of.
- Never give up.

Please Note that all the information is collected from different websites.

Contents

ISC Chapterwise Question Bank 2025-2001

Question Number 10, 11, 29, 31, 37 related to topic 'Redemption of debentures in annual instalments by draw of lots**' are not the part of latest syllabus.*

Latest Syllabus

Class XII (2025-26)

There will be two papers in the subject.

Paper I Theory : 3 Hours — 80 Marks

Paper II Project Work — 20 Marks

PAPER I THEORY — 80 Marks

There will be one paper of 3 hours duration of 80 marks divided into three Sections A, B and C.

It will be compulsory for all candidates to attempt **Section A.** Candidates will have a choice of attempting questions **either** from **Section B** or **Section C.**

S. No.	UNIT	TOTAL WEIGHTAGE
	SECTION A: 60 Marks	
1.	**Partnership Accounts**	
	A. Fundamentals of Partnership	11 Marks
	B. Goodwill C. Reconstitution of Partnership I. Admission II. Retirement and Death of a Partner	15 Marks
	III. Dissolution of a Partnership Firm	8 Marks
2.	**Joint Stock Company Accounts**	
	A. Issue of Shares	11 Marks
	B. Issue of Debentures C. Redemption of Debentures	8 Marks
	D. Final Accounts of Companies	7 Marks
	SECTION B (MANAGEMENT ACCOUNTING): 20 Marks	
3.	**Financial Statement Analysis**	4 Marks
4.	**Cash Flow Statement**	8 Marks
5.	**Ratio Analysis**	8 Marks
	OR **SECTION C (COMPUTERISED ACCOUNTING): 20 Marks**	
6.	Accounting Application of Electronic Spread Sheet	10 Marks
7.	Database Management System (DBMS)	10 Marks
	TOTAL	**80 Marks**

SECTION A

1. Partnership Accounts

A. Fundamentals of Partnership

(i) Definition, meaning and features of a Partnership.

(ii) Provisions of The Indian Partnership Act, 1932, with respect to books of accounts.

(iii) Preparation of Profit and Loss Appropriation Account and Partners' Capital and Current Accounts.

B. Goodwill

Concept of goodwill and mode of valuation.

C. Reconstitution of Partnership

I. Admission

(i) Calculation of new profit-sharing ratio, sacrificing ratio and gaining ratio.

(ii) Accounting treatment of goodwill on admission of a partner.

(iii) Preparation of Revaluation Account.

(iv) Accounting treatment of accumulated profits and losses.

(v) Adjustment of Capitals.

(vi) Change in Profit-Sharing Ratio.

II. Retirement and Death of a Partner

(i) Calculation of new profit-sharing ratio, gaining ratio and sacrificing ratio.

(ii) Adjustment with regard to goodwill including hidden goodwill.

(iii) Adjustment with regard to undistributed profits and losses.

(iv) Adjustment with regard to share of profits of the retiring or deceased partner from the date of the last Balance Sheet to the date of retirement or death (on the basis of time or turnover).

(v) Preparation of Revaluation Account on retirement or death of a partner.

(vi) Adjustment of capitals.

(vii) Calculation and payment of amount due to retiring partner.

(viii) Preparation of retiring partner's loan accounts and deceased partner's executor's loan account (with interest on loan accrued and due and interest on loan accrued but not due).

(ix) Change in Profit-Sharing Ratio.

III. Dissolution of a Partnership Firm

(i) Meaning of dissolution and settlement of accounts under Section 48 of The Indian Partnership Act 1932.

(ii) Preparation of Memorandum Balance Sheet, Realization Account, Partner's Loan Account, Partner's Capital Account and Cash/Bank Account.

2. Joint Stock Company Accounts

A. Issue of Shares

Problems on issue of shares.

(a) Issue of shares at par and premium under Companies Act, 2013.

(b) Issue of shares for consideration other than cash:

(i) To promoters (can be considered either through Goodwill account or Incorporation costs account).

(ii) To underwriters.

(iii) To vendors.

(c) Calls in arrears, calls in advance and interest thereon.

(d) Over and undersubscription (including pro-rata allotment).

(e) Preparation of Journal; Cash Book and Journal Proper; Ledger Accounts.

(f) Forfeiture and reissue of shares at par, premium or discount.

(g) Disclosure of Share capital in the company's Balance Sheet.

B. Issue of Debentures

Problems on issue of debentures (at par, at premium and at discount.)

C. Redemption of Debentures

D. Final Accounts of Companies

Preparation of the Balance Sheet of a company (along with notes to accounts) as per Schedule III Part I of Companies Act 2013.

SECTION B

MANAGEMENT ACCOUNTING

3. Financial Statement Analysis

Comparative Statements and Common Size Statements.

4. Cash Flow Statement (Only for Manufacturing Companies)

(i) Meaning, importance and preparation of a Cash Flow Statement.

(ii) Calculation of net cash flows from operating activities based on Indirect Method only.

(iii) Preparation of Cash Flow Statement on basis of operating, investing and financing activities.

5. Ratio Analysis

(i) Liquidity ratios

(ii) Solvency ratios

(iii) Activity ratios

(iv) Profitability ratios

PAPER II PROJECT WORK 20 Marks

Candidates will be expected to have completed two projects from any topic covered in Theory.

The project work will be assessed by the teacher and a Visiting Examiner appointed locally and approved by CISCE.

Mark allocation for each Project [10 marks]:

Overall format	1 Mark
Content	4 Marks
Findings	2 Marks
Viva-voce based on the Project	3 Marks

Analysis of Pupil's Performance:
ISC Accounts

Topics found difficult/confusing by candidates

TOPICS FOUND DIFFICULT BY CANDIDATES

- Mentioning the head and sub-head of the contingent liability.
- Calculation of subscribed capital.
- Calculation of interest on debentures.
- Calculation of net gain on reissue of forfeited shares.
- Gain on sale of DRI.
- Formula and valuation of goodwill by the Average Profit Method.
- Dissolution of partnership firm- treatment of realisation expenses and the realizable value of furniture.
- Determining the amount of Preference Dividend.
- Calculating the net gain on the reissue of forfeited shares.

CONCEPTS IN WHICH CANDIDATES GOT CONFUSED

- The term 'dissolution of partnership'.
- The journal entry for the amount due to the debenture holders.
- The journal entry for permanent withdrawal made by a partner.
- Adjusting the capital accounts of the continuing partners through cash / current account.
- Journal entry to close the partner's drawings account when the firm follows the fixed capital method.
- Calculating the depreciation charged on the machine sold while preparing the Cash Flow Statement.
- Calculating the number of shares issued for cash.

SUGGESTIONS FOR CANDIDATES

(i) To gain comprehensive knowledge of the subject

- Not to neglect the class XI syllabus
- Ensure that the accounting concepts are clear. This will help in answering the theory questions.

(ii) To perform better in the examination.

- Understand the concept before attempting any question.
- Do not resort to selective study. The entire syllabus must be done in totality.
- The scope of the syllabus should be strictly adhered to.
- Do not neglect Class XI syllabus.
- Do not write short forms in the formulae of the ratios.
- Do not write short forms in the particulars of ledger accounts.
- Write complete amounts in the ledger accounts.
- Always practice sums with proper formats drawn and correct dates/ years.
- All journal entries must be accompanied with narrations.
- Practice solving past years' question papers.
- Solve the sample papers and CFQs released by CISCE.
- Work on time management. Make effective use of the reading time.

01

Accounting for Partnership Firms : Fundamentals

TREND ANALYSIS 5 YEARS

Average No. of Questions Across all Sets

		Types of Questions	2023	2020	2019	2018	2017
01	Basics of Partnership, Capital Accounts and Profit and Loss Appropriation Account	1/2 Marks	—	1	1	1	1
		3 Marks	—	—	—	—	—
		6 Marks	—	—	—	1	—
		10 Marks	1	1	1	—	—
02	Past Adjustment	1/2 Marks	—	—	—	—	—
		3 Marks	—	1	—	1	1
		6 Marks	—	—	—	—	—
		10 Marks	1	—	—	—	—
03	Guarantee of Profits	1/2 Marks	—	—	—	—	—
		3 Marks	—	—	1	—	1
		6 Marks	—	—	—	—	—
		10 Marks	—	—	—	—	—
04	Goodwill	1/2 Marks	1	1	—	1	—
		3 Marks	—	—	—	—	—
		6 Marks	—	—	—	—	—
		10 Marks	—	—	—	—	—

Partnership

According to Section 4 of the Indian Partnership Act, 1932, 'Partnership is defined as the relation between persons, who have agreed to share the profits of a business, carried on by all or any of them acting for all'.

Nature of Partnership

Partnership is a separate business entity from accounting point of view, but from a legal view point, partnership firm is not a separate legal entity from its partners.

Characteristics/Features of Partnership

The essential characteristics/features of partnership are

(i) Two or more persons (ii) Agreement (iii) Legal business (iv) Mutual agency
(v) Sharing of profits (vi) Liability of partner (vii) Management and control (viii) Registration

Key Point

Minimum number of partners in a partnership business must be 2 and as per Section 464 of the Companies Act, 2013 maximum number of partners cannot exceed the number as prescribed in the rules, which at present is 50.

Partnership Deed

Partnership is the result of agreement between the partners. Therefore, it is essential that the terms defining the partnership must be mutually agreed on between the partners. Such agreement may be either oral or written. But, to avoid all misunderstandings and disputes, it is always better to have a written agreement. Such a written agreement containing the terms of partnership is called partnership deed.

Contents of Partnership Deed

The partnership deed contains a number of details, some of them are

(i) Names and addresses of all the partners and the firm, (ii) Principal place of business,
(iii) Nature of business, (iv) Date of commencement of the partnership,
(v) Capital to be contributed by each partner, etc.

Importance of Partnership Deed

A firm should have a partnership deed because

(i) It regulates the rights, duties and liabilities of the partners.
(ii) It avoids disputes in future, by acting as a proof or guiding document.
(iii) It helps to avoid any misunderstanding among the partners.

Rules Applicable in the Absence of Partnership Deed

In the absence of partnership deed, the relevant provisions of the Indian Partnership Act, 1932, apply which are as follows

(i) Sharing of profits/losses — Equally
(ii) Interest on capital — Not allowed
(iii) Salary/Commission to a partner — Not allowed
(iv) Interest on advances or loan by a partner — 6% per annum
(v) Interest on drawings — Not charged

Important Points to Remember

- Loan by a relative is not a loan from a partner. Hence, on such loan, this provision will not apply.
- In the absence of partnership deed, profits are to be shared equally, irrespective of the type of partner (active, sleeping) or the amount of capital contributed by them.
- Interest on capital is payable to a partner (if there is an agreement) but such interest is payable only out of profits except if it is allowed as a charge.

Maintenance of Capital Accounts of Partners

In a partnership firm, there are two methods by which partners' capital accounts may be maintained. These are

1. Fixed Capital Method

Under this method, the capital of the partners' shall remain fixed, unless additional capital is introduced or a part of the capital is withdrawn, permanently, as per the agreement among the partners.

Two accounts are maintained under this method

(i) Capital account (ii) Current account

(i) **Capital Account**

Dr **Partners' Capital Account** Cr

Particulars	X (₹)	Y (₹)	Particulars	X (₹)	Y (₹)
To Cash/Bank A/c (Capital withdrawn)	...	...	By Balance b/d (Opening credit balance)	...	...
To Balance c/d (Closing balance)	...	...	By Cash/Bank A/c (Additional capital introduced)	...	...
	...	...		...	...

(ii) **Current Account**

Dr **Partners' Current Account** Cr

Particulars	X (₹)	Y (₹)	Particulars	X (₹)	Y (₹)
To Balance b/d (Opening debit balance)	...	...	By Balance b/d (Opening credit balance)	...	...
To Drawings A/c (Out of profits)	...	...	By Interest on Capital A/c	...	...
To Interest on Drawings A/c	...	...	By Partner's Salary or Commission A/c	...	...
To Profit and Loss A/c (Share in losses)	...	...	By Profit and Loss Appropriation A/c (Share in profits)	...	...
To Balance c/d (Closing credit balance)	...	...	By Balance c/d (Closing debit balance)	...	...
	...	...		...	...

Notes • Transactions related to introduction and withdrawal of capital are recorded in capital accounts, rest are recorded in current account.

• Capital account will always have credit balance and current account may have credit or debit balance.

Interest on Current Account Interest on current account is provided to the partners with reference to the time, the current account balances have been used in the firm. Interest will be provided as per the partnership agreement.

2. Fluctuating Capital Method

Under this method, only one account, i.e. capital account of each partner is maintained.

All transactions are recorded in capital accounts. Generally, capital account has a credit balance but in exceptional cases, it may have debit balance due to heavy losses.

Dr **Partners' Capital Account** Cr

Particulars	X (₹)	Y (₹)	Particulars	X (₹)	Y (₹)
To Balance b/d (Opening debit balance)	...	...	By Balance b/d (Opening credit balance)	...	...
To Cash/Bank A/c (Capital withdrawn)	...	...	By Cash/Bank A/c (Additional capital introduced)	...	...
To Drawings A/c (Out of profits)	...	...	By Interest on Capital A/c	...	...
To Profit and Loss A/c (Share in losses)	...	...	By Partners' Salary or Commission A/c	...	...
To Balance c/d (Closing credit balance)	...	...	By Profit and Loss Appropriation A/c (Share in profits)	...	...
			By Balance c/d (Closing debit balance)	...	...
	...	...		...	...

Interest on Capital

It is a charge on capital provided by the partners to the firm. It is justified when profit sharing ratio and capital ratios are different. Interest on capital is allowed to compensate partners for contributing capital to the firm. It is paid only if the same has been provided in the agreement of partnership. The following formula is used to compute interest on capital

$$\text{Interest on Capital} = \text{Amount of Capital} \times \frac{\text{Rate}}{100} \times \text{Time}$$

Journal Entries to Record Interest on Capital

Interest on Capital A/c Dr
  To Partners' Capital/Current A/c

Profit and Loss Appropriation A/c Dr
  To Interest on Capital A/c

Different Cases Related to Interest on Capital

(i) When partnership deed is silent – Not allowed

(ii) When partnership deed provides that interest on capital is to be allowed, then

(a) **In case of loss** Not allowed.

(b) **In case of sufficient profit** Interest on capital is allowed in full.

(c) **In case of insufficient profit** Interest on capital is allowed proportionately to the extent of available profits. In such case, profits are distributed in capital ratio.

(iii) If interest on capital is to be provided as a charge, it is allowed in full, irrespective of profit or losses.

Key Points

- Interest on capital is calculated on the opening balance of the capital for the full year.
- Interest on additional capital will be calculated for the period, it remained with the firm i.e. from the date of introduction of additional capital to the last day of accounting year.
- If opening capital is not given, it can be calculated as

  Opening Capital = Closing Capital + Drawings – Profits – Additional Capital Introduced During the Year.

Interest on Partners' Drawings

The amount withdrawn by partners in cash or in kind for their personal use in anticipation of profits, is termed as drawings. When the partnership deed is silent, no interest on drawings is charged. Interest on drawings is calculated with reference to the time period for which money was withdrawn.

Journal Entries to Record Interest on Partners' Drawings

Partners' Capital/Current A/c	Dr
To Interest on Drawings A/c	
Interest on Drawings A/c	Dr
To Profit and Loss Appropriation A/c	

Different Cases Related to Interest on Drawings

(i) **If a partner withdraws a fixed amount in the beginning, middle and end of each period, then Value of time under different circumstances will be as under**

	Monthly Drawings for 12 Months	Quarterly Drawings for 12 Months	Half-yearly Drawings for 12 Months	Monthly Drawings for 6 Months
When drawings are made in the beginning of each period	6.5	7.5	9	3.5
When drawings are made in the middle of each period	6	6	6	3
When drawings are made at the end of each period	5.5	4.5	3	2.5

Formula will be used as follows

$$\text{Interest on Drawings} = \text{Total Drawings} \times \frac{\text{Rate}}{100} \times \frac{\text{Value of Time}}{12}$$

(ii) **When an unequal amount is withdrawn at different dates**

In this case, interest on drawings is calculated with the help of

(a) **Simple Method**

$$\text{Interest on Drawings} = \text{Amount of Drawings} \times \frac{\text{Rate}}{100} \times \frac{\text{Months Remaining}}{12}$$

(b) **Product Method**

$$\text{Interest on Drawings} = \text{Total of Product} \times \frac{\text{Rate}}{100} \times \frac{1}{365} \text{ or } \frac{1}{12}$$

(iii) **If the date of withdrawal is not given**

In this case, the interest on total drawings for the year is calculated for six months on an average basis. (By default, if nothing is specified, then this method is followed).

Salary or Commission to a Partner

Salary or commission to a partner is to be allowed, if the partnership agreement provides for the same. Salary or commission to a partner is an appropriation out of profits and not a charge against the profits, i.e. they are to be allowed only if there are profits and hence, must be transferred to the debit of profit and loss appropriation account and not to the debit of profit and loss account.

Journal Entries to Record Salary/Commission Payable to Partner

Partners' Salary/Commission A/c Dr
 To Partners' Capital/Current A/c

Profit and Loss Appropriation A/c Dr
 To Partners' Salary/Commission A/c

Calculation of Commission based on Profit

(i) Commission as percentage of net profit before charging such commission

$$= \text{Net Profit before Commission} \times \frac{\text{Rate of Commission}}{100}$$

(ii) Commission as percentage of net profit after charging such commission

$$= \text{Net Profit before Commission} \times \frac{\text{Rate of Commission}}{100 + \text{Rate of Commission}}$$

Interest on Partner's Loan to the Firm

Interest on partner's loan is a charge against the profits and not an appropriation out of profits and hence, must be transferred to the debit of profit and loss account and not to the debit of profit and loss appropriation account.

Journal Entries to Record Interest on Partner's Loan to the Firm

Interest on Partner's Loan A/c Dr
 To Partner's Loan A/c

Profit and Loss A/c Dr
 To Interest on Partner's Loan A/c

Important Points to Remember

- If there is an agreement as to the rate of interest, partner is entitled to an interest on loan at the agreed rate of interest. If there is no agreement as to the rate of interest, partner is entitled to interest on loan @ 6% per annum.
- Interest on partner's loan is not recorded in the partner's capital/current account but it should be recorded to the credit side of partner's loan account, if it is outstanding.

Rent Paid to a Partner

It is a charge against the profit and not an appropriation out of profits. It is therefore, debited to profit and loss account and credited to partners' current account (in case of fixed capitals) or to partners' capital account (when capitals are fluctuating).

Journal Entries to Record Rent Paid to a Partner

Rent Due to Partner A/c Dr
 To Partners' Current/Capital A/c

Profit and Loss A/c Dr
 To Rent Due to Partner A/c

Distribution of Profit Amongst Partners : Profit and Loss Appropriation Account

It is an extension of profit and loss account and shows appropriation or distribution of profit among partners. After the profit and loss account has been prepared, the profit for the year is transferred to the profit and loss appropriation account.

This account will show, how the net profit of the firm is being appropriated among the partners. It is a nominal account in nature.

Journal Entries Relating to the Profit and Loss Appropriation Account

1. **For transfer of balance of profit and loss account**	Profit and Loss A/c Dr To Profit and Loss Appropriation A/c
2. **For interest on capital**	(i) Interest on Capital A/c Dr To Partners' Capital A/c (or current, if capital accounts are fixed) (Individually)
	(ii) Profit and Loss Appropriation A/c Dr To Interest on Capital A/c Alternatively, only one entry may be passed, as follows Profit and Loss Appropriation A/c Dr To Partners' Capital A/c (or current, if capital accounts are fixed) (Individually)
3. **For interest on drawings**	(i) Partners' Capital A/c (or current, if capital accounts are fixed) (Individually) Dr To Interest on Drawings A/c
	(ii) Interest on Drawings A/c Dr To Profit and Loss Appropriation A/c
4. **For partners' salaries/commission**	(i) Partners' Salaries/Commission A/c Dr To Partners' Capital A/c (or current, if capital accounts are fixed) (Individually)
	(ii) Profit and Loss Appropriation A/c Dr To Partners' Salaries/Commission A/c
5. **For transfer to reserve**	Profit and Loss Appropriation A/c Dr To Reserve A/c
6. **For transfer of credit balance** (Being profit)	Profit and Loss Appropriation A/c Dr To Partners' Capital A/c (or current, if capital accounts are fixed) (Individually)

Format of Profit and Loss Appropriation Account

Profit and Loss Appropriation Account
for the year ended.........

Dr Cr

Particulars		Amt (₹)	Particulars		Amt (₹)
To Interest on Capital A/cs			By Profit and Loss A/c		......
A	......		(Ne profit subject to appropriations)		
B	......	......	By Interest on Drawings A/cs		
To Partners' Salaries A/c		......	A	......	
To Partners' Commission A/c		......	B	......	......
To Reserve A/c		......			
To Profit Transferred to					
*A's Capital A/c					
**or A's Current A/c	......				
*B's Capital A/c					
**or B's Current A/c	......	......			
		......			......

**Under fluctuating capital method* ***Under fixed capital method*

Note Charges such as interest on partners' loans, manager's salary and commission must be deducted from profit before transferring it to profit and loss appropriation account.

Past Adjustments

Sometimes, after the final accounts of a firm have been closed, it is found that certain transactions have been left out by mistake.

In such cases, instead of altering the final accounts which have already been closed, the firm rectifies the error or omission by passing an adjustment entry in the beginning of the next year.

Such adjustments, are called past adjustments, as they relate to past period.

Adjustments are required for the following omissions or errors

(i) When interest on capital or drawings have been omitted or charged at a different rate than that provided in partnership deed.
(ii) Profits/Losses have been distributed in a wrong proportion.
(iii) Change in profit sharing ratio retrospectively.
(iv) Salary/Commission payable has been omitted.

Guarantee of Profits

A partner may be admitted into the firm with a guarantee of minimum profit, which means that if his share of profit is less than that of guaranteed profit, then he would be paid the guaranteed share of profit.

The deficiency (difference between guaranteed profit and actual profit) is borne by firm or partner or partners who have guaranteed the profit in agreed ratio.

Different conditions regarding guarantee of profit are

(i) Guarantee by the firm to a partner.
(ii) Guarantee by one partner to another partner.
(iii) Guarantee given by a partner to the firm.
(iv) Simultaneous guarantee by the firm to a partner and by a partner to the firm.

Key Point

In case, a question contains guarantee of profits by one partner to another partner, by the firm to a partner and by a partner to the firm, then following sequence should by followed

First calculate the guarantee given by the partner to the firm, then calculate the guarantee given by the firm to a partner, then calculate the guarantee given by a partner to another partner.

Goodwill

It means the good name or reputation of a business earned by a businessman through his hardwork and honesty. This helps the business to earn more profits.

Nature of Goodwill

Goodwill is an intangible asset but not a fictitious asset because it has a realisable value. Fictitious assets don't have a realisable value.

Characteristics/Features of Goodwill

Characteristics or features of goodwill are

(i) It is an intangible and valuable asset.
(ii) It is helpful in earning excess profits.
(iii) Its value is liable to constant fluctuations.
(iv) It is relevant only when the entire business is sold.

Factors Affecting Goodwill

The various factors affecting goodwill are

(i) Nature of business
(ii) Efficiency of management
(iii) Location
(iv) Market situation
(v) Capital required

Classification of Goodwill

Goodwill can be classified into two categories

(i) **Purchased** (Acquired) **goodwill** It is the goodwill that is acquired by a business after paying consideration in cash or in other kind.

Note As per Accounting Standard (AS) 26, only purchased goodwill is recorded in the books of accounts.

(ii) **Self-generated goodwill** It is the internally generated or hard earned goodwill which arises due to continued hard work of the organisation, its better quality products, better customer service, etc.

Note As per Accounting Standard (AS) 26, self-generated goodwill is not recorded in the books because no consideration is paid for it.

Need for Valuation of Goodwill

Need for valuation of goodwill arises in the following circumstances

(i) At the time of change in profit sharing ratio.
(ii) At the time of admission of a new partner.
(iii) At the time of retirement or death of a partner.

Methods of Valuation of Goodwill

Following are the methods of valuing goodwill

1. Average Profit Method

Under this method, goodwill is valued on the basis of simple average or weighted average of profits of the firm multiplied by the number of years' purchase. In this method, goodwill can be calcualted in two ways

(i) **Simple Average Profit Method**

Value of Goodwill = Average Profit* × Number of Years' Purchase

*Average Profit =

$$\frac{\text{Total Actual Profits of Given Number of Years Before Abnormal and Non-business Items}}{\text{Given Number of Years}}$$

(ii) **Weighted Average Profit Method**

Value of Goodwill = Weighted Average Profit* × Number of Years' Purchase

$$\text{*Weighted Average Profit} = \frac{\text{Total of Products}}{\text{Total of Weights}}$$

Key Points

- Any abnormal gain or abnormal loss should not be taken into consideration while calculating the average profit.
- Number of years' purchase means for how many years the firm will continue to earn the same amount of profit because of its past efforts even after change of ownership.

2. Super Profit Method

In any business, a certain amount or percentage of profits is normally expected. But in practice, we may earn more than normal profit or we may earn less than that normal profit.

Excess of average (actual) profits over the normal profit is called super profit.

Value of Goodwill = Super Profit* × Number of Years' Purchase

*Super Profits = Average (Actual) Profits – Normal Profits**

$$\text{**Normal Profits} = \text{Capital Employed***} \times \frac{\text{Normal Rate of Return}}{100}$$

***Capital Employed (Net assets) = Total Assets (Excluding goodwill, non-trade investments and fictitious assets) – External Liabilities

3. Capitalisation Method

In this method, goodwill can be calculated in two ways

(i) **Capitalisation of average profit method** In this method, goodwill of the firm is calculated by deducting actual capital employed from the capitalised value of average (actual) profits on the basis of normal rate of return.

Value of Goodwill = Capitalised Value of Average Profit* – Capital Employed**

$$\text{Where, *Capitalised Value of Average Profit} = \frac{\text{Average Profit}}{\text{Normal Rate of Return}} \times 100$$

**Actual Capital Employed = Total Assets (Excluding goodwill non-trade investments and fictitious assets) – External Liabilities

(ii) **Capitalisation of super profit method** In this method, goodwill is calculated by the capitalisation of super profit on the basis of normal rate of return. This is done by using the given formula

$$\text{Value of Goodwill} = \frac{\text{Super Profit*}}{\text{Normal Rate of Return}} \times 100$$

*Super Profit = Average Profit – Normal Profit

Difference between Average Profit and Super Profit

Basis	Average profit	Super profit
Meaning	It is the average of the profits of past few years.	It is the excess of average profit over normal profit.
Normal rate of return	It is not relevant in the calculation of average profit.	It is considered while calculating the super profit.
Average capital employed	It is not considered while calculating average profit.	It is taken into account while calculating the super profit.
Formula	$\frac{\text{Sum of Profits of '}n\text{' years}}{n}$	Average/Annual/Actual Profits – Normal Profits

PYQs Previous Years' Questions

1/2 Marks Questions

1. Give the formula used for calculating goodwill of a partnership firm by the weighted average profit method. *ISC 2023*

2. Give any one important feature of non-purchased goodwill. *ISC Specimen 2023*

3. A firm follows the fluctuating capital method. One of its partners takes a loan from the firm on which, as per the partnership deed, the firm is entitled to receive interest. What will be the adjusting entry for this interest on loan? *ISC Sem I 2021*
   (a) Debit Interest on Loan A/c; Credit Profit and Loss Appropriation A/c
   (b) Debit Interest on Loan A/c; Credit Profit and Loss A/c
   (c) Debit Partner's Capital A/c; Credit Interest on Loan A/c
   (d) Debit Partner's Loan A/c; Credit Interest on Loan A/c

4. Arav, Rahil and Himmat are partners in a firm sharing profits and losses in the ratio of 5 : 3 : 2. Arav guaranteed a minimum profit of ₹ 30,000 to Himmat.
   The trading loss of the firm for the year ending 31st March, 2021, was ₹ 1,20,000. In order to meet the deficiency in Himmat's profits, Arav's capital will be *ISC Sem I 2021*
   (a) debited by ₹ 30,000 (b) credited by ₹ 54,000
   (c) debited by ₹ 54,000 (d) debited by ₹ 6,000

KEY IDEA

Since the firm is in loss, Arav will not only bear the losses of Himmat, but also pay for the guarantee provided by him.

5. What will be the formula to value the goodwill of a firm by the super profit method? *ISC Sem I 2021*
   (a) Capitalised Super Profit × Number of Years' Purchase
   (b) Super Profit × Number of Years' Purchase
   (c) Average Profit – Normal Profit
   (d) Super Profit + Normal Profit

6. To calculate goodwill, which one of the following items will the firm add back to its actual profit to get its normal profit? *ISC Sem I 2021*
   (a) Gain from speculation of ₹ 5,000 which was taken into account
   (b) Manager's salary of ₹ 10,000 which was omitted to be recorded
   (c) Undervalued closing stock of ₹ 3,000
   (d) Overvalued closing stock of ₹ 2,000

7. A partnership firm has assets worth ₹ 1,34,000. It earns an annual profit of ₹ 18,000. The normal rate of return in the industry is 10%. On the reconstitution of the firm, its goodwill, by capitalising the average profits of the firm, is valued at ₹ 70,000.
   What are the outside liabilities of the firm at the time of valuation of its goodwill? *ISC Sem I 2021*
   (a) ₹ 24,000 (b) ₹ 30,000
   (c) ₹ 40,000 (d) ₹ 36,000

8. Pick the odd one out from the following *ISC Sem I Specimen 2021*
   (a) Interest allowed on a loan taken by the firm from a partner
   (b) Rent due to a partner of the firm for using his premises for business purposes
   (c) Salary due to the manager of the firm
   (d) Salary due to a partner of the firm

9. The formula for valuing goodwill under the capitalisation of super profits method is *ISC Sem I Specimen 2021*
   (a) super profit made by the firm multiplied by the normal rate of return
   (b) capital employed by the firm mutiplied by the normal rate of return
   (c) capitalised profit of the firm divided by the rate of return
   (d) super profit made by the firm divided by the normal rate of return

10. Arif, Ravi and Ben are partners in a firm sharing profits and losses in the ratio of 6 : 4 : 1. Arif guaranteed a minimum profit of ₹ 16,000 to Ben. The trading profit of the firm for the year ending 31st March, 2021, was ₹ 1,32,000. Arif's share in the profits of the firm will be *ISC Sem I Specimen 2021*
    (a) ₹ 72,000 (b) ₹ 68,000
    (c) ₹ 69,600 (d) ₹ 16,000

11. Simi, Manu and Beena are partners in a firm sharing profits and losses in the ratio of 2:2:1. The balances of their fixed capital accounts on 1st April, 2020, were Simi ₹ 1,00,000, Manu ₹ 1,00,000 and Beena ₹ 80,000.
    After the accounts for the year ended 31st March, 2021, were prepared, it was discovered that interest on capital @ 10% per annum had been credited to the partners' current accounts even though it was not provided in the partnership deed.
    The error in Simi's capital account/current account will be rectified by *ISC Sem I Specimen 2021*

(a) debiting her capital account with ₹ 1,200
(b) crediting her current account with ₹ 1,200
(c) debiting her current account with ₹ 1,200
(d) crediting her capital account with ₹ 1,200

KEY IDEA
The question is asking for information regarding Simi's account, you are not required to show other partners details in the 'statement showing adjustment'.

12. How will a firm deal with a situation when its partnership deed provides for interest on capital, but the profit earned by it is not enough to do so, at the rate mentioned in the deed? **ISC 2020**

13. Why is goodwill considered to be an intangible asset and not a fictitious asset? **ISC 2020**

14. List any two items which may appear on the credit side of a partner's fixed capital account. **ISC 2019**

15. Give the adjusting entry and closing entry for interest on loan taken by a partner from the firm, when the firm follows the fluctuating capital method. **ISC 2018**

16. Give the formula for valuation of goodwill by the capitalisation of average profit method. **ISC 2018**

17. Give the adjusting entry for interest on capital allowed to a partner, when the firm follows the fixed capital method. **ISC 2017**

18. State one difference between partner's loan account and partner's capital account. **ISC 2015**

19. Give the adjusting entry and the closing entry for recording commission allowed to a partner, when the firm follows the fixed capital method. **ISC 2015**

20. State the provisions of the Indian Partnership Act, 1932, regarding charging of interest on drawings from a partner when **ISC 2014**
 (i) the firm has a partnership deed.
 (ii) the firm does not have a partnership deed.

21. What is meant by number of years' purchase in the valuation of a firm's goodwill? **ISC 2014**

22. Give two differences between fixed and fluctuating capital accounts. **ISC 2014, 2007**

23. The firm with X, Y and Z as partners earned a profit of ₹ 3,00,000 during the year ended 31st March, 2011. 20% of this profit was to be transferred to general reserve. Pass the necessary journal entry for the same. **ISC 2012**

24. List two instances when a partner's fixed capital may change. **ISC 2012**

25. State two differences between average profit and super profit. **ISC 2011**

26. How will you deal with the following items in the absence of a partnership deed?
 (i) Interest on capital
 (ii) Interest on drawings
 (iii) Interest on partner's loan to the firm
 (iv) Share in profit and loss **ISC 2010**

27. What is meant by 'super profit' in the context of valuation of goodwill in partnership accounts? **ISC 2009**

28. State two differences between interest on capital allowed to partners and interest on drawings charged from partners. **ISC 2008**

29. State the closing entries for
 (i) Rent paid to a partner
 (ii) Interest on loan allowed to partners **ISC 2008**

30. Name the provisions of the partnership act with respect to the interest on capital of partners and the profit sharing ratio between partners. **ISC 2006**

31. What is meant by guaranteed partnership? **ISC 2005**

32. Give one reason, why partners are charged interest on drawings? **ISC 2003**

33. Distinguish between drawings against profit and drawings against capital. **ISC 2002**

34. What is interest on capital? Give one reason, why it is allowed to partners? **ISC 2002**

35. What is the purpose of preparing a profit and loss appropriation account of a partnership firm? **ISC 2001**

36. State any four factors upon which the value of goodwill of a firm depends. **ISC 2001**

37. What is the adjustment and closing entry required at the time of finalisation of accounts for interest on capital allowed to partners assuming that accounts are maintained under fixed capital system? **ISC 2000**

3 Marks Questions

38. Xen, Sam and Tim are partners in a firm. For the year ended 31st March, 2019, the profits of the firm ₹ 1,20,000, were distributed equally amongst them, without providing for the following provisions of the partnership deed
 (i) Sam's guarantee to the firm that the firm would earn a profit of at least ₹ 1,35,000. Any shortfall in these profits would be personally met by him.
 (ii) Profits to be shared in the ratio of 2:2:1.

You are required to pass the necessary journal entries to rectify the error in accounting. **ISC 2020**

39. Peter, Max and Som were partners in a firm sharing profits and losses in the ratio of 4 : 2 : 1. Their fixed capitals were ₹ 40,000, ₹ 30,000 and ₹ 30,000 respectively. Som was guaranteed a profit of ₹ 39,000 by the firm.

It was decided that any loss arising because of guarantee would be shared by Peter and Max equally. The trading profit of the firm for the year ended 31st March, 2018 was ₹ 1,47,000.

You are required to prepare the profit and loss appropriation account for the year 2017-18, showing the distribution of profits. **ISC 2019**

40. The capital accounts of Amar and Harsh stood at ₹ 20,000 and ₹ 30,000 respectively after the necessary adjustments in respect of drawings and net profit for the year ended 31st March, 2017. It was subsequently ascertained that interest on capital @ 12% per annum was not taken into account while arriving at the divisible profits for the year.

During the year 2016-17, Amar had withdrawn ₹ 2,000 and Harsh's drawings were ₹ 1,000. The net profit for the year amounted to ₹ 15,000. The partners shared profit and loss in the ratio of 3: 2.

You are required to pass the necessary journal entries to rectify the error in accounting. **ISC 2018**

41. Mita, Rita and Sandra were partners in a firm, sharing profits and losses in the ratio of 2 : 2 : 1. Mita had personally guaranteed that in any year Sandra's share of profit, after allowing interest on capital to all the partners @ 5% per annum and charging interest on drawings @ 4% per annum, would not be less than ₹ 10,000.

The capitals of the partners on lst April, 2015 were Mita ₹ 80,000, Rita ₹ 50,000 and Sandra ₹ 30,000. The net profit for the year ended 31st March, 2016, before allowing or charging any interest amounted to ₹ 40,000. Mita had withdrawn ₹ 4,000 on lst April, 2015, while Sandra withdrew ₹ 5,000 during the year.

You are required to prepare the profit and loss appropriation account for the year 2015-16. **ISC 2017**

42. Roshan, Mahesh, Gopi and Jai are partners sharing profits and losses in the ratio of 3 : 3 : 2 : 2. The balances of capital accounts on lst April, 2015 were

Roshan ₹ 8,00,000, Mahesh ₹ 5,00,000, Gopi ₹ 6,00,000 and Jai ₹ 6,00,000. After the accounts for the year ended 31st March, 2016 were prepared, it was discovered that interest on capital @ 10% per annum as provided in the partnership deed had not been credited to the partners' capital accounts before the distribution of profits.

You are required to rectify the error by passing a single adjusting journal entry. **ISC 2017**

43. Veera and Sia are partners, sharing profits in the ratio of 3 : 2. Profit for the year 2013-14, amounting to ₹ 18,000 was distributed wrongly in the ratio of 2 : 3.

You are required to rectify the error by passing an adjusting journal entry. **ISC 2015**

6 Marks Questions

44. Asif and Ravi are partners in a firm, sharing profit and loss in the ratio of 3 : 2. Their fixed capital as on 1st April, 2016, were ₹ 6,00,000 and ₹ 4,00,000 respectively. Their partnership deed provides for the following

(i) Partners are to be allowed interest on their capital @ 10% per annum.

(ii) They are to be charged interest on drawings @ 4% per annum.

(iii) Asif is entitled to a salary of ₹ 2,000 per month.

(iv) Ravi is entitled to a commission of 5% of the correct net profit of the firm before charging such commission.

(v) Asif is entitled to a rent of ₹ 3,000 per month for the use of his premises by the firm.

The net profit of the firm for the year ended 31st March, 2017, before providing for any of the above clauses was ₹ 4,00,000. Both partners withdrew ₹ 5,000 at the beginning of every month for the entire year.

You are required to prepare a profit and loss appropriation account for the year ended 31st March, 2017. **ISC 2018**

45. The partnership agreement of Rohit, Ali and Sneh provides that

(i) Profits will be shared by them in the ratio of 2 : 2 : 1.

(ii) Interest on capital to be allowed at a rate of 6% per annum.

(iii) Interest on drawings to be charged at the rate of 3% per annum.

(iv) Ali to be given a salary of ₹ 500 per month.

(v) Ali's guarantee to the firm that the firm would earn a net profit of atleast ₹ 80,000 per annum and any shortfall in these profits would be personally met by him.

The capitals of the partners on 1st April, 2013, were Rohit = ₹ 1,20,000; Ali = ₹ 1,00,000; Sneh = ₹ 1,00,000

During the financial year 2013-14, all the three partners withdrew ₹ 1,000 each at the beginning of every month.

The net profit of the firm for the year 2013-14 was ₹ 70,000. You are required to prepare for the year 2013-2014 profit and loss appropriation account, partners' capital account. **ISC 2015**

46. Alex, John and Sam are partners in a firm. Their capital accounts on 1st April, 2011 stood at ₹ 1,00,000, ₹ 80,000 and ₹ 60,000 respectively. Each partner withdrew ₹ 5,000 during the financial year 2011-12.

As per the provisions of their partnership deed

(i) John was entitled to a salary of ₹ 1,000 per month.

(ii) Interest on capital was to be allowed @ 10% per annum.

(iii) Interest on drawings was to be charged @ 4% per annum.

(iv) Profits and losses were to be shared in the ratio of their capitals.

The net profit of ₹ 75,000 for the year ended 31st March, 2012 was divided equally amongst the partners without providing for the terms of the deed.

You are required to pass a single adjusting journal entry to rectify the error. (Show the working clearly) **ISC 2013**

KEY IDEA

In the absence of any information regarding time of drawings, it is assumed to be in the mid of every month. So, interest will be charged for 6 months.

10 Marks Questions

47. The fixed capital accouts of Shiv, Azeem and Angad, sharing profits and losses in the ratio of 2 : 2 : 1, stood at ₹ 4,00,000, ₹ 6,00,000 and ₹ 2,00,000 respectively. The accounts for the year ended 31st March, 2022, were drawn up and closed and the current account balances of the partners were determined to be Shiv ₹ 35,000. Azeeem ₹ 40,000 and Angad ₹ 25,000.

Subsequently, the following errors were discovered on 1st April, 2022

(i) Interest on capital @ 10% per annum had been allowed to the partners, although there was no provision for it in the partnership deed.

(ii) Salary of ₹ 16,000 per annum to Shiv and ₹ 20,000 per annum to Azeem was not allowed to them, despite a provision for salary in the partnership deed.

(iii) Commission of ₹ 24,000 was not allowed to Angad, despite a provision for commission in the partnership deed.

You are required to prepare the adjusted current accounts of the partners on 1st April, 2022, to rectify the lapse in acccounting. **ISC 2023**

48. Ruma and Neha started business on 1st April, 2021, with fixed capitals of ₹ 4,00,000 and ₹ 3,50,000 respectively.

On 1st October, 2021, they decided that their total capital (fixed) should be ₹ 8,00,000, in their profits sharing ratio of 3 : 2. Accordingly, they introduced extra capital or withdrew excess capital.

Their partnership deed provided for the following

(i) Interest on capital to be allowed @ 10% per annum.

(ii) A monthly salary of ₹ 1,000 each to be allowed to both Ruma and Neha.

(iii) Interest on drawings to be charged @ 18% per annum.

Ruma had withdrawn ₹ 12,000, during the year. As per the deed, the interest on her drawings amounting to ₹ 1,080 to be charged from her. During the year ending 31st March, 2022, the firm earned a net profit of ₹ 2,04,000 before charging manager's commission of ₹ 20,400 and interest on bank loan of ₹ 4,000.

You are required to

(a) Give the journal entry to close Ruma's drawings account.

(b) Prepare profit and loss appropriation account for the year ending 31st March, 2022. **ISC 2023**

49. Ajay and Vijay are in partnership sharing profits and losses in the ratio of 3 : 1. On 1st April, 2021, their capitals were ₹ 1,00,000 and ₹ 90,000.

The terms of their partnership are as follows

(i) Interest on capital to be allowed at @ 6% per annum.

(ii) Interest on drawings to be charged @ 4% per annum.

(iii) Partners to get a salary of ₹ 1,000 each per month.

(iv) Vijay to get a commission of 2% on the correct net profit.

(v) Any partner taking a loan from the firm to be charged interest on it @ 8% per annum.

Ajay had borrowed ₹ 10,000 from the firm on 1st October, 2021. Vijay had withdrawn ₹ 8,000 on 1st July, 2021. During the year ending 31st March, 2022, the firm earned a net profit of ₹ 60,000 before any of the provisions mentioned in the partnership deed.

You are required to prepare for the year ending 31st March, 2022

(a) Profit and loss appropriation account.

(b) Ajay's capital account. *ISC Specimen 2023*

50. The partnership agreement of Rohit, Ali and Sneh provides that

(i) Profits will be shared by them in the ratio of 2 : 2 : 1.

(ii) Interest on capital to be allowed at the rate of 6% per annum.

(iii) Interest on drawings to be charged at the rate of 3% per annum.

(iv) Ali to be given a salary of ₹ 500 per month.

(v) Ali's guarantee to the firm that the firm would earn a net profit of at least . 80,000 per annum and any shortfall in these profits would be personally met by him.

The capitals of the partners on 1st April, 2021, were

Rohit = ₹ 1,20,000; Ali = ₹ 1,00,000; Sneh = ₹ 1,00,000

All the three partners withdrew ₹ 1,000 each at the beginning of every month. The net profit for the year 2021-22 was ₹ 70,000.

You are required to prepare for the year 2021-2022

(a) Profit and loss appropriation account.

(b) Ali's capital account. *ISC Specimen 2023*

51. Anita and Tony, each doing business as sole proprietors, started a partnership on 1st April, 2018. Anita brought in plant and machinery valued at ₹ 5,00,000 whereas Tony brought in furniture costing ₹ 50,000 and ₹ 7,00,000 in cash.

Since the business needed more funds, Tony gave a loan of ₹ 2,00,000 to the firm on 30th June, 2018.

Their partnership deed provided for

(i) Interest on capital to be allowed @ 10% per annum.

(ii) Interest on drawings to be charged @ 6% per annum.

(iii) Anita to be given a commission of 4% on the corrected net profits before charging commission.

(iv) Tony to be given a salary of ₹ 12,000 per annum.

Tony withdrew ₹ 5,000 at the end of every month and Anita withdrew ₹ 30,000 on 1st August, 2018.

The net profit of the firm, for the year 2018-19, after debiting Tony's salary of ₹ 12,000 per annum but before considering any interest due to and due from the partners, was ₹ 4,00,000.

You are required to prepare for the year 2018-19

(a) Profit and loss appropriation account.

(b) Partners' capital account. *ISC 2020*

52. Ravi and Tiku are partners in a firm. According to their partnership deed

(i) Interest on capital will be allowed @ 5% per annum.

(ii) Interest on drawings will be charged @ 4% per annum.

(iii) Each partner will be given a salary of ₹ 1,000 per month.

(iv) Partners will share profits and losses in the ratio of 2 : 1.

Following are the particulars of the capitals and drawings of the partners

Particulars	Ravi (₹)	Tiku (₹)
Capital (1st April, 2017)	60,000	50,000
Drawings (made on 1st June, 2017)	3,000	6,000

Ravi had taken a loan of ₹ 10,000 from the firm on which interest of ₹ 200 was due by him to the firm. The accounts for the year 2017-18 showed that the firm had made a profit of ₹ 77,000 before taking into account any interest, partners' salaries and manager's salary of ₹ 18,000. You are required to prepare

(a) Profit and loss appropriation account for the year 2017-18.

(b) Partners' capital account. *ISC 2019*

53. Shankar and Manu are partners in a firm. On 1st April, 2014, their fixed capital accounts showed a balance of ₹ 2,00,000 and ₹ 4,00,000 respectively. On this date their current account balances were ₹ 50,000 and ₹ 1,00,000 respectively. On 1st January, 2015, Shankar introduced additional capital of ₹ 2,00,000 while Manu gave a loan of ₹ 1,50,000 to the firm.

The clauses of their partnership deed provided for

(i) Interest on capital to be allowed at the rate of 10% per annum.

(ii) Interest on drawings to be charged at the rate of 12% per annum.

(iii) Profits to be shared by them in the ratio of 3 : 2.

(iv) 10% of the correct net profit to be transferred to general reserve.

During the financial year 2014-15, both partners withdrew ₹ 6,000 each at the beginning of every quarter. The net profit of the firm, before any interest, for the financial year 2014-15 was ₹ 5,00,000.

You are required to prepare for the year 2014-15
(a) Profit and loss appropriation account.
(b) Partners' fixed capital account.
(c) Partners' current account.
(d) Partner's loan account. *ISC 2016*

54. Rahim and Sudesh, the two partners of a business firm, agreed to appropriate the profits of their firm on the following terms
(i) Interest is payable on capital @ 5% per annum.
(ii) Rahim will be entitled to a salary of ₹ 500 per month.
(iii) Interest on loan to be given by the firm to the partners @ 10% per annum.
(iv) Interest on drawings to be charged from the partners @ 5% per annum.
(v) Sudesh will get commission @ 1% on the sales made during the year.
(vi) Rahim is entitled to a rent of ₹ 25,000 per annum for allowing the firm to carry on the business in his premises.

The net profit of the firm for the year ended 31st March, 2013, was ₹1,80,000 before taking into account any of the above terms

	Rahim (₹)	Sudesh (₹)
Capital balances on 1st April, 2012	1,50,000	1,40,000
Loan advanced on 1st October, 2012	—	1,00,000
Drawings made during the year	40,000	30,000

During the year 2012-13, sales of the firm amounted to ₹ 7,00,000

From the above information, prepare
(a) Profit and loss appropriation account.
(b) Partners' capital account. *ISC 2014*

55. Basu, Harish and Jadav are partners in a firm with capital contributions of ₹ 50,000, ₹ 40,000 and ₹ 30,000 respectively.

Their partnership agreement provides for the following
(i) Interest on capitals to be allowed @ 10% per annum.
(ii) Interest on drawings to be charged @ 10% per annum.
(iii) Harish and Jadav are each to be paid salaries @ ₹ 500 per month.
(iv) Basu is to be paid a commission of 5% of the net profit.
(v) 10% of the net profit to be transferred to general reserve
(vi) The remaining profits are to be divided as 40% to Basu, 30% to Harish, 30% to Jadav.

The net profit for the year ended 31st December, 2008 was ₹ 50,000. Basu withdrew ₹ 1,000 per month at the beginning of each month, Harish withdrew ₹ 1,000 per month in the middle of each month and Jadav withdrew ₹ 1,000 per month at the end of each month.

You are required to prepare the profit and loss appropriation account for the year ended 31st December, 2008 only. *ISC 2009 (M)*

56. Anil, Kamal and Vimal are partners in a firm. Their capital accounts on 1st January, 2005 stood at ₹ 1,20,000, ₹ 60,000 and ₹ 60,000 respectively. Vimal advanced a sum of ₹ 20,000 to the firm on 1st January, 2005 in the form of a loan. The partners withdrew ₹ 4,000 each during the year.

The partnership deed provides for the following
(i) Interest of 5% per annum to be allowed on the loan taken from the partners.
(ii) Interest on capitals to be allowed @ 10% per annum.
(iii) Interest on drawings to be charged @ 5% per annum.
(iv) Kamal to be allowed an annual salary of ₹ 5,000.
(v) Profits and losses to be shared in the ratio of 5 : 3 : 2.

Ignoring all the terms of the deed, the net profit of ₹ 90,000 for the year ended 31st December, 2005 was divided equally among the partners. Pass a single journal entry to rectify the error. (Show the working clearly) *ISC 2006*

57. Ted, Phil and Gorden are partners in partnership sharing profits two-fifths, two-fifths and one-fifth and throughout the half year ended 31st December, 2001, their capital accounts have remained unchanged at ₹ 60,000, ₹ 40,000 and ₹ 30,000 respectively.

Their current account balances on 1st July, 2001 were

Phil	₹ 8,550 (Dr)	Gorden	₹ 6,550 (Dr)
Ted	₹ 12,000 (Cr)		

During 2001, Ted withdraws ₹ 200 at the beginning of each month, Gorden withdrew ₹ 400 at the end of each month while Phil withdrew ₹ 1,800 during the period of six months. Their partnership deed provides that
(i) Partners are allowed interest on capital @ 5% per annum.
(ii) Partners are allowed or charged interest on current account balances @ 4% per annum.
(iii) Interest on drawings @ 6% per annum.
(iv) Gorden is entitled to a salary of ₹ 500 per month.

(v) Ted is entitled to a commission of 5% of the correct net profit of the firm.

(vi) Phil is entitled to a commission of 5% of the correct net profit of the firm after charging such commission.

During the half year ended 2001, the net profit of the firm was ₹ 2,07,000 after charging Gorden's salary which had been debited to wages and salaries account.

You are required to prepare the profit and loss appropriation account of the firm only. **ISC 2002**

Case Based Questions

58. Deepa and Shweta are two partners sharing profits in the ratio of 1 : 2. Their balance sheet as at 31st March, 2021, is as follows

Balance Sheet of Deepa and Shweta
as at 31st March, 2021

Liabilities		Amt (₹)	Assets	Amt (₹)
Deepa's Loan		25,000	Sundry Assets	1,55,000
Capital A/cs				
Deepa	60,000			
Shweta	70,000	1,30,000		
		1,55,000		1,55,000

On 1st July, 2020, Deepa had introduced additional capital of ₹ 10,000 by converting a part of her loan into capital. The profits for the year ended 31st March, 2021, amounting to ₹ 30,000, were distributed between the partners before allowing interest on Deepa's capital @ 10% per annum as provided in the partnership deed. **ISC Sem I 2021**

(i) What was the interest on Deepa's capital for the year 2020-21, which was omitted to be credited to her capital account?
(a) ₹ 4,750
(b) ₹ 5,950
(c) ₹ 5,200
(d) ₹ 5,800

(ii) What will be the journal entry to convert Deepa's loan to her capital?
(a) Debit Cash A/c ₹ 10,000; Credit Deepa's Capital A/c ₹ 10,000
(b) Debit Deepa's Capital A/c ₹ 10,000; Credit Deepa's Loan A/c ₹ 10,000
(c) Debit Deepa' Loan A/c ₹ 15,000; Credit Deepa's Capital A/c ₹ 15,000
(d) Debit Deepa's Loan A/c ₹ 10,000; Credit Deepa's Capital A/c ₹ 10,000

59. The partnership deed of Sakshi and Tanu allowed an annual salary of ₹ 24,000 to Tanu. The trading profit of the firm for the year 2020-21, after debiting Tanu's salary, was ₹ 60,000. The partnership deed also provided for commission to Sakshi @ 5% of the correct trading profit of the firm before charging commission. **ISC Sem I 2021**

(i) What will be Sakshi's commission?
(a) ₹ 1,800 (b) ₹ 3,000 (c) ₹ 5,200 (d) ₹ 4,200

(ii) Another provision in the partnership deed was that partners are to be charged interest on drawings @ 4% per annum. Tanu withdrawn a fixed amount in the middle of every month and the interest on her drawings at the end of the year was ₹ 600. What were the total drawings made by Tanu?
(a) ₹ 6,000 (b) ₹ 30,000
(c) ₹ 15,000 (d) ₹ 24,000

(iii) What will be the entry to transfer the trading profit of the firm to the profit and loss appropriation account?
(a) Debit P & L Appropriation A/c; Credit Net Profit A/c
(b) Debit P & L Appropriation A/c; Credit P & L A/c
(c) Debit P & L A/c; Credit P & L Appropriation A/c
(d) Debit Trading Profit A/c; Credit P & L Appropriation A/c

60. On 1st April, 2020, Pixie, Nixie and Gypsy entered into a partnership with fixed capitals of ₹ 60,000, ₹ 50,000 and ₹ 30,000 respectively. On 1st October, 2020, Pixie gave a loan of ₹ 12,000 to the firm.
The partnership deed contained the following clauses
(i) Interest on drawings to be charged @ 4% per annum.
(ii) Pixie to be entitled to a rent of ₹ 2,000 per annum for allowing the firm to carry on the business in his premises.

Nixie withdrew ₹ 1,000 at the end of the month for the first six months. Net profit of the firm for the year ending 31st March, 2021 (before any interest but after rent on Pixie's premises) was ₹ 1,21,000. **ISC Sem I Specimen 2021**

(i) The net profit of the firm will be
(a) ₹ 1,21,000 (b) ₹ 1,20,640
(c) ₹ 1,18,640 (d) ₹ 96,640

(ii) Interest on drawings charged from Nixie will be
(a) ₹ 340 (b) ₹ 220 (c) ₹ 170 (d) ₹ 18.33

Explanations

1. Goodwill (as per Weighted Average Profit) = Weighted Average Profit × Number of Years' Purchase
Weighted Average Profit

$$= \frac{\text{Total of Weighted Average Profit}}{\text{Total of Weights}}$$

> **Concept Enhancer** Weighted average profit is more appropriate than simple average profit because it gives more weightage to recent profits.

2. One of the important features of non-purchased goodwill, is that it is generated internally and over the years.

3. (c) Debit Partner's Capital A/c; Credit Interest on Loan A/c

4. (c) Deficiency $= \left(1{,}20{,}000 \times \frac{2}{10}\right) + 30{,}000$

$= 24{,}000 + 30{,}000 = ₹\ 54{,}000$

5. (b) Super Profit × Number of Years' Purchase

6. (c) Undervalued closing stock of ₹ 3,000

> **Concept Enhancer** In order to calculate normal profit, any abnormal gain included in the profits will be subtracted and any abnormal loss included in the profits will be added to the profit.

7. (a) Capitalised value of average profits $= 18{,}000 \times \frac{100}{10}$

$= ₹\ 1{,}80{,}000$

Goodwill = Capitalised Value of Average Profit − Net Assets

$70{,}000 = 1{,}80{,}000 - \text{Net Assets}$

∴ Net Assets = ₹ 1,10,000

Now, Liabilities = Assets − Net Assets

$= 1{,}34{,}000 - 1{,}10{,}000 = ₹\ 24{,}000$

8. (d) Salary due to a partner of the firm

9. (d) super profit made by the firm divided by the normal rate of return

10. (b) Ben's Profit $= 1{,}32{,}000 \times \frac{1}{11} = 12{,}000$

(Gurantee ₹ 16,000)

Arift's Profit $\left(1{,}32{,}000 \times \frac{6}{11}\right)$ 72,000

(−) Transferred to Ben (4,000)

68,000

11. (b) **Statement Showing Adjustment**

Particulars	Simi (₹) Dr	Simi (₹) Cr	Firm (₹) Dr	Firm (₹) Cr
Interest on Capital (Not to be provided)	10,000	—	—	28,000
Profit		11,200	28,000	
	10,000	11,200	28,000	28,000
	(1,200) Cr		Nil	

Simi's current account will be credited.

12. In a situation of inadequate profits, the available profit will be distributed in the ratio of interest (or ratio of capital).

However, in case the interest is a charge as per partnership deed, interest will be allowed at the specified rate irrespective of profit.

13. Since goodwill doesn't have physical existence, it is considered as an intangible asset. It just has a capability to help businesses earn more.

It is not considered as a fictitious asset because fictitious assets are the expenses or losses which are still to be charged from the profit and they are neither tangible nor intangible assets.

14. Two items which may appear on the credit side of partner's fixed capital account are
(i) Opening credit balance of partners.
(ii) Additional capital introduced by partners.

15. **Adjusting entry**

Interest on Partner's Loan A/c Dr
To Partner's Loan A/c
(Being interest on partner's loan provided)

Closing entry

Profit and Loss A/c Dr
To Interest on Partner's Loan A/c

16. **Capitalisation of average profit method** In this method, goodwill of the firm is calculated by deducting actual capital employed from the capitalised value of average (actual) profits on the basis of normal rate of return.

Value of Goodwill = Capitalised Value of Average Profit − Capital Employed

Where, Capitalised Value of Average Profit

$$= \frac{\text{Average Profit}}{\text{Normal Rate of Return}} \times 100$$

Actual Capital Employed = Total Assets (Excluding goodwill) − External Liabilities

17. The adjusting entry for interest on capital allowed to a partner, when the firm follows fixed capital method is

Interest on Capital A/c Dr

To Partner's Current A/c

(Being interest on capital provided at x % per annum)

18. Difference between partner's loan account and partner's capital account

Basis	Partner's loan account	Partner's capital account
Interest	Interest on partner's loan is allowed at 6% per annum even is partnership deed is silent.	No interest on partner's capital will be allowed when deed is silent.

19. The adjusting entry and the closing entry for recording commission allowed to a partner, when the firm follows the fixed capital method are

Adjusting entry

Commission A/c Dr

To Partner's Current A/c

(Being commission allowed to partner)

Closing entry

Profit and Loss Appropriation A/c Dr

To Commission A/c

(Being commission to partner transferred)

20. (i) When the firm has a partnership deed, interest on drawings may be charged at the specified rate.

(ii) When the firm does not have a partnership deed, interest on drawings is not to be charged.

21. Number of years' purchase means for how many years the firm will continue to earn the same amount of profit because of its past efforts after change of ownership.

22. Difference between fixed capital account and fluctuating capital account

Basis	Fixed capital account	Fluctuating capital account
Number of accounts	Under this method, two separate accounts are maintained for each partner *viz*, capital account and current account.	Under this method, each partner has one account i.e., capital account.
Adjustments	All adjustments for drawings, salary, interest on capital, etc are made in the current accounts and not in the capital accounts.	All adjustments for drawings, salary, interest on capital, etc are made in the capital accounts.

23. Profit and Loss Appropriation A/c Dr 60,000

To General Reserve A/c 60,000

(Being 20% of profit transferred to general reserve)

24. Two circumstances under which fixed capital of a partner may be change are

(i) When additional capital is introduced.

(ii) When capital is withdrawn by partners permanently as per the agreement between them.

25. Difference between average profit and super profit

Basis	Average profit	Super profit
Meaning	It is average of the profits of past few years.	It is the excess of average profit over normal profit.
Normal rate of return	It is not relevant in the calculation of average profit.	It is considered while calculating the super profit.

26. (i) In the absence of partnership deed, interest on capital is not allowed.

(ii) In the absence of partnership deed, interest on drawings is not charged.

(iii) In the absence of partnership deed, interest on partner's loan is allowed @ 6% per annum.

(iv) In the absence of partnership deed, profits/losses are shared equally.

27. Super profit is the excess of average (actual) profits over the normal profits.

Value of Goodwill = Super Profit* × Number of Years' Purchase

*Super Profits = Average (Actual) Profits – Normal Profits**

Normal Profits = Capital Employed* $\times \dfrac{\text{Normal Rate of Return}}{100}$

***Capital Employed (Net assets) = Total Assets (Excluding goodwill) – External Liabilities

28. Difference between interest on capital and interest on drawings

Basis	Interest on capital	Interest on drawings
Objective	It is allowed to compensate those partners, who contribute capital.	It is charged to prevent withdrawal of cash in anticipation of profit.
Recorded	It is debited to profit and loss appropriation account and credited to partner's capital account.	It is credited to profit and loss appropriation account and debited to partner's capital account.

29. (i) Profit and Loss A/c Dr
To Rent Paid A/c
(Being rent charged)
(ii) Profit and Loss A/c Dr
To Interest on Loan A/c
(Being interest on loan charged)

30. Interest on capital is not allowed and profits and losses are to be shared equally in the absence of partnership deed.

31. Guaranteed partnership may be defined as a partnership in which a partner may be admitted into the firm with a guarantee of minimum profit, which means that if his share of profit is less than that of guaranteed profit, then he would be paid the guaranteed share of profit. The deficiency (difference between guaranteed profit and actual profit) is borne by partner or partners, who have guaranteed the profit in an agreed ratio.

32. The main reason of charging interest on drawings is to put an effective check on reckless withdrawals.

33. Difference between drawings against profits and drawings against capital

Basis	Drawings against profits	Drawings against capital
Meaning	It means drawings made out of profits earned by the firm during the year.	It means drawings made in excess of profits.
Effect	It does not reduce the capital of the firm.	It reduces the capital of the firm.

34. Interest on capital is a charge on capital provided by partners to the firm. It is justified when profit sharing ratio and capital ratios are different. Interest on capital is allowed to compensate partners for contributing capital to the firm.

35. Profit and loss appropriation account is prepared to show how the net profit as per the profit and loss account has been appropriated amongst the partners.

36. The four factors affecting goodwill are
(i) Nature of business
(ii) Efficiency of management
(iii) Location (iv) Market situation

37. Adjustment entry
Interest on Capital A/c Dr
To Partner's Current A/c
(Being interest on capital transferred to partner's current account under fixed capital method)

Closing entry
Profit and Loss Appropriation A/c Dr
To Interest on Capital A/c
(Being closing entry made for interest on capital)

38. **JOURNAL**

Date	Particulars	LF	Amt (Dr)	Amt (Cr)
	Sam's Capital A/cDr		1,000	
	Tim's Capital A/c Dr		13,000	
	To Xen's Capital A/c			14,000
	(Being adjustment entry passed)			

Adjustment Table

Particulars	Xen (₹)	Sam (₹)	Tim (₹)
Sam's decrease in capital (Dr) [to meet the deficiency of profit (1,35,000 – 1,20,000)]	—	15,000	—
Corrected profits distributed (₹ 1,35,000 in 2 : 2 : 1) (Cr)	54,000	54,000	27,000
Profits already credited (Dr)	40,000	40,000	40,000
Balance	14,000 (Cr)	1,000 (Dr)	13,000 (Dr)

39. **Profit and Loss Appropriation Account**
Dr for the year ending 2017-18 Cr

Particulars		Amt (₹)	Particulars	Amt (₹)
To Profit Tansferred to Partner Capital A/c			By Profit	1,47,000
Peter	84,000			
(–) Share to Som	(9,000)	75,000		
Max	42,000			
(–) Share to Som	(9,000)	33,000		
Som	21,000			
(+) Share from				
Peter and Max	18,000	39,000		
		1,47,000		1,47,000

Working Note	**Amt (₹)**
Guaranteed profit to Som	39,000
(–) Actual profit	(21,000)
Shortage to meet guaranteed profit	18,000

To be shared equally by Peter and Max, i.e. ₹ 9,000 each.

40. In the Books of Amor and Harsh

JOURNAL

Date	Particulars		LF	Amt (Dr)	Amt (Cr)
2017 Apr 1	Amar's Capital A/c	Dr		1,176	
	To Harsh's Capital A/c				1,176
	(Being an adjustment entry passed)				

Working Note

Calculation of Capital at the Beginning

Particulars	Amar (₹)	Harsh (₹)
Capital at the End	20,000	30,000
(+) Drawings	2,000	1,000
	22,000	31,000
(–) Net Profit	(9,000)	(6,000)
Capital at the Beginning	13,000	25,000
Interest on Capital @ 12% p.a.	1,560	3,000

Calculation of Amount to be Adjusted

Particulars	Amar (₹)	Harsh (₹)	Total (₹)
Interest on Capital to be Credited	1,560	3,000	4,560
Amount to be Debited (3 : 2)	2,736	1,824	4,560
	1,176 (Dr)	1,176 (Cr)	Nil

41. In the Books of Mita, Rita and Sandra

Profit and Loss Appropriation Account

for the year ended 2015-16

Dr | Cr

Particulars		Amt (₹)	Particulars		Amt (₹)
To Interest on Capital A/cs			By Profit and Loss A/c (Net Profit)		40,000
Mita $\left(80,000 \times \frac{5}{100}\right)$	4,000		By Interest on Drawings A/cs		
Rita $\left(50,000 \times \frac{5}{100}\right)$	2,500		Mita	160	
Sandra $\left(30,000 \times \frac{5}{100}\right)$	1,500	8,000	Sandra	100	260
To Profit Transferred to Capital A/cs					
Mita (12,904 – 3,548)	9,356				
Rita	12,904				
Sandra (6,452 + 3,548)	10,000	32,260			
		40,260			40,260

Working Notes

1. Interest on drawings by Mita $= 4{,}000 \times \frac{4}{100} =$ ₹ 160
2. Interest on drawings by Sandra $= 5{,}000 \times \frac{4}{100} \times \frac{6}{12} =$ ₹ 100
3. Distributable profits = 40,000 + 260 – 8,000 = ₹ 32,260; Sandra's share in profit $= 32{,}260 \times \frac{1}{5} =$ ₹ 6,452

   Deficiency to be borne by Mita = 10,000 – 6,452 = ₹ 3,548
4. Mita's share in profit $= 32{,}260 \times \frac{2}{5} = 12{,}904$

(–) Deficiency	(3,548)
Mita will be entitled to	9,356

42. **In the Books of Roshan, Mahesh, Gopi and Jai**

JOURNAL

Date	Particulars		LF	Amt (Dr)	Amt (Cr)
	Mahesh's Capital A/c	Dr		25,000	
	To Roshan's Capital A/c				5,000
	To Gopi's Capital A/c				10,000
	To Jai's Capital A/c				10,000
	(Being adjusting entry passed for interest on capital)				

Working Note

Analysis Table

Particulars	Roshan (₹)	Mahesh (₹)	Gopi (₹)	Jai (₹)	Total (₹)
Amount which should have been credited as interest on capital	80,000	50,000	60,000	60,000	2,50,000
(–) Adjusted loss of net effect ₹ 2,50,000 (80,000+50,000 +60,000+60,000) in the ratio of 3 : 3 : 2 : 2	75,000	75,000	50,000	50,000	2,50,000
	5,000 (Cr)	25,000 (Dr)	10,000 (Cr)	10,000 (Cr)	Nil

43. **In the Books of Veera and Sia**

JOURNAL

Date	Particulars		LF	Amt (Dr)	Amt (Cr)
	Sia's Capital A/c	Dr		3,600	
	To Veera's Capital A/c				3,600
	(Being profit wrongly distributed, now adjusted)				

Working Note

Adjustment Table

Particulars	Veera (₹)	Sia (₹)
Amount to be debited (₹ 18,000 in 2 : 3)	7,200	10,800
Amount to be credited (₹ 18,000 in 3 : 2)	10,800	7,200
Difference	3,600 (Cr)	3,600 (Dr)

44. **In the Books of Asif and Ravi**

Profit and Loss Appropriation Account

for the year ended 31st March, 2017

Dr | Cr

Particulars		Amt (₹)	Particulars		Amt (₹)
To Interest on Capital			By Profit and Loss A/c (4,00,000 – 36,000)		3,64,000
Asif's Current A/c	60,000		By Interest on Drawings		
Ravi's Current A/c	40,000	1,00,000	Asif's Current A/c	1,300	
To Asif's Salary A/c		24,000	Ravi's Current A/c	1,300	2,600
To Ravi's Commission A/c		18,200			
To Share of Profit Transferred to Current A/cs					
Asif	1,34,640				
Ravi	89,760	2,24,400			
		3,66,600			3,66,600

Working Notes

1. Rent to Asif is charged against the profit. Thus, it is debited to profit and loss account. After that correct net profit for the year is (4,00,000 – 36,000) = ₹ 3,64,000
2. Ravi's commission is calculated on net profit @ 5% p.a. = 3,64,000× 5 / 100= ₹ 18,200

3. Calculation of interest on drawings

$$\text{Total Drawings} \times \frac{\text{Rate}}{100} \times \frac{\text{Average Period}}{12} = 5{,}000 \times 12 \times \frac{4}{100} \times \frac{6.5}{12} = ₹\ 1{,}300 \text{ each}$$

Common Mistake Students usually ignore the information that the capitals are fixed and record everything in the partners' capital account. Since the capitals are fixed, all the transactions will be recorded in the current accounts of the partners.

45.

In the Books of Rohit, Ali and Sneh
Profit and Loss Appropriation Account
for the year ended 2013-14

Dr | | | | | Cr

Particulars		Amt (₹)	Particulars		Amt (₹)
To Interest on Capital A/cs			By Net Profit b/d		70,000
Rohit (1,20,000 × 6/100)	7,200		By Ali's Capital A/c (Shortfall)		10,000
Ali (1,00,000 × 6/100)	6,000		By Interest on Drawings A/c		
Sneh (1,00,000 × 6/100)	6,000	19,200	Rohit	195	
To Ali's Capital A/c			Ali	195	
Salary (500 × 12)		6,000	Sneh	195	585
To Net Profit Transferred to Capital A/c			$\left(12{,}000 \times \frac{3}{100} \times \frac{6.5}{12}\right)$		
Rohit	22,154				
Ali	22,154				
Sneh	11,077	55,385			
		80,585			80,585

Partners' Capital Account

Dr | | | | | | | | Cr

Particulars	Rohit (₹)	Ali (₹)	Sneh (₹)	Particulars	Rohit (₹)	Ali (₹)	Sneh (₹)
To Drawings	12,000	12,000	12,000	By Balance b/d	1,20,000	1,00,000	1,00,000
To Interest on Drawings	195	195	195	By Interest on Capital	7,200	6,000	6,000
To Profit and Loss Appropriation A/c	—	10,000	—	By Partner's Salary	—	6,000	—
To Balance c/d	1,37,159	1,11,959	1,04,882	By Profit Transferred to Profit and Loss Appropriation Account	22,154	22,154	11,077
	1,49,354	1,34,154	1,17,077		1,49,354	1,34,154	1,17,077

46.

In the Books of Alex, John and Sam
JOURNAL

Date	Particulars		LF	Amt (Dr)	Amt (Cr)
2012 Apr 1	Sam's Capital A/c	Dr		9,275	
	To Alex's Capital A/c				1,275
	To John's Capital A/c				8,000
	(Being adjustment entry for interest on capital, salary, interest on drawings and distribution of profit)				

Working Notes

1. **Statement of Adjustment**

Particulars	Alex (₹)	John (₹)	Sam (₹)	Total (₹)
Amount to be Debited				
Interest on Drawings (WN3)	100	100	100	300
Net Profit Wrongly Distributed	25,000	25,000	25,000	75,000
	25,100	25,100	25,100	75,300

Particulars	Alex (₹)	John (₹)	Sam (₹)	Total (₹)
Amount to be Credited				
Interest on Capital	10,000	8,000	6,000	24,000
Salary	—	12,000	—	12,000
Corrected Net Profit (WN2)	16,375	13,100	9,825	39,300
	26,375	33,100	15,825	75,300
Net Effect	1,275 (Cr)	8,000 (Cr)	9,275 (Dr)	Nil

2. **Profit and Loss Appropriation Account**
for the year ended 2011, 12

Dr | Cr

Particulars		Amt (₹)	Particulars		Amt (₹)
To John's Salary (1,000 × 12)		12,000	By Profit and Loss A/c (Net Profit)		75,000
To Interest on Capital A/cs			By Interest on Drawings A/cs		
Alex	10,000		Alex	100	
John	8,000		John	100	
Sam	6,000	24,000	Sam	100	300
To Profit Transferred to Capital A/cs					
Alex	16,375				
John	13,100				
Sam	9,825	39,300			
		75,300			75,300

3. Interest on drawings $= 5{,}000 \times \frac{4}{100} \times \frac{6}{12} = ₹\,100$

47. **Statement Showing Adjustments**

Particulars	Shiv (₹)	Azeem (₹)	Angad (₹)	Total (₹)
Interest on Capital (Dr)	40,000	60,000	20,000	1,20,000
Salary (Cr)	16,000	20,000	—	36,000
Commission (Cr)	—	—	24,000	24,000
	24,000 Dr	40,000 Dr	4,000 Cr	60,000 Dr
Profit (2 : 2 : 1)	24,000 Cr	24,000 Cr	12,000 Cr	—
	Nil	16,000 Dr	16,000 Cr	—

JOURNAL

Particulars		LF	Amt (Dr)	Amt (Cr)
Azeem's Current A/c	Dr		16,000	
To Angad's Current A/c				16,000
(Being rectifying entry passed)				

Partners' Current Account

Dr | Cr

Particulars	Shiv (₹)	Azeem (₹)	Angad (₹)	Particulars	Shiv (₹)	Azeem (₹)	Angad (₹)
To Angad's Current A/c	—	16,000	—	By Balance b/d	35,000	40,000	25,000
To Balance c/d	35,000	24,000	41,000	By Azeem's Current A/c	—	—	16,000
	35,000	40,000	41,000		35,000	40,000	41,000

48. (a) **JOURNAL**

Particulars		LF	Amt (Dr)	Amt (Cr)
Interest on Drawings A/c	Dr		1,080	
To Profit and Loss Appropriation A/c				1,080
(Being interest on drawings is transferred to profit and loss appropriation account)				

(b) Dr **Profit and Loss Appropriation Account** Cr

Particulars		Amt (₹)	Particulars	Amt (₹)
To Interest on Capital			By Net Profit (2,04,000 – 4,000 – 20,400)	1,79,600
Ruma's Current A/c	44,000		By Interest on Drawings	
Neha's Current A/c	33,500	77,500	Ruma's Current A/c	1,080
To Partner's Salary				
Ruma's Current A/c	12,000			
Neha's Current A/c	12,000	24,000		
To Profit Transferred to				
Ruma's Current A/c	47,508			
Neha's Current A/c	31,672	79,180		
		1,80,680		1,80,680

Working Note

Interest on capital

$$\text{Ruma} = \left(4{,}00{,}000\times\frac{10}{100}\times\frac{6}{12}\right)+\left(4{,}80{,}000\times\frac{10}{100}\times\frac{6}{12}\right)=20{,}000+24{,}000=₹\,44{,}000$$

$$\text{Neha} = \left(3{,}50{,}000\times\frac{10}{100}\times\frac{6}{12}\right)+\left(3{,}20{,}000\frac{10}{100}\times\frac{6}{12}\right)=17{,}500+16{,}000=₹\,33{,}500$$

49. (a) **Profit and Loss Appropriation Account as at 31st March, 2022**

Dr Cr

Particulars		Amt (₹)	Particulars	Amt (₹)
To Interest on Capital A/c			By Profit and Loss A/c	60,000
Ajay	6,000		By Interest on Drawings (Vijay)	240
Vijay	5,400	11,400	By Interest on Loan (Ajay)	400
To Salary A/c				
Ajay	12,000			
Vijay	12,000	24,000		
To Commission A/c (Vijay) (WN 1)		505		
To Net Profit Transferred to				
Ajay's Capital A/c	18,551			
Vijay's Capital A/c	6,184	24,735		
		60,640		60,640

(b) Dr **Ajay's Capital Account** Cr

Particulars	Amt (₹)	Particulars	Amt (₹)
To Interest on Loan A/c	400	By Balance b/d	1,00,000
To Balance c/d	1,36,151	By Interest on Capital A/c	6,000
		By Salary A/c	12,000
		By Profit and Loss appropriation A/c	18,551
	1,36,551		1,36,551

Working Notes

1. Profit before charging commission = 60,000 + 240 + 400 – 11,400 – 24,000 = ₹ 25,240

   $\text{Commission to Vijay} = 25{,}240\times\frac{2}{100}=₹\,504.8 \text{ or } ₹\,505$

2. Interest on capital $\quad$ Ajay = $1{,}00{,}000\times 6\% = ₹\,6{,}000$; $\quad$ Vijay = $90{,}000\times 6\% = ₹\,5{,}400$

3. Interest on drawings $\quad$ Vijay = $8000\times 4\%\times\frac{9}{12} = ₹\,240$

4. Interest on loan taken by Ajay = $10{,}000\times\frac{6}{12}\times\frac{8}{100}=₹\,400$

50. (a)

Profit and Loss Appropriation Account as at 31st March, 2022

Dr Particulars		Amt (₹)	Particulars		Cr Amt (₹)
To Interest on Capital A/c			By Profit and Loss A/c		70,000
Rohit	7,200		By Interest on Drawings		
Ali	6,000		Rohit	195	
Sneh	6,000	19,200	Ali	195	
To Partner's Salary A/c (Ali)		6,000	Sneh	195	585
To Net Profit Transferred to			By Ali's Capital A/c (WN 2)		34,615
Rohit	32,000				
Ali	32,000				
Sneh	16,000	80,000			
		1,05,200			1,05,200

(b)

Ali's Capital Account

Dr Particulars	Amt (₹)	Particulars	Cr Amt (₹)
To Profit and Loss Appropriation A/c	34,615	By Balance b/d	1,00,000
To Balance c/d	1,09,385	By Interest on Capital A/c	6,000
		By Partner's Salary A/c	6,000
		By Profit and Loss Appropriation A/c	32,000
	1,44,000		1,44,000

Working Notes

1. Interest on drawings $= (1,000 \times 12) \times \frac{6.5}{12} \times \frac{3}{100} =$ ₹ 195

2. Net profit before distribution $= (70,000 + 585) - (19,200 + 6,000) =$ ₹ 45,385
   Shortfall in profits $= 80,000 - 45,385 =$ ₹ 34,615

51. (a)

Profit and Loss Appropriation Account for the year ended 31st March, 2019

Dr Particulars		Amt (₹)	Particulars		Cr Amt (₹)
To Tony's Capital A/c (Salary)		12,000	By Profit and Loss A/c	4,12,000	
To Interest on Capitals			(4,00,000 + 12,000)		
Tony	75,000		(–) Interest on Loan (WN 1)	(9,000)	4,03,000
Anita	50,000	1,25,000			
To Anita's Capital A/c (Commission)		10,754	By Interest on Drawings (WN 2)		
(4% of ₹ 2,68,850)			Tony	1,650	
To Profits			Anita	1,200	2,850
Anita	1,29,048				
Tony	1,29,048	2,58,096			
		4,05,850			4,05,850

(b)

Partners' Capital Account

Dr Particulars	Anita (₹)	Tony (₹)	Particulars	Anita (₹)	Cr Tony (₹)
To P & L App. A/c (Int. on Drawings)	1,650	1,200	By Balance b/d	5,00,000	7,50,000
To Balance c/d	6,88,152	9,64,848	By P & L App. A/c (Salary)	—	12,000
			By P & L App. A/c (Int. on Capital)	50,000	75,000
			By P & L App. A/c (Commission)	10,754	—
			By P & L App. A/c	1,29,048	1,29,048
	6,89,802	9,66,048		6,89,802	9,66,048

Working Notes

1. Interest on Loan = 6% of ₹ 2,00,000 for 9 months = $\frac{6}{100} \times 2,00,000 \times \frac{9}{12}$ = ₹ 9,000

2. Interest on Drawings

Tony = $5,000 \times 12 \times \frac{5.5}{12} \times \frac{6}{100}$ = ₹1,650 ; Anita = $30,000 \times \frac{8}{12} \times \frac{6}{100}$ = ₹ 1,200

52. (a)

Profit and Loss Appropriation Account
for the year ended 31st March, 2018

Dr Particulars		Amt (₹)	Particulars		Cr Amt (₹)
To Interst on Capital			By Profit	77,000	
Ravi	3,000		(–) Manager Commission	(18,000)	59,000
Tiku	2,500	5,500	By Interest on Drawings		
To Salary to Partners			Ravi	100	
Ravi	12,000		Tiku	200	300
Tiku	12,000	24,000	By Interest on Loan given to Ravi		200
To Profit Transferred to Partners Capital A/c					
Ravi	20,000				
Tiku	10,000	30,000			
		59,500			59,500

(b) **Partners' Capital Account**

Dr Particulars	Ravi (₹)	Tiku (₹)	Particulars	Ravi (₹)	Cr Tiku (₹)
To Drawings	3,000	6,000	By Balance b/d	60,000	50,000
To Interest on Loan	200	–	By Interest on Capital	3,000	2,500
To Interest on Drawings	100	200	By Salary	12,000	12,000
To Balance c/d	91,700	68,300	By Profit and Loss Appropriation (Profit)	20,000	10,000
	95,000	74,500		95,000	74,500

Common Mistake Students usually forget to record the interest on loan. Since loan is given by the firm to partner, thus interest received on loan is an income to the firm. So, it will be recorded on the credit side of P & L App. A/c.

53. (a)

In the Books of Shankar and Manu
Profit and Loss Appropriation Account
for the year ended 2014-15

Dr Particulars		Amt (₹)	Particulars		Cr Amt (₹)
To Interest on Capital A/cs			By Net Profit for the Year (5,00,000 – 2,250)		4,97,750
Shankar	25,000				
Manu	40,000	65,000	By Interest on Drawings A/cs		
To Transfer to Reserve A/c (4,97,750 × 10%)		49,775	Shankar	1,800	
			Manu	1,800	3,600
To Profit Transferred to Current A/cs					
Shankar	2,31,945				
Manu	1,54,630	3,86,575			
		5,01,350			5,01,350

(b) **Partners' Capital Account**

Dr Particulars	Shankar (₹)	Manu (₹)	Particulars	Shankar (₹)	Cr Manu (₹)
To Balance c/d	4,00,000	4,00,000	By Balance b/d	2,00,000	4,00,000
			By Bank A/c	2,00,000	—
	4,00,000	4,00,000		4,00,000	4,00,000

(c) Dr **Partners' Current Account** Cr

Particulars	Shankar (₹)	Manu (₹)	Particulars	Shankar (₹)	Manu (₹)
To Interest on Drawings A/c	1,800	1,800	By Balance b/d	50,000	1,00,000
To Drawings A/c	24,000	24,000	By Interest on Capital A/c	25,000	40,000
To Balance c/d	2,81,145	2,68,830	By Profit and Loss Appropriation A/c (Profit)	2,31,945	1,54,630
	3,06,945	2,94,630		3,06,945	2,94,630

(d) Dr **Manu's Loan Account** Cr

Particulars	Amt (₹)	Particulars	Amt (₹)
To Balance c/d	1,52,250	By Bank A/c	1,50,000
		By Interest on Loan A/c	2,250
	1,52,250		1,52,250

Working Notes

1. Interest on capital Manu $= 4,00,000 \times \frac{10}{100} = ₹\ 40,000$

Shankar $=$ On ₹ 2,00,000 for full year $= 2,00,000 \times \frac{10}{100} \times 1 = 20,000$

$=$ On ₹ 2,00,000 for 3 months $= 2,00,000 \times \frac{10}{100} \times \frac{3}{12} = 5,000$

$25,000$

2. Interest on loan by Manu $= 1,50,000 \times \frac{6}{100} \times \frac{3}{12} = ₹\ 2,250$

3. Interest on drawings $= (6,000 \times 4) \times \frac{12}{100} \times \frac{7.5}{12} = ₹\ 1,800$

54. (a) **In the Books of Rahim and Sudesh**

Profit and Loss Account

Dr **for the year ended 31st March, 2013** Cr

Particulars	Amt (₹)	Particulars	Amt (₹)
To Interest on Loan A/c (Sudesh)	5,000	By Profit	1,80,000
To Rent (Rahim)	25,000		
To Profit Transferred to Profit and Loss Appropriation A/c	1,50,000		
	1,80,000		1,80,000

Profit and Loss Appropriation Account

Dr **for the year ended 31st March, 2013** Cr

Particulars		Amt (₹)	Particulars		Amt (₹)
To Interest on Capital A/cs			By Profit and Loss A/c		1,50,000
Rahim $\left(1,50,000 \times \frac{5}{100}\right)$	7,500		By Interest on Drawings A/cs		
Sudesh $\left(1,40,000 \times \frac{5}{100}\right)$	7,000	14,500	Rahim	1,000	
			Sudesh	750	1,750
To Salary to Rahim (500×12)		6,000			
To Commission to Sudesh		7,000			
To Profit Transferred to Partners' Capital A/cs					
Rahim	62,125				
Sudesh	62,125	1,24,250			
		1,51,750			1,51,750

(b) Dr **Partners' Capital Account** Cr

Particulars	Rahim (₹)	Sudesh (₹)	Particulars	Rahim (₹)	Sudesh (₹)
To Drawings A/c	40,000	30,000	By Balance b/d	1,50,000	1,40,000
To Interest on Drawings A/c	1,000	750	By Interest on Capital A/c	7,500	7,000
To Balance c/d	1,84,625	1,85,375	By Salary A/c	6,000	—
			By Commission A/c	—	7,000
			By Profit and Loss Appropriation A/c	62,125	62,125
	2,25,625	2,16,125		2,25,625	2,16,125

Working Notes

1. Commission to Sudesh = 1% on sales = $\frac{1}{100} \times 7{,}00{,}000 =$ ₹ 7,000
2. Interest on drawings

   Rahim = $40{,}000 \times \frac{5}{100} \times \frac{6}{12} =$ ₹ 1,000; Sudesh = $30{,}000 \times \frac{5}{100} \times \frac{6}{12} =$ ₹ 750
3. Interest on partner's loan has been treated as a charge against profit. It has been debited to profit and loss account and will be credited to a separate loan account.
4. Rent paid to partner has also been as charge against profit. It is also debited to profit and loss account and has been credited to rent payable account.

55.

In the Books of Harish and Jadav
Profit and Loss Appropriation Account
for the year ended 31st December, 2008

Dr Cr

Particulars		Amt (₹)	Particulars		Amt (₹)
To Interest on Capital A/cs			By Net Profit as per Profit and Loss A/c		50,000
Basu	5,000		By Interest on Drawings A/cs		
Harish	4,000		Basu	650	
Jadav	3,000	12,000	Harish	600	
To Salaries A/c			Jadav	550	1,800
Harish (500 × 12)	6,000				
Jadav (500 × 12)	6,000	12,000			
To Commission A/c					
Basu $\left(50{,}000 \times \frac{5}{100}\right)$		2,500			
To General Reserve $\left(50{,}000 \times \frac{10}{100}\right)$		5,000			
To Profit Transferred to Capital A/cs					
Basu (40%)	8,120				
Harish (30%)	6,090				
Jadav (30%)	6,090	20,300			
		51,800			51,800

Working Notes

1. Interest on drawings

   Basu (1,000 × 12) = $12{,}000 \times \frac{10}{100} \times \frac{6.5}{12} =$ ₹ 650; Harish (1,000 × 12) = $12{,}000 \times \frac{10}{100} \times \frac{6}{12} =$ ₹ 600

   Jadav (1,000 × 12) = $12{,}000 \times \frac{10}{100} \times \frac{5.5}{12} =$ ₹ 550
2. Interest on capital

   Basu = $50{,}000 \times \frac{10}{100} =$ ₹ 5,000; Harish = $40{,}000 \times \frac{10}{100} =$ ₹ 4,000; Jadav = $30{,}000 \times \frac{10}{100} =$ ₹ 3,000

56.

In the Books of Anil, Kamal and Vimal
JOURNAL

Date	Particulars		LF	Amt (Dr)	Amt (Cr)
	Kamal's Capital A/c	Dr		1,010	
	Vimal's Capital A/c	Dr		12,040	
	To Anil's Capital A/c				12,050
	To Vimal's Loan A/c				1,000
	(Being adjustment entry passed)				

Working Notes

1. **Statement of Adjustment**

Particulars	Anil (₹)		Kamal (₹)		Vimal (₹)		Total (₹)	
	Dr	Cr	Dr	Cr	Dr	Cr	Dr	Cr
Profit Wrongly Distributed	30,000	—	30,000	—	30,000	—	—	90,000
Interest on Capital	—	12,000	—	6,000	—	6,000	24,000	—
Salary	—	—	—	5,000	—	—	5,000	—
Interest on Drawings	100	—	100	—	100	—	—	300
Interest on Loan	—	—	—	—	—	—	1,000	—
Profit Distributed in 5:3:2 (WN2)	—	30,150	—	18,090	—	12,060	60,300	—
	30,100	42,150	30,100	29,090	30,100	18,060	90,300	90,300
Net Effect		12,050 (Cr)	1,010 (Dr)	12,040 (Dr)				

2. **Profit and Loss Appropriation Account**
for the year ended 31st December, 2005

Dr Cr

Particulars		Amt (₹)	Particulars		Amt (₹)
To Interest on Capital A/cs			By Profit and Loss A/c (Net Profit)		89,000
Anil (1,20,000 × 10%)	12,000		(90,000 – 1,000 being interest on loan)		
Kamal (60,000 × 10%)	6,000	24,000	By Interest on Drawings A/cs		
Vimal (60,000 × 10%)	6,000	5,000	Anil	100	
To Kamal's Salary			Kamal	100	
To Profit Transferred to Capital A/cs			Vimal	100	300
Anil	30,150				
Kamal	18,090				
Vimal	12,060	60,300			
		89,300			89,300

3. Interest on drawings

Anil $= 4{,}000 \times \frac{5}{100} \times \frac{6}{12} =$ ₹ 100 ; Kamal $= 4{,}000 \times \frac{5}{100} \times \frac{6}{12} =$ ₹ 100 ; Vimal $= 4{,}000 \times \frac{5}{100} \times \frac{6}{12} =$ ₹ 100

4. Interest on loan

Interest on Vimal's loan $= 20{,}000 \times \frac{5}{100} =$ ₹ 1,000

57.

In the Books of Ted, Phil and Gorden
Profit and Loss Appropriation Account
Dr for the half year ending 31st December, 2001 Cr

Particulars	Amt (₹)		Particulars	Amt (₹)	
To Interest on Capital A/cs			By Net Profit before Charging Gorden's Salary (2,07,000 + 3,000)		2,10,000
Ted $\left(60{,}000 \times \frac{5}{100} \times \frac{6}{12}\right)$	1,500		By Interest on Drawings A/cs		
			Ted	21	
Phil $\left(40{,}000 \times \frac{5}{100} \times \frac{6}{12}\right)$	1,000		Phil	27	
			Gorden	30	78
Gorden $\left(30{,}000 \times \frac{5}{100} \times \frac{6}{12}\right)$	750	3,250	By Interest on Current A/cs		
			Phil $\left(8{,}550 \times \frac{4}{100} \times \frac{6}{12}\right)$	171	
To Gorden's Salary (500×6)		3,000	Gorden $\left(6{,}550 \times \frac{4}{100} \times \frac{6}{12}\right)$	131	302
To Commission A/cs					
Ted $\left(2{,}10{,}000 \times \frac{5}{100}\right)$	10,500				
Phil $\left(2{,}10{,}000 \times \frac{5}{105}\right)$	10,000	20,500			
To Interest on Ted's Current A/c $\left(12{,}000 \times \frac{4}{100} \times \frac{6}{12}\right)$		240			
To Profit Transferred to Partners' Capital A/cs					
Ted	73,356				
Phil	73,356				
Gorden	36,678	1,83,390			
		2,10,380			2,10,380

Working Note

Calculation of interest on drawings

$$\text{Ted} = 1{,}200 \times \frac{6}{100} \times \frac{3.5}{12} = ₹\,21; \quad \text{Gorden} = 2{,}400 \times \frac{6}{100} \times \frac{2.5}{12} = ₹\,30; \quad \text{Phil} = 1{,}800 \times \frac{6}{100} \times \frac{6}{12} \times \frac{6}{12} = ₹\,27$$

Note Interest on drawings is calculated for half year.

58. (i) (a) Opening Capital of Deepa = Closing Capital – Additional Capital – Profit
= 60,000 – 10,000 – 10,000 = ₹ 40,000
Interest on Capital = (40,000 × 10/100) + (10,000 × 10/100 × 9/12) = 4,000 + 750 = ₹ 4,750

(ii) (d) Debit Deepa's Loan A/c ₹ 10,000; Credit Deepa's Capital A/c ₹ 10,000

59. (i) (d) Commission = (24,000 + 60,000) × 5% = ₹ 4,200

(ii) (b) $600 = x \times \frac{6}{12} \times \frac{4}{100}$; $\therefore$ $x = ₹\,30{,}000$

(iii) (c) Debit P & L A/c; Credit P & L Appropriation A/c

60. (i) (b) Net Profit = 1,21,000 – Interest on loan $= 1{,}21{,}000 - \left(12{,}000 \times \frac{6}{100} \times \frac{6}{12}\right) = 1{,}21{,}000 - 360 = ₹\,1{,}20{,}640$

Common Mistake Students sometimes ignore the fact that the loan was provided in the mid of the year. In the question, the loan is provided on 1st October thus interest will be charged for 6 months only.

(ii) (c) Interest on Nixie's Drawings $= \text{Drawings} \times \frac{\text{Rate}}{100} \times \frac{\text{Average Period}}{12} = 6{,}000 \times \frac{4}{100} \times \frac{8.5}{12} = ₹\,170$

CHAPTER TEST

01/02 Marks Questions

1. If the partners' capitals are fixed, which of the following will not appear in the partners' current account?
(a) Additional capital introduced
(b) Drawings
(c) Interest on capital
(d) All of the above

2. M, N and O are partners in a firm. They want to expand their business. In order to do that, they decided to admit more members in the firm. What is the maximum number of additional members they can admit?
(a) 50 (b) 02
(c) 45 (d) 47

3. A, Band C are partners in a firm sharing profits equally. B has drawn ₹ 500 per month in the middle of every month during the year. Interest on drawings amounted to ₹ 240. What is the rate of interest on drawings?
(a) 6% p.a. (b) 7% p.a.
(c) 7.5% p.a. (d) 8% p.a.

4. When a partner is given a guarantee of profit, any deficiency will be borne by
(a) all other partners
(b) the partner who has given the guarantee
(c) partner with the highest profit ratio
(d) firm

5. Following are the profits earned by LFT & Co. over the last five years ₹ 12,000, ₹ 13,000, ₹ 14,000, ₹ 18,000, ₹ (2,000). If goodwill is valued at 2 year's purchase of average profit of last 5 years, the goodwill of the firm is?
(a) ₹ 23,600 (b) ₹ 1,10,000
(c) ₹ 22,000 (d) ₹ 1,18,000

6. State any two essential characteristics of a partnership.

7. What is the formula for calculating goodwill by the super profit method?

8. Goodwill of a firm is ₹ 45,000 being 2 years purchase of average profit of the last 5 years. What is the average profit of the last five years of the firm?

03 Marks Questions

9. A and B entered into partnership on 1st April, 2009 without any partnership deed. They introduced capital of ₹ 5,00,000 and ₹ 3,00,000 respectively. On 31st October, 2009, A advanced ₹ 2,00,000 by way of loan to the firm without any agreement as to interest. The profit and loss accounts for the year ended 31st March, 2010 showed a profit of ₹ 4,30,000, but the partners could not agree upon the amount of interest on loan to be charged and the basis of division of profits.

Pass a journal entry for the distribution of the profit between the partners and prepare the capital accounts of both the partners and loan account of 'A'.

10. G, H and R were partners in a firm sharing profits in the ratio of 7 : 4 : 9. Their fixed capitals were G ₹ 2,00,000, H ₹ 75,000 and R ₹ 3,50,000.

Their partnership deed provided for the following
(i) Interest on capital @ 9% per annum.
(ii) Salary of ₹ 6,000 per month to H.
(iii) Interest on drawings @ 6% per annum.

During the year ended 31st December, 2009 the firm earned a profit of ₹ 1,70,000. Interest on G's drawings was ₹ 750, on H's drawings ₹ 450 and on R's drawings ₹ 1,250.

Prepare profit and loss appropriation account for the year ended 31st December, 2009.

11. Mohan, Neeraj and Peeyush are partners in a firm. They contributed ₹ 75,000 each as capital three years ago. At that time, Peeyush agreed to look after the business as Mohan and Neeraj were busy. The profits for the past three years were ₹ 45,000, ₹ 30,000 and ₹ 60,000 respectively. While going through the books of accounts, Mohan noticed that profit had been distributed in 1 : 1 : 2 ratio. When he enquired from Peeyush about this, Peeyush answered that since he looked after the business he should get more profit. Mohan disagreed and it was decided to distributed profits equally with retrospective effect for the last three years.

You are required to make necessary corrections in the books of accounts of Mohan, Neeraj and Peeyush by passing an adjustment entry.

06 Marks Question

12. A partnership firm earned net profits during the last 3 years as follows

Year	Net Profit (₹)
2007-08	1,90,000
2008-09	2,20,000
2010-11	2,50,000

The capital employed in the firm throughout the above mentioned period has been ₹ 4,00,000. Having regard to the risk involved, 15% is considered to be a fair return on the capital. The remuneration of all the partners during this period is estimated to be ₹ 1,00,000 per annum. Calculate the value of goodwill on the basis of

(i) 2 years' purchase of super profits earned on average basis during the above mentioned 3 years.

(ii) By capitalisation method.

10 Marks Questions

13. A, B and C were partners in a firm having capitals of ₹ 60,000, ₹ 60,000 and ₹ 80,000 respectively. Their current account balances were A ₹ 10,000, B ₹ 5,000 and C ₹ 2,000 (Dr). According to the partnership deed, the partners were entitled to interest on capital @ 5% per annum. C being the working partner was also entitled to a salary of ₹ 6,000 per annum. The profits were to be divided as follows

(i) The first ₹ 20,000 in proportion to their capitals.

(ii) Next ₹ 30,000 in the ratio of 5 : 3 : 2.

(iii) Remaining profits to be shared equally.

The firm made a profit of ₹ 1,56,000 before charging any of the above items.

Prepare the profit and loss appropriation account and pass necessary journal entry for appropriation of profit.

14. Ali, Bimal and Deepak are partners in a firm. On 1st April, 2011 their capital accounts stood at ₹ 4,00,000, ₹ 3,00,000 and ₹ 2,00,000 respectively. They shared profits and losses in the ratio of 5 : 3 : 2 respectively. Partners are entitled to interest on capital @ 10% per annum and salary to Bimal and Deepak ₹ 2,000 per month and ₹ 3,000 per quarter respectively as per the provisions of the partnership deed. Bimal's share of profit (excluding interest on capital but including salary) is guaranteed at a minimum of ₹ 50,000 per annum. Any deficiency arising on that account shall be met by Deepak.

The profits of the firm for the year ended 31st March, 2012 amount to ₹ 2,00,000. Prepare profit and loss appropriation account for the year ended on 31st March, 2012.

Answers

1. (a) Additional capital introduced

2. (d) 47

3. (d) 8% p.a

4. (b) the partner who has given the guarantee

5. (c) ₹ 22,000

8. ₹ 22,500

9. Profit Transferred to A's and B's Capital A/c = ₹ 2,12,500 each; Balance in Capital A/cs A = ₹ 7,12,500; B = ₹ 5,12,500

10. Profit Transferred to G's Current A/c = ₹ 15,470; H's Current A/c = ₹ 8,840; R's Current A/c = ₹ 19,890

11. Debit Peeyush by ₹ 22,500, Credit Mohan by ₹ 11,250 and Neeraj by ₹ 11,250

12. (i) Goodwill = ₹ 1,20,000
(ii) Goodwill = ₹ 4,00,000

13. Profit Transferred to A's Current A/c = ₹ 51,000; B's Current A/c = ₹ 45,000; C's Current A/c = ₹ 44,000

14. Profit Transferred to Ali's Capital A/c = ₹ 37,000; Bimal's Capital A/c = ₹ 26,000; Deepak's Capital A/c = ₹ 11,000

02

Reconstitution of a Partnership Firm : Admission of Partner

TREND ANALYSIS 5 YEARS

Average No. of Questions Across all Sets

	Types of Questions	2023	2020	2019	2018	2017
01 Treatment for Goodwill, Reserves, Accumulated Profits and Losses	1/2 Marks	—	—	—	—	—
	3 Marks	—	1	—	—	—
	6 Marks	1	—	1	—	1
	10 Marks	—	—	—	—	—
02 Revaluation of Assets and Reassessment of Liabilities	1/2 Marks	1	—	—	—	—
	3 Marks	—	—	—	—	—
	6 Marks	—	—	—	—	—
	10 Marks	—	—	—	1	—
03 Adjustment of Capital	1/2 Marks	—	—	—	—	—
	3 Marks	—	—	—	—	—
	6 Marks	—	—	—	—	—
	10 Marks	—	1	—	—	1

Change in Profit Sharing Ratio

When one or more existing partners acquire an interest in the business from another existing partner(s) then, it is said to be a **change in the profit sharing ratio** in a partnership firm. A change in the profit sharing ratio among the existing partners means the reconstitution of the firm without admission, retirement or death of a partner(s).

In this case, the aggregate amount of gain by one or more partners is equal to the aggregate amount of sacrifice made by the other partner(s).

Adjustments Required at the Time of Change in Profit Sharing Ratio

The adjustments required at the time of change in profit sharing ratio are

1. Determination of sacrificing ratio and gaining ratio.
2. Accounting treatment of goodwill.
3. Revaluation of assets and reassessment of liabilities.
4. Accounting treatment of reserves, accumulated profits and losses.

1. Determination of Sacrificing and Gaining Ratio

(i) **Sacrificing ratio** It is the ratio in which the partners sacrifice their share of profit in favour of another partner. It is calculated in the following manner

Sacrificing Ratio = Old Share – New Share

(ii) **Gaining ratio** It is the ratio in which the partners gain in profit from other partner(s). It is calculated in the following manner

Gaining Ratio = New Share – Old Share

(iii) **New profit sharing ratio** It is the ratio in which the partners are to share profits in future. It is calculated as follows

New Profit Sharing Ratio = Old Share – Sacrificing Share
or = Old Share – Gaining Share

Points to Remember

- Partner whose share in profit decreases as a result of reconstitution of firm is a **sacrificing partner**.
- Partner whose share in profit increases as a result of reconstitution of firm is a **gaining partner**.

2. Accounting Treatment of Goodwill

If the partners decide to change their profit sharing ratio, the gaining partner should compensate the sacrificing partner by way of payment to him as goodwill in the gaining ratio.

The entry to be passed for adjustment of goodwill, when there is a change in profit sharing ratio is

(i) **In Case of Fluctuating Capital**

Gaining Partners' Capital A/c	Dr	[In gaining ratio]
To Sacrificing Partners' Capital A/c		[In sacrificing ratio]

(ii) **In Case of Fixed Capital**

Gaining Partners' Current A/c	Dr	[In gaining ratio]
To Sacrificing Partners' Current A/c		[In sacrificing ratio]

Treatment of Existing Goodwill

Goodwill (if any) appearing in the books of the firm is written-off by debiting it to all partners' capital accounts in their old profit sharing ratio and by crediting the goodwill account. The entry is

All Partners' Capital/Current A/c	Dr	[In old ratio]
To Goodwill A/c		

Key Point

AS-26 'Intangible Assets' prescribes that goodwill should be recognised in the books of accounts only when consideration in money or money's worth is paid for it i.e. when goodwill is purchased.

3. Adjustment for Revaluation of Assets and Reassessment of Liabilities

At the time of change in profit sharing ratio, the assets are revalued and the liabilities are reassessed, since realisable or actual value of assets and liabilities may be different from those shown in balance sheet.

Revaluation of assets and reassessment of liabilities is necessary because the change in the value of assets and liabilities belongs to the period prior to change in the profit sharing ratio among the partners. Hence, any gain or loss on revaluation must be shared in their old profit sharing ratio by the partners.

Two alternatives available for this purpose are

(i) When Revised Values are to be Recorded in the Books of Accounts

An account titled 'revaluation account' or 'profit and loss adjustment account' is opened for this purpose.

The relevant journal entries are

Particulars	Entry		Amount
For increase in the value of asset	*Asset A/c To Revaluation A/c	Dr	Revised value – Book value
For decrease in the value of asset	Revaluation A/c To *Asset A/c	Dr	Book value – Revised value
For increase in the amount of liabilities	Revaluation A/c To *Liability A/c	Dr	Revised amount – Amount as per books
For decrease in the amount of liabilities	*Liability A/c To Revaluation A/c	Dr	Amount as per books – Revised amount
For recording an unrecorded asset	*Asset A/c To Revaluation A/c	Dr	(given amount)
For recording an unrecorded liability	Revaluation A/c To *Liability A/c	Dr	(given amount)
If there is profit on revaluation	Revaluation A/c To All Partners' Capital/Current A/c	Dr	In old ratio
If there is loss on revaluation	All Partners' Capital/Current A/c To Revaluation A/c	Dr	In old ratio

* = Particular

Format of Revaluation Account

Dr **Revaluation Account** Cr

Particulars	Amt (₹)	Particulars	Amt (₹)
To Decrease in Value of Assets	...	By Increase in Value of Assets	...
To Increase in Value of Liabilities	...	By Decrease in Value of Liabilities	...
To Unrecorded Liability	...	By Unrecorded Assets	...
To Profit Transferred to Old Partners' Capital A/c or Current A/c (Old ratio)	...	By Loss Transferred to Old Partners' Capital A/c or Current A/c (Old ratio)	...
	...		...

(ii) When Revised Values are not to be Recorded in the Books of Accounts

(Adjustments of profits/losses on revaluation of assets and reassessment of liabilities through the capital accounts only)

If partners decide to record the net effect of revaluation of assets and liabilities without affecting the old amount of assets and liabilities, a single adjusting entry involving the capital accounts of gaining partners and sacrificing partners is passed. In this regard, we take the following steps

Step 1 **Calculation of the net effect of revaluation**

Increase in the value of assets	....
(+) Decrease in amount of liabilities	....
(−) Decrease in value of assets	(....)
(−) Increase in amount of liabilities	(....)
Net effect of revaluation	....

Step 2 **To find share of sacrifice/gain by partners**

(i) Their old share	....
(ii) Their new share	....
Difference (i – ii)	....

***Step* 3 Calculation of proportional amount of net effect of revaluation**

For Gaining Partner

Proportional Amount of Net Effect of Revaluation = Share Gained × Net Effect of Revaluation

For Sacrificing Partner

Proportional Amount of Net Effect of Revaluation = Share Sacrificed × Net Effect of Revaluation

***Step* 4 Pass the following journal entries**

For Profit on Revaluation

Gaining Partners' Capital A/c Dr

To Sacrificing Partners' Capital A/c

For Net Loss on Revaluation

Sacrificing Partners' Capital A/c Dr

To Gaining Partners' Capital A/c

4. Accounting Treatment of Reserves, Accumulated Profits and Losses

The accounting treatment of reserves, accumulated profits or losses can be studied under two heads

(i) When Reserves and Accumulated Profits/Losses are not to be Transferred to Capital Accounts

When the partners decide to record net effect of reserves and accumulated profits/losses without affecting their old figures, a single adjusting entry involving the capital accounts of sacrificing and gaining partners is passed.

When reserves and accumulated profits/losses are adjusted through capital accounts only, then they appear in the balance sheet of the new firm at the old figures.

Steps involved in passing a journal entry

***Step* 1** Calculate the net effect of reserves and accumulated profits/losses

Accumulated profits	...
(+) Reserves	...
(–) Accumulated losses	(...)
Net effect	...

***Step* 2** Calculate sacrificing/(gaining) share

Sacrificing/(Gaining) share = Old share – New share

***Step* 3** Calculate share of gaining and sacrificing partners in the net reserves and accumulated profits/losses

For gaining partner = Net effect × Share gained

For sacrificing partner = Net effect × Share sacrificed

***Step* 4** Pass the single adjusting entry

In Case of Profit	In Case of Loss
Gaining Partner's Capital A/c Dr To Sacrificing Partner's Capital A/c	Sacrificing Partner's Capital A/c Dr To Gaining Partner's Capital A/c

Note Adjustment of the incoming (new) partner's share will be made through his current account.

(ii) When Reserves, Accumulated Profits/Losses are to be Transferred to Capital Accounts

At the time of change in profit sharing ratio, if any reserves or accumulated profits/losses exist in the books of the firm, they are transferred to partners' capital/current account in their old profit sharing ratio. The journal entries passed are

(a) **For Transfer of Reserves and Accumulated Profits**

Reserve/Profit and Loss A/c	Dr	
Workmen's Compensation Reserve A/c	Dr	[Excess of reserve over actual liability]
Investments Fluctuation Reserve A/c	Dr	[Excess of reserve over the difference between book value and market value]
To All Partners' Capital (or Current) A/c		[In old ratio]

(b) **For Transfer of Accumulated Losses**

All Partners' Capital (or Current) A/c Dr [In old ratio]
To Profit and Loss A/c
To Deferred Revenue Expenditure A/c

Admission of a Partner

Admission of a partner is one of the modes of reconstituting the firm under which old partnership comes to an end and a new one is constitute among all partners (including incoming partner).

According to Section 31 (1) of Indian Partnership Act, 1932, 'A new partner can be admitted only with the consent of all the existing partners'.

A new partner is admitted for the following purposes

(i) For procuring additional capital.
(ii) For acquiring additional managerial skills.

A newly admitted partner acquires following two main rights in the firm

(i) Proportionate share in the future profits of the firm.
(ii) Proportionate share in the assets of the firm.

Adjustments Required at the Time of Admission of a New Partner

Following adjustments are required at the time of admission of a new partner

1. Calculation of new profit sharing ratio and sacrificing ratio.
2. Accounting treatment of goodwill.
3. Accounting treatment of revaluation of assets and reassessment of liabilities.
4. Accounting treatment of reserves, accumulated profits and losses.
5. Adjustment of capital in new profit sharing ratio.

1. Determination of New Profit Sharing Ratio and Sacrificing Ratio

(i) **New Profit Sharing Ratio**

The ratio in which all the partners (including incoming partner) will share the future profits and losses is known as new profit sharing ratio.

New Profit Sharing Ratio = Old Share − Sacrificing Share (For old partners)

(ii) **Sacrificing Ratio**

It is the ratio in which the old partners have agreed to sacrifice their share of profits in favour of new or incoming partner.

Sacrificing Ratio = Old Share − New Share

2. Accounting Treatment of Goodwill

Different situations about the treatment of goodwill at the time of the admission of a new partner are

(i) **When premium for goodwill is paid privately by new partner** In case a new partner pays premium to the old partners privately or directly or outside the business, it will not be recorded because it is an out of business transaction.

(ii) **When premium for goodwill is brought in business by new partner in cash**

(a) **For bringing premium for goodwill and capital in cash**

Cash/Bank A/c Dr
To Premium for Goodwill A/c

(b) **For distributing premium to sacrificing** (old) **partners in their sacrificing ratio**
Premium for Goodwill A/c Dr
To Sacrificing Partners' Capital A/c

(c) **For withdrawing of premium by sacrificing** (old) **partners**
Sacrificing (old) Partners' Capital A/c Dr
To Cash/Bank A/c

(iii) **When premium for goodwill and capital is brought in kind**

(a) Assets A/c Dr
To Premium for Goodwill A/c

(b) Premium for Goodwill A/c Dr
To Sacrificing Partners' Capital A/c

(iv) **When the new partner is unable to bring his share of premium for goodwill in cash**
New Partner's Current A/c Dr (with the share of new partner in goodwill of the firm)
To Sacrificing (Old) Partners' Capital/Current A/c (in sacrificing ratio)

(v) **When a new partner brings only a part of premium for goodwill in cash**

(a) Cash/Bank A/c Dr
To Premium for Goodwill A/c (with the amount of goodwill brought in cash)

(b) Premium for Goodwill A/c Dr (with the amount of goodwill brought in cash)
New Partner's Current A/c Dr (with the amount of goodwill not brought in cash)
To Sacrificing (Old) Partners' Capital/Current A/c (in sacrificing ratio)

Note AS-26 'Intangible Assets' prescribes that goodwill should be recognised in the books of accounts only when consideration in money or money's worth is paid for it, i.e. when goodwill is purchased.

Writing-off Existing Goodwill

If goodwill is appearing in the balance sheet at the time of reconstitution (admission), then it will be written-off in old profit sharing ratio because it is belonged to the period prior to admission of a partner (reconstitution).

Old Partners' Capital A/c Dr
To Goodwill A/c

Hidden or Inferred Goodwill

Hidden or inferred goodwill is the excess of desired total capital of the firm over the actual combined capital of all partners.

In case the value of goodwill is not given at the time of admission of a new partner, it is required to be calculated on the basis of an inferred method of profit sharing ratio or capitalisation.

The following steps will be taken for calculating hidden goodwill

Step 1 Find out the total capital of the new firm on the basis of the capital brought in firm by the new partner for his share.

Step 2 Ascertain the existing total capital of the new firm by adding the capital of all partners, including new partner's capital after adjustments.

Step 3 Goodwill is assumed to be the excess of the total capital of the new firm on the basis of new partner's capital over the existing total capital of all the partners.

3. Revaluation of Assets and Reassessment of Liabilities

When a new partner is admitted, it is necessary to revalue the assets and liabilities of the firm. This is because the book value of the assets and liabilities may be different from their market value. It is done in the same manner as in case of change in profit sharing ratio.

4. Accounting Treatment of Reserves, Accumulated (Undistributed) Profits or Losses

The new partner is not entitled to have any share in undistributed profits or losses appearing in the balance sheet at the time of admission, as these are earned by the old partners. So, these should be transferred to old partners' capital/current account.

Journal entries are

(i) **For transfer of reserves, accumulated profits**

General Reserve A/c	Dr	
Reserve Fund A/c	Dr	
Contingency Reserve A/c	Dr	
Profit and Loss A/c	Dr	
Workmen's Compensation Fund A/c	Dr	(Excess of reserve over actual liability)
Investment Fluctuation Fund A/c	Dr	(Excess of reserve over the difference between book value and market value)
To Old Partners' Capital/Current A/c		(Old ratio)

(ii) **For transfer of accumulated losses**

Old Partners' Capital/Current A/c	Dr	(Old ratio)
To Profit and Loss A/c		
To Deferred Revenue Expenditure A/c		
To Advertisement Suspense A/c		

5. Adjustment of Capitals

At the time of admission of a new partner, the partners may agree that their capitals should also be adjusted so as to be proportionate to their profit sharing ratio.

The capitals of partners may be adjusted in any of the following ways

(i) **Adjusting the capitals of old partners on the basis of the capital of incoming partner** (When the total capital of the new firm is not given)

Steps involved in adjusting the capitals of old partners are

***Step* 1** Calculate total capital of firm on the basis of the capital of the new partner.

***Step* 2** Calculate the new capital of each partner, according to the new share.

***Step* 3** Ascertain the present capital of old partners (adjusted).

***Step* 4** Calculate the surplus/deficit capital by comparing step 1 and step 3.

***Step* 5** Surplus capital will be withdrawn and deficit capital will be brought by the partners.

(ii) **Determining the new partner's capital on the basis of combined capital of old partners**

Steps involved in the determination of capital of a new partner are

***Step* 1** Calculate the adjusted old capitals of old partners (after making all the adjustments).

***Step* 2** Calculate the total capital of new a firm.

***Step* 3** Calculate the total capital of a new partner as follows

Total Capital (Step 2) × Share of New Partner

PYQs Previous Years' Questions

1/2 Marks Questions

1. Pooja and Meher are partners in a firm. They admit Rati into the firm on the following terms
   (i) Unrecorded debtors of ₹ 1,000 to be brought into the books.
   (ii) Provision for doubtful debts to be created @ 5% on debtors.
   The recorded debtors in the balance sheet of Pooja and Meher on the date of Rati's admission were ₹ 25,000.
   What will be the net debtors to be shown in the balance sheet of the reconstituted firm? ***ISC 2023***

2. Joy and Deb were partners sharing profits and losses in the ratio of 2:1. They admitted Gopi into partnership for $\frac{1}{5}$ share. At the time of Gopi's admission, furniture (book value ₹ 2,50,000) was reduced by 40% and machinery (book value ₹ 1,50,000) was reduced to 40%. What was the net decrease in value of assets? ***ISC Specimen 2023***

3. Hemal and Rohan are two partners sharing profits and losses in the ratio of 4 : 3. An extract of their balance sheet as at 31st March, 2021, showed

Balance Sheet of Hemal and Rohan (An Extract)
as at 31st March, 2021

Liabilities		Amt (₹)	Assets	Amt (₹)
Workmen Compensation Reserve		28,000	Profit and Loss A/c	28,000
Capital A/cs				
Hemal	40,000			
Rohan	22,000	62,000		

They admit Tanay on 1st April, 2021, as a third partner for 1/3 share in the profits. On the date of Tanay's admission, the goodwill of the firm is valued at ₹ 21,000 and the gain on revaluation of assets and liabilities is ₹ 7,000. Tanay's capital contribution, which is decided as one-half of the combined capitals of Hemal and Rohan, will be ***ISC Sem I 2021***
(a) ₹ 45,000 (b) ₹ 38,000
(c) ₹ 52,000 (d) ₹ 59,000

4. Nitin and Mukul were partners in a business. An extract of the balance sheet of their firm showed

Balance Sheet of Nitin and Mukul (An Extract)
as at 31st March, 2021

Liabilities	Amt (₹)	Assets		Amt (₹)
Creditors	40,000	Land and Building		60,000
		Investments		25,000
		Sundry Debtors	41,000	
		(–) Provision for Doubtful Debts	(3,000)	38,000

On Ali's admission as a new partner on 1st April, 2021, the assets and liabilities of the firm were to be revalued as follows
(i) The investments to be valued at ₹ 27,000.
(ii) Bad debts of ₹ 2,000 to be written-off.
(iii) The provision for doubtful debts to be brought up to 10% of the debtors.
(iv) The value of land and building to be reduced to ₹ 50,000.
(v) Creditors to be discharged at a discount of 10%.

What will be the net effect of revaluation of assets and liabilities? ***ISC Sem I 2021***
(a) Loss of ₹ 8,900 (b) Loss of ₹ 11,900
(c) Loss of ₹ 6,900 (d) Loss of ₹ 7,100

5. Veena and Soma are partners in a firm. They admit Sara on 1st April, 2022, for $\frac{1}{4}$ share in the profits of the firm. Sara acquired her share as 1/12 from Veena and the remaining from Soma. The sacrificing ratio of the old partners will be **ISC Sem I Specimen 2021**

(a) 11 : 12 (b) 1 : 1
(c) 1 : 2 (d) 1 : 11

6. Runa and Ria were partners in a firm sharing profits and losses in the ratio of 3:1. On 1st April, 2020, Uday is admitted as a new partner in the firm for 3/8th share in the profits on various terms, one of them being his contribution of ₹ 42,000 as capital. The new profit sharing ratio amongst all the partners to be 3:2:3.

The capitals of Runa and Ria, after taking into account all the terms of admission were ₹ 61,625 and ₹ 25,375. It is decided that the capital accounts of Runa and Ria be adjusted in the ratio of their respective share in the profits after admission, any surplus to be adjusted through the current account while any deficiency through the cash account. The surplus capital adjusted through current account will be **ISC Sem I Specimen 2021**

(a) Ria's debit capital balance of ₹ 2,625 (b) Runa's credit capital balance of ₹ 2,625
(c) Ria's debit capital balance of ₹ 19,625 (d) Runa's credit capital balance of ₹ 19,625

7. What accounting steps are taken by a partnership firm when a new partner is unable to bring the business guaranteed by him? **ISC 2013, 2004**

8. What is the meaning of the word 'revaluation' in partnership accounts? **ISC 2009**

9. How is goodwill paid privately by an incoming partner treated in books of accounts? **ISC 2006**

10. What is hidden goodwill and how is it calculated? **ISC 2004**

11. Under what circumstances premium for goodwill paid by the incoming partner would never be recorded in the books of accounts? **ISC 2003**

12. What are the adjustments required when a change in the profit sharing ratio takes place in a partnership firm? **ISC 2002**

13. Why are assets and liabilities revalued at the time of admission of a partner? **ISC 2001**

14. Mention the accounting treatment required when the incoming partner brings personal goodwill into the business. **ISC 2000**

3 Marks Questions

15. Veena and Soma are partners in a firm. They admit Sara on 1st April, 2022, for $\frac{1}{4}$th share in the profits of the firm.

On an average, the profits earned by Veena and Soma are ₹ 21,000. The average capital employed by the firm is ₹ 1,50,000. The normal rate of return in the industry is 10%. It is decided to value goodwill on the basis of four years' purchase of profits in excess of profits @ 10% on the money invested.
You are required to
(i) Calculate the goodwill of the firm.
(ii) Pass the journal entries in the books of the firm if Sara brings into the firm her share of goodwill in cash. **ISC Specimen 2023**

16. From the following information, calculate goodwill of the firm of Anmol and Sujay at the time of admission of Dhruv **ISC 2020**

(i) At three years' purchase of super profit.
(ii) On the basis of capitalisation of super profit.
(a) Actual average profits of the firm for the last three years is ₹ 25,000.
(b) Normal rate of return is 10%.

(c)

Balance Sheet of Anmol and Sujay
as at 31st March, 2019

Liabilities		Amt (₹)	Assets	Amt (₹)
Sundry Creditors		40,000	Plant and Machinery	40,000
Bills Payable		10,000	Land and Building	80,000
General Reserve		20,000	Investments (Non-trade)	50,000
Capital A/cs			Sundry Debtors	15,000
Anmol	80,000		Bank	55,000
Sujay	90,000	1,70,000		
		2,40,000		2,40,000

6 Marks Questions

17. Benu and Leena are partners in a firm sharing profits and losses in the ratio of 5 : 3. They admit Deepa and Erica as two new partners. The new profit sharing ratio is decided to be 3 : 2 : 2 : 3. Both the new partners introduce ₹ 1,00,000 each as capital.

Deepa pays ₹ 40,000 in cash for her share of goodwill but Erica is unable to contribute any amount for her share of goodwill. At the time of Deepa's and Erica's admission, the firm had an advertisement suspense account of ₹ 56,000 which is written-off.

You are required to pass necessary journal entries to record the above adjustments at the time of admission of Deepa and Erica. ***ISC 2023***

18. Greg and Rohit are partners in a firm sharing profits and losses in the ratio of 2 : 3. Their balance sheet as at 31st March, 2022, is given below

Balance Sheet of Greg and Rohit
as at 31st March, 2022

Liabilities		Amt (₹)	Assets		Amt (₹)
Sundry Creditors		15,000	Goodwill		10,000
Outstanding Salary		5,000	Office Equipment		37,000
General Reserve		8,000	Sundry Debtors	6,400	
Capital A/cs			(−) Provision for Doubtful Debts	(400)	6,000
Greg	25,000		Cash		10,000
Rohit	10,000	35,000			
		63,000			63,000

On 1st April, 2022, they admit Kunal as a new partner on the following terms

(i) The new profit sharing ratio of Greg, Rohit and Kunal to be 5 : 3 : 2.

(ii) Kunal to bring his share of capital of ₹ 25,000 and his share of goodwill of ₹ 5,000 in cash.

(iii) Office equipment to be valued at ₹ 42,000.

You are required to prepare partners' capital account. ***ISC 2023***

19. Amit and Barun are partners sharing profits in the ratio of 4 : 1. Their balance sheet as at 31st March, 2022, was as under

Balance Sheet of Amit and Barun
as at 31st March, 2022

Liabilities		Amt (₹)	Assets		Amt (₹)
Sundry Creditors		51,000	Furniture		4,000
Capital A/cs			Building		45,000
Amit	20,000		Goodwill		1,000
Barun	15,000	35,000	Debtors	9,400	
			(–) Provision for Doubtful Debts	(400)	9,000
			Cash		27,000
		86,000			86,000

On 1st April, 2022, Charan is admitted as a new partner on the following terms
(i) The new profit sharing ratio of the partners to be 2 : 1 : 1.
(ii) Charan to bring in ₹ 16,000 as his capital but would be unable to bring his share of goodwill in cash.
(iii) The value of the goodwill of the firm to be calculated on the basis of Charan's share in the profits and the capital contributed by him.
(iv) Furniture, which had been undervalued by ₹ 600 to be brought up to its revised value.
(v) Out of the total insurance premium paid, ₹ 3,400 to be treated as prepaid insurance. The amount was earlier debited to profit and loss account.

You are required to prepare
(a) Revaluation account (b) Partners' capital account **ISC Specimen 2023**

20. Karan and Vijay are partners in a firm sharing profits and losses in the ratio of 4 : 3. They admit Shrey for 1/3 share in the profits.

On the date of Shrey's admission
(i) The capitals of Karan and Vijay are: ₹ 40,000 and ₹ 30,000 respectively.
(ii) Profit and loss account has a debit balance of ₹ 7,000.
(iii) General reserve shows a balance of ₹ 21,000 which is not to be disturbed.
(iv) Goodwill of the firm is valued at ₹ 42,000.
(v) The cash at bank is ₹ 15,000.
(vi) Shrey brings in proportionate capital and his share of goodwill in cash.

You are required to prepare
(a) Partners' capital account.
(b) Cash at bank account of the reconstituted firm on the date of Shrey's admission **ISC Specimen 2023**

21. Aditi and Parul are partners in a firm with capitals of ₹ 35,000 each. They shared profits and losses in the ratio of 3 : 1. On 1st April, 2017, they admit Chanda into their partnership with 1/5th share in the profits. Chanda brings in ₹ 40,000 as her capital and her share of goodwill in cash. Her share of godwill is calculated on the basis of her capital contribution and her share of profits in the firm.

At the time of Chanda's admission
(i) The firm had a workman compensation reserve of ₹ 60,000 against which there was a claim of ₹ 20,000.
(ii) Creditors of ₹ 8,000 were paid by Aditi privately for which she is not to be reimbursed.
(iii) There was no change in the value of other assets and liabilities.

You are required to, on the date of Chanda's admission
(a) Calculate the goodwill of the firm. (Show the workings clearly)
(b) Pass the necessary journal entries to record the above transactions **ISC 2019**

22. Anita, Asha and Bashir are partners sharing profits and losses in the ratio of 3 : 2 : 1 respectively. From lst April 2016, they decided to change their profit sharing ratio to 2 : 1 : 3. Their partnership deed provides that in the event of any change in the profit changing ratio, the goodwill of the firm should be valued at two years' purchase of the average super profits for the past three years. The actual profits and losses for the past three years were

2015-16	Profit ₹ 40,000
2014-15	Profit ₹ 30,000
2013-14	Loss ₹ 10,000

The average capital employed in the business was ₹ 1,10,000; the rate of interest expected from capital invested was 10%. You are required to

(i) Calculate the value of goodwill at the time of change in profit sharing ratio. (Show the workings clearly with the formulae).

(ii) Pass the journal entry to record the change. *ISC 2017*

23. Alf and Bert who are partners, decide to admit Steven into partnership on the basis of equal division of profits. The existing partners require some sort of compensation for the admission of Steven as a partner. Steven brings ₹ 5,000 as his capital but he is unable to pay his premium for goodwill, ₹ 1,000 in cash which is due from him.

Suggest various methods by which the existing partners can obtain the compensation they desire under such circumstances, assuming that no goodwill account appears in the books. Give the journal entries you would make to carry out your suggestion. *ISC 2002*

24. Alec and Ben are in partnership as bakers, sharing profits and losses in the ratio of 3 : 2 respectively. Their Balance Sheet on 31st December, 1999 was as follows

Liabilities		Amt (₹)	Assets	Amt (₹)
Capital A/cs			Goodwill	25,000
Alec	40,000		Other Net Assets	75,000
Ben	40,000	80,000		
General Reserve		12,000		
Current Liabilities		8,000		
		1,00,000		1,00,000

On 1st January, 2000 the partners agreed that as Alec wished to take a smaller part in the partnership business, the profit sharing ratio should change to 2 : 3 respectively with a salary of ₹ 10,000 a year to Alec. For the purpose of the change only, they did not however want to alter the book values of goodwill and reserve but recorded the change by passing one single journal entry. You are required to show that single journal entry as at 1st January, 2000. *ISC 2000*

10 Marks Questions

25. Smita and Punita are partners in a firm sharing profits and losses in the ratio of 3:2. Their balance sheet as at 31st March, 2019, is as follows

Balance Sheet of Smita and Punita
as at 31st March, 2019

Liabilities		Amt (₹)	Assets		Amt (₹)
Sundry Creditors		14,000	Cash in Hand		30,000
Bank Loan		6,000	Sundry Debtors	22,000	
General Reserve		10,000	(–) Provision for Doubtful Debts	(2,000)	20,000
Capital A/cs			Furniture		10,000
Smita	30,000		Stock		40,000
Punita	40,000	70,000			
		1,00,000			1,00,000

On 1st April, 2019, Mita is admitted as a new partner on the following terms

(i) The new profit sharing ratio of Smita, Punita and Mita to be 5:3:2.

(ii) Provision for doubtful debts to be raised to 10% of the debtors.

(iii) Punita to take over the firm's investments (not recorded in the books) at ₹ 3,000.

(iv) Goodwill of the firm to be valued at ₹ 50,000. Mita to bring in cash for her share of goodwill.

(v) 50% of the goodwill to be withdrawn by the old partners.

(vi) Mita to pay-off the bank loan on behalf of the firm. The amount due to her by the firm, to be considered as part of her capital contribution.

(vii) Mita to bring in the balance of her capital in cash, so as to make her capital equal to 1/5th of the total capital of the firm.

You are required to

(a) Pass journal entries at the time of Mita's admission.

(b) Prepare the balance sheet of the reconstituted firm.

ISC 2020

KEY IDEA

Partners' taking assets will be debited to partners' capital account.

26. Annie and Bonnie are partners in a firm, sharing profit and loss equally. Their balance sheet as at 31st March, 2017 was as follows

Balance Sheet of Annie and Bonnie
as at 31st March, 2017

Liabilities		Amt (₹)	Assets		Amt (₹)
Sundry Creditors		21,000	Cash at Bank		20,000
General Reserve		15,000	Sundry Debtors	22,000	
Capital A/cs			(–) Provision for Doubtful Debts	(1,000)	21,000
Annie	45,000		Stock		10,000
Bonnie	40,000	85,000	Plant and Machinery		60,000
			Goodwill		10,000
		1,21,000			1,21,000

Carl was to be taken as a partner for 1/4th share in the profits of the firm, with effect from 1st April, 2017, on the following terms

(i) Bad debts amounting to ₹ 1,500 to be written-off.

(ii) Stock to be taken over by Annie at ₹ 12,000.

(iii) Plant and machinery to be valued at ₹ 50,000.

(iv) Goodwill of the firm to be valued at ₹ 20,000.

(v) Carl has to bring in ₹ 50,000 as his capital. He was unable to bring in cash his share of goodwill.

(vi) General reserve not to be distributed. For this, it was decided that Carl would compensate the old partners through his current account.

You are required to

(a) Pass journal entries on the date of Carl's admission.

(b) Prepare the balance sheet of the reconstituted firm.

ISC 2018

KEY IDEA

General reserve not distributed will be debited to gaining partners' capital account and credited to sacrificing partners' capital account.

27. Juliet and Rabani are partners in a firm, sharing profits and losses in the ratio of 3 : 1. On 31st March, 2016, their balance sheet was as under

Balance Sheet of Juliet and Rabani
as at 31st March, 2016

Liabilities		Amt (₹)	Assets		Amt (₹)
Sundry Creditors		70,000	Plant and Machinery		1,76,000
General Reserve		30,000	Inventory		26,000
Provident Fund		40,000	Sundry Debtors	57,000	
Capital A/cs			(–) Provision for Doubtful Debts	(3,000)	54,000
Juliet	1,10,000		Cash at Bank		68,000
Rabani	90,000	2,00,000	Profit and Loss A/c		16,000
		3,40,000			3,40,000

Mike was taken as a partner for $\frac{1}{4}$th share, with effect from 1st April, 2016, subject to the following adjustments

(i) Plant and machinery was found to be overvalued by ₹ 16,000. It was to be shown in the books at the correct value.

(ii) Provision for doubtful debts was to be reduced by ₹ 2,000.

(iii) Creditors included an amount of ₹ 2,000 received as commission from Malini. The necessary adjustment was required to be made.

(iv) Goodwill of the firm was valued at ₹ 60,000. Mike was to bring in cash, his share of goodwill alongwith the capital of ₹ 1,00,000.

(v) Capital accounts of Juliet and Rabani were to be readjusted in the new profit sharing arrangement on the basis of Mike's capital, any surplus to be adjusted through current account and any deficiency through cash.

You are required to prepare

(a) Revaluation account (b) Partners' capital account

(c) Balance sheet of the reconstituted firm **ISC 2017**

> **KEY IDEA**
> Revenue included in creditors will not result in reassessment of liabilities.

28. Divya and Pooja are partners in a firm, sharing profits and losses in the ratio of 3 : 2. On 31st March, 2015, their balance sheet was as under

Balance Sheet
as at 31st March, 2015

Liabilities		Amt (₹)	Assets	Amt (₹)
Sundry Creditors		9,800	Goodwill	16,000
General Reserve		23,400	Land and Building	20,000
Profit and Loss A/c		4,000	Investments	66,000
Investment Fluctuation Fund		12,600	Sundry Debtors	18,600
Capital A/cs			Bills Receivables	7,400
Divya	60,000		Cash in Hand	11,100
Pooja	40,000	1,00,000	Advertisement Suspense A/c	10,700
		1,49,800		1,49,800

The partners decided that with effect from 1st April, 2015, they would share profits and losses equally.
For this purpose, they decided that

(i) Investments to be valued at ₹ 60,000. (ii) Goodwill to be valued at ₹ 24,000.

(iii) General reserve not to be distributed between the partners.

You are required to

(a) Pass journal entries. (b) Prepare the revised balance sheet of the firm. **ISC 2016**

29. Gautam and Rahul are partners in a firm, sharing profits and losses in the ratio of 2 : 3. Their balance sheet as at 31st March, 2014, was as follows

Balance Sheet
as at 31st March, 2014

Liabilities		Amt (₹)	Assets		Amt (₹)
Sundry Creditors		5,000	Goodwill		10,000
Bills Payable		15,000	Furniture		25,000
General Reserve		10,000	Stock		15,000
Capital A/cs			Sundry Debtors	12,000	
Gautam	30,000		(–) Provision for Doubtful Debts	(2,000)	10,000
Rahul	40,000	70,000	Cash in Hand		40,000
		1,00,000			1,00,000

Karim was to be taken as a partner with effect from 1st April, 2014, on the following terms

(i) The new profit sharing ratio of Gautam, Rahul and Karim would be 5:3:2.
(ii) Provision for doubtful debts would be raised to 20% of debtors.
(iii) Karim would bring in cash, his share of capital of ₹ 40,000 and his share of goodwill valued at ₹ 10,000.
(iv) Gautam would take over the furniture at ₹ 22,000.

You are required to

(a) Pass journal entries at the time of Karim's admission.
(b) Prepare the balance sheet of the reconstituted firm. *ISC 2015*

30. Sim, Tim and Jim are partners sharing profits and losses equally. Their Balance Sheet as at 31st March, 2012 stood as follows

Liabilities		Amt (₹)	Assets	Amt (₹)
Capital A/cs			Building	2,00,000
Sim	2,50,000		Plant and Machinery	1,00,000
Tim	2,00,000		Patent and Copyrights	1,50,000
Jim	1,50,000	6,00,000	Stock	1,25,000
Creditors		1,40,000	Debtors	1,50,000
General Reserve		60,000	Bank	75,000
		8,00,000		8,00,000

From 1st April, 2012 the partners decided to share profits and losses in the ratio of 3 : 2 : 1 and for that purpose, the following revised value of assets were agreed upon

Building ₹ 2,75,000, plant and machinery ₹ 90,000, patents and copyrights ₹ 1,32,500, stock ₹ 2,00,000, prepaid insurance ₹ 5,000 and debtors ₹ 1,42,500. Goodwill of the firm was valued at ₹ 60,000. Partners decide not to disturb the reserves. Also, they decide not to record the revised values of assets in the books of accounts.

You are required to prepare

(i) Partners' capital accounts.
(ii) Balance sheet of the re-constituted firm. (Show your workings clearly) *ISC 2013*

31. Neha and Tara are partners in a firm sharing profits and losses in the ratio of 3 : 2. Their balance sheet on 31st March, 2012, stood as follows

Balance Sheet
as at 31st March, 2012

Liabilities		Amt (₹)	Assets		Amt (₹)
Capital A/cs			Plant and Machinery		12,000
Neha	8,000		Land and Building		14,000
Tara	10,000	18,000	Debtors	19,000	
General Reserve		12,000	(–) Provision for Doubtful Debts	(4,000)	15,000

Liabilities	Amt (₹)	Assets	Amt (₹)
Workmen's Compensation Fund	5,000	Stock	6,000
Creditors	15,000	Cash	3,000
	50,000		50,000

They agreed to admit Prachi into partnership for 1/5th share of profits on 1st April, 2012, on the following terms

(i) All debtors to be considered as good and therefore the provision for doubtful debts to be written back.
(ii) Value of land and building to be increased to ₹ 18,000.
(iii) Value of plant and machinery to be reduced by ₹ 2,000.
(iv) The liability against workmen compensation fund is determined at ₹ 2,000 which is to be paid later in the year.
(v) Prachi to bring in her share of goodwill of ₹ 10,000 in cash.
(vi) She will further bring in cash so as to make her capital equal to 20% of the total capital of the new firm. (Show your workings clearly)

You are required to prepare

(a) Revaluation account.
(b) Partners' capital accounts.
(c) Balance sheet of the reconstituted firm. **ISC 2013**

32. David and Bimal are partners, sharing profits and losses in the ratio of 3 : 2. Their balance sheet as at 31st March, 2010, was as follows

Balance Sheet
as at 31st March, 2010

Liabilities		Amt (₹)	Assets		Amt (₹)
Sundry Creditors		82,000	Cash		32,000
General Reserve		3,000	Stock		15,000
Capital A/cs			Debtors	9,400	
David	18,000		(–) Provision for Doubtful Debts	(400)	9,000
Bimal	12,000	30,000	Building		55,000
			Furniture		4,000
		1,15,000			1,15,000

They admitted Chander as a new partner on 1st April, 2010 and the new profit sharing ratio became 5 :3 :2. Chander introduced a capital of ₹ 16,000. Chander was unable to bring any cash for goodwill and so it was decided to value the goodwill on the basis of his share in the profits and the capital contributed by him. The following revaluations were made at the time of Chander's admission

(i) Stock had been overvalued by ₹ 750 and furniture by ₹ 500.
(ii) Provision for doubtful debts to be increased by ₹ 100.
(iii) A creditor for ₹ 2,350 was paid off by Bimal privately for which he was not to be reimbursed.

Prepare the revaluation account, partners' capital accounts and a balance sheet of the new firm on the date of Chander's admission. Show your workings clearly. **ISC 2011**

33. Lucy, Rahul and Sanjay are partners sharing profits and losses in the ratio of 1 : 2 : 3. Arun is admitted as a partner who brings in ₹ 20,000 as his capital for 1/5th share in the profit. Goodwill of the firm is to be valued at an average of the last three years profits which were ₹ 25,000, ₹ 28,000 and ₹ 37,000 respectively. Arun is unable to bring in cash towards his share of premium for goodwill.

Give the journal entries if goodwill already appears in the books at ₹ 24,000. **ISC 2010**

34. The following is the Balance Sheet of James and Dias as at 31st December, 2007.

Liabilities		Amt (₹)	Assets	Amt (₹)
Capital A/cs			Land	6,000
James	60,000		Building	40,000
Dias	40,000	1,00,000	Furniture	4,000
Creditors		18,000	Stock	25,000
			Investment	16,000
			Bank	15,000
			Cash	12,000
		1,18,000		1,18,000

The partners shared profits and losses in the ratio of 3 : 2. From 1st January, 2008, they agreed to share profits and losses equally. For this purpose, the following particulars are provided

(i) Building is to be appreciated by 25%.

(ii) Current value of furniture is to be taken at ₹ 3,000.

(iii) Land is valued at ₹ 15,000.

(iv) Stock is valued at ₹ 30,000.

Prepare a revaluation account, partners' capital accounts and the revised balance sheet as at 1st January, 2008. *ISC 2008*

35. Angad and Vivek are partners in a firm sharing profits and losses in the ratio of 3 : 2. Their balance sheet as at 1st January, 2005 stood as follows

Balance Sheet
as at 1st January, 2005

Liabilities		Amt (₹)	Assets	Amt (₹)
General Reserve		10,000	Debtors	18,000
Creditors		15,000	Stock	20,000
Capital A/cs			Furniture	10,000
Angad	30,000		Plant	30,000
Vivek	25,000	55,000	Cash	2,000
		80,000		80,000

Gopal is admitted as a partner on the above date on the following terms

(i) He will pay ₹ 10,000 towards goodwill for 1/4th share in profits.

(ii) The assets are to be revalued as Plant ₹ 32,000; Stock ₹ 18,000.

(iii) A provision for bad debts at 5% on debtors has to be created.

(iv) A sum of ₹ 1,400 included in creditors is not to be paid. There is an unrecorded liability for ₹ 5,000 which is to be recorded in the books.

(v) Gopal is to bring in ₹ 20,000 as capital. The capitals of the other partners is to be adjusted in the new profit sharing ratio. For this purpose current accounts are to be opened.

Prepare

(a) The capital accounts of Angad, Vivek and Gopal.

(b) The balance sheet of the new firm. *ISC 2007*

36. X, Y and Z are partners sharing profits and losses in the ratio of 2 : 2 : 1 respectively. Their balance sheet as on 31st March, 2003 is as given below

Balance Sheet
as at 31st March, 2003

Liabilities		Amt (₹)	Assets	Amt (₹)
Sundry Creditors		51,400	Land and Building	1,00,000
Outstanding Liabilities		6,000	Furniture	26,000
General Reserve		26,000	Stock	47,000
Capital A/cs			Sundry Debtors	22,000
X	48,000		Cash	4,400
Y	48,000			
Z	20,000	1,16,000		
		1,99,400		1,99,400

The partners decided to admit Mr T as a partner with effect from 1st April, 2003, on the following terms

(i) Mr T will bring ₹ 20,000 as capital and ₹ 10,000 as his share of goodwill.
(ii) Mr T could bring only ₹ 2,500 as goodwill in cash.
(iii) The value of stock should be increased by ₹ 10,000. The furniture should be depreciated by 10% and the value of land and building should be enhanced by 20%.
(iv) Provision for doubtful debts should be made at 10% of the debtors.
(v) The outstanding liability includes ₹ 2,000 due to Mr R which has been paid by Mr X privately. Necessary entry is to be passed to reimburse Mr X before admitting the new partner.
(vi) The new profit sharing ratio between X, Y, Z and T is 5:5:3:2.
(vii) Creditors include ₹ 5,000 received as commission from Mr A.
(viii) Partners decided not to show goodwill in the books of the new firm.

Give necessary journal entries to incorporate the above changes. Also prepare capital accounts of partners and balance sheet of the new firm. ***ISC 2004 Modified***

Case Based Questions

37. Dev and Dhruv are partners sharing profits in the ratio of 5 : 4. An extract of the balance sheet of their firm showed

Balance Sheet of Dev and Dhruv (An Extract)
as at 31st March, 2021

Liabilities		Amt (₹)	Assets	Amt (₹)
Creditors		60,000	Advertisement Suspense A/c	9,000
Capital A/cs				
Dev	80,000			
Dhruv	79,000	1,59,000		

On Rahul's admission as a new partner, the new profit sharing ratio is agreed to be 3 : 2 : 1. Rahul brings in ₹ 60,000 as his capital but he is unable to bring his share of goodwill in cash. ***ISC Sem I 2021***

(i) What will be the value of non-purchased goodwill of the firm, based on Rahul's share in the profits and the capital contributed by him?
(a) ₹ 1,45,000 (b) ₹ 1,59,000 (c) ₹ 1,50,000 (d) ₹ 2,01,000

(ii) What will be the entry to record Rahul's share in the firm's goodwill?
(a) Debit Rahul's Current A/c; Credit the Current Accounts of Dev and Dhruv in the ratio of 5 : 4
(b) Debit Rahul's Current A/c; Credit the Capital Accounts of Dev and Dhruv in the ratio of 1 : 2
(c) Debit Rahul's Current A/c; Credit the Capital Accounts of Dev and Dhruv in the ratio of 5 : 4
(d) Debit Rahul's Capital A/c; Credit the Current Accounts of Dev and Dhruv in the ratio of 1 : 2

(iii) A bill of exchange for 3 months drawn by a creditor of ₹ 37,000 was accepted by the firm. What will be the entry to record this transaction?
(a) Debit Creditor's A/c ₹ 37,000; Credit Revaluation A/c ₹ 37,000
(b) Debit Creditor's A/c ₹ 37,000; Credit Bills Receivable A/c ₹ 37,000
(c) Debit Bills Payable A/c ₹ 37,000; Credit Creditor' A/c ₹ 37,000
(d) Debit Creditor's A/c ₹ 37,000; Credit Bills Payable A/c ₹ 37,000

(iv) Advertisement suspense account will be written-off from
(a) Dev's Current A/c ₹ 5,000; Dhruv's Current A/c ₹ 4,000
(b) Dev's Capital A/c ₹ 3,000; Dhruv's Capital A/c ₹ 6,000
(c) Dev's Capital A/c ₹ 5,000; Dhruv's Capital A/c ₹ 4,000
(d) Dev's Capital A/c ₹ 4,500; Dhruv's Capital A/c ₹ 3,000; Rahul's Capital A/c ₹ 1,500

38. Dev, Gautam and Kamal were three partners sharing profits and losses in the ratio of 2 : 1 : 2. On 1st April, 2020, their capital account balances stood at ₹ 90,000, ₹ 80,000 and ₹ 20,000 (Dr) respectively. On this date they admitted Naveen into the partnership with a capital of ₹ 50,000. Naveen is to have 1/4 share of the profits with a guaranteed minimum share of distributable profit of ₹ 40,000. The new profit sharing ratio among the partners being Dev : Gautam : Kamal : Naveen = 6 : 2 : 7 : 5. The profit of the firm for the year 2020-21 was ₹ 1,60,000 before the following adjustments were made

- Interest on capital @ 10% per annum to be allowed to the partners.
- Interest on drawings Dev ₹ 3,000; Kamal ₹ 6,000.
- Salary to Partners Gautam ₹ 7,000; Naveen ₹ 10,000. ***ISC Sem I Specimen 2021***

(i) The sacrificing ratio of Dev, Gautam and Kamal will be
(a) 2:1:2 (b) 2:2:1 (c) 2: -2: 1 (d) 2: -1:2

(ii) The total interest on capital allowed by the firm to the partners will be
(a) ₹ 22,000 (b) ₹ 23,000 (c) ₹ 21,400 (d) ₹ 23,100

(iii) Deficiency in Naveen's profits will be
(a) ₹ 8,000 (b) ₹ 7,500 (c) ₹ 12,500 (d) ₹ 12,000

39. Ritesh and Somesh are partners in a firm sharing profits and losses equally. They admit Satvik on 1st April, 2021 for 1/5th share in the profits of the firm, future profit shring ratio between Ritesh and Somesh would be 3 : 2.

At the time of reconstitution of a partnership firm, goodwill was valued at two years' purchase of the average profits of the preceeding four years which were as follows ***ISC Sem I Specimen 2021***

Year	Profit/Loss	
2017-18	Profit ₹ 70,000	(after debting loss of stock by fire ₹ 15,000)
2018-19	Profit ₹ 50,000	(including insurance claim of ₹ 5,000)
2019-20	Loss ₹ 40,000	(after debting voluntary retirement compensation paid ₹ 20,000)
2021-21	Profit ₹ 60,000	(excluding insurance premium of ₹ 10,000 on insurance of assets)

(i) The average profits of the firm from the year 2017-18 to the year 2020-21 were
(a) ₹ 30,000 (b) ₹ 60,000 (c) ₹ 37,500 (d) ₹ 40,000

(ii) The value of goodwill of the firm on Satvik's admission was
(a) ₹ 60,000 (b) ₹ 80,000 (c) ₹ 75,000 (d) ₹ 1,20,000

(iii) Satvik is unable to bring in cash his share of goodwill. The account to be debited to record his goodwill compensation will be
(a) Satvik's Capital A/c
(b) Satvik's Current A/c
(c) Premium for Goodwill A/c
(d) Old Partners' Capital A/c

40. Dhruv and Ansh are partners in a firm sharing profits and losses Dhruv 75% and Ansh 25%. Their balance sheet as at 31st March, 2021 is given below *ISC Sem I Specimen 2021*

Balance Sheet of Dhruv and Ansh
as at 31st March, 2021

Liabilities		Amt (₹)	Assets		Amt (₹)
Sundry Creditors		49,000	Cash		62,000
Workmen Compensation Reserve		5,000	Sundry Debtors	18,500	
Capital A/cs			(−) Provision for Doubtful Debts	(1,500)	17,000
Dhruv	30,000		Land and Building		25,000
Ansh	20,000	50,000			
		1,04,000			1,04,000

On 1st April, 2021, Kavi is admitted as a new partner on the following items
(a) Land and building is found to be valued at 25% above cost. It is decided to bring it to its cost.
(b) Bad debts amounting to ₹ 1,800 are to be written-off. The remaining debtors are good.
(c) Creditors include an amount of ₹ 5,000 received as commission from Amar. The necessary adjustment is required to be made.
(d) The liability on workmen compensation reserve is determined at ₹ 3,000.
(e) Kavi is to pay ₹ 15,000 to the existing partners as premium for goodwill for 20% of the future profits of the firm. He is also to bring in ₹ 25,000 as capital.

(i) At the time of Kavi's admission, the workmen compensation reserve of
(a) ₹ 5,000 will be credited to the capital accounts of all the partners
(b) ₹ 3,000 will be credited to the capital accounts of all the partners
(c) ₹ 2,000 will be credited to the capital accounts of all the partners
(d) ₹ 2,000 will be debited to the capital accounts of all the partners

(ii) The value of land and building in the balance sheet of the reconstituted firm will be
(a) ₹ 20,000
(b) ₹ 31,250
(c) ₹ 5,000
(d) ₹ 6,250

(iii) To adjust the creditors in adjustment (c)
(a) Commission account will be credited with ₹ 5,000
(b) Creditors account will be credited with ₹ 5,000
(c) Amar's account will be debited with ₹ 5,000
(d) Creditors account will be debited with ₹ 5,000

(iv) The provision for doubtful debts in the reconstituted firm will be
(a) ₹ 1,500
(b) ₹ 1,800
(c) ₹ Nil
(d) None of these

(v) The date of the balance sheet of the reconstituted firm will be
(a) Balance sheet for the year ending 31st March, 2022
(b) Balance sheet as at 31st March, 2021
(c) Balance sheet for the year ending 1st April, 2021
(d) Balance sheet as at 1st April, 2021

Explanations

1. Debtors after unrecorded debtors brought into the books $= 25{,}000 + 1{,}000 = ₹\,26{,}000$

Provision for doubtful debts $= 26{,}000 \times \frac{5}{100} = ₹\,1{,}300$

Net debtors $= 26{,}000 - 1{,}300 = ₹\,24{,}700$

2. Net decrease in the value of assets $= 2{,}50{,}000 \times \frac{40}{100} + 1{,}50{,}000 \times \frac{60}{100}$

$= 1{,}00{,}000 + 90{,}000$

$= ₹\ 1{,}90{,}000$

3. (b) Tanay's capital contribution $= \frac{40{,}000 + 22{,}000 + 7{,}000 + 7{,}000}{2}$

$= \frac{76{,}000}{2} = ₹\ 38{,}000$

4. (c) Net effect of revaluation $= 2{,}000 + (2{,}000) + (900) + (10{,}000) + 4{,}000 = ₹\ (6{,}900)$

5. (c) Veena's Sacrifice $= \frac{1}{12}$; Soma's Sacrifice $= \frac{1}{4} - \frac{1}{12} = \frac{2}{12}$; Sacrificing Ratio $= 1:2$

6. (d) Total Capital of the New Firm = New Partners' Capital × Reverse of His Share

$= 42{,}000 \times \frac{8}{3} = ₹\,1{,}12{,}000$

Runa's new capital $= 1{,}12{,}000 \times \frac{3}{8} = ₹\ 42{,}000$

Runa's old capital $= ₹\,61{,}625$

Runa's surplus capital $= 61{,}625 - 42{,}000 = ₹\,19{,}625$

7. In case a new partner is unable to bring the business guaranteed by him, his capital account is debited and profit and loss appropriation account is credited with the guaranteed amount or any shortfall in guaranteed amount. The journal entry is

New Partner's Capital A/c Dr

To Profit and Loss Appropriation A/c

8. Revaluation means revaluing the assets and liabilities of the partnership firm. Revaluation is done at the time of reconstitution of the partnership firm and it is done by preparing a revaluation account.

9. In case a new partner pays premium to the old partners privately or directly or outside the business, it will not be recorded in the books of accounts because it is an out of business transaction.

10. Hidden goodwill is the excess of desired total capital of the firm over the actual combined capital of all partners. The following steps will be taken for calculating hidden goodwill

Step 1 Find out the total capital of the new firm on the basis of the capital brought in by new partner, for his share.

Step 2 Ascertain the existing total capital of the new firm by adding the capital of all partners, including new partner's capital after adjustments.

Step 3 Goodwill is assumed to be the excess of the total capital of the new firm on the basis of new partner's capital over the existing total capital of all the partners.

11. When the incoming partner pays goodwill to old partners privately, it is never recorded in the books of accounts.

12. The adjustments required at the time of change in profit sharing ratio are

(i) Determination of sacrificing ratio and gaining ratio.

(ii) Accounting treatment of goodwill.

(iii) Revaluation of assets and reassessment of liabilities.

(iv) Accounting treatment of accumulated profits and reserves.

13. Assets and liabilities are revalued at the time of admission of a partner because the profit or loss arising on account of change in value of assets and liabilities belongs to the old partners. Thus, the result on account of such revaluation will be distributed only to the old partners in old profit sharing ratio.

14. When the incoming partner introduces personal goodwill in the firm, it will be treated as purchase of goodwill. Following entry will be passed for it

Goodwill A/c Dr

To New Partner's Capital A/c

However after recording the goodwill, it must be written-off. Thus, following entry will be passed for it

All Partners' Capital A/c (including new partner) Dr

To Goodwill A/c (in new ratio)

15. (i) Normal profit $= 1{,}50{,}000 \times \frac{10}{100} = ₹\ 15{,}000$

Goodwill = Super Profit × Number of Years' of Purchase $= (21{,}000 - 15{,}000) \times 4 = ₹\ 24{,}000$

(ii) Sara's share in goodwill $= 24{,}000 \times \frac{1}{4} = ₹\ 6{,}000$

JOURNAL

Date	Particulars		LF	Amt (Dr)	Amt (Cr)
	Cash A/c	Dr		6,000	
	To Goodwill A/c				6,000
	(Being goodwill brought in by Sara in cash)				

16. Capital Invested = Anmol's Capital + Sujay's Capital + General Reserve

$= 80{,}000 + 90{,}000 + 20{,}000 = ₹\ 1{,}90{,}000$

Normal Profit $= \frac{\text{Capital Invested} \times \text{Normal Rate}}{100} = \frac{1{,}90{,}000 \times 10}{100} = ₹\ 19{,}000$

Super Profit = Actual Average Profits − Normal Profit

$= 25{,}000 - 19{,}000 = ₹\ 6{,}000$

(i) Goodwill = Super Profit × No. of Years' Purchased $= 6{,}000 \times 3 = ₹\ 18{,}000$

(ii) Goodwill = Super Profit $\times \frac{100}{\text{Normal Rate of Return}} = ₹\ 60{,}000$

17. **JOURNAL**

Date	Particulars		LF	Amt (Dr)	Amt (Cr)
	Cash A/c	Dr		2,40,000	
	To Deepa's Capital A/c				1,00,000
	To Erica's Capital A/c				1,00,000
	To Premium for Goodwill A/c				40,000
	(Being new partners bring capital and goodwill in cash)				
	Erica's Current A/c	Dr		60,000	
	Premium for Goodwill A/c	Dr		40,000	
	To Benu's Capital A/c				65,000
	To Leena's Capital A/c				35,000
	(Being goodwill distributed among sacrificing partners)				
	Benu's Capital A/c	Dr		35,000	
	Leena's Capital A/c	Dr		21,000	
	To Advertisement Suspense A/c				56,000
	(Being advertisement suspense written-off)				

Working Notes

1. Goodwill of the firm = $40{,}000 \times \frac{10}{2}$ = ₹ 2,00,000; Erica's share of goodwill = $2{,}00{,}000 \times \frac{3}{10}$ = ₹ 60,000

2. **Sacrificing Ratio**

Benu = $\frac{5}{8}-\frac{3}{10}=\frac{25-12}{40}=\frac{13}{40}$; Leena = $\frac{3}{8}-\frac{2}{10}=\frac{15-8}{40}=\frac{7}{40}$

∴ Sacrificing ratio = 13 : 7

18. Dr **Partners' Capital Account** Cr

Particulars	Greg (₹)	Rohit (₹)	Kunal (₹)	Particulars	Greg (₹)	Rohit (₹)	Kunal (₹)
To Goodwill	4,000	6,000	—	By Balance b/d	25,000	10,000	—
To Rohit's Capital A/c (Goodwill)	2,500	—	—	By Cash A/c	—	—	25,000
To Balance c/d	23,700	19,300	25,000	By Premium for Goodwill	—	5,000	—
				By Revaluation A/c	2,000	3,000	—
				By General Reserve	3,200	4,800	—
				By Greg's Capital A/c (Goodwill)	—	2,500	—
	30,200	25,300	25,000		30,200	25,300	25,000

Working Notes

1. Dr **Revaluation Account** Cr

Particulars		Amt (₹)	Particulars	Amt (₹)
To Revaluation Profit			By Office Equipment	5,000
Greg's Capital A/c	2,000			
Rohit's Capital A/c	3,000	5,000		
		5,000		5,000

2. Sacrificing Ratio

Greg = $\frac{2}{5}-\frac{5}{10}=-\frac{1}{10}$ (Gain); Rohit = $\frac{3}{5}-\frac{3}{10}=\frac{3}{10}$ (Sacrifice)

3. Goodwill of the firm = $5{,}000 \times \frac{10}{2}$ = ₹ 25,000; Greg's Goodwill = $25{,}000 \times \frac{1}{10}$ = ₹ 2,500

19. Dr **Revaluation Account** Cr

Particulars		Amt (₹)	Particulars	Amt (₹)
To Profit on Revaluation			By Furniture A/c	600
Amit's Capital A/c	3,200		By Prepaid Insurance	3,400
Barun's Capital A/c	800	4,000		
		4,000		4,000

Dr **Partners' Capital Account** Cr

Particulars	Amit (₹)	Barun (₹)	Charan (₹)	Particulars	Amit (₹)	Barun (₹)	Charan (₹)
To Goodwill A/c	800	200	—	By Balance b/d	20,000	15,000	—
To Amit's Capital A/c	—	650	3,250	By Cash A/c	—	—	16,000
To Balance c/d	26,300	14,950	12,750	By Revaluation A/c	3,200	800	—
				By Charan's Capital A/c	3,250	—	—
				By Barun's Capital A/c	650	—	—
	27,100	15,800	16,000		27,100	15,800	16,000

Working Notes

1. **Calculation of Charan's Share of Goodwill**

$$\text{Goodwill} = \left(16{,}000 \times \frac{4}{1}\right) - (20{,}000 + 15{,}000 + 16{,}000) = ₹\ 13{,}000$$

$$\text{Charan's share} = 13{,}000 \times \frac{1}{4} = ₹\ 3{,}250$$

2. **Calculation of Sacrificing Ratio**

Sacrificing Ratio = Old Ratio – New Ratio

$$\text{Amit} = \frac{4}{5} - \frac{2}{4} = \frac{16-10}{20} = \frac{6}{20}; \qquad \text{Barun} = \frac{1}{5} - \frac{1}{4} = \frac{4-5}{20} = \left(\frac{1}{20}\right)$$

$\therefore$ Amount of goodwill to be paid by the gaining partner i.e. Barun $= 13{,}000 \times \frac{1}{20} = ₹\ 650$

JOURNAL

Date	Particulars		LF	Amt (Dr)	Amt (Cr)
	Charan's Capital A/c	Dr		3,250	
	Barun's Capital A/c	Dr		650	
	To Amit's Capital A/c				3,900
	(Being the goodwill credited to sacrificing partner in the sacrificing ratio)				

Common Mistake Students usually forget to write-off goodwill appearing in the balance sheet. Make sure to write-off goodwill appearing on the asset side of balance sheet.

20. (a) Dr **Partners' Capital Account** Cr

Particulars	Karan (₹)	Vijay (₹)	Shrey (₹)	Particulars	Karan (₹)	Vijay (₹)	Shrey (₹)
To Profit and Loss A/c	4,000	3,000	—	By Balance b/d	40,000	30,000	—
To Balance c/d	44,000	33,000	35,000	By Bank A/c	—	—	35,000
				By Goodwill A/c	8,000	6,000	—
	48,000	36,000	35,000		48,000	36,000	35,000

(b) Dr **Cash at Bank Account** Cr

Particulars	LF	Amt (₹)	Particulars	LF	Amt (₹)
To Balance b/d		15,000	By Balance c/d		64,000
To Shrey's Capital A/c		35,000			
To Goodwill A/c		14,000			
		64,000			64,000

Working Notes

1. Calculation of Total Capital of a Firm

$$\text{Remaining share of profits of firm} = 1 - \frac{1}{3} = \frac{2}{3}$$

$$\text{Total capital of a firm} = (40{,}000 + 30{,}000) \times \frac{3}{2} = ₹\ 1{,}05{,}000$$

2. Shrey's capital $= 1{,}05{,}000 \times \frac{1}{3} = ₹\ 35{,}000$

3. Shrey's share of goodwill $= 42{,}000 \times \frac{1}{3} = ₹\ 14{,}000$

4. Calculation of new profit sharing ratio

Karan $= \frac{4}{7} \times \frac{2}{3} = \frac{8}{21}$; Vijay $= \frac{3}{7} \times \frac{2}{3} = \frac{6}{21}$; Shrey $= \frac{1}{3} \times \frac{7}{7} = \frac{7}{21}$

New Ratio = 8 : 6 : 7

5. Calculation of sacrificing ratio

Karan $= \frac{4}{7} - \frac{8}{21} = \frac{12-8}{21} = \frac{4}{21}$; Vijay $= \frac{3}{7} - \frac{6}{21} = \frac{9-6}{21} = \frac{3}{21}$

Common Mistake Students usually get confused between debit and credit balance of profit and loss account. It should be remembered that debit balance of profit and loss account represents net loss.

21. (a) **Calculation of Goodwill**

$\frac{1}{5}$th share capital = ₹ 40,000

Total Capital = 40,000 × 5 = ₹ 2,00,000

Firms actual capital = 35,000 + 35,000 + 40,000 = ₹ 1,10,000

Firms goodwill = 2,00,000 – 1,10,000 = ₹ 90,000

Chanda's share of goodwill = $90{,}000 \times \frac{1}{5}$ = ₹18,000

(b) **JOURNAL**

Date	Particulars		LF	Amt (Dr)	Amt (Cr)
	Cash A/c	Dr		58,000	
	To Chanda's Capital A/c				40,000
	To Premium for Goodwill A/c				18,000
	(Being the amount brought in by Chanda as per capital and 1/5th share of goodwill)				
	Premium for Goodwill A/c	Dr		18,000	
	To Aditi's Capital A/c				13,500
	To Parul's Capital A/c				4,500
	(Being premium for goodwill distributed among old partner in sacrificing ratio)				
	Workmen Compensation Reserve A/c	Dr		40,000	
	To Aditi's Capital A/c				30,000
	To Parul's Capital A/c				10,000
	(Being amount of workmen compensation reserve credited to old partners)				
	Creditors A/c	Dr		8,000	
	To Aditi's Capital A/c				8,000
	(Being creditors taken over by Aditi)				

22. (i) **Valuation of Goodwill**

Average profits of last three years $= \frac{40{,}000 + 30{,}000 - 10{,}000}{3}$ = ₹ 20,000

Average capital employed = ₹ 1,10,000

Expected rate of interest = 10%

Normal Profit = Average Capital Employed × Expected Rate of Return = $1{,}10{,}000 \times \frac{10}{100}$ = ₹ 11,000

Super Profit = Average Profit – Normal Profit = 20,000 – 11,000 = ₹ 9,000

Goodwill = Super Profit × Number of Years' Purchase = 9,000 × 2 = ₹ 18,000

(ii)

In the Books of Anita, Asha and Bashir

JOURNAL

Date	Particulars		LF	Amt (Dr)	Amt (Cr)
2016 Apr 1	Bashir's Capital A/c	Dr		6,000	
	To Anita's Capital A/c				3,000
	To Asha's Capital A/c				3,000
	(Being goodwill adjusted at the time of change in profit sharing ratio)				

Working Note

Old ratio = 3:2:1; New ratio = 2:1:3

Sacrificing/(Gaining) Ratio = Old Share – New Share

Anita $= \frac{3}{6} - \frac{2}{6} = \frac{1}{6}$; Asha $= \frac{2}{6} - \frac{1}{6} = \frac{1}{6}$; Bashir $= \frac{1}{6} - \frac{3}{6} = \frac{2}{6}$

So, Bashir's capital account will be debited by ₹ 6,000 $(18{,}000 \times 2/6)$ and Anita's and Asha's capital accounts will be credited by ₹ 3,000 $(18{,}000 \times 1/6)$ each.

23.

In the Books of Alf and Bert

JOURNAL

Date	Particulars		LF	Amt (Dr)	Amt (Cr)
	Bank A/c	Dr		5,000	
	To Steven's Capital A/c				5,000
	(Being the amount brought in by Steven as capital)				
	Steven's Current A/c	Dr		1,000	
	To Alf's Capital A/c				500
	To Bert's Capital A/c				500
	(Being premium adjusted with old partner's capital account in sacrificing ratio)				

24.

In the Books of Alec and Ben

JOURNAL

Date	Particulars		LF	Amt (Dr)	Amt (Cr)
2000 Jan 1	Alec's Capital A/c	Dr		2,600	
	To Ben's Capital A/c				2,600
	(Being an adjustment entry made in respect of change in profit sharing ratio)				

Working Notes	**Amt (₹)**
1. Goodwill (Dr)	25,000
General Reserve (Cr)	12,000
Difference	13,000

2. **Calculation of Sacrifice or Gain**

Old ratio of Alec and Ben = 3 : 2; New ratio of Alec and Ben = 2 : 3

Sacrifice/(Gain) = Old Share – New Share

Alec $= \frac{3}{5} - \frac{2}{5} = \frac{3-2}{5} = \frac{1}{5}$ Sacrifice ; Ben $= \frac{2}{5} - \frac{3}{5} = \frac{2-3}{5} = \left(\frac{-1}{5}\right)$ Gain

Alec $= 13{,}000 \times \frac{1}{5}$ = ₹ 2,600 Dr ; Ben $= 13{,}000 \times \frac{1}{5}$ = ₹ 2,600 Cr

25. (a)

JOURNAL

Date	Particulars		LF	Amt (Dr)	Amt (Cr)
(i)	Revaluation A/c	Dr		200	
	To Provision for Doubtful Debts				200
	(Being provision for doubtful debts raised)				
(ii)	Investments A/c	Dr		3,000	
	To Revaluation A/c				3,000
	(Being investments recorded)				
(iii)	Revaluation A/c	Dr		2,800	
	To Smita's Capital A/c				1,680
	To Punita's Capital A/c				1,120
	(Being revaluation profit distributed)				
(iv)	Cash A/c	Dr		10,000	
	To Premium for Goodwill A/c				10,000
	(Being goodwill premium received)				
(v)	Premium for Goodwill A/c	Dr		10,000	
	To Smita's Capital A/c				5,000
	To Punita's Capital A/c				5,000
	(Being premium for goodwill distributed)				
(vi)	Smita's Capital A/c	Dr		2,500	
	Punita's Capital A/c	Dr		2,500	
	To Cash A/c				5,000
	(Being 50% goodwill withdrawn by old partners)				
(vii)	Punita's Capital A/c	Dr		3,000	
	To Investments A/c				3,000
	(Being investments taken over by Punita)				
(viii)	Bank Loan's A/c	Dr		6,000	
	To Mita's Capital A/c				6,000
	(Being bank loan paid by Mita on firm's behalf)				
(ix)	Cash A/c (WN 3)	Dr		15,200	
	To Mita's Capital A/c				15,200
	(Being capital amount brought by Mita)				

(b)

Balance Sheet
as at 1st April, 2019

Liabilities		Amt (₹)	Assets		Amt (₹)
Sundry Creditors		14,000	Cash in Hand (WN 2)		50,200
Capital A/cs (WN 1)			Sundry Debtors	22,000	
Smita	40,180		(–) Provision	(2,200)	19,800
Punita	44,620		Furniture		10,000
Mita	21,200	1,06,000	Stock		40,000
		1,20,000			1,20,000

Working Notes

1. Dr **Partners' Capital Account** Cr

Particulars	Smita (₹)	Punita (₹)	Mita (₹)	Particulars	Smita (₹)	Punita (₹)	Mita (₹)
To Cash A/c	2,500	2,500	—	By Balance b/d	30,000	40,000	—
To Investments A/c	—	3,000	—	By Revaluation A/c	1,680	1,120	—
To Balance c/d	40,180	44,620	21,200	By Premium for Goodwill A/c	5,000	5,000	—
				By Bank Loan	—	—	6,000
				By General Reserve A/c	6,000	4,000	—
				By Cash (WN 3)	—	—	15,200
	42,680	50,120	21,200		42,680	50,120	21,200

2. Dr **Cash Account** Cr

Particulars	Amt (₹)	Particulars	Amt (₹)
To Balance b/d	30,000	By Smita's Capital A/c	2,500
To Premium for Goodwill A/c	10,000	By Punita's Capital A/c	2,500
To Mita's Capital A/c	15,200	By Balance c/d	50,200
	55,200		55,200

3. Capital of Smita after all adjustments = ₹ 40,180

Capital of Punita after all adjustments = ₹ 44,620

Combined capital of Smita & Punita = ₹ 84,800

Combined share of Smita & Punita $= \frac{5}{10} + \frac{3}{10} = \frac{8}{10}$

$\therefore$ Total capital of firm $= 84{,}800 \times \frac{10}{8} =$ ₹ 1,06,000

$\therefore$ Mita's share $= \frac{2}{10} \times 1{,}06{,}000$ = ₹ 21,200

Adjusted through loan overtaken = (6,000)

Amount to be brought in = ₹ 15,200

26. (a)

In the Books of Annie, Bonnie and Carl
JOURNAL

Date	Particulars		LF	Amt (Dr)	Amt (Cr)
2017 Apr 1	Bank A/c	Dr		50,000	
	To Carl's Capital A/c				50,000
	(Being the amount brought in by Carl)				
Apr 1	Revaluation A/c	Dr		10,500	
	To Bad Debts A/c				500
	To Plant and Machinery A/c				10,000
	(Being the decrease in the value of assets)				
Apr 1	Stock A/c	Dr		2,000	
	To Revaluation A/c				2,000
	(Being the increase in the value of assets)				
Apr 1	Annie's Capital A/c	Dr		12,000	
	To Stock A/c				12,000
	(Being stock taken over)				
Apr 1	Annie's Capital A/c	Dr		4,250	
	Bonnie's Capital A/c	Dr		4,250	
	To Revaluation A/c				8,500
	(Being loss on revaluation transferred to capital account)				
Apr 1	Annie's Capital A/c	Dr		5,000	
	Bonnie's Capital A/c	Dr		5,000	
	To Goodwill A/c				10,000
	(Being goodwill written-off)				
Apr 1	Carl's Current A/c	Dr		5,000	
	To Annie's Capital A/c				2,500
	To Bonnie's Capital A/c				2,500
	(Being Carl's share of goodwill credited to old partners)				
Apr 1	Carl's Current A/c (2/8 Share)	Dr		3,750	
	To Annie's Capital A/c (1/8 Share)				1,875
	To Bonnie's Capital A/c (1/8 Share)				1,875
	(Being general reserve adjusted)				

(b)

Balance Sheet
as at 1st April, 2017

Liabilities		Amt (₹)	Assets		Amt (₹)
Creditors		21,000	Cash at Bank		70,000
General Reserve		15,000	Debtors	22,000	
Capital A/cs			(–) Bad Debts	(1,500)	20,500
Annie	28,125		Plant and Machinery		50,000
Bonnie	35,125		Carl's Current A/c		8,750
Carl	50,000	1,13,250			
		1,49,250			1,49,250

Working Note

Dr **Partners' Capital Account** Cr

Particulars	Annie (₹)	Bonnie (₹)	Carl (₹)	Particulars	Annie (₹)	Bonnie (₹)	Carl (₹)
To Stock A/c	12,000	—	—	By Balance b/d	45,000	40,000	—
To Revaluation A/c	4,250	4,250	—	By Bank A/c	—	—	50,000
To Goodwill A/c	5,000	5,000	—	By Carl's Current A/c	4,375	4,375	—
To Balance c/d	28,125	35,125	50,000				
	49,375	44,375	50,000		49,375	44,375	50,000

27. (a)

In the Books of Juliet, Rabani and Mike

Dr **Revaluation Account** Cr

Particulars	Amt (₹)	Particulars		Amt (₹)
To Plant and Machinery A/c	16,000	By Provision for Doubtful Debts A/c		2,000
		By Loss on Revaluation Transferred to		
		Juliet's Capital A/c	10,500	
		Rabani's Capital A/c	3,500	14,000
	16,000			16,000

(b) Dr **Partners' Capital Account** Cr

Particulars	Juliet (₹)	Rabani (₹)	Mike (₹)	Particulars	Juliet (₹)	Rabani (₹)	Mike (₹)
To Revaluation A/c	10,500	3,500	—	By Balance b/d	1,10,000	90,000	—
To Profit and Loss A/c	10,500	3,500	—	By General Reserve A/c	22,500	7,500	—
To Rabani's Current A/c (Balancing Figure)	—	19,250	—	By Bank A/c	—	—	1,00,000
To Balance c/d	2,25,000	75,000	1,00,000	By Premium for Goodwill A/c	11,250	3,750	—
				By Bank A/c (Balancing Figure)	1,02,250	—	—
	2,46,000	1,01,250	1,00,000		2,46,000	1,01,250	1,00,000

(c)

Balance Sheet of Juliet, Rabani and Mike
as at 1st April, 2016

Liabilities		Amt (₹)	Assets		Amt (₹)
Sundry Creditors		68,000	Plant and Machinery		1,60,000
Provident Fund		40,000	Inventory		26,000
Rabani's Current A/c		19,250	Sundry Debtors	57,000	
Capital A/cs			(–) Provision for Doubtful Debts	(1,000)	56,000
Juliet	2,25,000		Cash at Bank		2,85,250
Rabani	75,000				
Mike	1,00,000	4,00,000			
		5,27,250			5,27,250

Working Notes

1. Mike's share $= \frac{1}{4}$; Remaining share $= 1 - \frac{1}{4} = \frac{3}{4}$

   Juliet's new share $= \frac{3}{4} \times \frac{3}{4} = \frac{9}{16}$; Rabani's new share $= \frac{3}{4} \times \frac{1}{4} = \frac{3}{16}$

   Mike's share $= \frac{1}{4} \times \frac{4}{4} = \frac{4}{16}$

   ∴ New profit sharing ratio = 9 : 3 : 4

2. Necessary adjusting entries for commission received

Sundry Creditors A/c	Dr	2,000	
To Commission A/c			2,000
(Being creditors reduced by the amount of commission)			
Commission A/c	Dr	2,000	
To Profit and Loss A/c			2,000
(Being commission transferred to profit and loss account)			

   Alternatively, commission received (₹ 2,000) can be distributed among the old partners in old ratio.

Commission A/c	Dr	2,000	
To Juliet's Capital A/c			1,500
To Rabani's Capital A/c			500

   And ₹ 2,000 will be reduced from the value of creditors on the liabilities side of balance sheet (70,000 – 2,000) = ₹ 68,000

3. Profit and loss account has a debit balance of ₹ 16,000. Due to transfer of commission, the balance will be reduced by ₹ 2,000. Accordingly, ₹ 14,000 will be distributed amongst partners in old ratio.

4. Mike's share of goodwill $= 60{,}000 \times \frac{1}{4} =$ ₹ 15,000

   This will be distributed amongst Juliet and Rabani in the sacrificing ratio of 3 : 1.

5. Mike's capital for $\frac{1}{4}$ th share = ₹ 1,00,000

   Capital of the firm on the basis of Mike's capital $= 1{,}00{,}000 \times \frac{4}{1} =$ ₹ 4,00,000

   Juliet's capital $= 4{,}00{,}000 \times \frac{9}{16} =$ ₹ 2,25,000 ; Rabani's capital $= 4{,}00{,}000 \times \frac{3}{16} =$ ₹ 75,000

6. Dr **Cash Account** Cr

Particulars	Amt (₹)	Particulars	Amt (₹)
To Balance b/d	68,000	By Balance c/d	2,85,250
To Mike's Capital A/c	1,00,000		
To Juliet's Capital A/c	1,02,250		
To Premium for Goodwill A/c	15,000		
	2,85,250		2,85,250

28. (a)

In the Books of Divya and Pooja
JOURNAL

Date	Particulars		LF	Amt (Dr)	Amt (Cr)
	Divya's Capital A/c	Dr		9,600	
	Pooja's Capital A/c	Dr		6,400	
	To Goodwill A/c				16,000
	(Being goodwill written-off)				
	Pooja's Capital A/c	Dr		2,400	
	To Divya's Capital A/c				2,400
	(Being compensation given by Pooja due to change in profit sharing ratio)				
	Pooja's Capital A/c (23,400 × 1/ 10)	Dr		2,340	
	To Divya's Capital A/c (23,400 × 1/ 10)				2,340
	(Being the adjustment of general reserve on change in profit sharing ratio)				
	Profit and Loss A/c	Dr		4,000	
	To Divya's Capital A/c				2,400
	To Pooja's Capital A/c				1,600
	(Being transfer of accumulated profit to old partners in their old profit sharing ratio)				
	Investment Fluctuation Fund A/c	Dr		12,600	
	To Investment A/c				6,000
	To Divya's Capital A/c				3,960
	To Pooja's Capital A/c				2,640
	(Being the transfer of investment fluctuation fund to old partners in their old profit sharing ratio)				
	Divya's Capital A/c	Dr		6,420	
	Pooja's Capital A/c	Dr		4,280	
	To Advertisement Suspense A/c				10,700
	(Being the transfer of balance of advertisement suspense account to old partners in their profit sharing ratio)				

(b)

Balance Sheet (Revised)
as at 1st April, 2015

Liabilities		Amt (₹)	Assets	Amt (₹)
Sundry Creditors		9,800	Land and Building	20,000
General Reserve		23,400	Investments (66,000 – 6,000)	60,000
Capital A/cs			Sundry Debtors	18,600
Divya	55,080		Bills Receivable	7,400
Pooja	28,820	83,900	Cash in Hand	11,100
		1,17,100		1,17,100

Working Notes

1. Calculation of Sacrificing (Gaining) Ratio

Sacrificing/(Gaining) Ratio = Old Share – New Share

Divya $= \frac{3}{5} - \frac{1}{2} = \frac{6-5}{10} = \frac{1}{10}$ Sacrifice ; Pooja $= \frac{2}{5} - \frac{1}{2} = \frac{4-5}{10} = \left(\frac{-1}{10}\right)$ Gain

2. Dr **Partners' Capital Account** Cr

Particulars	Divya (₹)	Pooja (₹)	Particulars	Divya (₹)	Pooja (₹)
To Goodwill A/c	9,600	6,400	By Balance b/d	60,000	40,000
To Divya's Capital A/c	—	2,400	By Pooja's Capital A/c	2,400	—
To Divya's Capital A/c	—	2,340	By Pooja's Capital A/c	2,340	—
To Advertisement Suspense A/c	6,420	4,280	By Profit and Loss A/c	2,400	1,600
To Balance c/d	55,080	28,820	By Investment Fluctuation Fund A/c	3,960	2,640
	71,100	44,240		71,100	44,240

29. (a)

In the Books of Gautam, Rahul and Karim
JOURNAL

Date	Particulars		LF	Amt (Dr)	Amt (Cr)
	Gautam's Capital A/c	Dr		4,000	
	Rahul's Capital A/c	Dr		6,000	
	To Goodwill A/c				10,000
	(Being goodwill appearing in the books, is written-off in 2:3)				
	General Reserve A/c	Dr		10,000	
	To Gautam's Capital A/c				4,000
	To Rahul's Capital A/c				6,000
	(Being general reserve distributed in 2:3)				
	Revaluation A/c	Dr		400	
	To Provision for Doubtful Debts A/c				400
	(Being provision for doubtful debts raised to 20%)				
	Revaluation A/c	Dr		3,000	
	To Furniture A/c				3,000
	(Being reduction in the value of furniture)				
	Gautam's Capital A/c	Dr		1,360	
	Rahul's Capital A/c	Dr		2,040	
	To Revaluation A/c				3,400
	(Being loss on revaluation distributed in 2 : 3)				
	Gautam's Capital A/c	Dr		22,000	
	To Furniture A/c				22,000
	(Being furniture taken over at ₹ 22,000)				
	Cash A/c	Dr		50,000	
	To Karim's Capital A/c				40,000
	To Premium for Goodwill A/c				10,000
	(Being share of goodwill and capital brought in cash)				
	Premium for Goodwill A/c	Dr		10,000	
	Gautam's Capital A/c	Dr		5,000	
	To Rahul's Capital A/c				15,000
	(Being premium for goodwill adjusted)				

(b)

Balance Sheet
as at 1st April, 2014

Liabilities		Amt (₹)	Assets		Amt (₹)
Sundry Creditors		5,000	Stock		15,000
Bills Payable		15,000	Sundry Debtors	12,000	
Capital A/cs			(–) Provision for Doubtful Debts	(2,400)	9,600
Gautam	1,640		Cash in Hand (40,000 + 50,000)		90,000
Rahul	52,960				
Karim	40,000	94,600			
		1,14,600			1,14,600

Working Notes

1. **Calculation of Sacrificing Ratio**

Sacrificing Ratio = Old Share − New Share

Gautam's $= \frac{2}{5} - \frac{5}{10} = \frac{4-5}{10} = \left(\frac{-1}{10}\right)$ Gain; Rahul's $= \frac{3}{5} - \frac{3}{10} = \frac{6-3}{10} = \frac{3}{10}$

2. Since, Gautam is gaining 1/10th in profits, therefore he will also have to compensate Rahul proportionately. For 2/10th share Karim brought in ₹ 10,000 as premium.

Therefore, Gautam will compensate Rahul by $= 10{,}000 \times \frac{10}{2} \times \frac{1}{10} =$ ₹ 5,000

3. Dr **Partners' Capital Account** Cr

Particulars	Gautam (₹)	Rahul (₹)	Karim (₹)	Particulars	Gautam (₹)	Rahul (₹)	Karim (₹)
To Goodwill A/c (Written-off)	4,000	6,000	—	By Balance b/d	30,000	40,000	—
To Revaluation A/c (Loss)	1,360	2,040	—	By General Reserve A/c	4,000	6,000	—
To Furniture A/c	22,000	—	—	By Cash A/c	—	—	40,000
To Rahul's Capital A/c	5,000	—	—	By Premium for Goodwill A/c	—	10,000	—
To Balance c/d	1,640	52,960	40,000	By Gautam's Capital A/c	—	5,000	—
	34,000	61,000	40,000		34,000	61,000	40,000

30. (i) **In the Books of Sim, Tim and Jim**

Dr **Partners' Capital Account** Cr

Particulars	Sim (₹)	Tim (₹)	Jim (₹)	Particulars	Sim (₹)	Tim (₹)	Jim (₹)
To Jim's Capital A/c	40,000	—	—	By Balance b/d	2,50,000	2,00,000	1,50,000
To Balance c/d	2,10,000	2,00,000	1,90,000	By Sim's Capital A/c	—	—	40,000
	2,50,000	2,00,000	1,90,000		2,50,000	2,00,000	1,90,000

(ii) **Balance Sheet**
as at 1st April, 2012

Liabilities		Amt (₹)	Assets	Amt (₹)
Capital A/cs			Building	2,00,000
Sim	2,10,000		Plant and Machinery	1,00,000
Tim	2,00,000		Patents and Copyrights	1,50,000
Jim	1,90,000	6,00,000	Stock	1,25,000
Creditors		1,40,000	Debtors	1,50,000
General Reserve		60,000	Bank	75,000
		8,00,000		8,00,000

Working Notes

1. **Calculation of Net Adjustment to be Made**

	Amt (₹)
Increase in building	75,000
Decrease in plant and machinery	(10,000)
Decrease in patent and copyrights	(17,500)
Increase in stock	75,000
Prepaid insurance	5,000
Decrease in debtors	(7,500)
Profit on revaluation	1,20,000
Adjustment for general reserve	60,000
Adjustment for value of goodwill	60,000
	2,40,000

2. **Calculation of Sacrifice/Gain**

Sacrifice/(Gain) Ratio = Old Share – New Share

Sim $= \frac{1}{3} - \frac{3}{6} = \frac{2-3}{6} = \left(\frac{-1}{6}\right)$ Gain; Tim $= \frac{1}{3} - \frac{2}{6} = \frac{2-2}{6} = 0$; Jim $= \frac{1}{3} - \frac{1}{6} = \frac{2-1}{6} = \frac{1}{6}$ Sacrifice

Since, Sim has gained, he will be debited by $\left(\frac{1}{6} \text{of } 2,40,000\right)$ = ₹ 40,000

Since, Jim has sacrificed, he will be credited by $\left(\frac{1}{6} \text{of } 2,40,000\right)$ = ₹ 40,000

3. **JOURNAL**

Date	Particulars		LF	Amt (Dr)	Amt (Cr)
2012 Apr 1	Sim's Capital A/c	Dr		40,000	
	To Jim's Capital A/c				40,000
	(Being adjustment for goodwill)				

31. (a)

In the Books of Neha, Tara and Prachi

Revaluation Account

Dr | Cr

Particulars		Amt (₹)	Particulars	Amt (₹)
To Plant and Machinery A/c		2,000	By Provision for Doubtful Debts A/c	4,000
To Profit Transferred to Capital A/cs		6,000	By Land and Buildings A/c	4,000
Neha	3,600			
Tara	2,400			
		8,000		8,000

(b) **Partners' Capital Account**

Dr | Cr

Particulars	Neha (₹)	Tara (₹)	Prachi (₹)	Particulars	Neha (₹)	Tara (₹)	Prachi (₹)
To Balance c/d	26,600	22,400	12,250	By Balance b/d	8,000	10,000	—
				By General Reserve A/c	7,200	4,800	—
				By Workmen's Compensation Fund A/c	1,800	1,200	—
				By Revaluation A/c (Profit)	3,600	2,400	—
				By Cash A/c	—	—	12,250
				By Premium for Goodwill A/c	6,000	4,000	—
	26,600	22,400	12,250		26,600	22,400	12,250

(c) **Balance Sheet**

as at 1st April, 2012

Liabilities		Amt (₹)	Assets	Amt (₹)
Capital A/cs			Plant and Machinery (12,000 – 2,000)	10,000
Neha	26,600		Land and Building (14,000 + 4,000)	18,000
Tara	22,400		Debtors	19,000
Prachi	12,250	61,250	Stock	6,000
Workmen's Compensation Fund		2,000	Cash	25,250
Creditors		15,000		
		78,250		78,250

Working Notes

1. Goodwill brought in by Prachi is to be distributed in the sacrificing ratio 3 : 2 which is same as the old ratio, as the new ratio is not specified in the question.

Hence, Neha's share $= \frac{3}{5} \times 10,000 =$ ₹ 6,000; Tara's share $= \frac{2}{5} \times 10,000 =$ ₹ 4,000

2. **Calculation of Prachi's Capital**

Capital of Neha and Tara for $\frac{4}{5}$th share $= 26{,}600 + 22{,}400 =$ ₹ 49,000

Total capital of the firm $= 49{,}000 \times \frac{5}{4} =$ ₹ 61,250

$\therefore$ Prachi's share of capital $= \frac{1}{5} \times 61{,}250 =$ ₹ 12,250

3. **Cash Account**

Dr / Cr

Particulars	Amt (₹)	Particulars	Amt (₹)
To Balance b/d	3,000	By Balance c/d	25,250
To Premium for Goodwill A/c	10,000		
To Prachi's Capital A/c	12,250		
	25,250		25,250

32. **In the Books of David, Bimal and Chander**

Revaluation Account

Dr / Cr

Particulars		Amt (₹)	Particulars	Amt (₹)
To Stock A/c		750	By Creditors A/c	2,350
To Furniture A/c		500		
To Provision for Doubtful Debts A/c		100		
To Profit Transferred to Capital A/cs				
David	600			
Bimal	400	1,000		
		2,350		2,350

Partners' Capital Account

Dr / Cr

Particulars	David (₹)	Bimal (₹)	Chander (₹)	Particulars	David (₹)	Bimal (₹)	Chander (₹)
To Balance c/d	23,400	16,600	16,000	By Balance b/d	18,000	12,000	—
				By General Reserve A/c	1,800	1,200	—
				By Revaluation A/c	600	400	—
				By Cash A/c	—	—	16,000
				By Chander's Current A/c	3,000	3,000	—
	23,400	16,600	16,000		23,400	16,600	16,000

Balance Sheet
as at 1st April, 2010

Liabilities		Amt (₹)	Assets		Amt (₹)
Creditors		79,650	Cash		48,000
Capital A/cs			Stock		14,250
David	23,400		Debtors	9,400	
Bimal	16,600		(–) Provision for Doubtful Debts	(500)	8,900
Chander	16,000	56,000	Building		55,000
			Furniture		3,500
			Chander's Current A/c		6,000
		1,35,650			1,35,650

Working Notes

1. Sacrificing Ratio = Old Share – New Share

David $= \frac{3}{5} - \frac{5}{10} = \frac{6-5}{10} = \frac{1}{10}$; Bimal $= \frac{2}{5} - \frac{3}{10} = \frac{4-3}{10} = \frac{1}{10}$

Sacrificing ratio = 1 : 1

2. **Calculation of Hidden Goodwill**

Chander contributes ₹ 16,000 for $\frac{2}{10}$th share

$\therefore$ Total capital of the firm should be $= 16{,}000 \times \frac{10}{2} =$ ₹ 80,000

But the adjusted total capital of David, Bimal and Chander is (20,400 + 13,600 + 16,000) = ₹ 50,000

So, goodwill of the firm = 80,000 – 50,000 = ₹ 30,000

Chander's share of goodwill $= 30{,}000 \times \frac{2}{10} =$ ₹ 6,000,

which is distributed in sacrificing ratio of 1 : 1.

3. Dr **Cash Account** Cr

Particulars	Amt (₹)	Particulars	Amt (₹)
To Balance b/d	32,000	By Balance c/d	48,000
To Chander's Capital A/c	16,000		
	48,000		48,000

Concept Enhancer Liability paid by the firm will not be shown in revaluation account, but liability paid by the partner privately will be shown in the revaluation account.

33. **In the Books of Lucy, Rahul and Sanjay**
JOURNAL

Date	Particulars		LF	Amt (Dr)	Amt (Cr)
	Lucy's Capital A/c	Dr		4,000	
	Rahul's Capital A/c	Dr		8,000	
	Sanjay's Capital A/c	Dr		12,000	
	To Goodwill A/c				24,000
	(Being old goodwill written-off prior to Arun's admission)				
	Cash A/c	Dr		20,000	
	To Arun's Capital A/c				20,000
	(Being capital brought by Arun)				
	Arun's Current A/c	Dr		6,000	
	To Lucy's Capital A/c				1,000
	To Rahul's Capital A/c				2,000
	To Sanjay's Capital A/c				3,000
	(Being Arun's share of goodwill premium distributed among old partners)				

Working Notes

1. Calculation of Goodwill

$$\text{Average Profit} = \frac{\text{Total Profit of Given Number of Years}}{\text{Number of Years}} = \frac{25{,}000 + 28{,}000 + 37{,}000}{3} = \frac{90{,}000}{3}$$

Goodwill of firm = ₹ 30,000

2. Arun's share of goodwill $= 30{,}000 \times \frac{1}{5} =$ ₹ 6,000

34.

Dr **Revaluation Account** Cr

Particulars		Amt (₹)	Particulars	Amt (₹)
To Furniture A/c		1,000	By Building A/c	10,000
To Profit Transferred to Capital A/cs			By Land A/c	9,000
James	13,800		By Stock A/c	5,000
Dias	9,200	23,000		
		24,000		24,000

Dr **Partners' Capital Account** Cr

Particulars	James (₹)	Dias (₹)	Particulars	James (₹)	Dias (₹)
To Balance c/d	73,800	49,200	By Balance b/d	60,000	40,000
			By Revaluation A/c	13,800	9,200
	73,800	49,200		73,800	49,200

Balance Sheet (Revised)
as at 1st January, 2008

Liabilities		Amt (₹)	Assets	Amt (₹)
Creditors		18,000	Building (40,000 + 10,000)	50,000
Capital A/cs			Land (6,000 + 9,000)	15,000
James	73,800		Furniture (4,000 – 1,000)	3,000
Dias	49,200	1,23,000	Stock (25,000 + 5,000)	30,000
			Investment	16,000
			Bank	15,000
			Cash	12,000
		1,41,000		1,41,000

35. (a)

In the Books of Angad, Vivek and Gopal

Dr **Partners' Capital Account** Cr

Particulars	Angad (₹)	Vivek (₹)	Gopal (₹)	Particulars	Angad (₹)	Vivek (₹)	Gopal (₹)
To Revaluation A/c (Loss)	2,700	1,800	—	By Balance b/d	30,000	25,000	—
To Current A/c	3,300	7,200	—	By General Reserve A/c	6,000	4,000	—
(Balancing figure)				By Premium for Goodwill A/c	6,000	4,000	—
To Balance c/d	36,000	24,000	20,000	By Cash A/c	—	—	20,000
	42,000	33,000	20,000		42,000	33,000	20,000

(b)

Balance Sheet
as at 1st January, 2005

Liabilities		Amt (₹)	Assets		Amt (₹)
Capital A/cs			Cash at Bank		32,000
Angad	36,000		Plant (30,000 + 2,000)		32,000
Vivek	24,000		Stock (20,000 – 2,000)		18,000
Gopal	20,000	80,000	Debtors	18,000	
Current A/cs			(–) Provision for Doubtful Debts	(900)	17,100
Angad	3,300		Furniture		10,000
Vivek	7,200	10,500			
Creditors (15,000 – 1,400)		13,600			
Unrecorded Liability		5,000			
		1,09,100			1,09,100

Working Notes

1. Dr **Revaluation Account** Cr

Particulars	Amt (₹)	Particulars		Amt (₹)
To Stock A/c	2,000	By Plant A/c		2,000
To Provision for Doubtful Debts A/c	900	By Creditors A/c		1,400
To Unrecorded Liability A/c	5,000	By Loss Transferred to		4,500
		Angad's Capital A/c	2,700	
		Vivek's Capital A/c	1,800	
	7,900			7,900

2. Total share of a new firm is 1.

$\therefore$ Remaining share after Gopal's admission $= 1 - \frac{1}{4} = \frac{3}{4}$

Angad's share of profit $= \frac{3}{4} \times \frac{3}{5} = \frac{9}{20}$; Vivek's share of profit $= \frac{3}{4} \times \frac{2}{5} = \frac{6}{20}$

Gopal's share of profit $= \frac{1}{4} \times \frac{5}{5} = \frac{5}{20} = \frac{9}{20} : \frac{6}{20} : \frac{5}{20}$

$\therefore$ New ratio = 9 : 6 : 5

3. Total capital of the new firm taking Gopal's capital as base is $20{,}000 \times \frac{4}{1} =$ ₹ 80,000

Angad's share $= 80{,}000 \times \frac{9}{20} =$ ₹ 36,000 ; Vivek's share $= 80{,}000 \times \frac{6}{20} =$ ₹ 24,000

Gopal's share $= 80{,}000 \times \frac{5}{20} =$ ₹ 20,000

4. Dr **Cash Account** Cr

Particulars	Amt (₹)	Particulars	Amt (₹)
To Balance b/d	2,000	By Balance c/d	32,000
To Premium for Goodwill A/c	10,000		
To Gopal's Capital A/c	20,000		
	32,000		32,000

36. **In the Books of X, Y, Z and T**
JOURNAL

Date	Particulars		LF	Amt (Dr)	Amt (Cr)
	Cash A/c	Dr		22,500	
	To T's Capital A/c				20,000
	To Premium for Goodwill A/c				2,500
	(Being capital and premium brought in by T in cash)				
	Premium for Goodwill A/c	Dr		2,500	
	T's Current A/c	Dr		7,500	
	To X's Capital A/c				5,000
	To Y's Capital A/c				5,000
	(Being goodwill distributed in sacrificing ratio)				
	Stock A/c	Dr		10,000	
	To Revaluation A/c				10,000
	(Being value of stock increased)				
	Revaluation A/c	Dr		2,600	
	To Furniture A/c				2,600
	(Being furniture depreciated)				

Date	Particulars		LF	Amt (Dr)	Amt (Cr)
	Land and Building A/c	Dr		20,000	
	To Revaluation A/c				20,000
	(Being value of land and building increased)				
	Revaluation A/c	Dr		2,200	
	To Provision for Doubtful Debts A/c				2,200
	(Being provision for bad and doubtful debts created)				
	Revaluation A/c	Dr		25,200	
	To X's Capital A/c				10,080
	To Y's Capital A/c				10,080
	To Z's Capital A/c				5,040
	(Being revaluation profit distributed among partners)				
	Outstanding Liabilities A/c	Dr		2,000	
	To X's Capital A/c				2,000
	(Being outstanding liability paid by X)				
	X's Capital A/c	Dr		2,000	
	To Cash A/c				2,000
	(Being outstanding liability paid by X reimbursed)				
	Creditors A/c	Dr		5,000	
	To X's Capital A/c				2,000
	To Y's Capital A/c				2,000
	To Z's Capital A/c				1,000
	(Being commission included in creditors transferred to capital accounts of old partners in old ratio)				
	General Reserve A/c	Dr		26,000	
	To X's Capital A/c				10,400
	To Y's Capital A/c				10,400
	To Z's Capital A/c				5,200
	(Being general reserve distributed)				

Dr **Partners' Capital Account** Cr

Particulars	X (₹)	Y (₹)	Z (₹)	T (₹)	Particulars	X (₹)	Y (₹)	Z (₹)	T (₹)
To Cash A/c	2,000	—	—	—	By Balance b/d	48,000	48,000	20,000	—
To Balance c/d	75,480	75,480	31,240	20,000	By Cash A/c	—	—	—	20,000
					By Premium for Goodwill A/c	1,250	1,250	—	—
					By T's Current A/c	3,750	3,750	—	—
					By Revaluation A/c	10,080	10,080	5,040	—
					By Outstanding Liability A/c	2,000	—	—	—
					By General Reserve A/c	10,400	10,400	5,200	—
					By Creditors A/c	2,000	2,000	1,000	—
	77,480	75,480	31,240	20,000		77,480	75,480	31,240	20,000

Balance Sheet
as at 1st April, 2003

Liabilities		Amt (₹)	Assets		Amt (₹)
Outstanding Liabilities (6,000 – 2,000)		4,000	Cash		24,900
Sundry Creditors (51,400 – 5,000)		46,400	Land and Building (1,00,000 + 20,000)		1,20,000
Capital A/cs			Furniture (26,000 – 2,600)		23,400
X	75,480		Stock (47,000 + 10,000)		57,000
Y	75,480		Debtors	22,000	
Z	31,240		(–) Provision for Doubtful Debts	(2,200)	19,800
T	20,000	2,02,200	T's Current A/c		7,500
		2,52,600			2,52,600

Working Notes

1. Dr **Revaluation Account** Cr

Particulars		Amt (₹)	Particulars	Amt (₹)
To Furniture A/c		2,600	By Stock A/c	10,000
To Provision for Doubtful Debts A/c		2,200	By Land and Building A/c	20,000
To Profit Transferred to Capital A/cs				
X	10,080			
Y	10,080			
Z	5,040	25,200		
		30,000		30,000

2. Sacrificing Ratio = Old Share – New Share

$$X = \frac{2}{5} - \frac{5}{15} = \frac{6-5}{15} = \frac{1}{15}\ ;\ Y = \frac{2}{5} - \frac{5}{15} = \frac{6-5}{15} = \frac{1}{15}$$

$$Z = \frac{1}{5} - \frac{3}{15} = \frac{3-3}{15} = \frac{0}{15}$$

Only X and Y have sacrificed in the ratio of 1 : 1.

3. Dr **Cash Account** Cr

Particulars	Amt (₹)	Particulars	Amt (₹)
To Balance b/d	4,400	By X's Capital A/c	2,000
To T's Capital A/c	20,000	By Balance c/d	24,900
To Premium for Goodwill A/c	2,500		
	26,900		26,900

37. (i) (c) Value of goodwill of firm = 3,60,000 (60,000 × 6/1) – 2,10,000 (80,000 + 79,000 + 60,000 – 9,000) = ₹ 1,50,000

(ii) (b) Sacrificing ratio Dev $= \frac{5}{9} - \frac{3}{6} = \frac{3}{54}$; Dhruv $= \frac{4}{9} - \frac{2}{6} = \frac{6}{54}$ or 1 : 2

(iii) (d) Debit Creditor's A/c ₹ 37,000; Credit Bills Payable A/c ₹ 37,000

(iv) (d) Advertisement suspense account balance to be written-off from old partners capital account in old ratio.

38. (i) (b) Sacrificing Ratio = Old Ratio – New Ratio

Dev's sacrificing ratio $= \frac{2}{5} - \frac{6}{20} = \frac{8-6}{20} = \frac{2}{20}$

Gautam's sacrificing ratio $= \frac{1}{5} - \frac{2}{20} = \frac{4-2}{20} = \frac{2}{20}$

Kamal's sacrificing ratio $= \frac{2}{5} - \frac{7}{20} = \frac{8-7}{20} = \frac{1}{20}$

∴ Sacrificing ratio = 2 : 2 : 1

(ii) (a) Dev's interest on capital $= 90{,}000 \times \frac{10}{100} =$ ₹ 9,000

Gautam's interest on capital $= 80{,}000 \times \frac{10}{100} =$ ₹ 8,000

Naveen's interest on capital $= 50{,}000 \times \frac{10}{100} =$ ₹ 5,000

Total Interest on Capital = ₹ 22,000

(iii) (b) Divisible Profit = Net Profit + Interest on Drawings – Partners' Salaries – Interest on Capital

= 1,60,000 + 9,000 – 17,000 – 22,000 = ₹ 1,30,000

Naveen's share $= 1{,}30{,}000 \times \frac{1}{4} =$ ₹ 32,500, Naveen's guarantee = ₹ 40,000

Deficiency = 40,000 – 32,500 = ₹ 7,500

39. (i) (d) 2017-18 = 70,000 + 15,000 = ₹ 85,000

2018-19 = 50,000 – 5,000 = ₹ 45,000

2019-20 = (40,000) – 20,000 = ₹ (20,000)

2020-21 = 60,000 – 10,000 = ₹ 50,000

Average Profit $= \frac{85{,}000 + 45{,}000 - 20{,}000 + 50{,}000}{4} =$ ₹ 40,000

(ii) (b) Goodwill = Average Profit × Number of Years' Purchase

= 40,000 × 2 = ₹ 80,000

(iii) (b) ₹ Satvik's Current A/c

40. (i) (c) ₹ 2,000 will be credited to the capital accounts of the old partners

(ii) (a) Value of Land and Building $= \frac{25{,}000}{125} \times 100 =$ ₹ 20,000

(iii) (d) Creditors account will be debited with ₹ 5,000

(iv) (c) ₹ Nil

(v) (d) Balance sheet as at 1st April, 2021

CHAPTER TEST

01/02 Marks Questions

1. N and M are partners in a firm sharing profits in the ratio of 3 : 2. O is admitted into the partnership and he acquires his share $\frac{2}{10}$th from N and $\frac{1}{10}$ th from M. What is the profit share of O?

(a) $\frac{2}{10}$ (b) $\frac{1}{10}$ (c) $\frac{3}{10}$ (d) $\frac{4}{25}$

2. A, B and C are partners in a firm. They admitted D as new partner for $\frac{1}{5}$th share in profits. D gets his share equally from A and B. What is the new profit sharing ratio of A, B, C and D?

(a) 1 : 1 : 1 : 1 (b) 4 : 3 : 2 : 1 (c) 5 : 5 : 8 : 4 (d) 7 : 7 : 10 : 6

3. A and B are partners in a firm sharing with capital balances of ₹ 20,000 and ₹ 12,500 respectively. They admitted K into the firm who brings in ₹ 15,000 to have share in net assets and some amount of goodwill for $\frac{1}{5}$th share in profits. What is the share of goodwill of K?

(a) ₹ 45,000 (b) ₹ 50,000 (c) ₹ 5,500 (d) ₹ 27,500

4. In a partnership firm at the time of change in profit sharing ratio, the furniture is recorded in the books as ₹ 13,000. If the value of furniture is to be increased to 140%, what amount will be transferred to revaluation account?

(a) ₹ 18,200 (b) ₹ 13,000 (c) ₹ 5,200 (d) ₹ 4,800

5. What are the two rights that a newly admitted partner acquires?

6. Explain the term 'sacrificing ratio'.

7. Sanjeev, Mohan and Ashish are partners sharing profits and losses in the ratio of 2 : 3 : 4. They decide to share future profits and losses in the ratio of 4 : 3 : 2. They also decided to record the effect of the following without affecting their book values

General reserve	₹ 80,000
Profit and loss account	₹ 40,000
Advertisement suspense account	₹ 30,000

You are required to give the necessary single journal entry.

03 Marks Questions

8. Kartik and Aroha are partners in a firm, sharing profits in the ratio of 2 : 3. The balance sheet of the firm as on 31st March, 2012 is given below

Balance Sheet
as at 31st March, 2012

Liabilities		Amt (₹)	Assets	Amt (₹)
Creditors		6,200	Bills Receivable	3,600
Bills Payable		1,800	Stock	16,000
Capital A/cs			Machinery	18,400
Kartik	16,000		Land and Building	10,000
Aroha	24,000	40,000		
		48,000		48,000

The partners decided to share profits in equal ratio with effect from 1st April, 2012. The following adjustments were agreed upon

(i) Land and building was valued at ₹ 16,000 and machinery at ₹ 16,400 and was to appear at revalued amounts in the balance sheet.

(ii) The goodwill of the firm was valued at ₹ 800 but it was not to appear in books.

Pass the necessary journal entries to give effect the above.

9. Lalit, Rahul and Sumit are sharing profits and losses in the ratio of 5 : 3 : 2. They decided to share future profits and losses in the ratio of 2 : 3 : 5 with effect from 1st April, 2010. They also decide to record the effect of the following revaluations without affecting the book value of the assets and liabilities by passing a single adjusting entry.

Particulars	Book Figure (₹)	Revised Figure (₹)
Building	10,00,000	11,00,000
Machinery	5,00,000	4,80,000
Creditors	1,20,000	1,10,000
Outstanding Expenses	1,20,000	1,50,000

Pass the necessary single adjusting entry.

06 Marks Questions

10. Z, E and N are partners sharing profits and losses in the ratio of 3 : 2 : 1. Their balance sheet as on 31st December, 2012 was as follows

Balance Sheet
as at 31st December, 2012

Liabilities		Amt (₹)	Assets		Amt (₹)
Sundry Creditors		1,74,000	Cash and Bank		60,000
General Reserve		84,000	Sundry Debtors	1,24,000	
Profit and Loss A/c (Profits)		42,000	(–) Provision for Doubtful Debts	(4,000)	1,20,000
Capital A/cs			Stock		3,60,000
Z	6,00,000		Furniture		60,000
E	6,00,000		Plant and Machinery		4,00,000
N	1,00,000	13,00,000	Land and Building		6,00,000
		16,00,000			16,00,000

The partners agreed that from 1st January, 2012 they will share profits and losses in the ratio of 4 : 4 : 1. They agreed that

(i) Stock is to be valued at 20% less.

(ii) Provision for doubtful debts to be increased by ₹ 3,000.

(iii) Furniture is to be depreciated by 20% and plant and machinery by 15%.

(iv) ₹ 7,000 are outstanding for salaries.

(v) Land and building is to be valued at ₹ 7,00,000.

(vi) Goodwill is valued at ₹ 90,000.

Partners do not want to record the altered values of assets and liabilities in the books and want to leave the general reserves and profits undisturbed. They also decided not to show goodwill in the books.

You are required to pass a single journal entry to give effect to the above.

11. Sahaj and Nimish are partners in a firm. They share profits and losses in the ratio of 2 :1. Since, both of them are specially abled, sometimes they find it difficult to run the business on their own. Gauri, a common friend decides to help them. Therefore, they admitted her into partnership for a 1/3rd share. She brought her share of goodwill in cash and proportionate capital. At the time of Gauri's admission, the balance sheet of Sahaj and Nimish was as under

Balance Sheet
as at ...

Liabilities		Amt (₹)	Assets	Amt (₹)
Capital A/cs			Machinery	1,20,000
Sahaj	1,20,000		Furniture	80,000
Nimish	80,000	2,00,000	Stock	50,000
General Reserve		30,000	Sundry Debtors	30,000
Creditors		30,000	Cash	20,000
Employees' Provident Fund		40,000		
		3,00,000		3,00,000

It was decided to

(i) Reduce the value of stock by ₹ 5,000.

(ii) Depreciate furniture by 10% and appreciate machinery by 5%.

(iii) ₹ 3,000 of the debtors proved bad. A provision of 5% was to be created on sundry debtors for doubtful debts.

(iv) Goodwill of the firm was valued at ₹ 45,000.

Prepare revaluation account, partners' capital account and the balance sheet of the reconstituted firm.

10 Marks Questions

12. Atal and Madan were partners in a firm sharing profits in the ratio of 5 : 3. On 31st March, 2011, they admitted Mehra as a new partner for 1/5th share in the profit. The new profit sharing ratio was 5 : 3 : 2. On Mehra's admission, the balance sheet of the firm was as follows

Balance Sheet
as at 31st March, 2011

Liabilities		Amt (₹)	Assets	Amt (₹)
Capital A/cs			Land and Building	1,50,000
Atal	1,50,000		Machinery	40,000
Madan	90,000	2,40,000	Patents	5,000
Provision for Doubtful Debts		1,200	Stock	27,000
Creditors		20,000	Debtors	47,000
Workmen Compensation Fund		32,000	Cash	4,200
			Profit and Loss A/c	20,000
		2,93,200		2,93,200

On Mehra's admission, it was agreed that

(i) Mehra will bring ₹ 40,000 as his capital and ₹ 16,000 for his share of goodwill premium, half of which was withdrawn by Atal and Madan.

(ii) A provision of 2.5% for doubtful debts was to be created.

(iii) An item of ₹ 2,500 was included in the sundry creditors which was not to be paid.

(iv) A provision was to be made for an outstanding bill of electricity ₹ 3,000.

(v) A claim of ₹ 325 for damages against the firm was likely to be admitted. Provision for the same was to be made.

After the above adjustments, the capitals of Atal and Madan were to be adjusted on the basis of Mehra's capital. Actual cash was to be brought in or to be paid off to Atal and Madan, as the case may be. Prepare revaluation account, capital account of the partners and the balance sheet of the new firm.

13. The balance sheet of Madan and Mohan who share profits and losses in the ratio of 3 : 2, at 31st March, 2010 was as follows

Balance Sheet
as at 31st March, 2010

Liabilities		Amt (₹)	Assets		Amt (₹)
Creditors		28,000	Cash at Bank		10,000
Workmen's Compensation Fund		12,000	Debtors	65,000	
General Reserve		20,000	(–) Provision for Doubtful Debts	(5,000)	60,000
Capital A/cs			Stock		30,000
Madan	60,000		Investments		50,000
Mohan	40,000	1,00,000	Patents		10,000
		1,60,000			1,60,000

They decide to admit Gopal on 1st April, 2010 for 1/4th share on the following terms

(i) Gopal shall bring ₹ 25,000 as his share of premium for goodwill.
(ii) That unaccounted accrued income of ₹ 500 be provided for.
(iii) The market value of investments was ₹ 45,000.
(iv) A debtor whose dues of ₹ 1,000 were written-off as bad debt, paid ₹ 800 in full settlement.
(v) A claim of ₹ 2,000 on account of workmen compensation to be provided for.
(vi) Patents are undervalued by ₹ 5,000.
(vii) Gopal has to bring in capital equal to 1/4th of the total capital of a new firm after all adjustments.

Prepare the revaluation account, capital account of the partners and the balance sheet of the new firm.

Answers

1. (c) 3/10
2. (d) 7 : 7 : 10 : 6
3. (c) ₹ 5,500
4. (c) ₹ 5,200
7. Debit Sanjeev by ₹ 20,000 and Credit Ashish by ₹ 20,000.
8. Debit Kartik by ₹ 480 and Credit Aroha by ₹ 480.
9. Debit Sumit by ₹ 18,000 and Credit Lalit by ₹ 18,000.
10. Debit E by ₹ 18,000; Credit N by ₹ 9,000; Credit Z by ₹ 9,000.
11. Loss on Revaluation = ₹ 11,350; Balance in Partners Capital A/cs : Sahaj = ₹ 1,42,433, Nimish = ₹ 91,217, Gauri = ₹ 1,16,825, Balance Sheet Total = ₹ 4,20,475
12. Loss on Revaluation = ₹ 800, Balance in Partners Capital A/cs : Atal = ₹ 1,00,000, Madan = ₹ 60,000, Mehra = ₹ 40,000, Balance Sheet Total = ₹ 2,67,825
13. Profit on Revaluation = ₹ 1,300, Balance in Partners Capital A/cs : Madan = ₹ 93,780, Mohan = ₹ 62,520, Gopal = ₹ 52,100, Balance Sheet Total = ₹ 2,38,400

03

Reconstitution of a Partnership Firm : Retirement/Death of a Partner

TREND ANALYSIS 5 YEARS

		Average No. of Questions Across all Sets				
	Types of Questions	2023	2020	2019	2018	2017
01 Revaluation of Assets and Liabilities on Retirement	1/2 Marks	1	—	1	—	—
	3 Marks	—	—	—	—	—
	6 Marks	—	1	—	—	—
	10 Marks	—	—	1	1	—
02 Adjustment of Capital	1/2 Marks	—	—	—	—	—
	3 Marks	1	—	—	—	—
	6 Marks	—	—	—	—	—
	10 Marks	—	—	—	—	—
03 Death of a Partner	1/2 Marks	—	—	—	—	—
	3 Marks	2	—	—	1	—
	6 Marks	—	—	—	—	—
	10 Marks	—	—	—	—	1

Retirement

Retirement of a partner means ceasing to be a partner of the firm. When a partner leaves the firm due to various reasons (like old age, change of residence, ill health, misunderstanding with other partners, etc), it is called retirement of a partner.

The different ways by which a partner can retire from the firm are

(i) With the consent of all the partners.

(ii) By giving notice in writing to all other partners of his intention to retire, in case of partnership at will.

(iii) In accordance with the terms of agreement between the partners.

Adjustments Required at the Time of Retirement of a Partner

Various matters that need adjustment at the time of retirement are

1. Determination of new profit sharing ratio and gaining ratio.
2. Treatment of goodwill.
3. Revaluation of assets and reassessment of liabilities.
4. Adjustment for reserves, accumulated profits and losses.
5. Determination of the amount payable to the retiring partner.
6. Adjustment of capital.

1. New Profit Sharing Ratio and Gaining Ratio

(i) New Profit Sharing Ratio

The ratio in which the continuing partners will share future profits and losses is called new profit sharing ratio. It is the sum total of a partner's old share and that acquired from the share of retiring partner.

New Ratio = Old Share + Gaining Share

(ii) Gaining Ratio

The ratio in which the remaining i.e. continuing partners have acquired the share of the retiring partner is called gaining ratio.

Gaining Ratio = New Share – Old Share

Difference between Sacrificing Ratio and Gaining Ratio

Basis	Sacrificing ratio	Gaining ratio
Meaning	It is the ratio in which the old partners surrender a part of their share of profits in favour of a new partner.	It is the ratio in which the remaining partners acquire the outgoing partner's share of profit.
When calculated	At the time of admission of a new partner.	At the time of retirement or death of a partner.
Formula	Sacrificing Ratio = Old Share – New Share	Gaining Ratio = New Share – Old Share
Purpose	New partner's share of goodwill is divided between old partners in this ratio.	Retiring or deceased partner's share of goodwill is paid by the continuing partners in this ratio.

2. Treatment of Goodwill

Retiring partner's share in goodwill is paid to him by continuing partners in gaining ratio.

Adjustment for retiring partner's share of goodwill will be made through the following journal entry

Gaining Partners' Capital A/c (Individually) Dr
(Continuing partners in gaining ratio)

To Sacrificing Partner's Capital A/c
(Retiring/Deceased partner)

Goodwill Already Appearing in Books

Any goodwill already appearing in the books will be immediately written-off to old partners' capital account by passing the following journal entry

All Partners' Capital A/c (Individually) Dr
(in old ratio)

To Goodwill A/c

Hidden Goodwill

Sometimes the firm agrees to settle the retiring or deceased partners account by payment of a lumpsum amount. If such amount is in excess of his capital and share in reserves reserves of assets and reassessment of liabilities, etc., then the excess is treated as his share of goodwill.

3. Revaluation of Assets and Reassessment of Liabilities

Accounting treatment of revaluation of assets and reassessment of liabilities are to be done in the same way as in the case of change in profit sharing ratio of a new partner.

4. Accounting Treatment of Undistributed Profits/Loss and Reserves

Accounting treatment of adjustment of reserves and accumulated profits/losses are to be done in the same way as in the case of admission of a partner.

5. Calculation of Amount Payable to Retiring/Deceased Partner

The amount due to a retiring partner is ascertained by preparing retiring partner's capital account, after taking into account the following

(i) **Items to be Credited**

(a) Opening balance of capital and current account of retiring partner.
(b) His share in the profit of revaluation account.
(c) His share of reserve/accumulated profits.
(d) His share in the goodwill of the firm.
(e) His share of profit till the date of his retirement.
(f) His salary and/or interest on capital due to the retiring partner till the date of his retirement.

(ii) **Items to be Debited**

(a) Drawings and interest thereon of the retiring partner.
(b) Share in the accumulated losses of past year/years.
(c) Share in the loss of revaluation account.

6. Settlement of the Amount Due to the Retiring Partner

The amount due to retiring partner is either paid-off immediately or is transferred to his loan account.
The retiring partner's loan account will appear in the books of the new firm as a liability until it is paid-off fully.

The following journal entries are passed in this regard

(i) **If the amount is immediately paid-off**

Retiring Partner's Capital A/c Dr
To Cash/ Bank A/c

(ii) **In case, the amount is not immediately paid**

In this case, due amount is transferred to retiring partner's loan account by passing a following journal entry

Retiring Partner's Capital A/c Dr
To Retiring Partner's Loan A/c

(iii) **If amount due is partly paid in cash and the balance is to be treated as loan**

Retiring Partner's Capital A/c Dr
To Cash/Bank A/c
To Retiring Partner's Loan A/c

Interest on Loan

The partners may decide that the principal amount of the retiring partner will be paid in instalments. In that case interest will be paid on the outstanding amount of the loan. Accrued interest on loan will also be recorded while preparing loan account. There are two types of accrued interest

1. **Interest accrued but not due** When interest is recorded in the books of accounts, but its not due for payment, it is called interest accrued but not due. For example, when books are closing on 31st March, 2023, and interest is provided on half-yearly basis, i.e., on 30th June and 31st December, interest from January to March will be recorded on accrual basis in the loan account although the interest will become due for payment on 30th June, 2023.
2. **Interest accrued and due** When the interest is recorded in the loan account and its due for payment, is called interest accrued and due. For instance, in the previous example, interest from 1st January to 30th June, 2023 is due for payment and will be called interest accrued and due.

7. Adjustment of Capital

At the time of retirement of a partner, the remaining partners may decide to adjust their capital contributions in their profit sharing ratio. The capitals of the continuing partners may be required to be adjusted in the following three cases

Case I **When the total capital of the new firm is given**

The various steps involved in adjusting the capitals of the partners are given below

***Step* 1** Calculate the adjusted old capitals of continuing partners (i.e. after all other adjustment).

***Step* 2** Calculate the new capitals of continuing partners, according to the given capital.

***Step* 3** Calculate the surplus/deficit capital by comparing Step 1 and 2.

***Step* 4** Surplus amount will be withdrawn and deficit amount will be brought by the partners.

Case II **When the total capital of the new firm is not given**

The various steps involved in adjusting the capitals of the partners are given below

***Step* 1** Calculate the adjusted old capitals of continuing partners (i.e. after all other adjustments).

***Step* 2** Calculate total capital of the new firm by adding the adjusted capitals of the continuing partners.

***Step* 3** Calculate the new capitals of continuing partners on the basis of their new profit sharing ratio.

***Step* 4** Calculate the surplus/deficit capital by comparing Step 1 and 3.

***Step* 5** Surplus amount will be withdrawn and deficit amount will be brought by the partners.

Case III **When the outgoing partner is to be paid through cash brought by the continuing partners in such a way as to make their capitals proportionate to their new profit sharing ratio**

Steps involved in adjusting the capitals of partners are given below

***Step* 1** Calculate the adjusted old capitals of continuing partners after all other adjustments.

***Step* 2** Calculate total capital of the new firm by adding the adjusted capitals of continuing partners and amount to be paid to the retiring partner.

***Step* 3** Calculate the new capital of continuing partners, according to their new profit sharing ratio.

***Step* 4** Calculate the amount to be brought in by continuing partners by comparing Step 1 and Step 3.

Death of a Partner

The partnership comes to an end immediately whenever a partner dies, although the firm may continue with the remaining partners. The deceased partner is entitled to get his share in the firm as per the provisions of the partnership agreement. His share in the firm is calculated in the same manner as in the case of a retiring partner.

Calculation of Deceased Partner's Share in Profits

If a partner dies on any date after the date of the balance sheet, then his share of profit is calculated from the beginning of the year to the date of death on the basis of time or sales.

1. On Time Basis

When share of profit is calculated on the basis of time, it may be on the basis of previous year's profit or average profit of past years.

Profit from the date of last balance sheet to the date of death $= \frac{X}{Y} \times Z$

X = Number of days or months from the date of last balance sheet to the date of death
Y = 365 days or 12 months
Z = Previous year's profits or average profits of a given number of past years

2. On Sales Basis

Profit from the date of last balance sheet to the date of death $= \frac{X}{Y} \times Z$

X = Sales from the date of the last balance sheet to the date of death
Y = Previous year's sales or average sales of a given number of past years
Z = Previous year's profits or average profits of a given number of past years

Journal entries in both the cases are as follows

(i) **If profit sharing ratio of the remaining partners does not change**

In Case of Profit		In Case of Loss	
Profit and Loss Suspense A/c	Dr	Deceased Partner's Capital A/c	Dr
To Deceased Partner's Capital A/c		To Profit and Loss Suspense A/c	

(ii) **If profit sharing ratio of the remaining partners change**

In Case of Profit		In Case of Loss	
Gaining Partner's Capital A/c	Dr	Deceased Partner's Capital A/c	Dr
To Deceased Partner's Capital A/c		To Gaining Partner's Capital A/c	

Ascertainment of the Amount Due to the Deceased Partner

The deceased partner's share is also calculated in the same manner as in the case of retiring partner. Amount due to a deceased partner as shown by his capital account is transferred to his executor's account by passing the following journal entry

Deceased Partner's Capital A/c Dr
To Deceased Partner's Executor's A/c

Format of Deceased Partner's Capital Account

Dr **Deceased Partner's Capital Account** Cr

Particulars	Amt (₹)	Particulars	Amt (₹)
To Undistributed Losses A/c (Share in such losses)	...	By Balance b/d	...
To Revaluation A/c (Share in loss)	...	By Interest on Capital A/c	...

Particulars	Amt (₹)	Particulars	Amt (₹)
To Goodwill A/c (Written-off) (Share in goodwill)	...	By Salary and Commission A/c	...
To Drawings A/c	...	By Undistributed Profits (Share in such profits)	...
To Interest on Drawings A/c	...	By Revaluation A/c (Share in profit)	...
To Deceased Partner's Executor's A/c (Balancing figure)	...	By Gaining Partner's Capital A/c (Share of goodwill)	...
		By Profit and Loss Suspense A/c (Share in profits till death)	...
	...		...

Settlement of Deceased Partner's Executor Account

(i) **If payment is made in full/lumpsum**

Deceased Partner's Executor's A/c Dr

To Cash/ Bank A/c

(ii) **If payment is made in installment**

(a) Deceased Partner's Executor's A/c Dr

To Deceased Partner's Executor's Loan A/c

(b) Deceased Partner's Executor's Loan A/c Dr

To Cash/Bank A/c

PYQs Previous Years' Questions

1/2 Marks Questions

1. Nikhil, Akhil and Amber are partners in a firm. At the time of Akhil's retirement, Amber takes over furniture of ₹ 12,000 at ₹ 10,000.

Choose the correct journal entry from the following options to record this adjustment. *ISC 2023*

(a) Debit Furniture Account ₹ 10,000; Credit Amber's Capital Account ₹ 10,000

(b) Debit Furniture Account ₹ 12,000; Credit Amber's Capital Account ₹ 10,000; Credit Revaluation Account ₹ 2,000

(c) Debit Amber's Capital Account ₹ 10,000; Credit Furniture Account ₹ 10,000

(d) Debit Amber's Capital Account ₹ 10,000; Debit Revaluation Account ₹ 2,000; Credit Furniture Account ₹ 12,000

2. A firm has an unrecorded liability for workmen compensation of ₹ 10,000.

The firm was not prudent enough to create a workmen compensation reserve. How will this liability be treated in the books of the firm at the time of retirement of a partner? *ISC Specimen 2023*

(a) By debiting it to the capital accounts of all the partners

(b) By crediting it to revaluation account

(c) By debiting it to revaluation account

(d) By debiting it to workmen compensation reserve account

3. Punit, Sujit and Jiten are partners sharing profits and losses in the ratio of 4 : 3 : 1. Sujit retires from the firm, selling his share of profit to Punit and Jiten for ₹ 1,50,000; ₹ 80,000 being paid by Punit and ₹ 70,000 by Jiten.

What is the new profit sharing ratio between the remaining partners? *ISC Sem II 2022*

(a) 4 : 1 (b) 7 : 3

(c) 8 : 7 (d) 1 : 1

4. Ritu, Geetu and Sara are partners in a firm, sharing profits and losses in the ratio of 3 : 2 : 1. An extract of their balance sheet as at 31st March, 2021, is as under

Balance Sheet of Ritu, Geetu and Sara (Extract)
as at 31st March, 2021

Liabilities	Amt (₹)	Assets	Amt (₹)
		Plant and Machinery	90,000

On Geetu's retirement on 1st April, 2021, it was found that the value of machinery shown in the balance sheet was overvalued by $33\frac{1}{3}\%$.

What is the revised value of plant and machinery shown in the balance sheet of the reconstituted firm?
ISC Sem II 2022

KEY IDEA

Since the machinery is overvalued by 33.33%, its book value will be 133.33%.

5. Which of the following transactions is debited to revaluation account? **ISC Sem II Specimen 2022**

(a) Increase in the value of furniture
(b) Increase in provision for doubtful debts
(c) Creditors discharged at a discount
(d) Loss on revaluation of all assets and reassessment of all liabilities

6. Ravi, Vijay and Sujay were partners sharing profits in the ratio of 1/2 : 1/3 : 1/6. Vijay decided to retire, his share being taken up by the remaining partners in the ratio 1 : 4. On Vijay's retirement, a loss of ₹ 12,000 was determined upon revaluation of assets and liabilities.

Your are required to **ISC Sem II Specimen 2022**

(i) Calculate the new profit sharing ratio of the remaining partners.
(ii) Pass the journal entry to write-off the loss on revaluation of assets and liabilities.

7. Give the journal entry for closing the retiring partner's capital account when his share is paid to him privately by the remaining partners. **ISC 2019**

8. Give the formula for calculating the outgoing partner's share in the interim profits of the firm, on the basis of sales made by the firm. **ISC 2016**

9. List any four items that may have to be deducted from a deceased partner's capital account while computing the amount payable to his legal representatives. **ISC 2014**

10. How will the firm show the amount payable to the retiring partner, if it is not in a position to immediately pay the amount due to him on his retirement? **ISC 2013**

11. Give two differences between sacrificing ratio and gaining ratio. **ISC 2012, 2005**

12. What is a gaining ratio? **ISC 2007**

13. Name four items which are credited to the account of a deceased partner while calculating the amount due to his legal representatives. **ISC 2006**

14. What is the entitlement of the legal representative of a deceased partner in the subsequent profit of the firm? **ISC 2001**

3 Marks Questions

15. Pia, Sia and Jiya are partners in a frim sharing profits and losses in the ratio of 3 : 2: 1. Pia died on 31st October, 2021. Her capital as on 1st April, 2021, was ₹ 24,000 and her share of profit for the year 2021-22 till the date of her death, was assertained as ₹ 2,000.

Additional information

(i) Office equipment of the firm, the book value of which was ₹ 10,000 on 1st April, 2021, was revalued on the date of Pia's death at ₹ 13,600.
(ii) The amount of ₹ 35,000 due to Pia's executor in full settlement of the claim, was transferred to her executor's loan account.

You are required to prepare Pia's capital account to be rendered to her executor. **ISC 2023**

16. Vinay, Tarun and Arjun are partners in a firm sharing profits and losses in the ratio of 4 : 3: 2 respectively. On Tarun's retirement from the firm on 1st April, 2022, his capital account, after all adjustments, stood at ₹ 1,14,000.

The partners decided that

(i) Tarun to be paid 50% of the amount due to him immediately and the balance by accepting a bill of exchange (without interest) payable at the expiry of 3 months.
(ii) The continuing partners to re-adjust their capitals in their new profit sharing ratio in the reconstituted firm. Any surplus/deficit in their capital accounts to be adjusted through their current accounts.

Upon re-adjustment of their capitals, Vinay's capital showed a deficit of ₹ 1,000 while Arjun's capital had a surplus of ₹ 1,000.

You are required to pass journal entries to record

(i) The closing of the retiring partner's capital account.
(ii) Adjustment of surplus/deficit in the capital accounts of the continuing partners. **ISC 2023**

17. Viraj, Harsh and Akhil are partners in a firm sharing profits and losses in the ratio of 4/9 : 1/3 : 2/9. Akhil dies on 31st March, 2022. Viraj acquires 4/9 of Akhil's share and the balance is acquired by Harsh. On the date of Akhil's death, it was decided to value the goodwill of the firm on the basis of two years' purchase of average super profit.

The average net profit made by the firm is ₹ 49,000 per annum. The remuneration of the partners, considered as management cost, is estimated to be ₹ 9,000 per annum. The total value of assets and liabilities of the firm is ₹ 2,20,000 and ₹ 80,000 respectively. The normal rate of return in the industry is 15%.

Yor are required to calculate **ISC 2023**

(i) The gaining ratio of the continuing partners.

(ii) The value of non-purchased goodwill of the firm.

18. Kavi, Dhruv and Parth are partners in a firm sharing profits and losses in the ratio of 3:1:1.

Balance Sheet of Kavi, Dhruv and Parth (Extract)
as at 31st March, 2022

Liabilities	Amt (₹)	Assets	Amt (₹)
—	—	Bank	5,000

On Kavi's retirement from the firm on 1st April, 2022, the amount due to him is determined at ₹ 20,000. The firm took sufficient loan from the bank to pay the amount due to Kavi.

You are required to pass the necessary journal entries to pay the amount due to Kavi. **ISC Specimen 2023**

> **KEY IDEA**
> If loan is taken to repay the retiring partners' amount, initially bank balance will be increased and then payment will be made to retiring partner from that bank balance.

19. Gita, Sita and Meena were partners in a firm sharing profits and losses in the ratio of 2: 2:1. Gita died on 30th June, 2022. The firm closes its books on 31st March every year. According to their partnership deed, the representatives of the deceased partner would be entitled to get Gita's share in the interim profits of the firm calculated on sales basis.
Sales for the year 2020-21 were ₹ 6,00,000 and in the year 2021-22, till the date of her death, sales amounted to ₹ 1,20,000. The profits of the firm for the year 2020-21 were ₹ 1,80,000.

You are required to **ISC Specimen 2023**

(i) Calculate Gita's share of interim profit.

(ii) Pass the necessary journal entry for giving Gita's representative her share of interim profit.

20. Naresh, Dhruv and Azeem are partners sharing profits in the ratio of 5 : 3 : 7. Naresh retires from the firm. Dhruv and Azeem decided to share profits in the ratio of 2 : 3. The adjusted capital accounts of Dhruv and Azeem at the time of Naresh's retirement showed the balances of ₹ 33,000 and ₹ 70,500 respectively.
The total amount to be paid to Naresh is ₹ 90,500 which is paid in cash immediately by the firm, the cash being contributed by Dhruv and Azeem in such a way that their capitals become proportionate to their new profit sharing ratio and the firm maintains a minimum cash balance of ₹ 5,000 from its existing balance of ₹ 20,000. **ISC Sem II Specimen 2022**
You are required to pass journal entries to record

(i) Payment made to the retiring partner.

(ii) Cash brought in by the remaining partners to pay-off the retiring partner.

> **KEY IDEA**
> Total capital of the new firm will include remaining partner's capital balance, amount to be paid to retiring partner and minimum cash balance minus any existing cash balance.

21. Rita, Nina and Mita are partners in a firm sharing profit and loss in the ratio of 3 : 2 : 1. Mita dies on 1st April, 2017. On the date of her death, it was decided to value goodwill on the basis of two years' purchases of weighted average profit of the firm for the last three years.

The profit of the last three years and weights assigned were

Year	Profit (₹)	Weights Assigned
2014-15	30,000 (including gain from speculation ₹ 10,000)	1
2015-16	80,000	2
2016-17	1,00,000	3

You are required to

(i) Calculate the firm's goodwill on the date of Mita's death (Show the working with the formula).

(ii) Pass the necessary journal entry to credit Mita's capital account with her share of goodwill. **ISC 2018**

6 Marks Question

22. Manoj, Hari and Karan are partners in a firm sharing profits and losses in the ratio 4:2:1. Their balance sheet as at 31st March, 2019, was as follows

Balance Sheet of Manoj, Hari and Karan
as at 31st March, 2019

Liabilities		Amt (₹)	Assets	Amt (₹)
Sundry Creditors		32,600	Plant and Machinery	20,000
Bills Payable		4,000	Goodwill	7,000
General Reserve		8,400	Stock	38,000
Capital A/cs			Bank	20,000
Manoj	16,000			
Hari	14,000			
Karan	10,000	40,000		
		85,000		85,000

Hari retired from the business on 1st April, 2019. The remaining partners decided to carry on the business. The terms of retirement provided the following

(i) Out of the total insurance premium paid, ₹ 7,000 to be treated as prepaid insurance. The amount was earlier debited to profit and loss account.

(ii) General reserve not to be distributed.

(iii) Hari to be paid ₹ 24,400 in full settlement.

You are required to prepare partners' capital account. *ISC 2020*

10 Marks Questions

23. Mohit, Ali and John are partners in a firm, sharing profits and losses in the ratio of 3 : 1 : 1. Their balance sheet as at 31st March, 2018, was as follows

Balance Sheet of Mohit, Ali and John
as at 31st March, 2018

Liabilities		Amt (₹)	Assets		Amt (₹)
Trade Creditors		15,000	Cash at Bank		40,000
General Reserve		6,000	Sundry Debtors	30,000	
Investment Fluctuation Fund		9,000	(–) Provision for Doubtful Debts	(5,000)	25,000
Capital A/cs			Investments (Market value ₹ 40,000)		35,000
Mohit	70,000		Plant and Machinery		88,000
Ali	50,000		Goodwill		12,000
John	50,000	1,70,000			
		2,00,000			2,00,000

Mohit retired on 1st April, 2018, subject to the following adjustments

(i) Goodwill of the firm to be valued at ₹ 20,000.

(ii) Mohit to take over the investments at the market value.

(iii) 25% of the general reserve to be transferred to provision for doubtful debts and the balance to be distributed amongst all the partners.

(iv) Creditors to be paid ₹ 3,000 less.

(v) Investment fluctuation fund not to be distributed. For this, it was decided that the remaining partners would compensate the retiring partner through their capital accounts.

(vi) Mohit to be paid ₹ 20,000 immediately on retirement and the balance to be transferred to his loan account.

You are required to

(a) Pass journal entries on the date of Mohit's retirement.

(b) Prepare the balance sheet of the reconstituted firm. *ISC 2019*

KEY IDEA
Investment will be revalued at market value, then it will be debited to partner's capital account.

24. (i) Harish, Paresh and Mahesh were three partners sharing profit and loss in the ratio of 5 : 4 : 1. Paresh retired on 31st March, 2017. His capital as on 1st April, 2016, was ₹ 80,000. During the year 2016-17, he made drawings of ₹ 5,000. He was to be charged interest on drawings of ₹ 100.

The partnership deed provides that on the retirement of a partner, he will be entitled to

(a) His share of capital.

(b) Interest on capital @ 10% per annum.

(c) His share of profit in the year of retirement.

(d) His share of goodwill of the firm.

(e) His share in the profit/loss on revaluation of assets and liabilities.

Additional information

(a) Paresh's share in the profits of the firm for the year 2016-17, was ₹ 20,000.

(b) Goodwill of the firm was valued at ₹ 24,000.

(c) The firm suffered a loss of ₹ 12,000 on the revaluation of assets and liabilities.

(d) It was decided to transfer the amount due to Paresh to his loan account bearing interest @ 6% per annum. The loan was to be repaid in two equal annual installments, the first installment to be paid on 31st March, 2018.

You are required to prepare

(a) Paresh's capital account

(b) Paresh's loan account till it is finally closed.

(ii) Parth, Angad and Leesha are partners in a firm sharing profit and loss in the ratio of 3 : 2 : 1 respectively. Angad retires and his claim, including his capital and entitlements from the firm including his share of goodwill of the firm, is ₹ 50,000.

After this amount was determined, it was found that there was an unrecorded piece of furniture valued at ₹ 12,000 which had to be recorded. Upon recording this piece of furniture, the revised amount due to Angad was determined and settled by giving him this piece of furniture and the balance in cash.

You are required to give the journal entries for recording the payment to Angad in the books of the firm. *ISC 2018*

25. Karan, Ali and Deb are partners in a firm sharing profits and losses in the ratio of 3 : 2 : 1. On 31st March, 2016, their balance sheet was as under

Balance Sheet of Karan, Ali and Deb
as at 31st March, 2016

Liabilities		Amt (₹)	Assets		Amt (₹)
Capital A/cs			Building		1,00,000
Karan	1,00,000		Furniture		40,000
Ali	75,000		Investments		50,000
Deb	50,000	2,25,000	Debtors	30,000	
Investment Fluctuation Reserve		30,000	(–) Provision for Doubtful Debts	(1,000)	29,000
Bills Payable		10,000	Cash at Bank		43,000
Creditors		15,000	Goodwill		18,000
		2,80,000			2,80,000

Karan died on 1st July, 2016. An agreement was reached amongst Ali, Deb and Karan's legal representatives that

(i) Building be revalued at ₹ 93,500.
(ii) Furniture be appreciated by ₹ 10,000.
(iii) To write-off the provision for doubtful debts since all debtors were good.
(iv) Investments be valued at ₹ 38,000.
(v) Goodwill of the firm be valued at ₹ 1,20,000.
(vi) Karan's share of profit to the date of his death, to be calculated on the basis of previous year's profit which was ₹ 25,000.
(vii) Interest on capital to be allowed on Karan's capital @ 6% per annum.
(viii) Amount payable to Karan's legal representative to be transferred to his legal representative's loan account.

You are required to

(a) Pass journal entries on the date of Karan's death.
(b) Prepare the interim balance sheet of the reconstituted firm. **ISC 2017**

> **KEY IDEA**
> Loss from decrease in investments is initially written-off by investment fluctuation reserve and then deficiency (if any) will be written-off using revaluation account.

26. Pihu, Geeta and Nita are partners in a firm, sharing profits and losses in the ratio of 3 : 2 : 1. On 31st March, 2015, their balance sheet was as under

Balance Sheet
as at 31st March, 2015

Liabilities		Amt (₹)	Assets		Amt (₹)
Sundry Creditors		15,000	Cash at Bank		16,000
General Reserve		9,000	Sundry Debtors	25,000	
Capital A/cs			(–) Provision for Doubtful Debts	(1,300)	23,700
Pihu	79,000		Stock		14,300
Geeta	70,000		Plant and Machinery		60,000
Nita	61,000	2,10,000	Land and Building		1,20,000
		2,34,000			2,34,000

Nita retires on 1st April, 2015, subject to the following adjustments

(i) Land and building to be reduced by 10%.
(ii) Goodwill to be valued at ₹ 54,000.
(iii) Provision for doubtful debts to be raised to 10% of the debtors, the excess provision being created from general reserve. The balance of the general reserve to be distributed amongst the partners.
(iv) Creditors of ₹ 3,000 were paid by Pihu for which she is not to be reimbursed.
(v) The continuing partners to share profits and losses in future in the ratio of 5 : 4.
(vi) Nita to be paid ₹ 29,800 on retirement and the remaining amount in two equal annual installments together will interest @ 10% per annum on the outstanding balance. The first installment of Nita's loan to be paid on 31st March, 2016.

You are required to prepare

(a) Revaluation account.
(b) Partners' capital accounts.
(c) Nita's loan account till it is finally closed. **ISC 2016**

27. Ram, Krishna and Mohan are partners in a firm, sharing profits and losses in the ratio of 3 : 5 : 2. On 31st March, 2014, their balance sheet was as under

Balance Sheet
as at 31st March, 2014

Liabilities		Amt (₹)	Assets	Amt (₹)
Creditors		39,200	Land and Buildings	48,000
General Reserve		16,000	Plant	72,000
Capital A/cs			Inventory	34,000
Ram	76,800		Trade marks	26,400
Krishna	69,600		Bills Receivables	39,200
Mohan	54,000	2,00,400	Cash in Hand	24,000
			Advertisement Suspense	12,000
		2,55,600		2,55,600

Krishna died on 30th September, 2014. An agreement was reached amongst Ram, Mohan and Krishna's legal representative that

(i) Goodwill to be valued at 2 years purchase of the average profits of the previous three years, which were

Year	2011-12	2012-13	2013-14
Profit (₹)	31,200	28,800	36,000

(ii) Trademarks to be revalued at ₹ 19,200; plant at 80% of its book value and land and building at ₹ 57,600.
(iii) Krishna's share of profit to the date of his death to be calculated on the basis of previous year's profit.
(iv) Interest on capital to be provided @ 10% per annum.
(v) ₹ 60,080 to be paid in cash to Krishna's legal representative and balance to be transferred to the legal representative's loan account.

You are required to prepare
(a) Revaluation account.
(b) Krishna's capital account.
(c) Krishna's legal representative's account. *ISC 2015*

KEY IDEA
Interest on capital will be provided for 6 months only.

28. Angad, Kunal and Nitin were partners sharing profit and losses in the proportion of 2:2:1 respectively. The balance sheet of their firm as on 31st March, 2013, stood as follows

Balance Sheet
as at 31st March, 2013

Liabilities		Amt (₹)	Assets		Amt (₹)
Capital A/cs			Stock		12,500
Angad	12,500		Machinery		17,500
Kunal	15,000		Motor Van		4,000
Nitin	20,000	47,500	Buildings		22,500
Creditors		10,000	Bank		1,250
Bills Payable		2,000	Debtors	8,000	
General Reserve		6,000	(–) Provision for Doubtful Debts	(250)	7,750
		65,500			65,500

Kunal retires on 1st April, 2013, subject to the following adjustments
(i) Provision for doubtful debts to be increased by ₹ 975.
(ii) Stock to be appreciated by 20% and building by 10%.
(iii) Machinery to be depreciated by 10% and motor van by 15%.
(iv) Goodwill of the firm to be valued at ₹ 9,000.

(v) The capitals of the continuing partners are to be adjusted according to the new profit sharing ratio which is agreed between Angad and Nitin as 3 : 2 respectively.

(vi) Excess or shortfall in Angad's and Nitin's capital accounts to be transferred to their respective current accounts.

You are required to prepare

(a) Revaluation account.

(b) Partners' capital accounts.

(c) Balance sheet of the reconstituted firm.

ISC 2014

29. Bina and Anita are partners. Their partnership agreement provides for the following

(i) Accounts are to be balanced on 31st December each year.

(ii) Profits are to divided as follows

Bina : one-half, Anita : one third and carried to reserve account: one sixth.

(iii) That in the event of death of a partner, her executors will be entitled to the following

(a) The capital to her credit at the date of death.

(b) Proportionate profit to the date of death based on the average profits of the last three completed years.

(c) Share of goodwill based on three years' purchase of the average profits for the three preceding completed years.

The profit for the three years were : year 2005 — ₹ 42,000; year 2006 — ₹ 39,000 and year 2007 — ₹ 45,000. On 31st December, 2007, Anita's capital stood at ₹ 60,000 and firm's general reserve account stood at ₹ 30,000. Anita expired on 1st May, 2008.

From the above, prepare Anita's executors account as would appear in the firm's ledger by transferring the amount to her loan account with proper working notes.

ISC 2010, 2009

30. The balance sheet of Arun, Tarun and Varun who were sharing profits in the ratio of 4 : 3 : 2 stood as follows on 31st December, 2004.

Balance Sheet
as at 31st December, 2004

Liabilities		Amt (₹)	Assets	Amt (₹)
Creditors		19,000	Stock	25,000
Provident Fund		12,500	Cash at Bank	2,500
General Reserve		4,500	Debtors	15,500
Capital A/cs			Advertising Expenditure A/c	9,000
Arun	40,000		Plant and Machinery	34,000
Tarun	30,000		Building	45,000
Varun	25,000	95,000		
		1,31,000		1,31,000

Tarun retired on the above date on the following terms

(i) The assets and liabilities need not to be revalued.

(ii) The goodwill of the entire firm be fixed at ₹10,800 and Tarun's share of the same be adjusted into the accounts of Arun and Varun who are to share the profits in future in the ratio of 5 : 3.

(iii) The entire capital of the new firm be fixed at ₹ 56,000 and the capitals of Arun and Varun to be proportionate to their new profit sharing ratio. For this purpose actual cash is to be brought in or paid off.

Prepare

(a) The capital accounts of Arun and Varun after the retirement of Tarun.

(b) The balance sheet of Arun and Varun after the retirement of Tarun.

ISC 2006 (M)

31. A, B and C were equal partners. Their balance sheet as at 31st December, 2000 was as under

Balance Sheet
as at 31st December, 2000

Liabilities		Amt (₹)	Assets		Amt (₹)
Bills Payable		20,000	Bank		20,000
Creditors		40,000	Stock		20,000
General Reserve		30,000	Furniture		28,000
Profit and Loss A/c		6,000	Debtors	45,000	
Capital A/cs			(–) Provision for Doubtful Debts	(5,000)	40,000
A	60,000		Land and Building		1,20,000
B	40,000				
C	32,000	1,32,000			
		2,28,000			2,28,000

B retired on 1st January, 2001. A and C decided to continue the business as equal partners on the following terms

(i) Goodwill of the firm was valued at ₹ 57,600.
(ii) Provision for doubtful debts to be maintained at 10% on debtors.
(iii) Land and building to be increased to ₹ 1,32,000.
(iv) Furniture to be reduced by ₹ 8,000.
(v) Rent outstanding (not provided for as yet) was ₹ 1,500.

Remaining partners decided to bring sufficient cash in the business to pay-off B and to maintain a bank balance of ₹ 24,800. They also decided to re-adjust their capitals as per their new profit sharing ratio.

Prepare necessary ledger account and balance sheet. ***ISC 2001***

32. Albert, Boris and Cyril are partners sharing profits and losses in the ratio of 3 : 2 : 1 and their balance sheet as at 31st March, 1999 stood as under

Balance Sheet
as at 31st March, 1999

Liabilities		Amt (₹)	Assets	Amt (₹)
Capital A/cs			Building	70,000
Albert	50,000		Machinery	25,000
Boris	50,000		Stock	32,000
Cyril	50,000	1,50,000	Debtors	15,000
Creditors		17,000	Bank	25,000
		1,67,000		1,67,000

Albert died on 1st July, 1999 and the following decisions were taken by the surviving partners. According to the partnership deed, his executors were entitled to

(i) The deceased partner's capital as appearing in the last balance sheet and interest thereon at 6% per annum upto the date of death.
(ii) His share of profit for the period he was alive, based on the figure of 31st March, 1999.
(iii) Goodwill according to his share of profit to be calculated by taking twice the amount of the average profit of the last three years. The profits of the previous years were
31st March, 1999 — ₹ 11,000; 31st March, 1998 — ₹ 15,000 and 31st March, 1997 — ₹ 10,000
(iv) Assets were to be revalued.
Building — ₹ 80,000; Stock — ₹ 30,000; and Provision for doubtful debts @ 10%.

Assuming that all the above changes are to be incorporated in the new firm and are not to be written off, prepare the revaluation account, partners' capital account and a balance sheet as on 1st July, 1999. (All calculations are to be made to the nearest rupee). ***ISC Modified, 2000***

Explanations

1. (d) Debit Amber's Capital Account ₹ 10,000; Debit Revaluation Account ₹ 2,000; Credit Furniture Account ₹ 12,000
2. (c) By debiting it to revaluation account
3. (b) Calculation of new profit sharing ratio

   Sujit's share in profit on his retirement i.e., 3/8 will be distributed between Punit and Jiten in the ratio of 8 : 7.

   Profit share taken by Punit $= \frac{3}{8} \times \frac{8}{15} = \frac{1}{5}$

   Profit share taken by Jiten $= \frac{3}{8} \times \frac{7}{15} = \frac{7}{40}$

   Punit's new profit share $= \frac{4}{8} + \frac{1}{5} = \frac{20+8}{40} = \frac{28}{40}$

   Jiten's new profit share $= \frac{1}{8} + \frac{7}{40} = \frac{5+7}{40} = \frac{12}{40}$

   New profit sharing ratio = Punit : Jiten
   = 28 : 12
   = 14 : 6
   = 7 : 3
4. Calculation of revised value of plant and machinery

   $= \frac{90{,}000}{133.33} \times 100 = ₹\,67{,}500$
5. (b) Increase in provision for doubtful debts
6. (i) Old ratio of partners = Ravi : Vijay : Sujay

   $= \frac{1}{2} : \frac{1}{3} : \frac{1}{6} \Rightarrow 3:2:1$

   Now, Vijay's share taken by Ravi $= \frac{2}{6} \times \frac{1}{5} = \frac{2}{30}$

   Ravi's new share $= \frac{3}{6} + \frac{2}{30} = \frac{15+2}{30} = \frac{17}{30}$

   Vijay's share taken by Sujay $= \frac{2}{6} \times \frac{4}{5} = \frac{8}{30}$

   Sujay's new share $= \frac{1}{6} + \frac{8}{30} = \frac{5+8}{30} = \frac{13}{30}$

   ∴ New profit sharing Ratio = 17:13

   (ii) JOURNAL

Date	Particulars		LF	Amt (Dr)	Amt (Cr)
	Ravi's Capital A/c	Dr		6,000	
	Vijay's Capital A/c	Dr		4,000	
	Sujay's Capital A/c	Dr		2,000	
	To Revaluation A/c				12,000
	(Being the loss on account of revaluation adjusted between Ravi, Vijay and Sujay)				

7. JOURNAL

Date	Particulars		LF	Amt (Dr)	Amt (Cr)
	Retiring Partners' Capital A/c	Dr			
	To Remaining Partner's Capital A/c				
	(Being the amount of share of the retiring partner discharged)				

8. Profit from the date of last balance sheet to the date of death $= \frac{X}{Y} \times Z$

   X = Number of days or months from the date of last balance sheet to the date of death

   Y = 365 days or 12 months

   Z = Previous year's profits or average profits of a given number of past years
9. The items to be deducted from the account of a deceased partner are
   (i) Share in loss on the revaluation of assets and liabilities.
   (ii) Drawings up to the date of death.
   (iii) Interest on drawings charged in the year of death.
   (iv) Share in business losses till the date of death.
10. The amount payable to the retiring partner would be transferred to his loan account and reflected in the balance sheet as a liability.

    Concept Enhancer If a partner is retired, his dues can either be paid by the firm immediately in cash/bank or is transferred to partner's loan account.
11. Difference between sacrificing ratio and gaining ratio

Basis	Sacrificing ratio	Gaining ratio
Meaning	It is the ratio in which the old partners surrender a part of their share of profits in favour of a new partner.	It is the ratio in which the remaining partners acquire the outgoing partner's share of profit.
When calculated	At the time of admission of new partner.	At the time of retirement or death of a partner.

12. The ratio in which the remaining i.e. continuing partners have acquired the share from the retiring partner is called gaining ratio. It is calculated as follows

    Gaining Ratio = New Share − Old Share

13. The items credited to the account of a deceased partner are

(i) Opening balance of capital and current account of retiring partner.

(ii) His share in the profit of revaluation of assets and liabilities.

(iii) His share of reserve/accumulated profits.

(iv) His share of goodwill of the firm.

14. As per Section 37 of the Partnership Act, the deceased partner's executor would be entitled, at their discretion, to interest at 6% per annum on the amount due from the date of death to the date of actual payment or to that portion of profit which is earned by the firm with the help of the amount due to the deceased partner.

15. Dr **Pia's Capital Account** Cr

Particulars	Amt (₹)	Particulars	Amt (₹)
To Pia's Executors' A/c	35,000	By Balance b/d	24,000
		By Profit and Loss Suspense A/c	2,000
		By Revaluation A/c $\left(3{,}600 \times \frac{3}{6}\right)$	1,800
		By Sia and Jiya's Capital A/c (Balancing figure)	7,200
	35,000		35,000

16. **JOURNAL**

Date	Particulars		LF	Amt (Dr)	Amt (Cr)
(i)	Tarun's Capital A/c	Dr		1,14,000	
	To Bank A/c				57,000
	To Bills Payables A/c				57,000
	(Being Tarun's balance adjusted)				
(ii)	Bank A/c	Dr		1,000	
	To Vinay's Capital A/c				1,000
	(Being cash brought in by Vinay)				
(iii)	Arjun's Capital A/c	Dr		1,000	
	To Bank A/c				1,000
	(Being cash withdrawn by Arjun)				

17. (i) Viraj's Gain $= \frac{2}{9} \times \frac{4}{9} = \frac{8}{81}$; Harsh's Gain $= \frac{2}{9} \times \frac{5}{9} = \frac{10}{81}$; Gaining Ratio = 8 : 10 or 4: 5

(ii) Capital Employed = Assets – Liabilities = 2,20,000 – 80,000 = ₹ 1,40,000

Normal Profit $= 1{,}40{,}000 \times \frac{15}{100} =$ ₹ 21,000

Average Profit = 49,000 – 9,000 = ₹ 40,000

∴ Super Profit = 40,000 – 21,000 = ₹ 19,000

Goodwill = 19,000 × 2 = ₹ 38,000

Common Mistake Students usually do not deduct the expenses from the average profit. But management cost will be deducted from average profit in order to ascertain the actual average profit.

18. **JOURNAL**

Date	Particulars		LF	Amt (Dr)	Amt (Cr)
2022					
Apr 1	Bank A/c	Dr		15,000	
	To Bank Loan A/c				15,000
	(Being loan taken from bank)				
Apr 1	Kavi's Capital A/c	Dr		20,000	
	To Bank A/c				20,000
	(Being amount due to Kavi paid)				

Working Note

Dr **Kavi's Capital Account** Cr

Date	Particulars	JF	Amt (₹)	Date	Particulars	JF	Amt (₹)
2022 Apr 1	To Bank A/c		20,000	2022 Apr 1	By Balance b/d		20,000
			20,000				20,000

19. (i) Gita's share of interim profit

Percentage of profits on sales for the year 2020-2021 $= \frac{1,80,000}{6,00,000} \times 100 = 30\%$

Gita's share $= 1,20,000 \times \frac{30}{100} \times \frac{2}{5} =$ ₹ 14,400

(ii) **JOURNAL**

Date	Particulars		LF	Amt (Dr)	Amt (Cr)
	Gita's Capital A/c	Dr		14,400	
	To Gita's Executors A/c				14,400
	(Being the transfer of interim profit to Gita's executor account)				

20. Total capital of the new firm $= 33,000 + 70,500 + 90,500 + 5,000 - 20,000 =$ ₹ 1,79,000

Particulars	Dhruv (₹)	Azeem (₹)
I. New Capital (1,79,000 in new ratio i.e, 2 : 3)	71,600	1,07,400
II. Existing Capitals	33,000	70,500
III. Cash to be Brought in (I – II)	38,600	36,900

JOURNAL

Date	Particulars		LF	Amt (Dr)	Amt (Cr)
	Bank A/c	Dr		75,500	
	To Dhruv's Capital A/c				38,600
	To Azeem's Capital A/c				36,900
	(Being the cash brought in by partners)				
	Naresh's Capital A/c	Dr		90,500	
	To Bank A/c				90,500
	(Being the cash paid to Naresh)				

21. (i) **Calculation of Weighted Average Profit**

Year	Profit (₹) (X)	Weight (W)	Product (XW) (₹)
2014-15	(30,000 – 10,000) = 20,000	1	20,000
2015-16	80,000	2	1,60,000
2016-17	1,00,000	3	3,00,000
		6	4,80,000

Weighted Average Profit $= \frac{\text{Total of Product}}{\text{Total of Weights}} = \frac{4,80,000}{6} =$ ₹ 80,000

Goodwill = Weighted Average Profit × Number of Years' Purchase

$= 80,000 \times 2 =$ ₹ 1,60,000

(ii) **JOURNAL**

Date	Particulars		LF	Amt (Dr)	Amt (Cr)
	Rita's Capital A/c	Dr		16,000	
	Nina's Capital A/c	Dr		10,667	
	To Mita's Capital A/c				26,667
	(Being amount of goodwill adjusted)				

Notes
- Abnormal gain by speculation ₹ 10,000 will be deducted to get normal profit for the year 2014-15.
- Mita's share of goodwill $\left(\frac{1}{6} \times 1,60,000\right) =$ ₹ 26,667 will be distributed between continuous partner in gaining ratio.

22. Gaining ratio of partners = Old ratio (in absence of any other information)

∴ Gaining ratio of Manoj and Karan = 4 : 1

Dr **Partners' Capital Account** Cr

Particulars	Manoj (₹)	Hari (₹)	Karan (₹)	Particulars	Manoj (₹)	Hari (₹)	Karan (₹)
To Goodwill	4,000	2,000	1,000	By Balance bld	16,000	14,000	10,000
To Hari (WN 2)	1,920	—	480	By P & L A/c (WN 1)	4,000	2,000	1,000
To Hari (WN 3)	6,400	—	1,600	By Manoj (WN 2)	—	1,920	—
To Hari's Loan A/c	—	24,400	—	By Karan (WN 2)	—	480	—
To Balance c/d	7,680	—	7,920	By Manoj (WN 3)	—	6,400	—
				By Karan (WN 3)	—	1,600	—
	20,000	26,400	11,000		20,000	26,400	11,000

Working Notes

1. **Rectifying Entry for Insurance**

Date	Particulars		Amt (Dr)	Amt (Cr)
	Prepaid Insurance A/c	Dr	7,000	
	To P & L A/c			7,000
	P & L A/c	Dr	7,000	
	To Manoj			4,000
	To Hari			2,000
	To Karan			1,000

2. Share of general reserve

Hari's share = $\frac{2}{7} \times 8{,}400 =$ ₹ 2,400 to be adjusted in ratio of 4 : 1 (Manoj and Karan)

∴ Manoj = ₹ 1,920; Karan = ₹ 480

3. Share of Hari after all adjustments

= 14,000 + 2,000 + 1,920 + 480 – 2,000 = ₹ 16,400

Amount to be paid to Hari = ₹ 24,400

Hidden goodwill = ₹ 8,000

to be adjusted in ratio of 4 : 1 (Manoj and Karan)

Manoj = ₹ 6,400; Karan = ₹ 1,600

Common Mistake Students usually do nothing about the adjustment, 'General reserve not to be distributed'. But for this, gaining partners' capital account will be debited and sacrificing partners' capital account will be credited in gaining/sacrificing ratio.

23. (a) **JOURNAL**

Date	Particulars		LF	Amt (Dr)	Amt (Cr)
2018					
Apr 1	Investment A/c	Dr		5,000	
	Creditors A/c	Dr		3,000	
	To Revaluation A/c				8,000
	(Being assets and liabilities revalued)				
	Revaluation A/c	Dr		8,000	
	To Mohit's Capital A/c				4,800
	To Ali's Capital A/c				1,600
	To John's Capital A/c				1,600
	(Being profit on revaluation credited to partners capital account in old ratio)				

Date	Particulars		LF	Amt (Dr)	Amt (Cr)
	General Reserve A/c	Dr		6,000	
	To Mohit's Capital A/c				2,700
	To Ali's Capital A/c				900
	To John's Capital A/c				900
	To Provision for Doubtful Debts				1,500
	(Being general reserve distributed)				
	Ali's Capital A/c	Dr		6,000	
	John's Capital A/c	Dr		6,000	
	To Mohit's Capital A/c				12,000
	(Being amount of goodwill adjusted)				
	Mohit's Capital A/c	Dr		40,000	
	To Investment A/c				40,000
	(Being investment taken by Mohit)				
	Mohit's Capital A/c	Dr		7,200	
	Ali's Capital A/c	Dr		2,400	
	John's Capital A/c	Dr		2,400	
	To Goodwill A/c				12,000
	(Being goodwill written-off)				
	Ali's Capital A/c	Dr		2,700	
	John's Capital A/c	Dr		2,700	
	To Mohit's Capital A/c				5,400
	(Being amount of investment fluctuation fund adjusted in capital account)				
	Mohit's Capital A/c	Dr		20,000	
	To Cash A/c				20,000
	(Being cash paid to retiring partner)				
	Mohit's Capital A/c	Dr		27,700	
	To Mohit's Loan A/c				27,700
	(Being balance of capital transferred to Mohit's loan account)				

(b)

Balance Sheet
as at 1st April, 2018

Liabilities		Amt (₹)	Assets		Amt (₹)
Creditors		12,000	Cash at Bank		20,000
Investment Fluctuation Fund		9,000	Debtors	30,000	
Mohit's Loan A/c		27,700	(–) Provision for Doubtful Debts	(6,500)	23,500
Capital A/cs			Plant and Machinery		88,000
Ali	41,400				
John	41,400	82,800			
		1,31,500			1,31,500

24. (i) (a) Dr **Paresh's Capital Account** Cr

Particulars	Amt (₹)	Particulars	Amt (₹)
To Drawings A/c	5,000	By Balance b/d	80,000
To Interest on Drawings A/c	100	By Interest on Capital A/c	8,000
To Revaluation Loss A/c $\left(12{,}000 \times \frac{4}{10}\right)$	4,800	By Profit and Loss A/c	20,000
		By Harish's Capital A/c	8,000
To Paresh's Loan A/c (Balancing figure)	1,07,700	By Mahesh's Capital A/c	1,600
	1,17,600		1,17,600

(ii) Dr **Paresh's Loan Account** Cr

Date	Particulars	Amt (₹)	Date	Particulars	Amt (₹)
2018			2017		
Mar 31	To Bank A/c	53,850	Apr 1	By Paresh's Capital A/c	1,07,700
Mar 31	To Balance c/d	53,850			
		1,07,700			1,07,700
2019			2018		
Mar 31	To Bank A/c	53,850	Apr 1	By Balance b/d	53,850
		53,850			53,850

Note Interest on loan accrued and due and interest on loan accrued but not due is excluded from the syllabus.

Working Note

Firm's goodwill = ₹ 24,000

Paresh's share of goodwill $= 24{,}000 \times \frac{4}{10} =$ ₹ 9,600

Harish's sacrifice $= 9{,}600 \times \frac{5}{6} =$ ₹ 8,000 ; Mahesh's sacrifice $= 9{,}600 \times \frac{1}{6} =$ ₹ 1,600

(ii) **In the Books of Parth, Angad and Leesha**
JOURNAL

Date	Particulars		LF	Amt (Dr)	Amt (Cr)
	Furniture A/c	Dr		12,000	
	To Parth's Capital A/c				6,000
	To Angad's Capital A/c				4,000
	To Leesha's Capital A/c				2,000
	(Being an unrecorded asset now recorded)				
	Angad's Capital A/c (50,000 + 4,000)	Dr		54,000	
	To Furniture A/c				12,000
	To Cash A/c				42,000
	(Being cash and furniture given in final settlement)				

25. (a) **In the Books of Ali, Deb and Karan**
JOURNAL

Date	Particulars		LF	Amt (Dr)	Amt (Cr)
2016					
Jul 1	Revaluation A/c	Dr		6,500	
	To Building A/c				6,500
	(Being decrease in the value of building debited to revaluation account)				
Jul 1	Furniture A/c	Dr		10,000	
	To Revaluation A/c				10,000
	(Being increase in the value of furniture credited to revaluation account)				
Jul 1	Provision for Doubtful Debts A/c	Dr		1,000	
	To Revaluation A/c				1,000
	(Being provision for doubtful debts written-off)				
Jul 1	Revaluation A/c	Dr		4,500	
	To Karan's Capital A/c				2,250
	To Ali's Capital A/c				1,500
	To Deb's Capital A/c				750
	(Being profit on revaluation, transferred to partners' capital accounts)				

Date	Particulars		LF	Amt (Dr)	Amt (Cr)
Jul 1	Investment Fluctuation Reserve A/c	Dr		30,000	
	To Investment A/c				12,000
	To Karan's Capital A/c				9,000
	To Ali's Capital A/c				6,000
	To Deb's Capital A/c				3,000
	(Being investment revalued and excess balance of investment fluctuation reserve credited to partners' capital accounts)				
Jul 1	Karan's Capital A/c	Dr		9,000	
	Ali's Capital A/c	Dr		6,000	
	Deb's Capital A/c	Dr		3,000	
	To Goodwill A/c				18,000
	(Being existing goodwill written-off in old ratio)				
Jul 1	Ali's Capital A/c	Dr		40,000	
	Deb's Capital A/c	Dr		20,000	
	To Karan's Capital A/c				60,000
	(Being Karan's share of goodwill contributed by Ali and Deb in their gaining ratio)				
Jul 1	Profit and Loss Suspense A/c	Dr		3,125	
	To Karan's Capital A/c				3,125
	(Being Karan's share of profit upto the date of his death credited to his capital account)				
Jul 1	Interest on Capital A/c	Dr		1,500	
	To Karan's Capital A/c				1,500
	(Being interest on capital upto the date of Karan's death credited to his account)				
Jul 1	Profit and Loss Suspense A/c	Dr		1,500	
	To Interest on Capital A/c				1,500
	(Being interest on capital transferred to profit and loss suspense account)				
Jul 1	Karan's Capital A/c	Dr		1,66,875	
	To Karan's Legal Representative's Loan A/c				1,66,875
	(Being balance of Karan's capital account transferred to his representative's loan account)				

(b)

Balance Sheet of Ali and Deb
as at 1st July, 2016

Liabilities		Amt (₹)	Assets	Amt (₹)
Capital A/cs			Building	93,500
Ali	36,500		Furniture	50,000
Deb	30,750	67,250	Investments	38,000
Karan's Legal Representative's Loan		1,66,875	Debtors	30,000
Bills Payable		10,000	Cash at Bank	43,000
Creditors		15,000	Profit and Loss Suspense A/c	4,625
		2,59,125		2,59,125

Working Notes

1. Profit on revaluation can be ascertained by preparing revaluation account.

Dr **Revaluation Account** Cr

Particulars		Amt (₹)	Particulars	Amt (₹)
To Buildings A/c		6,500	By Furniture A/c	10,000
To Profit Transferred to			By Provision for Doubtful Debts A/c	1,000
Karan's Capital A/c	2,250			
Ali's Capital A/c	1,500			
Deb's Capital A/c	750	4,500		
		11,000		11,000

2. The value of investments has decreased by ₹ 12,000. So, investment fluctuation reserve will be maintained at ₹ 12,000 and the excess amount of ₹ 18,000 (30,000 – 12,000) will be distributed among partners in old ratio.
3. Existing goodwill of ₹ 18,000 will be written-off in old ratio.
4. Karan's share of goodwill $= 1{,}20{,}000 \times \frac{3}{6} =$ ₹ 60,000

   This will be contributed Ali and Deb in their gaining ratio of 2 : 1.
5. Karan's share of profit till the date of his death $= 25{,}000 \times \frac{3}{12} \times \frac{3}{6} =$ ₹ 3,125
6. Interest on Karan's capital upto the date of his death $= 1{,}00{,}000 \times \frac{6}{100} \times \frac{3}{12} =$ ₹ 1,500
7. Balance in Profit and Loss suspense Account = Share in Profit + Interest on Capital

   = 3,125 + 1,500 = ₹ 4,625
8. Amount payable to Karan's legal representative and balance of capital accounts of Ali and Deb can be ascertained by preparing partners' capital accounts.

Dr **Partners' Capital Account** Cr

Particulars	Karan (₹)	Ali (₹)	Deb (₹)	Particulars	Karan (₹)	Ali (₹)	Deb (₹)
To Goodwill A/c	9,000	6,000	3,000	By Balance b/d	1,00,000	75,000	50,000
To Karan's Capital A/c	—	40,000	20,000	By Revaluation A/c	2,250	1,500	750
To Karan's Legal Representative's Loan A/c	1,66,875	—	—	By Investment Fluctuation Reserve A/c	9,000	6,000	3,000
To Balance c/d	—	36,500	30,750	By Ali's Capital A/c	40,000	—	—
				By Deb's Capital A/c	20,000	—	—
				By Profit and Loss Suspense A/c	3,125	—	—
				By Interest on Capital A/c	1,500	—	—
	1,75,875	82,500	53,750		1,75,875	82,500	53,750

26. (a) **In the Books of Pihu, Geeta and Nita**

Dr **Revaluation Account** Cr

Particulars	Amt (₹)	Particulars		Amt (₹)
To Land and Building A/c	12,000	By Creditors		3,000
		By Loss Transferred to Capital A/c		
		Pihu	4,500	
		Geeta	3,000	
		Nita	1,500	9,000
	12,000			12,000

(b) Dr **Partners' Capital Account** Cr

Particulars	Pihu (₹)	Geeta (₹)	Nita (₹)	Particulars	Pihu (₹)	Geeta (₹)	Nita (₹)
To Revaluation A/c (Loss)	4,500	3,000	1,500	By Balance b/d	79,000	70,000	61,000
To Nita's Capital A/c	3,000	6,000	—	By General Reserve A/c	3,900	2,600	1,300
To Cash A/c	—	—	29,800	(9,000 – 1,200)			
To Nita's Loan A/c	—	—	40,000	By Pihu's Capital A/c	—	—	3,000
To Balance c/d	75,400	63,600	—	By Geeta's Capital A/c	—	—	6,000
	82,900	72,600	71,300		82,900	72,600	71,300

(c) **In the Books of Pihu and Geeta**

Dr **Nita's Loan Account** Cr

Date	Particulars	Amt (₹)	Date	Particulars	Amt (₹)
2016			2015		
Mar 31	To Bank A/c (20,000 + 4,000)	24,000	Apr 1	By Nita's Capital A/c	40,000
Mar 31	To Balance c/d	20,000	2016		
			Mar 31	By Interest A/c (40,000 × 10%)	4,000
		44,000			44,000
2017			2016		
Mar 31	To Bank A/c	22,000	Apr 1	By Balance b/d	20,000
			2017		
			Mar 31	By Interest A/c (20,000 × 10%)	2,000
		22,000			22,000

Note Though interest on loan accrued and due and interest on loan accrued but not due is excluded from the syllabus, however it is being shown in this question for knowledge purpose only.

Working Note

Gaining Ratio = New Share – Old Share

$$\text{Pihu} = \frac{5}{9} - \frac{3}{6} = \frac{1}{18}; \qquad \text{Neeta} = \frac{4}{9} - \frac{2}{6} = \frac{2}{18} \quad or \quad 1:2$$

27. (a) **In the Books of Ram, Krishna and Mohan**

Dr **Revaluation Account** Cr

Particulars	Amt (₹)	Particulars		Amt (₹)
To Trademark A/c	7,200	By Land and Building A/c		9,600
To Plant A/c	14,400	By Loss Transferred to		
		Ram's Capital A/c	3,600	
		Krishna's Capital A/c	6,000	
		Mohan's Capital A/c	2,400	12,000
	21,600			21,600

(b) Dr **Krishna's Capital Account** Cr

Particulars	Amt (₹)	Particulars	Amt (₹)
To Advertisement Suspense A/c (12,000 × 5/10)	6,000	By Balance b/d	69,600
		By General Reserve A/c (16,000 × 5/10)	8,000
To Revaluation A/c (Loss)	6,000	By Goodwill A/c (WN1)	32,000
To Krishna's Legal Representative's A/c (Balancing transfer)	1,10,080	By Interest on Capital A/c $\left(69{,}600 \times \frac{10}{100} \times \frac{6}{12}\right)$	3,480
		By Profit and Loss Suspense A/c $\left(36{,}000 \times \frac{6}{12} \times \frac{5}{10}\right)$	9,000
	1,22,080		1,22,080

(c) Dr **Krishna's Legal Representative's Account** Cr

Particulars	Amt (₹)	Particulars	Amt (₹)
To Cash A/c (Paid)	60,080	By Krishna's Capital A/c	1,10,080
To Legal Representative's Loan A/c (Transferred)	50,000		
	1,10,080		1,10,080

Working Note

Calculation of share of goodwill

$$\text{Goodwill of the firm} = \left(\frac{31{,}200 + 28{,}800 + 36{,}000}{3}\right) \times 2 = ₹\ 64{,}000$$

$$\text{Krishna's share} = 64{,}000 \times \frac{5}{10} = ₹\ 32{,}000$$

28. (a) **In the Books of Angad, Kunal and Nitin**

Dr **Revaluation Account** Cr

Particulars		Amt (₹)	Particulars	Amt (₹)
To Provision for Doubtful Debts A/c		975	By Stock A/c	2,500
To Machinery A/c		1,750	By Building A/c	2,250
To Motor Van A/c		600		
To Profit Transferred to Partners' Capital A/cs				
Angad	570			
Kunal	570			
Nitin	285	1,425		
		4,750		4,750

(b) Dr **Partners' Capital Account** Cr

Particulars	Angad (₹)	Kunal (₹)	Nitin (₹)	Particulars	Angad (₹)	Kunal (₹)	Nitin (₹)
To Kunal's Capital A/c (Goodwill)	1,800	—	1,800	By Balance b/d	12,500	15,000	20,000
				By Revaluation A/c	570	570	285
To Kunal's Loan A/c	—	21,570	—	By General Reserve	2,400	2,400	1,200
To Nitin's Current A/c (Balancing figure)	—	—	6,343	By Angad's Capital A/c (Goodwill)	—	1,800	—
To Balance c/d	20,013	—	13,342	By Nitin's Capital A/c (Goodwill)	—	1,800	—
				By Angad's Current A/c (Balancing figure)	6,343	—	—
	21,813	21,570	21,485		21,813	21,570	21,485

(c)

In the Books of Angad and Nitin
Balance Sheet
as at 1st April, 2013

Liabilities		Amt (₹)	Assets		Amt (₹)
Capital A/cs			Stock		15,000
Angad	20,013		Building		24,750
Nitin	13,342	33,355	Machinery		15,750
Nitin's Current A/c		6,343	Motor Van		3,400
Kunal's Loan		21,570	Debtors	8,000	
Creditors		10,000	(–) Provision for Doubtful Debts	(1,225)	6,775
Bills Payable		2,000	Angad's Current A/c		6,343
			Bank		1,250
		73,268			73,268

Working Notes

1. Gaining Ratio = New Share – Old Share

   Angad's gain $= \frac{3}{5} - \frac{2}{5} = \frac{1}{5}$; Nitin's gain $= \frac{2}{5} - \frac{1}{5} = \frac{1}{5}$; Gaining ratio = 1 : 1

2. **Treatment of Goodwill**

   Firm's goodwill = ₹ 9,000

   Kunal's share in goodwill $= \frac{2}{5} \times 9{,}000 =$ ₹ 3,600, to be paid by Angad and Nitin in gaining ratio.

3. **Calculation of New Capital of Remaining Partners**

	Amt (₹)
Adjusted capital of Angad	= 13,670
Adjusted capital of Nitin	= 19,685
Total capital of Angad and Nitin	33,355

   Hence, as per new profit sharing ratio

   Angad's capital $= 33{,}355 \times \frac{3}{5} =$ ₹ 20,013 ; Nitin's capital $= 33{,}355 \times \frac{2}{5} =$ ₹ 13,342

29.

In the Books of Bina

Dr **Anita's Executor's Account** Cr

Particulars	Amt (₹)	Particulars	Amt (₹)
To Anita's Executor's Loan A/c	1,28,000	By Anita's Capital A/c	60,000
		By General Reserve A/c $\left(30{,}000 \times \frac{2}{5}\right)$	12,000
		By Bina's Capital A/c (Goodwill)	50,400
		By Profit and Loss Suspense A/c (Profit)	5,600
	1,28,000		1,28,000

Working Notes

1. **Calculation of Profit**

   $$\text{Average Profit} = \frac{\text{Total Profits}}{\text{Number of Years}} = \frac{42{,}000 + 39{,}000 + 45{,}000}{3} = \frac{1{,}26{,}000}{3} = ₹\ 42{,}000$$

   Anita's share of profit $= 42{,}000 \times \frac{4}{12} \times \frac{2}{5} =$ ₹ 5,600

2. **Calculation of Goodwill**

   Goodwill = Average Profit × Number of Years' Purchase = 42,000 × 3 = 1,26,000

   Anita's share of goodwill $= 1{,}26{,}000 \times \frac{2}{5} =$ ₹ 50,400

30. (a)

Capital Accounts of Arun and Varun after the Retirement of Tarun

Particulars	Arun (₹)	Varun (₹)	Particulars	Arun (₹)	Varun (₹)
To Bank A/c	1,050	1,350	By Balance b/d	36,050	22,350
To Balance c/d	35,000	21,000			
	36,050	22,350		36,050	22,350

(b)

Balance Sheet
as at 31st December, 2004

Liabilities		Amt (₹)	Assets	Amt (₹)
Capital A/cs			Stock	25,000
Arun	35,000		Debtors	15,500
Varun	21,000	56,000	Plant and Machinery	34,000
Tarun's Loan		32,100	Building	45,000
Provident Fund		12,500	Cash at Bank	100
Creditors		19,000		
		1,19,600		1,19,600

Working Notes

1. **Calculation of Gaining Ratio**

Gaining Ratio = New Share – Old Share

Arun $= \frac{5}{8} - \frac{4}{9} = \frac{45-32}{72} = \frac{13}{72}$; Varun $= \frac{3}{8} - \frac{2}{9} = \frac{27-16}{72} = \frac{11}{72}$; Gaining ratio = 13 : 11

2. **Treatment of Goodwill**

Tarun's share of goodwill $= 10{,}800 \times \frac{3}{9} =$ ₹ 3,600

This goodwill will be paid by Arun and Varun in gaining ratio

Arun $= 3{,}600 \times \frac{13}{24} =$ ₹ 1,950 ; Varun $= 3{,}600 \times \frac{11}{24} =$ ₹ 1,650

3. Dr **Partners' Capital Account** Cr

Particulars	Arun (₹)	Tarun (₹)	Varun (₹)	Particulars	Arun (₹)	Tarun (₹)	Varun (₹)
To Advertising Expenditure A/c	4,000	3,000	2,000	By Balance b/d	40,000	30,000	25,000
				By General Reserve A/c	2,000	1,500	1,000
To Tarun's Capital A/c (Goodwill)	1,950	—	1,650	By Arun's Capital A/c (Goodwill)	—	1,950	—
To Tarun's Loan A/c	—	32,100	—	By Varun's Capital A/c (Goodwill)	—	1,650	—
To Balance c/d	36,050	—	22,350				
	42,000	35,100	26,000		42,000	35,100	26,000

4. **Calculation of New Capital**

Arun $= 56{,}000 \times \frac{5}{8} =$ ₹ 35,000 ; Varun $= 56{,}000 \times \frac{3}{8} =$ ₹ 21,000

5. Dr **Bank Account** Cr

Particulars	Amt (₹)	Particulars	Amt (₹)
To Balance b/d	2,500	By Arun's Capital A/c	1,050
		By Varun's Capital A/c	1,350
		By Balance c/d (Balancing figure)	100
	2,500		2,500

31.

In the Books of A, B and C

Revaluation Account

Dr					Cr
Particulars		**Amt (₹)**	**Particulars**		**Amt (₹)**
To Furniture A/c		8,000	By Provision for Doubtful Debts A/c		500
To Rent A/c		1,500	By Land and Building A/c		12,000
To Profit Transferred to				
A's Capital A/c	1,000			
B's Capital A/c	1,000			
C's Capital A/c	1,000	3,000		
		12,500			12,500

Partners' Capital Account

Dr Particulars	A (₹)	B (₹)	C (₹)	Particulars	A (₹)	B (₹)	C (₹) Cr
To B's Capital A/c (Goodwill)	9,600	—	9,600	By Balance b/d	60,000	40,000	32,000
To Cash A/c	—	72,200	—	By Profit and Loss A/c	2,000	2,000	2,000
To Balance c/d	87,900	—	87,900	By General Reserve	10,000	10,000	10,000
				By Revaluation A/c	1,000	1,000	1,000
				By A's Capital A/c (Goodwill)	—	9,600	—
				By C's Capital A/c (Goodwill)	—	9,600	—
				By Cash A/c	24,500	—	52,500
	97,500	72,200	97,500		97,500	72,200	97,500

In the Books of A and C

Balance Sheet

as at 1st January, 2001

Liabilities		Amt (₹)	Assets		Amt (₹)
Capital A/cs			Cash		24,800
A	87,900		Stock		20,000
C	87,900	1,75,800	Furniture		20,000
Creditors		40,000	Debtors	45,000	
Bills Payable		20,000	(–) Provision for Doubtful Debts	(4,500)	40,500
Outstanding Rent		1,500	Land and Building		1,32,000
		2,37,300			2,37,300

Working Notes

1. Gaining Ratio = New Share – Old Share

$$A = \frac{1}{2} - \frac{1}{3} = \frac{3-2}{6} = \frac{1}{6}; \qquad C = \frac{1}{2} - \frac{1}{3} = \frac{3-2}{6} = \frac{1}{6}$$

Gaining ratio = 1 : 1

2. **Treatment of Goodwill**

Firm's goodwill = ₹ 57,600; B's share $= 57{,}600 \times \frac{1}{3} =$ ₹ 19,200

The goodwill will be paid by A and B in gaining ratio

A's share $= 19{,}200 \times \frac{1}{2} = 9{,}600$; B's share $= 19{,}200 \times \frac{1}{2} = 9{,}600$

3. **Calculation of New Capital of Remaining Partners**

	Amt (₹)
A's adjusted capital	63,400
C's adjusted capital	35,400
(+) B's capital	72,200
(+) Cash to be kept	24,800
	1,95,800
(–) Cash in business	(20,000)
	1,75,800

$$\text{A's new capital} = 1,75,800 \times \frac{1}{2} = ₹\,87,900$$

$$\text{C's new capital} = 1,75,800 \times \frac{1}{2} = ₹\,87,900$$

4. Dr **Cash Account** Cr

Particulars	Amt (₹)	Particulars	Amt (₹)
To Balance b/d	20,000	By B's Capital A/c	72,200
To A's Capital A/c	24,500	By Balance c/d	24,800
To C's Capital A/c	52,500		
	97,000		97,000

32. **In the Books of Albert, Boris and Cyril**

Dr **Revaluation Account** Cr

Particulars		Amt (₹)	Particulars	Amt (₹)
To Stock A/c		2,000	By Building A/c	10,000
To Provision for Doubtful Debts A/c		1,500		
To Profit Transferred to Capital A/cs				
Albert	3,250			
Boris	2,167			
Cyril	1,083	6,500		
		10,000		10,000

Dr **Partners' Capital Account** Cr

Particulars	Albert (₹)	Boris (₹)	Cyril (₹)	Particulars	Albert (₹)	Boris (₹)	Cyril (₹)
To Albert's Executor A/c	67,375	—	—	By Balance b/d	50,000	50,000	50,000
To Albert's Capital A/c (Goodwill)	—	8,000	4,000	By Revaluation A/c	3,250	2,167	1,083
To Balance c/d	—	44,167	47,083	By Boris's Capital A/c (Goodwill)	8,000	—	—
				By Cyril's Capital A/c (Goodwill)	4,000	—	—
				By Profit and Loss Suspense A/c (Share of profit)	1,375	—	—
				By Profit and Loss Suspense A/c (Interest on capital)	750	—	—
	67,375	52,167	51,083		67,375	52,167	51,083

In the Books of Boris and Cyril
Balance Sheet
as at 1st July, 1999

Liabilities		Amt (₹)	Assets		Amt (₹)
Capital A/cs			Building		80,000
Boris	44,167		Plant and Machinery		25,000
Cyril	47,083	91,250	Stock		30,000
Albert's Executor A/c		67,375	Debtors	15,000	
Creditors A/c		17,000	(–) Provision for Doubtful Debts	(1,500)	13,500
			Bank		25,000
			Profit and Loss Suspense A/c		2,125
		1,75,625			1,75,625

Working Notes

1. **Calculation of Albert's Share of Goodwill**

$$\text{Average profit} = \frac{10,000 + 15,000 + 11,000}{3} = ₹\ 12,000$$

$$\text{Value of firm's goodwill} = 12,000 \times 2 = ₹\ 24,000$$

$$\text{Albert's share of goodwill} = 24,000 \times \frac{3}{6} = ₹\ 12,000$$

2. $\text{Interest on capital} = 50,000 \times \frac{6}{100} \times \frac{3}{12} = ₹\ 750$

3. $\text{Share of profit} = 11,000 \times \frac{3}{6} \times \frac{3}{12} = ₹\ 1,375$

4. **Profit and Loss Suspense Account**

	Amt (₹)
Interest on capital	750
Share of profit	1,375
	2,125

CHAPTER TEST

01 Mark Questions

1. M, N and O are partners sharing profits in the ratio of 3 : 4 : 1. M retired on 31st March, 2017 and surrenders 2/3rd of his partner in favour of N and the remaining share in favour of O. The new profit sharing ratio of N and O is

(a) 1 : 1 (b) 2 : 1 (c) 3: 1 (d) 2 : 3

2. A, B and C are partners in a firm. C decided to retire on 31st March, 2022 and the amount payable to C was ₹ 60,600. What will be the journal entry when the whole amount of C is treated as loan?

(a) Debit C's Capital A/c and Credit C's Loan A/c by ₹ 60,600
(b) Debit C's Loan A/c and Credit C's Capital A/c by ₹ 60,600
(c) Debit C's Capital A/c and Credit C's Loan A/c by ₹ 20,200
(d) Debit C's Loan A/c and Credit C's Capital A/c by ₹ 20,200

3. If, at the time of adjustment of capital, one of the remaining partners' new capital exceeds his/her contribution, the partner will

(a) withdraw cash
(b) bring cash
(c) Both (a) and (b)
(d) None of the above

4. The share of deceased partner is transferred to his

(a) captital account (b) loan account
(c) executors account (d) Either (a) or (c)

5. P, T and M are partners in a firm sharing profits in the ratio of 3 : 2 : 1. T died on 1st July, 2022. His share of profit of current year will be calculated on the basis of last year's profit which amounted to ₹ 14,000. During the year, bad debts amounted to ₹ 2,000 had to be adjusted. What will be the amount of profit transferred to T's capital account, if P and M decided to change their profit share to 3 : 1?

(a) ₹ 1,000 (b) ₹ 2,000 (c) ₹ 3,000 (d) ₹ 4,000

6. State a difference between sacrificing and gaining ratio.

7. A, S and D are partners in a firm with profit sharing ratio of 3:2:1. S retired, A and D decided to share future profits equally. Goodwill of the firm is valued at ₹ 30,000. What will be the journal entry for the treatment of goodwill of S?

8. How the amount payable to retiring partner is treated in partners' capital account?

03 Marks Questions

9. S, P and D are partners in a firm. D retires and the goodwill of the firm is valued at ₹ 30,000. S and P decide to share future profits in the ratio of 3 : 2. Pass necessary journal entries when goodwill account is raised and written-off from the books.

10. A, B and C were partners in a firm sharing profits in the ratio of 4 : 3 : 3. On 31st March, 2022 their Balance Sheet was as follows

Liabilities		Amt (₹)	Assets	Amt (₹)
Creditors		1,27,500	Cash	60,000
Bills Payable		90,000	Debtors	97,500
C's Loan		2,10,000	Bills Receivables	67,500
Capital A/cs			Furniture	2,02,500
A	5,25,000		Machinery	9,37,500
B	5,10,000	10,35,000	C's Capital	97,500
		14,62,500		14,62,500

On 30th September, 2022, C died. The partnership deed provided for the following to the executors of the deceased partner.

(i) His share in the goodwill of the firm calculated on the basis of three years' purchase of the average profits of the last four years.
The profits of the last four years were ₹ 14,25,000, ₹ 12,75,000, ₹ 13,50,000 and ₹ 12,00,000 respectively.
(ii) His share in the profits of the firm till the date of his death calculated on the basis of the average profits of the last four years.
(iii) Interest @ 8% p.a. on the credit balance, if any, in his capital account.
(iv) Interest on his loan @ 12% p.a.

Prepare C's capital account to be presented to his executors, assuming that his loan and interest on loan were transferred to his capital account.

06 Marks Questions

11. The balance sheet of Sudha, Rahim and Kartik who were sharing profits in the ratio of 3 : 3 : 4 as on 31st March, 2012 was as follows

Balance Sheet
as at 31st March, 2012

Liabilities		Amt (₹)	Assets	Amt (₹)
General Reserve		10,000	Cash	16,000
Bills Payable		5,000	Stock	44,000
Loan		12,000	Investments	47,000
Capital A/cs			Land and Building	60,000
Sudha	60,000		Sudha's Loan	10,000
Rahim	50,000			
Kartik	40,000	1,50,000		
		1,77,000		1,77,000

Sudha died on 30th June, 2012. The partnership deed provided for the following on the death of a partner

(i) Goodwill of the firm to be valued at two years' purchase of average profits for the last three years.
(ii) Sudha's share of profit or loss till the date of her death was to be calculated on the basis of sales. Sales for the year ended 31st March, 2012 amounted to ₹ 4,00,000 and that from 1st April to 30th June, 2012 to ₹1,50,000. The profit for the year ended 31st March, 2012 was ₹ 1,00,000.
(iii) Interest on capital was to be provided @ 6% per annum.
(iv) The average profits of the last three years were ₹ 42,000.
(v) According to Sudha's will, the executors should donate her share to 'Matri Chhaya, an orphanage for girls'.

Prepare Sudha's capital account to be rendered to her executor.

12. Indu and Hema were partners. The partnership deed provided for

(i) Profits to be divided as Indu 1/2, Hema 1/3 and 1/6th to be transferred to reserves.
(ii) The accounts are closed on 31st March each year.
(iii) In the event of the death of a partner the executors will be entitled to
 (a) Capital to be credited on the date of the death. (b) Interest on capital at 12% per annum.
 (c) Proportion of profit to the date of death based on the average profits credited for the last 3 years.
 (d) Share of goodwill based on three years' purchase of the average profits of the preceding 3 years.

The following information is provided to you

Indu's capital ₹1,20,000; Hema's capital ₹ 80,000; reserves ₹ 30,000; cash ₹ 1,10,000; investment ₹ 70,000.

Prepare Indu's capital account to be presented to her executor who died on 30th April, 2007. The profits for the three preceding years were ₹ 84,000, ₹ 90,000 and ₹ 99,000.

10 Marks Questions

13. The balance sheet of A, B and C on 31st March, 2007 was as follows

Balance Sheet
as at 31st March, 2007

Liabilities		Amt (₹)	Assets	Amt (₹)
Creditors		50,000	Profit and Loss A/c	30,000
Capital A/cs			Land and Buildings	80,000
A	80,000		Plant and Machinery	56,000
B	80,000		Motor Car	54,000
C	60,000	2,20,000	Debtors	48,000
			Cash	2,000
		2,70,000		2,70,000

The following terms were agreed upon for A's retirement

(i) Goodwill to be valued at ₹ 42,000 and not to be shown in the books of the firm after A's retirement.
(ii) Land and building to be appreciated by ₹ 20,000.
(iii) Plant and machinery to be reduced to ₹ 46,000.
(iv) Provision for doubtful debts to be created at 5% on debtors.
(v) Create a provision of ₹ 1,400 for discount on creditors.
(vi) The sum payable to A to be brought in by B and C in such a manner that their capitals are in proportion to their new profit sharing ratio.

Prepare the revaluation account, partners' capital account and the balance sheet of the new firm to give effect to the above terms.

14. A, B and C were in partnership, sharing profits in proportion to their capitals. Their balance sheet on 31st March, 2008 was as follows

Balance Sheet
as at 31st March, 2008

Liabilities		Amt (₹)	Assets		Amt (₹)
Creditors		15,600	Cash		16,000
Reserve		6,000	Debtors	20,000	
Capital A/cs			(–) Provision for Doubtful Debts	(400)	19,600
A	90,000		Stock		18,000
B	60,000		Machinery		48,000
C	30,000	1,80,000	Buildings		1,00,000
		2,01,600			2,01,600

On the above date, B retired owing to ill health and the following adjustments were agreed upon

(i) Buildings to be appreciated by 10%.
(ii) Provision for doubtful debts to be increased to 5% of debtors.
(iii) Machinery to be depreciated by 15%.
(iv) Goodwill of the firm be valued at ₹ 36,000 and be adjusted into the capital accounts of A and C who will share profits in the future in the ratio of 3 : 1.
(v) A provision to be made for outstanding repairs bill of ₹ 3,000.
(vi) ₹ 1,800 is included in the value of creditors for an outstanding legal claim, which is not likely to arise.
(vii) Out of the insurance premium paid, ₹ 2,000 is for the next year. The amount was debited to profit and loss account.
(viii) The partners decide to fix the capital of the new firm as ₹ 1,20,000 in the profit sharing ratios.
(ix) B to be paid ₹ 9,000 in cash and balance to be transferred to his loan account.

Prepare the revaluation account, partners' capital account and the balance sheet of the new firm after B's retirement.

Answers

1. (c) 3 : 1
2. (a) Debit C's Capital A/c and Credit C's Loan A/c by ₹ 60,000
3. (a) bring cash
4. (c) executors account
5. (b) ₹ 2,000
7. Debit D's Capital A/c and Credit S's Capital A/c by ₹ 10,000
10. C's executor account ₹ 15,03,225
11. Sudha's Executor's = ₹ 90,350
12. Indu's Executor's = ₹ 3,07,550
13. Profit on Revaluation = ₹ 9,000
    Balance in Partner's Capital A/cs B = ₹ 99,500
    C = ₹ 99,500
    Balance Sheet Total = ₹ 2,47,600
14. Profit on Revaluation = ₹ 3,000 ; Balance in Partner's Capital A/cs A = ₹ 90,000 ; C = ₹ 30,000
    Balance Sheet Total = ₹ 2,02,800

04

Dissolution of a Partnership Firm

TREND ANALYSIS 5 YEARS

Average No. of Questions Across all Sets

	Types of Questions	2023	2020	2019	2018	2017
01 Introduction	1/2 Marks	—	1	—	—	—
	3 Marks	—	—	—	—	—
	6 Marks	—	—	—	—	—
	10 Marks	—	—	—	—	—
02 Accounting Treatment on Dissolution	1/2 Marks	2	—	—	1	1
	3 Marks	—	—	—	—	—
	6 Marks	1	—	—	—	—
	10 Marks	—	1	1	1	1

Introduction

Dissolution means breaking up or extinction, i.e. discontinuance of existing relationship among the partners. Under the Indian Partnership Act, 1932, dissolution may be either of partnership or of a firm.

Dissolution of partnership changes the existing relationship between partners but the firm may continue its business.

Dissolution of firm means dissolution of partnership among all the partners of the firm. In this case, business of the firm also comes to an end.

Modes of Dissolution of Partnership Firm

Various modes of dissolution of a partnership firm are

(i) Dissolution by agreement
(ii) Compulsory dissolution
(iii) Dissolution on the happening of an event
(iv) Dissolution by notice (v) Dissolution by the court

Settlement of Accounts in Case of Dissolution of Firm

Settlement of accounts in case of dissolution is discussed below

(i) **Treatment of losses** [Section 48(a)] Losses shall be paid first out of profits, then out of partners' capital and lastly, by the partners individually in their profit sharing ratio, if necessary.

(ii) **Application of assets** [Section 48(b)] The assets of the firm, including amount contributed by the partners to make up deficiency of capital, is applied in the following order

(a) Payment to outsiders/creditors.
(b) Payment of loans and advances of partners.
(c) Payment of capital of partners.
(d) The remaining amount shall be divided among the partners in their profit sharing ratio.

Treatment of Firm Debts and Private Debts

Where both the debts of the firm and private debts of a partner co-exist, the following rules, as stated in Section 49 of the Act, shall apply

(i) Firm's property is applied first in payment of firm's debts and if there is any surplus, then the share of each partner is applied in the payment of his private debts or paid to him.

(ii) Partner's private property is applied first in payment of his private debts and the surplus (if any) in payment of firm's debts, if the firms liabilities exceed the firm's assets.

Accounting Treatment on Dissolution of Firm

On dissolution, the books of the firm are closed. The process is completed by opening the following accounts

1. Realisation account 2. Partners' capital account 3. Partners' loan account 4. Cash/Bank account

1. Realisation Account

It is a nominal account prepared at the time of dissolution of partnership firm to show profit or loss on realisation of assets and payment of liabilities.

Journal Entries

Transfer of assets (except cash and bank balance)	Realisation A/c To Sundry Assets A/c	Dr	At book value
Transfer of liabilities (except partners' loan, capital and undistributed profits)	Sundry Liabilities A/c To Realisation A/c	Dr	At book value
Sale of assets	Cash/Bank A/c To Realisation A/c	Dr	At selling price
Assets taken over by partner	Partners' Capital A/c To Realisation A/c	Dr	At agreed value
Sale of unrecorded assets	Cash/Bank A/c To Realisation A/c	Dr	Amount received on sale
Payment of liabilities	Realisation A/c To Cash/Bank A/c	Dr	Amount paid
Any liability taken over by thepartner	Realisation A/c To Partners' Capital A/c	Dr	At agreed value
Payment of realisation expenses	Realisation A/c To Cash/Bank A/c	Dr	Amount paid
Payment of unrecorded liability (which did not exist in the balance sheet)	Realisation A/c To Cash/Bank A/c	Dr	Amount paid
Payment of realisation expenses by any partner	Realisation A/c To Partners' Capital A/c	Dr	Amount paid
Credit balance of realisation account (Profit)	Realisation A/c To Partners' Capital/Current A/c	Dr	In profit sharing ratio
Debit balance of realisation account (Loss)	Partners' Capital/Current A/c To Realisation A/c	Dr	In profit sharing ratio

Points to Remember

- Goodwill appearing in the balance sheet is treated as any other asset. In case, question is silent about the realisation of goodwill, it is assumed the goodwill does not have any value and no amount is realised for it.
- When an asset is transferred to realisation account, its corresponding reserve or provision appearing on the liabilities side of balance sheet is also transferred to realisation account.
- In the absence of any information regarding realisation of assets, it should be assumed that tangible assets and investments have been realised at book value itself while intangible assets, accrued income and prepaid expenses have realised nothing.
- In the absence of any information regarding settlement of any outside liabilities, it should be assumed that an amount equal to the book value of such liability has been paid off.
- Bank overdraft is to be taken to the Bank/Cash A/c and not to be transferred to realisation account but bank loan must be transferred to realisation account.

Format of Realisation Account

Dr **Realisation Account** Cr

Particulars	Amt (₹)	Particulars	Amt (₹)
To Sundry Assets A/c {Excluding cash, bank, fictitious asset, accumulated losses, debit balance of partners' capital/current account, loan to partner(s)}	...	By Sundry Liabilities A/c {Excluding partners' capital, loan from partner(s), reserve, accumulated profit, etc}	...
To Provision on Any Liability A/c	...	By Provision on Any Assets A/c	...
To Bank/Cash A/c (Amount paid for discharging liabilities)	...	By Bank/Cash A/c (Amount received on realisation of assets)	...
To Bank/Cash A/c (Expenses on realisation)	...	By Bank/Cash A/c (Amount received from unrecorded assets)	...
To Partners' Capital/Current A/c (Liability taken over by a partner or remuneration/commission paid to him or any expenses borne by him)	...	By Partner's Capital A/c (Assets taken over by a partner recorded or unrecorded)	...
		By Partners' Capital/Current A/c (Loss on realisation)*	...
To Partners' Capital/Current A/c (Profit on realisation)*	...		
	...		...

Note *Any one of two amounts will appear.

Key Point

All provisions created against any asset or liabilities/provision for doubtful debts, provision for depreciation should be transferred to realisation account on credit or debit side as the case may be and it should be noted that those assets or liabilities should appear in realisation account at gross value.

Difference between Revaluation Account and Realisation Account

Basis	Revaluation account	Realisation account
Purpose	The purpose of preparing revaluation account is to ascertain profit or loss on the revaluation of assets and liabilities.	It is meant to ascertain profit or loss on the disposal of assets and payment of liabilities.
Situation	It is prepared in case of reconstitution of firm.	It is prepared in case of dissolution of firm.
Closing of Accounts	Accounts of assets and liabilities shown in this account, are not closed.	Account of assets and liabilities transferred here, are closed.

Accounting Treatment of Unrecorded Assets and Unrecorded Liabilities

(i) **Unrecorded assets** Assets which are owned by the firm but do not appear in the balance sheet of the firm, are known as unrecorded assets. These assets may have a market value and thus, either can be sold or be taken by a partner or by a creditor in settlement of his outstanding amount. Following entry is passed on its realisation

Cash/Bank A/c Dr (If sold for cash)
Partner's Capital A/c Dr (If taken by a partner)
    To Realisation A/c
(Being the unrecorded assets sold/taken by a partner)

Key Point

If the unrecorded assets are taken by a creditor, no entry is passed.

(ii) **Unrecorded liabilities** Liabilities which do not appear in the balance sheet of the firm, but are payable by the firm, are known as unrecorded liabilities. Such a liability may either be paid in cash or undertaken by a partner to be paid by him. Following entry is passed on its payment

Realisation A/c Dr
    To Cash A/c
    To Partner's Capital A/c (If partner has agreed to pay)
(Being an unrecorded liability paid/undertaken to be paid by a partner)

Key Point

It is to be noted that unrecorded assets and unrecorded liabilities are not transferred to realisation account (since, there is no account for such assets and liabilities, there is no case for their transfer). Only the amount paid or realised from them is recorded.

2. Partners' Capital Account

Balance of partners' capital and current account are recorded in this account. Any asset of the firm taken over by a partner is recorded on the debit side and liability taken over is recorded on the credit side. Undistributed profits and reserves are recorded on the credit side and undistributed losses or fictitious assets are recorded on the debit side. When capital accounts are maintained following fixed capital account method, partners have current accounts also. These current accounts may have credit or debit balance. Current accounts are closed by transferring them to concerned partners' fixed capital accounts.

The entries are as follows

(i) **In case of debit balance in the current account of a partner**

Concerned Partner's Capital A/c Dr
To Concerned Partner's Current A/c

(ii) **In case of credit balance in the current account of a partner**

Concerned Partner's Current A/c Dr
To Concerned Partner's Capital A/c

The balance of partners' capital account are closed in the following manner

(i) **For making final payment to a partner** (in case of credit balance)

Partner's Capital A/c Dr
To Cash/Bank A/c

(ii) **When a partner is required to bring in cash** (in case of a debit balance)

Cash/Bank A/c Dr
To Partner's Capital A/c

Format of Partners' Capital Account

Dr Partners' Capital Account Cr

Particulars	X (₹)	Y (₹)	Particulars	X (₹)	Y (₹)
To Balance b/d (Debit balance)	...	...	By Balance b/d (Credit balance)	...	...
To Profit and Loss A/c	...	...	By General Reserve A/c	...	...
To Advertisement Expenditure A/c	...	...	By Profit and Loss A/c	...	...
To Realisation A/c (Assets taken over)	...	...	By Workmen's Compensation Fund A/c	...	...
To Realisation A/c (Loss on realisation)	...	...	By Realisation A/c (Liabilities taken over)	...	...
To Cash/Bank A/c (Excess cash paid)	...	...	By Realisation A/c (Profit on realisation)	...	...
			By Cash/Bank A/c (Cash brought in)	...	...
	...	...		...	...

Points to Remember

- Loan taken from a partner will be passed through cash or bank account.
- Loan given to a partner will be transferred (debited) to his capital account.

3. Partners' Loan Account

Partners' loan will be paid after all outside liabilities are paid.

The following journal entry is passed

Partner's Loan A/c Dr
To Cash/Bank A/c

4. Bank or Cash Account

It is a real account. On debit side, opening balance, amount realised through sale of assets and any amount paid in by the partners are shown. On the credit side, all the payments for liabilities, realisation expenses and final settlement made to partners are shown. In case, both cash and bank balances appear in balance sheet, it is always better to open a single account.

Format of Cash/Bank Account

Dr **Cash/Bank Account** Cr

Particulars	Amt (₹)	Particulars	Amt (₹)
To Balance b/d (Cash in hand or cash at bank)	...	By Balance b/d (Bank overdraft)	...
To Realisation A/c (Assets realised)	...	By Realisation A/c (Liabilities paid)	...
To Partner's Capital A/c (Cash brought in by a partner)	...	By Realisation A/c (Realisation expenses paid)	...
		By Partner's Loan A/c (Partner's loan paid)	...
		By Partner's Capital A/c (Excess cash paid to partner)	...
	...		...

Preparation of Memorandum Balance Sheet

If a balance sheet, on the date of dissolution, is not given in the question, then it is always advisable to prepare memorandum balance sheet on the date of dissolution to ascertain the amount of missing figures.

Points to Remember

- In the absence of any other information, 'sundry assets' should be treated as balancing figure on the assets side of balance sheet.
- If the balance of partners' capital account are not given as on the date of dissolution, first we will find the balance of partners' capital accounts as on the date of dissolution by recasting the capital accounts.
- When 'sundry assets' are given in the question and nothing is specified about the difference on the asset side of balance sheet, the difference should be treated as debit balance of profit and loss account.

PYQs Previous Years' Questions

1/2 Marks Questions

1. On the dissolution of the firm, partner Rex agreed to take over the responsibility of completing the dissolution work at an agreed remuneration of ₹ 1,000 and to bear all realisation expenses. The actual realisation expenses amounted to ₹ 1,300 which were paid by the firm on Rex's behalf.
   What amount will be debited by the firm to the realisation account? *ISC 2023*
   (a) ₹ 1,000 (b) ₹ 2,300 (c) ₹ 1,300 (d) ₹ 300

2. A firm had given a loan to one of its partners. Give the journal entry to close this loan account at the time of dissolution of the partnership firm. *ISC 2023*

3. When a partnership firm dissolves, its losses including deficiencies of capital are to be paid first out of *ISC Specimen 2023*
   (a) the profits of the firm
   (b) the capitals of the partners
   (c) from the partners individually in their profit sharing ratio
   (d) from the proceeds from sale of assets

4. What is the accounting treatment of employees provident fund appearing in the balance sheet of a partnership firm at the time of dissolution of the firm? *ISC Specimen 2023*

5. Mita and Rita decided to dissolve their partnership firm. Their books showed goodwill of ₹ 5,000. How will the goodwill account be closed on the dissolution of the firm? *ISC Sem II 2022*
   (a) By transferring ₹ 5,000 to the debit side of the partners' capital accounts
   (b) By transferring ₹ 5,000 to the credit side of the partners' capital accounts
   (c) By transferring ₹ 5,000 to the debit side of the realisation account
   (d) By transferring ₹ 5,000 to the credit side of the realisation account

6. Tara and Anjali were partners in a firm sharing profits and losses equally. They dissolved their partnership firm on 31st March, 2021.
   On this date, the balance sheet of their firm, apart from the realisable assets and outside liabilities, showed the following

	Amt (₹)
Tara's Capital	35,000 (Cr)
Anjali's Capital	9,000 (Dr)
Tara's Loan	3,000 (Dr)
Bank Account	?

Additional information

On the dissolution of the firm

(i) The firm realised ₹ 22,000 from the sale of assets and paid ₹ 7,000 to discharge its outside liabilities.

(ii) The realisation account showed a profit of ₹ 6,000 which was shared by the partners in their profit sharing ratio.

(iii) The partners' capital accounts were closed, with a partner, either bringing in cash to cover the deficit of her capital or a partner being paid off her surplus capital.

(iv) The bank account was closed.

You are required to prepare the bank account on the date of dissolution of the firm to determine its balance at bank as shown in the balance sheet as at 31st March, 2021. ***ISC Sem II 2022***

7. Anita and Binita are partners in a firm. Anita had taken a loan of ₹ 15,000 from the firm. How will Anita's loan be closed in the event of dissolution of the firm? ***ISC Sem II Specimen 2022***

(a) By crediting it to Anita's capital account
(b) By debiting it to Anita's capital account
(c) By crediting it to realisation account
(d) By debting it to cash account

8. At the time of dissolution of a partnership firm, its balance sheet showed stock of ₹ 30,000 comprising easily marketable items, obsolete items and a few miscellaneous other items. These items were realised as

(i) Easily marketable items 65% of the total inventory in full.

(ii) Obsolete items 20% of the total inventory had to be discarded.

(iii) The miscellaneous other items in the stock at 40% of their book value.

You are required to pass the journal entry for the realisation of stock. ***ISC Sem II Specimen 2022***

9. (i) Mention any two circumstances which can lead to dissolution of partnership.

(ii) What is the status of the firm upon the dissolution of partnership? ***ISC 2020***

10. Give any two differences between a revaluation account and a realisation account. ***ISC 2018, 2014, 2010, 2006***

11. What will be the treatment of loan given to a partner by the firm at the time of its dissolution? ***ISC 2017***

12. How is workmen compensation fund, shown in the balance sheet of a partnership firm, treated at the time of its dissolution? ***ISC 2016***

13. How will the firm record the payment of realisation expenses which were to be borne by a partner, but paid by the firm on his behalf? ***ISC 2015***

14. What is the accounting treatment of employees provident fund appearing in the balance sheet of a partnership firm at the time of its dissolution? ***ISC 2013***

15. How are debts of the firm and private debts dealt with, in case of dissolution of partnership? ***ISC 2004***

16. How would you treat workmen's compensation fund and employees provident fund shown on the liabilities side of balance sheet, at the time of dissolution of partnership firm and why? ***ISC 2004***

3 Marks Question

17. Ritesh and Farhan are partners in a firm sharing profits and losses in the ratio of 3 : 1. They decided to dissolve their firm on 31st March, 2021. ***ISC Sem II 2022***

You are required to pass the necessary journal entries for the following, after the realisable assets and outside liabilities have been transferred to the realisation account.

(i) Creditors of ₹ 20,000 were paid the amount due to them, by giving them an unrecorded asset worth ₹ 4,000 and the balance in cash.

(ii) Bills payable of ₹ 30,000 were due to be paid on 30th April, 2021. They were paid on the date of dissolution of the firm at a rebate of 5% per annum.

(iii) Realisation expenses of ₹ 2,000 were to be borne by Farhan. These were paid by the firm on his behalf.

KEY IDEA

When a liability is paid by giving an asset to creaditors, no entry is passed for that.

6 Marks Questions

18. Mita and Sita, sharing profits in the ratio of 2 : 1, decided to dissolve their partnership firm on 31st March, 2022, on which date their balance sheet was as under

Balance Sheet of Mita and Sita
as at 31st March, 2022

Liabilities		Amt (₹)	Assets		Amt (₹)
Sundry Creditors		40,000	Land and Building		29,000
Sita's Son's Loan		2,000	Plant and Machinery		20,000
Bank Overdraft		8,000	Stock		3,000
Capital A/cs			Debtors	26,400	
Mita	20,000		(–) Provision for Doubtful Debts	(400)	26,000
Sita	10,000	30,000	Bank		2,000
		80,000			80,000

The partnership firm was dissolved on the date of the balance sheet subject to the following adjustments

(i) Trade creditors accepted plant and machinery at an agreed valuation of 10% less than the book value and the balance in cash in full settlement of their claims.

(ii) Debtors of ₹ 1,000 proved bad.

(iii) Sita took over the stock at a discount of 20%.

(iv) Realisation expenses of ₹ 1,100 were paid by the firm.

You are required to prepare the realisation account. *ISC 2023*

19. The balance sheet of Ravi and Kamal as at 31st March, 2022, was as follows

Balance Sheet of Ravi and Kamal
as at 31st March, 2022

Liabilities	Amt (₹)	Assets	Amt (₹)
Creditors	5,000	Cash	1,400
Investment Fluctuation Fund	300	Debtors	4,700
Capital A/cs		Stock	2,300
Ravi	3,500	Furniture	50
Kamal	2,750	Property	2,000
		Investment	1,100
	11,550		11,550

The partners shared profits in the ratio of 9 : 7. The partnership firm was dissolved on the date of the balance sheet subject to the following adjustments

(i) Property realised 75%.

(ii) Bad debts and discount amounted to ₹ 500.

(iii) Stock realised ₹ 2,525.

(iv) Creditors allowed a discount of 2%.

(v) Expenses of dissolution amounted to ₹ 75 which were paid by Ravi.

You are required to prepare the realisation account. *ISC Specimen 2023*

KEY IDEA

In the absence of any information, assume that furniture and investment have realised at book value.

20. Sita and Gita were partners sharing profits and losses in the ratio of 4 : 5. They dissolved their partnership on 31st March, 2021, when their balance sheet showed the following balances

	Amt (₹)
Sita's Capital	30,000
Gita's Capital	35,000
Gita's Current A/c (Dr)	2,000
Contingency Reserve	18,000
Profit and Loss A/c (Dr)	4,500

On the date of dissolution

(i) The firm, upon realisation of assets and settlement of liabilities, made a profit of ₹ 9,000.

(ii) Gita paid the realisation expenses of ₹ 2,000.

(iii) Gita discharged the outstanding salary of the manager of the firm of ₹ 1,000 which was unrecorded in the books.

You are required to prepare the partners' capital account. ***ISC Sem II Specimen 2022***

10 Marks Questions

21. Mike and Ajay are partners sharing profits and losses in proportion to their capitals, which on 31st March, 2019, stood at ₹ 6,00,000 and ₹ 4,00,000 respectively. On this date, the firm had ₹ 1,00,000 in its workmen compensation reserve and its outside liabilities amounted to ₹ 6,00,000, which included creditors of ₹ 2,00,000 and bills payable of ₹ 60,000.

The firm was dissolved on 31st March, 2019, on which date, the assets, apart from cash of ₹ 70,000, realised ₹ 14,00,000 and the liabilities were discharged as follows

(i) Creditors due on 31st May, 2019, were paid-off at a discount of 3% per annum.

(ii) Bills payable were discharged at a rebate of ₹ 1,000.

(iii) Workmen compensation claim of ₹ 40,000 was met.

(iv) Expenses of dissolution amounting to ₹ 30,000 were paid.

You are required to prepare

(a) Realisation account

(b) Partner's capital account ***ISC 2020***

22. Raina and Meena were partners in a firm sharing profits and losses equally. They dissolved their firm on 31st March, 2018. On this date, the balance sheet of the firm apart from realisable assets and outside liabilities showed the following

	Amt (₹)
Raina's Capital	40,000 (Cr)
Meena's Capital	20,000 (Dr)
Pofit and Loss Account	10,000 (Dr)
Raina's Loan to the firm	15,000
Contingency Reserve	7,000

On the date of dissolution of the firm

(i) Raina's loan was repaid by the firm alongwith interest of ₹ 500.

(ii) The dissolution expenses of ₹ 1,000 were paid by the firm on behalf of Raina who had to bear these expenses.

(iii) An unrecorded asset of ₹ 2,000 was taken over by Meena while Raina discharged an unrecorded liability of ₹ 3,000.

(iv) The dissolution resulted in a loss of ₹ 60,000 from the realisation of assets and settlement of liabilities.

You are required to prepare

(a) Partners' capital account (b) Raina's loan account ***ISC 2019***

KEY IDEA

When dissolution expense is paid by the firm on behalf of a partner, partners' capital account is debited.

23. Susan, Geeta and Rashi are partners sharing profit and loss in the ratio of 5 : 3 : 2. Their balance sheet as at 31st March, 2017 is as under

Balance Sheet of Susan, Geeta and Rashi
as at 31st March, 2017

Liabilities		Amt (₹)	Assets		Amt (₹)
Sundry Creditors		50,000	Cash at Bank		70,000
Workmen Compensation Reserve		25,000	Sundry Debtors	65,000	
Employees Provident Fund		5,000	(–) Provision for Doubtful Debts	(5,000)	60,000
Bank Loan		55,000	Goodwill		50,000
Capital A/cs			Furniture		1,00,000
Susan	2,20,000		Building		3,80,000
Geeta	1,70,000				
Rashi	1,35,000	5,25,000			
		6,60,000			6,60,000

The partners decided to dissolve their partnership on 31st March, 2017.
The following transactions took place at the time of dissolution
(i) Realisation expenses of ₹ 2,000 were paid by Susan on behalf of the firm.
(ii) Geeta took over the goodwill for her own business at ₹ 40,000.
(iii) Building was taken over by Rashi at ₹ 3,00,000.
(iv) Only 80% of the debtors paid their dues.
(v) Furniture was sold for ₹ 97,000.
(vi) Bank loan was settled alongwith interest of ₹ 5,000.
You are required to prepare the realisation account. *ISC 2018*

KEY IDEA
When the realisation expenses are paid by the partner on behalf of the firm, partners' capital account is credited.

24. Mehta and Menon were partners in a firm, sharing profits and losses in the ratio of 7 : 3. They decided to dissolve their partnership firm on 31st March, 2016. On that date, their books showed the following ledger account balances

Sundry Creditors	₹ 27,000
Profit and Loss A/c (Dr)	₹ 8,000
Cash in Hand	₹ 6,000
Bank Loan	₹ 20,000
Bills Payable	₹ 5,000
Sundry Assets	₹ 1,98,000
Capital A/cs	
Mehta	₹ 1,12,000
Menon	₹ 48,000

Additional information
Bills payable falling due on 31st May, 2016 were retired on the date of dissolution of the firm, at a rebate of 6% per annum.
The bankers accepted the furniture (included in sundry assets) having a book value of ₹ 18,000 in full settlement of the loan given by them.
Remaining assets were sold for ₹ 1,50,000.
Liability on account of outstanding salary not recorded in the books, amounting to ₹ 15,000 was met.

Menon agreed to take over the responsibility of completing the dissolution work and to bear all expenses of realisation at an agreed remuneration of ₹ 2,000. The actual realisation expenses were ₹ 1,500 which were paid by the firm on behalf of Menon.

Your are required to prepare

(i) Realisation account

(ii) Partners' capital account *ISC 2017*

25. Aman and Harsh were partners in a firm. They decided to dissolve their firm. Pass necessary journal entries for the following, after various assets (other than cash and bank) and third party liabilities have been transferred to realisation account.

(i) There was furniture worth ₹ 50,000. Aman took over 50% of the furniture at 10% discount and the remaining furniture was sold at 30% profit on book value.

(ii) Profit and loss account was showing a credit balance of ₹ 15,000 which was distributed between the partners.

(iii) Harsh's loan of ₹ 6,000 was discharged at ₹ 6,200.

(iv) The firm paid realisation expenses amounting to ₹ 5,000 on behalf of Harsh, who had to bear these expenses.

(v) There was a bill for ₹ 1,200 under discount. The bill was received from Sohan who proved insolvent and a first and final dividend of 25% was received from his estate.

(vi) Creditors, to whom the firm owed ₹ 6,000 accepted stock of ₹ 5,000 at a discount of 5% and the balance in cash.

(vii) The loss on dissolution was ₹ 8,000. *ISC 2014*

26. Following is the balance sheet of Ravi and Prakash as at 31st March, 2012.

Balance Sheet
as at 31st March, 2012

Liabilities		Amt (₹)	Assets		Amt (₹)
Sundry Creditors		60,000	Cash		25,000
Ravi's Loan		15,000	Debtors	42,000	
General Reserve		15,000	(–) Provision for Doubtful Debts	(6,000)	36,000
Investment Fluctuation Fund		2,000	Stock		12,000
Capital A/cs			Investments		18,000
Ravi	30,000		Plant and Machinery		41,000
Prakash	10,000	40,000			
		1,32,000			1,32,000

The firm was dissolved on 31st March, 2012, on the following terms

(i) Ravi took over stock at ₹ 8,000.

(ii) Creditors payable after two months were paid immediately at a discount of 6% per annum.

(iii) Debtors realised ₹ 35,000.

(iv) Plant and machinery and investments realised ₹ 60,000.

(v) An old computer completely written-off was taken over by Prakash at ₹ 1,200.

(vi) Realisation expenses of ₹ 2,000 were paid by Ravi.

You are required to prepare

(a) Realisation account (b) Partner's capital accounts

(c) Cash account *ISC 2013*

Explanations

1. (a) ₹ 1,000

2. Partners' Capital A/c Dr XXX
   To Loan to Partner A/c XXX
   (Being loan to partner transferred to his capital account)

Concept Enhancer If a partner has given a loan to the firm, it will be transferred to cash/bank account. But, if the firm has given loan to the partner, it will be transferred to debit side of that partner's capital account.

3. (a) Losses including deficiencies of capital shall be first paid out of profits, next from the capital and if necessary by the personal contribution of partners in their profit sharing ratio.
4. Employees provident fund is an outside liability for a business which is closed by transferring to the credit of realisation account.
5. (c) By transferring ₹ 5,000 to the debit side of the realisation account
6.

Dr **Bank Account** Cr

Particulars	Amt (₹)	Particulars	Amt (₹)
To Balance b/d	14,000	By Realisation A/c	7,000
To Realisation A/c	22,000	By Tara's Capital A/c	35,000
To Anjali's Capital A/c	6,000		
	42,000		42,000

Working Note

Dr **Partners' Capital Account** Cr

Particulars	Tara (₹)	Anjali (₹)	Paticulars	Tara (₹)	Anjali (₹)
To Balance b/d	—	9,000	By Balane b/d	35,000	—
To Tara's Loan A/c	3,000	—	By Realisation A/c (Profit)	3,000	3,000
To Bank A/c	35,000	—	By Bank A/c	—	6,000
	38,000	9,000		38,000	9,000

7. (b) By debiting it to Anita's capital account
8.

JOURNAL

Date	Particulars		LF	Amt (Dr)	Amt (Cr)
(i)	Cash A/c	Dr		21,300	
	To Realisation A/c				21,300
	(Being the stock realised)				

Working Note

Easily marketable items $= \frac{65}{100} \times 30{,}000 =$ ₹ 19,500 (realised in full)

Obsolete items = 20% of 30,000 = ₹ 6,000 (discarded)

Miscellaneous other items = 30,000 – (19,500 + 6,000) = ₹ 4,500

Realised amount from miscellaneous items = 40% of 4,500 = ₹ 1,800

Total amount realised = 1,800 + 19,500 = ₹ 21,300

9. (i) Cases of dissolution of partnership (any two)
   (a) In case of change in profit sharing ratio of existing partners.
   (b) In case of admission, retirement, death, expulsion of partner. (c) In case of expiry of period of partnership.

   (ii) After dissolution of partnership, the business or firm continues. However, the partnership is reconstituted. It does not involve the dissolution of the firm.

10. Difference between revaluation account and realisation account

Basis	Revaluation account	Realisation account
Purpose	The purpose of preparing revaluation account is to ascertain profit or loss on the revaluation of assets and liabilities.	It is meant to ascertain profit or loss on the disposal of assets and payment of liabilities.
Situation	It is prepared in case of reconstitution of firm.	It is prepared is case of dissolution of firm.

11. Loan given to a partner by the firm will be debited to his capital account at the time of dissolution. The journal entry passed will be

Partner's Capital A/c Dr
  To Loan to Partner A/c
(Being loan given to partner debited to his capital account)

12. At the time of dissolution, workmen compensation fund is credited to capital accounts of partners in their profit sharing ratio.

Workmen Compensation Reserve A/c Dr
  To Partners' Capital A/c
(Being workmen compensation reserve distributed among partners)

13. The entry for the payment of realisation expenses which were to be borne by a partner, but paid by the firm on his behalf is

Partner's Capital A/c Dr
  To Cash/Bank A/c
(Being realisation expenses paid on behalf of the partner)

14. Employees provident fund is a liability. Hence, it is transferred to the credit side of realisation account and will be paid of. For this, following entries are passed

Employee's Provident Fund A/c Dr
  To Realisation A/c
(Being employee provident fund transferred)

Realisation A/c Dr
  To Bank A/c
(Being employee provident fund paid)

15. Where both the debts of the firm and private debts of a partner co-exist, The following rules, as stated in Section 49 of the Act, shall apply

(i) Firm's property is applied first in payment of firm's debts and if there is any surplus, then the share of each partner is applied in the payment of his private debts or paid to him.

(ii) Partner's private property is applied first in payment of his private debts and the surplus (if any) in payment of firm's debts, if the firms liabilities exceed the firm's assets.

16. **Workmen's compensation fund** Refer to Q. No. 12 (1/2 Marks).

Employees provident fund Refer to Q. No. 14 (1/2 Marks).

17.

JOURNAL

Date	Particulars		LF	Amt (Dr)	Amt (Cr)
(i)	Realisation A/c	Dr		16,000	
	To Bank A/c				16,000
	(Being creditors worth ₹ 20,000 settled with ₹ 16,000 cash and assets worth ₹ 4,000)				
(ii)	Realisation A/c	Dr		29,875	
	To Bank A/c				29,875
	(Being bills payables paid $30,000 - 30,000 \times 5\% \times 1/2$)				

Date	Particulars		LF	Amt (Dr)	Amt (Cr)
(iii)	Farhan's Capital A/c	Dr		2,000	
	To Bank A/c				2,000
	(Being realisation expenses paid by the firm on behalf of Farhan)				

18. Dr **Realisation Account** Cr

Particulars	Amt (₹)	Particulars		Amt (₹)
To Land and Building	29,000	By Provision for Doubtful Debt		400
To Plant and Machinery	20,000	By Sundry Creditors		40,000
To Stock	3,000	By Sita's Son's Loan		2,000
To Debtors	26,400	By Bank Overdraft		8,000
To Bank A/c (Creditors)	22,000	By Bank A/c (Debtors)		25,400
To Bank A/c (Realisation expenses)	1,100	By Sita's Capital A/c (Stock)		2,400
To Bank A/c (Bank overdraft)	8,000	By Bank A/c (Land and Building)		29,000
To Bank A/c (Sita's son's loan)	2,000	By Realisation Loss		
		Mita's Capital A/c	2,867	
		Sita's Capital A/c	1,433	4,300
	1,11,500			1,11,500

19. Dr **Realisation Account** Cr

Particulars	Amt (₹)	Particulars		Amt (₹)
To Debtors	4,700	By Creditors		5,000
To Stock	2,300	By Investment Fluctuation Fund		300
To Furniture	50	By Cash A/c (Assets realised)		
To Property	2,000	Property	1,500	
To Investment	1,100	Stock	2,525	
To Cash A/c (Creditors)	4,900	Debtors	4,200	
To Ravi's Capital A/c	75	Furniture	50	
		Investment	1,100	9,375
		By Loss on Realisation Transferred to		
		Ravi's Capital A/c	253	
		Kamal's Capital A/c	197	450
	15,125			15,125

20. Dr **Partners' Capital Account** Cr

Particulars	Sita (₹)	Gita (₹)	Particulars	Sita (₹)	Gita (₹)
To Profit and Loss A/c	2,444	3,056	By Balance b/d	30,000	35,000
To Gita's Current A/c	—	2,000	By Realisation A/c	4,000	5,000
To Cash A/c	39,556	47,944	By Contingency Reserve A/c	8,000	10,000
			By Realisation A/c (Salary discharged by Gita)	—	1,000
			By Realisation A/c (Realisation expenses)	—	2,000
	42,000	53,000		42,000	53,000

Notes
- Assuming that expenses are paid by Gita but borne by the firm.
- Since outstanding salary of manager is not recorded it will be debited to profit and loss account.

21. (a) Dr **Realisation Account** Cr

Particulars		Amt (₹)	Particulars	Amt (₹)
To Sundry Assets (WN)		16,30,000	By Workmen Compensation Reserve A/c	40,000
To Bank A/c			By Sundry Liabilities	6,00,000
Bills Payable	59,000		By Bank A/c	14,00,000
Creditors	1,99,000		By Mike's Capital A/c	1,54,800
Workmen Compensation	40,000		By Ajay's Capital A/c	1,03,200
Other Liabilities	3,40,000			
Expenses	30,000	6,68,000		
		22,98,000		22,98,000

(b) Dr **Partners' Capital Account** Cr

Particulars	Mike (₹)	Ajay (₹)	Particulars	Mike (₹)	Ajay (₹)
To Realisation A/c	1,54,800	1,03,200	By Balance b/d	6,00,000	4,00,000
To Bank A/c (Balncing Figure)	4,81,200	3,20,800	By Workmen Compensation Reserve A/c	36,000	24,000
	6,36,000	4,24,000		6,36,000	4,24,000

Working Note

Balance Sheet (Before realisation)
as at 31st March, 2019

Liabilities		Amt (₹)	Assets	Amt (₹)
Capital A/cs			Cash	70,000
Mike	6,00,000		Sundry Assets (Balance)	16,30,000
Ajay	4,00,000	10,00,000		
Workmen Compensation Reserve		1,00,000		
Liabilities (Sundry)		6,00,000		
		17,00,000		17,00,000

Common Mistake Students usually forget to consider time factor while calculating discount. Discount will be calculated for 2 months only, i.e. April and May.

22. (a) Dr **Partners' Capital Account** Cr

Particulars	Raina (₹)	Meena (₹)	Particulars	Raina (₹)	Meena (₹)
To Balance b/d	—	20,000	By Balance b/d	40,000	—
To Cash A/c	1,000	—	By Realisation A/c (Liabilities)	3,000	—
To Realisation A/c (Assets)	—	2,000	By Contingency Reserve	3,500	3,500
To Realisation A/c (Loss)	30,000	30,000	By Cash A/c	—	53,750
To P & L A/c	5,250	5,250			
To Cash A/c	10,250	—			
	46,500	57,250		46,500	57,250

(b) Dr **Raina's Loan Account** Cr

Particulars	Amt (₹)	Pariculars	Amt (₹)
To Cash A/c	15,500	By Balance b/d	15,000
		By Profit and Loss (Interest) A/c	500
	15,500		15,500

23. **In the Books of Susan, Geeta and Rashi**

Realisation Account

Dr Particulars		Amt (₹)	Particulars		Cr Amt (₹)
To Sundry Assets A/c			By Sundry Liabilities A/c		
Debtors	65,000		Provision for Doubtful Debts	5,000	
Goodwill	50,000		Creditors	50,000	
Furniture	1,00,000		Employees Provident Fund	5,000	
Building	3,80,000	5,95,000	Bank Loan	55,000	1,15,000
To Susan's Capital A/c (Realisation expenses)		2,000	By Geeta's Capital A/c		40,000
To Bank A/c			By Rashi's Capital A/c		3,00,000
Bank Loan	60,000		By Bank A/c		
Creditors	50,000		Debtors	52,000	
Employees Provident Fund	5,000	1,15,000	Furniture	97,000	1,49,000
			By Loss Transferred to		
			Susan's Capital A/c	54,000	
			Geeta's Capital A/c	32,400	
			Rashi's Capital A/c	21,600	1,08,000
		7,12,000			7,12,000

24. (i) **In the Books of Mehta and Menon**

Realisation Account

Dr Particulars	Amt (₹)	Particulars		Cr Amt (₹)
To Sundry Assets	1,98,000	By Sundry Creditors		27,000
To Cash A/c (B/P retired)	4,950	By Bank Loan		20,000
To Cash A/c (Sundry creditors)	27,000	By Bills Payable A/c		5,000
To Cash A/c (Outstanding salary)	15,000	By Cash A/c (Assets sold)		1,50,000
To Menon's Capital A/c (Remuneration)	2,000	By Loss on Realisation Transferred to		
		Mehta's Capital A/c	31,465	
		Menon's Capital A/c	13,485	44,950
	2,46,950			2,46,950

(ii) **Partners' Capital Account**

Dr Particulars	Mehta (₹)	Menon (₹)	Particulars	Mehta (₹)	Cr Menon (₹)
To Profit and Loss A/c	5,600	2,400	By Balance b/d	1,12,000	48,000
To Realisation A/c	31,465	13,485	By Realisation A/c	—	2,000
To Cash A/c	—	1,500			
To Cash A/c (Balancing figure)	74,935	32,615			
	1,12,000	50,000		1,12,000	50,000

Working Note

Rebate on bills payable $= 5{,}000 \times \frac{6}{100} \times \frac{2}{12} =$ ₹ 50

25. **In the Books of Aman and Harsh**

JOURNAL

Date	Particulars		LF	Amt (Dr)	Amt (Cr)
(i)	Aman's Capital A/c	Dr		22,500	
	Cash A/c	Dr		32,500	
	To Realisation A/c				55,000
	(Being 50% furniture taken by Aman and remaining furniture sold at 30% profit)				

Date	Particulars		LF	Amt (Dr)	Amt (Cr)
(ii)	Profit and Loss A/c	Dr		15,000	
	To Aman's Capital A/c				7,500
	To Harsh's Capital A/c				7,500
	(Being profit distributed among partners)				
(iii)	Harsh's Loan A/c	Dr		6,000	
	Realisation A/c	Dr		200	
	To Bank A/c				6,200
	(Being Harsh's loan discharged)				
(iv)	Harsh's Capital A/c	Dr		5,000	
	To Bank A/c				5,000
	(Being realisation expenses paid by firm on account of Harsh)				
(v)	Bank A/c	Dr		300	
	To Realisation A/c				300
	(Being payment made to bank for dishonoured bill)				
	Realisation A/c	Dr		1,200	
	To Bank A/c				1,200
	(Being Sohan, become insolvent and 25% amount of bill received)				
(vi)	Realisation A/c	Dr		1,250	
	To Cash A/c				1,250
	(Being payment made to creditors)				
(vii)	Aman's Capital A/c	Dr		4,000	
	Harsh's Capital A/c	Dr		4,000	
	To Realisation A/c				8,000
	(Being transfer of loss on realisation to partners' capital account)				

Working Note

Value of furniture	**Amt (₹)**
Take over by Aman (50,000 × 50%)	= 25,000
(−) Discount (10%)	= (2,500)
	= 22,500
Sale (50,000 × 50%)	= 25,000
(+) Profit (30%)	= 7,500
	32,500

26. (a)

In the Books of Ravi and Prakash

Realisation Account

Dr | Cr

Particulars		Amt (₹)	Particulars		Amt (₹)
To Sundry Assets A/c			By Sundry Liabilities A/c		
Debtors	42,000		Creditors	60,000	
Stock	12,000		Investment Fluctuation Fund	2,000	
Investments	18,000		Provision for Doubtful Debts	6,000	68,000
Plant and Machinery	41,000	1,13,000	By Cash A/c		
To Cash A/c			Debtors	35,000	
Creditors (WN)		59,400	Plant and Machinery and Investments	60,000	95,000
To Ravi's Capital A/c (Realisation expenses)		2,000	By Ravi's Capital A/c (Stock)		8,000

Particulars	Amt (₹)	Particulars		Amt (₹)
		By Prakash's Capital A/c (Old computer)		1,200
		By Loss Transferred to Capital A/cs		
		Ravi	1,100	
		Prakash	1,100	2,200
	1,74,400			1,74,400

(b) Dr **Partners' Capital Account** Cr

Particulars	Ravi (₹)	Prakash (₹)	Particulars	Ravi (₹)	Prakash (₹)
To Realisation A/c (Loss)	1,100	1,100	By Balance b/d	30,000	10,000
To Realisation A/c (Stock)	8,000	—	By General Reserve	7,500	7,500
To Realisation A/c (Computer)	—	1,200	By Realisation A/c	2,000	—
To Cash A/c (Final settlement)	30,400	15,200	(Realisation expenses)		
	39,500	17,500		39,500	17,500

(c) Dr **Cash Account** Cr

Particulars	Amt (₹)	Particulars	Amt (₹)
To Balance b/d	25,000	By Ravi's Loan	15,000
To Realisation A/c (Sale of assets)	95,000	By Realisation A/c (Creditors)	59,400
		By Ravi's Capital A/c	30,400
		By Prakash's Capital A/c	15,200
	1,20,000		1,20,000

Working Note

	Amt (₹)
Creditors	60,000
(−) Discount $\left(60{,}000 \times \frac{6}{100} \times \frac{2}{12}\right)$	(600)
	59,400

Common Mistake Students distribute investment fluctuation fund among partners since it is a reserve. However, when both 'Investment' and 'Investment fluctuation fund' are given, then reserve will be transferred to realisation account.

CHAPTER TEST

01 Mark Questions

1. Which of the following will not come under compulsory dissolution?

(a) When all the partners or all but one partner, become insolvent

(b) When the business of the firm becomes illegal

(c) When a partner becomes permannently incapable of performing his duties

(d) When a partner who is a citizen of a country becomes an alien enemy

2. Which of the following will not be transferred to realisation account?

(a) Partners' loan (b) Partners' wife's loan

(c) Bank loan (d) Both (a) and (b)

3. In the absence of any information regarding payment of creditors, it will be treated as

(a) Never paid (b) Fully paid

(c) Partly paid (d) None of these

4. What account will be debited when realisation expeses are paid by the firm on behalf of a partner?

(a) Realisation account (b) Partners' capital account

(c) Partner's loan account (d) None of these

5. State any two situations where a court can order dissolution of a firm.

6. Manoj, a creditor of ₹ 10,000 was paid a furniture worth ₹ 14,000. He paid the difference amount. Pass necessary journal entry.

7. State the sequennce in which payment of losses is done in case of dissolution of partnership firm.

03 Marks Questions

8. A and B were partners in a firm sharing profits in the ratio of 2 : 3. On 28th February, 2022 the firm was dissolved. After transferring assets (other than cash) and outsiders liabilities to realisation account you are given the following information

(i) A creditors for ₹ 70,000 accepted building valued at ₹ 90,000 and paid to the firm ₹ 20,000.

(ii) A second creditor for ₹ 15,000 accepted machinery valued at ₹ 14,000 in full settlement of his claim.

Pass necessary journal entries for the above transactions in the books of the firm assuming that all payments were made by cheque.

9. G, D and P are partners. They decided to dissolve their firm. Pass necessary journal entries for the following after various assets (other than cash and bank) and the third party liabilities have been transferred to realisation account.

(i) G agreed to pay-off his wife's loan of ₹ 10,500 at a discount of 5%.

(ii) A laptop which was not recorded in the books was taken over by D at ₹ 4,500, whereas its expected value was ₹ 7,500.

(iii) A contingent liability (not provided for) of ₹ 6,000 was also discharged.

06 Marks Questions

10. Verma and Sharma were partners sharing profits in the ratio of 3 : 1. On 31st March, 2011, their balance sheet was as follows

Balance Sheet
as at 31st March, 2011

Liabilities		Amt (₹)	Assets	Amt (₹)
Capital A/cs			Land and Builiding	70,000
Verma	1,20,000		Machinery	60,000
Sharma	80,000	2,00,000	Debtors	80,000
Creditors		70,000	Bank	60,000
		2,70,000		2,70,000

The firm was dissolved on 1st April, 2011 and the assets and liabilities were settled as follows

(i) Creditors of ₹ 50,000 took over land and building in full settlement of their claim.

(ii) Remaining creditors were paid in cash.

(iii) Machinery was sold at a depreciation of 30%.

(iv) Debtors were collected at a cost of ₹ 500.

(v) Expenses on realisation were ₹ 1,700.

Pass necessary journal entries for dissolution of the firm.

11. Pass the necessary journal entries for the following transactions on the dissolution of the firm of P and Q after the various assets (other than cash) and outside liabilities have been transferred to realisation account.

(i) Bank loan ₹ 12,000 was paid.

(ii) Stock worth ₹ 16,000 was taken over by a partner Q.

(iii) Partner P paid a creditor ₹ 4,000.

(iv) An asset not appearing in the books of accounts realised ₹ 1,200.

(v) Expenses of realisation ₹ 2,000 were paid by partner Q.

(vi) Profit on realisation ₹ 36,000 was distributed between P and Q in 5 : 4 ratio.

10 Marks Questions

12. X, Y and Z were partners sharing profits in the ratio of 2 : 2 : 1. The balance sheet on 31st March, 2010, when they dissolved the firm was as follows

Balance Sheet
as at 31st March, 2010

Liabilities		Amt (₹)	Assets		Amt (₹)
Capital A/cs			Other Sundry Assets		1,17,000
X	1,27,500		Furniture		11,000
Y	1,10,000		Debtors	1,24,200	
Z	17,000	2,54,500	(–) Provision for Doubtful Debts	(1,200)	1,23,000
Loan		11,500	Stock		17,800
Creditors		16,000	Cash		13,200
		2,82,000			2,82,000

It was agreed that

(i) X to take over furniture at ₹ 8,000 and debtors amounting to ₹ 1,20,000 at ₹ 1,17,200 and the creditors of ₹ 16,000 were to be paid by him at this figure.

(ii) Y is to take over all stock for ₹ 17,000 and some sundry assets at ₹ 72,000 (being 10% less than the book value).

(iii) Z to take over remaining sundry assets at 80% of the book value and assume the responsibility of discharge of loan together with accrued interest of ₹ 2,300.

(iv) The expenses on realisation were ₹ 2,700. The remaining debtors were sold to a debt collecting agency at 50% of the value.

Prepare necessary accounts to close the books of the firm.

13. Y and Z were sharing profit and losses in the ratio of 3 : 1 respectively, decided to dissolve the firm on 31st March, 2012 at which date some of the balances were

Y's capital	₹ 50,000
Z's capital	₹ 5,000 (Debit balance)
Profit and loss account	₹ 4,000 (Debit balance)
Trade creditors	₹ 15,000
Loan form Mrs Y	₹ 5,000
Cash at bank	₹ 1,000

The assets (other than cash at bank) realised ₹ 55,000 and all creditors including loan from Mrs Y were paid off less 5% discount. Realisation expenses amounted to ₹ 500.

Prepare the realisation account, bank account and the capital accounts of the partners assuming that both the partners are solvent.

Answers

1. (c) When a partner becomes permanently incapable of performing his duties
2. (a) Partner's loan
3. (b) Fully paid
4. (b) Partners' capital account

10. Loss on Realisation = ₹ 40,200;
Payment to Partners' Capital A/cs Verma = ₹ 89,850,
Sharma = ₹ 69,950

12. Loss on Realisation = ₹ 27,900,
Cash Account Total = ₹ 19,680

13. Loss on Realisation = ₹ 4,500,
Bank Account Total = ₹ 63,125
Final Payment to Y = ₹ 43,625,
Cash Brought in by Z = ₹ 7,125

05

Issue of Shares

TREND ANALYSIS 5 YEARS

Average No. of Questions Across all Sets

	Types of Questions	2023	2020	2019	2018	2017
01 Introduction	1/2 Marks	—	—	—	—	—
	3 Marks	—	—	—	—	—
	6 Marks	1	—	—	—	—
	10 Marks	—	—	—	—	—
02 Issue of Shares	1/2 Marks	1	1	—	—	2
	3 Marks	—	—	—	—	—
	6 Marks	—	—	1	—	—
	10 Marks	—	—	—	—	—
03 Forfeiture and Reissue of Shares	1/2 Marks	—	—	1	1	—
	3 Marks	—	—	—	—	—
	6 Marks	—	—	—	—	—
	10 Marks	2	1	—	1	1

Company

A joint stock company is an incorporated association which is an artificial person, created by law, having a separate legal entity distinct from its members with a perpetual succession and a common seal.

According to Section 2(20) of the Companies Act, 2013, "Company means a company incorporated under this act or any previous company law".

Characteristics or Features of a Company

Main characteristics or features of a company are

(i) Artificial person (ii) Voluntary association
(iii) Created by law
(iv) Capital divisible into transferable shares
(v) Limited liability (vi) Perpetual succession
(vii) Separate legal entity from its members
(viii) Common seal (ix) May sue or be sued

Types of Companies

(i) **Private company** As per Section 2(68) of Companies Act, 2013, a private company is one which has a minimum paid-up capital as may be prescribed* and which by its articles

(a) Restricts the right to transfer its shares, if any.

(b) Except in case of one person company, limits the number of its members excluding its present and past employee members to 200. (If any share is hold jointly by two or more persons, they shall be treated as a single member).

(c) Prohibits any invitation to the public to subscribe for any securities of the company.

The name of a private company ends with the words, 'Private Limited'.

(ii) **Public company** As per Section 2 (71) of Companies Act, 2013, public company is a company which
   (a) is not a private company.
   (b) has minimum capital as may be prescribed*.
   (c) is a private company, being a subsidiary of a company which is not a private company.

   The name of the public company ends with the word 'Limited'.

(iii) **One person company** Section 2 (62) of the Companies Act, 2013 defines one person company as a company which has only one person as a member. It is a company incorporated as a private company which has only one member.

Note *Minimum paid-up capital is not prescribed. Private or public companies can have share capital as the promoters decide.

Share

The capital of a company is divided into a number of equal units. Each unit is called a share. A company may divide its capital into share of ₹ 100, ₹ 50, ₹ 10, ₹ 5 or even ₹ 1 each.

According to Section 2 (84) of the Companies Act, 2013, "Share means a share in the capital of a company and includes stock".

Nature of Shares

According to Sale of Goods Act, 1930, shares of a company are treated as goods. Share itself is an item of movable property which (sub company's articles) can be transferred by sale or gift.

Types of Shares

Shares are mainly classified into two categories

1. Preference Shares [Section 43(b)]

Preference shares are the shares that carry the following two rights

(i) Preferential right of dividend to be paid as fixed amount or an amount calculated at a fixed rate, which may either be free or subject to income tax.

(ii) Return of capital on the winding up of the company before that of equity shares.

Types of Preference Shares

There are different types of preference shares as follows

(i) Cumulative preference shares
(ii) Non-cumulative preference shares
(iii) Participating preference shares
(iv) Non-participating preference shares
(v) Redeemable preference shares
(vi) Irredeemable preference shares
(vii) Convertible preference shares
(viii) Non-convertible preference shares

2. Equity Shares [Section 43(a)]

Equity shares are the shares which are not preference shares. Thus, these shares do not carry any preferential right or in other words, equity shares are one which are entitled to dividend and repayment of capital after the claim on preference shares is satisfied.

Difference between Preference Shares and Equity Shares

Basis	Preference shares	Equity shares
Dividend rate	Preference shareholders are paid dividend at a fixed rate.	The rate of dividend on equity shares vary from year to year, depending upon the availability of profits.
Redemption	Preference shares can be redeemed as provided by the Articles and terms of issue.	Equity shares cannot be redeemed except, under a scheme involving reduction of capital.
Payment of dividend	These shares have a preferential right to receive dividend before any dividend is paid on equity shares.	Payment of dividend on equity shares is made only after satisfying the claim of preference shares.
Voting rights	Preference shareholders do not have any voting rights except when their interest is directly affected.	Equity shareholders enjoy voting rights.
Company's formation	A company with only preference shares cannot be formed.	A company may be formed only with equity shares.

Share Capital

It is that part of the capital of a company, which is represented by the total nominal value of issued shares.

Kinds of Share Capital

From accounting point of view, share capital can be classified as

1. Authorised Share Capital

According to Section 2(8) of Companies Act, 2013, 'authorised capital' or 'nominal capital' means such capital as is authorised by the memorandum of a company to be the maximum amount of share capital that a company can raise in its life.

It is the maximum amount of share capital which a company is authorised by its Memorandum of Association to issue to shareholders. The company cannot raise more than the amount of capital as specified in the Memorandum of Association. It is also called **nominal or registered capital**.

Key Point

The authorised share capital under each class (equity or preference) may be more or at most equal to the issued share capital, but cannot be less than the issued capital.

2. Issued Capital

According to Section 2(50) of the Companies Act, 2013, issued capital means such capital as the company issues from time-to-time for subscription. It is that part of the authorised capital which is actually issued to the public for subscription including the shares allotted for consideration other than cash, shares taken by directors as qualifying shares and the shares subscribed by the signatories to the company's memorandum.

Note Issued share capital cannot exceed the company's authorised share capital.

3. Subscribed Capital

According to Section 2(86) of the Companies Act, 2013, subscribed capital means such part of the issued capital which has been subscribed by the members of a company. It includes shares allotted for consideration other than cash, shares subscribed by the signatories to the company's memorandum and shares taken by directors as qualifying shares.

This capital can further be categorised as

(i) **Subscribed and fully paid-up** Shares are said to be 'subscribed and fully paid-up' when the entire nominal (face) value is called and also paid-up by the shareholders.

(ii) **Subscribed but not fully paid-up** Shares are said to be 'subscribed but not fully paid-up' under the following two situations

(a) **Company has called-up the entire nominal** (face) **value of the share but it has not been received** If the company has called-up the full nominal (face) value of the share but it has not received the full nominal (face) value, then it is classified or shown as 'shares subscribed but not fully paid-up'.

(b) **Company has not called-up full nominal** (face) **value of the share** If the company has not called-up the full nominal (face) value of the share, shares are not fully paid-up.

Notes
- There may be another situation, i.e. the company has not called the entire nominal (face) value of the share and also the shareholder has not paid the entire called-up amount.
- If a company is having 'reserve capital', the shares are shown as 'subscribed but not fully paid-up' because the company has not called the entire (face) value of the share.

4. Called-up Share Capital

According to Section 2 (15) of the Companies Act, 2013, 'called-up capital' means such part of the capital, which has been called for payment. Thus, it means the amount of nominal (face) value called-up by the company to be paid by the shareholders towards the share capital.

5. Paid-up Share Capital

According to Section 2 (64) of the Companies Act, 2013, 'paid-up share capital' or 'share capital paid-up' means such aggregate of money credited and paid-up as is equivalent to the amount received as paid-up in respect of shares issued and also includes any amount credited as paid-up in respect of such shares of a company but does not include any other amount received in respect of such shares, by whatever name called.

It means the amount that the shareholder has paid and the company has received against the amount 'called-up' against the shares towards share capital.

6. Reserve Capital

It is that portion of subscribed share capital, remaining uncalled, which is not capable of being called-up except in the event and for the purposes of the company being wound up.

Capital Reserve

'Capital reserve' is the reserve which is not free for distribution as dividend. It is mandatory to create capital reserve in case of capital profits earned by the company.

Reserves which are created out of capital profits, are not readily available for distribution as dividend among the shareholders, e.g. Premium on issue of shares or debentures, profits on re-issue of shares, profits prior to incorporation, premium on redemption of debentures, etc.

Difference between Reserve Capital and Capital Reserve

Basis	Reserve capital	Capital reserve
Meaning	It refers to that portion of uncalled share capital which shall not be called up except in the event of winding up.	It is that reserve which is created out of capital profits such as profit on sale of fixed assets, profit on revaluation of fixed assets, etc. These profits are not earned in the normal course of business.
Creation	It is not necessary to create reserve capital.	It is necessary to create capital reserve in case of capital profits.
Special resolution	A special resolution is required for its creation.	No special resolution is required for the creation of capital reserves.
With respect to amount	It refers to the amount which has not been received.	It refers to the amount which has already been received.
Disclosure	It is not shown in the company's balance sheet.	It is shown as the first item under the head, reserves and surplus on the liabilities side of the balance sheet.

Presentation of Share Capital in Company's Balance Sheet

As per Schedule III of Companies Act, 2013, share capital is to be disclosed in company's balance sheet in the following manner

Balance Sheet
as at......

Particulars	Note No.	Current Year (₹)	Previous Year (₹)
I. **EQUITY AND LIABILITIES**			
Shareholders' Funds			
Share Capital*	1	...	

Note *As per Schedule III, disclosure requirements pertaining to share capital are to be provided in notes to accounts and note number be put against the item in the balance sheet.

Notes to Accounts

Particulars		Amt (₹)
1. **Share Capital**		
Authorised Capital		
.... Shares of ₹........... each		...
Issued Capital		
.... Shares of ₹........... each		...
Subscribed Capital		
Subscribed and Fully Paid-up		
.... Shares of ₹........... each		...
Subscribed but not Fully Paid-up		
.... Shares of ₹...... each ...... Called-up	...	
(–) Calls-in-arrears (if any)	(...)	...
(+) Shares Forfeited A/c		...
Total		

Public Subscription of Shares

A company raises its capital by issue of shares. The important steps in the procedure of share issue are

(i) **Issue of prospectus** Prospectus is an invitation by the company to the public to subscribe its shares. It details the soundness of the business and profitability of the company, to attract the investing public.

(ii) **Receipt of applications** After reading the prospectus, persons desirous of purchasing shares, send their application alongwith the application money, which should not be less than 25% of the issue price of each share. The amount of application money should be deposited in a scheduled bank, which is mentioned in the prospectus.

(iii) **Allotment of shares** After the minimum subscription has been received by the company, it can proceed to allot shares.

Key Point

Minimum subscription According to Section 39 (1) of the Companies Act, 2013, it is the amount stated in the prospectus as the minimum amount that must be subscribed. No securities can be allotted, unless the sum payable on application for the sum so stated (minimum subscription) has been paid to and received by the company by cheque or any other instrument.

As per the guidelines of SEBI, a company must receive a minimum of 90% of the subscription against the entire issue before making any allotment of shares to the public.

(iv) **To make calls** The amount paid on application and allotment are not calls. After allotment of shares remaining part of share money when called-up is called call money. Call money may be collected in one or more installments.

If only one call is made then it is called first and final call in place of first call, otherwise the word final will be added to the last installment.

Issue of Shares for Cash

Shares can be issued for cash at par, at premium or at discount. However, it should be kept in mind that only sweat equity shares can be issued at discount.

1. Issue of Shares at Par

When shares are issued at their face value, the shares are said to have been issued at par i.e. issue price and face value are same.

2. Issue of Shares at Premium

When shares are issued at a value that is higher than the face value of the shares, the shares are said to have been issued at premium, i.e. issue price is more than the face value.

Utilisation of Securities Premium Reserve

Section 52 (2) of the Companies Act, 2013 restricts the use of the amount received as premium on securities for the following purposes

(i) In purchasing its own shares (buy back).

(ii) Issuing fully paid bonus shares to the members.

(iii) Writing-off preliminary expenses of the company.

(iv) Writing-off the expenses of, or the commission paid or discount allowed on any issue of securities or debentures of the company.

(v) Providing for the premium payable on the redemption of any redeemable preference shares or of any debentures of the company.

Accounting Entries for Issue of Shares for Cash

Journal Entries for Issue of Shares

(i)	**On Receipt of Application Money**		
	Bank A/c	Dr	(With application money received)
	To Share Application A/c		(Number of shares applied × Application money per share)
(ii)	**On Acceptance of Applications**		
	Share Application A/c	Dr	(With application money due on shares allotted)
	To Share Capital A/c		(Number of shares allotted × Application money per share)
(iii)	**On Making Allotment Money Due**		
	(a) **At Par**		
	Share Allotment A/c	Dr	(With allotment money due)
	To Share Capital A/c		(Number of shares allotted × Allotment money per share)

(b) **At Premium**

Share Allotment A/c	Dr	(with total money)
To Share Capital A/c		(With allotment money due)
To Securities Premium Reserve A/c		(With premium money due)

(iv) **On Receipt of Allotment Money**

Bank A/c	Dr	(With allotment money received)
To Share Allotment A/c		

(v) **On Making the First Call**

Share First Call A/c	Dr	(With first call money due)
To Share Capital A/c		(Number of shares allotted × First call money per share)

(vi) **On Receipt of the First Call**

Bank A/c	Dr	(With first call money received)
To Share First Call A/c		

Application and Allotment Account (Joint)

It is becoming a practice to record entries with respect to share application and share allotment in one account titled share application and allotment account. The following entries are passed

Bank A/c	Dr
To Share Application and Allotment A/c	
(Being application money received)	

Entries for disposition of application money received and recording of allotment money due are not passed separately but are combined as follows

Share Application and Allotment A/c	Dr	(Amount received as application money plus net amount receivable on allotment)
To Share Capital A/c		(Amount payable on application and allotment on allotted shares)
To Calls-in-advance A/c		(Surplus adjusted against calls)
To Bank A/c		(Excess amount refunded)

Full Subscription of Shares

When the number of shares applied for is equal to the number of shares offered for subscription, the shares are said to be fully subscribed. In this case, accounting entries are made on the basis of shares issued.

Over Subscription of Shares

When the number of shares applied for is more than the number of shares offered for subscription, the shares are said to be over subscribed.

In this case, allotment of shares cannot be made to all the applicants in full.

In case of over subscription, following three alternatives are available

(i) **Rejection of applications** Excess applications are rejected outrightly and their application money is refunded. This is known as rejection of application. The application money received from rejected applications is fully refunded.

(ii) **Partial or pro-rata allotment** In this case, no application for shares is refused and no applicant is alloted the shares in full. Each applicant receives the share in the same proportion which is the ratio of total number of shares offered to the total number of shares applied for. In this case, the excess application money received is normally adjusted towards the amount due on allotment. In case, the excess money is more than the amount due on allotment of shares, the excess amount may either be refunded or credited to calls-in-advance account.

(iii) **Combination of pro-rata allotment and rejection** Some applications are accepted in full, some applications are outrightly rejected and proportional allotment is made to the remaining.

Accounting Entries in Case of Over Subscription

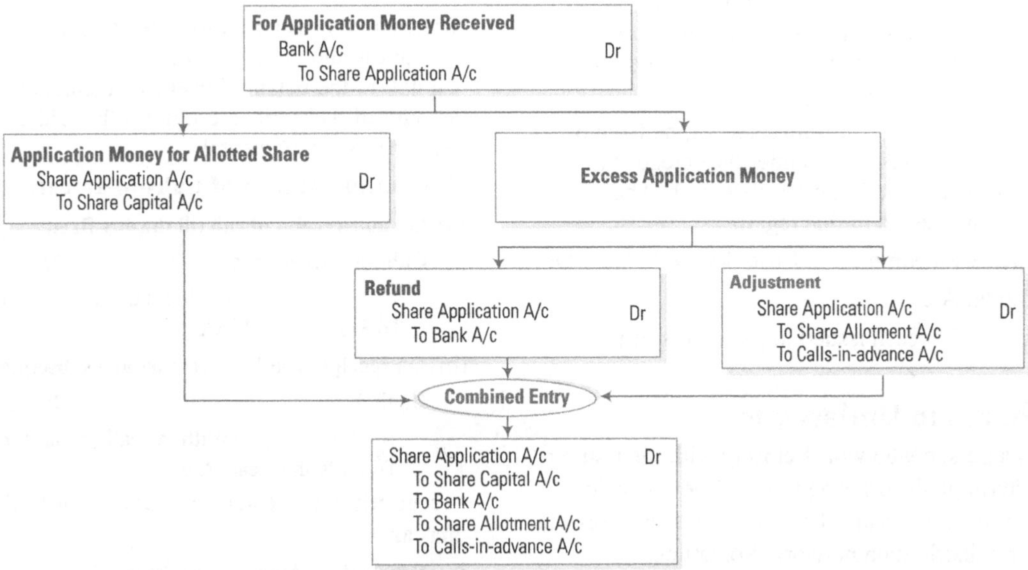

Under Subscription of Shares

When the number of shares applied for is less than the number of shares offered to the public, the shares are said to be under subscribed. In case of under subscription, accounting entries are made on the basis of shares applied for, since allotment is made in full to all the applicants.

Issue of Shares for Consideration Other than Cash

Sometimes a company issues shares in payment (consideration) against purchase of assets, business from vendors or to promoters/underwriters for their services, etc. In such cases, the payment is made in the form of fully paid shares of the company.

Cash is not received against issue of shares because consideration is received in the form of assets, business or services. These shares can also be issued either at par or at premium.

Issue of Shares to Vendors

In this regard, the purchase of assets and issue of shares are to be treated as two separate transactions. The following entries are passed in this regard

1. (i) **When assets are purchased**

   Assets A/c (individually) Dr
   To Vendor
   (Being assets purchased from ......)

   (ii) **When business is purchased**

   Sundry Assets A/c Dr
   *Goodwill A/c Dr
   To Sundry Liabilities A/c
   To Vendor
   *To Capital Reserve A/c
   (Being business purchased from vendor for purchase consideration of ₹ ....)

   Note 'Vendor' is credited with purchase consideration payable to him.
   *Either of the two will come, to balance out the debit and credit aspect.

2. **On Issue of Shares**

   (i) **Issue of shares at par**

   Vendor Dr
   To Share Capital A/c
   (Being ... shares of ₹ .... each issued to vendor)

   Note Number of Shares to be Issued $= \dfrac{\text{Amount Payable}}{\text{Issue Price (Face value)}}$

   (ii) **Issue of shares at premium**

   Vendor Dr
   To Share Capital A/c
   To Securities Premium Reserve A/c
   (Being ..... shares of ₹ ..... each at a premium of ₹ .... issued to vendor)

   Note Number of Shares to be Issued

   $= \dfrac{\text{Amount Payable}}{\text{Issue Price (Face value + Premium)}}$

Issue of Shares to Promoters

A promoter is one who undertakes to form a company with reference to a given purpose and takes necessary steps to accomplish that purpose. A promoter may be an individual, a firm, an association or a company.

Sometimes, companies pay their promoters in the form of shares. Such issue of shares is put under the category of issue of shares for consideration other than cash. The following entries are passed in this regard

Formation Expenses/Incorporation Cost/Goodwill A/c Dr

To Share Capital A/c

(Being ... shares of ₹ ... each issued to promoters of the company)

Issue of Shares to Underwriters

Underwriter is a person who works closely with the issuing company to determine the offering price of the securities, buys them from the issuer and sells them to the investors via the underwriter's distribution network. Sometimes underwriters are issued shares as their fees by the issuing companies. The following entries are passed in this regard

(i) **Making Underwriting Expenses Due**

Underwriting Expenses A/c Dr

To Underwriters A/c

(Being underwriting commission due)

(ii) **On Issuing Shares to Underwriters**

Underwriters A/c Dr

To Share Capital A/c

(Being ... shares issued @ ..... per share to underwriters)

(iii) **On Transferring Underwriting Expenses to Statement of Profit and Loss Account**

Statement of Profit and Loss Dr

To Underwriting Expenses A/c

(Being underwriting expenses charged to profit and loss account)

Calls-in-Arrears

When one or more shareholders fail to pay their dues at the time of allotment or call, it is technically called calls-in-arrears. Table F of the Companies Act, 2013 provides for the payment of interest on calls-in-arrears at a rate not exceeding 10% per annum.

Calls-in-arrears can be dealt in two ways

(i) **By opening calls-in-arrears account** In this method, the amount of calls-in-arrears is transferred to an account, namely calls-in-arrears account. The balance in calls-in-arrears account will show a debit balance equal to the total unpaid allotment and call money. Later on receipt of amount, it is credited to calls-in-arrears account.

Disclosure in the balance sheet Calls-in-arrears account is shown in the notes to accounts on 'share capital' to the balance sheet as a deduction from the amount of 'subscribed but not fully paid-up' under 'subscribed share capital'.

Accounting Entries of Calls-in-arrears

(a) **On non-receipt of call till the day fixed**

Calls-in-arrears A/c Dr

[With the amount not received]

To Relevant Calls A/c

(b) **On receipt of calls-in-arrears at a subsequent date**

Bank A/c Dr

[With the calls-in-arrears received]

To Calls-in-arrears A/c

Accounting Treatment of Interest on Calls-in-arrears

(a) **When the interest is received**

Bank A/c Dr

To Interest on Calls-in-arrears A/c

(Being interest on calls-in-arrears received)

(b) **On transfer to statement of profit and loss**

Interest on Calls-in-arrears A/c Dr

To Statement of Profit and Loss

(Being interest transferred to profit and loss account)

(ii) **Without opening calls-in-arrears account** In this method, the amount paid by the shareholders is credited to the call account and various call accounts will show debit balance equal to the total unpaid amount of each call. On receiving of calls-in-arrears amount, bank account is debited and relevant call account is credited.

Calls-in-Advance

When a company accepts money from the allottees against the calls not yet made, the amount reveived in advance is known as calls-in-advance.

In the case of calls-in-advance, the company pays interest at the rate stated in its Articles of Association. In the absence of the interest clause in the Articles of Association, provisions of Table F of the Companies Act, 2013 apply and the company is liable to pay interest at 12% per annum on calls-in-advance.

Disclosure in the balance sheet The amount received that is not yet due is a liability of the company. It is shown in the equity and liability part of the balance sheet under the head 'Current liabilities' and sub-head 'Other current liabilities'.

The journal entry passed to record this is

Bank A/c Dr
[With the amount of call money received in advance]
To Calls-in-advance A/c

It is adjusted when the respective call is made. The entry is

Calls-in-advance A/c Dr
To First Call A/c

Accounting Treatment of Interest on Calls-in-advance

(i) **When the interest is paid**

Interest on Calls-in-advance A/c Dr
To Bank A/c
(Being interest on calls-in-advance paid)

(ii) **On transfer to statement of profit and loss**

Statement of Profit and Loss Dr
To Interest on Calls-in-advance A/c
(Being interest transferred to profit and loss account)

Forfeiture of Shares

When a shareholder fails to pay the outstanding calls-in-arrears on his shares, the shares stand to be forfeited.

Forfeiture of shares means cancellation of shares and seizure of the amount already received from defaulting shareholders.

Upon forfeiture, the name of the original shareholder removed from the register of members. The following entries are passed in this case

(i) **Forfeiture of shares originally issued at par**

Share Capital A/c Dr (Called-up money)
To Forfeited Shares A/c (Paid-up money)
To Share Unpaid Calls A/c
(Unpaid money or calls-in-arrears)
(Being forfeiture of ...... shares for non-payment of call of ...... per share)

(ii) (a) **Forfeiture of shares originally issued at premium and premium was received**

Share Capital A/c Dr (Called-up money)
To Forfeited Shares A/c (Paid-up money)
To Share Allotment A/c
(Unpaid money excluding premium)
To Share Unpaid Call A/c
(Unpaid money or calls-in-arrears)
(Being forfeiture of ...... shares for non-payment of allotment and call of ...... per share)

(b) **Forfeiture of shares originally issued at premium and premium was not received**

Share Capital A/c Dr (Called-up money)
Securities Premium Reserve A/c Dr (Unpaid premium)
To Forfeited Shares A/c (Paid-up money)
To Share Allotment A/c
(Unpaid money including premium)
To Share Unpaid Call A/c
(Unpaid money or calls-in-arrears)
(Being forfeiture of ...... shares for non-payment of allotment and call of ......per share)

Re-issue of Shares

The directors can either cancel or re-issue the forfeited shares. Shares forfeited can be re-issued at par, at premium or at discount.

(i) **Re-issue of shares at par, if shares were originally issued at par or premium**

Bank A/c Dr (Amount received on re-issue)
To Share Capital A/c (Amount credited as paid-up)
(Being ...... forfeited shares re-issued @ ...... per share)

(ii) **Re-issue of shares at premium, if shares were originally issued at par or premium**

Bank A/c Dr (Amount received on re-issue)
To Share Capital A/c
(Amount credited as paid-up)
To Securities Premium Reserve A/c
(Amount of premium received)
(Being ...... forfeited shares re-issued @ ...... per share)

(iii) **Re-issue of shares at discount, if shares were originally issued at par**

Bank A/c Dr
(Amount received on re-issue)
Forfeited Shares A/c Dr
(Amount of discount allowed on re-issue)
To Share Capital A/c (Amount credited as paid-up)
(Being ... forfeited shares re-issued @...... per share)

(iv) **Balance amount of share forfeiture account must be transferred to capital reserve account related to those shares which are re-issued**

Forfeited Shares A/c Dr
To Capital Reserve A/c
(Being balance of share forfeiture account transferred to capital reserve account)

PYQs Previous Years' Questions

1/2 Marks Questions

1. ABC Ltd. offered 60,000 shares of ₹ 10 each to the public. The public applied for 1,00,000 shares. The company made pro-rata allotement in the ratio of 3 : 2 and the remaining applications were rejected and money refunded to the applicants. On how many shares did the company refund the application money? **ISC 2023**
   (a) 40,000 shares (b) 10,000 shares
   (c) 30,000 shares (d) 20,000 shares

2. A company forfeits 1,000 shares of ₹ 10 each. It had received ₹ 6,000 on these shares. What is the maximum discount that can be allowed by the company on the reissue of 400 shares? **ISC Specimen 2023**
   (a) ₹ 4,000 (b) ₹ 400
   (c) ₹ 1,600 (d) ₹ 2,400

3. Nickel Ltd. took over the business of Bronze Ltd. and agreed to pay for it by issuing 4,500 equity shares of ₹ 100 each at a premium of 20% along with a bankdraft of ₹ 60,000. What is the total agreed purchase consideration payable by Nickel Ltd. to Bronze Ltd.? **ISC Sem I 2021**
   (a) ₹ 4,50,000 (b) ₹ 5,40,000
   (c) ₹ 5,10,000 (d) ₹ 6,00,000

4. Vishesh Ltd. offered 50,000 equity shares of ₹ 10 each to the public for subscription. Applications for 45,000 equity shares were received and allotment was made to all the applicants. The first and final call of ₹ 2 per share was not received on 1,000 shares, which were forfeited by the company. What will be the subscribed capital of the company? **ISC Sem I 2021**
   (a) ₹ 4,48,000 (b) ₹ 4,50,000
   (c) ₹ 4,98,000 (d) ₹ 4,49,000

5. Joshua Ltd. forfeited 500 equity shares of ₹ 10 each, of ₹ 10 each, fully called up, on which ₹ 6 per share (including premium of ₹ 3 per share) was received. The company later reissued these shares at a discount. What is the maximum discount per share, which the company can give on their reissue? **ISC Sem I 2021**
   (a) ₹ 6 per share (b) ₹ 7 per share
   (c) ₹ 4 per share (d) ₹ 3 per share

6. The interest on calls-in-arrears account is closed by **ISC Sem I Specimen 2021**
   (a) crediting it to statement of profit and loss
   (b) crediting it to profit and loss appropriation account
   (c) debiting it to profit and loss appropriation account
   (d) debiting it to statement of profit and loss

7. Ronaldo Ltd. forfeited 300 equity shares of ₹ 10 each, fully called up, on which ₹ 5 per share (including premium of ₹ 1 per share) was received. It later reissued these shares at a discount. The maximum discount per share, which the company could have given on their reissue would be **ISC Sem I Specimen 2021**
   (a) ₹ 6 per share (b) ₹ 5 per share
   (c) ₹ 4 per share (d) ₹ 3 per share

8. ABC Ltd. forfeited 4,000 shares of ₹ 10 each, fully called up, on which application money of ₹ 3 had been paid. Out of these 2,000 shares were re-issued as fully paid up. Upon their reissue, the company transferred ₹ 4,000 to capital reserve. The rate at which these shares were reissued were **ISC Sem I Specimen 2021**
   (a) ₹ 10 per share (b) ₹ 4 per share
   (c) ₹ 9 per share (d) ₹ 8 per share

9. State with reason whether securities premium reserve can be used by a company to write-off the discount allowed to its debtors. **ISC 2020**

Or State with reason, whether securities premium reserve can be used to write-off bad debts. **ISC 2017**

10. In what way, if any, can the balance in shares forfeited account be used? **ISC 2019**

11. What is the minimum price at which a company can re-issue its forfeited shares which were originally issued at par? **ISC 2018, 2015**

12. State where will the non-cash transactions be recorded at the time of issue of shares, if all cash transactions are entered in the cash book. **ISC 2017**

13. Give any two differences between reserve capital and capital reserve. **ISC 2016, 2013**

14. State with reason whether a company can issue a share having a face value of ₹ 20 at ₹ 17. **ISC 2014**

15. Give the adjusting and closing entry for interest on calls-in-arrears due from a shareholder. **ISC 2014**

16. Give two differences between authorised capital and issued capital. **ISC 2013**

17. State any two uses of securities premium reserve as stated in Section 52 (2) of the Companies Act, 2013. **ISC 2012, 06, 01**

18. What are the closing entries for interest on calls-in-arrears account and interest on calls-in-advance account? **ISC 2011**

19. State two effects of forfeiture of shares. *ISC 2008*

20. What is meant by issue of shares for consideration other than cash? *ISC 2006*

21. What is meant by the term 'Reserve capital' in the context of joint stock companies? *ISC 2005*

22. What is the minimum time interval between two consecutive share calls according to 'Table F' of the Companies Act, 2013? *ISC 2005*

23. Explain minimum subscription. *ISC 2004*

24. Define share capital of a company. *ISC 2002*

25. Distinguish between nominal capital and paid-up capital. *ISC 2001*

26. Can fully paid-up shares be forfeited? If so, under what circumstances? *ISC 2000*

3 Marks Question

27. Sharp Ltd was formed on 1st December, 2013, with a capital of ₹ 5,00,000 divided into shares of ₹ 10 each. It offered 80% of the shares to the public.

The issue price was payable as follows

30% of the face value per share was payable with application.

20% of the face value per share was payable with allotment.

The balance as and when required. The company did not call for the balance during the year.

All the shares offered by the company were subscribed for. The company did not receive the allotment money on 3,000 shares.

You are required to

(i) Show the share capital in the balance sheet of the company (prepared as per Revised Schedule III of the Companies Act, 2013) at the end of the financial year.

(ii) Prepare notes to accounts. *ISC 2014*

6 Marks Questions

28. Sunrise Ltd. was formed on 1st November, 2021, with a capital of ₹ 20,00,000 divided into equity shares of ₹ 20 each.

It offered 95% shares to the public which were all subscribed for

- 60% amount was payable on application.
- 30% on allotment.
- And the balance on final call.

The applicants paid ₹ 11,40,000 on application and ₹ 5,40,000 on allotment. Final call was not made by the company till the balance sheet date.

You are required to prepare

(i) An extract of the balance sheet showing share capital.

(ii) Notes to accounts. *ISC 2023*

> **KEY IDEA**
>
> Since all calls are not made by the company, 'Subscribed and fully paid' will not appear in the balance sheet.

29. Meera Co. Ltd. invited applications for 50,000 equity shares of ₹ 10 each at a premium of ₹ 2 per share, payable as follows

On application on 1st May, 2017	₹ 2
On allotment on 1st July, 2017 (including premium)	₹ 5
On 1st and final call on 1st October, 2017	₹ 5

The company received applications for 62,500 shares. It was decided to

(i) Refuse allotment to the applicants of 2,500 shares.

(ii) Allot in full to the applicants of 10,000 shares.

(iii) Allot the balance of the shares applied on a pro-rata basis among the other applicants.

(iv) Utilise the excess application money in part payment of allotment money.

(v) Charge interest on calls-in-arrears, if any @10% per annum.

All the money due was received except from one shareholder to whom 200 shares had been allotted in full. The amount was due by him to the company even till the date of the balance sheet, which was 31st March, 2018. The company charged interest on calls-in-arrears from the shareholders from the date on which it was due till the balance sheet date.

You are required to, for the year 2017-18

(a) Prepare the cash book to record the above issue of shares.

(b) Pass journal entries in the journal proper (including entries for interest on calls-in-arrears). *ISC 2019*

10 Marks Questions

30. NH Ltd., with an authorised capital of ₹ 10,00,000 divided into 1,00,000 equity shares of ₹ 10 each, issued 50,000 shares to the public at a premium of ₹ 2 per share, payable as follows

₹ 5 on application (including premium)
₹ 3 on allotment
₹ 4 on first and final call.

The subscription was at par and the share money was received in full with the exception of the allotment money on 4,000 shares held by shareholder Ravi and the call money on 6,000 shares (including Ravi's shares).

The above 6,000 shares were forfeited by the company and 5,000 of these (including the shares which had been allotted to Ravi) were reissued at ₹ 8 per share as fully paid up.

You are required to pass journal entries to record the above transactions in the books of the company. ***ISC 2023***

31. MV Ltd. was registered with a capital of ₹ 2,00,000 divided into 10,000 equity shares of ₹ 20 each, payable as follows
On application ₹ 5 per share
On allotment ₹ 7 per share
On first and final call ₹ 8 per share

The company offered 5,000 shares to the public for subscription. It received applications for 6,700 shares.

From amongst the applicants

(i) Vimal, who had applied for 1,500 shares, paid ₹ 7,500 on application, but was alloted only 800 shares.
(ii) Abhay, who had applied for 2,000 shares, paid the full amount of ₹ 40,000 with his application, but was allotted only 1,000 shares.
(iii) Nitin, who had applied for and allotted 500 shares, did not pay the allotment and call money when due.
(iv) The remaining applicants paid as and when due.

The surplus money paid by both Vimal and Abhay was used towards allotment and call and any surplus beyond the call was refunded. The company forfeited Nitin's shares after the final call.

You are required to pass journal entries to record the above transactions in the books of the company. ***ISC 2023***

32. In the year 2021-22, Yamuna Limited Co. was registered with an authorised capital of ₹ 1,00,000 in ₹ 10 per equity share. Of these, 4,000 equity shares were issued as fully paid to vendor for the purchase of plant and machinery and 6,000 shares were subscribed for by the public.

During the first year, ₹ 6 per equity share was called up, payable ₹ 3 on application; ₹ 1 on allotment; ₹ 2 on the first call

The amounts received in respect of these shares were as follows
On 5,000 shares the full amount called
On 600 shares ₹ 4 per equity share
On 400 shares ₹ 3 per equity share

The company forfeited all those shares on which only ₹ 3 had been received and reissued them at ₹ 4 per share.

You are required to

(i) Pass journal entries to record the above transactions in the books of the company.
(ii) Prepare the calls-in-arrears account.

ISC Specimen 2023

33. Tapsi Ltd. invited applications from the public for the issue of 55,000 equity shares of ₹ 10 each payable as ₹ 3 on application; ₹ 5 on allotment; Balance on call.

The public applied for 50,000 shares which were duly allotted by the company. ₹ 2,49,000 were received by the company on allotment and ₹ 99,400 on call. The company forfeited those shares on which both, allotment and call money was not received. 70% of the forfeited shares were reissued at ₹ 7 per share, fully called up.

The company paid share issue expenses of ₹ 20,000 which were completely written-off at the end of the year. The company had ₹ 15,000 in its securities premium reserve account. You are required to pass journal entries to record the above transactions in the books of the company. ***ISC Specimen 2023***

34. Sudesh Ltd was registered with an authorised capital of ₹ 40,00,000 divided into 4,00,000 equity shares of ₹ 10 each.

The company offered 50,000 shares to the public at a premium of ₹ 2 per share, payable as follows
₹ 3 on application
₹ 6 on allotment (including premium)
₹ 3 on first and final call (due two months after allotment)

Applications were received for 60,000 shares and pro-rata allotment was made as follows

Category A: The applicants of 40,000 shares were allotted 30,000 shares.

Category B: The applicants of 20,000 shares were allotted in full.

Excess money paid on application was utilised towards allotment.

Nobby, a shareholder from Category A, who had applied for 1,200 shares failed to pay the allotmen and call money.

Vineet, a shareholder from Category B, who had been allotted 1,000 shares, paid the call money due, alongwith allotment.

The company forfeited Nobby's shares after the first and final call and paid interest on calls-in-advance to Vineet @ 12% per annum on the day of the final call.

Your are required to

(i) Pass journal entries to record the above transactions in the books of the company (including entries for interest on calls-in-advance).

(ii) Prepare calls-in-arrears account. **ISC 2020**

35. Saturn Ltd was registered with an authorised capital of ₹ 12,00,000, divided into 1,20,000 equity shares of ₹ 10 each. It issued 40,000 equity shares to the public at a premium of ₹ 5 per share, payable as follows

On application ₹ 6

On allotment ₹ 9 (including premium of ₹ 5)

All the shares were applied for and alloted. One shareholder holding 500 shares did not pay the allotment money and his shares were forfeited. Out of the forfeited shares, the company re-issued 400 shares at ₹ 7 per share fully called-up.

You are required to

(i) Pass journal entries in the books of company.

(ii) Prepare

(a) Securities premium reserve account

(b) Share capital account **ISC 2018**

> **KEY IDEA**
>
> Since all the forfeited shares are not reissued, the amount transferred to capital reserve will be calculated as
>
> $$\left[\left(\frac{\text{Profit on Forfeiture}}{\text{Forfeited Shares}} \times \text{Reissued Shares}\right) - \text{Loss on Reissue}\right]$$

36. Cargo Ltd invited applications for the issue of 20,000 equity shares of ₹ 10 each at a premium of ₹ 1 per share, payable as follows

On application ₹ 3

On allotment The balance (including premium ₹ 1)

Applications were received for 30,000 shares and pro-rata allotment was made to the remaining applicants after refunding application money to 5,000 share applicants.

Nicholas, who was allotted 3,000 shares, failed to pay the allotment money and his shares were forfeited. Out of these forfeited shares, 1,000 shares were re-issued as fully paid-up @ ₹ 8 per share.

You are required to

(i) Pass journal entries in the books of the company.

(ii) Prepare calls-in-arrears account.

(iii) Prepare share forfeiture account. **ISC 2017**

37. During the year 2014-15, ABC Ltd issued 10,000 equity shares of ₹ 50 each at ₹ 55 per share, payable as follows

On application ₹ 15

On allotment ₹ 20 (including premium ₹ 5)

On first and final call ₹ 20

All the issued shares were subscribed for by the public. One shareholder holding 500 shares did not pay the amount due on allotment and his shares were immediately forfeited. Another shareholder holding 100 shares paid the amount of the first and final call with allotment.

After the company had made the first and final call, 200 of the forfeited shares were re-issued as fully called up at ₹ 45 per share. The share issue expenses were ₹ 7,000 which were written-off at the end of the year.

You are required to pass journal entries in the books of the company for the year ending 31st March, 2015. **ISC 2016**

38. Pluto Ltd issued 20,000 equity shares of ₹ 10 each, payable as follows

On application	₹ 4
On allotment	₹ 1
On first call	₹ 3
On second and final call	₹ 2

Applications were received for 30,000 shares and pro-rata allotment was made to all the applicants. Excess money received on application was utilised towards allotment and subsequent calls.

One shareholder holding 100 shares did not pay the final call and his shares were forfeited. Of the forfeited shares, the company re-issued 70 shares as fully paid up at ₹ 12 per share.

You are required to pass journal entries in the books of the company for the year ending 31st March, 2014.

ISC 2015

> **KEY IDEA**
>
> Shares reissued as fully paid up at ₹ 12 per share basically means that the shares are issued at a premium of ₹ 2 per share.

39. Reliable Ltd was registered with an authorised capital of ₹ 20,00,000 in ₹ 10 per equity share. It invited applications for issuing 1,00,000 equity shares at a premium of ₹ 2 per share. The amount was payable as follows

On application ₹ 4 per share (including premium)
On allotment ₹ 3 per share
Balance on first and final call

Applications were received for 1,30,000 shares. Applications for 10,000 shares were rejected and the application money received on them was refunded. Pro-rata allotment was made to the remaining applications. Amount overpaid on these applications was adjusted towards the amount due on allotment.

Sameer, who had applied for 1,200 shares, failed to pay the allotment and call money. The company forfeited his shares, out of which, 800 shares were re-issued to Sanjay at ₹ 9 per share fully paid-up.

You are required to

(i) Pass the journal entries in the books of the company through calls-in-arrears account.
(ii) Prepare the share allotment account. *ISC 2013*

40. In 2010, Ganga Ltd was registered with an authorised capital of ₹ 1,00,000 equity shares of ₹ 10 each. Of these, 4,000 equity shares were issued as fully paid to vendors for the purchase of plant and machinery and the remaining 6,000 shares were subscribed for, by the public for cash.

During the first year, ₹ 6 per equity share was called-up, on these 6,000 shares, payable ₹ 3 on application, ₹ 1 on allotment and ₹ 2 on the first call. The amount received in respect of these shares were as follows

On 5,000 shares, the full amount called.
On 600 shares, ₹ 4 per share.
On 400 shares, ₹ 3 per share.

The company forfeited all those shares on which only ₹ 3 had been received and re-issued them at ₹ 4 per share, ₹ 6 called up.

Journalise the transactions in the books of the company and prepare calls-in-arrears account. *ISC 2012*

41. Sachdeva Tyres and Company Limited issued applications for 1,00,000 equity shares of ₹ 10 each at a premium of ₹ 3 per share. The amount was payable as follows

(i) On application ₹ 2
(ii) On allotment ₹ 5 (including premium)
(iii) Balance on the first and final call.

Applications were received for 1,50,000 shares. Allotment was made pro-rata to all applicants. Sudhir who had applied for 300 shares failed to pay allotment and call money. His shares were forfeited after the first and the final call. Of these, 170 shares were re-issued to Pramod at ₹ 9 per share fully paid.

Pass the necessary journal entries to show the above transactions. Show your working clearly. *ISC 2011*

42. The directors of Bhagat and Company Ltd issued 50,000 equity shares of ₹ 10 each at ₹ 12 per share, payable as ₹ 5 on application including the premium, ₹ 4 on allotment and the balance on final call.

Applications were received for 70,000 shares out of which applications for 8,000 shares were rejected and their money was refunded.

Money overpaid on application was applied towards sums due on allotment. All the money were duly received except from one shareholder holding 500 shares who failed to pay the final call money.

Pass the necessary journal entries to give effect to the above transactions. *ISC 2009*

43. Pioneer Ltd invited applications for 12,000 shares of ₹ 100 each to be issued at a premium of 10% payable as follows

On application ₹ 25
On allotment ₹ 40
On first and final call ₹ 35

Applications were received for 10,000 shares and all of these were accepted. All the money due was received except the first and final call on 100 shares which were forfeited. 60 of these forfeited shares were re-issued @ ₹ 90 per share credited as fully paid.

You are required to

(i) Pass the necessary journal entries.
(ii) Prepare the balance sheet of the company. *ISC 2007*

44. The Decoy Trading Company Ltd was registered with a nominal capital of ₹ 1,00,000 in shares of ₹ 10 each. 9,000 of which were issued payable as ₹ 1 on application, ₹ 2 on allotment, ₹ 3 on first call and the balance on final call.

All the shares were applied for and allotted and all cash was received on the due dates except that one shareholder holding 100 shares failed to pay the allotment money and another shareholder holding 200 shares paid the first and final call together with allotment money.

You are required to journalise the above transactions in the books of the company particularly through calls-in- arrears account and calls-in-advance account as and when necessary. *ISC 2002*

Case Based Questions

45. Pluto Ltd. with a registered capital of ₹ 20,00,000 in shares of ₹ 10 each, invited applications for 50,000 shares. The face value of the share was payable in three instalments. The company received ₹ 1,62,200 with applications, out of which it refunded ₹ 12,000 which it had received with the surplus applications.

ISC Sem I 2021

(i) What was the amount payable per share with application?
(a) ₹ 3 (b) ₹ 3.5
(c) ₹ 2 (d) ₹ 5

(ii) What were the number of shares applied for by the public?
(a) 81,000 (b) 50,000
(c) 40,000 (d) 54,000

(iii) The company received ₹ 2,25,000 with allotment. The calls in-arrears were ₹ 25,000. What was the amount payable per share with allotment?
(a) ₹ 5 (b) ₹ 4.5
(c) ₹ 3 (d) ₹ 6

(iv) The company immediately forfeits the shares on which it has not received the allotment. With which amount will the company debit share capital account to record the forfeiture of these shares?
(a) The total face value of these shares.
(b) The market value of these shares.
(c) The amount called up on these shares.
(d) The amount received by the company on these shares.

46. Xylo Ltd. was formed on 1st April, 2018, with an authorised capital of ₹ 12,00,000 divided into equity shares of ₹ 10 each.

It invited applications for 30,000 shares to be issued at par, in the year of its formation, all of which were subscribed for and the amount due on them fully received.

On 1st April, 2020, the company issued another 60,000 shares at a premium of ₹ 2 per share to be received with allotment. It received applications for 55,000 shares which were duly allotted. All amounts due on the allotted shares was received except the final call of ₹ 2 per share on 1,000 shares.

The company forfeited these shares and later reissued 800 of the forfeited shares @ ₹ 7 per share fully called up. The balance sheet of the company was prepared as at 31st March, 2021, as per Schedule III of the Companies Act, 2013. *ISC Sem I Specimen 2021*

(i) The issued capital of the company to be shown in notes to accounts as at 31st March, 2021, under 'Share capital' will be
(a) ₹ 12,00,000 (b) ₹ 9,00,000
(c) ₹ 8,50,000 (d) ₹ 8,49,600

(ii) The subscribed shares of the company at the end of the year 2020-21 will be
(a) 1,20,000 (b) 90,000
(c) 85,000 (d) 84,800

(iii) The amount of share capital to be shown in the balance sheet of the company as at 31st March, 2021, will be
(a) ₹ 12,00,000 (b) ₹ 9,00,000
(c) ₹ 8,50,000 (d) ₹ 8,49,600

(iv) The net gain made by the company on reissue of the 800 shares will be transferred to
(a) reserve capital account
(b) capital reserve account
(c) securities premium reserve account
(d) statement of profit and loss account

47. **Journal of Mekon Ltd.**

Date	Particulars		LF	Amt (Dr)	Amt (Cr)
	Share Capital A/c	Dr		...(i)...	
	Securities Premium Reserve A/c			2,000	
	To Share Forfeiture A/c				—
	To Calls-in-arrears A/c				7,000
	(Being ...... shares forfeited for non-payment of ₹ ...(ii)... including premium of ₹ 2 per share)				
	Bank A/c	Dr		—	
	Share Forfeiture A/c	Dr		...(iii)...	
	To Share Capital A/c				...(iv)...
	To ...(iii)... A/c				1,400
	(Being ... share reissued at ₹ 9 per share, fully paid @ ₹ 12 per share)				
	Share Forfeiture A/c	Dr		700	
	To Capital Reserve A/c				700
	(Being net gain on reissued shares transferred to capital reserve)				

Dr **Share Forfeiture Account** Cr

Particulars	Amt (₹)	Particulars	Amt (₹)
To Share Capital A/c	700	By Share Capital A/c	4,000
To Securities Premium Reserve A/c	1,400		
To Capital Reserve A/c	700		
To Balance c/d	1,200		
	4,000		4,000

Note Face value of share is ₹ 10 each. *ISC Sem I Specimen 2021*

(i) The share capital account was debited with
(a) ₹ 10,000 (b) ₹ 9,000
(c) ₹ 12,000 (d) ₹ 7,000

(ii) The shares were forfeited for non-payment of
(a) ₹ 10 per share
(b) ₹ 9 per share
(c) ₹ 12 per share
(d) ₹ 7 per share

(iii) At the time of reissue of shares, the share forfeiture account was debited with
(a) ₹ 6,300
(b) ₹ 7,000
(c) ₹ 2,100
(d) ₹ 1,400

(iv) At the time of reissue of shares, the share capital account was credited with
(a) ₹ 6,300 (b) ₹ 7,000
(c) ₹ 2,100 (d) ₹ 1,400

(v) At the time of reissue of shares, the account credited with ₹ 1,400 was
(a) calls-in-arrears account
(b) capital reserve account
(c) securities premium reserve account
(d) None of the above

KEY IDEA

As per the ledger account of share forfeiture, share forfeiture account will be credited by ₹ 4,000 in first entry.

Explanations

1. (b) Applied : Alloted
3 : 2
x : 60,000
$\therefore x = 90,000$

Applicants of 90,000 shares were issued 60,000 shares.
Rejected shares = 1,00,000 − 90,000 = 10,000 shares

2. (d) Maximum discount allowed on reissue of 400 shares $= \frac{6,000}{1,000} \times 400 =$ ₹ 2,400

Maximum discount that can be allowed on reissue of forfeited shares is the amount received on forfeited shares.

3. (d) Purchase consideration = (4,500 × 120) + 60,000
= 5,40,000 + 60,000 = ₹ 6,00,000

4. (a) Subscribed capital = (45,000 × 10) − (1,000 × 2)
= 4,50,000 − 2,000
= ₹ 4,48,000

5. (d) Company received ₹ 3 per share (excluding premium) on 500 shares before forfeiture, therefore company can reissue these shares at a maximum discount of ₹ 3 per share.

6. (a) crediting it to statement of profit and loss

7. (c) ₹ 4 per share

8. (c) Profit on forfeiture on 2,000 shares
$= \left(\frac{12,000}{4,000} \times 2,000\right)$
= ₹ 6,000

Transfer to reserve = 4,000
Profit on Forfeiture − Loss on Reissue = 4,000
6,000 − Loss on reissue = 4,000
∴ Loss on Reissue = ₹ 2,000
Amount received on reissue = 20,000 − 2,000 = ₹ 18,000
Reissue rate $= \frac{18,000}{2,000} =$ ₹ 9 per share

9. No, securities premium reserve cannot be used to write-off the discount allowed to its debtors. It is because the Companies Act, 2013 specifies the uses of security premium in Section 52, which are as follows
(i) Issuing fully paid bonus shares.
(ii) Writing-off preliminary expenses.
(iii) Writing-off expenses of, or commission paid, or discount allowed on issue of shares or debentures of company.
(iv) Providing for premium payable on redemption of any redeemable preference shares or debentures.
(v) For buy-back of shares.

10. The balance in shares forfeited account can be utilised for re-issue of forfeited shares at discount. However, if the shares are re-issued at a discount, then the amount doesn't exceed the amount forfeited on these shares.

11. The company, as per the provisions contained in its Articles can re-issue its shares at a price as per its own discretion. Generally, these shares are issued at a discount. However, the amount of discount cannot exceed the proportionate amount forfeited on these shares.

12. The non-cash transactions at the time of issue of shares, if cash book is maintained, will be recorded in journal proper.

13. Difference between reserve capital and capital reserve are

Basis	Reserve capital	Capital reserve
Meaning	It is that part of the uncalled capital which cannot be called-up except in the event of winding up.	It is that part of the reserves which is not free for distribution as dividend.
Disclosure	It is not disclosed in the company's balance sheet.	It is disclosed under the head 'reserves and surplus' in 'equity and liabilities' part of the company's balance sheet.

14. No, a company cannot issue a share having a face value of ₹ 20 at ₹ 17 because as per Companies Act, 2013, shares cannot be issued at discount. Any share except sweat equity share, issued by the company at a discounted price shall be void.

15. **Adjusting Entry**

Bank A/c Dr

To Interest on Calls-in-arrears A/c

(Being interest on calls-in-arrears received)

Closing Entry

Interest on Calls-in-arrears A/c Dr

To Statement of Profit and Loss

(Being interest on calls-in-arrears transferred to statement of profit and loss)

Concept Enhancer Calls-in-arrear is the amount which the company called but did not received. Since it is due but not received, the company is entitled to receive interest on calls-in-arrears

16. Difference between authorised capital and issued capital

Basis	Authorised capital	Issued capital
Meaning	It refers to that amount of capital which is stated in the Memorandum of Association of the company as registered capital.	It refers to that part of authorised capital of the company which is offered to the public for subscription.
Relation	It can exceed issued capital.	It cannot exceed authorised capital.

Concept Enhancer The other names of authorised capital are registered capital and nominal capital.

17. Section 52 (2) of the Companies Act, 2013 states the use of the amount received as premium for the following purposes

(i) In purchasing its own shares (buy back)

(ii) Issuing fully paid bonus shares to the members

18. **Closing entry for Calls-in-arrears**

Interest on Calls-in-arrear A/c Dr

To Statement of Profit and Loss

Closing entry for Calls-in-advance

Statement of Profit and Loss Dr

To Interest on Calls-in-advance A/c

19. The two effects of forfeiture of shares are

(i) Name of the shareholder is removed from the register of members.

(ii) Amount already received on these shares is forfeited by the company.

20. When a company issues shares in payment (consideration) against purchase of assets, business from vendors or to promoters/underwriters for their services, etc such an issue is said to be issue of shares for consideration other than cash.

In such cases, the payment is made in the form of fully paid shares of the company. Cash is not received against issue of shares because consideration is received in the form of assets, business or services.

21. It is that portion of subscribed share capital, remaining uncalled, which is not capable of being called up except in the event and for the purposes of the company being wound up.

22. As per Table F of the Companies Act, 2013 there must be an interval of atleast one month between two consecutive calls.

23. According to Section 39 (1) of the Companies Act, 2013, it is the amount stated in the prospectus as the minimum amount that must be subscribed. No securities cannot be allotted, unless the sum payable on application for the sum so stated (minimum subscription) has been paid to and received by the company by cheque or any other instrument.

As per the guidelines of SEBI, a company must receive a minimum of 90% of the subscription against the entire issue before making any allotment of shares to the public.

24. It refers to that part of the capital of a company, which is represented by the total nominal value of shares, which it has issued.

25. Difference between nominal capital and paid-up capital

Basis	Nominal capital	Paid-up capital
Meaning	It is the amount of share capital which a company is authorised to issue by its Memorandum of Association.	It is that part of called-up capital, which is actually paid by the shareholders.
Limit	It is the maximum limit on the number of shares. It can exceed paid-up capital.	It has to be less than nominal capital, i.e. it has to be within the limit set by authorised capital.

26. Fully paid-up shares can be forfeited in the following cases

(i) When there is a default in fulfilling any engagement between the members.

(ii) When there is expulsion of members, where the Articles specifically provide thereof.

27. (i)

In the Books of Sharp Ltd
Balance Sheet
as at 31st March, 2014

Particulars	Note No.	Amt (₹)
I. **EQUITY AND LIABILITIES**		
1. **Shareholders' Funds**		
(a) Share Capital	1	1,94,000
		1,94,000

(ii) **Notes to Accounts**

Particulars		Amt (₹)
1. **Share Capital**		
Authorised Capital		
50,000 Equity Shares of ₹ 10 each		5,00,000
Issued Capital		
40,000 Equity Shares of ₹ 10 each		4,00,000
Subscribed but not Fully Paid-up Capital		
40,000 Shares @ ₹ 5 each	2,00,000	
(–) Calls-in-arrears (3,000 × 2)	(6,000)	1,94,000
		1,94,000

28. (i)

Balance Sheet

Particulars	Note No.	Amt (₹)
I. **EQUITY AND LIABILITIES**		
1. **Shareholder's Funds**		
(a) Share Capital	1	16,80,000

(ii) **Notes to Accounts**

Particulars		Amt (₹)
1. **Share Capital**		
Authorised Capital		
1,00,000 Equity Shares of ₹ 20 each		20,00,000
Issued Capital		
95,000 Equity Shares of ₹ 20 each		19,00,000
Subscribed Capital		
Subscribed but not Fully Paid		
95,000 Shares of ₹ 20 each, ₹ 18 Called up	17,10,000	
(–) Calls-in-arrears (5,000 × 6)	(30,000)	16,80,000

29. JOURNAL

Date	Particulars		LF	Amt (Dr)	Amt (Cr)
2017					
May 1	Equity Share Application A/c	Dr		1,20,000	
	To Equity Share Capital A/c				1,00,000
	To Equity Share Allotment A/c				20,000
	(Being application money transferred to equity share capital account and excess money adjusted on allotment)				
Jul 1	Equity Share Allotment A/c	Dr		2,50,000	
	To Equity Share Capital A/c				1,50,000
	To Security Premium Reserve A/c				1,00,000
	(Being allotment money due with premium)				
Jul 2	Calls-in-arrears A/c	Dr		1,000	
	To Equity Share Allotment A/c				1,000
	(Being allotment money received on 49,800 shares)				
Oct 1	Equity Share First and Final Call A/c	Dr		2,50,000	
	To Equity Share Capital A/c				2,50,000
	(Being first call money due)				
Oct 1	Calls-in-arrears A/c	Dr		1,000	
	To Equity Share First and Final Call A/c				1,000
	(Being first call money received on 49,500 shares)				
2018					
Mar 31	Shareholder A/c	Dr		125	
	To Interest on Calls-in-arrears A/c				125
	(Being interest on calls-in-arrears due)				
Mar 31	Interest on Calls-in-arrears A/c	Dr		125	
	To Profit and Loss A/c				125
	(Being transfer of interest to profit and loss account)				

Dr **Cash Book** Cr

Date	Particulars	JF	Amt (₹)	Date	Particulars	JF	Amt (₹)
2017				2017			
May 1	To Equity Share Application A/c		1,25,000	May 1	By Equity Share Application A/c		5,000
Jul 1	To Equity Share Allotment A/c		2,29,000	2018 Mar 31	By Balance c/d		5,98,000
Oct 1	To Equity Share First and Final Call A/c		2,49,000				
			6,03,000				6,03,000

Working Note

Calculation of Interest on Calls-in-arrears

$$1{,}000 \times \frac{9}{100} \times \frac{9}{12} = ₹\ 75$$

$$1{,}000 \times \frac{9}{100} \times \frac{6}{12} = ₹\ 50$$

$$\underline{125}$$

Calculation of Amount Received at Allotment

Particulars	Amt (₹)
Allotment Money Due (50,000 × 5)	2,50,000
(–) Amount Received with Application	(20,000)
	2,30,000
(–) Calls-in-arrears (200 × 5)	(1,000)
	2,29,000

Common Mistake Students usually forget to transfer interest on calls-in-arrears to statement of profit and loss. Since interest is a revenue to the company, it will be transferred to profit and loss account.

30.

JOURNAL

Date	Particulars		LF	Amt (Dr)	Amt (Cr)
	Bank A/c	Dr		2,50,000	
	To Share Application A/c				2,50,000
	(Being application money received for 50,000 shares)				
	Share Application A/c	Dr		2,50,000	
	To Share Capital A/c				1,50,000
	To Securities Premium A/c				1,00,000
	(Being application money transferred to share capital account and securities premium)				
	Share Allotment A/c	Dr		1,50,000	
	To Share Capital A/c				1,50,000
	(Being allotment money due)				
	Bank A/c	Dr		1,38,000	
	Calls-in arrears A/c	Dr		12,000	
	To Share Allotment A/c				1,50,000
	(Being allotment received except on 4,000 shares)				
	Share First and Final Call A/c	Dr		2,00,000	
	To Share Capital A/c				2,00,000
	(Being first and final call money due)				
	Bank A/c	Dr		1,76,000	
	Calls-in-arrears A/c	Dr		24,000	
	To Share First and Final Call A/c				2,00,000
	(Being first and final call received except on 6,000 shares)				
	Share Capital A/c	Dr		60,000	
	To Share Forfeiture A/c				24,000
	To Calls-in-arrears A/c				36,000
	(Being 6,000 shares forfeited)				
	Bank A/c	Dr		40,000	
	Shares Forfeiture A/c	Dr		10,000	
	To Share Capital A/c				50,000
	(Being 5,000 shares on reissued)				
	Share Forfeiture A/c	Dr		8,000	
	To Capital Reseve A/c				8,000
	(Being transfer of gain on reissue)				
	$\left[12{,}000+\left(\frac{12{,}000}{2{,}000}\times 1{,}000\right)-10{,}000\right]$				

31.

JOURNAL

Date	Particulars	LF	Amt (Dr)	Amt (Cr)
	Bank A/c Dr To Share Application A/c (Being application money received for 6,700 shares)		63,500	 63,500
	Share Application A/c Dr To Share Capital A/c To Share Allotment A/c (3,500 + 7,000) To Bank A/c To Share First Call A/c (Being application money transferred to share capital account and excess amount adjusted)		63,500	 25,000 10,500 20,000 8,000
	Share Allotment A/c Dr To Share Capital A/c (Being allotment money due)		35,000	 35,000
	Bank A/c Dr Calls-in-arrears A/c Dr To Share Allotment A/c (Being allotment received except on 500 shares)		21,000 3,500	 24,500
	Share First and Final Call A/c Dr To Share Capital A/c (Being first and final call money due)		40,000	 40,000
	Bank A/c Dr Calls-in-arrears A/c Dr To Share First and Final Call A/c (Being first and final call received except on 500 shares)		28,000 4,000	 32,000
	Share Capital A/c Dr To Share Forfeiture A/c To Calls-in-arrears A/c (Being 6,000 shares forfeited)		10,000	 2,500 7,500

Common Mistake Students record advance received on application as calls-in-advance. It should be noted that advance received on application will be recorded by its name.

32. (i)

In the Books of Yamuna Ltd. Co.

JOURNAL

Date	Particulars	LF	Amt (Dr)	Amt (Cr)
	Plant and Machinery A/c Dr To Vendor A/c (Being plant and machinery purchased)		40,000	 40,000
	Vendor A/c Dr To Equity Share Capital A/c (Being issue of 4,000 equity shares of ₹ 10 each for consideration other than cash)		40,000	 40,000
	Bank A/c Dr To Equity Share Application A/c (Being application money received on 6,000 shares @ ₹ 3 each)		18,000	 18,000
	Equity Share Application A/c Dr To Equity Share Capital A/c (Being the application money transferred to equity share capital account)		18,000	 18,000
	Equity Share Allotment A/c Dr To Equity Share Capital A/c (Being allotment money due on 6,000 shares @ ₹ 1 each)		6,000	 6,000

Date	Particulars		LF	Amt (Dr)	Amt (Cr)
	Bank A/c (5,600 × 1)	Dr		5,600	
	Calls-in-arrear A/c (400 × 1)	Dr		400	
	To Equity Share Allotment A/c				6,000
	(Being allotment money received on 5,600 shares @ ₹ 1 each)				
	Equity Share First Call A/c	Dr		12,000	
	To Equity Share Capital A/c				12,000
	(Being first call money due)				
	Bank A/c (5,000 × 2)	Dr		10,000	
	Call-in-arrears A/c (1,000 × 2)	Dr		2,000	
	To Equity Share First Call A/c				12,000
	(Being first call money received on 5,000 shares @ ₹ 2 each)				
	Equity Share Capital A/c (400 × 6)	Dr		2,400	
	To Share Forfeiture A/c (400 × 3)				1,200
	To Calls-in-arrears A/c (400 × 3)				1,200
	(Being 400 shares forfeited for non-payment of allotment and first call money)				
	Bank A/c (400 × 4)	Dr		1,600	
	Share Forfeiture A/c (400 × 2)	Dr		800	
	To Equity Share Capital A/c (400 × 6)				2,400
	(Being the reissue of 400 shares out of the forfeited shares @ ₹ 4 each)				
	Share Forfeiture A/c	Dr		400	
	To Capital Reserve A/c				400
	(Being the profit on reissue transferred to capital reserve)				

(ii) Dr **Calls-in-arrears Account** Cr

Particulars	LF	Amt (₹)	Particulars	LF	Amt (₹)
To Equity Share Allotment A/c		400	By Equity Share Capital A/c		1,200
To Equity Share First Call A/c		2,000	By Balance b/d		1,200
		2,400			2,400

33.

In the Books of Tapsi Ltd.
JOURNAL

Date	Particulars		LF	Amt (Dr)	Amt (Cr)
	Bank A/c	Dr		1,50,000	
	To Equity Share Application A/c				1,50,000
	(Being application money received on 50,000 shares @ ₹ 3 each)				
	Equity Share Application A/c	Dr		1,50,000	
	To Equity Share Capital A/c				1,50,000
	(Being application money transferred to equity share capital account)				
	Equity Share Allotment A/c	Dr		2,50,000	
	To Equity Share Capital A/c				2,50,000
	(Being allotment money due)				
	Bank A/c	Dr		2,49,000	
	To Equity Share Allotment A/c				2,49,000
	(Being allotment money received on 49,800 shares @ ₹ 5 each)				
	Equity Share First and Final Call A/c	Dr		1,00,000	
	To Equity Share Capital A/c				1,00,000
	(Being first and final call money due)				
	Bank A/c	Dr		99,400	
	To Equity Share First and Final Call A/c				99,400
	(Being call money received on 49,700 shares @ ₹ 2 each)				

Date	Particulars		LF	Amt (Dr)	Amt (Cr)
	Equity Share Capital A/c (200 × 10)	Dr		2,000	
	To Share Forfeiture A/c (200 × 3)				600
	To Equity Share Allotment A/c (200 ×5)				1,000
	To Equity Share First and Final Call A/c (200 × 2)				400
	(Being 200 shares forfeited for non-payment of allotment and first and final call money)				
	Bank A/c (140 ×7)	Dr		980	
	Share Forfeiture A/c (140 × 3)	Dr		420	
	To Equity Share Capital A/c				1,400
	(Being the reissue of 70% of the forfeited shares)				
	Share Issue Expenses A/c	Dr		20,000	
	To Cash A/c				20,000
	(Being share issue expenses paid)				
	Securities Premium A/c	Dr		15,000	
	Profit and Loss A/c	Dr		5,000	
	To Share Issue Expenses A/c				20,000
	(Being share issue expenses write-off)				

Working Notes

1. Number of shares not paid the allotment money = $\frac{2,50,000 - 2,49,000}{5}$ = 200 shares

2. Number of shares not paid the first and final call money = $\frac{1,00,000 - 99,400}{2}$ = 300 shares

Common Mistake Students usually write-off share issue expenses directly from statement of profit and loss. However, securities premium should be utilised first to write-off share issue expense.

34. (i)

In the Books of Sudesh Ltd.
JOURNAL

S.No./Date	Particulars		LF	Amt (Dr)	Amt (Cr)
(a)	Bank A/c (60,000 ×₹ 3)	Dr		1,80,000	
	To Share Application A/c				1,80,000
	(Being money received on application)				
(b)	Share Application A/c	Dr		1,80,000	
	To Share Capital A/c (50,000 ×₹ 3)				1,50,000
	To Share Allotment A/c (10,000 ×₹ 3)				30,000
	(Being transfer of application money to share capital and excess of money transferred to allotment account)				
(c)	Share Allotment A/c (50,000 ×₹ 6)	Dr		3,00,000	
	To Share Capital A/c (50,000 ×₹ 4)				2,00,000
	To Security Premium A/c (50,000 ×₹ 2)				1,00,000
	(Being allotment due)				
(d)	Bank A/c (Balance)	Dr		2,68,500	
	Calls-in-arrears A/c (WN 1)	Dr		4,500	
	To Share Allotment A/c (3,00,000 – 30,000)				2,70,000
	To Calls-in-advance A/c (WN 2)				3,000
	(Being allotment money received after adjustment of money received on share application)				
(e)	Share First and Final Call A/c (50,000 ×₹ 3)	Dr		1,50,000	
	To Share Capital A/c				1,50,000
	(Being first and final call due)				

S.No./Date	Particulars		LF	Amt (Dr)	Amt (Cr)
(f)	Bank A/c	Dr		1,44,300	
	Calls-in-advance A/c (WN 2)	Dr		3,000	
	Calls-in-arrears A/c (900 ×₹ 3)	Dr		2,700	
	To Share First and Final Call A/c				1,50,000
	(Being last call received)				
(g)	Interest on Calls-in-advance A/c (WN 3)	Dr		60	
	To Bank A/c				60
	(Being interest on calls-in-advance)				
(h)	Profit and Loss A/c	Dr		60	
	To Interest on Calls-in-advance A/c				60
	(Being interest transferred to profit and loss account)				
(i)	Share Capital A/c (900 ×₹ 10)	Dr		9,000	
	Securities Premium A/c (900 ×₹ 2)	Dr		1,800	
	To Calls-in-arrears A/c (4,500 + 2,700)				7,200
	To Share Forfeiture A/c (Balance)				3,600
	(Being share forfeited of Nobby)				

(ii) **Ledger of Sudesh Ltd.**

Dr **Calls-in-Arrears Account** Cr

Particulars	JF	Amt (₹)	Particulars	JF	Amt (₹)
To Share Capital A/c		5,400	By Share Allotment A/c		4,500
To Security Premium A/c		1,800	By Share First and Final Call A/c		2,700
		7,200			7,200

Working Notes

1. Shares allotted to Nobby $= 1{,}200 \times \frac{30{,}000}{40{,}000} = 900$

   Excess money received on application $= (1{,}200 - 900) \times 3 = ₹\,900$

   Amount due on allotment $= 900 \times 6 =$ ₹ 5,400

   Already received on application = ₹ (900)

   Calls-in-arrears = ₹ 4,500

2. Calls-in-advance = 1,000 shares @ ₹ 3 = ₹ 3,000

3. Interest on calls-in-advance $=$ Calls-in-advance $\times$ Rate (in p.a.) $\times \frac{\text{Time Period (in months)}}{12}$

$$= 3{,}000 \times \frac{12}{100} \times \frac{2}{12} = ₹\,60$$

35. (i) **In the Books of Saturn Ltd**

JOURNAL

Date	Particulars		LF	Amt (Dr)	Amt (Cr)
	Bank A/c	Dr		2,40,000	
	To Equity Share Application A/c				2,40,000
	(Being share application money received)				
	Equity Share Application A/c	Dr		2,40,000	
	To Equity Share Capital A/c				2,40,000
	(Being share application money transferred to share capital account)				
	Equity Share Allotment A/c	Dr		3,60,000	
	To Equity Share Capital A/c				1,60,000
	To Securities Premium Reserve A/c				2,00,000
	(Being share allotment money due)				

Date	Particulars		LF	Amt (Dr)	Amt (Cr)
	Bank A/c	Dr		3,55,500	
	To Equity Share Allotment A/c				3,55,500
	(Being share allotment money received)				
	Equity Share Capital A/c	Dr		5,000	
	Security Premium Reserve A/c	Dr		2,500	
	To Share Forfeiture A/c				3,000
	To Equity Share Allotment A/c				4,500
	(Being 500 shares forfeited)				
	Bank A/c	Dr		2,800	
	Share Forfeiture A/c	Dr		1,200	
	To Equity Share Capital A/c				4,000
	(Being 400 shares re-issued @ ₹ 7 each full paid)				
	Share Forfeiture A/c	Dr		1,200	
	To Capital Reserve A/c				1,200
	(Being amount of share forfeiture transferred to capital reserve)				

(ii) (a) Dr **Security Premium Reserve Account** Cr

Particulars	Amt (₹)	Particulars	Amt (₹)
To Equity Share Allotment A/c	2,500	By Equity Share Allotment A/c	2,00,000
To Balance c/d	1,97,500		
	2,00,000		2,00,000

(b) Dr **Share Capital Account** Cr

Particulars	Amt (₹)	Particulars	Amt (₹)
To Share Forfeiture A/c	3,000	By Equity Share Application A/c	2,40,000
To Equity Share Allotment A/c	2,000	By Equity Share Allotment A/c	1,60,000
To Balance c/d	3,99,000	By Bank A/c	2,800
		By Share Forfeiture A/c	1,200
	4,04,000		4,04,000

Working Note Amt (₹)

Share forfeiture amount for 400 shares = $\frac{3,000}{500} \times 400$ = 2,400

Amount of share forfeiture adjusted on re-issue transferred to capital reserve = 1,200

1,200

36. (i)

In the Books of Cargo Ltd
JOURNAL

Date	Particulars		LF	Amt (Dr)	Amt (Cr)
	Bank A/c (30,000 × 3)	Dr		90,000	
	To Equity Share Application A/c				90,000
	(Being application money received on 30,000 equity shares @ ₹ 3 per share)				
	Equity Share Application A/c	Dr		90,000	
	To Equity Share Capital A/c (20,000 × 3)				60,000
	To Equity Share Allotment A/c				15,000
	To Bank A/c (5,000×3)				15,000
	(Being share application money transferred to share capital account and share allotment account and excess refunded)				
	Equity Share Allotment A/c	Dr		1,60,000	
	To Equity Share Capital A/c (20,000 ×7)				1,40,000
	To Securities Premium Reserve A/c (20,000 × 1)				20,000
	(Being allotment made due alongwith premium)				

Date	Particulars		LF	Amt (Dr)	Amt (Cr)
	Bank A/c	Dr		1,23,250	
	Calls-in-arrears A/c	Dr		21,750	
	To Equity Share Allotment A/c				1,45,000
	(Being allotment money received except on 3,000 shares)				
	Equity Share Capital A/c (3,000 × 10)	Dr		30,000	
	Securities Premium Reserve A/c (3,000 × 1)	Dr		3,000	
	To Calls-in-arrears A/c				21,750
	To Share Forfeiture A/c				11,250
	(Being Nicholas's share forfeited for non-payment of allotment money)				
	Bank A/c (1,000 × 8)	Dr		8,000	
	Share Forfeiture A/c	Dr		2,000	
	To Equity Share Capital A/c (1,000 × 10)				10,000
	(Being 1,000 shares re-issued at ₹ 8 per share as fully paid-up)				
	Share Forfeiture A/c	Dr		1,750	
	To Capital Reserve A/c				1,750
	(Being profit on re-issued shares transferred to capital reserve)				

(ii) Dr **Call-in-arrears Account** Cr

Particulars	Amt (₹)	Particulars	Amt (₹)
To Equity Share Allotment A/c	21,750	By Securities Premium Reserve A/c	3,000
		By Equity Share Capital A/c	18,750
	21,750		21,750

(iii) Dr **Share Forfeiture Account** Cr

Particulars	Amt (₹)	Particulars	Amt (₹)
To Equity Share Capital A/c	2,000	By Equity Share Capital A/c	11,250
To Capital Reserve A/c	1,750		
To Balance c/d	7,500		
	11,250		11,250

Working Notes

1. Shares applied by Nicholas = $\text{Shares Allotted} \times \frac{\text{Total Shares Applied}}{\text{Total Shares Allotted}} = 3{,}000 \times \frac{25{,}000}{20{,}000} = 3{,}750$ shares
2. Excess amount paid by Nicholas at the time of application = $(3{,}750 - 3{,}000) \times 3 =$ ₹ 2,250
3. | | Amt (₹) |
   |---|---|
   | Money due at the time of allotment (3,000 × 8) | 24,000 |
   | (−) Excess paid | (2,250) |
   | Calls-in-arrears | 21,750 |
4. Amount to be transferred to capital reserve = Amount forfeited on re-issued shares − Amount utilised at the time of re-issue

$$= \left(\frac{11{,}250}{3{,}000} \times 1{,}000\right) - 2{,}000 = 3{,}750 - 2{,}000 = ₹\ 1{,}750$$

37. **In the Books of ABC Ltd**

JOURNAL

Date	Particulars		LF	Amt (Dr)	Amt (Cr)
	Share Issue Expenses A/c	Dr		7,000	
	To Bank A/c				7,000
	(Being share issue expenses paid)				
	Bank A/c (10,000 × 15)	Dr		1,50,000	
	To Equity Share Application A/c				1,50,000
	(Being application money @ ₹ 15 per share received)				

Date	Particulars		LF	Amt (Dr)	Amt (Cr)
	Equity Share Application A/c	Dr		1,50,000	
	To Equity Share Capital A/c				1,50,000
	(Being application money 10,000 shares @ ₹ 15 each transferred to capital account)				
	Equity Share Allotment A/c (10,000 × 20)	Dr		2,00,000	
	To Equity Share Capital A/c (10,000 × 15)				1,50,000
	To Securities Premium Reserve A/c (10,000 ×5)				50,000
	(Being share allotment money due on 10,000 shares @ ₹ 20 each including ₹ 5 premium)				
	Bank A/c	Dr		1,92,000	
	Calls-in-arrears A/c (500 × 20)	Dr		10,000	
	To Equity Share Allotment A/c				2,00,000
	To Calls-in-advance A/c (100 × 20)				2,000
	(Being allotment money received on 9,500 shares and call money received in advance on 100 shares)				
	Equity Share Capital A/c (500 × 30)	Dr		15,000	
	Securities Premium Reserve A/c (500 ×5)	Dr		2,500	
	To Forfeited Shares A/c (500 × 15)				7,500
	To Equity Share Allotment A/c (500 × 20)				10,000
	(Being 500 equity shares forfeited for non-payment of allotment money)				
	Equity Share First and Final Call A/c (9,500 × 20)	Dr		1,90,000	
	To Equity Share Capital A/c				1,90,000
	(Being first and final call money due on 9,500 shares)				
	Bank A/c (9,400 × 20)	Dr		1,88,000	
	Calls-in-advance A/c (100 × 20)	Dr		2,000	
	To Equity Share First and Final Call A/c				1,90,000
	(Being first and final call money received on 9,400 shares @ ₹ 20 each and calls-in-advance on 100 shares adjusted)				
	Bank A/c (200 × 45)	Dr		9,000	
	Share Forfeiture A/c	Dr		1,000	
	To Equity Share Capital A/c (200 ×50)				10,000
	(Being 200 shares re-issued @ ₹ 45 per share)				
	Share Forfeiture A/c	Dr		2,000	
	To Capital Reserve A/c				2,000
	(Being the balance on re-issued shares transferred to capital reserve)				
	Securities Premium Reserve A/c	Dr		7,000	
	To Share Issue Expenses A/c				7,000
	(Being shares issue expenses written-off)				

Working Notes

1. Amount Received with Allotment

	Amt (₹)
On 9,500 shares @ ₹ 20 per share	1,90,000
(+) 100 shares @ ₹ 20 per share	2,000
	1,92,000

2. Amount to be transferred to capital reserve $\left(\frac{7,500}{500} \times 200\right)$ 3,000

Amount to be transferred to capital reserve $\left(\frac{7,500}{500} \times 200\right)$	3,000
(−) Amount utilised at the time of re-issue	(1,000)
	2,000

38.

In the Books of Pluto Ltd
JOURNAL

Date	Particulars		LF	Amt (Dr)	Amt (Cr)
	Bank A/c (30,000 × 4)	Dr		1,20,000	
	To Share Application A/c				1,20,000
	(Being application money on 30,000 shares @ ₹ 4 per share received)				
	Share Application A/c	Dr		1,20,000	
	To Share Capital A/c (20,000 × 4)				80,000
	To Share Allotment A/c (20,000 × 1)				20,000
	To Share First Call A/c				20,000
	(Being application money transferred to share capital on 20,000 shares @ ₹ 4 per share and excess adjusted)				
	Share Allotment A/c	Dr		20,000	
	To Share Capital A/c (20,000 × 1)				20,000
	(Being allotment money on 20,000 shares @ ₹ 1 per share transferred)				
	Share First Call A/c	Dr		60,000	
	To Share Capital A/c (20,000 × 3)				60,000
	(Being first call money on 20,000 shares @ ₹ 3 per share transferred)				
	Bank A/c	Dr		40,000	
	To Share First Call A/c				40,000
	(Being first call money received)				
	Share Final Call A/c	Dr		40,000	
	To Share Capital A/c (20,000 × 2)				40,000
	(Being final call money transferred on 20,000 shares @ ₹ 2 per share)				
	Bank A/c (19,900 × 2)	Dr		39,800	
	Calls-in-arrears A/c (100 × 2)	Dr		200	
	To Share Final Call A/c (20,000 × 2)				40,000
	(Being final call on 19,900 shares received @ ₹ per share)				
	Share Capital A/c (100 × 10)	Dr		1,000	
	To Share Forfeiture A/c (100 × 8)				800
	To Calls-in-arrears A/c (100 × 2)				200
	(Being 100 shares forfeited due to non-payment of final call)				
	Bank A/c (70 × ₹ 12)	Dr		840	
	To Share Capital A/c (70 × ₹ 10)				700
	To Securities Premium Reserve A/c (70 × ₹ 2)				140
	(Being 70 shares re-issued @ ₹ 12 per share fully paid-up)				
	Share Forfeited A/c	Dr		560	
	To Capital Reserve A/c				560
	(Being on forfeiture of 70 shares transferred to capital reserve)				

Working Note

	Amt (₹)
Profit on forfeiture of 100 shares	= 800
Profit on forfeiture of 70 shares = $\frac{800}{100} \times 70 =$	560
(–) Loss on re-issue of 70 shares	= Nil
Capital reserve	560

39. (i)

In the Books of Reliable Ltd
JOURNAL

Date	Particulars		LF	Amt (Dr)	Amt (Cr)
	Bank A/c	Dr		5,20,000	
	To Share Application A/c (1,30,000 × 4)				5,20,000
	(Being application amount received on 1,30,000 equity shares @ ₹ 4)				
	Share Application A/c	Dr		5,20,000	
	To Equity Share Capital A/c (1,00,000 × 2)				2,00,000
	To Securities Premium Reserve A/c (1,00,000 × 2)				2,00,000
	To Bank A/c (10,000 × 4)				40,000
	To Share Allotment A/c (20,000 × 4)				80,000
	(Being application amount on 1,00,000 equity shares @ ₹ 4 transferred to share capital and securities premium reserve, 10,000 shares refunded and on 20,000 shares adjusted)				
	Share Allotment A/c	Dr		3,00,000	
	To Equity Share Capital A/c (1,00,000 × 3)				3,00,000
	(Being allotment amount due on 1,00,000 equity shares @ ₹ 3)				
	Bank A/c (WN 1)	Dr		2,17,800	
	Calls-in-arrears A/c (WN 1)	Dr		2,200	
	To Share Allotment A/c				2,20,000
	(Being allotment amount received on 99,000 shares @ ₹ 3 after adjusting excess application amount)				
	Share First and Final Call A/c	Dr		5,00,000	
	To Equity Share Capital A/c (1,00,000 × 5)				5,00,000
	(Being final call due on 1,00,000 equity shares @ ₹ 5)				
	Bank A/c (99,000 × 5)	Dr		4,95,000	
	Calls-in-arrears A/c (1,000 × 5)	Dr		5,000	
	To Share First and Final Call A/c				5,00,000
	(Being first and final call amount received on 99,000 shares @ ₹ 5)				
	Equity Share Capital A/c (1,000 × 10)	Dr		10,000	
	To Calls-in-arrears A/c				7,200
	To Share Forfeiture A/c (WN 2)				2,800
	(Being 1,000 shares forfeited for non-payment of allotment and call money)				
	Bank A/c (800 × 9)	Dr		7,200	
	Share Forfeiture A/c (800 × 1)	Dr		800	
	To Equity Share Capital A/c				8,000
	(Being 800 shares re-issued @ ₹ 9)				
	Share Forfeiture A/c	Dr		1,440	
	To Capital Reserve A/c (WN 3)				1,440
	(Being profit on re-issue of 800 shares)				

(ii) Dr **Share Allotment Account** Cr

Date	Particulars	JF	Amt (₹)	Date	Particulars	JF	Amt (₹)
	To Equity Share Capital A/c		3,00,000		By Bank A/c		2,17,800
					By Calls-in-arrears A/c		2,200
					By Share Application A/c		80,000
			3,00,000				3,00,000

Working Notes

1. (i) Shares applied by Sameer = 1,200

$$\text{Shares allotted to Sameer} = \frac{1,200 \times 1,00,000}{1,20,000} = 1,000 \text{ shares}$$

Excess application money received from Sameer (1,200 – 1,000) = 200 shares @ ₹ 4 = ₹ 800

	Amt (₹)
(ii) Amount due from Sameer on allotment 1,000 shares @ ₹ 3	3,000
(–) Excess received from Sameer on application	(800)
Net amount not received from Sameer on allotment	2,200
(iii) Total amount due on allotment (1,00,000 × 3)	3,00,000
(–) Excess amount received on application	(80,000)
Amount due on allotment	2,20,000
(–) Amount not received from Sameer	(2,200)
Net amount received on allotment in cash	2,17,800

2. Amount of share forfeiture of Sameer = (1,200 × 4) – (1,000 × 2) (Securities premium)
= 4,800 – 2,000 = ₹ 2,800

(Premium once received cannot be cancelled)

	Amt (₹)
3. Amount forfeited on re-issued shares = $\frac{2,800}{1,000} \times 800$	= 2,240
(–) Amount utilised at the time of re-issue	= (800)
Amount transferred to capital reserve	= 1,440

40.

In the Books of Ganga Ltd

JOURNAL

Date	Particulars		LF	Amt (Dr)	Amt (Cr)
	Plant and Machinery A/c	Dr		40,000	
	To Vendor				40,000
	(Being plant and machinery purchased)				
	Vendor	Dr		40,000	
	To Equity Share Capital A/c (4,000 × 10)				40,000
	(Being 4,000 equity shares @ ₹ 10 issued as fully paid)				
	Bank A/c (6,000 × 3)	Dr		18,000	
	To Equity Share Application A/c				18,000
	(Being application amount received on 6,000 equity shares @ ₹ 3)				
	Equity Share Application A/c	Dr		18,000	
	To Equity Share Capital A/c				18,000
	(Being application amount transferred to equity share capital)				
	Equity Share Allotment A/c	Dr		6,000	
	To Equity Share Capital A/c (6,000 × 1)				6,000
	(Being allotment amount due on 6,000 equity shares @ ₹ 1)				
	Bank A/c	Dr		5,600	
	Calls-in-arrears A/c (400 × 1)	Dr		400	
	To Share Allotment A/c				6,000
	(Being allotment amount received on 5,600 shares @ ₹ 1)				

Date	Particulars		LF	Amt (Dr)	Amt (Cr)
	Share First Call A/c	Dr		12,000	
	To Equity Share Capital A/c (6,000 × 2)				12,000
	(Being first call due on 6,000 equity shares @ ₹ 2)				
	Bank A/c	Dr		10,000	
	Calls-in-arrears A/c (1,000 × 2)	Dr		2,000	
	To Share First Call A/c				12,000
	(Being first call amount received on 5,000 equity shares @ ₹ 2)				
	Equity Share Capital A/c (400 × 6)	Dr		2,400	
	To Calls-in-arrears A/c (400 × 3)				1,200
	To Share Forfeiture A/c (400 × 3)				1,200
	(Being 400 equity shares forfeited for non-payment of allotment and first call)				
	Bank A/c (400 × 4)	Dr		1,600	
	Share Forfeiture A/c (400 × 2)	Dr		800	
	To Equity Share Capital A/c				2,400
	(Being 400 forfeited equity shares re-issued @ ₹ 4, ₹ 6 called-up)				
	Share Forfeiture A/c	Dr		400	
	To Capital Reserve A/c				400
	(Being profit on re-issue of 400 equity shares transferred to capital reserve)				

Dr **Calls-in-arrears Account** Cr

Date	Particulars	JF	Amt (₹)	Date	Particulars	JF	Amt (₹)
	To Share Allotment A/c		400		By Equity Share Capital A/c		1,200
	To Share First Call A/c		2,000		By Balance c/d		1,200
			2,400				2,400

41. **In the Books of Sachdeva Tyres and Company Limited**

JOURNAL

Date	Particulars		LF	Amt (Dr)	Amt (Cr)
	Bank A/c (1,50,000 × 2)	Dr		3,00,000	
	To Share Application A/c				3,00,000
	(Being application money received)				
	Share Application A/c	Dr		3,00,000	
	To Share Capital A/c (1,00,000 × 2)				2,00,000
	To Share Allotment A/c (50,000 × 2)				1,00,000
	(Being excess application money transferred to allotment account)				
	Share Allotment A/c (1,00,000 × 5)	Dr		5,00,000	
	To Share Capital A/c (1,00,000 × 2)				2,00,000
	To Securities Premium Reserve A/c (1,00,000 × 3)				3,00,000
	(Being allotment money due)				
	Bank A/c (WN 3)	Dr		3,99,200	
	Calls-in-arrears A/c (WN 2)	Dr		800	
	To Share Allotment A/c				4,00,000
	(Being allotment amount received)				
	Share First and Final Call A/c	Dr		6,00,000	
	To Share Capital A/c (1,00,000 × 6)				6,00,000
	(Being calls amount due)				

Date	Particulars		LF	Amt (Dr)	Amt (Cr)
	Bank A/c (99,800 × 6)	Dr		5,98,800	
	Calls-in-arrears A/c (200 × 6)	Dr		1,200	
	To Share First and Final Call A/c				6,00,000
	(Being call amount received)				
	Share Capital A/c (200 × 10)	Dr		2,000	
	Securities Premium Reserve A/c (200 × 3)	Dr		600	
	To Share Allotment A/c				800
	To Share First and Second Call A/c (600 × 2)				1,200
	To Share Forfeiture A/c				600
	(Being 200 shares forfeited)				
	Bank A/c (170 × 9)	Dr		1,530	
	Share Forfeiture A/c (170 × 1)	Dr		170	
	To Share Capital A/c				1,700
	(Being 170 shares re-issued)				
	Share Forfeiture A/c	Dr		340	
	To Capital Reserve A/c (WN 4)				340
	(Being excess amount transfer to reserve account)				

Working Notes

1. Shares applied by Sudhir = 300, Shares allotted to Sudhir = $\frac{300 \times 1,00,000}{1,50,000}$ = 200 shares

   Excess application money received from Sudhir (300 − 200) = 100 shares @ ₹ 2 = ₹ 200

		Amt (₹)
2. Amount due from Sudhir on allotment (200 shares × 5)	=	1,000
(−) Excess received from Sudhir on application	=	(200)
Net amount due from Sudhir on allotment, which has not been received	=	800
3. Total amount due on allotment (1,00,000 × 5)	=	5,00,000
(−) Excess amount received on application (1,00,000 × 1)	=	(1,00,000)
Balance due		4,00,000
(−) Amount not received from Sudhir on allotment		(800)
Net amount received on allotment		3,99,200

4. Amount forfeited on re-issued shares $\left(\frac{600}{200} \times 170\right)$	510
(−) Amount utilised at the time of re-issue	(170)
Profit on re-issue transferred to capital reserve	340

42.

In the Books of Bhagat and Company Ltd

JOURNAL

Date	Particulars		LF	Amt (Dr)	Amt (Cr)
	Bank A/c (70,000 × 5)	Dr		3,50,000	
	To Share Application A/c				3,50,000
	(Being application money received on 70,000 shares @ ₹ 5)				
	Share Application A/c	Dr		3,50,000	
	To Share Capital A/c (50,000 × 3)				1,50,000
	To Securities Premium Reserve A/c (50,000 × 5)				1,00,000
	To Share Allotment A/c				60,000
	To Bank A/c (8,000 × 5)				40,000
	(Being application money transfer to share capital and adjustment made)				

Date	Particulars		LF	Amt (Dr)	Amt (Cr)
	Share Allotment A/c	Dr		2,00,000	
	To Share Capital A/c (50,000 x 4)				2,00,000
	(Being allotment money due)				
	Bank A/c	Dr		1,40,000	
	To Share Allotment A/c				1,40,000
	(Being allotment balance money received)				
	Share First and Final Call A/c	Dr		1,50,000	
	To Share Capital A/c (50,000 × 3)				1,50,000
	(Being call money due)				
	Bank A/c (49,500 × 3)	Dr		1,48,500	
	Calls-in-arrears A/c (500 × 3)	Dr		1,500	
	To Share First and Final Call A/c				1,50,000
	(Being call money received on 49,500 shares)				

Working Notes

1. Total number of shares applied = 70,000

Share application money received (70,000 × 5)	=	3,50,000
Money refunded (8,000 × 5)	=	(40,000)
		3,10,000
Money transferred to share capital (50,000 × 5)	=	(2,50,000)
Share application money adjusted towards allotment	=	60,000

2. Allotment money due (50,000 × 4) = 2,00,000

Allotment money due (50,000 × 4)	=	2,00,000
(–) Already received	=	(60,000)
Allotment money due on shares allotted	=	1,40,000

Calls-in-arrears (500 shares × 3) = ₹ 1,500

43. Since, it is not mentioned in the question as to when the premium is receivable, it will be assumed that the premium is due alongwith allotment money. Hence, the amount due on allotment will be ₹ 50 (including ₹ 10 premium).

(i)

In the Books of Pioneer Ltd

JOURNAL

Date	Particulars		LF	Amt (Dr)	Amt (Cr)
	Bank A/c (10,000 × 25)	Dr		2,50,000	
	To Share Application A/c				2,50,000
	(Being share application money received)				
	Share Application A/c	Dr		2,50,000	
	To Share Capital A/c				2,50,000
	(Being share application money transferred to share capital account)				
	Share Allotment A/c	Dr		5,00,000	
	To Share Capital A/c (10,000 × 40)				4,00,000
	To Securities Premium Reserve A/c (10,000 × 10)				1,00,000
	(Being share allotment money due on 10,000 shares @ ₹ 50)				
	Bank A/c	Dr		5,00,000	
	To Share Allotment A/c				5,00,000
	(Being share allotment money received on 10,000 shares @ ₹ 50)				
	Share First and Final Call A/c	Dr		3,50,000	
	To Share Capital A/c (10,000 × 35)				3,50,000
	(Being share first and final call money due on 10,000 shares @ ₹ 35)				
	Bank A/c (9,900 × 35)	Dr		3,46,500	
	Calls-in-arrears A/c (100 × 35)	Dr		3,500	
	To Share First and Final Call A/c				3,50,000
	(Being share first and final call money received on 9,900 shares @ ₹ 35)				

Date	Particulars		LF	Amt (Dr)	Amt (Cr)
	Share Capital A/c (100 × 100)	Dr		10,000	
	To Calls-in-arrears A/c (100 × 35)				3,500
	To Share Forfeiture A/c				6,500
	(Being 100 shares forfeited)				
	Bank A/c (60 × 90)	Dr		5,400	
	Share Forfeiture A/c	Dr		600	
	To Share Capital A/c (60 × 100)				6,000
	(Being 60 shares re-issued @ ₹ 90)				
	Share Forfeiture A/c	Dr		3,300	
	To Capital Reserve A/c				3,300
	(Being excess shares forfeited account transferred to capital reserve after adjustments)				

Working Note

	Amt (₹)
Amount forfeited on re-issued shares $\left(\frac{6,500}{100} \times 60\right)$	3,900
(–) Amount utilised at the time of re-issue	(600)
Amount transferred to capital reserve	3,300

(ii) **Balance Sheet**
as at ......

Particulars	Note No.	Amt (₹)
I. **EQUITY AND LIABILITIES**		
Shareholders' Fund		
Share Capital	1	9,98,600
Reserve and Surplus	2	1,03,300
Total		11,01,900
II. **ASSETS**		
Current Assets		
Cash and Cash Equivalents	3	11,01,900
Total		11,01,900

Notes to Accounts

Particulars		Amt (₹)
1. **Share Capital**		
Authorised Capital		
.... Shares of ₹ 100 each		—
Issued Capital		
12,000 Shares of ₹ 100 each		12,00,000
Subscribed Capital		
Subscribed and Fully Paid-up		
9,960 Shares of ₹ 100 each	9,96,000	
(+) Share Forfeited	2,600	9,98,600
2. **Reserves and Surplus**		
Capital Reserve		3,300
Securities Premium Reserve		1,00,000
		1,03,300
3. **Cash and Cash Equivalents**		
Cash at Bank		11,01,900

44. In the Books of Decoy Trading Company Ltd

JOURNAL

Date	Particulars		LF	Amt (Dr)	Amt (Cr)
	Bank A/c (9,000 × 1)	Dr		9,000	
	To Share Application A/c				9,000
	(Being application money @ ₹ 1 each share received)				
	Share Application A/c	Dr		9,000	
	To Share Capital A/c				9,000
	(Being application money due on 9,000 share @ ₹ 1 each share)				
	Share Allotment A/c	Dr		18,000	
	To Share Capital A/c (9,000 × 2)				18,000
	(Being share allotment money due on 9,000 shares @ ₹ 2 each)				
	Bank A/c (WN)	Dr		19,200	
	Calls-in-arrears A/c (100 × 2)	Dr		200	
	To Share Allotment A/c				18,000
	To Calls-in-advance A/c (200 × 7)				1,400
	(Being allotment money received on 8,900 shares and call money received in advance on 200 shares)				
	Share First Call A/c	Dr		27,000	
	To Share Capital A/c (9,000 × 3)				27,000
	(Being first call money due on 9,000 shares @ ₹ 3 each)				
	Bank A/c (8,700 × 3)	Dr		26,100	
	Calls-in-advance A/c (200 × 3)	Dr		600	
	Calls-in-arrears A/c (100 × 3)	Dr		300	
	To Share First Call A/c				27,000
	(Being first call money received on 8,700 shares @ ₹ 3 each and calls-in-advance on 200 shares adjusted)				
	Share Final Call A/c	Dr		36,000	
	To Share Capital A/c (9,000 × 4)				36,000
	(Being second call money due on 9,000 shares @ ₹ 4 each)				
	Bank A/c (8,700 × 4)	Dr		34,800	
	Calls-in-advance A/c (200 × 4)	Dr		800	
	Calls-in-arrears A/c (100 × 4)	Dr		400	
	To Share Final Call A/c				36,000
	(Being share final call money received on 8,700 shares @ ₹ 4 each and calls-in-advance on 200 shares adjusted)				

Working Note

Amount received with allotment		**Amt (₹)**
On 8,900 shares @ ₹2 per share	=	17,800
On 200 shares @ ₹7 per share	=	1,400
		19,200

45. (i) (a) Per share amount on application $= \frac{10}{3} = 333$ or 3.

(ii) (d) Number of shares applied $= \frac{1,62,000}{3} = 54,000$

(iii) (a) ₹ 5

(iv) (c) The amount called up on these shares.

46. (i) (b) 30,000 share @ ₹ 10 per share = 3,00,000
60,000 share @ ₹ 10 per share = 6,00,000
9,00,000

(ii) (d) 30,000 shares
(+) 54,000 shares
(+) 800 shares
84,800 shares

(iii) (d) 30,000 shares @ ₹10 per share = 3,00,000
54,800 shares @ ₹10 per share = 5,48,000
Share forfeiture 1,600
8,49,600

(iv) (b) capital reserve account

47. (i) (b) ₹ 9,000

(ii) (d) Number of Shares $= \frac{\text{Securities Premium}}{\text{Premium/Share}}$

$= \frac{2,000}{2}$

= 1,000 Shares

Calls-in-arrear = ₹ 7,000

Non-payment $= \frac{7,000}{1,000} =$ ₹ 7 per share

(iii) (c) Share forfeiture account

= 700 + 1,400 = ₹ 2,100

(iv) (b) Number of Shares $= \frac{\text{Securities Premium}}{\text{Premium/Share}}$

$= \frac{1,400}{2}$

= 700 shares

Share capital = 700 × 10

= ₹ 7,000

(v) (b) securities premium reserve account

CHAPTER TEST

01 Mark Questions

1. P Ltd. forfeited 400 shares of 10 each for non-payment of first call of 2 per share. The final call of 2 per share was not been called. On forfeiture of shares what amount will be transferred to share capital account?

(a) ₹ 4,000 (b) ₹ 3,400
(b) ₹ 3,200 (d) ₹ 2,800

2. BB Ltd. issued 10,000 equity shares of ₹ 50 each and had called-up ₹ 46 but received ₹ 40 per share, equity share capital account will be credited by

(a) ₹ 50 per share
(b) ₹ 44 per share
(b) ₹ 40 per share
(d) ₹ 46 per share

3. R&D Ltd. purchased a machinery from B & D Ltd. for ₹ 5,00,000, paid ₹ 5,000 immediately and balance by issuing equity shares of ₹ 10 each at a premium of ₹ 1 per share. What is the number of shares issued by R&D Ltd?

(a) ₹ 50,000 (b) ₹ 45,500
(b) ₹ 45,000 (d) None of these

4. Pea Tea Ltd. forfeited 10,000 equity shares of ₹ 10 each that were issued at a premium of ₹ 2 per share, for non-payment of final call of ₹ 4 per shate. The minimum reissue price of these shares can be

(a) ₹ 1,00,000 (b) ₹ 40,000
(b) ₹ 20,000 (d) ₹ 60,000

5. Dhara Ltd. forfeited 500 shares of ₹ 10 each for non-payment of first and final call of ₹ 2 per share each. At the time of forfeiture of shares, share forfeiture account will be credited with

(a) ₹ 3,000 (b) ₹ 2,000
(b) ₹ 4,000 (d) ₹ 1,000

6. State any two purposes where the company can use the amount of securities premium reserve.

7. PJ Ltd. invited applications for 10,000 shares of ₹ 10 each, payable as ₹ 3 on application, ₹ 4 on allotment and balance on final call. Applications for 14,000 shares were received.

The company decided to reject 2,000 applications and pro-rate allotment was made on the remaining shares. Rohan, a shareholder who has applied for 1,200 shares, paid the entire amount on allotment. Calculate the amount to be received on allotment.

03 Marks Questions

8. Jain Ltd purchased building for ₹ 10,00,000 from Gupta Ltd. 10% of the amount payable was paid by a cheque drawn in favour of Gupta Ltd. The balance was paid by issue of equity shares of ₹ 10 each. Pass necessary journal entries in the books of Jain Ltd.

9. SSP Ltd forfeited 300 shares of ₹ 10 each issued at a premium of ₹ 2 per share for the non-payment of allotment of ₹ 4 per share (including premium). The first and final call of ₹ 3 per share has not been made yet, 50% of the forfeited shares were re-issued at ₹ 8 per share fully paid-up. Pass necessary journal entries for the forfeiture and re-issue of shares.

10. Madhav Ltd issued fully paid equity shares of ₹ 80 per share for the purchase of a running business from Gupta Bros for a sum of ₹ 15,00,000.

The assets and liabilities consisted of the following

Plant ₹ 5,00,000, trucks ₹ 7,00,000; stock ₹ 3,00,000, machinery ₹ 6,00,000 and sundry creditors ₹ 5,00,000.

You are required to pass necessary journal entries for the above transactions in the books of Madhav Ltd.

11. The authorised capital of Suhani Ltd is ₹ 45,00,000, divided into 30,000 shares of ₹ 150 each .Out of these company issued 15,000 shares of ₹ 150 each at a premium of ₹ 10 per share. The amount was payable as follows

₹ 50 per share on application, ₹ 40 per share on allotment (including premium), ₹ 30 per share on first call and balance on final call. Public applied for 14,000 shares. All the money was duly received.

Prepare an extract of balance sheet of Suhani Ltd as per Schedule III, Part I of the Companies Act, 2013 disclosing the above information. Also, prepare 'notes to accounts' for the same.

06 Marks Questions

12. Shyam Ltd invited applications for issuing 80,000 equity shares of ₹ 10 each at a premium of ₹ 40 per share. The amount was payable as follows

On application – ₹ 35 per share
(including ₹ 30 premium)

On allotment – ₹ 8 per share (including ₹ 4 premium)
On first and final call – Balance

Applications for 77,000 shares were received. Shares were allotted to all the applicants. Sundram to whom 7,000 shares were allotted failed to pay the allotment money. His shares were forfeited immediately after allotment.

Afterwards the first and final call was made. Satyam, the holder of 500 shares failed to pay the first and final call.

His shares were also forfeited. Out of the forfeited shares 1,000 shares were re-issued at ₹ 50 per share fully paid-up. The re-issued shares included all the shares of Satyam.

Pass necessary journal entries for the above transactions in the books of Shyam Ltd.

13. Som Ltd invited applications for issuing 60,000 equity shares of ₹ 100 each at a premium of ₹ 50 per share. The amount was payable as follows

On application – ₹ 75 per share (including ₹ 25 premium)
On allotment – ₹ 50 per share (including ₹ 25 premium)
On first and final call – Balance amount

Applications for 55,000 shares were received. Allotment was made to all applicants and the company received all money due on allotment except 'K' who was allotted 500 shares and his shares were immediately forfeited.

Afterwards the first and final call was made. 'L' to whom 300 shares were allotted, failed to pay the first and final call. His shares were also forfeited. 300 shares of 'K' and 200 shares of 'L' were re-issued for 75,000 fully paid-up.

Pass necessary journal entries in the books of Som Ltd for the above transactions.

10 Marks Questions

14. Record the journal entries for forfeiture and re-issue in the following cases

(i) X Ltd forfeited 200 shares of ₹ 100 each, ₹ 70 called up, on which the shareholders had paid application and allotment money of ₹ 50 per share. Out of these,150 shares were re-issued to Naresh as ₹ 70 paid-up for ₹ 80 per share.

(ii) Y Ltd forfeited 180 shares of ₹ 10 each, ₹ 8 called-up, issued at a premium of ₹ 2 per share to R for non-payment of allotment money of ₹ 5 per share (including premium). Out of these, 160 shares were re-issued to Sanjay as ₹ 8 called up for ₹ 10 per share fully paid-up.

15. X Ltd issued 40,000 equity shares of ₹ 10 each at a premium of ₹ 2.50 per share. The amount was payable as follows

On application – ₹ 2 per share
On allotment – ₹ 4.50 per shar
On call – Balance ₹ 6 per share

Owing to heavy subscription, the allotment was made on pro-rata basis as follows

(i) Applications for 20,000 shares were allotted 10,000 shares.
(ii) Applications for 56,000 shares were allotted 14,000 shares.
(iii) Applications for 48,000 shares were allotted 16,000 shares.

It was decided that excess amount received on applications would be utilised on allotment and the surplus would be refunded. Ram, to whom 1,000 shares were allotted, who belongs to category (i), failed to pay allotment money. His shares were forfeited after the call.

Pass necessary journal entries in the books of X Ltd for the above transactions.

Answers

1. (c) ₹ 3,200
2. (d) ₹ 46 per share
3. (c) 45,000
4. (b) ₹ 40,000
5. (a) ₹ 3,000
7. ₹ 37,000 received on allotment
8. Number of Shares Issued = 90,000
9. Capital Reserve = ₹ 450
10. Capital Reserve = ₹ 20,000
11. Number of Equity Shares Issued = 18,750
13. Capital Reserve = ₹ 7,000
14. Capital Reserve = ₹ 30,000
15. (i) Capital Reserve = ₹ 7,500
(ii) Capital Reserve = ₹ 480

06

Issue and Redemption of Debentures

TREND ANALYSIS 5 YEARS

	Types of Questions	2023	2020	2019	2018	2017
01 Issue of Debentures and Interest	1/2 Marks	2	—	1	—	—
	3 Marks	—	1	—	—	—
	6 Marks	—	—	—	—	—
	10 Marks	—	—	—	—	—
02 Cases from Point of View of Redemption	1/2 Marks	—	—	—	—	—
	3 Marks	1	—	—	—	—
	6 Marks	—	—	—	—	—
	10 Marks	—	—	1	—	—
03 Redemption of Debentures	1/2 Marks	1	—	1	—	—
	3 Marks	2	—	—	—	—
	6 Marks	—	1	—	—	—
	10 Marks	—	—	—	1	—

Average No. of Questions Across all Sets

Debenture

A debenture is a document under company's seal which provides for the repayment of a principal sum and interest thereon at regular intervals which is usually secured by a fixed or floating charge on the company's property and which acknowledges loan of a company.

According to Section 2 (30) of the Companies Act, 2013, "Debenture includes debenture, stock, bonds and any other instrument of a company evidencing a debt, whether constituting a charge on the assets of the company or not".

Debentures shall be shown in the equity and liabilities part of the balance sheet under the major head 'non-current liabilities' and sub head 'long-term borrowings'.

Characteristics/ Features of Debentures

Characteristics of debentures are as follows

(i) It is a certificate or document acknowledging debt of a company.

(ii) Mode and period of repayment of principal and interest is fixed.

(iii) It is issued under the common seal of the company.

(iv) It may or may not be secured.

(v) It is considered as external equity or long-term borrowings of the company.

(vi) Rate of interest on debentures is fixed. It is usual to prefix 'debentures' with the rate of interest payable.

Types or Kinds of Debentures

Following are the types of debentures

(i) **Secured or mortgage debentures** These are those debentures which are secured by either a fixed charge or a floating charge. A regular mortgage deed or trust deed is entered into between the company and the representatives (called trustees) of the debentureholders.

(ii) **Unsecured or naked debentures** These debentures are not secured against any asset or otherwise. They do not have a security.

(iii) **Registered debentures** These debentures have a record of name, address and particulars of holdings of debentureholders. These debentures are not freely transferable. The transfer of debentures in this case requires the execution of regular transfer deed.

(iv) **Bearer debentures** These debentures are transferable by mere delivery. The company keeps no record of such debentureholders. Payment of interest is made on the production of coupons attached to the debenture.

(v) **Redeemable debentures** These debentures are repaid at the end of specified time or by installments during the lifetime of the company.

(vi) **Irredeemable/Perpetual debentures** These debentures are not repayable during the existence of the company and hence repaid at the time of liquidation of the company.

(vii) **Convertible debentures** These can be converted into equity shares or other securities after a specified period, at the option of the debentureholders.

Difference between Shares and Debentures

Basis	Shares (Equity)	Debentures
Meaning	Shares are the denomination (parts) of share capital.	Debentures are the denomination of loan.
Return	Dividend is received on shares.	Interest is received on debentures.
Assured return	Rate of dividend on equity shares is not assured.	Rate of interest on debentures is assured.
Security	Shares are not secured.	Debentures are generally secured.
Repayment	Money received on equity shares is not required to be returned except in dissolution.	Money received through debentures has to be repaid as per the terms of their issue.
Status	The holders of equity shares are the owners of the company.	The holders of debentures are the creditors of company.
Convertibility	Shares cannot be converted into debentures.	Debentures can be converted into shares.

Issue of Debentures

Debentures can be issued for cash or for consideration other than cash.

Issue of Debentures for Cash

Debentures, when issued for cash, can be issued at par, at premium or at discount.

(i) **Issue of debentures at par** Debentures are said to be issued at par when the issue price and face value of the debentures is same.

(ii) **Issue of debentures at a premium** Debentures are said to be issued at premium when the issue price is more than the face value.

(iii) **Issue of debentures at a discount** Debentures are said to be issued at discount when they are issued at a price below its nominal price or face value.

Accounting Entries for Issue of Debentures for Cash

(i) On Receipt of Applications	Bank A/c To Debenture Application A/c	Dr	[With the application money received]
(ii) (a) On Acceptance of Applications	Debenture Application A/c To X % Debentures A/c	Dr	[With the amount of application money on the allotted debentures]
(b) On Adjustment of Excess Debenture Application Money	Debenture Application A/c To Debenture Allotment A/c	Dr	[With the surplus application money on partially accepted applications]
(c) On Refund of Excess Debenture Application Money	Debenture Application A/c To Bank A/c	Dr	[With the application money on rejected applications]

(d) On Making Allotment Money Due	**At Par**	
	Debenture Allotment A/c Dr	[With the amount due on allotment of the debentures]
	To X% Debentures A/c	
	At Premium	
	Debenture Allotment A/c Dr	[With the money due on allotment]
	To X% Debentures A/c	[With the nominal value of debentures due at the time of allotment]
	To Securities Premium Reserve A/c	[With the premium money received]
	At Discount	
	Debenture Allotment A/c Dr	[With the amount due on allotment]
	Discount on Issue of Debentures A/c Dr	[With the amount of discount]
	To X% Debentures A/c	[With the face value]
(e) On Receipt of Allotment Money	Bank A/c Dr	[With the amount actually received on allotment]
	To Debenture Allotment A/c	
(iii) (a) On Making Calls	Debenture Call A/c Dr	[With the money due on a particular call]
	To X % Debentures A/c	
(b) On Receipt of Call Money	Bank A/c Dr	[With the amount received on a particular call]
	To Debenture Call A/c	

Issue of Debentures for Consideration Other than Cash

When debentures are issued to vendors/promoters/underwriters against purchase of assets or against purchase of business, it is termed as issue of debentures for consideration other than cash. In this case, consideration for issue of debentures is not cash but the assets or business. In this case also debentures can be issued at par, premium or discount.

Issue of Debentures to Vendors

Following journal entries will be passed in this case

(i) **On purchase of assets or business**

(a) **When assets are purchased**

Sundry Assets A/c Dr
    To Vendor

(b) **When business is purchased**

Sundry Assets A/c Dr
*Goodwill A/c Dr
    To Sundry Liabilities A/c
    To Vendor's
    *To Capital Reserve A/c

*Either of the two will come to balance out the debit and credit aspect.

Issue of Debentures to Promoters

Persons like individuals, firms or companies which promote the company are called promoters. A company may pay its promoters in the form of debentures. Such issue of debentures is put under the category of 'Issue of Debentures for Consideration Other than Cash'.

The following entry is passed

Formation Expenses/Incorporation Cost/Goodwill A/c Dr
    To Debentures A/c
(Being .... debentures of ₹ ...... each issued to promoters of the company)

Issue of Debentures to Underwriters

Sometimes, underwriters are also issued debentures as their fees by the issuing company. The following entries are passed

(i) **Making underwriting expenses due**

Underwriting Expenses A/c Dr
To Underwriters A/c
(Being underwriting commission due)

(ii) **Issuing debentures to underwriters**

Underwriters A/c Dr
To Debentures A/c
(Being debentures issued @ ₹ ...... per debenture to underwriters)

(iii) **Transferring underwriting expenses to statement of profit and loss**

Statement of Profit and Loss Dr
To Underwriting Expenses A/c
(Being underwriting expenses charged to profit and loss)

Issue of Debentures as Collateral Security

When a company takes a loan, it may provide a primary security on its assets. However, the lending institution may insist on some more assets as secondary or collateral security. In such a situation, the company may issue debentures to the lender as secondary or collateral security, such an issue of debentures is known as 'Debentures Issued as Collateral Security'.

If the company fails to repay the loan alongwith the interest and the primary security is insufficient to repay the loan, only in that case the lender is entitled to use the debentures issued as collateral security. The lender may either present such debentures for redemption or sell them in open market.

Debentures issued as collateral security can be recorded in two ways

(i) First Method (Without Passing Journal Entry)

In this method, no journal entry is passed in the books for issue of debentures as collateral security.

However, the fact that debentures have been issued as collateral security is disclosed by way of information below debentures, which are shown as long-term borrowings under non-current liabilities or as short-term borrowings under current liabilities.

(a) **Debentures issued as collateral security for long-term loan from bank.**

Balance Sheet
as at...

Particulars	Note No.	Amt (₹)
I. **EQUITY AND LIABILITIES**		
Non-current Liabilities		
Long-term Borrowings		

Notes to Accounts

Particulars	Amt (₹)
1. **Long-term Borrowings**	
Term Loan from Bank	
(Secured by issue of X% debentures of ₹ ... each as collateral security)	

(b) **Debentures issued as collateral security for short-term loan from bank.**

Balance Sheet
as at........

Particulars	Note No.	Amt (₹)
I. **EQUITY AND LIABILITIES**		
Current Liabilities		
Short-term Borrowings		

Notes to Accounts

Particulars	Amt (₹)
1. **Short-term Borrowings**	
Loan from Bank	
(Secured by issue of X% debentures of ₹.... each as collateral security)	

(ii) Second Method (With Journal Entry)

Debentures issued as collateral security may be recorded in the books of accounts.

Following journal entry will be passed for issue of debentures as collateral security

Debenture Suspense A/c Dr
To X% Debentures A/c

When the loan is paid, the above entry is cancelled by passing its reverse entry. In balance sheet, debentures issued as collateral security must be shown separately from other debentures.

As debenture issued as collateral security is related to the loan of the company, therefore, it is shown in the note in which the loan secured by debenture is shown.

Balance Sheet
as at ...

Particulars	Note No.	Amt (₹)
I. **EQUITY AND LIABILITIES**		
1. **Non-current Liabilities**		
Long-term Borrowings		

Notes to Accounts

Particulars		Amt (₹)
1. **Long-term Borrowings**		
Term Loan from Bank		...
X% Debentures of ₹ .... each issued as Collateral Security	...	
(–) Debenture Suspense	(...)	...
		...

When the loan is paid back, the above mentioned entry will be reversed as follows

X% Debentures A/c Dr
To Debentures Suspense A/c
(Being debentures issued as collateral security, now cancelled on payment of loan)

Interest on Debentures

Interest on debentures is calculated at a fixed rate on its face value and is usually payable half yearly. Interest on debentures is payable even if the company suffers a loss. Debenture interest is a charge on profit and it is not an appropriation of profit.

According to Income Tax Act, 1961, a company paying interest on debentures is required to deduct income tax at the prescribed rate from the gross amount of debenture interest before any payment is made to debentureholders, which is called Tax Deducted at Source (TDS).

Entries for interest on debentures are as follows

(i) **When interest is due and tax is deducted at source**

Debentures Interest A/c Dr [With gross interest]
To Debentureholders' [With net interest]
To TDS/Income Tax Payable A/c [With income tax deducted]

(ii) **When interest is paid**

Debentureholders' Dr [With net interest]
To Bank or Cash A/c

(iii) **When TDS is deposited in government account**

TDS/ Income Tax Payable A/c Dr [With the amount of income tax deducted at source]
To Bank A/c

(iv) **On transfer of interest on debentures to profit and loss account**

Statement of Profit and Loss Dr [With the amount of interest]
To Debenture Interest A/c

Points to Remember

- Interest on debentures is a charge against the profits of the company and is payable irrespective of the fact whether there are profits or not.
- Interest is not payable on debentures issued as collateral security.

Various Cases from the Point of View of Redemption

As the issue can be made at par, at premium or at discount, the redemption of debentures can be either at par or at premium.

Combining various conditions/terms of issue and redemption of debentures, there may be the following possibilities

(Journal entries to be passed at the time of issue)

(i) **When debentures are issued at par and redeemable at par**

(a) Bank A/c Dr
To Debenture Application and Allotment A/c

(b) Debenture Application and Allotment A/c Dr
To X% Debentures A/c

(ii) **When debentures are issued at discount and redeemable at par**

(a) Bank A/c Dr
To Debenture Application and Allotment A/c

(b) Debenture Application and Allotment A/c Dr
Discount on Issue of Debentures A/c Dr
To X% Debentures A/c

(iii) **When debentures are issued at premium and redeemable at par**

(a) Bank A/c Dr
To Debenture Application and Allotment A/c

(b) Debenture Application and Allotment A/c Dr
To X% Debentures A/c
To Securities Premium Reserve A/c

(iv) **When debentures are issued at par and redeemable at premium**

(a) Bank A/c Dr
To Debenture Application and Allotment A/c

(b) Debenture Application and Allotment A/c Dr
Loss on Issue of Debentures A/c Dr
To X% Debentures A/c
To Premium on Redemption of Debentures A/c

(v) **Basically discount on issue of debentures should be merged is loss on issue of debentures**

(a) Bank A/c Dr
To Debenture Application and Allotment A/c

(b) Debenture Application and Allotment A/c Dr
Loss on Issue of Debentures A/c Dr
To X% Debentures A/c
To Premium on Redemption of Debentures A/c

(vi) **When debentures are issued at premium and redeemable at premium**

(a) Bank A/c Dr
To Debenture Application and Allotment A/c

(b) Debenture Application and Allotment A/c Dr
Loss on Issue of Debentures A/c Dr
To X% Debentures A/c
To Securities Premium Reserve A/c
To Premium on Redemption of Debentures A/c

Writing-off Discount/ Loss on Issue of Debentures

As per ISC Council's instructions, discount or loss on issue of debentures are to be written-off from securities premium reserve (if any) or from general reserve or surplus, i.e. balance in statement of profit and loss under the head 'reserves and surplus' in the year in which they occur. The following entry will be passed

Entry

Securities Premium Reserve A/c Dr
and/or
General Reserve A/c Dr
and/or
Statement of Profit and LossDr
To Discount/Loss on Issue of Debentures A/c

Redemption of Debentures

Redemption of debentures refers to extinguishing or discharging the liability on account of debentures in accordance with the terms of issue. In other words, redemption of debentures means repaying or returning the amount of debentures to the debentureholders after the period for which they were issued.

Sources of Redemption of Debentures

The debentures may be redeemed

(i) Out of capital

(ii) Out of profits

(iii) By converting them into shares or new debentures (not in syllabus)

Debenture Redemption Reserve (DRR)

It is the amount set aside out of surplus, (i.e., balance in statement of profit and loss) for redeeming the debentures. Section 71(4) of the Companies Act, 2013, requires the company to create debenture redemption reserve out of the profits available for payment of dividend.

The amount so credited to DRR shall not be utilised by the company except for the redemption of debentures. DRR is required to be created for Non-Convertible Debentures (NCD) and non-convertible part of Partly Convertible Debentures (PCD).

In view of Section 71(4) of the Companies, Act, 2013 and SEBI guidelines, unlisted companies (other than NBFCs and HFCs) are required to create DRR equivalent to atleast 10% of the nominal (face) value of outstanding debentures.

The following companies are exempted to create DRR (For both public as well as privately placed debentures)

(i) All India Financial Institutions, regulated by Reserve Bank of India (RBI).

(ii) Banking companies.

(iii) Other financial institutions within the meaning of Section 2(72) of the Companies Act, 2013.

(iv) Listed companies including

(a) Non-Banking Financing Companies (NBFCs), registered with RBI.

(b) Housing Finance Companies (HFCs), registered with National Housing Bank (NHB).

(c) Other listed companies.

(v) Unlisted non-banking financing companies registered with RBI.

(vi) Unlisted housing finance companies registered with national housing bank.

Debenture Redemption Investment (DRI)

Rule 18 (7)(b) of the Companies (Share capital and debentures) Rules, 2014 (as amended) prescribes that all listed as well as unlisted companies, that are to redeem debentures (except the companies which are exempted from creating DRI), shall on or before 30th April of the each year, invest or deposit in specified securities, a sum at least equal to 15% of the amount of debentures maturing for payment during the year ended 31st March of the next year.

The following companies are not required to make DRI

(i) All India Financial Institutions, regulated by Reserve Bank of India (RBI).

(ii) Banking companies.

(iii) Other financial institutions within the meaning of Section 2 (72) of the companies Act, 2013.

(iv) Unlisted non-banking financing companies registered with RBI.

(v) Unlisted housing finance companies registered with national housing bank.

Thus, following companies are required to deposit or invest at least 15% of the nominal or face value of its debentures maturing during the year

(i) Listed companies (including NBFCs registered with RBI and HFCs registered with NHB).

(ii) Unlisted companies (other than NBFCs and HFCs mentioned above).

Disclosure of DRR in the Balance Sheet

Debenture redemption reserve is shown in the equity and liabilities part of the balance sheet under the head 'shareholders' funds' and sub-head 'reserves and surplus'. When all the debentures have been redeemed, debenture redemption reserve account is closed by transferring the amount to general reserve. The entry will be passed

Debenture Redemption Reserve A/c	Dr
To General Reserve A/c	

Methods of Redemption of Debentures

The methods of redemption of debentures are

(i) Redemption of debentures in lumpsum on maturity.

(ii) Redemption of debentures in instalments by draw of lots.

(iii) Redemption of debentures by purchase in open market.

(iv) Redemption of debentures by conversion.

Note Redemption of debentures by purchase in open market and conversion are not in syllabus, therefore, they are not discussed.

1. Redemption of Debentures in Lumpsum on Maturity

When all the debentures are redeemed by paying in lumpsum at a specified time, it is called redemption in lumpsum. In this method, all the debentures are redeemed at the end of the specified time. A company may adopt any of the following two options for redeeming debentures

(i) **Redemption of debentures out of capital** When, before or at the time of redemption, profits are neither required by law nor otherwise transferred to DRR, such redemption is said to be out of capital. Section 71 of the Companies Act, 2013, restricts redemption of debentures out of capital by requiring every company (except All India Financial Institutions and Banking Companies) to create a Debenture Redemption Reserve (DRR) out of profit available for dividend.

(ii) **Redemption of debentures out of profits** It means amount specified in Section 71(4) of the Companies Act, 2013 is transferred to debenture redemption reserve out of the profits available for dividend.

Section 71(4) of the Companies Act, 2013 alongwith rules requires that an amount equal to atleast 100% of the value of debentures is to be transferred to **'Debenture Redemption Reserve Account'** before the redemption of debentures. Further, every company that is required to create DRR is also required to invest or deposit in specified securities by 30th April a sum which is atleast equal to 15% of the amount of debentures maturing for payment during the year ending on 31st March of the next year.

The journal entries passed in this case are

Transaction	Entry		Amount
(a) **On creation of debenture redemption reserve**	Surplus, i.e. Balance in Statement of Profit and Loss To Debenture Redemption Reserve A/c	Dr	
(b) **On investment or deposit being made in specified securities**	Debenture Redemption Investment (DRI) A/c To Bank A/c	Dr	
(c) **On encashing investment**	Bank A/c To Debenture Redemption Investment A/c	Dr	[With the amount paid]
(d) **On the amount being due to debentureholders on redemption**	▪ **If the debentures are to be redeemed at par** X% Debentures A/c To Debentureholders	Dr	[With nominal value]
	▪ **If the debentures are to be redeemed at a premium** X% Debentures A/c Premium on Redemption of Debentures A/c To Debentureholders	Dr Dr	[With nominal value] [With premium payable] [With total]
(e) **On payment to debentureholders**	Debentureholders' To Bank A/c	Dr	[With the amount paid]
(f) **When all debentures are redeemed**	Debenture Redemption Reserve A/c To General Reserve A/c	Dr	[With the amount of DRR]
(g) **DRI shall earn income which may be subjected to Tax Deducted at Source** (TDS).	Bank A/c TDS Collected A/c To Interest Earned A/c	Dr Dr	

Point to Remember

When all the debentures are redeemed, the amount of debenture redemption reserve account is transferred to general reserve account.

2. Redemption of Debentures in Instalments by Draw of Lots

In this method, the company may redeem its debentures in instalments beginning from a particular year. The actual debentures to be redeemed are selected usually by draw of lots. The holders are repaid the amount at par or at a premium as per the terms of issue.

The journal entries required to be passed are the same as discussed when debentures are repayable in lumpsum.

Note DRR must be created before commencing redemption of debentures under this method also.

PYQs Previous Years' Questions

1/2 Marks Questions

1. Select the correct statement from the following options. *ISC 2023*
   (a) A debentureholder is entitled to receive dividend on his debentures from the company even if the company has incurred losses.
   (b) A debentureholder is entitled to receive interest on his debentures from the company only if the company has made profits.
   (c) A debentureholder is entitled to receive interest on his debentures from the company only after dividend has been paid by the company to its shareholders.
   (d) A debentureholder is entitled to receive interest on his debentures from the company even if the company has incurred losses.

2. Sunrise Ltd, a listed NBFC, had outstanding 20,000, 7% debentures of ₹ 100 each, due for redemption on 31st March, 2022. As per the provisions of the Companies Act, 2013, what amount, if any, does the company need to transfer to debenture redemption reserve, before it can redeem the debentures? *ISC 2023*

3. On 1st April, 2021, Bhim Ltd. issued 2,000, 5% debentures of ₹ 100 each as follows
   (i) For cash at a discount of 5% ₹ 80,000 (Nominal)
   (i) To a vendor for ₹ 60,000 in satisfaction of his claim ₹ 70,000 (Nominal)
   (iii) To bankers for a loan of ₹ 40,000 as collateral security ₹ 50,000 (Nominal)

   The interest on these debentures was to be paid annually on 31st March every year by the company. You are required to calculate interest on these debentures payable by the company on 31st March, 2022. *ISC 2023*

4. Neptune Ltd., an unlisted manufacturing company has to redeem its 3,000, 7% debentures of ₹ 100 each on 30th September, 2022.

   As per the provisions of the Companies Act, 2013, on which date should the company invest in specified securities? *ISC Specimen 2023*
   (a) On or before 30th September, 2021
   (b) On or before 30th September, 2022
   (c) On or before 30th April, 2021
   (d) On or before 30th April, 2022

5. Give any one difference between securities premium reserve and premium on redemption of debentures. *ISC Specimen 2023, 2006*

6. Gabby Ltd. (a listed NBFC) has 30,000, 5% debentures of ₹100 each due for redemption at par on 31st March, 2022.
   The debenture redemption investment which was purchased on 30th April, 2021, was realised on the date of redemption at 102% less 0.5% brokerage and the debentures were redeemed.

   You are required to calculate the sale price of the debenture redemption investment. *ISC Specimen 2023*

7. Which one of the following can be used by a company to write-off any loss on issue of debentures? *ISC Sem II 2022*
   (a) Investment fluctuation fund
   (b) Machinery replacement fund
   (c) Workmen compensation reserve
   (d) General reserve

8. On 1st April, 2018, Halogen Ltd, issued 4,000, 8% debentures of ₹ 100 each, to be redeemed in four equal annual instalments beginning from 31st March, 2020. The interest on these debentures was payable half yearly, on 30th September and 31st March every year. What is the journal entry to close the interest on debentures account on 31st March, 2021? *ISC Sem II 2022*
   (a) Debit Statement of P&L ₹ 32,000; Credit Interest on Debentures A/c ₹ 32,000.
   (b) Debit Statement of P&L ₹ 16,000; Credit Interest on Debentures A/c ₹ 16,000.
   (c) Debit Statement of P&L ₹ 24,000; Credit Interest on Debentures A/c ₹ 24,000.
   (d) Debit Statement of P&L ₹ 8,000; Credit Interest on Debentures A/c ₹ 8,000.

9. Give the adjusting entry for interest on calls in arrears due from the debentureholders. *ISC Sem II 2022*

10. Phantom Ltd. (a listed NBFC) redeemed its 6,000, 10% debentures of ₹ 100 each in instalments, as follows

Date of Redemption	Debentures to be redeemed
31st March, 2019	3,000
31st March, 2020	1,500
31st March, 2021	1,500

On the basis of the above details, you are required to pass journal entries to record the purchase/sale of debenture redemption investment, from the year of the redemption of the first instalment of debentures to the date of the redemption of the final instalment. *ISC Sem II 2022*

Note The entire DRI purchased for the redemption of the instalment of debentures is not sold by the company at the end of the year but sold/further purchased to the extent to maintain an amount required, as per the provisions of the Companies Act, 2013, for debentures to be redeemed in the next instalment.

11. Relay Ltd. (an unlisted Non-NBFC) redeems its 8,000, 10% debentures of ₹ 100 each in instalments as follows

Date of Redemption	Debentures to be Redeemed
31st March, 2019	2,000
31st March, 2020	5,000
31st March, 2021	1,000

On the basis of the above details, what will be the amount of debenture redemption reserve which the company will transfer to general reserve on 31st March, 2021? **ISC Sem II Specimen 2022**

(a) ₹ 20,000 (b) ₹ 50,000
(c) ₹ 10,000 (d) ₹ 80,000

12. Orange Ltd. took over assets of ₹ 7,00,000 and liabilities of ₹ 60,000 of Purple Ltd. for a purchase consideration of ₹ 6,30,000 payable by the issue of 10% debentures of ₹ 100 each at a premium of 10% and if need be, a part of the purchase consideration in cash. How will the company meet the purchase consideration? **ISC Sem II Specimen 2022**

(a) By the issue of ₹ 5,72,727, 10% debentures at a premium of ₹ 57,272 with no cash.
(b) By the issue of ₹ 5,72,000, 10% debentures at a premium of ₹ 57,200 and cash of ₹ 800.
(c) By the issue of ₹ 5,72,720, 10% debentures at a premium of ₹ 57,272 and cash of ₹ 8.
(d) By the issue of ₹ 5,72,700, 10% debentures at a premium of ₹ 57,270 and cash of ₹ 30.

13. What is the maximum amount of debentures which an unlisted company, other than a NBFC and HFC, can redeem out of its capital? **ISC Sem II Specimen 2022**

14. Suhas Ltd. issued 1,000, 7% debentures of ₹ 100 each to be redeemed after three years at a premium of 5%. The face value of the debentures was payable as

₹ 20 on application
₹ 30 on allotment (on 1st May, 2020)
₹ 30 on first call (on 1st October, 2020)
₹ 20 on final call (on 1st January, 2021)

All the debentures were applied and allotted. Ali, to whom 20 debentures were allotted, paid the allotment money and the two calls on 31st March, 2021.

The Articles of Association of the company provided for interest on calls-in-arrear to be charged @ 10% per annum, which Ali paid on 31st March, 2021.

You are required to pass journal entries in the books of Suhas Ltd. to record

(i) The adjustment and receipt of interest on calls-in-arrear.
(ii) The entry to close the interest on calls-in-arrear account. **ISC Sem II Specimen 2022**

15. Give the journal entries to be passed when
(i) Interest is due on debentures.
(ii) Interest is paid to debentureholders. **ISC 2019**

16. Enumerate any two methods of redemption of debentures. **ISC 2019**

17. Give the adjusting entry and closing entry for interest on debentures due to the debentureholders of a company. **ISC 2016**

18. What is accounting treatment when debentures are issued as collateral security? **ISC 2014**

19. Why is premium on issue of debentures considered a capital profit? **ISC 2014, 2007**

20. When does loss on issue of debenture arise? **ISC 2013**

21. Explain the nature of interest on debentures. **ISC 2011**

22. What is meant by issue of debentures as collateral security? **ISC 2010**

23. State two difference between share capital and loan capital. **ISC 2009**

24. Explain any two ways of amortising the discount on issue of debentures. **ISC 2008**

25. Interest on debentures has to be paid even if the company is not earning a profit. Justify. **ISC 2007**

26. What is meant by irredeemable debentures? **ISC 2002**

3 Marks Questions

27. On 1st April, 2022, Lighthouse Ltd. purchased land from Bricks Ltd. The payment was made on the same day by

(i) Issuing a bank draft for ₹ 20,00,000;
(ii) Drawing a promissory note in favour of Bricks Ltd. for ₹ 10,00,000,
(iii) Issuing 8,000, 10% debentures of ₹ 100 each at par, redeemable at a premium of 10%, after three years.

You are required to pass necessary journal entries in the books of Lighthouse Ltd. on the date of purchase of land. **ISC 2023**

KEY IDEA
Promissory note will be recorded as bills payables.

28. Jerome Ltd., an unlisted manufacturing company, had 20,000, 6% debentures of ₹ 100 each due for redemption at par on 31st March, 2022. On this date the company had the required amount of ₹ 2,00,000 in its debenture redemption reserve. The debenture redemption investment which was purchased on 30th April, 2021, was realised at 98% on the date of redemption and the debentures were redeemed on the due date.

You are required to pass journal entries in the books of the company for the year 2021-22. (Ignore interest on debentures). *ISC 2023*

> **KEY IDEA**
> Investments realised at 98% means that the investment is sold at a loss.

29. On 1st April, 2017, Gabriel Ltd., a listed company, issued 3,000, 8% debentures of ₹ 100 each. One-third of the debentures were redeemed at par on 31st March, 2021, and the remaining two-third on 31st March, 2022. The company paid interest on debentures annually on 31st March.

After meeting the requirements of the Companies Act, 2013, regarding debenture redemption investment, the debentures were redeemed by the company. You are required to record necessary journal entries in the books of the company only on 31st March, 2022, including entries for interest on debentures. *ISC 2023*

30. On 31st March, 2021, the books of Pragya Ltd. (an unlisted manufacturing company) showed the following closing balances

7% Debentures (redeemable on 30th September, 2022)	₹ 60,00,000
Debenture redemption reserve	₹ 2,00,000

In order to meet the provisions of the Companies Act, 2013, the company transferred the required balance amount to debenture redemption reserve account on 31st March, 2022. It met the requirements of debenture redemption investment. *ISC Specimen 2023*

You are required to prepare the debenture redemption reserve account for the years 2021-22, 2022-23.

31. Barua Ltd. (a listed NBFC) redeems its 9,000, 10% debentures of ₹ 100 each in instalments as follows

Date of Redemption	Debentures to be Redeemed
31st March, 2020	3,000
31st March, 2021	5,000
31st March, 2022	1,000

You are required to prepare the debenture redemption investment account for the years 2020-21, 2021-22. *ISC Specimen 2023*

32. On 1st February, 2022, Swadesh Ltd. issued to the public 12,000, 10% debentures of ₹100 each at a discount of 3% payable ₹ 20 on application.

The balance on allotment being made on 1st May, 2022. The public applied for 20,000 debentures. Pro-rata allotment was made on 15,000 debentures. The debentures were to be redeemed at par after four years.

You are required to pass journal entries for the year 2021-2022. *ISC Specimen 2023*

33. On 1st July, 2018, Astrex Ltd. (an unlisted construction company) issued 1,000, 8% debentures, of ₹ 100 each, to be redeemed at a premium of 6% on 31st December, 2020. The company transferred ₹ 6,000 to the debenture redemption reserve account on 31st March, 2019, and the balance on 31st March, 2020.

The company met the requirement regarding the purchase of debenture redemption investment. The debentures were redeemed on the due date.

You are required to prepare

(i) Debenture redemption reserve account for the years 2019-20 and 2020-21.

(ii) Debentureholders account for the year 2020-21. *ISC Sem II 2022*

Note Ignore interest on debentures due to the debentureholders.

34. On 1st April, 2020, Venus Ltd. acquired fixed assets of the value of ₹ 7,50,000 and current liabilities of ₹ 90,000 from Jupiter Ltd., for a purchase consideration of ₹ 6,40,000. Venus Ltd. met the purchase consideration due to Jupiter Ltd., by issuing to it, 10% debentures of ₹ 100 each at a discount of 5%. These 10% debentures were redeemable at par on 31st March, 2025.

Note Venus Ltd. writes-off its capital losses in the year in which they occur.

You are required to pass the necessary journal entries in the books of Venus Ltd. for the year 2020-21. (Ignore interest on debentures). *ISC Sem II 2022*

35. Zee Ltd. purchased a running business from Rainbow Ltd. for a sum of ₹ 6,60,000. Zee Ltd. paid 5% of the purchase consideration by drawing a promissory note in favour of Rainbow Ltd. and the balance by the issue of fully paid 7% debentures of ₹ 100 each at a premium of 10%. The assets and liabilities of Rainbow Ltd. consisted of fixed assets ₹ 6,50,000, Sundry creditors ₹ 80,000.

You are required to pass the necessary journal entries in the books of Zee Ltd. *ISC 2020*

6 Marks Questions

36. On 1st April, 2012, Neptune Finance Company (a listed NBFC) issued 4,000, 9 % debentures of ₹ 100 each to be redeemed at a premium of 5% on 31st March, 2021.

You are required to pass necessary journal entries for the issue and redemption of debentures.

ISC Sem II Specimen 2022

37. On 1st April, 2016, the following balances appeared in the books of Shikhar Ltd.

10% Debentures	₹ 14,00,000
Premium on Redemption of Debentures	₹ 1,40,000
Debenture Redemption Reserve	₹ 75,000

The debentures were to be redeemed at a premium of 10% in two equal annual instalments beginning from 31st March, 2018. To meet the requirements of the Companies Act, 2013, the company transferred the balance amount to debenture redemption reserve on 31st March, 2017. On 30th April, 2017, it met the requirements of the Companies Act, 2013 regarding debenture redemption Investment and redeemed the debentures on the scheduled dates. You are required to pass necessary journal entries to record the above transactions in the books of Shikhar Ltd. (Ignore interest on debentures). *ISC 2020*

Note Assume that company is an unlisted company.

10 Marks Questions

38. You are required to pass journal entries to record the following issues of debentures and to write-off any capital losses.

(i) Zoom Ltd. issues 6,000, 12% debentures of ₹ 100 each at par redeemable after 5 years also at par.

(ii) Zola Ltd. issues 5,000, 13% debentures of ₹ 100 each at a discount of 10% to be redeemed at par after 7 years.

(iii) Zubic Ltd. issues 11% debentures of the total face value of ₹ 12,00,000 at a premium of 5% to be redeemed at par after 6 years.

(iv) Ruby Ltd. issues 5,00,000, 12% debentures at a premium of 5% to be redeemed at 10% premium after 10 years.

(v) Emerald Ltd. issues 3,000, 9% debentures of ₹ 100 each at a discount of 7% to be redeemed at a premium of 10% after 4 years. *ISC 2019*

Note All the companies write-off their capital losses in the year in which they occur.

39. (i) On 1st April, 2013, Rayon Ltd issued 2,000, 9% debentures of ₹ 100 each at a discount of 10%, redeemable at par on 31st March, 2017. The issue was fully subscribed. To meet the provisions of the Companies Act, 2013, the Board of Directors decided to transfer ₹ 30,000 to debenture redemption reserve on 31st March, 2014 and the balance on 31st March, 2015. On 1st April, 2016, the company made the required investment in government securities.

The investments were encashed and the debentures were redeemed on the due date. It is the policy of the company to write-off capital losses in the year in which they occur.

You are required to pass journal entries for issue and redemption of debentures (Ignore interest on debentures).

Note Assume that company is an unlisted company.

(ii) On 1st April, 2016, Krayon Ltd issued 8,000, 12% debentures of ₹ 100 each, redeemable at par after 5 years.

The issue was fully subscribed. According to the terms of issue, interest on debentures is payable annually on 31st March. Tax deducted at source is 20%.

You are required to pass journal entries for the year 2016-17 regarding issue of debentures and interest on debentures. *ISC 2018 (M)*

40. During the year 2014-15, Anderson Ltd issued 12% debentures of ₹ 100 each, as per the details given below

(i) 900 debentures issued as collateral security to a bank against a loan of ₹ 60,000.

(ii) The underwriters were to be paid a commission of ₹ 48,000. 25% of the amount was paid to them in cash and the balance was paid by the issue of debentures at a discount of 10%, to be redeemed at par.

(iii) A machine was purchased for ₹ 2,18,500. The vendor was paid by the issue of debentures at a premium of 15%, to be redeemed at par.

(iv) 5,000 debentures were issued to the public at 5% premium, to be redeemed at a premium of 5%.

The company wrote-off all capital losses arising from the issue of debentures at the end of the year from its capital profits and if need be from its revenue profits.

You are required to journalise the above transactions in the books of Anderson Ltd. *ISC 2016*

41. On 1st April, 2013, Sunshine Ltd issued ₹ 10,00,000, 15% debentures of ₹ 100 each at 8% discount payable as ₹ 40 on application, the balance on allotment. These debentures were to be redeemed at a premium of 5% after five years. All the debentures were subscribed for by the public.

Interest on these debentures was to be paid half-yearly which was duly paid by the company.

You are required to

(i) Pass journal entries in the first year of debenture issue (including entries for debenture interest).

(ii) Prepare the 15% debenture account for the year ending 31st March, 2014. ***ISC 2015***

42. You are required to pass journal entries for the issue of debentures in the following conditions

(i) Ben Ltd issued 5,000, 12% debentures of ₹ 100 each at par, redeemable at 5% premium after five years.

(ii) Rex Ltd issued ₹ 2,00,000, 12% debentures of ₹ 100 each at a discount of 2%, redeemable at a premium of 5% after 10 years.

(iii) Josh Ltd issued 6,000, 12% debentures of ₹ 100 each at a premium of 5%, redeemable at a premium of 10% after 6 years.

(iv) Oxygen Ltd issued ₹ 30,000, 7% debentures of ₹ 100 each to a creditor for ₹ 25,000 in full satisfaction of his claim. The company had purchased machinery from him. ***ISC 2014***

43. On 1st January, 2000 Star Ltd issued 1,000, 12% debentures of ₹100 each at a discount of 5% repayable as follows

	Amt (₹)
On 31st December, 2002	20,000
On 31st December, 2003	60,000
On 31st December, 2004	20,000

The company pays interest on debentures annually. You are required to

(i) Pass the journal entries (including interest) for the year beginning 1st January, 2000 to 31st December, 2000.

(ii) Prepare the 'discount on issue of debenture account', till it is finally closed. ***ISC 2012***

44. (i) Gurung Ltd took over assets of ₹ 6,00,000 and liabilities of ₹ 60,000 from Batra Ltd for the purchase consideration of ₹ 5,50,000. It paid the purchase consideration by issuing 8% debentures of ₹ 100 each at 10% premium.

(ii) Gurung Ltd purchased land from Jaiswal Ltd for ₹ 4,50,000. The consideration was paid by issuing 5% debentures at a discount of 10%.

(iii) Gurung Ltd issued 1,000, 6% debentures of ₹ 100 each at a discount of 7% repayable after 5 years at a premium of 10%.

From the above particulars, pass journal entries in the books of Gurung Ltd to record the transactions. ***ISC 2011***

45. Show by means of journal entries, how you would record the following issues. Also show how they would appear in their respective balance sheets.

(i) B Ltd issues 30,000, 12% debentures of ₹ 100 each at a discount of 5% to be repaid at par at the end of 5 years.

(ii) C Ltd issues 12% debentures of the total face value of ₹ 40,00,000 at a premium of 5% to be redeemed at par.

(iii) D Ltd issues ₹ 50,00,000, 12% debentures at par but redeemable at the end of 10 years at 105%.

(iv) E Ltd issues ₹ 60,00,000, 12% debentures at a discount of 5% repayable at a premium of 10% at the end of 5 years. ***ISC 2004***

Explanations

1. (d) A debenture holder is entitled to receive interest on his debentures from the company even if the company has incurred losses.

2. Listed NBFCs are exempted from preparing DRR as per Section 71(4) of the Companies Act, 2013 and SEBI guidelines.

Concept Enhancer Although Listed NBFCs and HFCs are exempted from creating debenture redemption reserve, they are required to create debenture redemption investment.

3. Interest on debentures $= (80{,}000 + 70{,}000)\dfrac{5}{100} =$ ₹ 7,500

4. (d) As per the provisions of Companies Act, 2013, the company will have to invest on or before 30th April, 2022.

5. Securities premium reserve arises when debentures are issued for a price more than the nominal or face value of a debenture whereas premium on redemption of debenture implies that the company is paying more than what it received at the time of issue of the debenture, to the debentureholders at the time of redemption.

6. Sale price of the debenture redemption investment $= 30{,}000 \times 100 \times \dfrac{15}{100} \times \left(\dfrac{102 - 0.5}{100}\right) =$ ₹ 4,56,750

7. (d) General reserve

8. (d) Debit Statement of P&L ₹ 8,000; Credit Interest on Debentures A/c ₹ 8,000.

9. Interest on Calls-in-arrears A/c Dr
   To Calls-in-arrears A/c

10. **JOURNAL**

Date	Particulars		LF	Amt (Dr)	Amt (Cr)
2018 Apr 30	Debenture Redemption Investment A/c	Dr		45,000	
	To Bank A/c				45,000
	(Being debenture redemption investment made)				
2019 Mar 31	Bank A/c	Dr		22,500	
	To Debenture Redemption Investment A/c				22,500
	(Being excess DRI incashed)				
2021 Mar 31	Bank A/c	Dr		22,500	
	To Debenture Redemption Investment A/c				22,500
	(Being DRI encashed)				

11. (c) DRR will be transferred to general reserve as follows

On 31st March, 2019 $= 80{,}000 \times \dfrac{2{,}00{,}000}{8{,}00{,}000} =$ ₹ 20,000; On 31st March, 2020 $= 80{,}000 \times \dfrac{5{,}00{,}000}{8{,}00{,}000} =$ ₹ 50,000

On 31st March, 2021, $= 80{,}000 \times \dfrac{1{,}00{,}000}{8{,}00{,}000} =$ ₹ 10,000

12. (d) **JOURNAL**

Date	Particulars		LF	Amt (Dr)	Amt (Cr)
	Sundry Assets A/c	Dr		7,00,000	
	To Sundry Liabilities A/c				60,000
	To Vendor A/c				6,30,000
	To Capital Reserve A/c				10,000
	(Being the assets and liabilities purchased)				

Date	Particulars		LF	Amt (Dr)	Amt (Cr)
	Vendor A/c	Dr		6,30,000	
	To 10% Debentures A/c (5,727 × 100)				5,72,700
	To Securities Premium Reserve A/c (5,727 × 10)				57,270
	To Cash A/c				30
	(Being the purchase consideration discharged)				

$$\text{Number of debentures} = \frac{6,30,000}{110} = 5,727 \text{ debentures}$$

13. Unlisted company can redeem 90% of its debentures out of capital.

Concept Enhancer Unlisted companies are required to create debenture redemption reserve out of profits or general reserves, which should be at least 10% of the nominal face value of the debentures which are to be redeemed.

14. JOURNAL

Date	Particulars		LF	Amt (Dr)	Amt (Cr)
2021 Mar 31	Bank A/c	Dr		95	
	To Interest on Calls-in-arrear A/c				95
	(Being the interest on calls-in-arrear received)				
	Interest on Calls-in-arrear A/c	Dr		95	
	To Statement of Profit and Loss				95
	(Being the interest on calls-in-arrear transferred)				

Working Note

$$\text{Interest on calls-in-arrear} = 600\times\frac{10}{100}\times\frac{11}{12} + 600\times\frac{10}{100}\times\frac{6}{12} + 400\times\frac{10}{100}\times\frac{3}{12} = 55 + 30 + 10 = ₹\,95$$

15. JOURNAL

Date	Particulars		LF	Amt (Dr)	Amt (Cr)
(i)	Debenture Interest A/c	Dr		...	
	To Debentureholders' A/c				...
	To TDS/Income Tax Payable A/c				...
	(Being interest due on debentures)				
(ii)	Debentureholders' A/c	Dr		...	
	To Bank A/c				...
	(Being interest paid to debentureholders')				

16. The methods of redemption of debentures are (any two)

(i) Redemption of debentures in lumpsum on maturity.

(ii) Redemption of debentures in instalments by draw of lots.

(iii) Redemption of debentures by purchase in open market.

17. **Adjusting Entry**

Interest on Debentures A/c Dr
 To Debentureholders'
 To Tax Payable A/c

Closing Entry

Statement of Profit and Loss Dr
 To Interest on Debentures A/c

18. Debentures issued as collateral security can be dealt in two ways

(i) **First Method** (without passing journal entry) No entry is passed in the books for issue of debenture as collateral security. The fact that debentures have been issued as collateral security must be clearly mentioned in the balance sheet by way of a note under the item 'Debentures'.

(ii) **Second Method** (with journal entry)

Following journal entry will be passed for issue of debentures as collateral security

Debenture Suspense A/c Dr

To X% Debentures A/c

When the loan is paid back, the above mentioned entry is reversed.

X% Debentures A/c Dr

To Debenture Suspense A/c

19. It is considered as a capital profit because it is not an income arising from the normal course of business operations.

20. Loss on issue of debentures arises at the time of issue of debentures when they are redeemable at premium.

21. Interest on debentures is a charge against the profit.

22. When debentures are issued as a subsidiary security or secondary security in addition to primary security against a loan raised by the company, such an issue of debentures is known as 'debentures issued as collateral security'.

23. Difference between share capital and loan capital

Basis	Share capital	Loan capital
Position	Providers of share capital, i.e. shareholders are the owners of the company.	Providers of loan capital, e.g. debentureholders are the creditors of the company.
Return	Shareholders get dividend from the company.	Debentureholders get interest from the company.

24. Discount or loss on issue of debentures are to be written-off from securities premium reserve (if it exists) or from general reserve or surplus, i.e. balance in the statement of profit and loss.

25. Interest payable on debentures constitutes a charge against profits and is to be paid even if the company is not earning profit. It is justified because debenture is an acknowledgement of a debt. Debentureholders are not the owners of the company and will not get higher interest in the periods when the company will be earning huge profits, therefore it is not justified to burden them with losses.

26. These debentures are not repayable during the existence of the company and hence repaid at the time of liquidation of the company.

27.

JOURNAL

Date	Particulars		LF	Amt (Dr)	Amt (Cr)
	Land A/c	Dr		38,00,000	
	To Bricks Ltd. A/c				38,00,000
	(Being land purchased from Bricks Ltd.)				
	Bricks Ltd. A/c	Dr		38,00,000	
	Loss on Issue of Debentures A/c	Dr		80,000	
	To Bank A/c				20,00,000
	To Bills Payables A/c				10,00,000
	To 10% Debentures A/c				8,00,000
	To Premium on Redemption of Debentures A/c				80,000
	(Being payment made to Bricks Ltd. by issuing bankdraft, promissory note and 10% debentures)				

28.

JOURNAL

Date	Particulars		LF	Amt (Dr)	Amt (Cr)
2021 Apr 30	Debenture Redemption Investment A/c	Dr		3,00,000	
	To Bank A/c				3,00,000
	(Being debentures redemption investment made)				
2022 Mar 31	Bank A/c	Dr		2,94,000	
	Loss on Sale of Investment A/c	Dr		6,000	
	To Debenture Redemption Investment A/c				3,00,000
	(Being DRI encashed)				

Date	Particulars		LF	Amt (Dr)	Amt (Cr)
Mar 31	6% Debenture A/c	Dr		20,00,000	
	To Debentureholder A/c				20,00,000
	(Being debentures due)				
Mar 31	Debentureholder A/c	Dr		20,00,000	
	To Bank A/c				20,00,000
	(Being payment to debentureholders)				
Mar 31	Debenture Redemption Reserve A/c	Dr		2,00,000	
	To General Reserve A/c				2,00,000
	(Being DRR Transferred)				

29.

JOURNAL

Date	Particulars		LF	Amt (Dr)	Amt (Cr)
2022					
Mar 31	Debenture Interest A/c	Dr		16,000	
	To Debentureholder A/c				16,000
	(Being interest on debenture due)				
Mar 31	Debentureholder A/c	Dr		16,000	
	To Bank A/c				16,000
	(Being interest paid)				
Mar 31	8% Debenture A/c	Dr		2,00,000	
	To Debentureholder A/c				2,00,000
	(Being debentures due)				
Mar 31	Debentureholder A/c	Dr		2,00,000	
	To Bank A/c				2,00,000
	(Being payment to debentureholder)				

Common Mistake Students usually don't read the requirements of the question. The question is asking for entries in the books 'only on 31st March, 2022'.

30. Dr **Debenture Redemption Reserve Account** Cr

Date	Particulars	LF	Amt (₹)	Date	Particulars	LF	Amt (₹)
2022				2022			
Mar 31	To Balance c/d		6,00,000	Apr 1	By Balance b/d		2,00,000
				Apr 1	By P & L Appropriation A/c		4,00,000
			6,00,000				6,00,000
2022				2022			
Sep 30	To General Reserve A/c		6,00,000	Apr 1	By Balance b/d		6,00,000
			6,00,000				6,00,000

31. Dr **Debenture Redemption Investment Account** Cr

Date	Particulars	LF	Amt (₹)	Date	Particulars	LF	Amt (₹)
2019				2020			
Apr 30	To Bank A/c		45,000	Mar 31	By Balance c/d		45,000
			45,000				45,000
2020				2021			
Apr 1	To Balance b/d		45,000	Mar 31	By Bank A/c		60,000
Apr 1	To Bank A/c		30,000	Mar 31	By Balance c/d		15,000
			75,000				75,000

Date	Particulars	LF	Amt (₹)	Date	Particulars	LF	Amt (₹)
2021				2022			
Apr 1	To Balance b/d		15,000	Mar 31	By Bank A/c		15,000
			15,000				15,000

32.

JOURNAL

Date	Particulars		LF	Amt (Dr)	Amt (Cr)
2022					
Feb 1	Bank A/c	Dr		4,00,000	
	To Debenture Application A/c				4,00,000
	(Being amount received on application of 20,000 debentures)				
Feb 1	Debenture Application A/c	Dr		4,00,000	
	To 10% Debentures A/c				2,40,000
	To Debenture Allotment A/c				60,000
	To Bank A/c				1,00,000
	(Being application money adjusted and surplus refunded)				
May 1	Debenture Allotment A/c	Dr		9,24,000	
	Discount on Issue of Debentures A/c	Dr		36,000	
	To 10% Debentures A/c				9,60,000
	(Being allotment money due)				
May 1	Bank A/c	Dr		8,64,000	
	To Debenture Allotment A/c				8,64,000
	(Being allotment money received after adjustment)				
2023					
Mar 31	Statement of Profit and Loss	Dr		36,000	
	To Discount on Issue of Debentures A/c				36,000
	(Being capital loss written-off)				

33. (i) Dr **Debenture Redemption Reserve Account** Cr

Date	Particulars	Amt (₹)	Date	Particulars	Amt (₹)
2019			2019		
Mar 31	To Balance c/d	6,000	Mar 31	By Statement of P & L	6,000
2020					
Mar 31	To Balance c/d	10,000	Apr 1	By Balance b/d	6,000
			2020		
			Mar 31	By Statement of P & L	4,000
		10,000			10,000
2020					
Dec 31	To General Reserve	10,000	Apr 1	To Balance b/d	10,000
		10,000			10,000

(ii) Dr **Debentureholders Account** Cr

Date	Particulars	Amt (₹)	Date	Particulars	Amt (₹)
2020			2020		
Mar 31	To Bank A/c	1,06,000	Dec 31	By 8% Debentures A/c	1,00,000
				By Premium on Redemption A/c	6,000
		1,06,000			1,06,000

34.

JOURNAL

Date	Particulars		LF	Amt (Dr)	Amt (Cr)
	Assets A/c	Dr		7,50,000	
	To Liabilities A/c				90,000
	To Vendor A/c				6,40,000
	To Capital Reserve A/c (Bal fig)				20,000
	(Being business purchased)				
	Vendor A/c	Dr		6,40,000	
	Discount on Debentures A/c	Dr		33,700	
	To 10% Debentures A/c				6,73,700
	(Being purchase consideration paid)				
	Statement of Profit and Loss	Dr		33,700	
	To Discount on Debentures A/c				33,700
	(Being discount on debentures adjusted)				

Working Note

Number of Debentures issued $= \frac{6,40,000}{95} = 6,737$ debentures

Common Mistake Students usually take ₹ 100 (base price) for calculating number of debentures. It should be noted that the formula of calculating number of debentures is 'Purchase Consideration/Issue price', and in the given question, issue price is ₹ 95.

35.

In the Books of Zee Ltd.

JOURNAL

Date	Particulars		LF	Amt (Dr)	Amt (Cr)
(i)	Fixed Assets A/c	Dr		6,50,000	
	Goodwill A/c (Balance)	Dr		90,000	
	To Sundry Creditors A/c				80,000
	To Rainbow Ltd. A/c				6,60,000
	(Being running business purchased)				
(ii)	Rainbow Ltd. A/c	Dr		6,60,000	
	To Bills Payable A/c				33,000
	To 7% Debentures A/c				5,70,000
	To Security Premium A/c				57,000
	(Being purchase consideration paid)				

Working Note

Number of debentures to be issued $= \frac{6,60,000 - 33,000}{100 + 10} = 5,700$ debentures

36.

JOURNAL

Date	Particulars		LF	Amt (Dr)	Amt (Cr)
2012					
Apr 1	Bank A/c	Dr		4,00,000	
	To Debenture Application and Allotment A/c (4,000 × 100)				4,00,000
	(Being the debenture application and allotment money received)				
Apr 1	Debenture Application and Allotment A/c	Dr		4,00,000	
	Loss on Issue of Debentures A/c (4,000 × 5)	Dr		20,000	
	To 9% Debentures A/c				4,00,000
	To Premium on Redemption of Debentures A/c				20,000
	(Being the 4,000, 9% debentures issued at par, redeemed at premium)				

Date	Particulars		LF	Amt (Dr)	Amt (Cr)
2020					
Mar 31	Debenture Redemption Investment A/c	Dr		60,000	
	To Bank A/c				60,000
	(Being the investment made @ 15% of face value of debentures)				
2021					
Mar31	Bank A/c	Dr		60,000	
	To Debenture Redemption Investments A/c				60,000
	(Being the DRI encashed)				
Mar 31	9% Debentures A/c	Dr		4,00,000	
	Premium on Redemption A/c	Dr		20,000	
	To Debentureholders' A/c				4,20,000
	(Being the amount due for redemption)				
Mar 31	Debentureholders' A/c	Dr		4,20,000	
	To Cash A/c				4,20,000
	(Being the cash paid to debentureholders)				

Note Listed NBFC is not required to transfer 10% of the face value of debentures to DRR, but they are required to make DRI @ 15% of face value of debentures.

37.

Books of Shikhar Ltd.

JOURNAL

Date	Particulars		LF	Amt (Dr)	Amt (Cr)
2017					
Mar 31	Surplus in Statement of Profit and Loss	Dr		65,000	
	To Debenture Redemption Reserve A/c				65,000
	(Being required DRR created, i.e. 1,40,000 – 75,000)				
Apr 30	Debenture Redemption Investment A/c (WN)	Dr		30,000	
	To Bank A/c				30,000
	(Being investment in DRI entered)				
2018					
Mar 31	10% Debentures A/c	Dr		7,00,000	
	Premium on Redemption of Debentures A/c	Dr		70,000	
	To Debentureholders A/c				7,70,000
	(Being debentures due)				
Mar 31	Debentureholders A/c	Dr		7,70,000	
	To Bank A/c				7,70,000
	(Being payment to debentureholders)				
Mar 31	Debenture Redemption Reserve A/c	Dr		70,000	
	To General Reserve (1/2 × 1,40,000)				70,000
	(Being DRR transferred)				
2019					
Mar 31	Bank A/c	Dr		1,05,000	
	To Debenture Redemption Investment A/c				1,05,000
	(Being DRI realised)				
Mar 31	10% Debentures A/c	Dr		7,00,000	
	Premium on Redemption of Debentures A/c	Dr		70,000	
	To Debentureholder A/c				7,70,000
	(Being debentures due)				

Date	Particulars		LF	Amt (Dr)	Amt (Cr)
Mar 31	Debentureholders A/c	Dr		7,70,000	
	To Bank A/c				7,70,000
	(Being payment to debentureholders)				
Mar 31	Debenture Redemption Reserve A/c	Dr		70,000	
	To General Reserve A/c				70,000
	(Being DRR transferred)				

Working Note

DRI = 15% of amount redeemable in first instalment

= 15% × 7,00,000 = ₹ 1,05,000

Already Existing = ₹ (75,000)

Invested in DRI = ₹ 30,000

38. **JOURNAL**

Date	Particulars		LF	Amt (Dr)	Amt (Cr)
(i)	Bank A/c	Dr		6,00,000	
	To Debenture Application and Allotment A/c				6,00,000
	(Being application money received)				
	Debenture Application and Allotment A/c	Dr		6,00,000	
	To 12% Debentures A/c				6,00,000
	(Being application money transferred to debentures account, issued at par and redeemable at par)				
(ii)	Bank A/c	Dr		4,50,000	
	To Debenture Application and Allotment A/c				4,50,000
	(Being application money received)				
	Debenture Application and Allotment A/c	Dr		4,50,000	
	Discount on Issue of Debenture A/c	Dr		50,000	
	To 13% Debentures A/c				5,00,000
	(Being application money transferred to debentures account issued at 10% discount and redeemable at par)				
(iii)	Bank A/c	Dr		12,60,000	
	To Debenture Application and Allotment A/c				12,60,000
	(Being application money received)				
	Debenture Application and Allotment A/c	Dr		12,60,000	
	To 11% Debentures A/c				12,00,000
	To Securities Premium Reserve A/c				60,000
	(Being application money transferred to debentures acount issued at premium and redeemable at par)				
(iv)	Bank A/c	Dr		5,25,000	
	To Debenture Application and Allotment A/c				5,25,000
	(Being application money received)				

Date	Particulars		LF	Amt (Dr)	Amt (Cr)
	Debenture Application and Allotment A/c	Dr		5,25,000	
	Loss on Issue of Debentures A/c	Dr		50,000	
	To 12% Debentures A/c				5,00,000
	To Securities Premium Reserve A/c				25,000
	To Premium on Redemption of Debentures A/c				50,000
	(Being application money transferred to debentures account issued at premium and redeemable at premium)				
(v)	Bank A/c	Dr		2,79,000	
	To Debenture Application and Allotment A/c				2,79,000
	(Being application money received)				
	Debenture Application and Allotment A/c	Dr		2,79,000	
	Loss on Issue of Debentures A/c (21,000 + 30,000)	Dr		51,000	
	To 9% Debentures A/c				3,00,000
	To Premium on Redemption of Debentures A/c				30,000
	(Being application money transferred to debentures account issued at discount and redeemable at premium)				

39. (i)

In the Books of Rayon Ltd
JOURNAL

Date	Particulars		LF	Amt (Dr)	Amt (Cr)
2013 Apr 1	Bank A/c	Dr		1,80,000	
	To Debenture Application and Allotment A/c				1,80,000
	(Being application money received on 2,000, 9% debentures @₹ 90 at a discount of 10%)				
Apr 1	Debenture Application and Allotment A/c	Dr		1,80,000	
	Discount on Issue of Debenture A/c	Dr		20,000	
	To 9% Debentures A/c				2,00,000
	(Being 2,000, 9% debentures allotted)				
2014 Mar 31	Statement of Profit and Loss	Dr		10,000	
	To Debenture Redemption Reserve A/c				10,000
	(Being DRR created for ₹ 10,000)				
Mar 31	Statement of Profit and Loss	Dr		20,000	
	To Discount on Issue of Debenture A/c				20,000
	(Being discount on issue of debentures written-off)				
2015 Mar 31	Statement of Profit and Loss	Dr		10,000	
	To Debenture Redemption Reserve A/c				10,000
	(Being DRR created for ₹ 10,000)				
2016 Apr 1	Debenture Redemption Investment	Dr		30,000	
	To Bank A/c				30,000
	(Being investment made in specified securities being 15% of face value of the debentures to be redeemed)				

Date	Particulars		LF	Amt (Dr)	Amt (Cr)
2017 Mar 31	Bank A/c	Dr		30,000	
	To Debenture Redemption Investment A/c				30,000
	(Being the investment realised)				
Mar 31	9% Debentures A/c	Dr		2,00,000	
	To Debentureholders'				2,00,000
	(Being amount due to debentureholders)				
Mar 31	Debentureholders'	Dr		2,00,000	
	To Bank A/c				2,00,000
	(Being amount paid to debentureholders)				
Mar 31	Debenture Redemption Reserve A/c	Dr		20,000	
	To General Reserve A/c				20,000
	(Being amount of DRR transferred to general reserve)				

(ii)

In the Books of Krayon Ltd
JOURNAL

Date	Particulars		LF	Amt (Dr)	Amt (Cr)
2016 Apr 1	Bank A/c	Dr		8,00,000	
	To Debenture Application and Allotment A/c				8,00,000
	(Being the application money received on 8,000, 12% debentures @₹ 100 each)				
Apr 1	Debenture Application and Allotment A/c	Dr		8,00,000	
	To 8% Debentures A/c				8,00,000
	(Being 8,000, 12% debentures allotted to debenture application)				
2017 Mar 31	Interest on Debentures A/c	Dr		96,000	
	To Debentureholders' A/c				76,800
	To TDS Payable A/c				19,200
	(Being the interest due and TDS deducted @ 20%)				
Mar 31	Debentureholders' A/c	Dr		76,800	
	To Bank A/c				76,800
	(Being the interest paid to debentureholders)				
Mar 31	TDS Payable A/c	Dr		19,200	
	To Bank A/c				19,200
	(Being the TDS deposited in government account)				
Mar 31	Statement of Profit and Loss (Finance cost)	Dr		96,000	
	To Interest on Debentures A/c				96,000
	(Being the interest on debentures transferred to statement of profit and loss account)				

40.

In the Books of Anderson Ltd
JOURNAL

Date	Particulars		LF	Amt (Dr)	Amt (Cr)
(i)	Bank A/c	Dr		60,000	
	To Bank Loan A/c				60,000
	(Being loan taken from bank)				

Date	Particulars		LF	Amt (Dr)	Amt (Cr)
	Debenture Suspense A/c	Dr		90,000	
	To X% Debentures A/c				90,000
	(Being 900 debentures of ₹ 100 each issued as collateral security for loan from bank)				
(ii)	Underwriting Commission A/c	Dr		48,000	
	To Underwriters				48,000
	(Being underwriting commission payable to underwriters credited to their account)				
	Underwriters	Dr		48,000	
	Discount on Issue of Debentures A/c (400 × 10)	Dr		4,000	
	To Cash A/c				12,000
	To X% Debentures A/c (400 × 100)				40,000
	(Being debentures issued to underwriter at a discount of 10%)				
(iii)	Machinery A/c	Dr		2,18,500	
	To Vendor				2,18,500
	(Being machinery purchased)				
	Vendor	Dr		2,18,500	
	To X% Debentures A/c (1,900 × 100)				1,90,000
	To Securities Premium Reserve A/c (1,900 × 15)				28,500
	(Being debentures issued at 15% premium)				
(iv)	Bank A/c (5,000 × 105)	Dr		5,25,000	
	To Debenture Application and Allotment A/c				5,25,000
	(Being application money received)				
	Debenture Application and Allotment A/c	Dr		5,25,000	
	Loss on Issue of Debentures A/c (5,000 × 5)	Dr		25,000	
	To X % Debentures A/c (5,000 × 100)				5,00,000
	To Securities Premium Reserve A/c (5,000 × 5)				25,000
	To Premium on Redemption of Debentures A/c (5,000 × 5)				25,000
	(Being transfer of application money to debentures account issued at 5% premium and redeemable at 5% premium)				
	Securities Premium Reserve A/c	Dr		53,500	
	Statement of Profit and Loss	Dr		23,500	
	To Discount on Issue of Debentures A/c				4,000
	To Loss on Issue of Debentures A/c				25,000
	To Underwriting Commission A/c				48,000
	(Being capital losses on the issue of debentures written-off from capital profits and revenue profits)				

Working Notes

1. Number of debentures issued $= \dfrac{36,000}{90\,(100-10)} = 400$ debentures

2. Number of debentures issued $= \dfrac{\text{Purchase Consideration}}{\text{Issue Price}} = \dfrac{2,18,500}{115\,(100+15)} = 1,900$ debentures

3. Total capital losses = 77,000 (4,000 + 25,000 + 48,000)

   Capital profits available (Securities premium reserve) = 28,500 + 25,000 = ₹ 53,500

   Remaining capital losses i.e. (77,000 − 53,500) = 23,500 will be written-off from revenue profits i.e. statement of profit and loss.

41. (i)

In the Books of Sunshine Ltd
JOURNAL

Date	Particulars		LF	Amt (Dr)	Amt (Cr)
2013					
Apr 1	Bank A/c	Dr		4,00,000	
	To Debenture Application A/c				4,00,000
	(Being debenture application received on 10,000 debentures @₹40 per debenture)				
Apr 1	Debenture Application A/c	Dr		4,00,000	
	To 15% Debentures A/c				4,00,000
	(Being transfer of debenture application money)				
Apr 1	Debenture Allotment A/c	Dr		5,20,000	
	Loss on Issue of Debentures A/c	Dr		1,30,000	
	To 15% Debentures A/c				6,00,000
	To Premium on Redemption of Debentures A/c				50,000
	(Being debenture allotment money due)				
Apr 1	Bank A/c	Dr		5,20,000	
	To Debenture Allotment A/c				5,20,000
	(Being debenture allotment money received)				
Sep 30	Debenture Interest A/c	Dr		75,000	
	To Debentureholders'				75,000
	(Being interest on debenture due)				
Sep 30	Debentureholders'	Dr		75,000	
	To Bank A/c				75,000
	(Being interest on debentures paid)				
2014					
Mar 31	Debentures Interest	Dr		75,000	
	To Debentureholders' A/c				75,000
	(Being interest on debentures due)				
Mar 31	Debentureholders'	Dr		75,000	
	To Bank A/c				75,000
	(Being interest on debentures paid)				
Mar 31	Statement of Profit and Loss	Dr		1,50,000	
	To Debentures Interest A/c				1,50,000
	(Being interest on debentures transferred)				

(ii)

15% Debentures Account

Dr for the year ending 31st March, 2014 Cr

Date	Particulars	Amt (₹)	Date	Particulars	Amt (₹)
2014			2013		
Mar 31	To Balance c/d	10,00,000	Apr 1	By Debenture Application A/c	4,00,000
			Apr 1	By Debenture Allotment A/c	5,20,000
			Apr 1	By Discount on Issue of Debenture A/c	80,000
		10,00,000			10,00,000

Working Note

$$10{,}00{,}000 \times \frac{15}{100} \times \frac{6}{12} = ₹\ 75{,}000$$

42. (i)

In the Books of Ben Ltd
JOURNAL

Date	Particulars		LF	Amt (Dr)	Amt (Cr)
	Bank A/c (5,000 × 100)	Dr		5,00,000	
	To Debenture Application and Allotment A/c				5,00,000
	(Being application money received)				
	Debenture Application and Allotment A/c	Dr		5,00,000	
	Loss on Issue of Debentures A/c (5,000 ×5)	Dr		25,000	
	To 12% Debentures A/c (5,000 × 100)				5,00,000
	To Premium on Redemption of Debentures A/c (5,000 ×5)				25,000
	(Being transfer of application money to debentures account issued at par but redeemable at a premium of 5%)				

(ii)

In the Books of Rex Ltd
JOURNAL

Date	Particulars		LF	Amt (Dr)	Amt (Cr)
	Bank A/c (2,000 × 98)	Dr		1,96,000	
	To Debenture Application and Allotment A/c				1,96,000
	(Being debentures issued at discount)				
	Debenture Application and Allotment A/c	Dr		1,96,000	
	Loss on Issue of Debentures A/c (2,000 × 2) + (2,000 ×5)	Dr		14,000	
	To 12% Debentures A/c (2,000 × 100)				2,00,000
	To Premium on Redemption of Debentures A/c (2,000 ×5)				10,000
	(Being transfer of application money to debentures account issued at 2% discount and redeemable at a premium of 5%)				

(iii)

In the Books of Josh Ltd
JOURNAL

Date	Particulars		LF	Amt (Dr)	Amt (Cr)
	Bank A/c (6,000 × 105)	Dr		6,30,000	
	To Debentures Application and Allotment A/c				6,30,000
	(Being application money received)				
	Debenture Application and Allotment A/c	Dr		6,30,000	
	Loss on Issue of Debentures A/c (6,000 × 10)	Dr		60,000	
	To 12% Debentures A/c (6,000 × 100)				6,00,000
	To Securities Premium Reserve A/c (6,000 ×5)				30,000
	To Premium on Redemption of Debentures A/c (6,000 × 10)				60,000
	(Being transfer of application money to debentures account, issued at 5% premium and redeemable at 10% premium)				

(iv)

In the Books of Oxygen Ltd
JOURNAL

Date	Particulars		LF	Amt (Dr)	Amt (Cr)
	Machinery A/c	Dr		25,000	
	To Vendor				25,000
	(Being machinery purchased by Oxygen Ltd)				
	Vendor	Dr		25,000	
	Discount on Issue of Debentures A/c	Dr		5,000	
	To 7% Debentures A/c (3,000 × 10)				30,000
	(Being amount of ₹ 25,000 settled by issue of ₹ 30,000 debentures)				

43. (i)

In the Books of Star Ltd
JOURNAL

Date	Particulars		LF	Amt (Dr)	Amt (Cr)
2000 Jan 1	Bank A/c	Dr		95,000	
	To Debenture Application A/c				95,000
	(Being application amount received on 1,000 debentures @ ₹ 95)				
	Debenture Application A/c	Dr		95,000	
	Discount on Issue of Debentures A/c	Dr		5,000	
	To 12% Debentures A/c				1,00,000
	(Being 1,000, 12% debentures of ₹100 each issued @ 5% discount)				
Dec 31	Interest on Debentures A/c	Dr		12,000	
	To Debentureholders' A/c				12,000
	(Being interest paid due on 1,000 debentures ₹ 100 each at 12%)				
	Debentureholders' A/c	Dr		12,000	
	To Bank A/c				12,000
	(Being interest paid on 1,000 debentures of ₹ 100 each at 12%)				
	Statement of Profit and Loss	Dr		17,000	
	To Interest on Debentures A/c				12,000
	To Discount on Issue of Debentures A/c				5,000
	(Being interest on debentures transferred to profit and loss account)				

(ii) Dr **Discount on Issue of Debentures Account** Cr

Date	Particulars	JF	Amt (₹)	Date	Particulars	JF	Amt (₹)
2000 Jan 1	To 12% Debenture A/c		5,000	2000 Dec 31	By Statement of Profit and Loss		5,000
			5,000				5,000

Note As per latest guidelines, discount on issue of debentures is to be written-off completely in the year of issue of debentures itself.

44.

In the Books of Gurung Ltd
JOURNAL

Date	Particulars		LF	Amt (Dr)	Amt (Cr)
(i)	Assets A/c	Dr		6,00,000	
	Goodwill A/c	Dr		10,000	
	To Liabilities A/c				60,000
	To Batra Ltd				5,50,000
	(Being assets and liabilities taken over)				
	Batra Ltd Co.	Dr		5,50,000	
	To 8% Debentures A/c (5,000 × 100)				5,00,000
	To Securities Premium Reserve A/c (5,000 × 10)				50,000
	(Being purchase consideration paid by issue of debentures)				
(ii)	Land A/c	Dr		4,50,000	
	To Jaiswal Ltd				4,50,000
	(Being land purchased)				
	Jaiswal Ltd	Dr		4,50,000	
	Discount on Issue of Debentures A/c (5,000 × 10)	Dr		50,000	
	To 5% Debentures A/c (5,000 × 100)				5,00,000
	(Being consideration paid for land)				

Date	Particulars		LF	Amt (Dr)	Amt (Cr)
(iii)	Bank A/c	Dr		93,000	
	To Debentures Application and Allotment A/c				93,000
	(Being debentures issued @ 7% discount)				
	Debenture Application and Allotment A/c	Dr		93,000	
	Loss on Issue of Debentures A/c	Dr		17,000	
	To 6% Debentures A/c				1,00,000
	To Premium on Redemption of Debentures A/c				10,000
	(Being provision for loss on debenture and discount made)				

Working Notes

1. Number of Debentures Issued to Batra Ltd = $\frac{\text{Purchase Consideration}}{\text{Issue Price}} = \frac{5,50,000}{110\ (100+10)} = 5,000$ debentures

2. Number of Debentures Issued to Jaiswal Ltd = $\frac{\text{Purchase Consideration}}{\text{Issue Price}} = \frac{4,50,000}{90(100-10)} = 5,000$ debentures

45. (i)

In the Books of B Ltd
JOURNAL

Date	Particulars		LF	Amt (Dr)	Amt (Cr)
	Bank A/c	Dr		28,50,000	
	Discount on Issue of Debentures A/c	Dr		1,50,000	
	To 12% Debentures A/c				30,00,000
	(Being 30,000, 12% debentures of ₹ 100 each issued at discount of 8% to be repaid at the end end of 5 years)				

Balance Sheet
as at...

Particulars	Note No.	Amt (₹)
I. **EQUITY AND LIABILITIES**		
Shareholders' Funds		
Reserve and Surplus	1	(1,50,000)
Non-current Liabilities		
Long-term Borrowings	2	30,00,000
Total		28,50,000
II. **ASSETS**		
Current Assets		
Cash and Cash Equivalents	3	28,50,000
Total		28,50,000

Notes to Accounts

Particulars	Amt (₹)
1. **Reserves and Surplus**	
Balance in Statement of Profit and Loss (Discount on issue of debentures)	(1,50,000)
2. **Long-term Borrowings**	
30,000, 12% Debentures of ₹100 each	30,00,000
3. **Cash and Cash Equivalent**	
Cash at Bank	28,50,000

(ii)

In the Books of C Ltd
JOURNAL

Date	Particulars		LF	Amt (Dr)	Amt (Cr)
	BankA/c	Dr		42,00,000	
	To 12% Debentures A/c				40,00,000
	To Securities Premium Reserve A/c				2,00,000
	(Being 12% debentures application transferred with 5% premium)				

Balance Sheet
as at...

Particulars	Note No.	Amt (₹)
I. **EQUITY AND LIABILITIES**		
Shareholders' Funds		
Reserves and Surplus	1	2,00,000
Non-current Liabilities		
Long-term Borrowings	2	40,00,000
Total		42,00,000
II. **ASSETS**		
Current Assets		
Cash and Cash Equivalents	3	42,00,000
Total		42,00,000

Notes to Accounts

Particulars	Amt (₹)
1. **Reserves and Surplus**	
Securities Premium Reserve	2,00,000
2. **Long-term Borrowings**	
40,000, 12% Debentures of ₹100 each	40,00,000
3. **Cash and Cash Equivalents**	
Cash at Bank	42,00,000

(iii)

In the Books of D Ltd
JOURNAL

Date	Particulars		LF	Amt (Dr)	Amt (Cr)
	Bank A/c	Dr		50,00,000	
	Loss on Issue of Debentures A/c	Dr		2,50,000	
	To 12% Debentures A/c				50,00,000
	To Premium on Redemption of Debentures A/c				2,50,000
	(Being issue of 12% debentures at par but redeemable at premium of 5%)				

Balance Sheet
as at...

Particulars	Note No.	Amt (₹)
I. **EQUITY AND LIABILITIES**		
Shareholders' Funds		
Reserve and Surplus		(2,50,000)
Non-current Liabilities		
Long-term Borrowings		52,50,000
Total		50,00,000
II. **ASSETS**		
Current Assets		
Cash and Cash Equivalents		50,00,000
Total		50,00,000

Notes to Accounts

Particulars	Amt (₹)
1. **Reserves and Surplus**	
Balance in Statement of Profit and Loss (Loss on issue of debentures)	(2,50,000)
2. **Long-term Borrowings**	
50,000, 12% Debentures of ₹100 each	50,00,000
Premium on Redemption	2,50,000
	52,50,000
3. **Cash and Cash Equivalents**	
Cash at Bank	50,00,000

(iv)

In the Books of E Ltd
JOURNAL

Date	Particulars		LF	Amt (Dr)	Amt (Cr)
	Bank A/c	Dr		57,00,000	
	Loss on Issue of Debentures A/c	Dr		9,00,000	
	To 12% Debentures A/c				60,00,000
	To Premium on Redemption of Debentures A/c				6,00,000
	(Being 12% debentures issued at a discount of 5% and redeemable at a premium of 10%)				

Balance Sheet
as at...

Particulars	Note No.	Amt (₹)
I. **EQUITY AND LIABILITIES**		
Shareholders' Funds		
Reserves and Surplus	1	(9,00,000)
Non-current Liabilities		
Long-term Borrowings	2	66,00,000
Total		57,00,000
II. **ASSETS**		
Current Assets		
Cash and Cash Equivalents	3	57,00,000
Total		57,00,000

Notes to Accounts

Particulars	Amt (₹)
1. **Reserves and Surplus**	
Balance in Statement of Profit and Loss (Loss on issue of debentures)	(9,00,000)
2. **Long-term Borrowings**	
60,000, 12% Debentures of ₹100 each	60,00,000
Premium on Redemption	6,00,000
	66,00,000
3. **Cash and Cash Equivalents**	
Cash at Bank	57,00,000

CHAPTER TEST

01 Mark Questions

1. Interest payable on debentures is
   (a) debited to capital reserve
   (b) credited to general reserve
   (c) a charge against profit
   (d) an appropriation of profit

2. What type of debentures can be transferred only by executing a regular transfer deed?
   (a) Convertible debentures (b) Redeemable debentures
   (c) Secured debentures (d) Registered debentures

3. Debentures can be redeemed out of
   (a) capital
   (b) profit
   (c) Both (a) and (b)
   (d) None of the above

4. After the redemption of all the debentures, the debenture redemption reserve is transferred to
   (a) statement of profit and loss
   (b) general reserve
   (c) capital reserve
   (d) debentureholders

5. What journal entry will be passed when the debentures are issued as collateral security?

6. Name two advantages of redemption of debentures by purchase in the open market.

7. List two companies which are exempted from creating debenture redemption reserve.

03 Marks Questions

8. Narain Laxmi Ltd invited applications for issuing 7,500, 12% debentures of ₹ 100 each at a premium of ₹ 35 per debenture. The full amount was payable on application.
   Applications were received for 10,000 debentures. Applications for 2,500 debentures were rejected and the application money was refunded. Debentures were allotted to the remaining applicants.
   Pass necessary journal entries for the above transactions in the books of Narain Laxmi Ltd.

9. X Ltd obtained a loan of ₹ 3,00,000 from IDBI Bank. The company issued 4,000, 9% debentures of ₹ 100 each as a collateral security for the same. Show how these items will be presented in the balance sheet of the company.

10. Well Flo Ltd took over assets of ₹ 9,80,000 and liabilities of ₹ 40,000 of HDR Ltd at an agreed value of ₹ 9,00,000. Well Flo Ltd paid to HDR Ltd by issue of 9% debentures of ₹ 100 each at a premium of 20%. Pass necessary journal entries to record the above transactions in the books of Well Flo Ltd.

11. Give journal entries in each of the following cases, if the face value of the debenture is ₹ 100.
    (i) A debenture issued at ₹ 105 repayable at ₹ 100.
    (ii) A debenture issued at ₹ 100 repayable at ₹ 105.
    (iii) A debenture issued at ₹ 110 repayable at ₹ 105.

12. Y Ltd purchased machinery ₹ 55,000 from Z Ltd. 10% was paid by Y Ltd by accepting a bill of exchange in favour of Z Ltd and the balance was paid by issue of 9% debentures of ₹ 100 each at par, redeemable after 5 years.
    Pass necessary journal entries in the books of Y Ltd.

13. Pass necessary journal entries for the issue and redemption of debentures in the following cases 10,000, 12% debentures of ₹ 50 each were issued and to be redeemed as follows
    (i) Issued at par and redeemed at a premium of 10%.
    (ii) Issued at a premium of 10% and redeemable at a premium of 20%.

06 Marks Questions

14. Suresh Ltd on 1st April, 2006 acquired assets of the value of ₹ 6,00,000 and liabilities worth ₹ 70,000 from P & Co. at an agreed value of ₹ 5,50,000. Suresh Ltd issued 12% debentures of ₹ 100 each at a premium of 10% in full satisfaction of purchase consideration. The debentures were redeemable 3 years later at a premium of 5%. Pass entries to record the above including redemption of debentures.

15. A Ltd issued 5,000, 10% debentures of ₹ 100 each, at a premium of ₹ 10 per debenture payable as follows

On application	₹ 25
On allotment	₹ 45 (including premium)
On first and final call	₹ 40

The debentures were fully subscribed and all money was duly received. Record the necessary entries in the books of the company. Show how the amounts as they will appear in the balance sheet.

10 Marks Questions

16. Pass the necessary journal entries for the issue of debentures in the following cases

(i) 40,000, 15% debentures of ₹ 100 each issued at par, redeemable at 10% premium.

(ii) 90,000, 15% debentures of ₹ 100 each issued at a discount of 5%, redeemable at premium of 10%.

(iii) 70,000, 13% debentures of ₹ 100 each issued at a premium of 10% redeemable at 5% premium.

(iv) 30,000, 12% debentures of ₹ 100 each issued at a discount of 5% redeemable at par.

(v) 60,000, 12% debentures of ₹ 100 each issued at a discount of 5% redeemable at ₹ 105.

17. On lst April, 2019, Rakoon Ltd. (an unlisted company) issued 40,000, 11% debentures of ₹ 100 each at a discount of 10% redeemable at par on 31st March, 2023. The issue was fully subscribed.

To meet the provisions of the Companies Act, 2013, the Board of Directors decided to transfer ₹ 2,40,000 to debenture redemption reserve on 31st March, 2020, and the balance on 31st March, 2021. On 1st April, 2022, the company made the required investment in government securities. The investments were encashed and the debentures were redeemed on the due date. It is the policy of the company to write-off capital losses in the year in which they occur.

You are required to pass journal entries for issue and redemption of debentures (ignore interest on debentures).

Answers

1. (c) a charge against profit

2. (d) Registered debentures

3. (c) Both (a) and (b)

4. (b) general reserve

07

Final Accounts of Companies

TREND ANALYSIS 5 YEARS

01 Balance Sheet

Average No. of Questions Across all Sets

Types of Questions	2023	2020	2019	2018	2017
1/2 Marks	1	1	—	1	1
3 Marks	—	1	—	—	—
6 Marks	—	—	—	—	—
10 Marks	—	1	1	1	1

Financial Statements

The statements which are prepared to ascertain the profit earned or loss suffered and position of assets and liabilities at a particular date are known as financial statements. These are the final product of accounting process. Financial statements are generally divided in the following parts

(i) Balance sheet i.e., position statement
(ii) Statement of profit and loss i.e., income statement
(iii) Cash flow statement
(iv) Statement of changes in equity
(v) Notes to accounts

Objectives of Financial Statements

Main objectives of financial statements are

(i) Financial statements provide the information about the earning capacity of the business.
(ii) Financial statements provide the information about the economic resources and obligation of an enterprise.
(iii) Financial statements also provide the information about the cash flows.

Characteristics of Financial Statements

Characteristics of financial statements are as follows

(i) Financial statements are historical documents as they relate to past period.
(ii) Financial statements are prepared in monetary terms.
(iii) Balance sheet reveals the financial position and statement of profit and loss shows the profitability of the business organisation.

Nature of Financial Statements

Nature of financial statements is as follows

(i) Recorded facts
(ii) Accounting conventions
(iii) Postulates
(iv) Personal judgements

Balance Sheet

It may be defined as a statement of assets and liabilities of the company, at a particular date. It must exhibit a true and fair view of the financial position at the closing of the year. It is prepared and presented in the horizontal form prescribed in Schedule III, Part I of the Companies Act, 2013.

Proforma of Balance Sheet

Name of the Company
Balance Sheet
as at ......

(₹ in ......)

Particulars	Note No.	Figures as at the End of Current Reporting Period (₹)	Figures as at the End of Previous Reporting Period (₹)
I. **EQUITY AND LIABILITIES**			
1. **Shareholders' Funds**			
(a) Share Capital			
(b) Reserves and Surplus			
*(c) Money Received Against Share Warrants			
*2. **Share Application Money Pending Allotment**			
3. **Non-current Liabilities**			
(a) Long-term Borrowings			
*(b) Deferred Tax Liabilities (Net)			
*(c) Other Long-term Liabilities			
(d) Long-term Provisions			
4. **Current Liabilities**			
(a) Short-term Borrowings			
(b) Trade Payables			
(c) Other Current Liabilities			
(d) Short-term Provisions			
Total			
II. **ASSETS**			
1. **Non-current Assets**			
(a) Property, Plant and Equipment and Intangible Assets			
(i) Property, Plant and Equipment			
(ii) Intangible Assets			
*(iii) Capital Work-in-Progress			
*(iv) Intangible Assets Under Development			
(b) Non-current Investments			
*(c) Deferred Tax Assets (Net)			
(d) Long-term Loans and Advances			
(e) Other Non-current Assets			
2. **Current Assets**			
(a) Current Investments			
(b) Inventories			
(c) Trade Receivables			
(d) Cash and Cash Equivalents			
(e) Short-term Loans and Advances			
(f) Other Current Assets			
Total			

Note As per the guidelines issued by the Board, students will not be examined on the star marked items.

Statement of Profit and Loss

The title of 'Profit and Loss Account' has been changed to 'Statement of Profit and Loss'. It shows the net result of business operations. Its form is prescribed in Schedule III, Part II of the Companies Act, 2013.

Proforma of Statement of Profit and Loss

Name of the Company ...
Statement of Profit and Loss
for the year ending ...

(₹ in......)

Particulars	Note No.	Figures for the Current Reporting Period (₹)	Figures for the Previous Reporting Period (₹)
I. Revenue from Operations			
II. Other Income			
III. Total Revenue (I + II)			
IV. **Expenses**			
Cost of Materials Consumed			
Purchases of Stock-in-trade			
Changes in Inventories of Finished Goods			
Work-in-progress and Stock-in-trade			
Employees Benefits Expenses			
Finance Costs			
Depreciation and Amortisation Expenses			
Other Expenses			
Total Expenses			
V. **Profit before Tax** (III – IV)			
VI. Tax			
VII. **Profit after Tax** (V – VI)			

Note Schedule III, Part II of Companies Act, 2013 (Statement of Profit and Loss) is excluded for the purpose of preparing final accounts of a company. However, for the preparation of comparative and common size income statements, the extent and format of statement of profit and loss is to be studied.

PYQs Previous Years' Questions

1/2 Marks Questions

1. Mention the heading and sub-heading under which vehicles are shown in the balance sheet of a company prepared as per Schedule III of the Companies Act, 2013. ***ISC 2023***

2. Mention the heading and sub-heading under which calls-in-arrears and calls-in-advance are shown in the balance sheet of a company prepared as per Schedule III of the Companies Act, 2013. ***ISC Specimen 2023, 08***

3. If the operating cycle of a company cannot be identified, it is assumed to be ***ISC Sem I Specimen 2021***
   (a) 18 months
   (b) 12 months
   (c) 10 months
   (d) 15 months

4. Which of the following is not shown as a current liability in the balance sheet of a company prepared as per Schedule III of the Companies Act, 2013? ***ISC Sem I Specimen 2021***
   (a) Trade payable (b) Short-term borrowings
   (c) Deferred tax liabilities (d) Short-term provisions

5. List any four items that are shown under the sub-head 'Other Current Assets' in the balance sheet of a company prepared as per Schedule III of the Companies Act, 2013. ***ISC 2020***

6. Mention whether the following trade payables are current liabilities or non-current liabilities ***ISC 2018***

	Operating Cycle	Expected Period of Payment
(i)	12 months	14 months
(ii)	15 months	12 months

7. Give any two differences between a company's balance sheet and a firm's balance sheet. **ISC 2017**

8. What is a contingent liability? How are contingent liabilities shown in the balance sheet of a company prepared as per Schedule III of the Companies Act, 2013? **ISC 2016**

9. What are trade investments? **ISC 2012**

10. Give four examples of property, plant and equipment as per Schedule III, Part I of the Companies Act, 2013. **ISC 2010**

11. What are 'fictitious assets'? Give one example. **ISC 2010**

12. Give two examples of intangible fixed assets. **ISC 2009**

13. State two differences between current assets and current liabilities (without giving any example). **ISC 2003**

14. Give two differences between tangible fixed assets and intangible fixed assets (without giving any example). **ISC 2003**

15. What is a contingent liability? Give one example. **ISC 2002**

16. Name the major headings into which the liability side of a company's balance sheet is organised and presented. **ISC 2002**

17. Give two examples of a contingent liability. **ISC 2000**

3 Marks Questions

18. Under which heads and sub-heads will the following items appear in the balance sheet of a company as per Schedule III of the Companies Act, 2013?
    (i) Trade Debtors
    (ii) Marketable Securities
    (iii) Finished Goods
    (iv) Patents **ISC 2020**

19. Under which heads and sub-heads will the following items appear in the balance sheet of a company as per Schedule III of the Companies Act, 2013?
    (i) Bills receivable
    (ii) Interest accrued and due on debentures
    (iii) Trade creditors
    (iv) Provision for taxation
    (v) Stores and spares **ISC 2014**

6 Marks Question

20. From the information of Prudence Ltd. given below, you are required to show how the relevant items will appear in the company's balance sheet (an extract) as at 31st March, 2022. The authorised capital of Prudence Ltd. consisted of 3,000, 10% preference shares of ₹ 100 each and 8,000 equity shares of ₹ 100 each, out of which **ISC Specimen 2023**
    (i) 1,000, 6% preference shares were issued to the public, fully called and paid-up
    (ii) 3,000 equity shares were issued which were fully called-up.
    (iii) There were arrears of ₹ 20 per share on 400 equity shares.

Liabilities	Amt (₹)
Mortgage Debentures	50,000
Bank Overdraft	25,000
Balance in Statement of Profit and Loss (Dr)	76,000
Freehold Property	50,000

KEY IDEA
Debit balance of statement of profit and loss means 'net loss'.

10 Marks Questions

21. Xylo Ltd. was formed on 1st April, 2017, with an authorised capital of ₹ 12,00,000 divided into equity shares of ₹ 10 each. It issued a prospectus inviting applications for 30,000 shares to be issued at par. The issue was fully subscribed and the amount due on the shares was received by the company.

On 1st April, 2018, the company issued another 60,000 shares at a premium of ₹ 2 per share to be received with allotment. Applications for 55,000 shares were received which were duly allotted.

All the amounts due on these shares were received except the final call of ₹ 2 per share on 1,000 shares. On 1st October, 2018, the company also issued 2,000, 6% Debentures of ₹ 100 each at par, to be redeemed at par in five equal annual instalments beginning from 1st October, 2019. The entire issue price of these debentures was received by the company with application.

Half-yearly interest on the debentures of ₹ 6,000 was paid by the company to the debenture holders on 31st March, 2019.

You are required to show the relevant items under

(i) Equity and liabilities in the balance sheet of the company as at 31st March, 2019 (prepared as per Schedule III of the Companies Act, 2013).

(ii) Notes to accounts. *ISC 2020*

22. The trainee accountant of Rudra Ltd. drafted the following balance sheet. He did not prepare it according to the format prescribed as per Schedule III of the Companies Act, 2013. He also classified a few items incorrectly.

Balance Sheet of Rudra Ltd.
for the year ending 31st March, 2018

Assets	Amt (₹)	Liabilities	Amt (₹)
General Reserve	1,20,000	Capital (1,30,000 Equity shares @ ₹ 10 each)	13,00,000
Plant and Machinery	6,00,000	Share Forfeiture	10,000
Land and Building	8,00,000	Goodwill	1,00,000
Profit and Loss (Debit Balance)	1,50,000	Trade Receivables	20,000
Cash and Bank Balances	2,50,000	Trade Payables	50,000
Unclaimed Dividend	30,000	Inventories	30,000
Calls-in-arrears (₹ 4 per share)	40,000	Fixed Deposit Accepted	4,50,000
		Calls-in-advance	30,000
	19,90,000		19,90,000

Foot note: The company had an authorised capital of 2,00,000 equity shares of ₹ 10 each.

You are required to prepare, as at 31st March, 2018

(i) The balance sheet of Rudra Ltd. as per Schedule III of the Companies Act, 2013.

(ii) Notes to accounts. *ISC 2019*

23. The following balances have been extracted from the books of Vanity Ltd as at 31st March, 2017.

Trial Balance
as at 31st March, 2017

Particulars	Amt (Dr)	Amt (Cr)
Equity Share Capital (5,000 shares of ₹ 100 each fully paid)	—	5,00,000
Property, Plant and Equipment and Intangible Assets	7,30,000	—
Reserves and Surplus	—	2,00,000
Inventories	50,000	—
Cash and Bank Balance	1,58,000	—
Creditors	—	40,000
Bills Payable	—	20,000
Underwriting Commission on issue of shares	10,000	—
5% Debentures (1/5 of the Debentures to be redeemed on 31st March, 2018)	—	2,00,000
Interest accrued and due on 5% Debentures	—	8,000
Trade Receivables	20,000	—
Total	9,68,000	9,68,000

You are required to prepare as at 31st March, 2017

(i) The balance sheet of Vanity Ltd as per Schedule III of the Companies Act, 2013.

(ii) Notes to accounts. *ISC Modified, 2018*

KEY IDEA

1/5th of the debentures which will be redeemed in current year will come under the head 'other currrent liabilities'.

24. Following balances have been extracted from the books of Universe Ltd as at 31st March, 2016

Particulars	Amt (₹)
Equity Share Capital (Fully paid shares of ₹ 100 each)	4,00,000
Unclaimed Dividend	10,000
Bank Balance	40,000
Securities Premium Reserve	75,000
Statement of Profit and Loss (Dr)	50,000
Tangible Assets (at cost)	3,50,000
Accumulated Depreciation till date	25,000
Trademarks	70,000

You are required to prepare as at 31st March, 2016

(i) The balance sheet of Universe Ltd as per Schedule III of the Companies Act, 2013.

(ii) Notes to accounts **ISC 2017**

KEY IDEA

Accumulated depreciation will be deducted from tangible assets since their cost price is provided.

25. (i) Pinnacle Instruments Ltd registered itself with a capital of ₹ 20,00,000 divided into equity shares of ₹ 100 each. On 1st June, 2014, the company issued 5,000 equity shares, as fully paid to Mila Herbals, as purchase consideration for the purchase of plant and machinery.

The remaining shares were issued to the public at par. Till the date of the balance sheet, the directors had called from the public, 60% of the nominal value of the shares.

The amount called was received by the company.

You are required to prepare as at 31st March, 2015

(a) The balance sheet of Pinnacle Instruments Ltd as per Schedule III of the Companies Act, 2013.

(b) Notes to accounts.

(ii) Under which heads and sub-heads will the following items appear in the balance sheet of a company as per Schedule III of the Companies Act, 2013

(a) Public deposits (b) Calls-in-advance

(c) Building under construction **ISC 2016**

26. From the given trial balance, prepare the balance sheet of Moon Light Limited as at 31 st March, 2014 **ISC 2015**

Trial Balance
as at 31st March, 2014

Particulars	Debit (₹)	Credit (₹)
Share Capital (40,000 Equity Shares of ₹ 10 each)	—	4,00,000
Bills Receivable	90,000	—
16% Mortgage Loan	—	1,70,000
Stores and Spares	1,15,000	—
Debtors	1,66,000	—
Plant and Machinery	2,90,000	—
Goodwill	40,000	—
Provision for Tax	—	26,000
General Reserve	—	1,30,000
Cash in Hand	18,000	—
Calls-in-arrears	2,000	—
Marketable Securities	5,000	—
	7,26,000	7,26,000

27. The following balance have been extracted from the books of King Furnishings Ltd as at 31st March, 2011

Equity Share Capital (Fully paid shares of ₹ 100 each)	4,00,000	Accumulated Depreciation	30,000
		Provision for Taxation	25,000
Property, Plant and Equipment	6,60,000	Reserves and Surplus	1,00,000
Inventories	40,000	5% Debentures (Secured against land)	2,00,000
Cash and Bank Balance	50,000	Unsecured Loan from Subsidiaries	50,000
Creditors	30,000	Underwriting Commission	5,000
Bills Receivable	20,000	Investments	70,000
		Interest Accrued and Due	10,000

You are required to prepare a balance sheet of King Furnishings Ltd as at 31st March, 2011 in the form, as prescribed under Schedule III, of the Companies Act, 2013. ***ISC 2012***

28. The following balances have been extracted from the books of Robin Ltd as at 31st December, 2008

	Amt (₹)
Share Capital	10,00,000
Securities Premium	1,00,000
12% Debentures	5,00,000
Creditors	2,00,000
Proposed Dividend	50,000
Statement of Profit and Loss (Dr)	50,000
Livestock	9,00,000
Investment in Government Bonds	4,00,000
Work-in-progress	3,50,000
Discount on Issues of 12% Debentures	1,00,000
Patents	40,000
Unclaimed Dividend	10,000
Account Receivable	20,000
Fixed Deposits	50,000

Prepare the balance sheet of the company as per Schedule III, Part I of the Companies Act, 2013. ***ISC Modified, 2009***

29. From the following balances extracted on 31st March, 2003 from the books of Modern Ltd, prepare a balance sheet in the form prescribed under the Companies Act, 2013.

Particulars	Amt (Dr)	Amt (Cr)
Land	80,000	—
Cash in Mill	7,000	—
Share Capital	—	6,30,000
Building	2,12,500	—
Calls-in-arrears	25,000	—
Creditors	—	6,18,000
Capital Reserve	—	1,54,000
Preliminary Expenses	30,000	—
Brokerage on Shares	12,000	—
Stores	90,000	—
Wages Due	—	29,000
Godown Rent Due	—	3,600
Stock-in-trade	2,50,000	—
Unexpired Insurance	8,200	—
Cash in Office	1,25,000	—
Employee Benefit Fund	—	15,000

Particulars	Amt (Dr)	Amt (Cr)
Salaries Due	—	3,500
Bad Debts Provision	—	6,500
Cash at Bank	62,000	—
Livestock	4,900	—
Machinery	5,08,000	—
Loose Tools	1,30,000	—
Debtors	1,20,000	—
Unclaimed Dividends	—	5,000
Profit and Loss A/c	—	2,00,000
15% Debentures	—	1,00,000
Bank Loan A/c	—	1,50,000
Investments	2,50,000	
	19,14,600	19,14,600

Note Bill discounted but not matured ₹ 40,000.

ISC 2004

30. The trainee accountant of John Smith and Company Ltd, who has gained a little knowledge of accounts, has drafted the following balance sheet

Balance Sheet
for the year ended 31st December, 2002

Assets	Amt (₹)	Liabilities	Amt (₹)
Land and Building	1,09,500	Capital (18,000 equity shares of ₹ 10 each fully called up)	1,80,000
Fixed Deposit Accepted	15,000		
Furniture	30,000	General Reserve	40,000
Goodwill	10,000	Preliminary Expenses	12,000
Stock	24,000	10% Debentures	35,000
Creditors	9,000	Provision for Taxation	22,000
Machinery	25,000	Discount on Issue of Shares	10,000
Cash	24,000	Profit and Loss A/c (Cr)	8,000
Bills Payable	7,000	Investment in Zee Ltd	15,000
Bank	72,000	Bills Receivable	7,000
Capital Reserve	12,000	Debtors	9,000
Calls-in-arrears	2,000	Unclaimed Dividends	11,000
Share Premium	10,000	Authorised Capital (20,000 equity shares, of ₹ 10 each)	—
		Share Forfeiture	500
	3,49,500		3,49,500

Additional Information

Proposed dividend ₹ 14,000

You are required to redraft the above balance sheet as per Schedule III, Part I of Companies Act, 2013.

ISC Modified, 2003

Case Based Questions

31. The accountant of Biren Ltd. is preparing the balance sheet of the company as per Schedule III of the Companies Act, 2013. *ISC Sem I 2021*

(i) The company has an operating cycle of 15 months. It has accounts payables (creditors and bills payable) amounting to ₹ 1,20,000. ₹ 20,000 of these are payable within 14 months, while the expected period of payment of the remaining account payables is between 16-18 months.

How will the company show its accounts payables in the balance sheet?

(a) Current Liability of ₹ 1,20,000
(b) Non-current Liability of ₹ 1,20,000
(c) Current Liability of ₹ 20,000 and Non-current Liability of ₹ 1,00,000
(d) Current Liability of ₹ 1,00,000 and Non-current Liability of ₹ 20,000

(ii) Which of the following will be shown as a sub-head in the balance sheet?

(a) Debtors
(b) Stock-in-trade
(c) Current investments
(d) Prepaid expenses

32. Following is an extract of the balance sheet of Vitamin Ltd. prepared incorrectly by a trainee accountant

Balance Sheet of Vitamin Ltd. (An Extract)
for the year ended 31st March, 2021

Assets	Amt (₹)	Liabilities	Amt (₹)
Statement of Profit and Loss (Dr)	2,10,000	Bills Receivable	50,000
Securities Premium	10,000	Provision for Tax	1,00,000
Bills Receivable maturing on 30th June, 2021, discounted with the bank	1,50,000	Equity Share Capital (90,000 shares of ₹ 10 each)	9,00,000
		Provision for Doubtful Debts	40,000
Proposed Dividend for 2020-21	1,10,000	Share Issue Expenses	25,000
Sundry Debtors	3,30,000	Underwriting Commission	5,000
Calls-in-advance	20,000		

Note Apart from preparing on incorrect format of the balance sheet, the accountant also did not follow the company's policy of writing-off the capital losses in the year in which they occur.

If this balance sheet was prepared as per Schedule III of the Companies, Act, 2013, it would show. *ISC Sem I 2021*

(i) The date of the balance sheet as

(a) Mentioned by the trainee accountant
(b) Balance Sheet of Vitamin Ltd. as at 31st March, 2021
(c) Balance Sheet of Vitamin Ltd. as on 31st March, 2021
(d) Balance Sheet of Vitamin Ltd. for the year 2020-21

(ii) The head 'Shareholders' Fund' of amount

(a) ₹ 6,70,000
(b) ₹ 10,95,000
(c) ₹ 6,00,000
(d) ₹ 7,05,000

(iii) The sub-head 'Trade Receivables' of amount

(a) ₹ 4,90,000
(b) ₹ 5,30,000
(c) ₹ 3,40,000
(d) ₹ 3,80,000

(iv) The item 'Bills Receivable maturing on 30th June, 2021, discounted with the bank' as a

(a) current liability
(b) current asset
(c) non-current liability
(d) contingent liability

Explanations

1.

Particulars	Main head	Sub-head
Vehicle	Non-current Assets	Property, Plant and Equipment and Intangible Assets

2.

S.No.	Particulars	Heading	Sub-heading
(i)	Calls-in-arrears	Shareholder's Fund	Subscribed Capital (Shown by way of deduction)
(ii)	Calls-in-advance	Current Liabilities	Other Current Liabilities

3. (b) 12 months

4. (c) Deferred Tax Liabilities

5. Other current assets include
   (i) Advances paid to employees or suppliers.
   (ii) Piece of property that is being readied for sale.
   (iii) Restricted cash or investments.
   (iv) Cash surrender value of life insurance policies.

6. (i) Non-current liabilities as expected period of payment is more than 12 months.
   (ii) Current liabilities as expected period of payment is less than or equal to 12 months.

7. Differences between a company's balance sheet and a firm's balance sheet are

Basis	Company's balance sheet	Firm's balance sheet
Form	As per Schedule III, of Companies Act, 2013, a company's balance sheet can be presented in horizontal form only.	A firm's balance sheet can be presented in horizontal form, as well as, vertical form.
Supplement	A company's balance sheet is supplemented with 'notes to accounts'.	A firm's balance sheet is not supplemented with 'notes to accounts'.

8. Contingent liabilities are those liabilities which may or may not arise because they are dependent on an event, happening in future.

   Contingent liabilities can be classified as claims against the company not acknowledged as debt, guarantees, other money for which the company is contingently liable, it is not recorded in the books of accounts, but is disclosed in the notes to accounts for the information of the user.

9. The term 'trade investments' is reffered to as an investment made by a company in shares or debentures of another company, not being its subsidiary to promote its own trade and business.

10. Land, buildings, machinery and leaseholds are the examples of property, plant and equipment.

11. Fictitious assets are the assets which cannot be realised in cash or no further benefit can be derived from these assets. These assets are not really assets and shall be written-off in the same year in which they occur. e.g. Preliminary expenses.

12. The two examples of intangible fixed assets are patents and goodwill.

13. Difference between current assets and current liabilities

Basis	Current assets	Current liabilities
Meaning	These are those assets which are expected to be realised in or intended for sale or consumption in normal operating cycle of the company.	These are those liabilities which are expected to be settled in company's normal operating cycle.
Purpose	Current assets are acquired for the purpose of reselling.	Current liabilities helps to raise working capital to finance day-to-day operations of business.

14. Difference between tangible fixed assets and intangible fixed assets

Basis	Tangible fixed assets	Intangible fixed assets
Meaning	These are those assets which can be physically seen and touched.	These are those assets which cannot be seen and touched.
Valued	These are valued at their cost less depreciation.	They are valued on the basis of benefit available to business from such assets.

15. Those liabilities which may or may not arise because they are dependent on a happening in future. e.g. Claims against the company not acknowledged as debts.

Concept Enhancer Contingent liability is not recorded in the books of accounts, but it is disclosed in the notes to accounts.

16. The major headings are
   (i) Shareholder's funds
   (ii) Share application money pending allotment
   (iii) Non-current liabilities
   (iv) Current liabilities

17. Two examples of a contingent liability are
(i) Bills discounted but not matured. (ii) Guarantees given by the company.

18.

S. No.	Particulars	Heads	Sub-heads
(i)	Trade Debtors	Current Assets	Trade Receivables
(ii)	Marketable Securities	Current Assets	Current Investments
(iii)	Finished Goods	Current Assets	Inventories
(iv)	Patents	Non-current Assets	Intangible Assets

Concept Enhancer Marketable securities are taken as cash equivalent while preparing cash flow statement.

19.

S.No.	Particulars	Headings	Sub-headings
(i)	Bills Receivable	Current Assets	Trade Receivables
(ii)	Interest Accrued and Due on Debentures	Current Liabilities	Other Current Liabilities
(iii)	Trade Creditors	Current Liabilities	Trade Payables
(iv)	Provision for Taxation	Current Liabilities	Short-term Provision
(v)	Stores and Spares	Current Assets	Inventories

20. **Balance Sheet of Prudence Ltd.** (Extract)
as at 31st March, 2022

Particulars	Note No.	Amt (₹)
I. **EQUITY AND LIABILITIES**		
1. **Shareholder's Funds**		
(i) Share Capital	1	3,92,000
(ii) Reserves and Surplus	2	(76,000)
2. **Non-current Liabilities**		
Long-term Borrowings	3	50,000
3. **Current Liabilities**		
Short-term Borrowings	4	25,000
II. **ASSETS**		
1. **Non-current Assets**		
(i) Property, Plant and Equipment and Intangible Assets		
(a) Property, Plant and Equipment	5	50,000

Notes to Accounts

	Particulars		Amt (₹)
1.	**Share Capital**		
	Authorised Share Capital		
	3,000, 10% Preference Shares of ₹ 100 each		3,00,000
	8,000 Equity Shares of ₹ 100 each		8,00,000
	Issued Share Capital		
	1,000, 10% Preference Shares of ₹ 100 each		1,00,000
	3,000 Equity Share of ₹ 100 each		3,00,000
	Subscribed Share Capital		
	1,000, 10% Preference Shares of ₹ 100 each	1,00,000	
	3,000 Equity Share of ₹ 100 each	3,00,000	
	(–) Calls-in-arrears	(8,000)	3,92,000
2.	**Reserves and Surplus**		
	Profit and Loss (Dr)		(76,000)

Particulars	Amt (₹)
3. **Long-term Borrowings**	
Mortgage Debentures	50,000
4. **Short-term Borrowings**	
Bank Overdraft	25,000
5. **Property, Plant and Equipment**	
Freehold Property	50,000

21. (i)

Balance Sheet of Xylo Ltd.
as at 31st March, 2019

Particulars	Note No.	Current Year (₹)	Previous Year (₹)
I. EQUITY AND LIABILITIES			
1. **Shareholder's Fund**			
(a) Share Capital	1	8,48,000	
(b) Reserves and Surplus	2	1,10,000	
2. **Non-Current Liabilities**			
Long-term Borrowings	3	2,00,000	

(ii) Notes to Accounts

Particulars		Amt (₹)
1. **Share Capital**		
Authorised Share Capital		
1,20,000 Equity Shares @ ₹ 10 each		12,00,000
Issued Capital		
90,000 Equity Shares @ ₹ 10 each		9,00,000
Subscribed Capital		
Subscribed and Full Paid Capital		
84,000 Equity Shares @ ₹ 10 each		8,40,000
Subscribed but not full paid		
1,000 Equity Shares @ ₹ 10 each	10,000	
(–) Calls-in-arrears	(2,000)	8,000
		8,48,000
2. **Reserves and Surplus**		
Security Premium		
₹ 2 for 55,000 Shares		1,10,000
3. **Long-term Borrowings**		
6% Debentures, 2,000 @ ₹ 100 each		2,00,000

Common Mistake Students usually classify stores and spares as other current asset. But, stores and spares is a part of inventories.

22. (i)

Balance Sheet of Rudra Ltd.
as at 31st March, 2018

Particulars	Note No.	Amt (₹)
I. EQUITY AND LIABILITIES		
1. **Shareholders' Funds**		
(a) Share Capital	1	12,70,000
(b) Reserve and Surplus	2	(30,000)
2. **Non-current Liabilities**		
(a) Long-term Borrowings	3	4,50,000
3. **Current Liabilities**		
(a) Trade Payables	4	50,000
(b) Other Current Liabilities	5	60,000
Total		18,00,000
II. ASSETS		
1. **Non-current Assets**		
(a) Property, Plant and Equipment and Intangible Assets		
(i) Property, Plant and Equipment	6	14,00,000
(ii) Intangible Assets	7	1,00,000
2. **Current Assets**		
(a) Inventories	8	30,000
(b) Trade Receivables	9	20,000
(c) Cash and Cash Equivalents	10	2,50,000
Total		18,00,000

(ii) **Notes to Accounts**

Particulars		Amt (₹)
1. **Share Capital**		
Authorised Capital		
2,00,000 equity shares of ₹ 10 each		20,00,000
Issued Capital		
Equity shares of ₹ 10 each		—
Subscribed Capital		
Subscribed and Fully Paid-up		
1,20,000 equity shares of ₹ 10 each		12,00,000
Subscribed but not Fully Paid-up		
10,000 equity shares of ₹ 10 each	1,00,000	
(–) Calls-in-arrears (10,000 × 4)	(40,000)	60,000
		12,60,000
(+) Forfeited Shares		10,000
		12,70,000
2. **Reserves and Surplus**		
General Reserve	1,20,000	
(–) Profit and Loss (Debit Balance)	(1,50,000)	(30,000)
3. **Long-term Borrowings**		
Fixed Deposit Accepted		4,50,000
4. **Trade Payables**		50,000

Particulars	Amt (₹)
5. **Other Current Liabilities**	
Calls-in-advance	30,000
Unclaimed Dividend	30,000
	60,000
6. **Property, Plant and Equipment**	
Plant and Machinery	6,00,000
Land and Building	8,00,000
	14,00,000
7. **Intangible Assets**	
Goodwill	1,00,000
8. **Current Assets**	
Inventories	30,000
9. **Current Assets**	
Trade Receivables	20,000
10. **Cash and Cash Equivalents**	2,50,000

23. (i)

Balance Sheet of Vanity Ltd
as at 31st March, 2017

Particulars	Note No.	Amt (₹)
I. **EQUITY AND LIABILITIES**		
1. **Shareholder's Funds**		
(a) Share Capital	1	5,00,000
(b) Reserve and Surplus	2	1,90,000
2. **Share Application Money Pending Allotment**		
3. **Non-current Liabilities**		
Long-term Borrowings	3	1,60,000
4. **Current Liabilities**		
Trade Payables	4	60,000
Other Current Liabilities	5	48,000
Total		9,58,000
II. **ASSETS**		
1. **Non-current Assets**		
Property, Plant and Equipment and Intangible Assets		7,30,000
2. **Current Assets**	6	2,28,000
Total		9,58,000

Additional Information

Proposed Dividend ₹ 12,000

(ii) **Notes to Accounts**

Particulars	Amt (₹)
1. **Share Capital**	
Subscribed and Fully Paid Capital	
5,000 Equity Shares of ₹ 100 each	5,00,000
2. **Reserves and Surplus**	2,00,000
(–) Underwriting Commission	(10,000)
	1,90,000

Particulars	Amt (₹)
3. **Long-term Borrowings**	
5% Debentures	1,60,000
4. **Trade Payables**	
Creditors	40,000
Bills Payable	20,000
	60,000
5. **Other Current Liabilities**	
5% Debentures	40,000
Interest accrued and due on 5% debentures	8,000
	48,000
6. **Current Assets**	
Inventories	50,000
Cash and Bank	1,58,000
Trade Receivable	20,000
	2,28,000

24. (i)

In the Books of Universe Ltd
Balance Sheet
as at 31st March, 2016

Particulars	Note No.	Figures at the End of the Current Reporting Period (₹)	Figures at the End of the Previous Reporting Period (₹)
I. **EQUITY AND LIABILITIES**			
1. **Shareholders' Funds**			
(a) Share Capital	1	4,00,000	—
(b) Reserves and Surplus	2	25,000	—
2. **Current Liabilities**			
Other Current Liabilities	3	10,000	—
Total		4,35,000	—
II. **ASSETS**			
1. **Non-current Assets**			
(a) Property, Plant and Equipment and Intangible Assets			
(i) Property, Plant and Equipment	4	3,25,000	—
(ii) Intangible Assets	5	70,000	—
2. **Current Assets**			
Cash and Cash Equivalents	6	40,000	—
Total		4,35,000	—

(ii) Notes to Accounts

Particulars	Amt (₹)
1. **Share Capital**	
Subscribed and Fully Paid up 4,000 Equity Shares of ₹ 100 each	4,00,000
2. **Reserves and Surplus**	
Securities Premium	75,000
(–) Statement of Profit and Loss (Dr)	(50,000)
	25,000
3. **Other Current Liabilities**	
Unclaimed Dividend	10,000

Particulars	Amt (₹)
4. **Property, Plant and Equipment and Intangible Assets**	
Property, Plant and Equipment (at cost)	3,50,000
(–) Accumulated Depreciation till date	25,000
	3,25,000
5. **Intangible Assets**	
Trademarks	70,000
6. **Cash and Cash Equivalents**	
Bank Balance	40,000

25. (i)

Balance Sheet (Extract)
as at 31st March, 2015

Particulars	Note No.	Amt (₹)
I. **EQUITY AND LIABILITIES**		
1. **Shareholders' Funds**		
(a) Share Capital	1	14,00,000
II. **ASSETS**		
1. **Non-Current Assets**		
Plant and Machinery		5,00,000
2. **Current Assets**		
Cash and Bank		9,00,000
Total		14,00,000

Notes to Accounts

Particulars	Amt (₹)
1. **Share Capital**	
Authorised Share Capital	
20,000 Equity Shares of ₹ 100 each	20,00,000
Issued Share Capital	
5,000 Equity Shares of ₹ 100 each as Fully Paid for Consideration other than Cash	5,00,000
15,000 Equity Shares of ₹ 100 each	15,00,000
	20,00,000
Subscribed Capital	
Subscribed and Fully Paid up	
5,000 Equity Shares of ₹ 100 each	5,00,000
Subscribed but not Fully Paid up	
15,000 Equity Shares of ₹ 60 each	9,00,000
	14,00,000

(ii)

S.No.	Particulars	Main Head	Sub-head
(a)	Public Deposits	Non-current Liabilities	Long-term Borrowings
(b)	Calls-in-advance	Current Liabilities	Other Current Liabilities
(c)	Building under Construction	Non-current Assets	Property, Plant and Equipment

26.

In the Books of Moon Light Ltd
Balance Sheet
as at 31st March, 2014

Particulars	Note No.	31st March, 2014 (₹)
I. **EQUITY AND LIABILITIES**		
1. **Shareholders' Funds**		
(a) Share Capital	1	3,98,000
(b) Reserves and Surplus	2	1,30,000
2. **Non-current Liabilities**		
Long-term Borrowings	3	1,70,000
3. **Current Liabilities**		
Short-term Provision	4	26,000
Total		7,24,000
II. **ASSETS**		
1. **Non-current Assets**		
Property, Plant and Equipment and Intangible Assets		
(a) Property, Plant and Equipment	5	2,90,000
(b) Intangible Assets	6	40,000
2. **Current Assets**		
(a) Current Investments	7	5,000
(b) Inventories	8	1,15,000
(c) Trade Receivables	9	2,56,000
(d) Cash and Cash Equivalents	10	18,000
Total		7,24,000

Notes to Accounts

Particulars		Amt (₹)
1. **Share Capital**		
Subscribed Capital (Subscribed but not fully paid)		
40,000 Equity Shares of ₹ 10 each	4,00,000	
(–) Calls-in-arrears	(2,000)	3,98,000
		3,98,000
2. **Reserves and Surplus**		
General Reserve		1,30,000
3. **Long-term Borrowings**		
16% Mortage Loan		1,70,000
4. **Short-term Provisions**		
Provision for Tax		26,000
5. **Property, Plant and Equipment**		
Plant and Machinery		2,90,000
6. **Intangible Assets**		
Goodwill		40,000
7. **Current Investments**		
Marketable Securities		5,000
8. **Inventories**		
Stores and Spares		1,15,000
9. **Trade Receivables**		
Bills Receivables		90,000
Debtors		1,66,000
		2,56,000
10. **Cash and Cash Equivalents**		
Cash in Hand		18,000

27.

In the Books of King Furnishings Ltd
Balance Sheet
as at 31st March, 2011

Particulars	Note No.	Amt (₹)
I. EQUITY AND LIABILITIES		
1. **Shareholders' Funds**		
(a) Share Capital		4,00,000
(b) Reserves and Surplus	1	95,000
2. **Non-current Liabilities**		
(a) Long-term Borrowings	2	2,50,000
3. **Current Liabilities**		
(a) Property, Plant and Equipment	3	30,000
(b) Other Current Liabilities	4	10,000
(c) Short-term Provisions	5	25,000
Total		8,10,000
II. ASSETS		
1. **Non-current Assets**		
(a) Property, Plant and Equipment	6	6,30,000
2. **Current Assets**		
(a) Short-term Investments		70,000
(b) Inventories		40,000
(c) Trade Receivables	7	20,000
(d) Cash and Cash Equivalents	8	50,000
Total		8,10,000

Notes to Accounts

Particulars	Amt (₹)
1. **Reserves and Surplus**	1,00,000
(–) Underwriting Commission	(5,000)
	95,000
2. **Long-term Borrowings**	
5% Debentures	2,00,000
Unsecured Loan from Subsidiaries	50,000
	2,50,000
3. **Trade Payables**	
Creditors	30,000
4. **Other Current Liabilities**	
Interest Accrued and Due on 5% Debentures	10,000
5. **Short-term Provisions**	
Provision for Taxation	25,000
6. **Property, Plant and Equipment**	
Cost	6,60,000
(–) Accumulated Depreciation	(30,000)
	6,30,000
7. **Trade Receivables**	
Bills Receivable	20,000
8. **Cash and Cash Equivalents**	
Cash and Bank Balance	50,000

28.

In the Books of Robin Ltd
Balance Sheet
as at 31st March, 2011

Particulars	Note No.	Amt (₹)
I. **EQUITY AND LIABILITIES**		
1. **Shareholders' Funds**		
(a) Share Capital		10,00,000
(b) Reserves and Surplus	1	(50,000)
2. **Non-current Liabilities**		
(a) Long-term Borrowings	2	5,50,000
3. **Current Liabilities**		
(a) Trade Payables	3	2,00,000
(b) Other Current Liabilities	4	10,000
Total		17,10,000
II. **ASSETS**		
1. **Non-current Assets**		
(a) Property, Plant and Equipment and Intangible Assets		
(i) Property, Plant and Equipment	5	9,00,000
(ii) Intangible Assets	6	40,000
(iii) Trade Receivables	7	4,00,000
2. **Current Assets**		
(a) Inventories	8	3,50,000
(b) Trade Receivables	9	20,000
Total		17,10,000

Additional Information

Proposed Dividend ₹ 50,000

Notes to Accounts

Particulars	Amt (₹)
1. **Reserves and Surplus**	
Securities Premium	1,00,000
(–) Discount on Issue of 12% Debentures	(1,00,000)
Debit Balance in Statement of Profit and Loss	(50,000)
	(50,000)
2. **Long-term Borrowings**	
12% Debentures	5,00,000
Fixed Deposits	50,000
	5,50,000
3. **Trade Payables**	
Creditors	2,00,000
4. **Other Current Liabilities**	
Unclaimed Dividend	10,000
5. **Property, Plant and Equipment**	
Livestock	9,00,000
6. **Intangible Assets**	
Patents	40,000
7. **Non-current Investments**	
Investment in Government Bonds	4,00,000

Particulars	Amt (₹)
8. **Inventories**	
Work-in-progress	3,50,000
9. **Trade Receivables**	
Accounts Receivable	20,000

Common Mistake Students usually record proposed dividend as short-term provisions in the balance sheet. However, current year's proposed dividend is not shown in the balance sheet of the company.

29.

In the Books of Modern Ltd
Balance Sheet
as at 31st March, 2003

Particulars	Note No.	Amt (₹)
I. **EQUITY AND LIABILITIES**		
1. **Shareholders' Funds**	1	6,05,000
(a) Share Capital	2	3,12,000
(b) Reserves and Surplus		
2. **Share Application Money Pending Allotment**		
3. **Non-current Liabilities**		
(a) Long-term Borrowings	3	2,50,000
(b) Long-term Provisions	4	15,000
4. **Curent Liabilities**		
(a) Trade Payables		6,18,000
(b) Other Current Liabilities	5	41,100
(c) Short-term Provisions	6	6,500
Total		18,47,600
II. **ASSETS**		
1. **Non-current Assets**		
(a) **Property, Plant and Equipment and Intangible Assets**		
(i) Property, Plant and Equipment	7	8,05,400
(ii) Non-current Investments		2,50,000
2. **Current Assets**		
(a) Inventories	8	4,70,000
(b) Trade Receivables		1,20,000
(c) Cash and Cash Equivalents	9	1,94,000
(d) Other Current Assets	10	8,200
Total		18,47,600

Notes to Accounts

Particulars		Amt (₹)
1. **Share Capital**		
Subscribed Capital		
Subscribed and Fully Paid Capital		
53,000 Shares of ₹ 10 each		5,30,000
Subscribed but not Fully Paid Capital		
10,000 Shares of ₹ 10 each	1,00,000	
(–) Calls-in-arrears	(25,000)	75,000
		6,05,000

Particulars			Amt (₹)
2. **Reserves and Surplus**			
General Reserve		1,54,000	
(–) Preliminary Expenses	30,000		
Brokerage on Shares	12,000	(42,000)	1,12,000
Statement of Profit and Loss Balance			2,00,000
			3,12,000
3. **Long-term Borrowings**			
15% Debentures			1,00,000
Bank Loan			1,50,000
			2,50,000
4. **Long-term Provisions**			
Employees Benefit Fund			15,000
(It is assumed that employees benefit fund is for more than 12 months)			
5. **Other Current Liabilities**			
Wages Due			29,000
Godown Rent Due			3,600
Salaries Due			3,500
Unclaimed Dividends			5,000
			41,100
6. **Short-term Provisions**			
Provision for Bad Debts			6,500
7. **Property, Plant and Equipment**			
Land			80,000
Building			2,12,500
Machinery			5,08,000
Livestock			4,900
			8,05,400
8. **Inventories**			
Stores			90,000
Stock-in-trade			2,50,000
Loose Tools			1,30,000
			4,70,000
9. **Cash and Cash Equivalents**			
Cash at Bank			62,000
Cash in Mill			7,000
Cash in Office			1,25,000
			1,94,000
10. **Other Current Assets**			
Unexpired Insurance			8,200

Note Bill discounted but not matured ₹ 4,00,000.

30.

In the Books of ...
Balance Sheet
as at 31st March, 2002

Particulars	Note No.	Amt (₹)
I. **EQUITY AND LIABILITIES**		
1. **Shareholders' Funds**		
(a) Share Capital	1	1,78,500
(b) Reserves and Surplus	2	48,000
2. **Share Application Money Pending Allotment**		
3. **Non-current Liabilities**		
(a) Long-term Borrowings	3	50,000

Particulars	Note No.	Amt (₹)
4. **Current Liabilities**		
Trade Payables	4	16,000
Other Current Liabilities	5	11,000
Short-term Provisions	6	22,000
Total		3,25,500
II. **ASSETS**		
1. **Non-current Assets**		
(a) Property, Plant and Equipment and Intangible Assets		
(i) Property, Plant and Equipment	7	1,64,500
(ii) Intangible Assets	8	10,000
(b) Non-current Investments	9	15,000
2. **Current Assets**		
(a) Inventories		24,000
(b) Trade Receivables	10	16,000
(c) Cash and Cash Equivalents	11	96,000
Total		3,25,500

Additional Information

Proposed Dividend ₹ 14,000

Notes to Accounts

Particulars			Amt (₹)
1. **Share Capital**			
Authorised			
20,000 Equity Share of ₹ 10 each			2,00,000
Issued			
.... Equity Shares of ₹ 10 each			
Subscribed Capital			
Subscribed and Fully Paid Share Capital			
17,000 Equity Shares of ₹ 10 each			1,70,000
Subscribed but not Fully Paid Capital			
1,000 Equity Shares of ₹ 10 each Fully Called Up		10,000	
(–) Calls-in-arrears		(2,000)	8,000
			1,78,000
(+) Share Forfeiture A/c			500
			1,78,500
2. **Reserves and Surplus**			
General Reserve		40,000	
Securities Premium		10,000	
Capital Reserve		12,000	
		62,000	
(–) Preliminary Expenses	(12,000)		
Discount on Issue of Shares	(10,000)	(22,000)	40,000
Statement of Profit and Loss Balance			8,000
			48,000

	Particulars	Amt (₹)
3.	**Long-term Borrowings**	
	10% Debentures	35,000
	Fixed Deposits Accepted (Assumed for more than 12 months)	15,000
		50,000
4.	**Trade Payables**	
	Bills Payable	7,000
	Sundry Creditors	9,000
		16,000
5.	**Other Current Liabilities**	
	Unclaimed Dividend	11,000
6.	**Short-term Provisions**	
	Provision for Taxation	22,000
		22,000
7.	**Property, Plant and Equipment**	
	Land and Building	1,09,500
	Machinery	25,000
	Furniture	30,000
		1,64,500
8.	**Intangible Assets**	
	Goodwill	10,000
9.	**Non-current Investments**	
	Investment in Zee Ltd	15,000
10.	**Trade Receivables**	
	Bills Receivables	7,000
	Debtors	9,000
		16,000
11.	**Cash and Cash Equivalents**	
	Bank	72,000
	Cash	24,000
		96,000

31. (i) (c) Payment period of creditor of ₹ 1,00,000 exceeds the operating cycle.

(ii) (c) Current investments

32. (i) (b) Balance sheet of Vitamin Ltd. as at 31st March, 2021.

(ii) (a)

Particulars		Amt (₹)
Share Capital	9,00,000	
Reserves and Surplus		
Statement of Profit and Loss	(2,10,000)	
Securities Premium	10,000	
Share Issue Expenses	(25,000)	
Underwriting commission	(5,000)	6,70,000

(iii) (c) ₹ 3,40,000

(iv) (d) contingent liability

CHAPTER TEST

01 Mark Questions

1. While preparing balance sheet of a company, 'deposit with custom authorities' is shown under which sub-head
(a) long-term loans and advances
(b) other non-current assets
(c) other non-current liabilities
(d) None of the above

2. If a company's operating cycle is 15 months, a creditor payable after 13.5 months will be classified as
(a) non-current liabilities
(b) current liabilities
(c) other current liabilities
(d) other non-current liabilities

3. Which of the following is not a sub-head under current assets?
(a) Cash and cash equivalents
(b) Short-term loans and advances
(c) Current investments
(d) Short-term provisions

4. Which of the following is not a part of cash and cash equivalents under current assets?
(a) Marketable securities
(b) Cheque-on-hand
(c) Draft-on-hand
(d) Bank balance

5. While preparing balance sheet of a company, provision for doubtful debts is recorded as
(a) a provision under short-term provisions
(b) a provision under long-term provisions
(c) Either (a) or (b)
(d) None of the above

6. Name the major heads under equity and liabilities.

7. Name three items that are shown under the head property, plant and equipment.

8. Explain any two limitations of financial statements.

03 Marks Questions

9. Under what heads and sub-heads, will the following items appear in the balance sheet of a company as per Schedule III, Part I of the Companies Act, 2013.
(i) Stores and spares
(ii) Proposed dividend
(iii) Computer software
(iv) Debentures
(v) Loose tools

10. Under what heads and sub-heads, will the following items appear in the balance sheet of a company as per Schedule III, Part I of the Companies Act, 2013.
(i) Calls-in-advance
(ii) Mining rights
(iii) Encashment of employees earned leave payable on retirement
(iv) Vehicles
(v) Tax reserve

06 Marks Questions

11. Under what heads and sub-heads will the following items appear in the balance sheet of a company as per Schedule III, Part I of the Companies Act, 2013.
(i) Premium on redemption of debentures
(ii) Subsidy reserves
(iii) Provision for doubtful debts
(iv) Long-term investments
(v) Bills of exchange
(vi) Discount on issue of shares
(vii) Unclaimed dividend
(viii) Securities premium
(ix) Preliminary expenses
(x) Provision for tax

12. Prepare the balance sheet for Rishant Ltd as at 31st March, 2012 from the following information as per provisions of Schedule III, Part I of the Companies Act, 2013.

Particulars	Amt (₹)
General Reserve	300
8% Debentures	300
Balance of Statement of Profit and Loss (credit)	120
Depreciation of Property, Plant and Equipment	70
Property, Plant and Equipment (cost)	900
Current Liabilities	250
Preference Share Capital	500
Current Assets	640

10 Marks Questions

13. From the list of following assets and liabilities, prepare the balance sheet of the company as per Schedule III, Part I of the Companies Act, 2013.

Vishal Co. Ltd

Liabilities		Amt (₹)	Assets		Amt (₹)
Sundry Creditors		1,00,000	Cash at Bank		79,800
Securities Premium		50,000	Cash in Hand		1,500
Interest on Debentures		28,000	Investments		95,000
Authorised Share Capital			Preliminary Expenses		9,000
1,20,000 Shares of ₹ 10 per Share		12,00,000	Loans and Advances to Staff		95,000
Subscribed Capital			Goodwill		50,000
Shares of ₹ 10 each	8,00,000		Buildings		6,00,000
(–) Calls-in-arrears	(15,000)		Plant and Machinery	6,60,000	
(₹ 3 per share on 5,000 shares)		7,85,000	(–) Depreciation	(66,000)	5,94,000
Statement of Profit and Loss Balance		75,000	Inventories		10,000
6% Debentures		6,00,000	Debtors	1,74,000	
Bills Payable		76,000	(–) Provision for Doubtful Debts	(8,700)	1,65,300
			Furniture		14,400

14. The following balance sheet is prepared by XYZ Ltd. You are required to redraft it as per Schedule III, Part I of Companies Act, 2013.

Balance Sheet
for the year ended 31st March, 2014

Liabilities	Amt (₹)	Assets	Amt (₹)
12% Debentures	2,00,000	Land and Buildings	7,80,000
Provision for Taxation	1,50,000	Stock-in-trade	1,20,000
Securities Premium	50,000	Proposed Dividend	1,49,800
Investments in Shares of Ravi Ltd	11,20,000	Debtors	90,000
General Reserve	1,40,000	Loose Tools	1,45,000
Creditors	1,00,000	Cash and Bank	75,000
Bills Payable	62,000	Capital Redemption Reserve	9,70,200
Unclaimed Dividends	28,000	Leasehold Premises	6,00,000
Balance of Statement of Profit and Loss (Cr)	70,000	Preliminary Expenses	10,000
Share Capital (15,000 Shares of ₹ 100 each)	15,00,000	Bills Receivable	2,00,000
Calls-in-arrears (on 500 shares)	2,000	Discount on Issue of 12% Debentures	5,000
		Vehicles	2,75,000
		Share Forfeiture	2,000
	34,22,000		34,22,000

Answers

1. (a) long-term loans and advances
2. (b) current liabilities
3. (d) Short-term provisions
4. (a) Marketable securities
5. (c) Either (a) or (b)

08

Financial Statement Analysis

TREND ANALYSIS 5 YEARS

Average No. of Questions Across all Sets

Topic	Types of Questions	2023	2020	2019	2018	2017
01 Introduction to Financial Statement Analysis	1/2 Marks	1	—	1	1	—
	3 Marks	—	—	—	—	—
	6 Marks	—	—	—	—	—
	10 Marks	—	—	—	—	—
02 Comparative Statements	1/2 Marks	—	—	—	—	—
	3 Marks	1	—	—	—	—
	6 Marks	—	1	—	—	1
	10 Marks	—	—	—	—	—
03 Common Size Statements	1/2 Marks	—	—	—	—	—
	3 Marks	—	—	—	—	—
	6 Marks	—	—	1	1	—
	10 Marks	—	—	—	—	—

Meaning of Financial Statement Analysis

It is the systematic numerical representation and study of the relationship of one financial fact with the other to measure the profitability, operational efficiency, solvency and the growth potential of the business.

Tools of Financial Statement Analysis

There are different tools of financial statements analysis available to the analyst. These tools are used to measure the operational efficiency and financial soundness of an enterprise.

The most common used techniques of financial analysis are

1. Comparative financial statements
2. Common size statements
3. Ratio analysis
4. Cash flow statements

Note In this chapter, comparative statements and common size statements are discussed.

Comparative Statements

Statements used to compare the items of income statement, i.e. statement of profit and loss and position statement, i.e. balance sheet across a given number of years for ascertaining the trend of the performance and profitability of an enterprise are known as comparative statements.

Objectives or Significance of Comparative Statements

Main objectives of comparative statements are

(i) Data presentation becomes simple and comparable
(ii) Indicates trend
(iii) Indicates strengths and weaknesses
(iv) Facilitates comparison with other firms and industry
(v) Helps in forecasting and planning
(vi) Provides key financial statistics

Limitations of Comparative Statements

Limitations of comparative statements are

(i) Based on historical records
(ii) Affected by personal judgement
(iii) Ignores qualitative elements
(iv) Ignores price level changes

Types of Comparative Statements

There are two types of comparative statements, *viz.* comparative income statement and comparative balance sheet.

Comparative Statement of Profit and Loss

It is a statement which shows in absolute as well as percentage term the total of income earned and expenses incurred during two or more accounting periods.

Objectives or Significance of Comparative Statement of Profit and Loss

The main objectives or significance of comparative income statement are

(i) Analyse the income and expenditure for two or more years.
(ii) Analyse the increase or decrease in the income and expenditure in terms of rupees and also in terms of percentage.
(iii) Review the business operations of the last year and its likely effect on the current year's operations.

Format of Comparative Statement of Profit and Loss

Comparative Statement of Profit and Loss
for the year ended ...

Particulars	Previous Year (₹)	Current Year (₹)	Absolute Change (Increase or Decrease) (₹)	Percentage Change (Increase or Decrease) (%)
I. Revenue from Operations	...	...		...
II. Other Income	...	...	...	...
III. Total Revenue (I + II)	...	...	...	...
IV. Expenses				
(a) Cost of Materials Consumed	...	...	...	...
(b) Purchases of Stock-in-trade	...	...	...	...
(c) Changes in Inventories of Finished Goods, Work-in-progress and Stock-in-trade	...	...	...	...
(d) Employees Benefit Expenses	...	...	...	...
(e) Finance Cost	...	...	...	...
(f) Depreciation and Amortization	...	...	...	...
(g) Other Expenses	...	...	...	...
Total Expenses	...	...	...	...
V. Profit before Tax (III – IV)	...	...	...	...
(–) Income Tax	...	...	...	...
VI. Profit after Tax	...	...	...	...

Comparative Balance Sheet

It is a statement showing assets and liabilities of the business for two or more accounting periods. It shows the absolute change as well as percentage change in the monetary value of the assets and liabilities.

Objectives or Significance of Comparative Balance Sheet

The objectives or significance of comparative balance sheet are

(i) It shows the balances of accounts as at different dates but also the extent of their increase or decrease between these dates.

(ii) Comparative balance sheet emphasises on change.

(iii) Comparative balance sheet contains data not only of single balance sheet but also data which may be helpful in studying the trend in the enterprise.

(iv) Comparative balance sheet is a link between the balance sheet and the statement of profit and loss. It shows the effects of business operations on its assets, liabilities and capital.

Format of Comparative Balance Sheet

Comparative Balance Sheet
as at ...

Particulars	Previous Year (₹)	Current Year (₹)	Absolute Change (Increase or Decrease) (₹)	Percentage Change (Increase or Decrease) (%)
I. EQUITY AND LIABILITIES				
1. Shareholders' Funds				
(a) Share Capital				
(i) Equity Share Capital	...	...	...	...
(ii) Preference Share Capital	...	...	...	...
(b) Reserves and Surplus	...	...	...	...
2. Non-current Liabilities				
(a) Long-term Borrowings	...	...	...	...
(b) Long-term Provisions	...	...	...	...
3. Current Liabilities				
(a) Short-term Borrowings	...	...	...	...
(b) Trade Payables	...	...	...	...
(c) Other Current Liabilities	...	...	...	...
(d) Short-term Provisions	...	...	...	...
Total	...	...	...	...
II. ASSETS				
1. Non-current Assets				
(a) Property, Plant and Equipment and Intangible Assets				
(i) Property, Plant and Equipment	...	...	...	...
(ii) Intangible Assets	...	...	...	...
(b) Non-current Investments	...	...	...	...
(c) Long-term Loans and Advances	...	...	...	...
2. Current Assets				
(a) Current Investments	...	...	...	...
(b) Inventories	...	...	...	...
(c) Trade Receivables	...	...	...	...
(d) Cash and Cash Equivalents	...	...	...	...
(e) Short-term Loans and Advances	...	...	...	...
(f) Other Current Assets	...	...	...	...
Total	...	...	...	...

Common Size Statements

The statement wherein figures reported are converted into percentage to some common base is known as a common size statement. Each percentage shows the relation of the individual item to its respective total.

Objectives or Significance of Common Size Statements

Objectives or significance of common size statement are

(i) To presents the change in various items in relation to revenue from operations, total assets or total liabilities.

(ii) To establish a relationship.

(iii) To provide for a common base for comparison.

Limitations of Common Size Statements

The limitations of common size statements are as follows

(i) It can be misleading for a business that is impacted by seasonal fluctuations.

(ii) In such statement, time value of money is not considered.

(iii) This analysis does not prove to be very useful for important decision-making.

(iv) It does not provide meaningful disclosure while comparing common size statements of two or more years.

Types of Common Size Statements

There are two types of common size statements, *viz.* common size of profit and loss or income statement and common size balance sheet.

Common Size Statement of Profit and Loss

The statement in which net sales figure is assumed to be 100 and all other figures are expressed as a percentage of sales is known as common size income statement.

Objectives of Common Size Statement of Profit and Loss

The objectives of common size income statement is as follows

(i) It helps in analysing the changes in individual item of income statement.

(ii) It helps to study the trend in different items of income and expenditure.

Format of Common Size Statement of Profit and Loss

Common Size Statement of Profit and Loss
for the year ended ...

Particulars	Absolute Amounts		Percentage of Revenue from Operations (Net Sales)	
	Previous Year (₹)	Current Year (₹)	Previous Year (%)	Current Year (%)
(1)	(3)	(2)	(4)	(5)
I. Revenue from Operations (Net sales)	...	...	...	...
II. Other Income	...	...	...	...
III. Total Revenue (I + II)	...	...	...	...
IV. Expenses				
(a) Cost of Materials Consumed	...	...	...	...
(b) Purchases of Stock-in trade	...	...	...	...
(c) Changes in Inventories of Finished Goods, Work-in-progress and Stock-in-trade	...	...	...	...
(d) Employess Benefit Expenses	...	...	...	...
(e) Finance Cost	...	...	...	...
(f) Depreciation and Amortization	...	...	...	...
(g) Other Expenses	...	...	...	...
Total Expenses	...	...	...	...
V. Profit before Tax (III – IV)	...	...	...	...
VI. (–) Income Tax	...	...	...	...
VII. Profit after Tax (V – VI)	...	...	...	...

Common Size Balance Sheet

In common size balance sheet, the total of assets and liabilities is assumed to be 100 and all figures are expressed as a percentage of the total assets or total liabilities.

Objectives of Common Size Balance Sheet

The objectives of common size balance sheet are as follows

(i) It helps in analysing the changes in individual item of balance sheet.

(ii) It helps to see the trend of different items of assets, equity and liabilities.

Format of Common Size Balance Sheet

Common Size Balance Sheet
as at ...

Particulars	Absolute Amounts		Percentage of Balance Sheet Total	
	Previous Year (₹)	Current Year (₹)	Previous Year (%)	Current Year (%)
(1)	(2)	(3)	(4)	(5)
I. **EQUITY AND LIABILITIES**				
1. **Shareholders' Funds**				
(a) Share Capital				
(i) Equity Share Capital	...	...	...	...
(ii) Preference Share Capital	...	...	...	...
(b) Reserves and Surplus	...	...	...	...
2. **Non-current Liabilities**				
(a) Long-term Borrowings	...	...	...	...
(b) Long-term Provisions	...	...	...	...
3. **Current Liabilities**				
(a) Short-term Borrowings	...	...	...	...
(b) Trade Payables	...	...	...	...
(c) Other Current Liabilities	...	...	...	...
(d) Short-term Provisions	...	...	...	...
Total	...	...	100	100
II. **ASSETS**				
1. **Non-current Assets**				
(a) Property, Plant and Equipment and Intangible Assets				
(i) Property, Plant and Equipment	...	...	...	...
(ii) Intangible Assets	...	...	...	...
(b) Non-current Investments	...	...	...	...
(c) Long-term Loans and Advances	...	...	...	...
2. **Current Assets**				
(a) Current Investments	...	...	...	...
(b) Inventories	...	...	...	...
(c) Trade Receivables	...	...	...	...
(d) Cash and Cash Equivalents	...	...	...	...
(e) Short-term Loans and Advances	...	...	...	...
(f) Other Current Assets	...	...	...	...
Total	...	...	100	100

PYQs Previous Years' Questions

1/2 Marks Questions

1. What is meant by inter-firm analysis? *ISC 2023*

2. Which one of the following is not a tool for analysing the financial statements of a company? *ISC Sem II 2022*
   (a) Comparative statements
   (b) Revaluation account
   (c) Cash flow statement
   (d) Ratio analysis

3. From the following particulars of Supreme Ltd., you are required to prepare its common size balance sheet as at 31st March, 2021. *ISC Sem II 2022*

Particulars	31st March, 2021 (₹)
Shareholders' Funds	6,00,000
Non-current Assets	8,00,000
Working Capital	1,00,000
Current Liabilities	1,00,000
Total Debt	4,00,000

KEY IDEA

'Total debt' is the sum of non-current liabilities and current liabilities.

4. Which one of the following analysis is considered as a dynamic analysis? *ISC Sem II Specimen 2022*
   (a) Vertical analysis
   (b) Horizontal analysis
   (c) Internal analysis
   (d) External analysis

5. You are required to prepare a comparative statement of profit and loss from the following particulars of Nishant Ltd. *ISC Sem II Specimen 2022*

Particulars	Note No.	31st March 2021 (₹)	31st March 2020 (₹)
Revenue from Operations		4,00,000	3,00,000
Cost of Raw Materials Consumed		2,00,000	1,50,000
Changes in Inventories of Raw Materials		25,000	(12,500)

KEY IDEA

Changes in inventories of raw materials will be calculated as 25,000 – (12,500) = ₹ 37,500

6. Mention any two commonly used tools for comparison of financial statements. *ISC 2019*

7. Give any two differences between horizontal analysis and vertical analysis of financial statements. *ISC 2018*

8. What is a common size balance sheet? *ISC 2016*

9. Give any two objectives of preparing common size statements. *ISC 2015*

3 Marks Questions

10. From the following data of Horizon Ltd. you are required to prepare a comparative statement of profit and loss. ***ISC 2023***

Particulars	31st March, 2022	31st March, 2021
Revenue from Operations (% of Other income)	100%	100%
Other Income	₹ 1,00,000	₹ 50,000
Cost of Materials Consumed	₹ 50,000	₹ 20,000
Depreciation and Amortization Expenses	₹ 10,000	₹ 5,000

11. From the following particulars of Bharti Ltd., you are required to prepare a common size balance sheet as at 31st March, 2022. ***ISC Specimen 2023***

Particulars	31st March, 2022 (₹)
Shareholders' Funds	14,00,000
Current Liabilities	2,00,000
Total Equity and Liabilities	20,00,000
Non-current Assets	15,00,000

KEY IDEA

Total equity and liabilities means total of the balance sheet.

12. From the following data, prepare a comparative statement of profit and loss of Simon Ltd. ***ISC 2015***

Particulars	31st March, 2014 (₹)	31st March, 2013 (₹)
Revenue from Operations	15,00,000	12,00,000
Other Income	30,000	20,000
Cost of Materials Consumed	7,00,000	5,50,000

13. From the following data, prepare common size balance sheet of Mint Ltd. ***ISC 2015***

Particulars	31st March, 2014 (₹)	31st March, 2013 (₹)
Share Capital	1,50,000	1,20,000
Reserves and Surplus	30,000	30,000
Trade Payables	20,000	40,000
Property, Plant and Equipment	2,00,000	1,90,000

6 Marks Questions

14. Prepare a comparative statement of profit and loss of cosmos Ltd. from the following information. ***ISC 2020***

Particulars	31st March, 2019	31st March, 2018
Revenue from Operations	₹ 20,00,000	₹ 10,00,000
Purchases of Stock-in-trade	₹ 12,00,000	₹ 6,00,000
Charge in Inventories of Stock-in-trade	25% of purchases of stock-in-trade	20% of purchases of stock-in-trade
Other Expenses	₹ 1,00,000	₹ 80,000
Tax Rate	40%	40%

KEY IDEA

Tax will be calculated on 'Profit before tax'. Profit before tax can be computed by deducting total revenue from total expenses.

15. From the following data, prepare a common size balance sheet of Palms Ltd. as at 31st March, 2018 *ISC 2019*

(All calculations upto two decimal places)

Particulars	31st March, 2018 (₹)
Share Capital	24,00,000
Trade Payables	2,40,000
Property, Plant and Equipment	20,00,000
Fixed Assets (Intangible)	2,00,000
Reserves and Surplus	3,60,000
Cash and Bank Balances	8,00,000
Short-term Loans and Advances	2,00,000
Short-term Borrowings	40,000
Long-term Borrowings	1,60,000

16. From the following information, prepare a common size statement of profit and loss of Prudence Ltd for the year ending 31st March, 2017 *ISC 2018*

Particulars	31st March, 2017 (₹)
Revenue from Operations	20,00,000
Purchases	15,00,000
Changes in Inventories	1,00,000
Other Income (Dividend received)	40,000
Depreciation and Amortization Expenses	60,000
Tax Rate @ 40%	

17. From the following information, prepare a comparative statement of profit and loss of Matrix Ltd. *ISC 2017*

Particulars	31st March, 2016 (₹)	31st March, 2015 (₹)
Revenue from Operations	3,00,000	2,50,000
Cost of Material Consumed	1,70,000	1,50,000
Interest from Investments	20,000	20,000
Employee Benefit Expenses	10,000	10,000
Tax Rate	50%	50%

18. From the following data, prepare a common size statement of profit and loss of Nicholson Ltd. *ISC 2016*

Particulars	31st March, 2015	31st March, 2014
Revenue from Operations	₹ 6,00,000	₹ 4,00,000
Cost of Materials Consumed	60% of Revenue from Operations	50% of Revenue from Operations
Finance Cost	₹ 10,000	₹ 8,000
Tax Rate	40% of Profit before Tax	40% of Profit before Tax

10 Marks Question

19. From the following data, prepare a common size balance sheet of Teak Wood Ltd. *ISC 2014*

Note Current year's figures appear in the first column and the previous year's figures are in the second column.

Particulars	31st March, 2013 (₹)	31st March, 2012 (₹)
Share Capital	3,00,000	2,40,000
Reserves and Surplus	80,000	70,000
Trade Payables	1,00,000	1,10,000
Trade Receivables	1,90,000	1,80,000
Short-term Provision	40,000	15,000
Property, Plant and Equipment and Intangible Assets	2,90,000	2,30,000
Long-term Provision	80,000	65,000
Current Investments	10,000	8,000
Inventory	1,01,000	72,000
Cash and Cash Equivalents	9,000	10,000

Additional Questions

1. From the statement of profit and loss, prepare comparative income statement or statement of profit and loss of Sai Ram Ltd

Particulars	2013 (₹)	2012 (₹)
I. **Income**		
Revenue from Operations	66,00,000	60,00,000
Other Income	1,20,000	1,20,000
Total	67,20,000	61,20,000
II. **Expenses**		
Purchases of Stock-in-trade	48,00,000	46,00,000
Changes in Inventories of Stock-in-trade	2,40,000	2,00,000
Employees Benefit Expenses	1,80,000	1,40,000
Finance Cost	1,20,000	1,20,000
Other Expenses	1,80,000	1,60,000
Total	55,20,000	52,20,000
III. **Profit** (I – II)		
Tax is Payable @ 50%	12,00,000	9,00,000

2. From the following balance sheet of Saransh Ltd, as at 31st March, 2012 and 2011, prepare a comparative balance sheet

Particulars	Note No.	2011-12 (₹)	2010-11 (₹)
I. **EQUITY AND LIABILITIES**			
1. **Shareholders' Funds**			
(a) Share Capital		2,80,000	1,80,000
(b) Reserves and Surplus		1,00,000	1,00,000
2. **Non-current Liabilities**			
Long-term Borrowings		80,000	20,000
3. **Current Liabilities**			
Trade Payables		50,000	30,000
Total		5,10,000	3,30,000

Particulars	Note No.	2011-12 (₹)	2010-11 (₹)
II. **ASSETS**			
1. **Non-current Assets**			
(a) Property, Plant and Equipment and Intangible Assets			
(i) Property, Plant and Equipment		2,80,000	1,80,000
(ii) Intangible Assets		50,000	30,000
(b) Non-current Investments		80,000	50,000
2. **Current Assets**			
(a) Inventories		70,000	30,000
(b) Cash and Cash Equivalents		30,000	40,000
Total		5,10,000	3,30,000

3. From the following balance sheet of Sun Ltd, as at 31st March, 2012 and 2011, prepare a common size balance sheet

Particulars	Note No.	2011-12 (₹)	2010-11 (₹)
I. **EQUITY AND LIABILITIES**			
1. **Shareholders' Funds**			
(a) Share Capital		40,00,000	30,00,000
(b) Reserves and Surplus		6,00,000	4,00,000
2. **Non-current Liabilities**			
Long-term Borrowings		12,00,000	10,00,000
3. **Current Liabilities**			
Trade Payables		2,00,000	6,00,000
Total		60,00,000	50,00,000
II. **ASSETS**			
1. **Non-current Assets**			
(a) Property, Plant and Equipment and Intangible Assets			
(i) Property, Plant and Equipment		40,00,000	30,00,000
(ii) Intangible Assets		2,00,000	6,00,000
2. **Current Assets**			
(a) Inventories		12,00,000	10,00,000
(b) Cash and Cash Equivalents		6,00,000	4,00,000
Total		60,00,000	50,00,000

4. Prepare common size statement of profit and loss from the following statement of profit and loss

Particulars	31st March, 2013 (₹)	31st March, 2012 (₹)
I. **Income**		
Revenue from Operations (Net sales)	5,00,000	5,00,000
Other Income	5,500	5,000
Total	5,05,500	5,05,000
II. **Expenses**		
Purchases of Stock-in-trade	3,50,000	3,25,000
Changes in Inventories of Stock-in-trade	24,000	25,000
Employees Benefit Expenses	49,000	40,000
Other Expenses	45,000	58,750
Total	4,68,000	4,48,750
III. **Profit** (I – II)	37,500	56,250

Additional information

	2013 (₹)	2012 (₹)
Other Expenses Include		
Provision for Tax	37,500	56,250

Explanations

1. This analysis is a comparison of financial statements of two or more enterprises for the same accounting period.

Common Mistake Students usually get confused in the words intra-firm and inter-firm. Intra-firm means within the firm and inter-firm means outside the firm.

2. (b) Revaluation account

3.

Common Size Balance Sheet

Particulars	31st March, 2021 (₹)	% of Balance Sheet
I. **EQUITY AND LIABILITIES**		
Shareholders' Funds	6,00,000	60%
Non-current Liabilities	3,00,000	30%
Current Liabilities	1,00,000	10%
Total	10,00,000	100%
II. **Assets**		
Current Assets (WN)	2,00,000	20%
Non-current Assets	8,00,000	80%
	10,00,000	100%

Working Note

Working Capital = Current Assets – Current Liabilities

1,00,000 = Current Assets – 1,00,000

∴ Current Assets = ₹ 2,00,000

4. (b) Horizontal analysis

Concept Enhancer In such type of analysis, financial statements for a number of years are reviewed and analysed.

5.

Comparative Statement of Profit and Loss
for the years ended 31st March, 2021 and 2020

Particulars	31st March, 2020 (₹)	31st March, 2021 (₹)	Absolute Change (₹)	Percentage Change (%)
I. Revenue from Operations	3,00,000	4,00,000	1,00,000	33.33 %
II. Expenses				
(i) Cost of Raw Material	1,50,000	2,00,000	50,000	33.33 %
(ii) Changes in Inventories of Raw Material	(12,500)	25,000	37,500	300 %
Total Expenses	1,37,500	2,25,000	87,500	63.63 %
III. Profit before Tax (I – II)	1,62,500	1,75,000	12,500	7.692 %
(–) Tax	(–)	(–)	(–)	(–)
IV. Profit after Tax	1,62,500	1,75,000	12,500	7.692 %

6. Two commonly used tools for comparison of financial statements are (any two)

(i) Comparative financial statements
(ii) Common size statements
(iii) Ratio analysis
(iv) Cash flow statements

7. Difference between horizontal and vertical analysis

Basis	Horizontal analysis	Vertical analysis
Meaning	Horizontal analysis is a procedure in the fundamental analysis in which the amount of financial information over a certain period of time is compared line by line in order to make related decisions.	Vertical analysis is the method of analysis of financial statements where each line item is listed as a percentage of another item to assist decision-making.
Objective	The main purpose of horizontal analysis is to compare line items to calculate the changes over time.	Main purpose of vertical analysis is to compare changes in percentage terms.

8. Common size balance sheet shows the percentage relation of each asset/liability to total assets/liabilities including capital. In this, total assets or total equity and liabilities are taken as 100 and all figures are expressed as percentage of the total.

9. The objectives of preparing common size statements are as under
   (i) To analyse change in individual item of the financial statements.
   (ii) To study the trend in different items of financial statements.

10.

Comparative Statement of Profit and Loss
for the years ended 31st March, 2021 and 2022

	Particulars	Note No.	31st March, 2021(₹) (A)	31st March, 2022 (₹) (B)	Absolute Change (₹) (Increase/ Decrease) (C= B– A)	Percentage (Increase/ Decrease) (%) $\left(D=\frac{C}{A}\times 100\right)$
I.	Revenue from Operations		1,00,000	1,00,000	—	—
II.	Other Income (Note)		1,00,000	1,00,000	—	—
III.	**Total Revenue** (I + II)		2,00,000	2,00,000	—	—
IV.	**Expenses**					
	(a) Cost of Materials Consumed		20,000	50,000	30,000	150%
	(b) Depreciation and Amortization		5,000	10,000	5,000	100%
	Total Expenses		25,000	60,000	35,000	140%
V.	**Profit before Tax** (III – IV)		1,75,000	1,40,000	(35,000)	20%

11.

Common Size Balance Sheet of Bharti Ltd.
as at 31st March, 2022

Particulars	31st March, 2022 (₹)	% of Balance Sheet Total
I. **EQUITY AND LIABILITIES**		
1. Shareholders' Funds	14,00,000	70
2. Non-current Liabilities	4,00,000	20
3. Current Liabilities	2,00,000	10
Total	20,00,000	100
II. **ASSETS**		
1. Non-current Assets	15,00,000	75
2. Current Assets	5,00,000	25
Total	20,00,000	100

12.

In the Books of Simon Ltd

Comparative Statement of Profit and Loss

for the year ended 31st March, 2014

Particulars	31st March, 2013 (₹)	31st March, 2014 (₹)	Absolute Value (₹)	Percentage (%)
I. Revenue from Operations	12,00,000	15,00,000	3,00,000	25
II. Other Income	20,000	30,000	10,000	50
III. Total Revenue (I + II)	12,20,000	15,30,000	3,10,000	25.41
IV. Expenses				
Cost of Materials Consumed	5,50,000	7,00,000	1,50,000	27.27
V. Profit before Tax (III – IV)	6,70,000	8,30,000	1,60,000	23.88

13.

In the Books of Mini Ltd

Common Size Balance Sheet

as at 31st March, 2014

Particulars	Absolute Amount		Percentage of Balance Sheet Total	
	31st March, 2013 (₹)	31st March, 2014 (₹)	31st March, 2013 (%)	31st March, 2014 (%)
I. **EQUITY AND LIABILITIES**				
1. **Shareholders' Funds**				
(a) Share Capital	1,20,000	1,50,000	63.16	75
(b) Reserves and Surplus	30,000	30,000	15.79	15
2. **Current Liabilities** (Trade payables)	40,000	20,000	21.05	10
Total	1,90,000	2,00,000	100	100
II. **ASSETS**				
1. **Non-current Assets**				
(a) Property, Plant and Equipment	1,90,000	2,00,000	100	100
Total	1,90,000	2,00,000	100	100

14.

Comparative Statement of Profit and Loss of Cosmos Ltd.

Particulars	Note No.	2017-18 (₹)	2018-19 (₹)	Absolute Change (₹)	Percentage Change (%)
I. Revenue from Operations		10,00,000	20,00,000	10,00,000	100
		10,00,000	20,00,000	10,00,000	100
II. Expenses					
(a) Purchases of Stock-in-trade		6,00,000	12,00,000	6,00,000	100
(b) Change in Inventories of Stock-in-trade		1,20,000	3,00,000	1,80,000	150
(c) Other Expenses		80,000	1,00,000	20,000	25
		8,00,000	16,00,000	8,00,000	100
III. Profit before Tax (I – II)		2,00,000	4,00,000	2,00,000	100
IV. (–) Tax @ 40%		(80,000)	(1,60,000)	(80,000)	(100)
V. Profit after Tax		1,20,000	2,40,000	1,20,000	100

15.

Common Size Balance Sheet
as at 31st March, 2018

Particulars	Note No.	Absolute Amount 2018 (₹)	% of Balance Sheet Total 2018 (₹)
I. **EQUITY AND LIABILITIES**			
1. **Shareholders' Fund**			
(a) Share Capital		24,00,000	75
(b) Reserve and Surplus		3,60,000	11.25
2. **Non-current Liabilities**			
(a) Long-term Borrowings		1,60,000	5
3. **Current Liabilities**			
(a) Short-term Borrowings		40,000	1.25
(b) Trade Payables		2,40,000	7.50
Total		32,00,000	100
II. **ASSETS**			
1. **Non-current Assets**			
(a) Property, Plant and Equipment and Intangible Assets			
(i) Property, Plant and Equipment		20,00,000	62.50
(ii) Intangible Assets		2,00,000	6.25
2. **Current Assets**			
(a) Cash and Cash Equivalents		8,00,000	25
(b) Short-term Loans and Advances		2,00,000	6.25
Total		32,00,000	100

16.

In the Books of Prudence Ltd
Common Size Statement of Profit and Loss
for the year ending 31st March, 2017

Particulars	Note No.	Absolute Amount (₹)	Percentage of Revenue from Operations
I. Revenue from Operations (Net sales)		20,00,000	100
II. Other Income (Dividend received)		40,000	2
III. Total Revenue (I + II)		20,40,000	102
IV. Expenses			
(a) Purchase		15,00,000	75
(b) Changes in Inventories		1,00,000	5
(c) Depreciation and Amortization Expenses		60,000	3
Total Expenses		16,60,000	83
V. Profit before Tax (III – IV)		3,80,000	19
VI. (–) Tax @ 40%		(1,52,000)	(7.6)
VII. Profit after Tax (V – VI)		2,28,000	11.4

17.

In the Books of Matrix Ltd
Comparative Statement of Profit and Loss
for the year ended at 31st March, 2015 and 2016

Particulars	Absolute Value		Change	
	2014-15 (₹)	2015-16 (₹)	Absolute Change (₹)	Percentage Change (%)
I. Revenue from Operations	2,50,000	3,00,000	50,000	20
II. Other Incomes	20,000	20,000	—	—
III. Total Revenue (I + II)	2,70,000	3,20,000	50,000	18.52

Particulars	Absolute Value		Change	
	2014-15 (₹)	2015-16 (₹)	Absolute Change (₹)	Percentage Change (%)
IV. Expenses				
(a) Cost of Material Consumed	1,50,000	1,70,000	20,000	13.33
(b) Employee Benefit Expenses	10,000	10,000		—
Total Expenses	1,60,000	1,80,000	20,000	12.5
V. Profit before Tax (III–IV)	1,10,000	1,40,000	30,000	27.27
VI. (–) Tax @ 50%	55,000	70,000	15,000	27.27
VII. Profit after Tax (V – VI)	55,000	70,000	15,000	27.27

18. **In the Books of Nicholson Ltd**
Common Size Statement of Profit and Loss
for the year ended 31st March, 2014 and 2015

Particulars	Absolute Amount		Percentage of Revenue from Operations	
	2014 (₹)	2015 (₹)	2014 (%)	2015 (%)
I. Revenue from Operations	4,00,000	6,00,000	100	100
II. Expenses				
(a) Cost of Materials Consumed	2,00,000	3,60,000	50.00	60.00
(b) Finance Cost	8,000	10,000	2.00	1.67
Total Expenses	2,08,000	3,70,000	52.00	61.67
III. Profit before Tax (I – II)	1,92,000	2,30,000	48.00	38.33
IV. (–) Tax @ 40%	(76,800)	(92,000)	(19.20)	(15.33)
V. Profit after Tax (III – IV)	1,15,200	1,38,000	28.80	23

19. **In the Books of Teak Wood Ltd**
Common Size Balance Sheet
as at 31st March, 2012 and 31st March, 2013

Particulars	Note No.	Absolute Amount		% of Balance Sheet Total	
		2012 (₹)	2013 (₹)	2012 (%)	2013 (%)
I. **EQUITY AND LIABILITIES**					
1. **Shareholders' Funds**					
(a) Share Capital		2,40,000	3,00,000	48	50.00
(b) Reserves and Surplus		70,000	80,000	14	13.33
2. **Non-current Liabilities**					
(a) Long-term Provision		65,000	80,000	13	13.33
3. **Current Liabilities**					
(a) Trade Payables		1,10,000	1,00,000	22	16.67
(b) Short-term Provisions		15,000	40,000	3	6.67
Total		5,00,000	6,00,000	100	100
II. **ASSETS**					
1. **Non-current Assets**					
(a) Property, Plant and Equipment and Intangible Assets		2,30,000	2,90,000	46	48.33
2. **Current Assets**					
(a) Current Investments		8,000	10,000	1.6	1.67
(b) Inventory		72,000	1,01,000	14.4	16.83
(c) Trade Receivables		1,80,000	1,90,000	36	31.67
(d) Cash and Cash Equivalents		10,000	9,000	2	1.50
Total		5,00,000	6,00,000	100	100

Additional Questions

1.

In the Books of Sai Ram Ltd
Comparative Statement of Profit and Loss
for the years ended 31st March, 2012 and 2013

Particulars	31st March, 2012 (₹)	31st March, 2013 (₹)	Absolute Change (Increase or Decrease) (₹)	Percentage Change (Increase or Decrease) (%)
I. Revenue from Operations (Sales)	60,00,000	66,00,000	6,00,000	10.00
II. Other Income	1,20,000	1,20,000	—	—
III. Total Revenue (I + II)	61,20,000	67,20,000	6,00,000	9.80
IV. Expenses				
(a) Purchases of Stock-in-trade	46,00,000	48,00,000	2,00,000	4.35
(b) Changes in Inventories of Stock-in-trade	2,00,000	2,40,000	40,000	20.00
(c) Employess Benefit Expenses	1,40,000	1,80,000	40,000	28.57
(d) Finance Costs	1,20,000	1,20,000	—	—
(e) Other Expenses	1,60,000	1,80,000	20,000	12.50
Total Expenses	52,20,000	55,20,000	3,00,000	5.75
V. Profit before Tax (III – IV)	9,00,000	12,00,000	3,00,000	33.33
(–) Income Tax @ 50%	(4,50,000)	(6,00,000)	(1,50,000)	(33.33)
VI. Profit after Tax	4,50,000	6,00,000	1,50,000	33.33

2.

In the Books of Saransh Ltd
Comparative Balance Sheet
as at 31st March, 2011 and 2012

Particulars	2010-11 (₹)	2011-12 (₹)	Absolute Change (Increase or Decrease) (₹)	Percentage Change (Increase or Decrease) (%)
I. EQUITY AND LIABILITIES				
1. **Shareholders' Funds**				
(a) Share Capital	1,80,000	2,80,000	1,00,000	55.55
(b) Reserves and Surplus	1,00,000	1,00,000	—	—
2. **Non-current Liabilities**				
Long-term Borrowings	20,000	80,000	60,000	300
3. **Current Liabilities**				
Trade Payables	30,000	50,000	20,000	66.67
Total	3,30,000	5,10,000	1,80,000	54.54
II. ASSETS				
1. **Non-current Assets**				
(a) Property, Plant and Equipment and Intangible Assets				
(i) Property, Plant and Equipment	1,80,000	2,80,000	1,00,000	55.55
(ii) Intangible Assets	30,000	50,000	20,000	66.67
(b) **Non-current Investments**	50,000	80,000	30,000	60.00
2. **Current Assets**				
(a) Inventories	30,000	70,000	40,000	133.33
(b) Cash and Cash Equivalents	40,000	30,000	(10,000)	(25)
Total	3,30,000	5,10,000	1,80,000	54.54

3.

In the Books of Sun Ltd
Common Size Balance Sheet
as at 31st March, 2011 and 2012

Particulars	Absolute Amount 2010-11 (₹)	Absolute Amount 2011-12 (₹)	Percentage of Total Revenue 2010-11	Percentage of Total Revenue 2011-12
I. **EQUITY AND LIABILITIES**				
1. **Shareholders' Funds**				
(a) Share Capital	30,00,000	40,00,000	60	66.7
(b) Reserves and Surplus	4,00,000	6,00,000	8	10.0
2. **Non-current Liabilities**				
Long-term Borrowings	10,00,000	12,00,000	20	20.0
3. **Current Liabilities**				
Trade Payables	6,00,000	2,00,000	12	3.3
Total	50,00,000	60,00,000	100	100.0
II. **ASSETS**				
1. **Non-current Assets**				
(a) Property, Plant and Equipment and Intangible Assets				
(i) Property, Plant and Equipment	30,00,000	40,00,000	60	66.7
(ii) Intangible Assets	6,00,000	2,00,000	12	3.3
2. **Current Assets**				
(a) Inventories	10,00,000	12,00,000	20	20.0
(b) Cash and Cash Equivalents	4,00,000	6,00,000	8	10.0
Total	50,00,000	60,00,000	100	100

4.

In the Books of ...
Common Size Statement of Profit and Loss
for the year ended 31st March, 2012 and 2013

Particulars	Absolute Amount		Percentage of Revenue from Operations (Net sales)	
	2012 (₹)	2013 (₹)	2012 (%)	2013 (%)
I. Revenue from Operations (Net sales)	5,00,000	5,00,000	100.00	100.00
II. Other Income	5,000	5,500	1.00	1.10
III. Total Revenue (I + II)	5,05,000	5,05,500	101.00	101.10
IV. Expenses				
(a) Purchases of Stock-in-trade	3,25,000	3,50,000	65.00	70.00
(b) Changes in Inventories of Stock-in-trade	25,000	24,000	5.00	4.80
(c) Employees Benefit Expenses	40,000	49,000	8.00	9.80
(d) Other Expenses	2,500	7,500	0.50	1.50
Total Expenses	3,92,500	4,30,500	78.50	86.10
V. Profit before Tax (III – IV)	1,12,500	75,000	22.50	15.00
VI. Tax	56,250	37,500	11.25	7.50
VII. Profit after Tax (V – VI)	56,250	37,500	11.25	7.50

CHAPTER TEST

01 Mark Questions

1. Which of the following is not a technique of financial statements analysis?
(a) Ratio analysis
(b) Statement of profit and loss
(c) Common size balance sheet
(d) None of these

2. Which of the following analysis reviews and analyses the financial statements for a number of years?
(a) Inter-firm anaysis
(b) Static analysis
(c) External analysis
(d) Dynamic analysis

3. Which of the following analysis deals with different items of the same period?
(a) Horizontal analysis
(b) Vertical analysis
(c) External analysis
(d) Internal analysis

4. If non-current assets of a company are ₹ 5,00,000 and its current assets are ₹ 3,00,000, at what percentage current assets will be shown in the common size balance sheet?
(a) 60%
(b) 62.5%
(c) 37.5%
(d) None of these

5. List any one advantage and limitation of financial statements analysis.

6. Name two objectives of preparing comparative statement of profit and loss.

7. Which item is assumed 100% while preparing common size balance sheet?

03 Marks Questions

8. Prepare comparative statement of profit and loss from the following

Particulars	Note No.	31st March 2022 (₹)	31st March 2021 (₹)
Revenue from Operations		3,00,000	2,00,000
Expenses		2,10,000	1,20,000
Other Income		36,000	40,000

9. Prepare common size balance sheet from the following information

Particulars	Note No.	31st March, 2022 (₹)	31st March, 2021 (₹)
Shareholders' Funds		9,00,000	6,00,000
Non-current Liabilities		3,00,000	3,00,000
Current Liabilities		3,00,000	1,00,000
Non-current Assets		10,50,000	7,00,000
Current Assets		4,50,000	3,00,000

06 Marks Questions

10. Convert the following statements of profit and loss into common size statement of profit and loss

Particulars	Note No.	31st March, 2013 (₹)	31st March, 2012 (₹)
I. **Income**			
Revenue from Operations		18,01,000	15,00,000
Other Income		20,000	15,000
Total		18,21,000	15,15,000

Particulars	Note No.	31st March, 2013 (₹)	31st March, 2012 (₹)
II. **Expenses**			
Purchases of Stock-in-trade		10,22,500	9,00,000
Changes in Inventories of Stock-in-trade		(10,000)	10,000
Employees Benefit Expenses		3,30,000	3,00,000
Other Expenses		2,00,000	1,70,000
Total		15,42,500	13,80,000
III. **Net Profit** (I – II)		2,78,500	1,35,000

11. Prepare comparative statement of profit and loss from the following

Particulars	31st March, 2012 (₹)	31st March, 2011 (₹)
Revenue from Operations (Sales)	30,00,000	20,00,000
Cost of Material Consumed	1,00,000	2,00,000
Other Expenses	20,00,000	10,00,000
Other Income	3,60,000	4,00,000
Income Tax	50%	50%
Purchases of Stock-in-trade	2,00,000	2,00,000

12. The balance sheet of Saraswati Ltd as at 31st March, 2012 and 2013 are given below

Balance Sheet
as at 31st March, 2013 and 2012

Particulars	2013 (₹)	2012 (₹)
I. **EQUITY AND LIABILITIES**		
1. **Shareholders' Funds**		
(a) Share Capital	27,400	27,400
(b) Reserves and Surplus	7,000	15,200
2. **Non-current Liabilities**		
Long-term Borrowings: Secured Loans	23,200	10,000
Unsecured Loans	20,600	59,600
3. **Current Liabilities**		
(a) Short-term Borrowings (Secured bank overdraft)	5,000	12,500
(b) Trade Payables	2,000	10,000
(c) Other Current Liabilities	300	5,000
(d) Short-term Provisions	500	2,300
Total	86,000	1,42,000
II. **ASSETS**		
1. **Non-current Assets**		
(a) Property, Plant and Equipment	43,000	56,800
(b) Non-current Investments	400	600
2. **Current Assets**		
(a) Inventories	21,600	42,600
(b) Trade Receivables	14,000	33,000
(c) Cash and Cash Equivalents	7,000	9,000
Total	86,000	1,42,000

Prepare common size balance sheet for Saraswati Ltd for 2013 and 2012 and comment on the changes.

13. From the following balance sheet of Suhana as on 31st March, 2012 and 2011, prepare a comparative balance sheet.

(₹ in Lakh)

Particulars	Note No.	2011-12 (₹)	2010-11 (₹)
I. **EQUITY AND LIABILITIES**			
1. **Shareholders' Funds**			
(a) Share Capital		40	30
(b) Reserves and Surplus		6	8
2. **Non-current Liabilities**			
Long-term Borrowings		18	12
3. **Current Liabilities**			
Trade Payables		6	4
Total		70	54
II. **ASSETS**			
1. **Non-current Assets**			
Property, Plant and Equipment and Intangible Assets			
(i) Property, Plant and Equipment		40	30
(ii) Intangible Assets		18	12
2. **Current Assets**			
(a) Inventories		6	8
(b) Cash and Cash Equivalents		6	4
Total		70	54

Answers

1. (b) Statement of profit and loss
2. (d) Dynamic analysis
3. (b) Vertical analysis
4. (c) 37.5%

09

Cash Flow Statement

TREND ANALYSIS 5 YEARS

Average No. of Questions Across all Sets

	Types of Questions	2023	2020	2019	2018	2017
01 Operating Activity	1/2 Marks	1	—	—	—	—
	3 Marks	—	—	—	—	—
	6 Marks	—	—	—	—	—
	10 Marks	—	—	—	—	—
02 Investing Activity	1/2 Marks	—	1	—	—	—
	3 Marks	—	—	—	—	—
	6 Marks	—	—	—	—	—
	10 Marks	—	—	1	—	—
03 Financing Activity	1/2 Marks	1	—	1	—	—
	3 Marks	—	—	—	—	—
	6 Marks	—	—	—	—	—
	10 Marks	—	—	—	—	1
04 Cash Flow Statement	1/2 Marks	—	—	1	—	1
	3 Marks	—	—	—	—	—
	6 Marks	2	—	—	—	—
	10 Marks	—	1	—	1	—

Meaning of Cash Flow Statement

Cash flow statement is a statement showing the changes in financial position of a business concern during different intervals of time in terms of cash and cash equivalents.

The Revised Accounting Standard-3 has made it mandatory for all listed companies to prepare and present a cash flow statement alongwith other financial statements on annual basis.

Cash means cash in hand and demand deposits with the bank.

Cash = Cash in Hand + Cash at Bank

Cash equivalents means 'short-term highly liquid investments that are readily convertible into known amount of cash and which are subject to an insignificant risk of change in value'.

Objectives/Importance of Cash Flow Statement

Objectives of cash flow statement are as follows

(i) Tool useful in financial planning.

(ii) Useful in efficient cash management.

(iii) Helpful in formulation of business policies.
(iv) Assists in preparation of cash budget.
(v) Used for assessment of cash flow from various activities *viz* operating, investing and financing activities.

Limitations of Cash Flow Statement

Limitations for using cash flow statement are

(i) Based on historical cost principle.
(ii) Based on secondary data.
(iii) Ignores non-cash transactions.
(iv) No adherence to basic accounting principles.
(v) Cash flow statement is not a substitute for income statement.

Classification of Business Activities to Assess Cash Flows

Accounting Standard-3 (Revised) requires that the changes resulting in inflows and outflows of cash and cash equivalents will be classified into following three activities

(i) Cash flow from operating activities
(ii) Cash flow from investing activities
(iii) Cash flow from financing activities

Cash Flow from Operating Activities

Operating activities are the principal revenue producing activities of the enterprise and other activities that are not investing or financing activities.

Cash flow from operating activities is exhibited as follows

Operating Activities

Cash Inflow
(a) Cash sales
(b) Cash received from debtors
(c) Cash received from commission and fees
(d) Royalty

Cash Outflow
(a) Cash purchases
(b) Payment to creditors
(c) Cash operating expenses
(d) Payment of wages
(e) Income tax

Calculation of Cash Flow from Operating Activities

Particulars		Amt (₹)
Cash Flow from Operating Activities		
Net Profit before Taxation (Working Note)		...
Adjustment for Non-cash and Non-operating Items		
(+) Items to be Added		
Depreciation	...	
Amortised Expenses (Such as discount on issue of shares, share issue expenses and loss on issue of debentures, etc)	...	
Goodwill Written-off, Patents and Trademarks Amortised	...	
Interest on Borrowings and Debentures	...	
Loss on Sale of Property, Plant and Equipment and Intangible Assets	...	...
(–) Items to be Deducted		
Interest Income	...	
Dividend Income	...	
Rental Income	...	
Profit on Sale of Property, Plant and Equipment and Intangible Assets	...	(...)
Operating Profit before Working Capital Changes		...

Particulars	Amt (₹)
(+) Decrease in Current Assets and Increase in Current Liabilities	
Decrease in Stock/Inventories	...
Decrease in Debtors/Bills Receivable (Trade receivables)	...
Decrease in Accrued Incomes	...
Decrease in Prepaid Expenses	...
Increase in Creditors/Bills Payable (Trade payables)	...
Increase in Outstanding Expenses	...
Increase in Advance Incomes	...
Increase in Provision for Doubtful Debts	... ...
(–) Increase in Current Assets and Decrease in Current Liabilities	
Increase in Stock/Inventories	...
Increase in Debtors/Bills Receivable (Trade receivables)	...
Increase in Accrued Incomes	...
Increase in Prepaid Expenses	...
Decrease in Creditors/Bills Payable (Trade payables)	...
Decrease in Outstanding Expenses	...
Decrease in Advance Incomes	...
Decrease in Provision for Doubtful Debts	... (...)
Cash Generated from Operations	...
(–) Income Tax Paid (Net of tax refund received)	(...)
Net Cash from (or used in) Operating Activities	...

Note Bracket denotes minus items.

Working Note

Calculation of Net Profit before Tax

Particulars	Amt (₹)
Net Profit as per Statement of Profit and Loss or Difference between Closing Balance and Opening Balance of Statement of Profit and Loss	...
(+) Transfer to Reserves	...
Proposed Dividend for Previous Year	...
Interim Dividend Paid During the Year	...
Provision for Tax made During the Current Year	...

Difference between Net Profit and Cash from Operations

Basis	Net profit	Cash from operations
Meaning	It indicates the net result of activities carried out during an accounting year.	It indicates the cash flow as a result of operating activities.
Non-cash operating items	It is calculated after taking into account the effect of non-cash operating items such as depreciation.	It is calculated after excluding the effect of non-cash operating items, since these items represent merely the book entries.
Non-operating items	It is calculated after taking into account the effect of non-operating items such as goodwill written-off.	It is calculated after excluding the effect of non-operating items, since these items do not relate to operating activities.
Basis of calculation	It is calculated on accrual basis.	It is calculated on cash basis.
Working capital changes	For calculating net profit, changes in working capital are not considered.	For calculating cash from operations, changes in working capital are considered.

Cash Flow from Investing Activities

As per Accounting Standard-3, investing activities are the acquisition and disposal of the long-term assets and other investments, not included in cash equivalents.

Cash flow from investing activities is exhibited as follows

Investing Activities

Cash Inflow

(a) Sale of Property, Plant and Equipment and Intangible Assets
(b) Sale of investments
(c) Interest received
(d) Dividend received

Cash Outflow

(a) Purchase of Property, Plant and Equipment and Intangible Assets
(b) Purchase of investments

Cash Flow from Financing Activities

Financing activities are the activities which result in change in the size and composition of the owner's capital (including preference share capital) and borrowings (including debentures) of the enterprise from other sources.

Cash flow arising from financing activities is exhibited as follows

Financing Activities

Cash Inflow

(a) Issue of shares in cash
(b) Issue of debentures in cash
(c) Proceeds from long-term borrowings
(d) Securities premium received
(e) Interest received on calls-in-arrears
(f) Increase in balance of bank overdraft or cash credit

Cash Outflow

(a) Payment of loans
(b) Redemption of preference shares, debentures
(c) Buy-back of equity shares
(d) Payment of dividends
(e) Payment of interest
(f) Premium paid on redemption of preference shares, debentures
(g) Share issue expenses/Underwriting commission paid

Format of Cash Flow Statement

Indirect Method [As per Accounting Standard-3 (Revised)]
for the year ended...

Particulars		Amt (₹)
I. **Cash Flow from Operating Activities**		
Net Profit before Taxation		...
Adjustment for Non-cash and Non-operating Items		
(+) Items to be Added		
Depreciation	...	
Amortised Expenses (Such as discount on issue of shares, share issue expenses and loss on issue of debentures, etc)	...	
Goodwill Written-off, Patents and Trademarks Amortised	...	
Interest on Borrowings and Debentures	...	
Loss on Sale of Property, Plant and Equipment and Intangible Assets	...	...
(–) Items to be Deducted		
Interest Income	...	
Dividend Income	...	
Rental Income	...	
Profit on Sale of Property, Plant and Equipment and Intangible Assets	...	(...)
Operating Profit before Working Capital Changes		...
(+) Decrease in Current Assets and Increase in Current Liabilities		...
(–) Increase in Current Assets and Decrease in Current Liabilities		(...)
Cash Generated from Operations		...
(–) Income Tax Paid (Net of tax refund received)		(...)
Net Cash Flow from Operating Activities (or used in)		...
II. **Cash Flow from Investing Activities**		
Proceeds from Sale of Property, Plant and Equipment and Intangible Assets	...	
Proceeds from Sale of Investments	...	

Particulars		Amt (₹)
Proceeds from Sale of Intangible Assets	...	
Interest and Dividend Received (For non-financial companies only)	...	
Rent Income	...	
Purchase of Property, Plant and Equipment and Intangible Assets	(...)	
Purchase of Investments	(...)	
Purchase of Intangible Assets like Goodwill	(...)	
Net Cash from Investing Activities (or used in)		...
III. **Cash Flow from Financing Activities**		
Proceeds from Issue of Shares and Debentures	...	
Proceeds from Other Long-term Borrowings	...	
Increase/Decrease in Bank Overdraft and Cash Credit	(...)	
Final Dividend Paid	(...)	
Interim Dividend Paid	(...)	
Interest on Debentures and Loans Paid	(...)	
Repayment of Loans	(...)	
Redemption of Debentures/Preference Shares	(...)	
Share Issue Expenses	(...)	
Net Cash from Financing Activities (or used in)		...
IV. **Net Increase/Decrease in Cash and Cash Equivalents** (I + II + III)		...
V. (+) **Cash and Cash Equivalents in the Beginning of the Year**		
Cash in Hand	...	
Cash at Bank	...	
Short-term Investments	...	
Marketable Securities	...	...
		...
VI. **Cash and Cash Equivalents at the End of the Year**		
Cash in Hand	...	
Cash at Bank	...	
Short-term Investments	...	
Marketable Securities	...	...

PYQs Previous Years' Questions

1/2 Marks Questions

1. During the year 2021-22, SM Ltd. issued 10,000, 10% debentures of ₹ 100 each at a discount of 10% to be redeemed after three years. The company had a balance of ₹ 60,000 in its securities premium. What amount will be added under operating activities as discount on issue of debentures written-off in the cash flow statement of SM Ltd. for the year 2021-22? ***ISC 2023***

(a) ₹ 10,00,000
(b) ₹ 60,000
(c) ₹ 1,00,000
(d) ₹ 40,000

2. While preparing its cash flow statement, will a company consider an increase in its bank overdraft as an operating activity or as a financing activity? ***ISC 2023***

3. How is interest paid on debentures considered in a cash flow statement? ***ISC Specimen 2023***

(a) As an operating activity (b) As a financing activity
(c) As an investing activity
(d) Both as an operating activity and a financing activity

4. Mention the accounting basis on which a cash flow statement is prepared. ***ISC Specimen 2023***

5. Mention whether interest due on debentures would result in inflow, outflow or no flow of cash. ***ISC Sem II 2022***

6. State with reason whether old furniture written-off would lead to inflow, outflow or no flow of cash and cash equivalents. *ISC Sem II Specimen 2022*

7. From the following extract of the balance sheet of Regal Ltd., taking into consideration the additional information, you are required to calculate the amounts of the following items to be shown in the company's cash flow statement for the year 2018-19
   (i) Property, plant and equipment and intangible assets purchased
   (ii) Property, plant and equipment and intangible assets sold
   (iii) Profit/Loss on sale property, plant and equipment and intangible assets.
   (iv) Depreciation charged on property, plant and equipment and intangible assets.

Particulars	31st March, 2019 (₹)	31st March, 2018 (₹)
Property, Plant and Equipment and Intangible Assets	6,00,000	4,90,000

Additional information
   (i) The provision for depreciation on property, plant and equipment and intangible assets stood at ₹ 1,40,000 on 31st March, 2018 and ₹ 1,80,000 on 31st March, 2019.
   (ii) During the year 2018-19, property, plant and equipment and intangible assets costing ₹ 60,000 (book value ₹ 30,000) was sold for ₹ 20,000. *ISC 2020*

8. While preparing a cash flow statement, identify the following transactions as belonging to operating activities, investing activities, financing activities, cash and cash equivalents
   (i) Bank overdraft repaid.
   (ii) Purchase of marketable securities to be sold within 90 days. *ISC 2019*

9. Mention whether the following would result in inflow, outflow or no flow of cash
   (i) Issue of fully paid bonus shares
   (ii) Cash withdrawn from bank *ISC 2019*

10. What is meant by the term cash equivalents as per Accounting Standard-3? *ISC 2017*

11. While preparing a cash flow statement, identify the following transactions as belonging to operating activities, investing activities, financing activities.
   (i) Goodwill written-off.
   (ii) Interest received by a company on its investments. *ISC 2016*

12. What is meant by an operating cycle? *ISC 2015*

13. Give two difference between net profit and cash from operations. *ISC 2013*

14. List any two types of operating activities. *ISC 2011*

15. What is meant by cash equivalents? *ISC 2010*

16. What is meant by cash flow statement? *ISC 2009*

17. List any two types of financing activity. *ISC 2008*

18. List any four types of investing activities. *ISC 2007*

6 Marks Questions

19. From the following information of Hoopla Ltd., you are required to prepare a cash flow statement (as per AS-3) for the year 2021-22. *ISC 2023*

S. No.		Particulars	Amt (₹)
(i)		Profit for the year 2021-22, before considering dividend and tax but after taking into account the following items	15,80,000
	(a)	Depreciation on Property, Plant and Equipment	5,50,000
	(b)	Interest Payable on Bank Loan	3,80,000
	(c)	Profit on Sale of Investments, the Book Value of which was ₹ 2,20,000	1,00,000
(ii)		During the year 2021-22	
	(a)	The Company	
		Paid Tax (which was provided in 2020-21)	4,40,000
		Issued 66,000 Equity Shares of ₹ 10 each	6,60,000
		Repaid Bank Loan	15,00,000
		Paid Interest on Bank Loan	3,00,000
		Paid Dividend	5,00,000
	(b)	Trade Payables Decreased by	10,000
	(c)	Cash at Bank Increased from ₹ 60,000 on 1st April, 2021 to ₹ 7,00,000 on 31st March, 2022	

20. From the following balance sheets of Rainbow Ltd., you are required to prepare a cash flow statement (as per AS-3) for the year 2021-22.

Balance Sheets of Rainbow Ltd.
as at 31st March, 2022 and 31st March, 2021

Particulars	Note No.	31st March, 2022 (₹)	31st March, 2021 (₹)
I. **EQUITY AND LIABILITIES**			
1. **Shareholders' Funds**			
(a) Share Capital (Equity)		4,00,000	4,00,000
(b) Reserves and Surplus	1	1,60,000	1,20,000
2. **Non-current Liabilities**			
Long-term Borrowings (5% Debentures)		3,50,000	2,60,000
3. **Current Liabilities**			
Short-term Provision (Provision for Tax)		30,000	25,000
Total		9,40,000	8,05,000
II. **ASSETS**			
1. **Non-current Assets**			
Property, Plant and Equipment and Intangible Assets			
Property, Plant and Equipment : Plant and Machinery		6,00,000	7,80,000
2. **Current Assets**			
Cash and Bank Balance (Cash at Bank)		3,40,000	25,000
Total		9,40,000	8,05,000

Notes to Accounts

	Particulars	31st March, 2022 (₹)	31st March, 2021 (₹)
1.	**Reserves and Surplus**		
	General Reserve	30,000	20,000
	Balance in Statement of Profit and Loss	1,30,000	1,00,000

Additional information

During the year 2021-22, the company

(i) Sold a machine for ₹ 90,000 at a loss of ₹ 10,000.

(ii) Issued the 5% debentures on 31st March, 2022, at a discount of 10%. The discount was written-off from general reserve. *ISC 2023*

21. From the following extracts of a company's balance sheet, you are required to calculate

(i) Cash from investing activities

(ii) Cash from financing activities

Particulars	31st March, 2022 (₹)	31st March, 2021 (₹)
Equity Share Capital	15,00,000	12,00,000
5% Debentures	10,00,000	8,00,000
Securities Premium	50,000	10,000
Plant and Machinery (At Cost)	10,90,000	9,00,000
Accumulated Depreciation	3,00,000	4,00,000
10% Investments	60,000	50,000
Goodwill	1,00,000	70,000

Note Dividend proposed in the years 2020-21 and 2021-22 were ₹ 42,000 and ₹ 40,000 respectively.

Additional information

During the year 2021-22, the company

(a) Issued the 5% debentures at a discount of 10% on 1st April, 2021. The discount on issue of debentures was written-off from securities premium.

(b) Provided depreciation of ₹ 1,00,000 on plant and machinery.

(c) Sold plant and machinery, the book value of which was ₹ 5,00,000 for ₹ 4,50,000. ***ISC Specimen 2023***

KEY IDEA

Assume that the investment was purchased at the beginning of the year.

22. You are required to prepare a cash flow statement of Bruno Ltd. (as per AS-3) for the year 2021-22 from the following balance sheets.

Balance Sheets of Bruno Ltd.

as at 31st March, 2022 and 31st March, 2021

Particulars	Note No.	31st March, 2022 (₹)	31st March, 2021 (₹)
I. **EQUITY AND LIABILITIES**			
1. **Shareholders' Funds**			
(i) Share Capital (Equity)		5,00,000	3,50,000
(ii) Reseves and Surplus (Statement of Profit and Loss)		1,20,000	88,000
2. **Non-current Liabilities**			
Long-term Borrowings (7% Debentures)		1,50,000	2,10,000
3. **Current Liabilities**			
(i) Short-term Borrowings		39,000	46,000
(ii) Short-term Provision (Provision for Tax)		40,000	30,000
Total		8,49,000	7,24,000
II. **ASSETS**			
1. **Non-current Assets**			
(i) Property, Plant and Equipment and Intangible Assets			
(a) Property, Plant and Equipment (Plant and Machinery)		3,80,000	3,30,000
2. **Current Assets**			
Cash and Bank Balances (Cash at Bank)		4,69,000	3,94,000
Total		8,49,000	7,24,000

Notes to Accounts

Particulars	31st March, 2022 (₹)	31st March, 2021 (₹)
1. **Contingent Liability**		
Proposed Dividend	30,000	—

Additional information

During the year 2021-22

(i) Plant and machinery of ₹ 1,20,000 was purchased and some machinery was sold at a loss of ₹ 12,000.

(ii) The company charged ₹ 38,000 as depreciation on its plant and machinery.

(iii) Interest of ₹ 18,000 was paid on all borrowings. (iv) Tax paid was ₹ 25,000. ***ISC Specimen 2023***

KEY IDEA

Since there is no dividend in the previous year, dividend will not be recorded in the cash flow statement.

23. From the following particulars of Phantom Ltd., you are required to calculate

(i) Cash from operating activities (ii) Cash from investing activities

Particulars	31st March, 2021 (₹)	31st March, 2020 (₹)
Plant and Machinery (At Cost)	4,00,000	4,20,000
Accumulated Depreciation	1,30,000	1,10,000
Goodwill	70,000	90,000
Inventory	20,000	10,000
Trade Payables	15,000	25,000
Provision for Tax	30,000	20,000
Balance of Statement of Profit and Loss	1,00,000	(90,000)

Additional information

During the year 2020-21, a machine with a book value of ₹ 50,000 (accumulated depreciation ₹ 20,000) was sold at a loss of ₹ 6,000.

ISC Sem II 2022

24. From the following extracts of a company's balance sheets and the additional information, you are required to calculate cash from operating activities for the year ending 31st March, 2021. **ISC Sem II Specimen 2022**

Anjan Ltd. reported a profit of ₹ 80,000 for the year ended 31st March, 2021, after considering the following

	Amt (₹)
(i) Tax Provided During the Year	4,000
(ii) Amortisation of Patents	10,000
(iii) Profit on Sale of Vehicle	3,000
(iv) Writing-off Preliminary Expenses	2,000

(v) During the year, machinery costing ₹ 40,000 (accumulated depreciation thereon being ₹ 18,000) was sold for ₹ 6,000.

	31st March, 2021 (₹)	31st March, 2020 (₹)
Trade Receivable	20,000	16,000
Inventory	12,000	15,000
Cash at Bank	8,000	10,000
Trade Payable	9,000	11,000
Marketable Securities	5,000	2,000
Plant and Machinery	88,000	1,30,000

25. From the following extracts of a company's balance sheets and the additional information, you are required to calculate cash from financing activities for the year ending 31st March, 2021.

Particulars	31st March, 2021 (₹)	31st March, 2020 (₹)
Equity Share Capital	9,00,000	7,00,000
10% Preference Share Capital	3,00,000	5,00,000
Securities Premium	30,000	5,000
12% Debentures	4,00,000	3,00,000
Cash Credit	12,000	10,000

Additional information

(i) During the year 2020-21

(a) Dividend proposed on equity shares in 2019-20 of ₹ 65,000 was declared and paid.

(b) Debentures were issued on 1st July, 2020, at a discount of 10%.

(c) Interest on cash credit of ₹ 500 was paid.

(d) Underwriting commission of ₹ 25,000 was paid to the underwriters.

(e) The equity shares were issued at a premium.

(ii) The 10% preference shares were redeemed on 31st March, 2021. **ISC Sem II Specimen 2022**

10 Marks Questions

26. You are required to prepare a cash flow statement (as per AS-3) for the year 2018-19 from the following balance sheets

Balance Sheets of Hillock Ltd.
as at 31st March, 2018 and 31st March, 2019

Particulars	Note No.	31st March, 2019 (₹)	31st March, 2018 (₹)
I. **EQUITY AND LIABILITIES**			
1. **Shareholder's Funds**			
(a) Equity Share Capital		2,50,000	2,00,000
(b) Reserves and Surplus	1	90,000	50,000
2. **Current Liabilities**			
(a) Short-term Borrowings (Bank Overdraft)		—	10,000
(b) Trade Payables		20,000	15,000
(c) Other Current Liabilities	2	5,000	5,000
(d) Short-term Provisions (Provision for Tax)		25,000	20,000
Total		3,90,000	3,00,000
II. **ASSETS**			
1. **Non-current Assets**			
(a) Property, Plant and Equipment and Intangible Assets			
Property, Plant and Equipment		2,55,000	2,35,000
2. **Current Assets**			
(a) Current Investments		30,000	—
(b) Inventories		15,000	25,000
(c) Trade Receivables		40,000	10,000
(d) Cash and Bank Balances		50,000	30,000
Total		3,90,000	3,00,000

Notes to Accounts

Particulars	31st March, 2019 (₹)	31st March, 2018 (₹)
1. **Reserves and Surplus**		
Balance in Statement of Profit and Loss	70,000	40,000
Securities Premium	20,000	10,000
	90,000	50,000
2. **Other Current Liabilities**		
Outstanding Expenses	1,000	5,000
Unclaimed Dividend	4,000	—
	5,000	5,000
3. **Contingent Liability**		
Proposed Dividend	5,000	10,000

Additional information

During the year 2018-19,

(i) Property, plant and equipment costing ₹ 50,000 was purchased.

(ii) Tax paid ₹ 15,000.

(iii) Interest of ₹ 1,000 was paid on the bank overdraft. *ISC 2020*

KEY IDEA

Unclaimed dividend is a current liability but it will be deducted from dividend paid in financing activity.

27. From the following information and extracts of balance sheets of Pioneer Ltd. as at 31st March, 2017 and 31st March, 2018, calculate for the year 2017-18

(i) Cash from operating activities (ii) Cash from investing activities

Particulars	31st March, 2018 (₹)	31st March, 2017 (₹)
General Reserve	40,000	30,000
Balance in Statement of Profit and Loss	2,40,000	1,40,000
Provision for Tax	1,20,000	90,000
Trade Payables	32,000	44,000
Plant and Machinery (at cost)	2,90,000	2,45,000
Accumulated Depreciation on Plant and Machinery	30,000	40,000
Patents	50,000	1,50,000
10% Debentures	1,20,000	10,000
Goodwill	15,000	12,000

Note Proposed dividends for the years 2016-17 and 2017-18 were ₹ 40,000 and ₹ 50,000 respectively.

Additional information

During the year 2017-18

(a) The company provided depreciation on plant and machinery amounting to ₹ 24,000.

(b) A machine had been condemned and scrapped.

(c) Interest of ₹ 12,000 paid on debentures.

(d) Tax paid ₹ 50,000.

(e) Patents worth ₹ 30,000 were written-off while some patents were sold for ₹ 75,000 at a profit of ₹ 5,000. No new patents were purchased.

(f) Dividend proposed in 2016-17 was approved by the shareholders and paid by the company. *ISC 2019*

KEY IDEA

Decrease in the value of goodwill will be recorded as 'goodwill written-off' in operating activity, whereas increase in the value of goodwill will be recorded as 'purchase of goodwill' in investing activity.

28. (i) You are required to prepare a cash flow statement (as per AS-3) for the year 2016-17 from the following balance sheet.

Balance Sheets of Honesty Ltd
as at 31st March, 2017 and 31st March, 2016

Particulars	Note No.	31st March, 2017 (₹)	31st March, 2016 (₹)
I. **EQUITY AND LIABILITIES**			
1. **Shareholders' Funds**			
(a) Share Capital (Equity Share Capital)		14,00,000	10,00,000
(b) Reserve and Surplus (Statement of P & L)		5,00,000	4,00,000

Particulars	Note No.	31st March, 2017 (₹)	31st March, 2016 (₹)
2. **Non-current Liabilities**			
Long-term Borrowings (10% Debentures)		5,00,000	1,40,000
3. **Current Liabilities**			
(a) Short-term Borrowings (Bank Overdraft)		20,000	30,000
(b) Trade Payables (Creditors)		1,00,000	60,000
(c) Short-term Provisions	1	60,000	30,000
Total		25,80,000	16,60,000
II. **ASSETS**			
1. **Non-current Assets**			
Property, Plant and Equipment and Intangible Assets			
Property, Plant and Equipment	2	16,00,000	9,00,000
Intangible (Goodwill)		1,40,000	2,00,000
2. **Current Assets**			
(a) Inventories		2,50,000	2,00,000
(b) Trade Receivables		5,00,000	3,00,000
(c) Cash and Bank Balance (Cash at Bank)		90,000	60,000
Total		25,80,000	16,60,000

Notes to Accounts

	Particulars	31st March, 2017 (₹)	31st March, 2016 (₹)
1.	**Short-term Provisions**		
	Provision for Taxation	60,000	30,000
2.	**Property, Plant and Equipment**		
	Plant and Machinery	17,60,000	10,00,000
	(−) Accumulated Depreciation	(1,60,000)	(1,00,000)
		16,00,000	9,00,000

Additional information

During the year 2016-17

(a) A part of the machine, costing ₹ 50,000 accumulated depreciation thereon being ₹ 20,000, was sold for ₹ 18,000.

(b) Tax paid ₹ 20,000.

(c) Interest of ₹ 50,000 paid on debentures.

(ii) State whether the following would result in inflow, outflow or no flow of cash

(a) Bill receivable endorsed to creditors (b) Old vehicle written-off. *ISC 2018*

29. From the following information of Purity Ltd, calculate

(i) Cash from operating activities (ii) Cash from financing activities

Particulars	31st March, 2016 (₹)	31st March, 2015 (₹)
Trade Receivables	17,000	20,000
Inventories	25,000	30,000
Prepaid Expenses	12,000	10,000
Expenses Outstanding	9,000	7,000
Provisions for Tax	15,000	10,000
Cash in Hand	50,000	75,000

Particulars	31st March, 2016 (₹)	31st March, 2015 (₹)
Furniture (At Book Value)	1,20,000	1,60,000
General Reserve	50,000	40,000
10% Debentures	40,000	30,000
Goodwill	60,000	70,000
Trade Payable	21,000	25,000
Balance of Statement of Profit and Loss (Cr)	1,30,000	1,20,000
Proposed Dividend	5,000	4,000
Share Capital	5,00,000	3,00,000

Additional information

During the year 2015-16

(a) A piece of furniture costing ₹ 30,000 (accumulated depreciation ₹ 3,000) was sold for ₹ 25,000.

(b) Tax of ₹ 9,000 was paid.

(c) Interim dividend of ₹ 4,000 was paid.

(d) The company paid ₹ 3,000 as interest on debentures. ***ISC 2017***

30. You are required to prepare a cash flow statement (as per AS-3) for the year 2014-15 from the following balance sheets.

Balance Sheets

as at 31st March, 2015 and 2014

Particulars	Note No.	31st March, 2015 (₹)	31st March, 2014 (₹)
I. EQUITY AND LIABILITIES			
1. **Shareholders' Funds**			
(a) Share Capital (Equity Share Capital)		3,00,000	2,00,000
(b) Reserves and Surplus (Statement of profit and loss)		1,20,000	70,000
2. **Non-current Liabilities**			
(a) Long-term Borrowings (8% Debentures)		1,50,000	1,20,000
3. **Current Liabilities**			
(a) Short-term Borrowings (Bank Overdraft)		19,000	5,000
(b) Trade Payables (Creditors)		31,000	20,000
(c) Short-term Provisions	1	80,000	60,000
Total		7,00,000	4,75,000
II. ASSETS			
1. **Non-current Assets**			
(a) Property, Plant and Equipment	2	2,04,200	1,83,000
(b) Non-current Investments		1,30,000	1,20,000
2. **Current Assets**			
(a) Inventories		91,500	65,000
(b) Trade Receivables	3	62,600	62,900
(c) Cash and Bank Balances (Cash at Bank)		2,11,700	44,100
Total		7,00,000	4,75,000

Additional information	**2015 (₹)**	**2014 (₹)**
Proposed Dividend	50,000	60,000

Notes to Accounts

Particulars	31st March, 2015 (₹)	31st March, 2014 (₹)
1. **Short-term Provisions**		
Provision for Taxation	80,000	60,000
	80,000	60,000
2. **Property, Plant and Eqipment** (Tangible)		
Plant and Machinery	2,43,000	2,23,000
(–) Accumulated Depreciation	(38,800)	(40,000)
	2,04,200	1,83,000
3. **Trade Receivables**		
Debtors	64,600	64,500
(–) Provision for Doubtful Debts	(2,000)	(1,600)
	62,600	62,900

Additional information

During the year 2014-15

(i) A part of the machine was sold for ₹ 21,000 at a profit of ₹ 4,000.

(ii) The company charged ₹ 3,000 as depreciation on its plant and machinery.

(iii) New debentures were issued on 31st March, 2015, at a discount of 10%.

(iv) Interest of ₹ 9,600 was paid on debentures. *ISC 2016*

31. (i) State with reason whether the following would result in inflow, outflow or no flow of cash

(a) Charging depreciation on furniture.

(b) Cash withdrawn from bank for office use.

(ii) From the following extracts of a company's balance sheet, calculate for the year ending 31st March, 2013.

(a) Cash from investing activities (b) Cash from financing activities

Note Current year's figures appear in the first column and the previous year's figures are in the second column.

Particulars	2012-13 (₹)	2011-12 (₹)
Equity Share Capital	13,00,000	12,00,000
Long-term Borrowings (10% Bank Loan)	60,000	1,00,000
Proposed Dividend	20,000	21,000
Property, Plant and Equipment and Intangible Assets		
Plant and Machinery	1,70,000	1,40,000
(–) Accumulated Depreciation	(24,000)	(40,500)
	1,46,000	99,500
Non-current Investments	1,00,000	20,000
Land (at cost)	5,00,000	7,00,000
Goodwill	30,000	40,000

Additional information

(i) The loan instalment and interest on loan was paid at the end of the financial year.

(ii) During the year 2012-13

(a) The company provided depreciation on plant and machinery amounting to ₹ 13,500.

(b) The company sold 70% of its non-current investments which it held at the beginning of the year, at a profit of 20% on its book value. *ISC 2014 (M)*

32. Arthur Ltd reported a profit of ₹ 90,000 for the year ended 31st March, 2012 after considering the following

	Amt (₹)
(i) Tax provided during the year	3,000
(ii) Amortisation of goodwill	12,000
(iii) Profit on sale of land	5,000
(iv) Writing-off preliminary expenses	2,000

(v) Machinery costing ₹ 40,000 (Accumulated depreciation thereon being ₹ 18,000) was sold during the year at a loss of ₹ 17,000.

Extracts of its balance sheets at the beginning and at the end of the year are given below

Particulars	31st March, 2012 (₹)	1st April, 2011 (₹)
Accounts Receivable	20,000	16,000
Stock	12,000	15,000
Cash at Bank	8,000	10,000
Accounts Payable	9,000	11,000
Expenses Payable	6,000	5,000
Provision for Taxation	4,000	6,000
Investments (Short-term)	5,000	2,000
Plant and Machinery (Net value)	94,000	1,30,000
Proposed Dividend	12,000	10,000

You are required to calculate cash from operating activities as per Accounting Standard-3. (Show your working clearly) *ISC 2013*

33. The balance sheet of Cooper and Company as at 31st December, 2010 and 2011 are given below

Particulars	Note No.	31st December, 2011 (₹)	31st December, 2010 (₹)
I. **EQUITY AND LIABILITIES**			
1. **Shareholders' Funds**			
(a) Share Capital	1	1,80,000	1,50,000
(b) Reserves and Surplus	2	1,00,000	80,000
2. **Non-current Liabilities**			
Long-term Borrowings	3	1,89,000	1,31,000
3. **Current Liabilities**			
Trade Payable	4	14,000	14,000
Total		4,83,000	3,75,000
II. **ASSETS**			
1. **Non-current Assets**			
(i) Property, Plant and Equipment and Intangible Assets			
(a) Property, Plant and Equipment	5	3,20,000	2,30,000
(b) Intangible Assets	6	5,000	10,000
2. **Current Assets**			
(a) Inventories		75,000	60,000
(b) Trade Receivable	7	26,000	28,000
(c) Cash and Cash Equivalents	8	49,000	37,000
(d) Other Current Assets	9	8,000	10,000
Total		4,83,000	3,75,000

Notes to Accounts

Particulars	31st December, 2011 (₹)	31st December, 2010 (₹)
1. **Share Capital**		
Equity Share Capital	1,80,000	1,50,000
2. **Reserves and Surplus**		
General Reserve	30,000	30,000
Statement of Profit and Loss	70,000	50,000
	1,00,000	80,000
3. **Long-term Borrowings**		
12% Debentures	1,89,000	1,31,000
4. **Trade Payables**		
Creditors	10,000	8,000
Bills Payable	4,000	6,000
	14,000	14,000
5. **Property, Plant and Equipment**		
Building	2,20,000	1,50,000
Plant	1,00,000	80,000
	3,20,000	2,30,000
6. **Intangible Assets**		
Goodwill	5,000	10,000
7. **Trade Receivable**		
Bills Receivable	26,000	28,000
8. **Cash and Cash Equivalents**		
Cash	50,000	40,000
Cash Credit	(1,000)	(3,000)
	49,000	37,000
9. **Other Current Assets**		
Accrued Income	6,000	10,000
Prepaid Expenses	2,000	—
	8,000	10,000

Additional information

(i) Depreciation charged on building ₹ 10,000. (ii) Depreciation charged on plant ₹ 5,000.

(iii) Interest paid on debentures ₹ 7,200. (iv) Interest paid on public deposit ₹ 9,600 for the year.

From the above information, prepare a cash flow statement as per Accounting Standard-3 for the year ended 31st December, 2011. *ISC 2012*

34. Given below is the balance sheet of Gurmeet and Company Ltd as at 31st December, 2009 and 2010

Particulars	Note No.	31st December, 2010 (₹)	31st December, 2009 (₹)
I. **EQUITY AND LIABILITIES**			
1. **Shareholders' Funds**			
(a) Share Capital		3,50,000	3,00,000
(b) Reserves and Surplus	1	2,20,000	1,55,000
2. **Non-current Liabilities**			
Long-term Borrowings	2	2,50,000	1,50,000
3. **Current Liabilities**			
Trade Payables	3	1,25,000	85,000
Total		9,45,000	6,90,000

Particulars	Note No.	31st December, 2010 (₹)	31st December, 2009 (₹)
II. **ASSETS**			
1. **Non-current Assets**			
Property, Plant and Equipment and Intangible Assets			
(a) Property, Plant and Equipment	4	4,10,000	3,20,000
(b) Intangible Assets	5	80,000	1,00,000
(c) 12% Non-current Investment		80,000	30,000
2. **Current Assets**			
(a) Inventories		55,000	40,000
(b) Trade Receivables	6	1,90,000	80,000
(c) Cash and Cash Equivalents		1,30,000	1,20,000
Total		9,45,000	6,90,000

Notes to Accounts

Particulars	31st December, 2010 (₹)	31st December, 2009 (₹)
1. **Reserves and Surplus**		
General Reserve	1,50,000	1,00,000
Statement of Profit and Loss	70,000	60,000
Discount on Debentures	—	(5,000)
	2,20,000	1,55,000
2. **Long-term Borrowings**		
11% Debenture	2,50,000	1,50,000
3. **Trade Payables**		
Creditors	1,10,000	75,000
Bills Payable	15,000	10,000
	1,25,000	85,000
4. **Property, Plant and Equipment**		
Machinery	4,10,000	3,20,000
5. **Intangible Assets**		
Goodwill	80,000	1,00,000
6. **Trade Receivables**		
Debtors	1,90,000	80,000

Additional information

(i) Investments costing ₹ 36,000 were sold for ₹ 30,000 during the year 2010.
(ii) New debentures have been issued at the end of the current accounting year.
(iii) New investment have been purchased at the end of the current accounting year.
(iv) Depreciation charged on machinery during the current accounting year was ₹ 10,000.

From the above information, prepare a cash flow statement as per Accounting Standard-3. *ISC 2011*

35. The balance sheet of Amarnath and Company Ltd as at 31st March, 2006 and 2007 are as follows

Particulars	Note No.	31st March, 2007 (₹)	31st March, 2006 (₹)
I. **EQUITY AND LIABILITIES**			
1. **Shareholders' Funds**			
(a) Share Capital	1	72,000	50,000
(b) Reserve and Surplus	2	14,500	9,000
2. **Non-current Liabilities**			
Long-term Borrowings	3	20,000	10,000

Particulars	Note No.	31st March, 2007 (₹)	31st March, 2006 (₹)
3. **Current Liabilities**			
Trade Payables	4	11,000	8,000
Total		1,18,000	77,700
II. **ASSETS**			
1. **Non-current Assets**			
Property, Plant and Equipment		83,000	46,700
2. **Current Assets**			
(a) Inventories		35,500	29,500
(b) Cash and Cash Equivalents		2,500	2,500
Total		1,18,000	77,700

Notes to Accounts

Particulars	31st March, 2007 (₹)	31st March, 2006 (₹)
1. **Share Capital**		
Equity Share Capital	72,500	50,000
2. **Reserves and Surplus**		
Statement of Profit and Loss	15,000	10,000
Preliminary Expenses	(500)	(1,000)
	14,500	9,000
3. **Long-term Borrowings**		
11% Debentures	20,000	10,000
4. **Trade Payable**		
Creditors	11,000	8,700

Additional information

(i) Depreciation on property, plant and equipment for year 2006-07 was ₹ 11,700.

(ii) Interest paid on debentures ₹ 1,100.

From the above information, prepare a cash flow statement as per Accounting Standard-3. (No other version will be considered for evaluation)

ISC 2008

Explanations

1. (d) Discount on issue of debentures = $10,00,000 \times \frac{10}{100} = ₹ 1,00,000$

₹ 60,000 will be written-off using securities premium reserve, remaining ₹ 40,000 will be shown under operating activity.

2. Bank overdraft is a loan from bank and is considered as a part of financing activity.
3. (b) Interest paid on debentures is a financing activity because debentures are issued by the company to fulfill the financial need or a company can raise the long-term funds by issue of debentures.
4. Cash flow statement is based upon the cash basis of accounting. The cash flow statement is a cash basic report on three types of financial activities, *viz* operating, investing and financing activities.

Concept Enhancer There are two basis of accounting, cash basis and accrual basis. While cash basis records only the cash transactions, accrual basis records cash as well as credit transactions.

5. Interest due on debentures would result in no flow of cash.
6. Old furniture written-off does not effect flow of cash and cash equivalents as it is written-off from the books but not sold and their is no cash realised from this transaction.
7. (i) Property, Plant and Equipment and Intangible Assets Purchased = ₹ 1,70,000 (Outflow – Investing activities)
   (ii) Property, Plant and Equipment and Intangible Assets Sold = ₹ 20,000 (Inflow – Investing activities)
   (iii) Profit/Loss on Sale of Property, Plant and Equipment and Intangible Assets = ₹ 10,000 (Loss)
   (iv) Depreciation Charged on Property, Plant and Equipment and Intangible Assets = ₹ 70,000

Working Notes

1. Dr **Property, Plant and Equipment and Intangible Assets Account** Cr

Particulars	Amt (₹)	Particulars	Amt (₹)
To Balance b/d	4,90,000	By Bank A/c	20,000
To Bank A/c (Balance)	1,70,000	By Provision for Depreciation	30,000
		By Loss	10,000
		By Balance c/d	6,00,000
	6,60,000		6,60,000

2. Dr **Provision for Depreciation Account** Cr

Particulars	Amt (₹)	Particulars	Amt (₹)
To Property, Plant and Equipment and Intangible Assets A/c	30,000	By Balance b/d	1,40,000
To Balance c/d	1,80,000	By Depreciation (Balance)	70,000
	2,10,000		2,10,000

8. (i) Bank overdraft repaid – Cash and cash equivalent
   (ii) Purchase of marketable securities to be sold within 90 days – Cash and cash equivalent
9. (i) No flow of cash (ii) No flow of cash
10. As per Accounting Standard-3, cash equivalents means short-term highly liquid investments that are readily convertible into known amounts of cash and which are subject to an insignificant risk of changes in value. e.g. Short-term marketable securities.

11. (i) Operating activity (ii) Investing activity

12. Operating cycle is the time between the acquisition of an asset for processing and its realisation into cash and cash equivalents. If operating cycle cannot be identified, it is assumed to be of 12 months.

Concept Enhancer The operating cycle of a business can exceed 12 months as well.

13. Difference between net profit and cash from operations

Basis	Net profit	Cash from operations
Meaning	It indicates the net result of activities carried out during an accounting year.	It indicates cash flow as a result of operating activities.
Basis of calculation	It is calculated on accrual basis.	It is calculated on cash basis.

14. The two types of operating activities are
(i) Cash receipts from the sale of goods and rendering of services.
(ii) Cash payment to suppliers of goods and services.

15. Cash equivalents means 'short-term highly liquid investments that are readily convertible into known amount of cash and which are subject to an insignificant risk of change in value'.

16. Cash flow statement is a statement showing the changes in financial position of a business concern during different intervals of time in terms of cash and cash equivalents.

17. The two types of financing activities are
(i) Issue of shares (ii) Redemption of debentures

18. Four types of investing activities are
(i) Sale of fixed assets (ii) Purchase of fixed assets
(iii) Interest received (iv) Dividend received

19. **Cash Flow Statement of Hoopla Ltd.**
for the year ended......

	Particulars		Amt (₹)
A	**Cash Flow from Operating Activities**		
	Net Profit before Tax and Dividend		15,80,000
	(+) Adjustment for Non-cash and Non-operating Items		
	Depreciation of Assets	5,50,000	
	Interest on Bank Loan	3,80,000	9,30,000
			25,10,000
	(–) Gain on Sales of Investment		(1,00,000)
	Operating Profit before Working Capital Changes		24,10,000
	(–) Decrease in Current Liabilities: Trade Payable		(10,000)
	Cash Generated from Operation		24,00,000
	(–) Tax Paid		(4,40,000)
	Net Cash Flow from Operating Activities		19,60,000
B	**Cash Flow from Investing Activities**		
	Sales Proceeds from Investment	3,20,000	
	Net Cash Flow from Investing Activities		3,20,000
C	**Cash Flow from Financing Activities**		
	Proceeds from Issue of Shares	6,60,000	
	(–) Repayment of Bank loan	(15,00,000)	
	(–) Interest Paid on Bank Loan	(3,00,000)	
	(–) Dividend Paid	5,00,000	

Particulars	Amt (₹)
Net Cash Used in Financing Activities	(16,40,000)
Net Increase in Cash and Cash Equivalent (A + B + C)	6,40,000
(+) Opening Balance of Cash and Cash Equivalent	60,000
Closing Balance of Cash and Cash Equivalent	7,00,000

20. **Cash Flow Statement**

For the year ended.....:

	Particulars		Amt (₹)
A	**Cash Flow from Operating Activities**		
	Net Profit before Tax and Dividend		79,000
	(+) Adjustment for Non-cash and Non-operating Items		
	Depreciation on Plant and Machinery	80,000	
	Loss on Sales of Plant and Machinery	10,000	90,000
	Operating Profit before Working Capital Changes		1,69,000
	(–) Tax Paid		(25,000)
	Net Cash Flow from Operating Activities		1,44,000
B	**Cash Flow from Investing Activities**		
	Sales Proceeds of Plant and Machinery	90,000	
	Net Cash Flow from Investing Activities		90,000
C.	**Cash Flow from Financing Activities**		
	Proceeds from Issue of Debentures	81,000	
	Net Cash Flow from Financing Activities		81,000
	Net Increase in Cash and Cash Equivalent (A + B + C)		3,15,000
	(+) Opening Balance of Cash and Cash Equivalent		25,000
	Closing Balance of Cash and Cash Equivalent		3,40,000

21. (i) **Cash from Investing Activities**

Particulars		Amt (₹)
Cash from Investing Activities		
(+) Interest on Investment Received	6,000	
(+) Proceeds from Sale of Plant and Machinery	4,50,000	
(–) Purchase of Plant and Machinery	(7,90,000)	
(–) Purchase of Investments	(10,000)	
(–) Purchase of Goodwill	(30,000)	
Net Cash Used in Investing Activities		(3,74,000)

Working Notes

1. Dr **Plant and Machinery Account** Cr

Particulars	Amt (₹)	Particulars	Amt (₹)
To Balance b/d	9,00,000	By Accumulated Depreciation A/c	1,00,000
To Bank A/c (Purchase of Machinery)	7,90,000	By Bank A/c	4,50,000
		By Loss on Sale of Plant and Machinery	50,000
		By Balance c/d	10,90,000
	16,90,000		16,90,000

2. Dr **Accumulated Depreciation Account** Cr

Particulars	Amt (₹)	Particulars	Amt (₹)
To Plant and Machinery A/c	1,00,000	By Balance b/d	4,00,000
To Balance c/d	3,00,000		
	4,00,000		4,00,000

(ii) **Cash from Financing Activities**

Particulars		Amt (₹)
Cash from Financing Activities		
(+) Proceeds from Issue of Equity Share Capital	3,00,000	
(+) Proceeds from Issue of 5% Debentures	2,00,000	
(–) Interest Paid on Debentures	(50,000)	
(–) Dividend Paid	(42,000)	
Net Cash from Financing Activities		4,08,000

22. **Cash Flow Statement of Bruno Ltd.**
for the year ended 31st March, 2022

Particulars		Amt (₹)
A. **Cash Flow from Operating Activities**		
Net Profit as per Profit and Loss Account		32,000
(+) Provision made for Tax During the Year		35,000
Net Profit before Tax		67,000
Adjustments for Non-cash and Non-operating Items		
(+) Items to be Added		
Depreciation	38,000	
Loss on Sale of Machinery	12,000	
Interest on Borrowings	18,000	68,000
(–) Items to be Deducted		—
Operating Profit before Working Capital Changes		1,35,000
(–) Decrease in Short-term Borrowings		(7,000)
Cash Generated from Operations		1,28,000
(–) Tax paid During the Year		(25,000)
Net Cash from Operating Activities		1,03,000
B. **Cash Flow from Investing Activities**		
(+) Proceeds from Sale of Plant and Machinery	20,000	
(–) Purchase of Plant and Machinery	(1,20,000)	
Net Cash Used in Investing Activities		(1,00,000)
C. **Cash Flow from Financing Activities**		
(+) Proceeds from Issue of Shares	1,50,000	
(–) Interest paid	(18,000)	
(–) Redemption of Debentures	(60,000)	
Net Cash Flow from Financing Activities		72,000
Net Increase in Cash and Cash Equivalents (A + B + C)		75,000
(+) Cash and Cash Equivalents in the Beginning of the Year (Cash at Bank)		3,94,000
Cash and Cash Equivalents at the End of the Year		4,69,000

Working Notes

1. Dr **Provision for Tax Account** Cr

Particulars	Amt (₹)	Particulars	Amt (₹)
To Bank A/c	25,000	By Balance b/d	30,000
To Balance b/d	40,000	By Profit and Loss A/c (Provision made)	35,000
	65,000		65,000

2. Dr **Plant and Machinery Account** Cr

Particulars	Amt (₹)	Particulars	Amt (₹)
To Balance b/d	3,30,000	By Deprecation A/c	38,000
To Bank A/c	1,20,000	By Loss on Sale of Machinery	12,000
		By Bank A/c (Sale of Machinery)	20,000
		By Balance c/d	3,80,000
	4,50,000		4,50,000

23. (i) **Cash Flow from Operating Activities**

Particulars		Amt (₹)
Net Profit before Tax (WN)		2,20,000
(+) Adjustment for		
Loss on Sale of Assets		6,000
Goodwill Written-off		20,000
Depreciation		40,000
Operation Profit before Working Capital Changes		2,86,000
(–) Increase in Current Assets and Decrease in Current Liabilities		
Inventory	(10,000)	
Trade Payables	(10,000)	(20,000)
Cash Generated from Operations		2,66,000
(–) Tax Paid		(20,000)
Cash Flow from Operating Activities		2,46,000

Working Note

Calculation of net profit before tax	Amt (₹)
Net Profit of the Year 1,00,000 – (90,000)	1,90,000
(+) Provision for Tax	30,000
	2,20,000

(ii) **Cash Flow from Investing Activities**

Particulars	Amt (₹)
Purchase of Plant and Machinery	(30,000)
Sale of Plant and Machinery	24,000
Cash used in Investing Activities	6,000

24. **Cash Flow from Operating Activities**

Particulars	Amt (₹)
Net Profit before Tax (WN)	84,000
Adjustments for Non-cash and Non-operating Items	
(+) Amortisation of Patents	10,000
Preliminary Expenses Written-off	2,000
Accumulated Depreciation	18,000
Loss on Sale of Machinery	16,000
(–) Profit on Sale of Vehicle	(3,000)
Operating Profit before Working Capital Changes	1,27,000
(+) Decrease in Current Assets and Increase in Current Liabilities	
Inventory	3,000
	1,30,000

Particulars		Amt (₹)
(–) Increase in Current Assets and Decrease in Current Liabilities		
Trade Receivables	(4,000)	
Trade Payables	(2,000)	(6,000)
Cash Generated from Operations		1,24,000
(–) Income Tax Paid		(4,000)
Net Cash Inflow from Operating Activities		1,20,000

Working Note

Calculation of Net Profit before Tax		Amt (₹)
Profit made during the Year	=	80,000
(+) Tax Provided	=	4,000
	=	84,000

25. **Cash Flow from Financing Activities**

Particulars	Amt (₹)
Issue of Equity Shares	2,00,000
Securities Premium on Issue of Shares	25,000
Dividend Proposed Paid	(65,000)
Dividend on Preference Shares Paid	(50,000)
Redemption of Preference Shares	(2,00,000)
Underwriting Commission Paid	(25,000)
Cash Credit Taken	2,000
Interest Paid on Cash Credit	(500)
Issue of Debentures at 10% Discount	90,000
Interest on Debentures @12% $\left(3,00,000 \times 12\% + 1,00,000 \times 12\% \times \frac{9}{12}\right)$	(45,000)
Cash Used in Financing Activities	(68,500)

Common Mistake Students usually put cash credit in operating activity. But cash credit will be recorded under the head 'Financing Activity'.

26. **Cash Flow Statement**
for the year ended 31st March, 2019

	Particulars		Amt (₹)
A	**Cash Flow from Operating Activities**		
	Net Profit before Tax		30,000
	(+) Adjustments for Non-cash and Non-operating Items		
	Depreciation (WN 1)	30,000	
	Interest on Bank Overdraft	1,000	
	Tax Provision made	20,000	
	Provision for Dividend	10,000	61,000
	Operating Profit before Working Capital Changes		91,000
	(+) Decrease in Current Assets and Increase in Current Liabilities		
	Increase in Trade Payable	5,000	
	Decrease in Inventories	10,000	15,000
			1,06,000
	(–) Decrease in Current Liabilities and Increase in Current Assets		
	Increase in Current Investments	(30,000)	
	Decrease in Outstanding Expenses	(4,000)	
	Increase in Trade Receivables	(30,000)	(64,000)

	Particulars		Amt (₹)
	Cash Generated from Operations		42,000
	(–) Tax Paid		(15,000)
	Cash Flow from Operating Activities		27,000
B	**Cash Flow from Investing Activities**		
	Purchase of Property, Plant and Equipment	(50,000)	
	Cash used in Investing Activities		(50,000)
C	**Cash Flow from Financial Activities**		
	Issue from Equity Share Capital (50,000 + 10,000)	60,000	
	Interest on Bank Overdraft Paid	(1,000)	
	Dividend Paid (10,000 – 4,000)	(6,000)	
	Repayment of Bank Overdraft	(10,000)	
	Cash Flow from Financial Activities		43,000
	Net Increase/Decrease in Cash and Cash Equivalents (A + B + C)		20,000
	(+) Opening Balance of Cash and Cash Equivalents		30,000
	Closing Balance of Cash and Cash Equivalents		50,000

Working Notes

1. Dr **Property, Plant and Equipment Account** Cr

Particulars	Amt (₹)	Particulars	Amt (₹)
To Balance b/d	2,35,000	To Depreciation (Balance)	30,000
To Bank A/c	50,000	To Balance c/d	2,55,000
	2,85,000		2,85,000

2. Dr **Provision for Tax Account** Cr

Particulars	Amt (₹)	Particulars	Amt (₹)
To Bank A/c	15,000	By Balance b/d	20,000
To Balance c/d	25,000	By Surplus of P & L	20,000
	40,000		40,000

3. Current investments are taken as 'current assets'. 4. Bank overdraft is taken as a part of financing activities.

27. (i) **Calculation of Cash Flow from Operating Activities**

Particulars		Amt (₹)
Cash Flow from Operating Activities		
Net Profit before Taxation		2,30,000
Adjustment for Non-cash and Non-operating Items		
(+) Items to be Added		
Patents Written-off	30,000	
Interest on Debentures	12,000	
Depreciation on Plant and Machinery	24,000	66,000
		2,96,000
(–) Items to be Deducted-Profit on Sale of Patents		(5,000)
		2,91,000
(+) Increase in Current Liabilities and Decrease in Current Assets		
(–) Decrease in Current Liabilities and Increase in Current Assets		
Trade Payables		(12,000)
Cash Generated from Operations		2,79,000
(–) Tax Paid		(50,000)
Net Cash from Operating Activities		2,29,000

Working Notes

1. **Calculation of Net Profit before Tax and Extraordinary Items**

	Amt (₹)
Net profit as per statement of profit and loss (2,40,000 – 1,40,000)	1,00,000
(+) Transfer to general reserve	10,000
Proposed dividend	40,000
Provision for tax made during the year	80,000
	2,30,000

2. Dr **Plant and Machinery Account** Cr

Particulars	Amt (₹)	Particulars	Amt (₹)
To Balance b/d	2,45,000	By Accumulated Depreciation	34,000
To Bank A/c (Purchase) (Bal. Fig.)	79,000	By Balance c/d	2,90,000
	3,24,000		3,24,000

3. Dr **Accumulated Depreciation Account** Cr

Particulars	Amt (₹)	Particulars	Amt (₹)
To Plant and Machinery A/c	34,000	By Balance b/d	40,000
To Balance c/d	30,000	By Profit and Loss A/c	24,000
	64,000		64,000

4. Dr **Patents Account** Cr

Particulars	Amt (₹)	Particulars	Amt (₹)
To Balance b/d	1,50,000	By Profit and Loss A/c (Write-off)	30,000
To Profit on Sale	5,000	By Bank A/c (Sale)	75,000
		By Balance c/d	50,000
	1,55,000		1,55,000

5. Dr **Provision for Tax** Cr

Particulars	Amt (₹)	Particulars	Amt (₹)
To Cash A/c	50,000	By Balance b/d	90,000
To Balance c/d	1,20,000	By Profit and Loss A/c	80,000
	1,70,000		1,70,000

(ii) **Calculation of Cash Flow from Investing Activities**

Particulars	Amt (₹)
Cash Flow from Investing Activities	
Purchase of Plant and Machinery	(79,000)
Sale of Patent	75,000
Purchase of Goodwill	(3,000)
Net Cash used in Investing Activities	(7,000)

28. (i) **In the Books of Honesty Ltd**
Cash Flow Statement
for the year ended 31st March, 2017

Particulars	Amt (₹)
A **Cash Flow from Operating Activities**	
Net Profit before Taxation (WN 1)	1,50,000
(+) Adjustment for Non-cash and Non-operating Items	
Goodwill Written-off	60,000
Loss on Sale of Machinery	12,000
Depreciation on Machinery	80,000
Interest Paid on Debentures	50,000
Operating Profit before Working Capital Changes	3,52,000
(+) Decrease in Current Assets and Increase in Current Liabilities Creditors	40,000
	3,92,000

Particulars	Amt (₹)
(–) Increase in Current Assets and Decrease in Current Liabilities	
Stock	(50,000)
Trade Receivable	(2,00,000)
	1,42,000
(–) Tax Paid	(20,000)
Net Cash from Operating Activities	1,22,000
B. **Cash Flow from Investing Activities**	
Sale of Machinery	18,000
Purchase of Machinery	(8,10,000)
Net Cash Used in Investing Activities	(7,92,000)
C. **Cash Flow from Financing Activities**	
Issue of Equity Share Capital	4,00,000
Issue of 10% Debentures	3,60,000
Interest Paid on Debentures	(50,000)
Decrease in Bank Overdraft	(10,000)
Net Cash from Financing Activities	7,00,000
Net Increase in Cash and Cash Equivalent (A + B + C)	30,000
(+) Opening Balance of Cash and Cash Equivalent	60,000
Closing Balance of Cash and Cash Equivalent	90,000

Working Notes

	Amt (₹)
1. Calculation of net profit before tax reserve and surplus balance on 31st March, 2017	5,00,000
(–) Reserve and surplus balance on 31st March, 2016	(4,00,000)
	1,00,000
(+) Provision for tax made during the year	50,000
	1,50,000

2. Dr **Plant and Machinery Account** Cr

Particulars	Amt (₹)	Particulars	Amt (₹)
To Balance b/d	10,00,000	By Bank A/c	18,000
To Bank A/c (Balancing Figure being Purchase)	8,10,000	By Accumulated Depreciation A/c	20,000
		By Statement of Profit and Loss	12,000
		By Balance c/d	17,60,000
	18,10,000		18,10,000

3. Dr **Accumulated Depreciation Account** Cr

Particulars	Amt (₹)	Particulars	Amt (₹)
To Machine A/c	20,000	By Balance b/d	1,00,000
To Balance c/d	1,60,000	By Statement of Profit and Loss (Balancing Figure)	80,000
	1,80,000		1,80,000

4. Dr **Provision for Taxation Account** Cr

Particulars	Amt (₹)	Particulars	Amt (₹)
To Cash A/c	20,000	By Balance b/d	30,000
To Balance c/d	60,000	By Statement of Profit and Loss (Balancing Figure)	50,000
	80,000		80,000

(ii) (a) Bill receivable endorsed to creditors – No Flow of Cash

(b) Old vehicle written-off – No Flow of Cash

29. (i)

In the Books of Purity Ltd
Cash Flow from Operating Activities

Particulars		Amt (₹)
Net Profit before Tax (WN1)		42,000
Adjustments for Non-cash and Non-operating Expenses		
(+) Depreciation on Furniture	13,000	
Loss on Sale of Furniture	2,000	
Goodwill Amortised	10,000	
Interest on Debentures	4,000	29,000
Operating Profit before Working Capital Changes		71,000
(+) Decrease in Current Assets and Increase in Current Liabilities		
Trade Receivables	3,000	
Inventories	5,000	
Expenses Outstanding	2,000	
(–) Increase in Current Assets and Decrease in Current Liabilities		
Prepaid Expenses	(2,000)	
Trade Payable	(4,000)	4,000
Net Cash Flow from Operating Activities before Tax		75,000
(–) Tax Paid		(9,000)
Net Cash Inflow from Operating Activities after Tax		66,000

(ii) **Calculation of Net Cash Flow from Financing Activities**

Particulars	Amt (₹)
Issue of Shares	2,00,000
Issue of Debentures	10,000
	2,10,000
(–) Dividend Paid	(4,000)
(–) Interim Dividend Paid	(4,000)
(–) Interest on Debentures Paid	(3,000)
Net Cash Flow from Financing Activity	1,99,000

Working Notes

1. **Calculation of Net Profit before Tax**

	Amt (₹)
Net Profit as per statement of profit and loss (1,30,000 – 1,20,000)	10,000
(+) Transfer to reserve (50,000 – 40,000)	10,000
(+) Proposed dividend	4,000
(+) Interim dividend	4,000
(+) Provisions for tax	14,000
Net profit befor tax	42,000

2. Dr **Provision for Tax Account** Cr

Particulars	Amt (₹)	Particulars	Amt (₹)
To Cash A/c	9,000	By Balance b/d	10,000
To Balance c/d	15,000	By Statement of Profit and Loss (Balancing Figure)	14,000
	24,000		24,000

3. Dr **Furniture Account** Cr

Particulars	Amt (₹)	Particulars	Amt (₹)
To Balance b/d	1,60,000	By Bank A/c (Sale)	25,000
		By Loss on Sale A/c	2,000
		By Depreciation A/c (Balancing Figure)	13,000
		By Balance c/d	1,20,000
	1,60,000		1,60,000

	Amt (₹)
4. Value of Furniture Sold	30,000
(−) Depreciation	(3,000)
	27,000
(−) Sale Value	(25,000)
Loss on Sale	2,000

5. Interest on Debenture = 40,000 × 10/100 = ₹ 4,000

30.

In the Books of ......
Cash Flow Statement
for the year ended 31st March, 2015

Particulars		Amt (₹)
A **Cash Flow from Operating Activities**		
Net Profit before Tax		1,90,000
(+) **Adjustments for**		
Depreciation	1,800	
Interest Paid on Debentures	9,600	
Discount on Issue of Debentures Written-off	3,000	
(−) Profit on Sale	(4,000)	10,400
Operating Profit before Working Capital Changes		2,00,400
(+) Decrease in Current Assets and Increase in Current Liabilities		
Creditors	11,000	
Provision for Doubtful Debts	400	11,400
(−) Increase in Current Assets and Decrease in Current Liabilities		
Inventories	26,500	
Debtors	100	(26,600)
Cash Generated from Operations		1,85,200
(−) Tax Paid		(60,000)
Cash Flow from Operating Activities		1,25,200
B **Cash Flow from Investing Activities**		
Proceeds from Sale of Machinery	21,000	
Purchase of Machinery	(40,000)	
Purchase of Investments	(10,000)	
Net Cash used in Investing Activities		(29,000)
C **Cash Flow from Financing Activities**		
Issue of Shares	1,00,000	
Issue of Debentures (30,000 − 3,000)	27,000	
Interest on Debentures	(9,600)	
Increase in Bank Overdraft	(14,000)	
Proposed Dividend	(60,000)	

Particulars	Amt (₹)
Net Cash Flow from Financing Activities	71,400
Net Increase in Cash and Cash Equivalent (A + B + C)	1,67,600
(+) Opening Cash and Cash Equivalent	44,100
Closing Cash and Cash Equivalent	2,11,700

Working Notes

1. **Calculation of Net Profit before Tax and Extraordinary Items**

Particulars	Amt (₹)
Net Profit During the Year (1,20,000 – 70,000)	50,000
(+) Proposed Dividend	60,000
(+) Provision for Tax	80,000
	1,90,000

2. Dr **Plant and Machinery Account** Cr

Particulars	Amt (₹)	Particulars	Amt (₹)
To Balance b/d	2,23,000	By Bank A/c (Sale)	21,000
To Statement of Profit and Loss (Profit)	4,000	By Depreciation A/c	3,000
To Bank A/c (Balancing Figure being Purchase)	40,000	By Balance c/d	2,43,000
	2,67,000		2,67,000

3. Dr **Accumulated Depreciation Account** Cr

Particulars	Amt (₹)	Particulars	Amt (₹)
To Machinery A/c	3,000	By Balance b/d	40,000
To Balance c/d	38,800	By Depreciation A/c (Balancing Figure) (Depreciation for Current Year)	1,800
	41,800		41,800

31. (i) (a) **No flow** There will be no flow of cash as depreciation is a non-cash expense.

(b) **No flow** There will be no flow of cash as it is simply a movement between two components of cash and cash equivalents.

(ii) (a) **Cash Flow from Investing Activities** (AS-3)

Particulars		Amt (₹)
Sale of Investment	16,800	
Sale of Land	2,00,000	
Purchase of Plant and Machinery	(60,000)	
Purchase of Investment	(94,000)	
Net Cash from Investing Activities		62,800

(b) **Calculation of Cash Flow from Financing Activities**

Particulars		Amt (₹)
Issue of Equity Share Capital	1,00,000	
Repayment of Bank Loan	(40,000)	
Payment of Interest on Loan	(10,000)	
Payment of Dividend	(21,000)	
Net Cash from Financing Activities		29,000

Working Notes

1. Dr **Plant and Machinery Account** Cr

Particulars	Amt (₹)	Particulars	Amt (₹)
To Balance b/d	1,40,000	By Accumulated Depreciation A/c	30,000
To Bank A/c (Purchases)	60,000	By Balance c/d	1,70,000
	2,00,000		2,00,000

2. Dr **Accumulated Depreciation Account** Cr

Particulars	Amt (₹)	Particulars	Amt (₹)
To Machinery A/c	30,000	By Balance b/d	40,500
To Balance c/d	24,000	By Statement of Profit and Loss (Current Year)	13,500
	54,000		54,000

3. Dr **Investment Account** Cr

Particulars	Amt (₹)	Particulars	Amt (₹)
To Balance b/d	20,000	By Bank A/c (Sale)	16,800
To Statement of Profit and Loss (Profit on Sale)	2,800	By Balance c/d	1,00,000
To Bank A/c (Purchases)	94,000		
	1,16,800		1,16,800

4. Sale of Investment **Amt (₹)**

Value of investment $= \frac{70}{100} \times 20,000$ $= 14,000$

(+) Gain 20% $= \frac{20}{100} \times 14,000$ $= 2,800$

16,800

32.

In the Books of Arthur Ltd
Cash from Operating Activities
for the year ended 31st March, 2012

Particulars		Amt (₹)
Net Profit before Tax (WN1)		1,03,000
Adjustment for Non-cash and Non-operating Items		
(+) Amortisation of Goodwill	12,000	
Preliminary Expenses Written-off	2,000	
Loss on Sale of Machinery	17,000	
Depreciation on Machinery	14,000	45,000
(–) Profit on Sale of Land		(5,000)
Operating Profit before Change in Working Capital		1,43,000
(+) **Decrease in Current Assets and Increase in Current Liabilities**		
Stock	3,000	
Expenses Payable	1,000	4,000
(–) **Increase in Current Assets and Decrease in Current Liabilities**		
Accounts Receivable	4,000	
Accounts Payable	2,000	(6,000)
Cash from Operating Activities before Tax		1,41,000
(–) Tax Paid		(5,000)
Net Cash Flow from Operating Activities		1,36,000

Working Notes

1. Calculation of Net Profit before Tax

	Amt (₹)
Profit and loss balance on 31st March, 2012	90,000
(+) Provision for tax made during the year	3,000
Proposed dividend for current year	10,000
	1,03,000

2. Dr **Provision for Taxation Account** Cr

Date	Particulars	Amt (₹)	Date	Particulars	Amt (₹)
	To Bank A/c (Tax Paid) (Balancing Figure)	5,000		By Balance b/d	6,000
	To Balance c/d	4,000		By Statement of Profit and Loss A/c (Tax Provided)	3,000
		9,000			9,000

3. Dr **Plant and Machinery Account** Cr

Particulars	Amt (₹)	Particulars	Amt (₹)
To Balance b/d	1,30,000	By Bank A/c (Sale)	5,000
		By Statement of Profit and Loss (Loss on Sale)	17,000
		By Depreciation A/c (Balancing Figure)	14,000
		By Balance c/d	94,000
	1,30,000		1,30,000

33.

In the Books of Cooper and Company Ltd
Cash Flow Statement
for the year ended 31st December, 2011

Particulars		Amt (₹)
A **Cash from Operating Activities**		
Net Profit before Tax (1,00,000 – 80,000)		20,000
Adjustments for Non-cash and Non-operating Items		
(+) Goodwill Written-off	5,000	
Depreciation on Buliding	10,000	
Depreciation on Plant	5,000	
Interest on Debentures	7,200	
Interest on Public Deposits	9,600	36,800
Operating Profit before Changes in Working Capital		56,800
(+) **Decrease in Current Assets and Increase in Current Liabilities**		
Debtors	3,000	
Accrued Income	4,000	
Creditors	2,000	9,000
(–) **Increase in Current Assets and Decrease in Current Liabilities**		
Stock	15,000	
Bills Receivable	1,000	
Prepaid Expenses	2,000	
Bills Payable	2,000	(20,000)
Cash from Operating Activities before Income Tax		45,800
(–) Income Tax Paid		—
Net Cash from Operating Activities		45,800

Particulars		Amt (₹)
B. **Cash from Investing Activities**		
Purchase of Building	80,000	
Purchase of Plant	25,000	(1,05,000)
Net Cash Used in Investing Activities		(1,05,000)
C. **Cash from Financing Activities**		
Issue of Shares	30,000	
Issue of Debentures	18,000	
Public Deposits Raised	40,000	
Interest Paid on Debentures	(7,200)	
Decrease in Cash Credit	(2,000)	
Interest Paid on Public Deposits	(9,600)	
Net Cash from Financing Activities		69,200
Net Change in Cash and Cash Equivalents (A + B + C)		10,000
(+) Cash and Cash Equivalents at the Beginning		40,000
Cash and Cash Equivalents at the End		50,000

Working Notes

1. Dr **Building Account** Cr

Date	Particulars	JF	Amt (₹)	Date	Particulars	JF	Amt (₹)
2011				2011			
Jan 1	To Balance b/d		1,50,000	Dec 31	By Depreciation A/c		10,000
Dec 31	To Cash A/c (Balancing Figure being Purchase)		80,000	Dec 31	By Balance c/d		2,20,000
			2,30,000				2,30,000

2. Dr **Plant Account** Cr

Date	Particulars	JF	Amt (₹)	Date	Particulars	JF	Amt (₹)
2011				2011			
Jan 1	To Balance b/d		80,000	Dec 31	By Depreciation A/c		5,000
Dec 31	To Cash A/c (Balancing Figure being Purchase)		25,000	Dec 31	By Balance c/d		1,00,000
			1,05,000				1,05,000

34. **In the Books of Gurmeet and Company Ltd**

Cash Flow Statement

for the year ended 31st December, 2010

Particulars		Amt (₹)
A **Cash Flow from Operating Activities**		
Net Profit before Tax (WN1)		60,000
Adjustment for Non-cash and Non-operating Items		
(+) Depreciation	10,000	
Goodwill Written-off	20,000	
Loss on Sale of Investment	6,000	
Discount on Debenture	5,000	
Interest on Debenture	16,500	
(–) Interest on Investment	(3,600)	53,900
Operating Profit before Working Capital Changes		1,13,900
(+) **Increase in Current Liabilities and Decrease in Current Assets**		
Creditors	35,000	
Bills Payable	5,000	40,000

Particulars		Amt (₹)
(–) **Increase in Current Assets and Decrease in Current Liabilities**		
Stock	15,000	
Debtors	1,10,000	(1,25,000)
Net Cash from Operating Activities		28,900
B **Cash Flow from Investing Activities**		
Purchase of Machinery	(1,00,000)	
Sale of Investment	30,000	
Interest on Investment	3,600	
Purchase of Investment	(86,000)	
Net Cash used in Investing Activities		(1,52,400)
C. **Cash Flow from Financing Activities**		
Issue of Shares	50,000	
Issue of Debentures	1,00,000	
Interest on Debenture	(16,500)	
Net Cash from Financing Activities		1,33,500
Net Increase in Cash and Cash Equivalents (A + B + C)		10,000
Cash and Cash Equivalents at the Beginning		1,20,000
Cash and Cash Equivalents at the End		1,30,000

Working Notes

1. **Calculation of Net Profit before Tax**

	Amt (₹)
Statement of profit and loss on 31st December, 2010	70,000
(–) Statement of profit and loss on 31st December, 2009	60,000
	10,000
(+) Transfer to general reserve (1,50,000 – 1,00,000)	50,000
	60,000

2. Dr **Machinery Account** Cr

Particulars	Amt (₹)	Particulars	Amt (₹)
To Balance b/d	3,20,000	By Depreciation A/c	10,000
To Bank A/c (Balancing Figure being Purchase)	1,00,000	By Balance c/d	4,10,000
	4,20,000		4,20,000

3. Dr **Investment Account** Cr

Particulars	Amt (₹)	Particulars	Amt (₹)
To Balance b/d	30,000	By Bank A/c	30,000
To Bank A/c (Balancing Figure being Purchase)	86,000	By Loss on Sale A/c	6,000
		By Balance c/d	80,000
	1,16,000		1,16,000

35.

In the Books of Amarnath and Company Ltd
Cash Flow Statement
for the year ended 31st March, 2007

Particulars		Amt (₹)
A **Cash Flow from Operating Activities**		
Net Profit before Taxation		5,000
(+) **Adjustment for Non-cash and Non-operating Items**		
Preliminary Expenses Written-off	500	
Interest Paid on Debenture	1,100	
Depreciation on Property, Plant and Equipment and Intangible Assets	11,700	13,300
Operating Profit before Working Capital Changes		18,300
(+) **Decrease in Current Assets and Increases in Current Liabilities**		
Creditors		2,300
(–) **Increase in Current Assets and Decrease in Current Liabilities**		
Stock		(3,500)
Net Cash from Operating Activities		17,100
B **Cash Flow from Investing Activities**		
Purchase of Property, Plant and Equipment and Intangible Assets		(48,000)
Net Cash Used in Investing Activities		(48,000)
C **Cash Flow from Financing Activities**		
Issue of Equity Shares	22,500	
Issue of Debentures	10,000	
Interest Paid on Debentures	(1,100)	31,400
Net Cash from Financing Activities		31,400
Net Increase in Cash and Cash Equivalents (A + B + C)		500
Cash and Cash Equivalents at the Beginning		2,000
Cash and Cash Equivalents at the End		2,500

Working Note

Dr **Property, Plant and Equipment and Intangible Assets Account** Cr

Particulars	Amt (₹)	Particulars	Amt (₹)
To Balance b/d	46,700	By Depreciation A/c	11,700
To Bank A/c (Balancing Figure being Purchase)	48,000	By Balance c/d	83,000
	94,700		94,700

CHAPTER TEST

01 Mark Questions

1. Which of the following is an operating activity of a manufacturing business?
(a) Dividend paid to the shareholders
(b) Cash received from trade receivables
(c) Buy back of equity shares
(d) Redemption of debentures

2. Which of the following is not a financing activity?
(a) Dividend paid to the shareholders
(b) Interest paid on borrowings
(c) Purchase of shares of a company
(d) Decrease in bank overdraft

3. Which of the following will result in no flow of cash and cash equivalents?
(a) Purchase of land and building against issue of shares
(b) Sale of plant and machinery (book value ₹ 1,00,000) at a profit of 23,000
(c) Declaration of interim dividend
(d) Cash received from debtors

4. Which of the following will result in outflow of cash and cash equivalents?
(a) Cash received from debtors
(b) Cash withdrawn from bank
(c) Writing-off bad debts against the provision for doubtful debts
(d) Purchase of stock-in-trade

5. What will be the amount of cash flow from financing activities of PDF Ltd. if they redeemed ₹ 2,00,000, 12% debentures at 10% premium?
(a) ₹ 2,24,000 (outflow)
(b) ₹ 2,24,000 (inflow)
(c) ₹ 2,00,000 (outflow)
(d) ₹ 24,000 (outflow)

6. Give any two examples of cash flow from operating activity.

7. Increase in the value of goodwill is a part of which activity?

03 Marks Questions

8. The profit of Polo Ltd. after all the appropriations was ₹ 5,00,000. This profit was arrived at after taking into consideration the following items

Particulars	Amt (₹)
Depreciation on Property, Plant and Equipment (Machinery)	40,000
Loss on Sale of Property, Plant and Equipment (Furniture)	4,000
Goodwill Written-off	18,000
Provision for Taxation	70,000
Transfer to General Reserve	35,000
Gain on Sale of Property, Plant and Equipment (Machinery)	16,000

Additional information

Particulars	31st March 2018 (₹)	31st March, 2017 (₹)
Debtors (All Good)	1,24,000	1,00,000
Creditors	1,10,000	90,000
Stock	16,000	24,000
Interest Received in Advance	—	16,000
Outstanding Salary	6,000	12,000
Prepaid Rent	10,000	—

You are required to calculate cash from operating activities.

9. From the following information calculate the amount of cash flows from investing activities

Particulars	31st March, 2023 (₹)	31st March, 2022 (₹)
Plant and Machinery	2,00,000	1,70,000
Goodwill	20,000	8,000
Land (At Cost)	20,000	40,000

Additional information

(i) Depreciation charged on plant and machinery was ₹ 10,000.

(ii) Plant and machinery with a book value of ₹ 12,000 was sold for ₹ 8,000.

(iii) Land was sold at a gain of ₹ 12,000.

06 Marks Questions

10. From the following balance sheet of Vijay as on 31st March, 2011 and 2012, prepare a cash flow statement.

Particulars	Note No.	31st March, 2012 (₹)	31st March, 2011 (₹)
I. **EQUITY AND LIABILITIES**			
1. **Shareholder's Funds**			
(a) Share Capital		65,000	45,000
(b) Reserve and Surplus	1	42,000	24,000
2. **Current Liabilities**			
Trade Payables	2	11,000	8,700
Total		1,18,000	77,700
II. **ASSETS**			
1. **Non-current Assets**			
Property, Plant and Equipment		83,000	46,700
2. **Current Assets**			
(a) Inventories		13,000	11,000
(b) Trade Receivables	3	19,500	18,000
(c) Cash		2,500	2,000
Total		1,18,000	77,700

Notes to Accounts

Particulars	31st March, 2012 (₹)	31st March, 2011 (₹)
1. **Reserves and Surplus**		
General Reserve	27,500	15,000
Balance of Statement of Profit and Loss	15,000	10,000
Preliminary Expenses	(500)	(1,000)
	42,000	24,000
2. **Trade Payables**		
Creditors	11,000	8,700
3. **Trade Receivables**		
Debtors	19,500	18,000

Additional information

(i) Depreciation on fixed assets for the year 2011-12 was ₹ 14,700.

(ii) An interim dividend ₹ 7,000 has been paid to the shareholders during the year.

11. From the following balance sheet of Ramesh Ltd as at 31st March, 2011 and 2012, prepare a cash flow statement.

Particulars	Note No.	31st March, 2012 (₹)	31st March, 2011 (₹)
I. **EQUITY AND LIABILITIES**			
1. **Shareholders' Funds**			
(a) Equity Share Capital		3,60,000	3,00,000
(b) Reserves and Surplus	1	2,00,000	1,60,000
2. **Non-current Liabilities**			
Long-term Borrowings	2	3,78,000	2,62,000
3. **Current Liabilities**			
(a) Trade Payables	3	28,000	28,000
(b) Other Current Liabilities (Outstanding expenses)		2,000	6,000
Total		9,68,000	7,56,000
II. **ASSETS**			
1. **Non-current Assets**			
(a) Property, Plant and Equipment and Intangible Assets			
(i) Property, Plant and Equipment	4	6,40,000	4,60,000
(ii) Intangible Assets		10,000	20,000
2. **Current Assets**			
(a) Inventories		34,000	40,000
(b) Trade Receivables	5	1,68,000	1,36,000
(c) Cash and Cash Equivalents (Cash at Bank)		1,00,000	80,000
(d) Other Current Assets		16,000	20,000
Total		9,68,000	7,56,000

Notes to Accounts

Particulars	31st March, 2012 (₹)	31st March, 2011 (₹)
1. **Reserves and Surplus**		
General Reserve	60,000	60,000
Balance of Statement of Profit and Loss	1,40,000	1,00,000
	2,00,000	1,60,000
2. **Long-term Borrowings**		
12% Debentures	1,38,000	1,02,000
12% Public Deposits	2,40,000	1,60,000
	3,78,000	2,62,000
3. **Trade Payables**		
Creditors	20,000	16,000
Bills Payables	8,000	12,000
	28,000	28,000
4. **Property, Plant and Equipment**		
Building	4,40,000	3,00,000
Plant	2,00,000	1,60,000
	6,40,000	4,60,000
5. **Trade Receivables**		
Debtors	1,50,000	1,20,000
Bills Receivables	18,000	16,000
Total	1,68,000	1,36,000

Additional information

(i) Depreciation charged on building ₹ 20,000 and plant ₹ 10,000.

(ii) Interest paid on debentures ₹ 14,400. New debentures of ₹ 36,000 were issued on 1st October, 2011.

(iii) Interest paid on deposits from public ₹ 19,200 for the year.

Answers

1. (b) Cash received from trade receivables
2. (c) Purchase of shares of a company
3. (a) Purchase of land and building against issue of shares
4. (d) Puchase of stock-in-trade
5. (a) ₹ 2,24,000 (outflow)

10. Cash Flow from Operating Activities = ₹ 38,500
Cash Used in Investing Activities = ₹ (51,000)
Cash Flow from Financing Activities = ₹ 13,000

11. Cash Flow from Operating Activities = ₹ 87,600
Cash Used in Investing Activities = ₹ (2,10,000)
Cash Flow from Financing Activities = ₹ 1,42,400

10

Ratio Analysis

TREND ANALYSIS 5 YEARS

	Average No. of Questions Across all Sets					
	Types of Questions	2023	2020	2019	2018	2017
01 Liquidity and Solvency Ratios	1/2 Marks	2	2	—	1	1
	3 Marks	—	—	—	—	—
	6 Marks	—	—	—	—	—
	10 Marks	—	—	—	—	—
02 Activity Ratios	1/2 Marks	—	—	—	—	—
	3 Marks	—	—	—	—	—
	6 Marks	1	1	—	—	—
	10 Marks	—	—	—	—	—
03 Profitability Ratios	1/2 Marks	—	1	1	—	—
	3 Marks	—	—	—	—	—
	6 Marks	—	—	—	—	—
	10 Marks	—	—	1	1	1

Ratio

It is an arithmetical expression of relationship between two related or interdependent items.

Accounting Ratios

It is a mathematical expression that shows the relationship between various items or groups of items shown in financial statements. When ratios are calculated on the basis of accounting information, they are called accounting ratios.

Ratio Analysis

It is a technique which involves re-grouping of data by application of arithmetical relationship.

Objectives of Ratio Analysis

Following are the objectives of ratio analysis

(i) To know the areas of an enterprise which need more attention.

(ii) To know about the potential areas which can be improved on.

(iii) To facilitate inter-firm comparison.

(iv) To facilitate planning and control and thus, decision-making.

(v) To provide analysis of the liquidity, solvency, activity and profitability of an enterprise.

(vi) To provide information useful for making estimates and preparing the plans for future.

Advantages of Ratio Analysis

Main advantages of ratio analysis are as follows

(i) It is useful in analysis of financial statements.

(ii) Helps in simplifying accounting figures.

(iii) Useful in judging the operating efficiency of business.

(iv) Helps in identification of problem areas.

(v) Helpful in comparative analysis.

Limitations of Ratio Analysis

Various limitations of ratio analysis are

(i) Accounting ratios ignore qualitative factors.
(ii) Absence of universally accepted terminology.
(iii) Ratios are affected by window-dressing.
(iv) Effects of inherent limitations of accounting.
(v) Misleading results in the absence of absolute data.
(vi) Price level changes are ignored.
(vii) Impressed by personal bias and ability of the analyst.

Classification of Accounting Ratios

In view of the requirements of various users, the accounting ratios may be classified as under

1. Liquidity Ratios

Liquidity ratios measure the firm's ability to fulfill its short-term financial obligations.

Liquidity ratio are further classified as

(i) Current Ratio/Working Capital Ratio

This ratio establishes relationship between current assets and current liabilities and is used to assess the short-term financial position of the business concern. Current ratio of 2:1 is considered to be satisfactory.

$$\text{Current Ratio/Working Capital Ratio} = \frac{\text{Current Assets}}{\text{Current Liabilities}}$$

Items Included in Current Assets

(a) Current investments
(b) Inventories (excluding loose tools and spare parts)
(c) Trade receivables (bills receivable and sundry debtors less provision for doubtful debts)
(d) Cash and cash equivalents (cash in hand, cash at bank, cheques/drafts in hand)
(e) Short-term loans and advances
(f) Other current assets (prepaid expenses, interest receivable, etc)

Items Included in Current Liabilities

(a) Short-term borrowings
(b) Trade payables (bills payable and sundry creditors)
(c) Other current liabilities (current maturities of long-term debts, interest accrued but not due on borrowings, interest accrued and due on borrowings, outstanding expenses, unclaimed dividend, calls-in-advance, etc)
(d) Short-term provisions.

(ii) Liquid Ratio/Quick Ratio/Acid Test Ratio

This ratio establishes relationship between liquid assets and current liabilities and is used to measure the firm's ability to pay the claims of creditors immediately. This ratio is a better indicator of liquidity and 1:1 is considered to be satisfactory.

$$\text{Liquid Ratio/Quick Ratio/Acid Test Ratio} = \frac{\text{Liquid Assets or Quick Assets}^*}{\text{Current Liabilities}}$$

*Liquid/Quick Assets = All Current Assets − Inventories (excluding loose tools and spare parts) − Prepaid Expenses

2. Solvency Ratios

Solvency ratios judge the long-term financial position of an enterprise, i.e. whether business is able to pay its long-term liabilities or not.

The various solvency ratios are

(i) Debt to Equity Ratio/Debt Worth Ratio

It establishes the relationship between long-term debt (external equities) and the equity (internal equities) i.e. shareholders' funds. It is computed to ascertain soundness of the long-term financial position of the firm.

Generally, the ratio of 2 : 1 is considered as an ideal ratio

$$\text{Debt to Equity Ratio} = \frac{\text{Debt (Long-term debt)}}{\text{Equity (Shareholders' fund)}}$$

Items Included in Long-term Debts

It includes long-term borrowings and long-term provisions.

Items Included in Equity or Shareholders' Funds

Equity/Shareholders' Funds = Share Capital + Reserves and Surplus

or = Non-current Assets + (Current assets − Current liabilities) − Non-current Liabilities

= Non-current Assets + Working Capital − Non-current Liabilities

or = (Tangible Assets + Intangible Assets + Non-current investments + Long-term loans and advances) + Working Capital − (Long-term borrowings + Long-term provisions)

(ii) Proprietary Ratios

It establishes the relationship between proprietors' funds and total assets.

$$\text{Proprietary Ratio} = \frac{\text{Proprietors' Funds or Shareholders' Funds / Equity}}{\text{Total Assets}}$$

Total Assets = Non-current Assets + Current Assets
= Tanglible Assets + Intangible Assets + Non-current Investments +Long-term Loans and Advances + Current Investments + Inventories (including loose tools and spare parts) + Trade Receivables + Cash and Cash Equivalents + Short-term Loans and Advances + Other Current Assets

(iii) Debt to Total Assets Ratio

It establishes a relationship between total long-term debts and total assets.

$$\text{Debt to Total Assets Ratio} = \frac{\text{Long-term Debts}}{\text{Total Assets}}$$

(iv) Interest Coverage Ratio

This ratio expresses the relationship between net profit before interest and tax and interest payable on long-term debts. The ideal coverage ratio is 6 to 7 times as net profit.

$$\text{Interest Coverage Ratio} = \frac{\text{Net Profit before Interest and Tax}}{\text{Interest on Long-term Debts}}$$

3. Turnover or Performance or Activity Ratios

These ratios measure how efficiently a company is using its assets to generate sales.
The various activity ratios are

(i) Inventory Turnover Ratio

The ratio indicates the number of times, the stock is turned in sales during the accounting period. i.e., it measures how fast the stock is moving through the firm and generating sales.

Stock or Inventory Turnover Ratio

$$= \frac{\text{Cost of Goods Sold (i.e. Cost of Revenue from Operations)}}{\text{Average Inventory}}$$

Note In case of cost of goods sold, i.e. (cost of revenue from operations) is not available, the amount of sales, i.e. (revenue from operations) may be used for computing the ratio.

Cost of Revenue from Operations (i.e. Cost of goods sold)
= Cost of Materials Consumed (including direct expenses) + Changes in Inventories of Finished Goods and Work-in-progress
or = Opening Inventories + Net Purchases + Direct Expenses – Closing Inventories
or = Revenue from Operations – Gross Profit

$$\text{Average Inventory} = \frac{\text{Opening Inventory} + \text{Closing Inventory}}{2}$$

(ii) Trade Receivables/Debtors Turnover Ratio

Trade receivable turnover ratio indicates economy and efficiency in the collection of amount due from debtors. The lower the ratio the better it is.

Debtors/Receivables Turnover Ratio

$$= \frac{\text{Credit Revenue from Operations}}{\text{Average Trade Receivables}}$$

Credit Revenue from Operations
= Revenue from Operations – Cash Revenue from Operations

Average Trade Receivables

$$= \frac{\text{Opening Receivables (Debtors + Bills receivable)} + \text{Closing Receivables (Debtors + Bills receivable)}}{2}$$

Average Collection Period

$$= \frac{\text{Number of Days/Weeks/Months in a Year}}{\text{Trade Receivable Turnover Ratio}}$$

(iii) Trade Payables/Creditors Turnover Ratio

Trade payables turnover ratio indicates the speed with which the amount is being paid to creditors. The higher the ratio, the better it is.

Creditors/Payables Turnover Ratio

$$= \frac{\text{Net Credit Purchase}}{\text{Average Trade Payables}}$$

Average Payables

$$= \frac{\text{Opening Payables (Creditors + Bills payable)} + \text{Closing Payables (Creditors + Bills payable)}}{2}$$

In the absence of opening creditors and bills payable, closing creditors and bills payable can be used in the above formula.

Average Payment Period

$$= \frac{\text{Number of Days/Weeks/Months in a Year}}{\text{Trade Payables Turnover Ratio}}$$

(iv) Working Capital Turnover Ratio

This ratio shows the number of times the working capital has been employed in the process of carrying of business.

Working Capital Turnover Ratio

$$= \frac{\text{Cost of Goods Sold or Revenue from Operations (Net sales)}}{\text{Working Capital}}$$

Working Capital = Current Assets – Current Liabilities

4. Profitability Ratios

These ratios measure the profitability of a business and helps in assessing the overall efficiency of the business. The various profitability ratios are

(i) Gross Profit Ratio

Gross profit ratio shows the relationship between the gross profit to net sales (revenue from operations).

$$\text{Gross Profit Ratio} = \frac{\text{Gross Profit}}{\text{Revenue from Operations (Net sales)}} \times 100$$

Gross Profit = Revenue from Operations (i.e. Sales) − Cost of Revenue from Operations *or* Cost of Goods Sold

Cost of Revenue from Operations
= Cost of Material Consumed (including direct expenses) + Change in Inventories of WIP and Finished Goods

or

Opening Inventory + Net Purchases + Direct Expenses − Closing Inventory

(ii) Net Profit Ratio

Net profit ratio shows the relationship between net profit and net sales (revenue from operations). Net profit ratio is an indicator of overall operational efficiency of the business.

$$\text{Net Profit Ratio} = \frac{\text{Net Profit}}{\text{Net Sales (Revenue from operations)}} \times 100$$

Net Profit = Gross Profit + Other Income − Indirect Expenses − Tax

(iii) Operating Ratio

Operating ratio establishes the relationship between operating cost and net sales (revenue from operations).

$$\text{Operating Ratio} = \frac{\text{Cost of Revenue from Operations} + \text{Operating Expenses}}{\text{Revenue from Operations (Net sales)}} \times 100$$

Operating Expenses = Employee Benefit Expenses + Depreciation and Amortisation Expenses + Selling and Distribution Expenses + Office and Administrative Expenses

(iv) Operating Profit Ratio

Operating profit ratio establishes the relationship between the operating profit and net sales (revenue from operations).

Operating profit ratio is an indicator of operational efficiency of the business.

$$\text{Operating Profit Ratio} = \frac{\text{Net Operating Profit}}{\text{Revenue from Operations (Net sales)}} \times 100$$

Net Operating Profit = Net Profit after Tax + Non-operating Expenses − Non-operating Income

or

Gross Profit − Operating Expenses + Operating Incomes

Non-operating Expenses = Interest on Debentures/ Long-term Loans + Loss on Sale of Non-current Assets

Non-operating Incomes = Interest Received on Investment + Profit on Sale of Non-current Assets

(v) Earning Per Share

This ratio measures the earnings available to equity shareholders after tax and preference dividend on per equity share basis.

$$\text{Earning Per Share (EPS)} = \frac{\text{Net Profit (after interest, tax and dividend on preference shares)}}{\text{Number of Equity Shares}}$$

(vi) Price Earning Ratio

The price earning ratio is the ratio of the market price of a company's stock to its earnings per share.

$$\text{Price Earning Ratio} = \frac{\text{Market Value of an Equity Share}}{\text{Earning per Share}}$$

(vii) Return on Investments (RoI) or Return on Capital Employed

This ratio establishes the relationship between **net profit before interest, tax** and preference dividend and **capital employed** (equity + debts).

This ratio shows how efficiently the internal (equity) sources and external (debts) sources are being used or employed in business.

$$\text{Return on Investments (RoI)} = \frac{\text{Net Profit before Interest and Tax}}{\text{Capital Employed}} \times 100 = \ldots\ldots\%$$

Capital Employed = Shareholders' Fund + Non-current Liabilities

or

= Non-current Assets + Working Capital

PYQs Previous Years' Questions

1/2 Marks Questions

1. A company had current assets of ₹ 3,00,000 and current liabilities of ₹ 1,50,000, having a current ratio of 2 : 1.

   What will be the company's revised current ratio after it collects ₹ 20,000 cash from its debtors of ₹ 25,000, the remaining debtors being bad? **ISC 2023**

   (a) 2.56 : 1 (b) 2.03 : 1 (c) 2.13 : 1 (d) 1.97 : 1

2. State with reason whether provision for doubtful debts is subtracted from trade receivables while computing current ratio. **ISC 2023**

3. What will be the operating ratio of Zenia Ltd. from the particulars given below? **ISC Specimen 2023**

   Revenue from Operations ₹ 9,00,000

   Gross Profit 20% on cost

   Operating Expenses ₹ 60,000

   (a) 86.67% (b) 90%
   (c) 76.67% (d) 20%

4. State the objective of calculating liquidity ratios. **ISC Specimen 2023**

5. What is gross profit + cost of materials consumed? **ISC Specimen 2023**

6. Sumo Ltd. had a current ratio of 0.8 : 1, its current assets being ₹ 2,00,000 and current liabilities being ₹ 2,50,000.

   What will be the revised current ratio of Sumo Ltd, after one of its endorsed bills receivable of ₹ 30,000 gets dishonoured? **ISC Sem I 2021**

   (a) 0.71 : 1 (b) 0.92 : 1 (c) 0.72 : 1 (d) 0.82 : 1

7. The debt-equity ratio of a company is 1.7 : 1. Which one of the following transactions will reduce the debt-equity ratio? **ISC Sem I 2021**

   (a) Plant and machinery worth ₹ 1,20,000 sold at a loss of ₹ 10,000
   (b) Interest of ₹ 5,000 received on calls-in-arrears
   (c) A loan of ₹ 10,00,000 taken from a bank
   (d) Interest of ₹ 10,000 paid on the bank loan

8. The particulars of Mars Ltd. are given below

Particulars	Amt (₹)
Opening Debtors	50,000
Cash received from debtors	2,20,000
Closing Debtors	30,000

   What will be the trade receivables turnover ratio of the company? **ISC Sem I 2021**

   (a) 4.75 times (b) 5.5 times
   (c) 5 times (d) 6.75 times

9. The net revenue from operations of Gama Ltd. is ₹ 14,00,000.

   Its gross profit is ₹ 9,00,000; Operating expenses are ₹ 75,000; Commission received is ₹ 5,000; Profit from sale of fixed asset is ₹ 10,000.

   The operating profit ratio of Gama Ltd will be **ISC Sem I Specimen 2021**

   (a) 59.29% (b) 56.29%
   (c) 60% (d) 58.93%

10. Which of the following four companies is not deriving the benefit of 'trading on equity'? **ISC Sem I Specimen 2021**

    (a) Mars Ltd., which has a debt-equity ratio of 0.49:1
    (b) Venus Ltd., which has a debt-equity ratio of 1.54:1
    (c) Saturn Ltd., which has a debt-equity ratio of 1.62:1
    (d) Pluto Ltd.. which has a debt-equity ratio of 2.32:1

KEY IDEA

Company with high debt-equity ratio will derive more benefit of 'trade on equity'.

11. From the given particulars of Zee Ltd., the trade receivables turnover ratio of the company will be **ISC Sem I Specimen 2021**

Particulars	Amt (₹)
Revenue from Operations	12,00,000
Cash Revenue form Operations	25% of Credit Revenue from Operations
Gross Debtors	1,90,000
Bills Receivable	50,000
Provision for Doubtful Debts	10,000

    (a) 3.75 times (b) 4 times
    (c) 4.17 times (d) 8 times

12. The correct formula for computing earning per share is **ISC Sem I Specimen 2021**

    (a) $\frac{\text{Net Profit after Tax}}{\text{No. of Shares}}$

    (b) $\frac{\text{Net Profit after Tax and Preference Dividend}}{\text{No. of Shares}}$

    (c) $\frac{\text{Net Profit after Tax and Preference Dividend}}{\text{No. of Equity Shares}}$

    (d) $\frac{\text{Net Profit after Tax and Preference Dividend}}{\text{No. of Preference Shares}}$

13. The current ratio of a company is 1.8 : 1 and its quick ratio is 1.6 : 1.
From the following transactions, pick out the transaction which involves an increase in both the current ratio and quick ratio *ISC Sem I Specimen 2021*
(a) Goods worth ₹ 10,000 sold at a loss of ₹ 2,000.
(b) Insurance premium of ₹ 3,000 paid in advance.
(c) Plant and machinery purchased for ₹ 9,000.
(d) Bills payable of ₹ 2,000 honoured on the due date.

KEY IDEA
If current asset and current liability will reduce with equal amount, it will increase current ratio and quick ratio.

14. State the objective of calculating liquidity ratios. *ISC 2020*

15. Assuming that the current ratio of company is 0.7: 1, mention whether this ratio would increase, decrease or not change after the following transactions *ISC 2020*
(i) Payment of ₹ 15,000 made to a creditor.
(ii) Purchase of inventory worth ₹ 1,00,000 on credit.

16. From the following information, calculate earnings per share (upto two decimal places) *ISC 2020*

Particulars	Amt (₹)
10% Peference Share Capital	₹ 6,00,000
Equity Share Capital (3,00,000 Shares of ₹ 10 each)	₹ 30,00,000
Profit before Tax	₹ 15,00,000
Tax Rate	30%

17. Calculate the gross profit ratio from the following information *ISC 2019*

Particulars	Amt (₹)
Opening Inventory	80,000
Closing Inventory	1,00,000
Revenue from Operations	9,00,000
Inventory Turnover Ratio	8 times

18. The quick ratio of a company is 0.8 : 1. State whether the quick ratio will improve, decline or will not change in the following cases *ISC 2018*
(i) Cash collected from debtors ₹ 50,000.
(ii) Creditors of ₹ 20,000 paid-off.

19. The current ratio of a company is 2 : 1. State whether the current ratio will improve, decline or will not change in the following cases *ISC 2017*
(i) Bill receivable of ₹ 2,000 endorsed to a creditor is dishonoured.
(ii) ₹ 8,000 cash collected from debtors of ₹ 8,500 in full and final settlement.

20. The current ratio of a company is 2 : 1. State whether the following will increase, reduce or not change the ratio *ISC 2015*
(i) Bills payable ₹ 5,000 discharged.
(ii) Purchase of inventory ₹ 20,000 on credit.

21. Give the formulae for calculating *ISC 2015*
(i) Earning per share.
(ii) Trade payables turnover ratio.

22. Assuming that the debt-equity ratio of a company is 2 : 1, state whether this ratio would increase, decrease or not change in the following cases *ISC 2012*
(i) Issue of new shares for cash
(ii) Repayment of a long-term bank loan

23. State two difference between current ratio and quick ratio. *ISC 2011*

24. How is 'cost of goods sold' i.e., cost of revenue from operations calculated? *ISC 2009*

25. What is gross profit ratio and net profit ratio? *ISC 2009*

26. Name any two balance sheet ratios. *ISC 2008*

27. When calculating the acid test ratio, name two items that are excluded from current assets. *ISC 2008*

28. What is quick ratio? State its significance. *ISC 2005*

6 Marks Questions

29. Answer any three of the following questions *ISC 2023*
(i) Calculate debt to total assets ratio of Moonlight Ltd. (up-to two decimal places) from the following information

Particulars	Amt (₹)
Property, Plant and Equipment and Intangible Assets	20,00,000
Shares of XYZ Bank Ltd.	1,00,000
Long-term Loans and Advances	1,00,000
Current Assets	10,00,000
Current Liabilities	4,00,000
Total Debt	12,00,000

(ii) Calculate trade payables turnover ratio (up-to two decimal places) from the following information

Particulars	Amt (₹)
Trade Payables at the beginning of the year	70,000
Trade Payables at the end of the year	80,000
Payment to Trade Payables	3,20,000
Returns to Credit Suppliers	30,000

(iii) Calculate quick ratio (up-to two decimal places) from the following information

Particulars	Amt (₹)
Total Current Assets	90,000
Working Capital	60,000
Prepaid Expenses	30,000

(iv) In the year 2021-22, Kartik Ltd. carried an average stock of ₹ 40,000. Its inventory turnover ratio was 8 times. It sold goods at a profit of 25% on the cost of revenue from operations. Calculate the profit made by Kartik Ltd. in the year 2021-22.

30. From the following statement of profit and loss of Swatantra Ltd. for the year 2020-21, calculate any three ratios (upto two decimal places) ***ISC Specimen 2023***

(i) Gross profit ratio
(ii) Net profit ratio
(iii) Operating profit ratio
(iv) Inventory turnover ratio

Statement of Profit and Loss of Swatantra Ltd.
for the year ending 31st March, 2022

Particulars	Note No.	Amt (₹)
Revenue from Operations		5,00,000
Other Income (Profit on Sale of Machinery)		40,000
Total Revenue		5,40,000
Expenses		
Purchases		2,50,000
Changes in Inventories	1	(10,000)
Employee Benefit Expenses	2	26,000
Depreciation		14,000
Finance Cost (Interest on Debentures)		30,000
Other Expenses	3	20,000
Total Expenses		3,30,000
Profit before Tax		2,10,000
Provision for Tax		(84,000)
Profit after Tax		1,26,000

Notes to Accounts

Particulars	Amt (₹)
1. **Changes in Inventories**	
Opening Inventory	40,000
Closing Inventory	50,000
2. **Employee Benefit Expenses**	
Wages	16,000
Salaries	10,000
3. **Other Expenses**	
Carriage Inward	8,000
Loss on Sale of Furniture	12,000

31. From the following information calculate the following ratios (upto two decimal places) ***ISC 2020***

(i) Debt to total assets ratio
(ii) Proprietary ratio
(iii) Inventory turnover Ratio

Particulars	Amt (₹)
Property, Plant and Equipment and Intangible Assets	14,00,000
Current Assets (including inventory of ₹ 2,00,000)	10,00,000
Shareholders' Funds	14,40,000
Non-current Liabilities (10% Long-term Bank Loan)	8,00,000
Current Liabilities	5,00,000
Revenue from Operations	15,00,000
Gross Profit	6,00,000

32. From the following information calculate (upto two decimal places) ***ISC 2015***

(i) Gross profit ratio (ii) Inventory turnover ratio
(iii) Net profit ratio

Particulars	Amt (₹)
Cash Revenue from Operations	70,000
Net Purchases	2,97,000
Credit Revenue from Operations	2,80,000
Closing Inventory	80,000
Opening Inventory	60,000
Carriage Inward	3,000
Selling Expenses	5,000
Administrative Expenses	40,000
Loss on Sale of Property, Plant and Equipment and Intangible Assets	10,000
Dividend Received	7,000

10 Marks Questions

33. From the following statement of profit and loss of Gama Ltd. for the year 2017-18, calculate (upto two decimal places)

(i) Net profit ratio (ii) Operating profit ratio
(iii) Current ratio (iv) Quick ratio

Statement of Profit and Loss of Gama Ltd.
for the year ending 31st March, 2018

Particulars	Note No.	Amt (₹)
Revenue from Operations		3,00,000
Other Income (Dividend received)		40,000
Total Revenue		3,40,000
Expenses		
Purchases		1,80,000
Change in Inventories	1	(4,000)

Particulars	Note No.	Amt (₹)
Employee Benefit Expenses (Salaries)		10,000
Depreciation and Amortisation (Depreciation of Property, Plant and Equipment and Intangible Assets)		28,000
Other Expenses	2	6,000
Total Expenses		2,20,000
Profit before Tax		1,20,000
(–) Provision for Tax		(48,000)
Profit after Tax		72,000

Notes to Accounts

Particulars	Amt (₹)
1. **Change in Inventories**	
Opening Inventory	8,000
Closing Inventory	12,000
	(4,000)
2. **Other Expenses**	
Carriage Outward	4,000
Rent	2,000
	6,000

Additional information

Total current liabilities as on 31st March, 2018 ₹ 50,000
Current assets (other than inventory) as on 31st March, 2018 ₹ 70,000 *ISC 2019*

34. (i) Calculate the net profit ratio (upto two decimal places) from the following information

Particulars	Amt (₹)
Gross Profit	80,000
Salary and Rent	30,000
Interest on Debentures	5,000
Gain on Sale of Furniture	2,000
Revenue from Operations	4,00,000

(ii) From the following information calculate the following ratio (upto two decimal places)

(a) Earning per share (b) Price earning ratio
(c) Return on investments
(d) Working capital turnover ratio

Particulars	Amt (₹)
Net Profit after Interest and Tax	2,40,000
Tax	1,60,000
Property, Plant and Equipment and Intangible Assets	10,00,000
Non-current Investments (Non-trade)	1,00,000
Equity Share Capital (face value ₹ 10 per share)	5,00,000
15% Preference Share Capital	1,00,000
Reserves and Surplus (including surplus of the year under consideration)	2,00,000
10% Debentures	4,00,000
Revenue from Operations	10,00,000
Working Capital	1,00,000

Note The market value of an equity share is ₹ 40. *ISC 2018*

KEY IDEA

Net Profit = Gross Profit + Other Incomes – Indirect Expenses – Tax

35. From the information given below, calculate (upto two decimal places) *ISC 2017*

(i) Operating ratio (ii) Quick ratio
(iii) Debt to equity ratio
(iv) Proprietary ratio
(v) Working capital turnover ratio

Particulars	Amt (₹)
Net Revenue from Operations	12,00,000
Cost of Revenue from Operation	9,00,000
Operating Expenses	15,000
Inventory	20,000
Other Current Assets	2,00,000
Current Liabilities	75,000
Paid-up Share Capital	4,00,000
Statement of Profit and Loss (Dr)	47,500
Total Debt	2,50,000

KEY IDEA

Shareholders' fund includes share capital and reserves and surplus. So, debit balance of statement of profit and loss will be deducted from paid-up share capital.

36. (i) Calculate liquid ratio from the following (upto two decimal places)

Current assets	₹ 1,26,000
Inventories	₹ 2,000
Current ratio	3 : 2

(ii) From the following statement of profit and loss of Dixon Ltd for the year 2014-15, calculate (upto two decimal places)

(a) Trade receivables turnover ratio
(b) Inventory turnover ratio
(c) Net profit ratio
(d) Operating profit ratio

Statement of Profit and Loss
for the year ending 31st March, 2015

Particulars	Note No.	Amt (₹)
Revenue from Operations		2,00,000
Other Income (Rent received)		10,000
Total Revenue		2,10,000
Expenses		
Purchases		55,000
Change in Inventories	1	3,000
Employee Benefit Expenses	2	5,000
Depreciation		2,000
Other Expenses	3	5,000
Total Expenses		70,000
Profit before Tax		1,40,000
(–) Tax		(56,000)
Profit after Tax		84,000

Notes to Accounts

Particulars	31st March, 2015 (₹)
1. **Change in Inventories**	
Opening Inventory	6,000
Closing Inventory	(3,000)
	3,000
2. **Employee Benefit Expenses**	
Wages	2,000
Salaries	3,000
	5,000
3. **Other Expenses**	
Carriage Inward	2,000
Carriage Outward	3,000
	5,000

Additional information

Debtors (as on 31st March, 2015)	₹ 7,000
Bills receivable (as on 31st March, 2015)	₹ 5,000
Cash revenue from operations	₹ 50,000

ISC 2016

37. (i) How does the quality of ratio analysis of a business depend upon the accuracy of its financial statements?

(ii) From the following information, calculate trade receivable turnover ratio

Credit Revenue from Operations	₹ 9,60,000
Gross Debtors	₹ 1,90,000
Bills Receivable	₹ 50,000
Provision for Doubtful Debts	₹ 10,000

(iii) From the following information, calculate the following ratio (upto two decimal places)

(a) Debt equity ratio (b) Interest coverage ratio (c) Proprietary ratio

	Amt (₹)
Equity Share Capital	2,00,000
5% Preference Share Capital	60,000
General Reserve	1,20,000
Property, Plant and Equipment and Intangible Assets	5,05,000
Current Assets	1,20,000
Current Liabilities	40,000

Loan @10% Interest	5,00,000
Tax paid During the Year	30,000
Profit for the Current Year after Interest and Tax (available for the shareholders)	90,000

ISC 2014

38. (i) The following information is available from the books of Greg Goods Ltd

Particulars	Amt (₹)
Equity Share Capital	1,00,000
8% Preference Share Capital	40,000
Reserves and Surplus	60,000
Investments	30,000
Current Assets	70,000
Proprietary Ratio is 0.8 : 1	

Assuming that there are no fictitious assets, calculate the value of the property, plant and equipment and intangible assets of the company.

(ii) The following figures have been extracted from the records of Allen Cosmetics Ltd

Particulars	Amt (₹)
Cost of Revenue from Operations (Cost of goods sold)	4,00,000
Current Liabilities	90,000
Profit Margin is equal to 20% on Revenue from Operations	
Working Capital Turnover Ratio is equal to 10 times.	

Determine the value of the current assets of the company.

(iii) The following details are available from the books of Simon Gadgets Ltd

Particulars	Amt (₹)
Revenue from Operations (Sales)	8,00,000
Opening Inventory	40,000
Closing Inventory	50,000
Gross Profit Ratio is 20%	

Calculate the stock turnover ratio of the company (upto two decimal places).

KEY IDEA

In the absence of information, gross profit will be considered as percentage of revenue from operations (Net sales).

(iv) The following data is available from the records of Johnson and Company Ltd

Particulars	Amt (₹)
Stock	50,000
Sundry Debtors	40,000
Bills Receivable	10,000
Advances Paid	4,000
Cash in Hand	30,000
Sundry Creditors	60,000
Bills Payable	40,000
Bank Overdraft	4,000
Reserves	70,000
10% Preference Share Capital	5,00,000
Equity Share Capital	7,00,000
Net Profit after Tax	1,40,000

Calculate the following (upto two decimal places)

(a) Current ratio (b) Quick ratio

ISC 2013

39. From the following information, calculate (upto two decimal places) *ISC 2012*

(i) Liquid ratio
(ii) Current ratio
(iii) Proprietary ratio
(iv) Working capital turnover ratio
(v) Gross profit ratio
(vi) Operating ratio
(vii) Net profit ratio

Particulars	Amt (₹)
Cost of Revenue from Operations	6,00,000
Operating Expenses	50,000
Revenue from Operations	8,00,000
Sales Returns	10,000
Total Current Assets	3,00,000
Total Current Liabilities	1,00,000
Total Assets	7,00,000
Closing Stock	30,000
Prepaid Insurance	5,000
Preliminary Expenses	6,000
Share Capital	5,60,000
Reserves and Surplus	40,000

40. The following figure have been extracted from the books of Arvind and Company Ltd

Particulars	Amt (₹)
Net Sales (Revenue from operations)	12,00,000
Net Purchases	5,00,000
Administrative Expenses	65,000
Selling and Distribution Expenses	35,000
Gross Profit	20% on sales
Net Profit after Tax	10,00,000
Total Assets	40,00,000
Equity Share Capital of ₹ 10 each	10,00,000
10% Preference Share Capital for ₹ 10 each	3,00,000
Reserves and Surplus	2,00,000
8% Debentures	8,00,000
Opening Debtors	1,20,000
Closing Debtors	80,000
Opening Bills Receivable	60,000
Closing Bills Receivable	40,000
Opening Creditors	1,30,000
Closing Creditors	70,000
Closing Bills Payable	50,000
Opening Bills Payable	1,10,000

From the above information, calculate the following
(i) Total assets to debt ratio
(ii) Debt equity ratio (iii) Operating ratio
(iv) Operating profit ratio (v) Earning per share
(vi) Debtors turnover ratio
(vii) Creditors turnover ratio

Note All calculations are to be made to two places of decimal
. *ISC 2011*

41. From the given information, calculate the following ratios *ISC 2009*

(i) Debt equity ratio
(ii) Total assets to debt ratio
(iii) Operating ratio
(iv) Debtors turnover ratio
(v) Creditors turnover ratio

Particulars	Amt (₹)
Shareholders' Funds	50,000
10% Debentures	25,000
Total Assets	1,75,000
Credit Sales (Revenue from operations)	2,70,000
Credit Purchases	1,80,000
Average Debtors	30,000
Average Creditors	16,000
Cost of Goods Sold (Cost of revenue from operations)	2,16,000
Operating Expenses	24,000

Note All calculations are to be made to two places of decimal.

42. Calculate the following ratios from the given information *ISC 2007*

(i) Acid test ratio (ii) Gross profit ratio
(iii) Stock turnover ratio (iv) Operating ratio
(v) Debt equity ratio

Statement of Profit and Loss
for the year ended...

Particulars	Note No.	Amt (₹)
I. **Revenue from Operations**		5,00,000
II. **Expenses**		
Purchase of Stock-in-trade		2,00,000
Change in Inventories	1	(30,000)
Other Expenses	2	1,25,000
Total Expenses		2,95,000
III. Profit before Tax (I – II)		2,05,000
IV. Provision for Tax		40,000
V. Profit after Tax (III – IV)		1,65,000

Notes to Accounts

Particulars		Amt (₹)
1. **Changes in Inventories**		
Opening Inventory	50,000	
(–) Closing Inventory	(80,000)	(30,000)
2. **Other Expenses**		
Administrative Expenses		20,000
Selling Expenses		30,000
Finance Expenses (Interest on long-term loan)		25,000
Direct Expenses		50,000
		1,25,000

Balance Sheet
as at 31st March, 2012

Particulars	Note No.	Amt (₹)
I. **EQUITY AND LIABILITIES**		
1. **Shareholders' Funds**		
(a) Share Capital	1	7,00,000
(b) Reserves and Surplus	2	1,11,000
2. **Non-current Liabilities**		
Long-term Borrowings		1,50,000
3. **Current Liabilities**		
Trade Payables	3	24,000
Total		9,85,000
II. **ASSETS**		
1. **Non-current Assets**		
Property, Plant and Equipment		7,20,000
2. **Current Assets**		
(a) Inventory		80,000
(b) Trade Receivables		1,20,000
(c) Cash and Cash Equivalents	4	60,000
(d) Other Current Assets	5	5,000
Total		9,85,000

Notes to Accounts

Particulars	Amt (₹)
1. **Share Capital**	
Equity Share Capital	
4,000 Equity Shares of ₹ 100 each	4,00,000
Preference Share Capital	
3,000, 5% Preference Shares of ₹ 100 each	3,00,000
	7,00,000
2. **Reserve and Surplus**	
Reserves	5,000
Statement of Profit and Loss	1,06,000
	1,11,000
3. **Trade Payables**	
Creditors	20,000
Bills Payable	4,000
	24,000
4. **Cash and Cash Equivalents**	
Cash Balance	15,000
Bank Balance	45,000
	60,000
5. **Other Current Assets**	
Prepaid Expenses	5,000

43.

Statement of Profit and Loss
for the year ending 31st March

Particulars	Note No.	Amt (₹)
I. Revenue from Operations		1,00,100
II. Other Income	1	1,200
III. **Total Revenue**		1,01,300
IV. **Expenses**		
Purchase of Stock-in-trade		63,050
Changes in Inventories	2	(4,350)
Employee Benefit Expenses	3	1,000
Other Expenses	4	24,800
Total Expenses		84,500
V. Profit before Tax (III – IV)		16,800

Notes to Accounts

Particulars		Amt (₹)
1. **Other Income**		
Non-operating Income		1,200
2. **Changes in Inventories**		
Opening Inventory	15,250	
(–) Closing Inventory	(19,600)	(4,350)
3. **Employee Benefit Expenses**		
Wages		1,000
4. **Other Expenses**		
Administrative Expenses	20,200	
Selling and Distribution Expenses	2,400	
Finance Expenses	1,400	
Non-operating Expenses	400	
Carriage Inward	400	24,800

Balance Sheet

Particulars	Note No.	Amt (₹)
I. **EQUITY AND LIABILITIES**		
1. **Shareholders' Funds**		
(a) Share Capital		70,000
(b) Reserves and Surplus	1	18,000

Particulars	Note No.	Amt (₹)
2. **Current Liabilities**		
Trade Payables (Creditors)		3,700
Total		91,700
II. **ASSETS**		
Non-current Assets		
Property, Plant and Equipment		60,100
Current Assets		
(a) Inventories		19,600
(b) Trade Receivables (Debtors)		9,000
(c) Cash and Cash Equivalents		3,000
Total		91,700

Notes to Accounts

Particulars	Amt (₹)
1. **Reserves and Surplus**	
Reserves	1,200
Statement of Profit and Loss	16,800
	18,000

From the above, calculate the following ratios
(i) Gross profit ratio (%) (ii) Net profit ratio (%)
(iii) Stock turnover ratio
(iv) Proprietary ratio
(v) Current ratio
(vi) Quick ratio *ISC 2005*

Note All calculations are to be made to two places of decimal.

Case Based Questions

44. The particulars of Barua Ltd are given below *ISC Sem I 2021*

Particulars	Amt (₹)
Revenue from Operations	10,00,000
Purchase of Stock-in-trade	6,00,000
Changes in Inventory of Stock-in-trade	(60,000)
(Opening Inventory ₹ 1,20,000, Closing Inventory ₹ 1,80,000)	
Employee Benefit Expenses (Salaries)	40,000
Provision for Tax	1,00,000
Sundry Creditors	2,00,000
Cash at Bank	5,00,000
Marketable Securities	50,000

(i) What will be the current ratio of the company?
(a) 2.23 : 1 (b) 3.65 : 1
(c) 2.43 : 1 (d) 1.83 : 1

(ii) What will be the net profit ratio of the company?
(a) 32% (b) 30%
(c) 42% (d) 36%

45. The particular of Alpha Ltd are given below *ISC Sem I Specimen 2021*

Particulars	Amt (₹)
Equity Share Capital	2,00,000
5% Preference Share Capital	60,000
General Reserve	1,20,000
Property, Plant and Equipment and Intangible Assets	5,05,000
Current Assets	1,20,000
Current Liabilities	40,000
Loan @ 10% Interest	5,00,000
Tax Provided During the Year	30,000
Profit for the Current Year after Interest and Tax (available for the shareholders)	90,000

(i) The interest coverage ratio of the company will be
(a) 1.8 times (b) 2.8 times
(c) 3.4 times (d) 2.4 times

(ii) The proprietary ratio of the company will be
(a) 0.47 : 1 (b) 0.75 : 1
(c) 0.61 : 1 (d) 0.38 : 1

Explanations

1. (d) New current ratio $= \frac{3,00,000 + 20,000 - 25,000}{1,50,000}$

$= 1.97 : 1$

2. Yes, provision for doubtful debts is deducted from the trade receivables in order to ascertain the reasonable value of trade receivables while calculating current ratio.

3. (b) Cost of Revenue from Operations = Revenue from Operations − Gross Profit

$x = 9,00,000 - 20\%x$

$\therefore x = ₹ 7,50,000$

$\Rightarrow$ Operating ratio $= \frac{7,50,000 + 60,000}{9,00,000} \times 100 = 90\%$

4. A liquid ratio is a type of financial ratio used to determine a company's ability to pay its short-term debt obligations. The ratio helps to determine if a company can use its current or liquid assets to cover its current liabilities.

Concept Enhancer Liquidity ratio helps in calculating the short-term solvency of a company. Liquidity ratios tell us whether the company is solvent in short- term or not.

5. If the gross profit and cost of materials consumed are added, then we can get the value of revenue from operations.

6. (d) Current Ratio of Sumo Ltd. $= \frac{0.8}{1} = \frac{2,00,000}{2,50,000}$

Endorsed bill dishonoured will increase both debtor and creditor

Revised Current Ratio $= \frac{2,00,000 + 30,000}{2,50,000 + 30,000}$

$= \frac{2,30,000}{2,80,000} = 0.82 : 1$

7. (b) Interest of ₹ 5,000 received on calls-in-arrears will reduce the debt-equity ratio.

8. (c) Trade Receivable Turnover Ratio

$= \frac{\text{Credit Sales}}{\text{Average Trade Receivables}} = \frac{2,00,000}{40,000} = 5 \text{ times}$

Average Trade Receivable $= \frac{\text{Opening Trade Receivable} + \text{Closing Trade Receivable}}{2}$

$= \frac{50,000 + 30,000}{2} = ₹ 40,000$

Credit Sales = Closing Debtors + Cash Received − Opening Debtors

$= 30,000 + 2,20,000 - 50,000$

$= ₹ 2,00,000$

9. (a) Operation Profit Ratio

$= \frac{\text{Operating Profit*}}{\text{Revenue from operation}} \times 100$

$= \frac{8,30,000}{14,00,000} \times 100 = 59.29\%$

*Operating profit = Gross Profit − Operating Expenses + Operating income

$= 2,00,000 - 75,000 + 5,000$

$= 8,30,000$

10. (a) Man Ltd. which has a debt-equity ratio of 0.49:1

11. (b) Trade Receivables Turnover Ratio

$= \frac{\text{Credit Sales*}}{\text{Average Trade Receivable}}$

$= \frac{9,60,000}{(1,90,000 + 50,000)}$

$= 4$ times

Net Sales = Cash Sales + Credit Sales*

12,00,000 = 25% of Credit Sales + Credit Sales

$\therefore$ Credit Sales = 9,60,000

12. (c) $\frac{\text{Net Profit after Tax and Preference Dividend}}{\text{No. of Equity Shares}}$

13. (d) Bills payable of ₹ 2,000 honoured on the due date.

14. Liquidity is defined as the ability of a company to meet its financial obligations when they become due. Thus, liquidity ratio is used to pay its short-term debts. It includes current ratio, acid-test ratio and cash ratio.

15. (i) **Decrease** Since numerator [current assets (cash)] and denominator [current liabilities (creditor)] reduces by same amount, the ratio decreases.

(ii) **Increase** Since numerator [current assets (inventories)] and denominator [current liabilities (creditor)] increases by same amount, the ratio increases.

16.

Profit before Tax	= ₹ 15,00,000
(−) Tax Rate @ 30%	= ₹ (4,50,000)
	₹ 10,50,000
(−) Preference Dividend	= ₹ (60,000)
	₹ 9,90,000

Outstanding Equity Shares = 3,00,000

$$\text{Earning per Share} = \frac{9,90,000}{3,00,000} = 3.3$$

17. Average Inventory

$$= \frac{\text{Opening Inventory} + \text{Closing Inventory}}{2}$$

$$= \frac{80,000 + 1,00,000}{2} = ₹\,90,000$$

Cost of Revenue from Operations

$$= \text{Inventory Turnover Ratio} \times \text{Average Inventory}$$

$$= 8 \times 90,000 = ₹\,7,20,000$$

Gross Profit = Revenue from Operations – Cost of Revenue from Operations

$$= 9,00,000 - 7,20,000 = ₹\,1,80,000$$

$$\text{Gross Profit Ratio} = \frac{\text{Gross Profit}}{\text{Revenue from Operations}} \times 100$$

$$= \frac{1,80,000}{9,00,000} \times 100 = 20\%$$

18. (i) Cash collected from debtors will not change the total of quick assets because one quick asset will be replaced by another. Therefore, the quick ratio will not change.

(ii) Payment to creditors will reduce the quick assets as well as current liabilities by the same amount. Therefore, the quick ratio will decline.

19. (i) Bill receivable endorsed to a creditor is dishonoured. It will reduce the current assets as well as current liabilities by the same amount. Therefore, the current ratio will decline.

(ii) Cash collected from debtors will not change the total of current assets because one current asset will be replaced by another. But discount allowed reduces the account receivable, thus reducing current assets. Therefore, the current ratio will decline.

20. (i) Bills payable discharged will reduce current assets as well as current liabilities by the same amount. Therefore, current ratio will increase.

(ii) Purchase of inventory on credit will increase current assets as well as current liabilities by the same amount. Therefore, current ratio will reduce.

21. (i) Earning Per Share

$$= \frac{\text{Net Profit available to Equity Shareholders}}{\text{Number of Equity Shares}}$$

(ii) Trade Payables Turnover Ratio

$$= \frac{\text{Net Credit Purchases}}{\text{Average Trade Payables}}$$

22. (i) Issue of new shares for cash will increase the equity. Therefore, debt-equity ratio will decrease.

(ii) Repayment of a long-term bank loan will reduce debt as well as shareholders' fund, i.e. current assets by the same amount. Therefore, debt-equity ratio will decrease.

23. Difference between current ratio and quick ratio

Basis	Current ratio	Quick ratio
Meaning	This ratio establishes relationship between current assets and current liabilities and is used to assess the short-term financial position of the business concern.	This ratio establishes relationship between liquid assets and current liabilities and is used to measure the firm's ability to pay the claims of creditors immediately.
Ideal ratio	Current ratio of 2 : 1is considered to be satisfactory.	This ratio is a better indicator of liquidity and 1 : 1 is considered to be satisfactory.

24. Cost of Revenue from Operations

= Opening Inventory + Net Purchases + Direct Expenses – Closing Inventory

or

= Revenue from Operations (Net sales) – Gross Profit

25. **Gross profit ratio** Gross profit ratio shows the relationship between gross profit to net sales (revenue from operations).

Gross Profit Ratio

$$= \frac{\text{Gross Profit}}{\text{Revenue from Operations (Net sales)}} \times 100$$

Net profit ratio Net profit ratio shows the relationship between net profit and net sales (revenue from operations). Net profit ratio is an indicator of overall operational efficiency of the business.

Net Profit Ratio

$$= \frac{\text{Net Profit}}{\text{Revenue from Operations (Net sales)}} \times 100$$

26. The two balance sheet ratios are

(i) Current ratio (ii) Quick ratio

27. Inventories and prepaid expenses are the items, which are excluded.

28. This ratio establishes relationship between liquid assets and current liabilities and is used to measure the firm's ability to pay the claims of creditors immediately.

This ratio is a better indicator of liquidity and a quick ratio of 1 : 1 is considered to be satisfactory.

Liquid Ratio/Quick Ratio/Acid Test Ratio

$$= \frac{\text{Liquid Assets or Quick Assets *}}{\text{Current Liabilities}}$$

*Liquid/Quick Assets = All Current Assets – Inventories (excluding loose tools and spare parts) – Prepaid Expenses

29. (i) Total Assets = 20,00,000 + 1,00,000 + 1,00,000 + 10,00,000 = ₹ 32,00,000

Debt = 12,00,000 – 4,00,000 = 8,00,000

$$\text{Debt to Total Assets Ratio} = \frac{\text{Debt}}{\text{Total Assets}}$$

$$= \frac{8,00,000}{32,00,000} = 1:4 = 0.25:1$$

(ii) $$\text{Average Trade Receivable} = \frac{70,000 + 80,000}{2}$$

= ₹ 75,000

Dr **Trade Payables Account** Cr

Particulars	Amt (₹)	Particulars	Amt (₹)
To Bank A/c	3,20,000	By Balance b/d	70,000
To Purchase Return	30,000	By Purchases	3,60,000
To Balance c/d	80,000		
	4,30,000		4,30,000

Trade Payables Turnover Ratio

$$= \frac{\text{Credit Purchases}}{\text{Average Trade Payables}}$$

$$= \frac{3,60,000 - 30,000}{75,000} = 4.4 \text{ times}$$

(iii) Working Capital = Current Assets – Current Liabilities

Current Liabilities = 90,000 – 60,000 = ₹ 30,000

Quick Assets = Current Assets – Prepaid Expenses = 90,000 – 30,000 = ₹ 60,000

$$\text{Quick Ratio} = \frac{\text{Quick Assets}}{\text{Current Liabilities}} = \frac{60,000}{30,000} = 2:1$$

(iv) $$\text{Inventory Turnover Ratio} = \frac{\text{Cost of Goods Sold}}{\text{Average Inventory}}$$

Cost of goods sold = 40,000 × 8 = 3,20,000

$$\text{Profit for the year} = 3,20,000 \times \frac{25}{100} = ₹\ 80,000$$

30. (i) Cost of Goods Sold = Opening Stock + Purchases + Direct Expenses – Closing Stock

= 40,000 + 2,50,000 + (16,000 + 8,000) – 50,000

= ₹ 2,64,000

Gross Profit = Revenue from Operations – COGS

= 5,00,000 – 2,64,000 = ₹ 2,36,000

$$\text{Gross Profit Ratio} = \frac{\text{Gross Profit}}{\text{Revenue from Operations}} \times 100$$

$$= \frac{2,36,000}{5,00,000} \times 100 = 47.20\%$$

(ii) $$\text{Net Profit Ratio} = \frac{\text{Net Profit after Tax}}{\text{Revenue from Operations}} \times 100$$

$$= \frac{1,26,000}{5,00,000} \times 100 = 25.20\%$$

(iii) Operating Profit = Gross Profit – Operating Expense + Operating Income

= 2,36,000 – (10,000 + 14,000) + 0

= ₹ 2,12,000

Operating Profit Ratio

$$= \frac{\text{Operating Profit}}{\text{Revenue from Operations}} \times 100$$

$$= \frac{2,12,000}{5,00,000} \times 100 = 42.40\%$$

(iv) $$\text{Average Inventory} = \frac{\text{Opening Stock} + \text{Closing Stock}}{2}$$

$$= \frac{40,000 + 50,000}{2} = ₹\ 45,000$$

$$\text{Inventory Turnover Ratio} = \frac{\text{COGS}}{\text{Average Inventory}}$$

$$= \frac{2,64,000}{45,000} = 5.87 \text{ times}$$

31. (i) Long-term Debt = ₹ 8,00,000

Total Assets = 14,00,000 + 10,00,000 = ₹ 24,00,000

$$\text{Debt to Total Assets Ratio} = \frac{\text{Long-term Debt}}{\text{Total Assets}}$$

$$= \frac{8,00,000}{24,00,000} = 0.33:1$$

(ii) $$\text{Proprietary Ratio} = \frac{\text{Shareholders' Funds}}{\text{Total Assets}}$$

$$= \frac{14,40,000}{24,00,000}$$

= 0.6 : 1

(iii) $$\text{Inventory Turnover Ratio} = \frac{\text{COGS}}{\text{Average Inventory}}$$

Cost of Goods Sold (COGS) = Revenue from Operations – Gross Profit

= 15,00,000 – 6,00,000

= ₹ 9,00,000

Average Inventory = ₹ 2,00,000

$$\text{Now, Inventory Turnover Ratio} = \frac{9,00,000}{2,00,000}$$

= 4.5 times

32. (i) Gross Profit Ratio $= \frac{\text{Gross Profit}}{\text{Revenue from Operations}} \times 100$

$= \frac{70,000}{3,50,000} \times 100 = 20\%$

Working Notes

1. Cost of Revenue from Operations

$= \text{Opening Inventory} + \text{Net Purchases} + \text{Carriage Inward} - \text{Closing Inventory}$

$= 60,000 + 2,97,000 + 3,000 - 80,000$

$= ₹\ 2,80,000$

2. Gross Profit = Revenue from Operations (Cash + Credit) – Cost of Revenue from Operations

$= (70,000 + 2,80,000) - 2,80,000$

$= 3,50,000 - 2,80,000 = ₹\ 70,000$

(ii) Inventory Turnover Ratio

$= \frac{\text{Cost of Revenue from Operations}}{\text{Average Inventory}}$

$= \frac{2,80,000}{70,000} = 4 \text{ times}$

Average Inventory $= \frac{\text{Opening Inventory} + \text{Closing Inventory}}{2}$

$= \frac{60,000 + 80,000}{2} = ₹\ 70,000$

(iii) Net Profit Ratio $= \frac{\text{Net Profit}}{\text{Revenue from Operations}} \times 100$

$= \frac{22,000}{3,50,000} \times 100 = 6.29\%$

Working Note

Net Profit = Gross Profit – Indirect Expenses + Indirect Incomes

$= 70,000 - (10,000 + 40,000 + 5,000) + 7,000$

$= 77,000 - 55,000 = ₹\ 22,000$

33. (i) Net Profit Ratio $= \frac{\text{Net Profit after Tax}}{\text{Revenue from Operations}} \times 100$

$= \frac{72,000}{3,00,000} \times 100 = 24\%$

(ii) Operating Profit Ratio

$= \frac{\text{Operating Profit}}{\text{Revenue from Operations}} \times 100$

$= \frac{1,20,000}{3,00,000} \times 100 = 40\%$

Operating Profit = Revenue from Operations + Other Income – Purchase – Change in Inventories – Employee Benefit Expenses (salary) – Depreciation – Other Expenses

$= 3,00,000 + 40,000 - 1,80,000 - (-4,000) - 10,000 - 28,000 - 6,000$

$= ₹\ 1,20,000$

(iii) Current Ratio $= \frac{\text{Current Assets}}{\text{Current Liabilities}} = \frac{70,000 + 12,000}{50,000}$

$= 1.64 : 1$

(iv) Quick Ratio $= \frac{\text{Quick Assets}}{\text{Current Liabilities}} = \frac{70,000}{50,000} = 1.4 : 1$

34. (i) Net Profit after Tax = Gross Profit – Salary and Rent – Interest on Debentures + Gain on Sale of Furniture

$= 80,000 - 30,000 - 5,000 + 2,000 = ₹\ 47,000$

Net Profit Ratio $= \frac{\text{Net Profit after Tax}}{\text{Revenue from Operations}} \times 100$

$= \frac{47,000}{4,00,000} \times 100 = 11.75\%$

(ii) (a) Earning Per Share

$= \frac{\text{Net Profit (after interest, tax and dividend on preference share)}}{\text{Number of Equity Shares}}$

$= \frac{2,40,000 - 15,000}{50,000} = ₹\ 4.50$

(b) Price Earning Ratio

$= \frac{\text{Market Value of an Equity Share}}{\text{Earning Per Share}}$

$= \frac{40}{4.5} = 8.88$

(c) Return on Investment

$= \frac{\text{Net Profit before Interest and Tax}}{\text{Capital Employed}} \times 100$

$= \frac{4,40,000}{12,00,000} \times 100 = 36.67\%$

(d) Working Capital Turnover Ratio

$= \frac{\text{Revenue from Operations}}{\text{Working Capital}} = \frac{10,00,000}{1,00,000} = 10 \text{ times}$

Working Note

	Particulars	Amt (₹)
1.	Net Profit after Interest and Tax	2,40,000
	(+) Tax	1,60,000
		4,00,000
	(+) Interest	40,000
	Net Profit before Interest and Tax	4,40,000
2.	Capital Employed	
	Equity Share Capital	5,00,000
	(+) Reserve and Surplus	2,00,000
		7,00,000
	(+) Preference Share Capital	1,00,000
	Shareholders' Fund	8,00,000
	(+) Long-term Borrowings (10% Debentures)	4,00,000
		12,00,000

35. (i) Operating Ratio

$$= \frac{\text{Cost of Revenue from Operations} + \text{Operating Expenses}}{\text{Net Revenue from Operations}} \times 100$$

$$= \frac{9,00,000 + 15,000}{12,00,000} \times 100 = 76.25\%$$

(ii) Quick Ratio $= \frac{\text{Liquid Assets}}{\text{Current Liabilities}} = \frac{2,00,000}{75,000} = 2.67 : 1$

Note Other current assets are treated as liquid assets.

(iii) Debt to Equity Ratio $= \frac{\text{Debt}}{\text{Shareholders' Funds}}$

$$= \frac{2,50,000}{3,52,500} = 0.71 : 1$$

Working Note

Shareholders' Fund = Paid-up Share Capital − Statement of Profit and Loss (Dr)

= 4,00,000 − 47,500 = ₹ 3,52,500

(iv) Proprietary Ratio $= \frac{\text{Shareholders' Funds}}{\text{Total Assets}} \times 100$

$$= \frac{3,52,500}{6,02,500} \times 100 = 58.51\%$$

Working Note

Total Assets = Shareholders' Funds + Total Debt

= 3,52,500 + 2,50,000 = ₹ 6,02,500

(v) Working Capital Turnover Ratio

$$= \frac{\text{Net Revenue from Operations}}{\text{Working Capital}}$$

Working Capital Turnover Ratio $= \frac{12,00,000}{1,45,000}$

= 8.28 times

Working Note

Working Capital = Current Assets − Current Liabilities

= (20,000 + 2,00,000) − 75,000

= ₹ 1,45,000

36. (i) Liquid Ratio $= \frac{\text{Liquid Assets}}{\text{Current Liabilities}} = \frac{1,24,000}{84,000}$

= 1.48

Working Notes

1. Current Ratio $= \frac{\text{Current Assets}}{\text{Current Liabilities}}$

$$= \frac{3}{2} = \frac{1,26,000}{CL}$$

3 CL = ₹ 2,52,000

Thus, Current Liabilities = ₹ 84,000

2. Liquid Assets = Current Assets − Inventories

= 1,26,000 − 2,000 = ₹ 1,24,000

(ii) (a) Trade Receivables Turnover Ratio

$$= \frac{\text{Credit Revenue from Operations}}{\text{Average Trade Receivables}} = \frac{1,50,000}{12,000} = 12.5 \text{ times}$$

Working Notes

1. Credit Revenue from Operations = Revenue from Operations − Cash Revenue from Operations

= 2,00,000 − 50,000 = ₹ 1,50,000

2. Opening receivables is not given therefore, closing receivable is taken as average trade receivables

Average Trade Receivables = Closing Debtors + Closing Bills Receivable

= 7,000 + 5,000 = ₹ 12,000

(b) Inventory Turnover Ratio

$$= \frac{\text{Cost of Revenue from Operations}}{\text{Average Inventory}}$$

$$= \frac{62,000}{1,500} = 41.33 \text{ times}$$

Working Notes

1. Cost of Revenue from Operations

= Purchases + Changes in Inventories + Direct Expenses (Wages + Carriage inward)

⇒ = 55,000 + 3,000 + (2,000 + 2,000) = ₹ 62,000

2. Average Inventory

$$= \frac{\text{Opening Inventory} + \text{Closing Inventory}}{2}$$

$$= \frac{6,000 + (-3,000)}{2} = ₹\ 1,500$$

(c) Net Profit Ratio $= \frac{\text{Net Profit after Tax}}{\text{Revenue from Operations}} \times 100$

$$= \frac{84,000}{2,00,000} \times 100 = 42\%$$

(d) Operating Profit Ratio

$$= \frac{\text{Operating Profit}}{\text{Revenue from Operations}} \times 100$$

$$= \frac{1,32,000}{2,00,000} \times 100 = 66\%$$

Working Note

Operating Profit = Revenue from Operations − Cost of Revenue from Operations − Other Expenses

= 2,00,000 − 62,000 − (3,000 + 3,000) = ₹ 1,32,000

37. (i) The quality of ratio analysis of a business depends upon the accuracy of its financial statements because ratios are calculated on the basis of data given in profit and loss statement and balance sheet. Therefore, they will be only as correct as the accounting data on which they are based.

(ii) Trade Receivables Turnover Ratio

$$= \frac{\text{Credit Revenue from Operations}}{\text{Trade Receivables (Gross Debtors + Bills receivables)}}$$

$$= \frac{9,60,000}{1,90,000+50,000} = \frac{9,60,000}{2,40,000} = 4 \text{ times}$$

(iii) (a) Debt Equity Ratio $= \frac{\text{Long-term Debts}}{\text{Shareholders' Funds}}$

$$= \frac{5,00,000}{4,70,000} = 1.06:1$$

Working Notes

1. Shareholders' Funds = Equity Share Capital + Preference Share Capital + General Reserve + Profit
   = 2,00,000 + 60,000 + 1,20,000 + 90,000
   = ₹ 4,70,000
2. Long-term Debts = Loan = ₹ 5,00,000

(b) Interest Coverage Ratio

$$= \frac{\text{Profit before Interest and Tax}}{\text{Total Interest}} = \frac{1,70,000}{50,000} = 3.4 \text{ times}$$

Working Note

Profit before Interest and Tax = Profit after Interest and Tax + Interest + Tax

$$= 90,000 + (5,00,000 \times 10\%) + 30,000 = ₹\ 1,70,000$$

(c) Proprietary Ratio $= \frac{\text{Shareholders' Funds}}{\text{Total Assets}}$

$$= \frac{4,70,000}{6,25,000} = 0.75:1$$

Working Note

Total Assets = Property, Plant and Equipment and Intangbile Assets + Current Assets

= 5,05,000 + 1,20,000 = ₹ 6,25,000

Common Mistake Students usually deduct provision for doubtful debts from gross debtors to calculate average trade receivables. If provision is deducted from debtors, it may give a false impression that trade receivables are collected quickly.

38. (i) Proprietary Ratio $= \frac{\text{Shareholders' Funds}}{\text{Total Assets}}$

Working Notes

1. Shareholders' Funds = Equity Share Capital + 8% Preference Share Capital + Reserve and Surplus
   = 1,00,000 + 40,000 + 60,000 = ₹ 2,00,000
2. As, proprietary ratio = 0.8 : 1

$$\Rightarrow \quad 0.8 = \frac{2,00,000}{\text{Total Assets}}$$

$$\text{Total Assets} = \frac{2,00,000}{0.8} = ₹\ 2,50,000$$

3. Total Assets = Property, Plant and Equipment and Intangbile Assets + Current Assets + Investments

   2,50,000 = Property, Plant and Equipment and Intangbile Assets + 70,000 + 30,000

   Property, Plant and Equipment and Intangbile Assets
   = 2,50,000 – 1,00,000 = ₹ 1,50,000

(ii) Working Capital Turnover Ratio

$$= \frac{\text{Revenue from Operations (Net sales)}}{\text{Working Capital}}$$

$$= \frac{4,00,000}{50,000}$$

$$= \frac{8}{1} = 8:1$$

Working Notes

1. Revenue from Operations = Cost of Revenue from Operations + Gross Profit
2. Cost of revenue from operations or Cost of goods sold = ₹ 4,00,000
3. Profit margin = 20% on selling price
   20% on selling price = 25% on cost price
   Hence, Gross profit $= \frac{25}{100} \times 4,00,000 = ₹\ 1,00,000$
4. Revenue from Operations (Net sales)
   = 4,00,000 + 1,00,000 = ₹ 5,00,000
5. Working capital turnover ratio = 10 times
   $$10 = \frac{5,00,000}{\text{Working Capital}}$$
   Working capital $= \frac{5,00,000}{10} = ₹\ 50,000$
6. Working Capital = Current Assets – Current Liabilities
   50,000 = Current Assets – 90,000
   Current Assets = ₹ 1,40,000

(iii) Inventory Turnover Ratio

$$= \frac{\text{Cost of Revenue from Operations}}{\text{Average Inventory}}$$

$$\text{Inventory Turnover Ratio} = \frac{6,40,000}{45,000} = 14.22 \text{ times}$$

Working Notes

1. Cost of Revenue from Operations = Revenue from Operations – Gross Profit
   Gross Profit $= \frac{20}{100} \times 8,00,000 = 1,60,000$
   ∴ Cost of Revenue from Operations
   = 8,00,000 – 1,60,000
   = ₹ 6,40,000

2. Average Inventory

$$= \frac{\text{Opening Inventory} + \text{Closing Inventory}}{2}$$

$$= \frac{40{,}000 + 50{,}000}{2} = ₹45{,}000$$

(iv) (a) Current Ratio $= \frac{\text{Current Assets}}{\text{Current Liabilities}}$

$$= \frac{1{,}34{,}000}{1{,}04{,}000} = 1.29 : 1$$

Working Notes

1. Current Assets = Stock + Debtors + Bills Receivable + Advances Paid + Cash
   = 50,000 + 40,000 + 10,000 + 4,000 + 30,000
   = ₹ 1,34,000
2. Current Liabilities = Bills Payable + Overdraft + Creditors
   = 40,000 + 4,000 + 60,000
   = ₹ 1,04,000

(b) Quick Ratio $= \frac{\text{Quick Assets}}{\text{Current Liabilities}}$

$$= \frac{80{,}000}{1{,}04{,}000} = -0.77 : 1$$

Working Note

Quick Assets = Debtors + Bill Receivable + Cash
= 40,000 + 10,000 + 30,000 = ₹ 80,000

39. (i) Liquid Ratio $= \frac{\text{Liquid Assets}}{\text{Current Liabilities}} = \frac{2{,}65{,}000}{1{,}00{,}000} = 2.65 : 1$

Working Note

Liquid Assets = Current Assets – Closing Inventory – Prepaid Insurance
= 3,00,000 – 30,000 – 5,000 = ₹ 2,65,000

(ii) Current Ratio $= \frac{\text{Current Assets}}{\text{Current Liabilities}} = \frac{3{,}00{,}000}{1{,}00{,}000} = 3 : 1$

(iii) Proprietary Ratio

$$= \frac{\text{Shareholders' Funds}}{\text{Total Assets}} = \frac{5{,}94{,}000}{7{,}00{,}000} \times 100 = 84.86\%$$

Working Notes

Shareholders' Funds = Share Capital + Reserves and Surplus
= 5,60,000 + 34,000
= ₹ 5,94,000

(iv) Working Capital Turnover Ratio

$$= \frac{\text{Revenue from Operations (Net sales)}}{\text{Working Capital}}$$

$$= \frac{7{,}90{,}000}{2{,}00{,}000} = 3.95 \text{ times}$$

Working Notes

1. Revenue from Operations (Net sales)
   = Revenue from Operations – Sales Return
   = 8,00,000 – 10,000 = ₹ 7,90,000
2. Working Capital = Current Assets – Current Liabilities
   = 3,00,000 – 1,00,000 = ₹ 2,00,000

(v) Gross Profit Ratio

$$= \frac{\text{Gross Profit}}{\text{Revenue from Operations (Net sales)}} \times 100$$

$$= \frac{1{,}90{,}000}{7{,}90{,}000} \times 100 = 24.05\%$$

Working Note

Gross Profit = Revenue from Operations (Net sales) – Cost of Goods Sold (Cost of revenue from operations)
= 7,90,000 – 6,00,000 = ₹ 1,90,000

(vi) Operating Ratio

$$= \frac{\text{Operating Cost}}{\text{Revenue from Operations (Net sales)}} \times 100$$

$$= \frac{6{,}50{,}000}{7{,}90{,}000} \times 100 = 82.28\%$$

Working Note

Operating Cost = Cost of Revenue from Operations + Operating Expenses
= 6,00,000 + 50,000 = ₹ 6,50,000

(vii) Net Profit Ratio

$$= \frac{\text{Net Profit}}{\text{Revenue from Operations (Net sales)}} \times 100$$

$$= \frac{1{,}40{,}000}{7{,}90{,}000} \times 100 = 17.72\%$$

Working Note

Net Profit = Gross Profit – Operating Expenses
= 1,90,000 – 50,000 = ₹ 1,40,000

40. (i) Total Assets to Debts Ratio $= \frac{\text{Total Assets}}{\text{Long-term Debts}}$

$$= \frac{40{,}00{,}000}{8{,}00{,}000} = 5 : 1$$

(ii) Debt Equity Ratio $= \frac{\text{Debt / Long-term Debts}}{\text{Equity / Shareholders' Funds}}$

$$= \frac{8{,}00{,}000}{15{,}00{,}000} = 0.53 : 1$$

Working Note

Shareholders' Funds = Equity Share Capital + Preference Share Capital + Reserve and Surplus
= 10,00,000 + 3,00,000 + 2,00,000 = ₹ 15,00,000

(iii) Operating Ratio

$$= \frac{\text{Operating Cost}}{\text{Revenue from Operations (Net sales)}}$$

$$or \quad = \frac{\text{Cost of Revenue from Operations + Operating Expenses}}{\text{Revenue from Operations (Net sales)}} \times 100$$

$$= \frac{10,60,000}{12,00,000} \times 100 = 88.33\%$$

Working Notes

1. Cost of Revenue from Operations = Net Revenue from Operations – Gross Profit
= 12,00,000 – (20% of 12,00,000)
= 12,00,000 – 2,40,000 = ₹ 9,60,000

2. Operating Cost = Cost of Revenue from Operations + Operating Expenses
= 9,60,000 + (65,000 + 35,000) = ₹ 10,60,000

(iv) Operating Profit Ratio

$$= \frac{\text{Operating Profit}}{\text{Revenue from Operations (Net Sales)}} \times 100$$

$$= \frac{1,40,000}{12,00,000} \times 100 = 11.67\%$$

Working Note

Operating Profit = Net Revenue from Operations – Operating Cost
= 12,00,000 – 10,60,000 = ₹ 1,40,000

(v) Earning Per Share

$$= \frac{\text{Net Profit Available to Equity Shareholders}}{\text{Number of Equity Shares}}$$

$$= \frac{10,00,000 - 30,000}{1,00,000} = ₹\ 9.70$$

(vi) Debtors Turnover Ratio

$$= \frac{\text{Revenue from Operations (Net credit sales)}}{\text{Average Trade Receivable}}$$

$$= \frac{12,00,000}{1,50,000} = 8 \text{ times}$$

Working Note

Average Trade Receivables

$$= \frac{\text{Opening Debtors + Closing Debtors + Opening Bills Receivable + Closing Bills Receivable}}{2}$$

$$= \frac{1,20,000 + 60,000 + 80,000 + 40,000}{2} = ₹\ 1,50,000$$

(vii) Credit Turnover Ratio $= \frac{\text{Net Credit Purchases}}{\text{Average Trade Payables}}$

$$= \frac{5,00,000}{1,80,000}$$

= 2.77 : 1

Working Note

Average Trade Payables

$$= \frac{\text{Opening Creditors + Opening Bills Payable + Closing Creditors + Closing Bills Payable}}{2}$$

$$= \frac{1,30,000 + 1,10,000 + 70,000 + 50,000}{2}$$

= ₹ 1,80,000

41. (i) Debt Equity Ratio $= \frac{\text{Debt /Long-term Debts}}{\text{Equity / Shareholders' Funds}}$

$$= \frac{25,000}{50,000} = 1:2$$

Working Note

Long-term Debts = 10% Debenture = ₹ 25,000

(ii) Total Assets to Debt Ratio $= \frac{\text{Total Assets}}{\text{Long-term Debts}}$

$$= \frac{1,75,000}{25,000} = 7 : 1$$

(iii) Operating Ratio

$$= \frac{\text{Cost of Revenue from Operations + Operating Expenses}}{\text{Revenue from Operations}} \times 100$$

$$= \frac{2,16,000 + 24,000}{2,70,000} \times 100$$

$$= \frac{2,40,000}{2,70,000} \times 100 = 88.89\%$$

(iv) Debtors Turnover Ratio

$$= \frac{\text{Revenue from Operations (Net credit sales)}}{\text{Average Trade Receivables}}$$

$$= \frac{2,70,000}{30,000} = 9 \text{ times}$$

Working Note

Average Trade Receivable = Average Debtors
= ₹ 30,000

(v) Creditors Turnover Ratio $= \frac{\text{Net Credit Purchase}}{\text{Average Trade Payable}}$

$$= \frac{1,80,000}{16,000} = 11.25 \text{ times}$$

Working Note

Average Trade Payable = Average Creditors
= ₹ 16,000

42. (i) Acid Test Ratio $= \frac{\text{Liquid Assets}}{\text{Liquid Liabilities}}$

$$= \frac{1,80,000}{24,000}$$

= 7.5 : 1

Working Notes

1. Liquid Assets = Trade Receivables + Cash + Bank

$= 1,20,000 + 15,000 + 45,000$

$= ₹\ 1,80,000$

2. Liquid Liabilities = Creditors + Bills Payable

$= 20,000 + 4,000$

$= ₹\ 24,000$

(ii) Gross Profit Ratio

$$= \frac{\text{Gross Profit}}{\text{Revenue from Operations (Net sales)}} \times 100$$

$$= \frac{2,80,000}{5,00,000} \times 100 = 56\%$$

Working Notes

1. Gross Profit = Revenue from Operations – Cost of Revenue from Operations (WN2)

$= 5,00,000 - 2,20,000 = 2,80,000$

2. Cost of Revenue from Operations

= Opening Inventory + Purchases + Direct Expenses – Closing Inventory

$= 50,000 + 2,00,000 + 50,000 - 80,000$

$= ₹\ 2,20,000$

(iii) Stock Turnover Ratio

$$= \frac{\text{Cost of Revenue from Operations (Cost of goods sold)}}{\text{Average Inventory}}$$

$$= \frac{2,20,000}{65,000} = 3.38 \text{ times}$$

Working Note

Average Inventory

$$= \frac{\text{Opening Inventory} + \text{Closing Inventory}}{2}$$

$$= \frac{50,000 + 80,000}{2} = ₹\ 65,000$$

(iv) Operating Ratio

$$= \frac{\text{Cost of Revenue from Operations + Operating Expenses}}{\text{Revenue from Operations (Net sales)}} \times 100$$

$$= \frac{2,20,000 + (20,000 + 30,000)}{5,00,000} \times 100 = 54\%$$

(v) Debt Equity Ratio

$$= \frac{\text{Debt/Long-term Debts}}{\text{Equity/Shareholders' Funds}}$$

$$= \frac{1,50,000}{8,11,000}$$

$= 0.18 : 1$

Working Note

Shareholders' Funds

= Equity Share Capital + Preference Share Capital + Reserves + Statement of Profit and Loss

$= 3,00,000 + 4,00,000 + 5,000 + 1,06,000$

$= ₹\ 8,11,000$

43. (i) Gross Profit Ratio

$$= \frac{\text{Gross Profit}}{\text{Revenue from Operations (Net sales)}} \times 100$$

$$= \frac{40,000}{1,00,100} \times 100 = 39.96\%$$

Working Notes

1. Gross Profit = Revenue from Operations – Cost of Revenue from Operations

$= 1,00,100 - 60,100$

$= ₹\ 40,000$

2. Cost of Revenue from Operations

= Opening Inventory + Purchases – Closing Inventory + Direct Expenses (Carriage inwards + Wages)

$= 15,250 + 63,050 - 19,600 + (400 + 1,000)$

$= ₹\ 60,100$

(ii) Net Profit Ratio

$$= \frac{\text{Net Profit}}{\text{Revenue from Operations (Net sales)}} \times 100$$

$$= \frac{16,800}{1,00,100} \times 100 = 16.78\%$$

(iii) Stock Turnover Ratio

$$= \frac{\text{Cost of Revenue from Operations (Cost of goods sold)}}{\text{Average Inventory}}$$

$$= \frac{60,100}{17,425} = 3.44 \text{ times}$$

Working Note

Average Inventory

$$= \frac{\text{Opening Inventory} + \text{Closing Inventory}}{2}$$

$$= \frac{15,250 + 19,600}{2} = ₹\ 17,425$$

(iv) Proprietary Ratio $= \dfrac{\text{Shareholders' Funds}}{\text{Total Assets}}$

$$= \frac{88,000}{91,700} = 0.96 \text{ times}$$

Working Notes

1. Shareholders' Funds = Share Capital + Reserves + Statement of Profit and Loss

$= 70,000 + 1,200 + 16,800$

$= ₹\ 88,000$

2. Total Assets = Non-current Assets + Current Assets

$$= 60,100 + (19,600 + 9,000 + 3,000)$$

$$= ₹\,91,700$$

(v) $\text{Current Ratio} = \dfrac{\text{Current Assets}}{\text{Current Liabilities}} = \dfrac{31,600}{3,700} = 8.54 : 1$

Working Note

Current Assets = Inventory + Debtors + Bank
= 19,600 + 9,000 + 3,000 = ₹ 31,600

(vi) $\text{Quick Ratio} = \dfrac{\text{Quick Assets}}{\text{Current Liabilities}}$

$$= \frac{12,000}{3,700} = 3.24 : 1$$

Working Note

Quick Assets = Debtors + Bank
= 9,000 + 3,000 = ₹ 12,000

44. (i) (c) $\text{Current Ratio} = \dfrac{\text{Current Assets}}{\text{Current Liabilities}}$

$$= \frac{7,30,000}{3,00,000} = 2.43 : 1$$

(ii) (a) $\text{Net Profit Ratio} = \dfrac{\text{Net Profit}}{\text{Net Sales}} \times 100$

$$\text{Net Profit} = \frac{3,20,000}{10,00,000} \times 100 = 32\%$$

45. (i) (c) $\text{Interest Coverage Ratio} = \dfrac{\text{EBIT}^*}{\text{Interest}}$

$$= \frac{1,70,000}{50,000} = 3.4 \text{ times}$$

EAT = ₹ 90,000

*EBIT = 90,000 + Tax + Interest
= 90,000 + 30,000 + 50,000
= ₹ 1,70,000

(ii) $\text{Proprietary Ratio} = \dfrac{\text{Equity}}{\text{Total Assets}}$

$$= \frac{2,00,000 + 60,000 + 1,20,000 + 90,000}{5,05,000 + 1,20,000}$$

$$= \frac{4,70,000}{6,25,000}$$

$$= 0.75 : 1$$

CHAPTER TEST

01 Mark Questions

1. What will be the operating ratio of DLF Ltd. if their revenue from operations is ₹ 4,50,000, gross profit on cost is 25%, and operating expenses are ₹ 45,000?

(a) 100% (b) 50%
(c) 90% (d) 110%

2. Which of the following ratios measures the ability of the business to quickly convert various accounts into revenue from operations or cash?

(a) Activity
(b) Liquidity
(c) Debt
(d) Profitability

3. The other name of quick ratio is

(a) liquid ratio (b) current ratio
(c) acid test ratio (d) Both (a) and (c)

4. The current ratio of GULF Ltd. is 1.5 : 1. They want to increase it to 2 : 1. They can

(a) repay the bills payables
(b) purchase goods on credit
(c) take a short-term loan
(d) withdraw cash from bank

5. The credit terms of SET Ltd. was 52 days. The credit collection would be considered as poor if the average collection period was:

(a) less than 30 days
(b) 40 days
(c) 52 days
(d) 56 days

6. Define current assets with examples.

7. What is an ideal debt-to-equity ratio?

8. List any three activity ratios.

06 Marks Questions

9. On the basis of information given below, calculate:

(i) Gross profit ratio
(ii) Inventory turnover ratio
(iii) Working capital turnover ratio

Additional Information

Revenue from operations ₹ 15,75,000; Cost of revenue from operations ₹ 7,91,200; Current liabilities ₹ 4,74,000; Current assets ₹ 7,98,000; and Average inventory ₹ 3,95,000.

10. Following is the statement of profit and loss of Shyam Ltd for the year ended 31st March, 2013 and the balance sheet of the company as at that date

Statement of Profit and Loss
for the year ended 31st March, 2013

Particulars	Note No.	Amt (₹)
Revenue from Operations (Sales)		2,00,000
Expenses		
Purchases of Stock-in-Trade		1,00,000
Changes in Inventories	1	(5,000)
Employees Benefit Expenses (Salaries)	2	17,000
Other Expenses		18,000
		(1,30,000)
Net Profit		70,000

Notes to Accounts

Particulars		Amt (₹)
1. **Changes in Inventories**		
Opening Inventory	25,000	
(–) Closing Inventory	(30,000)	(5,000)
2. **Other Expenses**		
Direct Expenses	8,000	
Loss on Sale of Furniture	10,000	18,000

Balance Sheet
as at 31st March, 2013

Particulars	Amt (₹)
I. **EQUITY AND LIABILITIES**	
1. **Shareholders' Funds**	
(a) Share Capital	1,00,000
(b) Reserves and Surplus	70,000
2. **Current Liabilities**	
(a) Trade Payables	95,000
(b) Other Current Liabilities	35,000
Total	3,00,000
II. **ASSETS**	
1. **Non-current Assets**	
Property, Plant and Equipment	2,00,000
2. **Current Assets**	
(a) Inventories	30,000
(b) Trade Receivables	50,000
(c) Cash and Cash Equivalents	20,000
Total	3,00,000

Calculate the following ratios
(i) Quick ratio
(ii) Inventory turnover ratio

10 Marks Questions

11. From the following information, calculate
(i) Gross profit ratio
(ii) Inventory turnover ratio
(iii) Current ratio
(iv) Net profit ratio and
(v) Working capital turnover ratio

	Amt (₹)
Revenue from Operations	12,60,000
Net Profit	1,80,000
Cost of Revenue from Operations	9,60,000
Long-term Debts	4,50,000
Trade Payables	1,00,000
Average Inventory	4,00,000
Current Assets (Other than inventory)	3,80,000
Property, Plant and Equipment and Intangbile Assets	7,20,000
Current Liabilities	3,00,000
Net Profit before Interest and Tax	4,00,000

12. Following is the balance sheet of Arvind Mills Ltd, as at 31st March, 2012

Balance Sheet
as at 31st March, 2012

Particulars	Amt (₹)
I. EQUITY AND LIABILITIES	
1. **Shareholders' Funds**	
(a) Share Capital	6,00,000
(b) Reserves and Surplus	4,00,000
2. **Non-current Liabilities**	
Long-term Borrowings	7,00,000
3. **Current Liabilities**	
(a) Trade Payables	1,60,000
(b) Other Current Liabilities	10,000
(c) Short-term Provision (Tax)	1,30,000
Total	20,00,000
II. ASSETS	
1. **Non-current Assets**	
Property, Plant and Equipment	13,00,000
2. **Current Assets**	
(a) Short-term Investments	1,50,000
(b) Inventories	3,00,000
(c) Trade Receivables	2,00,000
(d) Cash and Cash Equivalents	50,000
Total	20,00,000

Other Information

	Amt (₹)
Revenue from Operations, i.e. sales	30,00,000
Cost of Revenue from Operations	25,80,000
Net Income before Tax	2,00,000
Net Income after Tax	1,00,000
Depreciation on Fixed Assets	5,00,000

You are required to calculate
(i) Liquid ratio
(ii) Proprietary ratio
(iii) Current ratio
(iv) Gross profit ratio and net profit ratio

Answers

1. (c) 90%
2. (a) Activity
3. (d) Both (a) and (c)
4. (a) repay the bills payables
5. (d) 56 days

9. (i) 49.76%
(ii) 2 times
(iii) 2.44 times

10. (i) Quick Ratio = 0.54:1
(ii) Inventory Turnover Ratio = 3.74 times

11. (i) 23.81%
(ii) 2.4 times
(iii) 2.6 : 1
(iv) 14.29 %
(v) 2.625 times

12. (i) Liquid Ratio = 1.33:1
(ii) Proprietary Ratio = 0.5:1
(iii) Current Ratio = 2.33:1
(iv) Gross Profit Ratio = 14%
(v) Net Profit Ratio = 6.67%

Assertion/Reasoning Based MCQs

Chapter 1 Accounting for Partnership Firms : Fundamentals

Direction (Q. No. 1 to 5) *There are two statements marked as Assertion (A) and Reason (R). Read the statements and choose the appropriate option from the options given below*

(a) Both Assertion (A) and Reason (R) are true and Reason (R) is the correct explanation for Assertion (A)

(b) Both Assertion (A) and Reason (R) are true, but Reason (R) is not the correct explanation for Assertion (A)

(c) Assertion (A) is true, but Reason (R) is false

(d) Assertion (A) is false, but Reason (R) is true

1. **Assertion** (A) If percentage of interest on capital is not mentioned in partnership deed, partners will not receive any interest on capital.

   Reason (R) The interest on capital is charged on the capital invested by the partners.

Ans (b) The interest on capital is charged in accordance with the partnership deed, and if not mentioned, it will not be charged.

2. **Assertion** (A) Partnership deed is a legal document signed by all the partners.

   Reason (R) Any type of charitable institution running as a not-for-profit organisation, will not be considered as a business.

Ans (b) Partnership deed is a legal document as it helps to resolve any dispute or conflict which arises between the partners regarding the partnership norms.

3. **Assertion** (A) When the partners brings in additional capital, it is recorded in the credit side of the current account.

   Reason (R) Current account records all the transactions relating to the interest on capital, drawings, commission to partners, etc. when the capital is to be remained fixed.

Ans (d) When a partner brings in additional capital, it is shown in the capital account even if fixed capital method is to be followed.

4. **Assertion** (A) Goodwill of the firm is affected by the reputation of the firm.

   Reason (R) The goodwill of the firm is dependent on the management capacity of the firm.

Ans (b) Goodwill of the firm is affected by the reputation of the firm as firm will be able to earn more profit if its reputation is good.

5. **Assertion** (A) Commission payable to the partner on sales or on the net profit of the firm, will be shown in the profit and loss appropriation account.

   Reason (R) All appropriations are shown in the profit and loss appropriation account.

Ans (a) Both Assertion (A) and Reason (R) are true and Reason (R) is the correct explanation for Assertion (A)

Chapter 2 Reconstitution of a Partnership Firm : Admission of a Partner

Direction (Q. No. 1 to 5) *There are two statements marked as Assertion (A) and Reason (R). Read the statements and choose the appropriate option from the options given below*

(a) Both Assertion (A) and Reason (R) are true and Reason (R) is the correct explanation for Assertion (A)

(b) Both Assertion (A) and Reason (R) are true, but Reason (R) is not the correct explanation for Assertion (A)

(c) Assertion (A) is true, but Reason (R) is false

(d) Assertion (A) is false, but Reason (R) is true

1. **Assertion** (A) When the new partner brings his share of goodwill in cash and it is to be paid to the existing partners privately, no entry is passed in the books.

   Reason (R) The intention of the partners is not to show any amount or transaction relating to goodwill for any of the reasons.

Ans (a) Both Assertion (A) and Reason (R) are true and Reason (R) is the correct explanation for Assertion (A)

2. **Assertion** (A) An increase in the value of assets and a decrease in the value of the liability at the time of admission of a partner is debited to the revaluation account.

Reason (R) Revaluation account is nominal in nature.

Ans (d) Increase in value of assets and decrease in value of liabilities are credited to revaluation account.

3. **Assertion** (A) A partner can admit a new partner.

Reason (R) A new partner can be admitted only when the existing partners unanimously agree to it.

Ans (d) To admit a new partner, all partners' consent is needed.

4. **Assertion** (A) A and B are partners sharing profits in the ratio of 3 : 2. They admit C as a new partner for 1/4th share. Goodwill is valued at ₹ 1,00,000 and the new partner C will compensate both A and B by crediting ₹ 25,000 in the ratio of 3 : 2.

Reason (R) C has taken 1/4th share in profits and therefore, he will bring 1/4th goodwill, i.e. ₹ 25,000. Since, sacrificing ratio or the new profit sharing ratio is not given, A and B have sacrificed in the ratio of 3 : 2. Therefore, they will be compensated in the ratio of 3 : 2.

Ans. (a) Both Assertion (A) and Reason (R) are true and Reason (R) is the correct explanation for Assertion (A)

5. **Assertion** (A) The new partner brings in a premium for goodwill.

Reason (R) The new partner is required to compensate the old partners for their loss of share in the profits of the firm.

Ans (a) Both Assertion (A) and Reason (R) are true and Reason (R) is the correct explanation for Assertion (A)

Chapter 3 Reconstitution of a Partnership Firm : Retirement/Death of a Partner

Direction (Q. No. 1 to 5) *There are two statements marked as Assertion (A) and Reason (R). Read the statements and choose the appropriate option from the options given below*

(a) Both Assertion (A) and Reason (R) are true and Reason (R) is the correct explanation for Assertion (A)
(b) Both Assertion (A) and Reason (R) are true, but Reason (R) is not the correct explanation for Assertion (A)
(c) Assertion (A) is true, but Reason (R) is false
(d) Assertion (A) is false, but Reason (R) is true

1. **Assertion** (A) Death of partner means partnership comes to an end and new partnership becomes operative.

Reason (R) Death of partner leads to reconstitution of partnership as the firm continues.

Ans (a) Both Assertion (A) and Reason (R) are true and Reason (R) is the correct explanation for Assertion (A)

2. **Assertion** (A) At the time of death of a partner, the deceased partner will get his share in general reserve and credit balance in profit and loss account.

Reason (R) Deceased partner will get his share of workmen compensation reserve remaining after claim, if any.

Ans (b) Both Assertion (A) and Reason (R) are true, but Reason (R) is not the correct explanation for Assertion (A)

3. **Assertion** (A) In the absence of partnership deed or agreement, interest on amount due to deceased partner is paid @ 6% p.a. on the outstanding amount.

Reason (R) Unpaid amount is a loan to the firm. The Partnership Act, 1932 (Section 37) prescribes that interest is payable @ 6% p.a. in the absence of agreement.

Ans (a) Both Assertion (A) and Reason (R) are true and Reason (R) is the correct explanation for Assertion (A)

4. **Assertion** (A) Sacrificing ratio is always calculated at the time of death of a partner.

Reason (R) At the time of death of a partner, gaining ratio may or may not be calculated.

Ans (d) Sacrificing ratio is calculated at the time of admission of a new partner for dispersing goodwill.

5. **Assertion** (A) Ramesh, Suresh and Mahesh share profits in the ratio 2 : 3 : 5. Ramesh decides to retire. The new profit sharing ratio is 3 : 5. If the profit earned was ₹ 1,50,000 before retirement, then Suresh's share is ₹ 45,000.

Reason (R) In case of retirement of a partner, profits are shared in new profit sharing ratio among existing partners.

Ans (c) Whenever a partner retires from a firm, his share of profit is acquired either by all the remaining partners or some/one of them. Thus, a new profit sharing ratio for each remaining partner is determined.

Chapter 4 Dissolution of a Partnership Firm

Direction (Q. No. 1 to 5) *There are two statements marked as Assertion (A) and Reason (R). Read the statements and choose the appropriate option from the options given below*

(a) Both Assertion (A) and Reason (R) are true and Reason (R) is the correct explanation for Assertion (A)
(b) Both Assertion (A) and Reason (R) are true, but Reason (R) is not the correct explanation for Assertion (A)
(c) Assertion (A) is true, but Reason (R) is false
(d) Assertion (A) is false, but Reason (R) is true

1. **Assertion** (A) Dissolution of the firm means the dissolution of the partnership between all the partners of the firm.

   Reason (R) Dissolution of the firm means the closure of business and therefore means dissolution of partnership also.

Ans (b) Dissolution of partnership firm is a process in which relationship between partners of firm is dissolved or terminated.

2. **Assertion** (A) A loan from a partner is not transferred to realisation account.

   Reason (R) A loan from a partner is not an external liability but is discharged after repayment of capital.

Ans (c) Loan from a partner to firm is not transferred to realisation account, it remains in its account itself. At the time of settlement, i.e., payment of liabilities, partner's loan is paid after paying the outside liabilities but before payment of capital.

3. **Assertion** (A) Realisation account is prepared at the time of dissolution of the partnership firm.

   Reason (R) Dissolution of partnership firm involves the partners selling the assets and settling the liabilities. Thus, various amounts are recovered or paid by selling assets or settling liabilities.

Ans (a) Both Assertion (A) and Reason (R) are true and Reason (R) is the correct explanation for Assertion (A)

4. **Assertion** (A) A firm is dissolved compulsorily when all the partners or all but one partner, become insolvent.

   Reason (R) Dissolution of partnership and dissolution of firm both are the same.

Ans (c) Dissolution of partnership and dissolution of firm are different. In the event of dissolution of partnership, business continues, but the partnership is reconstituted, while in the event of dissolution of firm, the firm ceases to exist.

5. **Assertion** (A) At the time of dissolution of partnership firm, the amount received from realisation of all the assets of the firm is used first of all to pay the external liabilities of the firm.

   Reason (R) As per the Partnership Act, outside liability should be paid first of all at the time for dissolution of partnership firm.

Ans (a) Both Assertion (A) and Reason (R) are true and Reason (R) is the correct explanation for Assertion (A)

Chapter 5 Issue of Shares

Direction (Q. No. 1 to 5) *There are two statements marked as Assertion (A) and Reason (R). Read the statements and choose the appropriate option from the options given below*

(a) Both Assertion (A) and Reason (R) are true and Reason (R) is the correct explanation for Assertion (A)
(b) Both Assertion (A) and Reason (R) are true, but Reason (R) is not the correct explanation for Assertion (A)
(c) Assertion (A) is true, but Reason (R) is false
(d) Assertion (A) is false, but Reason (R) is true

1. **Assertion** (A) A company is formed through the process of incorporation under the Companies Act, 2013.

   Reason (R) A company is an artificial person which is a separate legal entity from its members.

Ans (b) The Companies Act, 2013 regulates the company incorporation procedure and the provision of the company registration certificate.

2. **Assertion** (A) Proportionate allotment or pro-rata allotment is made in case of oversubscription of shares.

Reason (R) In case of oversubscription, it is not possible for the company to allot shares to every applicant in the number that he desires.

Ans (a) Both Assertion (A) and Reason (R) are true and Reason (R) is the correct explanation for Assertion (A)

3. **Assertion** (A) The company has to get a minimum subscription within 30 days from the date of issue of prospectus.

Reason (R) If the company fails to receive the minimum subscription, the company can proceed with the allotment of shares and application money only after 130 days of the date of issue of prospectus.

Ans (c) Shares can not be alloted unless 90% of the sum payable on application for shares issued to the public for subscription, is received by the company.

4. **Assertion** (A) The forfeited shares can not be re-issued at a loss.

Reason (R) The forfeited shares can be re-issued at a discount provided the amount of discount allowed does not exceed the credit balance of the share forfeiture account relating to shares being re-issued.

Ans (a) Forfeited shares can be re-issued at discount upto the amount of forfeiture.

5. **Assertion** (A) The liability of a shareholder is limited upto the nominal price of shares subscribed by one.

Reason (R) Paid-up capital is the amount of nominal value of shares that have been called-up by the company for payment by the subscriber towards the shares.

Ans (c) Paid-up capital is the part of called-up capital that actually has been paid by the subscriber.

Chapter 6 Issue and Redemption of Debentures

Direction (Q. No. 1 to 5) *There are two statements marked as Assertion (A) and Reason (R). Read the statements and choose the appropriate option from the options given below*

(a) Both Assertion (A) and Reason (R) are true and Reason (R) is the correct explanation for Assertion (A)
(b) Both Assertion (A) and Reason (R) are true, but Reason (R) is not the correct explanation for Assertion (A)
(c) Assertion (A) is true, but Reason (R) is false
(d) Assertion (A) is false, but Reason (R) is true

1. **Assertion** (A) Debentureholders are the creditors of the company carrying a fixed rate of interest.

Reason (R) Debentures are short-term loan taken from the public.

Ans (c) Debentures are long-term debt instrument that large companies use to borrow money.

2. **Assertion** (A) Issue of debentures does not result in dilution of interest of equity shareholders.

Reason (R) Debentureholders have voting rights.

Ans (c) Issue of debentures does not result in dilution of interest of equity shareholders as they do not have the right either to vote or to take part in the management of the company.

3. **Assertion** (A) ABC Ltd. issued 10%, 5,000 debentures at par @ ₹ 100 per debenture. The company suffered a loss but still the directors of the company paid interest on debentures.

Reason (R) Interest on debentures is a charge against profits and therefore, its payment is not subject to the earning of profit.

Ans (a) Both Assertion (A) and Reason (R) are true and Reason (R) is the correct explanation for Assertion (A)

4. **Assertion** (A) Debentureholders do not enjoy any voting rights.

Reason (R) A debentureholder just lends money but does not become an owner of the company with the purchase of debentures.

Ans (a) Debentureholders are only the creditors of the company as debentures are the part of loan.

5. **Assertion** (A) When all the debentures have been redeemed, Debenture Redemption Reserve (DRR) account is closed by transferring the amount to general reserve.

Reason (R) Debentures may be redeemed out of capital or out of profit or both.

Ans (b) The amount of debenture redemption reserve shall not be utilised by the company except for the debentures redemption, thus after redeeming all the debentures, this account is closed.

Chapter 7 Final Accounts of Companies

Direction (Q. No. 1 to 5) *There are two statements marked as Assertion (A) and Reason (R). Read the statements and choose the appropriate option from the options given below*

(a) Both Assertion (A) and Reason (R) are true and Reason (R) is the correct explanation for Assertion (A)
(b) Both Assertion (A) and Reason (R) are true, but Reason (R) is not the correct explanation for Assertion (A)
(c) Assertion (A) is true, but Reason (R) is false
(d) Assertion (A) is false, but Reason (R) is true

1. **Assertion** (A) Financial statements are the basic source of information to the shareholders and other external parties for understanding the profitability and financial position of any business concern.

Reason (R) The primary objective of financial statement is to assist the users in their decision-making.

Ans (a) Both Assertion (A) and Reason (R) are true and Reason (R) is the correct explanation for Assertion (A)

2. **Assertion** (A) Surplus is the another name for statement of profit and loss.

Reason (R) Surplus is an item of the balance sheet that shows accumulated profits or losses whereas statement of profit and loss shows the net profit or net loss for the year.

Ans (d) A surplus is the amount of retained earnings, recorded in the balance sheet of a business entity.

3. **Assertion** (A) Borrowings that are payable after 12 months or after the period of the operating cycle from the date of balance sheet, are long-term borrowings.

Reason (R) Current liabilities are those liabilities that are payable within 12 months or within the period of the operating cycle from the date of the balance sheet. Thus, loans that are not payable within the above said period, are long-term borrowings.

Ans (a) Both Assertion (A) and Reason (R) are true and Reason (R) is the correct explanation for Assertion (A)

4. **Assertion** (A) A trading company sells its fixed assets through an agent. The agent is to be paid ₹ 50,000 as fee which can be shown as trade payables in the balance sheet.

Reason (R) Trade payables are defined as the amount payable against purchase of goods or services taken in the normal course of business and includes both sundry creditors and bills payable.

Ans (d) Fees paid to an agent is an expense for a company. It is not listed on a balance sheet but appear on a company's income statement instead.

5. **Assertion** (A) Money received against share warrants' is to be disclosed as a separate line item under 'shareholder's fund'.

Reason (R) It is the amount received by the company which is converted into shares at a specified date on a specified rate.

Ans (a) Both Assertion (A) and Reason (R) are true and Reason (R) is the correct explanation for Assertion (A)

Chapter 8 Financial Statement Analysis

Direction (Q. No. 1 to 5) *There are two statements marked as Assertion (A) and Reason (R). Read the statements and choose the appropriate option from the options given below*

(a) Both Assertion (A) and Reason (R) are true and Reason (R) is the correct explanation for Assertion (A)
(b) Both Assertion (A) and Reason (R) are true, but Reason (R) is not the correct explanation for Assertion (A)
(c) Assertion (A) is true, but Reason (R) is false
(d) Assertion (A) is false, but Reason (R) is true

1. **Assertion** (A) Financial statement analysis is a systematic process of analysing the financial data for its easy understanding and decision-making.

Reason (R) Financial statements are analysed using analytical tools such as comparative statements, common size statements, ratios and cash flow statements.

Ans (a) Both Assertion (A) and Reason (R) are true and Reason (R) is the correct explanation for Assertion (A)

2. **Assertion** (A) Common size statement is a statement in which individual items of financial statements of two or more years are converted into a percent of a common base for comparison.

Reason (R) Common size balance sheet is prepared to place each item thereof and to convert them into percent of total of liabilities part or assets part.

Ans (b) Common size statements help to analyse and compare a company's performance over several periods with varying sales figures.

3. **Assertion** (A) Comparative balance sheet provides information regarding progress of the business firm.

   Reason (R) The comparative balance sheet shows increase and decrease in absolute terms as well as in percentage in various assets, liabilities and capital.

Ans (a) Both Assertion (A) and Reason (R) are true and Reason (R) is the correct explanation for Assertion (A)

4. **Assertion** (A) The analysis of financial statements does not disclose the current worth of the business.

   Reason (R) Financial statements are prepared on cost principle basis.

Ans (a) Both Assertion (A) and Reason (R) true and Reason (R) is the correct explanation for Assertion (A)

5. **Assertion** (A) Financial statement analysis is undertaken by investors, lenders and creditors for assessing the safety of the amount invested in the company.

   Reason (R) Investors, lenders and creditors undertake the analysis of the financial statements because they have invested their money in the company and have either indirect control or no control over the affairs of the company.

Ans (a) Both Assertion (A) and Reason (R) are true and Reason (R) is the correct explanation for Assertion (A)

Chapter 9 Cash Flow Statement

Direction (Q. No. 1 to 5) *There are two statements marked as Assertion (A) and Reason (R). Read the statements and choose the appropriate option from the options given below*

(a) Both Assertion (A) and Reason (R) are true and Reason (R) is the correct explanation for Assertion (A)

(b) Both Assertion (A) and Reason (R) are true, but Reason (R) is not the correct explanation for Assertion (A)

(c) Assertion (A) is true, but Reason (R) is false

(d) Assertion (A) is false, but Reason (R) is true

1. **Assertion** (A) Cash flow statement shows inflow and outflow of cash and cash equivalents under operating, investing and financing activities of a company during a specified period.

   Reason (R) The cash flow statement traces the flow of cash and cash equivalents into and out of the business during an accounting period under operating, investing and financing activities.

Ans (a) Both Assertion (A) and Reason (R) are true and Reason (R) is the correct explanation for Assertion (A)

2. **Assertion** (A) Cash flow statement is a substitute for income statement.

   Reason (R) Cash flow statement does not show profit and loss.

Ans (d) Cash flow statement is not a substitute for an income statement. Just like income statement, a cash flow statement does not take both cash and non-cash transactions into account.

3. **Assertion** (A) Cash equivalents are short-term, highly liquid investments that are readily convertible into known amounts of cash and which are subject to an insignificant risk of change in value.

   Reason (R) Cash equivalents are held for the purpose of meeting short-term cash commitments rather than for investment or other purposes.

Ans (b) A cash equivalent is a highly liquid investment that can be converted into cash speedily, say in three months or less.

4. **Assertion** (A) Depreciation is added back to net profit while calculating cash flows from operating activities.

   Reason (R) Depreciation is a non-cash expense. It had reduced the net profit while there is no cash flow.

Ans (a) Both Assertion (A) and Reason (R) are true and Reason (R) is the correct explanation for Assertion (A)

5. **Assertion** (A) Sale of fixed asset is shown under the investing activities.

   Reason (R) Sale of fixed asset leads to inflow of cash.

Ans (b) Investing activities include purchases of physical assets, investments in securities, or the sale of securities or assets.

Chapter 10 Ratio Analysis

Direction (Q. No. 1 to 5) *There are two statements marked as Assertion (A) and Reason (R). Read the statements and choose the appropriate option from the options given below*

(a) Both Assertion (A) and Reason (R) are true and Reason (R) is the correct explanation for Assertion (A)

(b) Both Assertion (A) and Reason (R) are true, but Reason (R) is not the correct explanation for Assertion (A)

(c) Assertion (A) is true, but Reason (R) is false

(d) Assertion (A) is false, but Reason (R) is true

1. **Assertion** (A) Accounting ratio is an arithmetic relationship between two independent variables.

   Reason (R) Accounting ratios can be expressed in pure form, percentage, times or fraction.

Ans (d) Accounting ratio is a relationship between two figures obtained from the account statement.

2. **Assertion** (A) An ideal current ratio of 2 : 1 indicates good financial health of a company.

   Reason (R) Increased current ratio is an indicator of ideal funds.

Ans (b) The current ratio describes the relationship between a company's assets and liabilities.

So, a higher ratio means the company has more assets than liabilities.

3. **Assertion** (A) Activity ratios are the ratios that are calculated for measuring the efficiency of operations of business based on effective utilisation of resources.

   Reason (R) Current ratio and quick ratio are liquidity ratios.

Ans (b) Activity ratio is used to determine the efficiency of the organisation in generating revenue from the assets.

4. **Assertion** (A) If the debt-equity ratio is 1 : 2, it is considered to be safe.

   Reason (R) From a security point of view, a capital structure with less debt and more equity is considered favourable as it reduces the changes of bankruptcy.

Ans (d) If the debt-equity ratio is 2 : 1, then it is considered to be ideal as it is manageable.

5. **Assertion** (A) Higher trade receivable turnover means speedy collections from trade receivable.

   Reason (R) Trade receivable turnover ratio indicates the number of times the receivable are turned over and converted into cash in an accounting period.

Ans (a) Both Assertion (A) and Reason (R) are true and Reason (R) is the correct explanation for Assertion (A)

ISC

Examination Paper 2024

Time : 3 hrs
Marks : 80

Accounts XII

General Instructions

1. Candidates are allowed additional 15 minutes for only reading the paper. They must not start writing during this time.
2. Section-A is compulsory for all candidates.
3. Candidates have to attempt all questions from either Section-B or Section-C*.
4. There are internal choices provided in each section.
5. The intended marks for questions or parts of questions are given in the brackets [ ].
6. All calculations should be shown clearly.
7. All working, including rough work, should be done on the same page as and adjacent to, the rest of the answer.

* Section-C has not been covered.

Section A

(60 Marks)

(Answer all questions)

1. In sub-parts (i) to (iv), choose the correct option and in sub-parts (v) to (x) answer the questions as instructed.

(i) On the date of admission of Ajay as a partner, the balance sheet of the firm of Nita and Rita showed a balance of ₹ 80,000 in the workmen compensation reserve.

Choose the correct option to record the effect of a workmen compensation claim of ₹ 90,000 on the accounts of the partnership firm. **[1]**

(a) The revaluation account to be credited with ₹ 10,000
(b) The revaluation account to be debited with ₹ 10,000
(c) The capital accounts of Nita and Rita to be debited with ₹ 90,000
(d) The capital accounts of Nita and Rita to be credited with ₹ 90,000

(ii) CreditAccess Grameen Ltd., a listed NBFC-MFI (Micro Finance Institution), is all set to enter the bond market next week to raise up to ₹ 1,000 crore in non-convertible debentures, as it looks to diversify its liability profile.

Source *Economic Times, 20th August, 2023*

According to the provisions of the Companies Act, 2013, what is the maximum amount of these non-convertible debentures which CreditAccess Grameen Ltd. will redeem out of its capital? **[1]**

(a) ₹ 100 crore (b) ₹ 150 crore
(c) ₹ 900 crore (d) ₹ 1,000 crore

(iii) Choose the correct order in which a partnership firm at the time of its dissolution, will apply the amount realised from the sale of its assets, including any amount contributed by the partners, towards the payment of **[1]**

P – Partners' loan
Q – Firm's debts
R – Balance of partners' capital
S – Surplus divided amongst the partners in their profit sharing ratio

(a) P, Q, R, S (b) Q, P, S, R
(c) S, P, Q, R (d) Q, P, R, S

(iv) Tulip Ltd. allotted 45,000 equity shares of ₹ 10 each to the public. The first and final call of ₹ 2 per share was not received on 1,000 shares, which were forfeited by the company. Later, 600 of the forfeited shares were re-issued at ₹ 7 fully paid-up.
What is the subscribed capital of the company? **[1]**
(a) ₹ 4,49,200 (b) ₹ 4,50,000
(c) ₹ 4,40,000 (d) ₹ 4,46,000

(v) **Assertion** (A) A revaluation account is prepared at the time of dissolution of a partnership.
Reason (R) A revaluation account is prepared to determine the net gain/loss on realisation of assets and settlement of liabilities. **[1]**
Alternatives
(a) Both Assertion (A) and Reason (R) are true and Reason (R) is the correct explanation of Assertion (A)
(b) Both Assertion (A) and Reason (R) are true, but Reason (R) is not the correct explanation of Assertion (A)
(c) Both Assertion (A) and Reason (R) are false
(d) Assertion (A) is true, but Reason (R) is false

(vi) A firm having a debtor of ₹ 30,000 from whom the amount was due on 30th June, 2023, gets dissolved on 31st March, 2023. The debtor cleared his dues on the date of dissolution of the firm at a discount of 4% per annum.
Give the journal entry passed by the firm to realise the payment from the debtor. **[1]**

(vii) Xylo Ltd. issued 9,000, 7% debentures of ₹ 100 each at a certain rate of discount. After writing-off the discount on the issue of debentures, the company was left with a balance of ₹ 35,000 in its securities premium out of the original amount of ₹ 71,000.
At what rate of discount did the company issue these debentures? **[1]**

(viii) The Annual Report of ITC Ltd., for the financial year 2021-22, showed claims against the company not acknowledged as debts of ₹ 880.58 crores including third party claims arising from disputes relating to contracts aggregating ₹ 29.22 crores.
Source *Annual Report of ITC Ltd. 2021-22*
Mention the heading and the sub-heading under which this item would have been shown in the notes to accounts accompanying the balance sheet of ITC Ltd. as at 31st March, 2022. **[1]**

(ix) Deepa and Pia are in partnership sharing profits and losses in the ratio of 3 : 2. They admit Charu as a partner for 1/5 share in the profits. The capitals of Deepa and Pia, before adjusting the loss of ₹ 5,000 on revaluation of assets and liabilities are ₹ 30,000 and ₹ 20,000 respectively.
It is decided that Charu will contribute 25% of the combined capitals of Deepa and Pia.
What is Charu's capital contribution? **[1]**

(x) The balance sheet of Anjum Ltd. as at 31st March, 2022, had outstanding 1,000, 8% debentures of ₹ 100 each. These debentures were to be redeemed by the company on 31st March, 2023.
Give the journal entry for the amount due to the debentureholders on 31st March, 2023, including the interest on debentures due to them. **[1]**

2. The balance sheet of Hari, Jacob and James as at 31st March, 2023, stood as follows

Balance Sheet of Hari, Jacob and James
as at 31st March, 2023

Liabilities		Amt (₹)	Assets	Amt (₹)
Capital A/cs			Fixed Assets	3,50,000
Hari	3,40,000		Debtors	2,50,000
Jacob	1,90,000		Bank	1,50,000
James	2,20,000	7,50,000		
		7,50,000		7,50,000

Jacob died on 30th June, 2023.
His drawings from 1st April, 2023, up to the date of his death amounted to ₹ 1,00,000.
According to the partnership deed, Jacob was
(i) To be charged with interest on drawings @ 4% per annum.
(ii) Entitled to his share of interim profits for which his capital account was credited with ₹ 1,10,000.
(iii) Entitled to his share in the non-purchased goodwill of the firm.
The firm's non-purchased goodwill on the date of Jacob's death had no value.
The final amount due to Jacob by the firm was transferred to his executor's loan account.
You are required to prepare the interim balance sheet of the reconstituted firm as at 30th June, 2023. **[3]**

Or

Kamal, Ali and John are partners in a firm. On Kamal's retirement from the firm on 30th June, 2023, his capital account stood at ₹ 40,000 after all adjustments.
The partners decided that Kamal be paid 50% of the amount due to him immediately and the balance, along with interest @ 6% per annum, be paid on 30th June, 2024.
The firm closes its books on 31st March every year.
You are required to prepare Kamal's loan account till it is finally closed.

3. On 1st April, 2022, Harbour Ltd. issued 50,000, 6% debentures of ₹ 100 each to the public at a discount of 5% to be redeemed after three years at a premium of 7%.

On this date, the company also issued 1,00,000 equity shares of ₹ 10 each at a premium of ₹ 2 per share.

Both the issues were fully subscribed.

You are required to prepare the following accounts for the year 2022-23 in the books of Harbour Ltd.

(i) 6% Debentures account

(ii) Loss on issue of debentures account **[3]**

4. On 1st April, 2022, the following balances appeared in the books of Alpha Pvt. Ltd.

9% Debentures (redeemable on 31st March, 2023, at a premium of 2%)	₹ 50,00,000
Debenture Redemption Reserve	₹ 5,00,000

The debenture redemption investment, which was purchased by the company on 1st April, 2022, was realised at 101% on the date of redemption and the debentures were redeemed on the due date.

You are required to prepare the following accounts for the year 2022-23 in the books of Alpha Pvt. Ltd.

(i) Debentureholders' account.

(ii) Debenture redemption investment account. **[3]**

Or

On 1st April, 2022, Resorts Ltd. (a listed construction company) had 60,000,5% debentures of ₹ 100 each due for redemption at par on 31st March, 2023.

As per the law, investment was made in a fixed deposit of a bank on 30th April, 2022, earning interest @ 5% per annum.

Tax @ 10% was deducted by the bank on the interest.

You are required to pass necessary journal entries in the year of redemption of debentures, including entries for interest on debenture redemption investment. (Ignore the interest on debentures).

5. On 1st April, 2020, Anish started a business with a capital of ₹ 3,00,000.

During the three years ending 31st March, 2023, the results of his business were

Year		Amt (₹)
2020-21	Loss	20,000
2021-22	Profit	34,000
2022-23	Profit	46,000

From the year 2020-21 to the year 2022-23, Anish withdrew ₹ 30,000 from the firm for his personal use.

On 1st April, 2023, he admitted Danish into partnership on the following terms

(i) Goodwill of the firm to be valued at two years' purchase of the average profits of the last three years.

(ii) Danish to have 1/4 share in the future profits.

(iii) Danish's capital to be equal to 1/4 of Anish's capital determined on 1st April, 2023, after the goodwill compensation has been taken into account.

You are required to give

(a) The formula to calculate goodwill by the average profit method.

(b) The value of self-generated goodwill of the firm.

(c) Danish's capital contribution. **[3]**

6. The following balances have been extracted from the books of Meadow Ltd. as at 31st March, 2023.

Particulars	Amt (₹)	Particulars	Amt (₹)
Capital Reserve	1,20,000	Bank Overdraft	40,000
Plant and Machinery (At cost)	6,00,000	Bills Receivables	20,000
		Patents	80,000
Land and Building	6,80,000	Sundry Debtors	90,000
Statement of Profit and Loss (Dr)	1,70,000	Provision for Doubtful Debts	10,000
Short-term Loans and Advances	50,000	Inventories	30,000
		Share Capital	12,20,000
Cash and Bank Balances	1,60,000	5% Debentures	3,00,000
Trade Payables	90,000	(1/5 of the debentures to be redeemed on 31st March, 2024)	
Accumulated Depreciation on Plant and Machinery	1,00,000		

Additional Information

- The company had issued 1,25,000 equity shares of ₹ 10 each which were all applied for and allotted to the public. These shares were fully called-up by the company.
- There were calls-in-arrears @ ₹ 2 per share on 15,000 shares out of which 5,000 shares were forfeited by the company.

You are required to

(i) Show the share capital in the notes to accounts.

(ii) Give the amount for each of the following

(a) Short-term borrowings

(b) Current assets

(c) Property, plant & equipment and intangible assets

- Property, plant and equipment **[6]**

7. Amay and Sujoy are partners sharing profits and losses in the ratio of 3 : 1. Their balance sheet as at 31st March, 2023, is given below

Balance Sheet of Amay and Sujoy
as at 31st March, 2023

Liabilities		Amt (₹)	Assets		Amt (₹)
Bills Payable		70,000	Land and Building		1,65,000
Capital A/cs			Stock		60,000
Amay	1,30,000		Sundry Debtors	70,000	
Sujoy	1,25,000	2,55,000	(–) Provision for Doubtful Debts	(10,000)	60,000
			Cash in Hand		40,000
		3,25,000			3,25,000

On 1st April, 2023, they admit Malay as a new partner for 1/4 share in the profits on the following terms

(i) Malay to bring his share of capital of ₹ 1,20,000 and to pay ₹ 10,000 in cash for his share of goodwill.

(ii) Stock worth ₹ 45,000 to be taken over by Amay at ₹ 25,000.

(iii) Bills payable of ₹ 20,000 to be honoured by Sujoy, for which he is not to be reimbursed.

(iv) The capitals of Amay and Sujoy to be adjusted on the basis of Malay's capital and his share in the profits, any surplus to be readjusted through current account and deficiency through cash.

You are required to prepare the partners' capital account. **[6]**

Or Mitu and Ritu are partners sharing profits and losses in the ratio of 2 : 3. An extract of their balance sheet as at 31st March, 2023, is given below

Balance Sheet of Mitu and Ritu (An extract)
as at 31st March, 2023

Liabilities	Amt (₹)	Assets	Amt (₹)
Workmen Compensation Reserve	30,000	Investments (Market value ₹ 76,000)	80,000
		Sundry Debtors	1,00,000
General Reserve	40,000	Profit and Loss Account	55,000
Investment Fluctuation Reserve	10,000		

On 1st April, 2023, they admit Nitu as a new partner for 1/5 share in the profits on the following terms regarding the treatment of the reserves and the accumulated losses.

(i) Accumulated losses, if any, to be written-off.

(ii) A workmen compensation claim of ₹ 10,000 to be adjusted against the workmen compensation reserve. The balance of the reserve is not to be distributed.

(iii) Any loss in the value of investments to be adjusted against the investment fluctuation reserve. The balance of the investment fluctuation reserve is to be distributed.

(iv) Provision for doubtful debts to be created to the extent of 10% of the debtors from the general reserve. The remaining amount in the general reserve is to be distributed.

You are required to pass necessary journal entries to record the above adjustments at the time of Nitu's admission.

8. Adit and Shiv were partners sharing profits and losses in the ratio of 5:4. They dissolved their partnership firm on 31st March, 2023, when their balance sheet showed the following balances

Particulars	Amt (₹)
Adit's Capital	40,000
Shiv's Capital	30,000
Adit's Current A/c (Cr)	3,000
Shiv's Current A/c (Dr)	6,000
Loan by the Firm to Shiv	22,000
Profit and Loss Account (Dr)	4,500

On the date of dissolution of the firm

(i) The firm suffered a loss of ₹18,000 upon realisation of assets and settlement of liabilities.

(ii) The expenses of dissolution of ₹ 3,000, to be borne by Shiv, were paid by the firm on his behalf.

(iii) The firm had furniture of ₹ 15,000. Adit took over some pieces of the furniture at ₹ 9,000 (being 10% less than the book value). Shiv took over the remaining furniture at 80% of its book value.

You are required to prepare the partners' capital account. **[6]**

9. Tanuj and Ravi are partners in a business with capital balances of ₹ 1,50,000 and ₹ 1,00,000 respectively on 1st April, 2022.

Their partnership deed contains the following clauses

(i) Interest on capital to be allowed @ 10% per annum.

(ii) Interest on drawings to be charged @ 4% per annum.

(iii) Tanuj to be allowed a commission @ 5% of the trading profit after charging his commission.

(iv) Ravi to be allowed an annual commission of ₹ 10,000.

Additional Information

During the year 2022-23

- Tanuj withdrew ₹ 6,000 at the end of every quarter.
- The trading profit of the firm was ₹ 84,000.
- The firm's divisible profit was ₹ 46,360.
- On 1st October, 2022, Ravi permanently withdrew ₹ 20,000 from his capital.

You are required to do the following

(a) Pass the journal entries to record **[6]**

(i) The permanent withdrawal made by Ravi.

(ii) The distribution of the divisible profits between the partners.

(iii) The adjusting entry for commission due to Ravi.

(b) Calculate the interest on capital allowed to **[2]**

(i) Tanuj (ii) Ravi

(c) Calculate the commission allowed to Tanuj. **[1]**

(d) Calculate the interest on drawings charged from Tanuj. **[1]**

Or Amit and Iqbal are partners in a business. Their partnership deed contained the following clauses

(i) Interest on drawings to be charged @ 6% per annum.

(ii) Amit to get a salary of ₹ 1,000 per month.

(iii) Iqbal to get an annual commission of ₹ 10,000.

(iv) Any partner taking a loan from the firm to be charged interest on it @ 8% per annum.

Additional Information

Particulars	Amit (₹)	Iqbal (₹)
Drawings made on 1st May, 2022	—	30,000
Borrowed from the Firm on 1st July, 2022	10,000	—
Capital Balances on 31st March, 2023	75,000	10,000 (Dr)
Divisible Profits for the Year 2022-23 Credited to the Partners' Capital Account	9,000	9,000

You are required to

(a) Give the closing journal entry for interest on loan due from Amit. **[1]**

(b) Find the opening capital balance of the partners on 1st April, 2022 by preparing the partners' capital account for the year 2022-23. **[9]**

10. Gama Ltd. issued 20,000 equity shares of ₹ 10 each to the public, payable as follows

₹ 2 on Application

₹ 3 on Allotment (on 1st November, 2022)

₹ 5 on First and Final Call (on 1st March, 2023)

Applications were received for 25,000 shares. The directors of the company accepted applications for 20,000 shares and refunded the application money on the remaining shares.

One shareholder who was allotted 30 shares paid the first and final call with allotment.

Another shareholder did not pay his allotment on 20 shares when due but paid it with the first and final call along with interest on calls-in-arrears.

The directors of the company charged interest on calls-in-arrears at the rate provided in Table F of the Companies Act, 2013. No interest was allowed on calls-in-advance.

You are required to pass journal entries to record the above transactions in the books of Gama Ltd. **[10]**

Or (i) Roxy Ltd. issued equity shares of ₹ 10 each payable as ₹ 4 on application and allotment ; ₹ 2 on first call; ₹ 4 on second and final call. Following is an extract of the journal of Roxy Ltd.

Journal of Roxy Ltd. (An extract)

Date	Particulars		LF	Amt (Dr)	Amt (Cr)
	Share First Call A/c	Dr		28,000	
	To Share Capital A/c				28,000
	(Being first call due on .... shares @ ₹ 2 each)				
	Bank A/c	Dr		...	
	Calls-in-arrears A/c	Dr		2,000	
	To Share First Call A/c				28,000
	(Being first call received on ...... shares)				
	Share Capital A/c	Dr		...	
	To Shares Forfeited A/c				4,000
	To Calls-in-arrears A/c				...
	(Being...shares of ₹ 10 each forfeited for non-payment of first call)				
	Share Second and Final Call A/c	Dr		52,000	
	To Share Capital A/c				52,000
	(Being second and final call due on ...... shares @ ₹ 4 each)				
	Bank A/c	Dr		...	
	Calls-in-arrears A/c	Dr		10,000	
	To Share Second and Final Call A/c				52,000
	(Being second call received on ...... shares)				
	Share Capital A/c	Dr		...	
	To Shares Forfeited A/c				...
	To Calls-in-arrears A/c				10,000
	(Being ... shares of ₹ 10 each forfeited for non-payment of final call)				
	Bank A/c	Dr		...	
	Shares Forfeited A/c	Dr		...	
	To Share Capital A/c				...
	(Being 1,500 forfeited shares, including those on which the first call was not received, re-issued @ ₹ 6 per share fully called-up)				
	Share Forfeiture A/c	Dr		...	
	To Capital Reserve A/c				...
	(Being ....)				

You are required to complete the journal entries by filling up the missing information represented by '...', including the number of shares and narration, if any. **[9]**

(ii) Savi Ltd. forfeited 50 shares of ₹ 100 each issued at a premium of 10%, on which allotment money of ₹ 30 per share (including premium) and first and final call of ₹ 40 per share were not received.

What is the minimum amount per share at which the company can re-issue these shares? **[1]**

Section B

(Answer all questions) **(20 Marks)**

11. In sub-parts (i) and (ii) choose the correct option and in sub-parts (iii) to (v) answer the questions as instructed.

(i) What is the difference between total assets and current liabilities? **[1]**

(a) Total liabilities
(b) Shareholders' funds
(c) Total debt
(d) Capital employed

(ii) While preparing its cash flow statement, which of the following will be classified by a company as its cash outflow from investing activities? **[1]**

P – Investment in government securities.
Q – Investment in bank deposits (having maturity of six months).
R – Proceeds from redemption of liquid mutual fund units.
S – Proceeds from bank deposits with original maturity of less than three months.

(a) P and Q (b) R and S
(c) Only P (d) Only R

(iii) A company has a quick ratio of 1.8 : 1. Mention whether this ratio will improve/ reduce / not change after it sells a machine worth ₹ 1,20,000 at a loss of ₹ 30,000. **[1]**

(iv) State whether creditors would prefer lending to a company with a high debt-equity ratio or a low debt-equity ratio. Give a reason. **[1]**

(v) An extract of the balance sheet of Nova Ltd. shows

Particulars	31st March, 2023 (₹)	31st March 2022 (₹)
Share Capital (Equity shares @ ₹ 10 each)	8,00,000	5,00,000
Securities Premium	70,000	1,70,000

During the year 2022-23, the company raised its share capital by issuing bonus shares to the shareholders at the beginning of the year in the ratio of 1 : 5 (one bonus share was issued for every five equity shares). The balance shares were issued for cash to the public.

How many shares were issued for cash by the company? **[1]**

12. Following is the comparative income statement of Violet Ltd. for the years ending 31st March, 2023 and 31st March, 2022.

You are required to present the comparative income statement in its complete form after calculating the missing information represented by "...". **[3]**

Comparative Income Statement of Violet Ltd.
for the years ending 31st March, 2023 and 31st March, 2022

Particulars	31st March, 2023 (₹)	31st March, 2022 (₹)	Absolute Change	% Change
Revenue from Operations	...	7,098	364	...
Expenses	8,998	7,931	...	...
Net Profit	...	(833)	(703)	...

13. Based on the following information of Neon Ltd, answer the questions given below in relation to the cash flow statement of the company for the year 2022-23.

Particulars	31st March, 2023 (₹)	31st March, 2022 (₹)
Provision for Tax	80,000	50,000
7% Debentures	8,00,000	3,00,000
Unclaimed Dividend	6,000	—
Plant and Machinery (At book value)	1,00,000	1,00,000
Land	4,50,000	6,00,000

Note *Dividend proposed in the years 2021-22 and 2022-23 were ₹ 30,000 and 40,000 respectively.*

Additional Information

During the year 2022-23, the company

(i) Provided ₹ 75,000 for tax.
(ii) Issued 7% debentures at a discount of 5%.
(iii) Purchased plant and machinery for ₹ 40,000.

(a) What is the amount of tax paid by the company? **[1]**

(b) Give the reason for the opening book value and closing book value of plant and machinery remaining the same, despite the purchase of a machine during the year. **[1]**

(c) What is the inflow of cash from the issue of 7% debentures? **[1]**

(d) Give the company's outflow of cash for dividend paid to the shareholders. **[1]**

(e) State with reason whether Neon Ltd. will consider the decrease in the amount of land as an operating activity or as an investing activity, while preparing its cash flow statement. **[2]**

Or From the following balance sheets of Halogen Ltd. you are required to prepare a cash flow statement (as per AS-3) for the year 2022-23.

Balance Sheet of Halogen Ltd.
as at 31st March, 2023 and 31st March, 2022

Particulars	Note No.	31st March, 2023 (₹)	31st March, 2022 (₹)
I. **EQUITY AND LIABILITIES**			
1. **Shareholders' Funds**			
(i) Share Capital (Equity shares @ ₹ 10 each)		4,50,000	4,00,000
(ii) Reserves and Surplus (Statement of P and L)		1,06,000	(20,000)
2. **Non-current Liabilities**			
Long-term Borrowings (15% debentures)		6,00,000	4,00,000
3. **Current Liabilities**			
Short-term Provisions (Provision for tax)		50,000	70,000
Total		12,06,000	8,50,000
II. **ASSETS**			
1. Non-current Assets			
(i) Property, Plant & Equipment and Intangible Assets			
(a) Property, Plant and Equipment	1	4,80,000	7,00,000
2. **Current Assets**			
(i) Current Investments		2,56,000	10,000
(ii) Cash and Bank Balances		4,70,000	1,40,000
Total		12,06,000	8,50,000

Notes to Accounts

Particulars	31st March, 2023 (₹)	31st March, 2022 (₹)
1. **Property, Plant and Equipment**		
Plant and Machinery	7,42,000	9,00,000
(–) Accumulated Depreciation	(2,62,000)	(2,00,000)

Additional Information

During the year 2022-23, the company

(i) Issued additional debentures on 1st October, 2022.

(ii) Sold plant and machinery, the book value of which was ₹ 1,20,000 (accumulated depreciation ₹ 38,000) for ₹ 50,000. **[6]**

14. Answer any three of the following questions. **[6]**

(i) From the following particulars of Hind Ltd. calculate the preference dividend paid by the company.

Particulars	Amt (₹)
Net Profit before Tax	20,00,000
Equity Shares of ₹ 10 each (Market value ₹ 15)	40,00,000
Tax Rate	30%
Earning Per Share	2.75

(ii) Calculate the current ratio (upto two decimal places) of Windlas Biotech Ltd. from the following extract of its annual report of 2021-22.

Particulars	Amt (₹) (in millions)
Opening Inventory of Consumables (Raw materials)	264.79
Closing Inventory of Consumables (Raw materials)	389.85
Opening Inventory of Finished Goods and Work-in-progress	149.82
Closing Inventory of Finished Goods and Work-in-progress	197.24
Current Assets (Other than inventory of consumables and of finished goods and work-in-progress)	3,229.23
Current Liabilities	936.52

Source *Annual Report 2021-22 of Windlas Biotech Ltd.*

(iii) For the year 2022-23, the return on investment of Yolo Ltd. was 20%; its capital employed being ₹ 50,00,000.

(a) You are required to give the formula used by Yolo Ltd., to calculate the return on investment.

(b) You have been provided with two components for calculating return on investment. Calculate the missing third component.

(iv) Calculate the working capital turnover ratio of Moonlight Ltd., (upto two decimal places) from the following particulars

Particulars	Amt (₹)
Cash	10,00,000
Short-term Loans and Advances	3,00,000
Inventory	2,00,000
Trade Payables	5,00,000
Cost of Revenue from Operations	12,00,000
Gross Profit on Cost of Revenue from Operations	25%

Answers

1. (i) (b) The excess claim i.e. 90,000 – 80,000 = ₹ 10,000 will be debited to revaluation account as increase in liability.

(ii) (d) CreditAccess is a listed NBFC, so they are exempted from creating DRR.

(iii) (d) The assets of the firm, including amount contributed by the partners to make up deficiency of capital, is applied in the following order

- Payment to outsiders/creditors.
- Payment of loans and advances of partners.
- Payment of capital of partners.
- The remaining amount shall be divided among the partners in their profit sharing ratio.

(iv) (a)

Subscribed Share Capital	**Amt (₹)**
Subscribed and Fully Paid-up (44,600 × 10)	4,46,000
(+) Share Forfeiture Account (400 × 8)	3,200
	4,49,200

(v) (c) Both Assertion (A) and Reason (R) are false

(vi) JOURNAL

Date	Particulars		LF	Amt (Dr)	Amt (Cr)
	Cash A/c	Dr		29,700	
	To Realisation A/c				29,700
	(Being cash received from debtors)				

Working Note

$$\text{Discount to Debtors} = 30,000 \times \frac{4}{100} \times \frac{3}{12} = ₹\ 300$$

(vii) Discount written-off from Securities Premium = 71,000 – 35,000 = ₹ 36,000

$$\text{Percentage of Discount} = \frac{\text{Discount}}{\text{Face Value}} \times 100$$

$$= \frac{36,000}{9,00,000} \times 100 = 4\%$$

(viii) The amount will be shown as contingent liability because it is not acknowledged as debts.

(ix)

Deepa's Capital after Adjustment of Loss (30,000 – 3,000)	₹ 27,000
Pia's Capital after Adjustment of Loss (20,000 – 2,000)	₹ 18,000
Total Capital	₹ 45,000

Charu's Capital = 45,000 × 25/100 = ₹ 11,250

(x) JOURNAL

Date	Particulars		LF	Amt (Dr)	Amt (Cr)
	8% Debentures A/c	Dr		1,00,000	
	Debentures Interest A/c	Dr		8,000	
	To Debentureholders' A/c				1,08,000
	(Being 8% debentures due for redemption)				

2. Balance Sheet
as at 30th June, 2023

Liabilities		Amt (₹)	Assets	Amt (₹)
Capital A/cs			Fixed Assets	3,50,000
Hari	3,40,000		Debtors	2,50,000
James	2,20,000	5,60,000	Bank (1,50,000 – 1,00,000)	50,000
Jacob's Executor A/c		1,99,500	Profit and Loss Suspense A/c	1,09,500
		7,59,500		7,59,500

Working Notes

1. Dr **Jacob's Capital Account** Cr

Particulars	Amt (₹)	Particulars	Amt (₹)
To Bank A/c (Drawings)	1,00,000	By Balance b/d	1,90,000
To Profit and Loss Suspense A/c (Interest on drawings)	500	By Profit and Loss Suspense A/c	1,10,000
To Jacob's Executor A/c	1,99,500		
	3,00,000		3,00,000

2. Interest on Jacob's Drawings = $1{,}00{,}000 \times \frac{4}{100} \times \frac{1.5}{12}$ = ₹ 500

3. Profit and Loss Suspense Account = 1,10,000 – 500 = ₹ 1,09,500

Or

Dr **Kamal's Loan Account** Cr

Date	Particulars	Amt (₹)	Date	Particulars	Amt (₹)
2024 Mar 31	To Balance c/d	20,900	2023 Jun 30	By Kamal's Capital A/c	20,000
			2024 Mar 31	By Interest A/c $\left(20{,}000 \times \frac{6}{100} \times \frac{9}{12}\right)$	900
		20,900			20,900
2024 Jun 30	To Bank A/c (20,000 + 900 + 300)	21,200	2024 Apr 1	By Balance b/d	20,900
			Jun 30	By Interest A/c $\left(20{,}000 \times \frac{6}{100} \times \frac{3}{12}\right)$	300
		21,200			21,200

3. (i) Dr **6% Debentures Account** Cr

Particulars	Amt (₹)	Particulars	Amt (₹)
To Balance c/d	50,00,000	By Debentures Application and Allotment A/c	47,50,000
		By Discount on Issue of Debentures A/c	2,50,000
	50,00,000		50,00,000

(ii) Dr **Loss on Issue of Debentures Account** Cr

Particulars	Amt (₹)	Particulars	Amt (₹)
To 6% Debentures A/c	2,50,000	By Securities Premium A/c	2,00,000
To Premium on Redemption of Debentures A/c	3,50,000	By Statement of Profit and Loss (Balancing Figure)	4,00,000
	6,00,000		6,00,000

4. (i) Dr **Debentureholders' Account** Cr

Date	Particulars	Amt (₹)	Date	Particulars	Amt (₹)
2023 Mar 31	To Bank A/c	51,00,000	2023 Mar 31	By 9% Debentures A/c	50,00,000
			Mar 31	By Premium on Redemption of Debentures A/c $\left(50{,}00{,}000 \times \frac{2}{100}\right)$	1,00,000
		51,00,000			51,00,000

(ii) Dr **Debenture Redemption Investment Account** Cr

Date	Particulars	Amt (₹)	Date	Particulars	Amt (₹)
2022 Apr 1	To Bank A/c $\left(50{,}00{,}000 \times \frac{15}{100}\right)$	7,50,000	2023 Mar 31	By Bank A/c	7,57,500
2023 Mar 31	To Profit on Sale of Investment $\left(7{,}50{,}000 \times \frac{1}{100}\right)$	7,500			
		7,57,500			7,57,500

Or

JOURNAL

Date	Particulars		LF	Amt (Dr)	Amt (Cr)
2022 Apr 30	Debenture Redemption Investment A/c	Dr		9,00,000	
	To Bank A/c (60,00,000 × 15%)				9,00,000
	(Being 15% of the face value is invested)				
2023 Mar 31	Bank A/c	Dr		9,37,125	
	TDS Deposited A/c	Dr		4,125	
	To Debenture Redemption Investment A/c				9,00,000
	To Interest on Investment A/c $\left(9,00,000 \times \frac{5}{100} \times \frac{11}{12}\right)$				41,250
	(Being investment bearing 5% p.a. interest encashed)				
Mar 31	5% Debentures A/c	Dr		60,00,000	
	To Debentureholders' A/c				60,00,000
	(Being amount due to debentures)				
Mar 31	Debentureholders' A/c	Dr		60,00,000	
	To Bank A/c				60,00,000
	(Being amount paid on redemption)				
Mar 31	Interest on Investment A/c	Dr		41,250	
	To Statement of Profit and Loss				41,250
	(Being interest on investment transferred to statement of profit and loss)				

5. (a) **Simple Average Profit Method**

Value of Goodwill = Average Profit* × Number of Years' Purchase

$$\text{*Average Profit} = \frac{\text{Total Actual Profits of Given Number of Years Before Abnormal and Non-business Items}}{\text{Given Number of Years}}$$

(b) $\text{Average Profit} = \frac{(20,000) + 34,000 + 46,000}{3} = \frac{60,000}{3} = ₹\ 20,000$

Goodwill = 20,000 × 2 = ₹ 40,000

(c) $\text{Danish's share of goodwill} = 40,000 \times \frac{1}{4} = ₹\ 10,000$

Anish's Capital on 1st April, 2023	**Amt (₹)**
Opening Capital of Anish	3,00,000
(+) Profit/Loss of Last 3 Years	(20,000)
	34,000
	46,000
(−) Drawings	(30,000)
(+) Premium for Goodwill	10,000
Anish's Capital	3,40,000

Danish's Capital = 3,40,000 × 1/4 = ₹ 85,000

6. (i) **Notes to Accounts**

Particulars	Amt (₹)
Share Capital	
Authorised Share Capital	
.........Equity Shares of ₹ 10 each	—
Issued Share Capital	
1,25,000 Equity Shares of ₹ 10 each	12,50,000
Subscribed Share Capital	
Subscribed and Fully Paid-up	
1,10,000 Equity Shares of ₹ 10 each	11,00,000

Particulars		Amt (₹)
Subscribed but not Fully Paid-up		
10,000 Equity Share of ₹ 10 each	1,00,000	
(–) Calls-in-arrears (10,000 × 2)	(20,000)	80,000
(+) Share Forfeiture Account (5,000 × 8)		40,000
		12,20,000

(ii) (a) **Short-term Borrowings**

	Amt (₹)
Bank Overdraft	40,000
(+) Matured Debentures (1/5 × 3,00,000)	60,000
	1,00,000

(b) **Current Assets**

		Amt (₹)
Short-term Loans and Advances		50,000
Cash and Bank Balances		1,60,000
Inventories		30,000
Bills Receivables		20,000
Debtors	90,000	
(–) Provision	(10,000)	80,000
		3,40,000

(c) **Property, Plant and Equipment**

		Amt (₹)
Plant and Machinery	6,00,000	
(–) Accumulated Depreciation	(1,00,000)	5,00,000
Land and Building		6,80,000
		11,80,000

7. Dr **Partners' Capital Account** Cr

Particulars	Amay (₹)	Sujoy (₹)	Malay (₹)	Particulars	Amay (₹)	Sujoy (₹)	Malay (₹)
To Stock	25,000	—	—	By Balance b/d	1,30,000	1,25,000	—
To Sujoy's Current A/c	—	37,500	—	By Cash A/c	—	—	1,20,000
To Balance c/d	2,70,000	90,000	1,20,000	By Premium for Goodwill A/c	7,500	2,500	—
				By Cash A/c (Cash bought in)	1,57,500	—	—
	2,95,000	1,27,500	1,20,000		2,95,000	1,27,500	1,20,000

Working Notes

1. **JOURNAL**

Date	Particulars		LF	Amt (Dr)	Amt (Cr)
	Cash A/c	Dr		1,30,000	
	To Malay's Capital A/c				1,20,000
	To Premium for Goodwill A/c				10,000
	(Being goodwill and capital brought in by new partner)				
	Premium for Goodwill A/c	Dr		10,000	
	To Amay's Capital A/c				7,500
	To Sujoy's Capital A/c				2,500
	(Being goodwill distributed between sacrificing partner)				

2. Dr **Revaluation Account** Cr

Particulars	Amt (₹)	Particulars	Amt (₹)
To Stock A/c	20,000	By Bills Payable A/c	20,000
	20,000		20,000

3. **Adjustment of Capital**

New Firm's Capital = $1,20,000 \times \frac{4}{1}$ = ₹ 4,80,000

New Profit Sharing Ratio

Let profit be ₹ 1

Remaining Share = $1 - \frac{1}{4} = \frac{3}{4}$; Amay's New Share = $\frac{3}{4} \times \frac{3}{4} = \frac{9}{16}$

Sujoy's New Share = $\frac{1}{4} \times \frac{3}{4} = \frac{3}{16}$; Malay's Share = $\frac{1}{4} \times \frac{4}{4} = \frac{4}{16}$

New Ratio = 9 : 3 : 4

Amay's New Capital = $4,80,000 \times \frac{9}{16}$ = ₹ 2,70,000

Sujoy's New Capital = $4,80,000 \times \frac{3}{16}$ = ₹ 90,000

Or

JOURNAL

Date	Particulars		LF	Amt (Dr)	Amt (Cr)
(i)	Mitu's Capital A/c	Dr		22,000	
	Ritu's Capital A/c	Dr		33,000	
	To Profit and Loss A/c				55,000
	(Being balance of profit and loss account adjusted)				
(ii) (a)	Workmen Compensation Reserve A/c	Dr		10,000	
	To Outstanding Workmen Claim A/c				10,000
	(Being workmen claim adjusted)				
(b)	Nitu's Capital A/c	Dr		4,000	
	To Mitu's Capital A/c				1,600
	To Ritu's Capital A/c				2,400
	(Being adjustment of workmen compensation reserve)				
(iii)	Investment Fluctuation Reserve A/c	Dr		10,000	
	To Investment A/c				4,000
	To Mitu's Capital A/c				2,400
	To Ritu's Capital A/c				3,600
	(Being transfer of excess investment fluctuation reserve to partners' capital account)				
(iv)	General Reserve A/c	Dr		40,000	
	To Provision for Doubtful Debts				10,000
	To Mitu's Capital A/c				12,000
	To Ritu's Capital A/c				18,000
	(Being transfer of excess general reserve to partners' capital account)				

8. Dr **Partners' Capital Account** Cr

Particulars	Adit (₹)	Shiv (₹)	Particulars	Adit (₹)	Shiv (₹)
To Shiv's Current A/c	—	6,000	By Balance b/d	40,000	30,000
To Profit and Loss (Debit Balance)	2,500	2,000	By Adit's Current A/c	3,000	—
To Loan to Shiv	—	22,000	By Cash A/c	—	15,000
To Realisation Loss	10,000	8,000			
To Cash A/c (Dissolution Expenses)		3,000			
To Realisation A/c (Furniture)	9,000	4,000			
To Cash A/c	21,500	—			
	43,000	45,000		43,000	45,000

Working Note

Let the book value of furniture taken over by Adit be x

$$9{,}000 = x - 10\% \text{ of } x \Rightarrow 9{,}000 = 0.9x \Rightarrow x = \frac{9{,}000}{0.9} = ₹\ 10{,}000$$

Total value of furniture = ₹ 15,000 ; Remaining furniture = 15,000 – 10,000 = ₹ 5,000

Furniture taken over by Shiv = $5{,}000 \times \frac{80}{100}$ = ₹ 4,000

9. (a)

JOURNAL

Date	Particulars		LF	Amt (Dr)	Amt (Cr)
2022					
(i) Jan 10	Ravi's Capital A/c	Dr		20,000	
	To Cash A/c				20,000
	(Being permanent withdrawal of capital by Ravi)				
2023					
(ii) Mar 31	Profit and Loss Appropriation A/c	Dr		46,360	
	To Tanuj's Capital A/c				23,180
	To Ravi's Capital A/c				23,180
	(Being divisible profit distributed)				
(iii) Mar 31	Ravi's Commission A/c	Dr		10,000	
	To Ravi's Capital A/c				10,000
	(Being commission due to Ravi)				

(b) (i) Interest on Tanuj's Capital = $1{,}50{,}000 \times \frac{10}{100}$ = ₹ 15,000

(ii) Interest on Ravi's Capital = $\left[\left(1{,}00{,}000 \times \frac{10}{100} \times \frac{6}{12}\right) + \left(80{,}000 \times \frac{10}{100} \times \frac{6}{12}\right)\right]$ = 5,000 + 4,000 = ₹ 9,000

(c) Tanuj's Commission = $\frac{\text{Trading Profit} \times \text{Rate}}{100 + \text{Rate}} = 84{,}000 \times \frac{5}{105}$ = ₹ 4,000

(d) Interest on Tanuj's Drawings = Drawings $\times \frac{\text{Rate}}{100} \times \frac{\text{Average Period}}{12} = 24{,}000 \times \frac{4}{100} \times \frac{4.5}{12}$ = ₹ 360

Or (a)

JOURNAL

Date	Particulars		LF	Amt (Dr)	Amt (Cr)
	Interest on Amit's Loan A/c $\left(10{,}000 \times \frac{8}{100} \times \frac{9}{12}\right)$	Dr		600	
	To Profit and Loss A/c				600
	(Being interest on loan transferred to profit and loss account)				

(b) Dr **Partners' Capital Account** Cr

Particulars	Amit (₹)	Iqbal (₹)	Particulars	Amit (₹)	Iqbal (₹)
To Drawings A/c	—	30,000	By Balance b/d (Bal. Figure)	54,600	2,650
To Interest on Amit's Loan A/c	600	—	By Partner's Salary A/c	12,000	—
To Interest on Drawings $\left(30{,}000 \times \frac{6}{100} \times \frac{11}{12}\right)$	—	1,650	By Divisible Profits A/c	9,000	9,000
			By Partners' Commission A/c	—	10,000
To Balance c/d	75,000	—	By Balance c/d	—	10,000
	75,600	31,650		75,600	31,650

10.

JOURNAL

Date	Particulars		LF	Amt (Dr)	Amt (Cr)
	Bank A/c	Dr		50,000	
	To Equity Share Application A/c				50,000
	(Being application money received on 25,000 shares @ ₹ 2 each)				

Date	Particulars	LF	Amt (Dr)	Amt (Cr)
	Equity Share Application A/c Dr		50,000	
	To Equity Share Capital A/c			40,000
	To Bank A/c			10,000
	(Being 20,000 equity shares allotted and excess application money on 5,000 shares refunded)			
	Equity Share Allotment A/c Dr		60,000	
	To Equity Share Capital A/c			60,000
	(Being allotment money made due to 20,000 equity shares @ ₹ 3 per share)			
	Bank A/c Dr		60,090	
	Calls-in-arrears A/c (20 × 3) Dr		60	
	To Equity Share Allotment A/c			60,000
	To Calls-in-advance A/c (30 × 5)			150
	(Being allotment money received except for 20 shares, along with first and final call money on 30 shares)			
	Equity Share First and Final Call A/c Dr		1,00,000	
	To Equity Share Capital A/c			1,00,000
	(Being first and final call money made due on 20,000 equity shares @ ₹ 5 each)			
	Bank A/c Dr		99,910	
	Calls-in-advance A/c Dr		150	
	To Equity Share First and Final Call A/c			1,00,000
	To Calls-in-arrears A/c			60
	(Being first and final call money received on 20,000 equity shares along with allotment money on 20 shares and calls-in-advance on 30 shares adjusted)			
	Sundry Members A/c Dr		2	
	To Interest on Calls-in-arrears A/c (60 × 10 / 100 × 4 × 12)			2
	(Being interest on calls-in-arrears due)			
	Bank A/c Dr		2	
	To Sundry Members A/c			2
	(Being interest on calls-in-arrears paid)			
	Interest on Calls-in-arrears A/c Dr		2	
	To Statement of Profit and Loss			2
	(Being interest on calls-in-arrears transferred to statement of profit and loss)			

Or (i)

JOURNAL of Roxy Ltd. (An extract)

Date	Particulars	LF	Amt (Dr)	Amt (Cr)
	Share First Call A/c Dr		28,000	
	To Share Capital A/c			28,000
	(Being first call due on **14,000** shares @ ₹ 2 each)			
	Bank A/c (13,000 × 2) Dr		**26,000**	
	Calls-in-arrears A/c (1,000 × 2) Dr		2,000	
	To Share First Call A/c			28,000
	(Being first call received on **13,000** shares)			
	Share Capital A/c (1,000 × 6) Dr		**6,000**	
	To Shares Forfeited A/c (1,000 × 4)			4,000
	To Calls-in-arrears A/c (1,000 × 2)			**2,000**
	(Being **1,000** shares of ₹ 10 each forfeited for non-payment of first call)			
	Share Second and Final Call A/c Dr		52,000	
	To Share Capital A/c			52,000
	(Being second and final call due on **13,000** shares @ ₹ 4 each)			
	Bank A/c (10,500 × 4) Dr		**42,000**	
	Calls-in-arrears A/c (2,500 × 4) Dr		10,000	
	To Share Second and Final Call A/c			52,000
	(Being second call received on **10,500** shares)			

Date	Particulars		LF	Amt (Dr)	Amt (Cr)
	Share Capital A/c (2,500 × 10)	Dr		**25,000**	
	To Shares Forfeited A/c (2,500 × 6)				**15,000**
	To Calls-in-arrears A/c (2,500 × 4)				10,000
	(Being **2,500** shares of ₹ 10 each forfeited for non-payment of final call)				
	Bank A/c (1,500 × 6)	Dr		**9,000**	
	Shares Forfeited A/c (1,500 × 4)	Dr		**6,000**	
	To Share Capital A/c (1,500 × 10)				**15,000**
	(Being 1,500 forfeited shares, including those on which the first call was not received , re-issued @ ₹ 6 per share fully called-up)				
	Share Forfeiture A/c	Dr		**1,000**	
	To Capital Reserve A/c (W.N.)				**1,000**
	(Being **profit on 1,500 forfeited shares transferred to capital reserve**)				

Working Note

Amount of Capital Reserve

$$= \left[\text{Profit on Forfeiture} + \left(\frac{\text{Profit on Forfeiture}}{\text{Forfeited Shares}} \times \text{Re-issued Shares}\right)\right] - \text{Loss on Re-issue}$$

$$= \left[4{,}000 + \left(\frac{15{,}000}{2{,}500} \times 500\right)\right] - 6{,}000 = 7{,}000 - 6{,}000 = ₹\ 1{,}000$$

(ii) Amount (per share) received on forfeited shares = ₹ 40

The maximum amount of discount the company can allow is ₹ 40. Therefore, the minimum amount at which the company can re-issue these shares is ₹ 60.

11. (i) (d) Capital Employed = Total Assets – Current Liabilities

(ii) (a) P and Q

(iii) Sale of machinery will increase bank (current asset) and will not put any impact on current liabilities. The ratio will improve.

(iv) Creditors would prefer to lend a low debt–equity ratio, because low debt-equity ratio means the company's debt burden is low and the company is in better position to pay back its debts.

(v)

Total shares issued by the company (8,00,000 – 5,00,000)	= ₹	3,00,000
(–) Total securities premium used to issue bonus shares	= ₹	(1,00,000)
Total amount received in cash	=	₹ 2,00,000

Face value of share = ₹ 10

Number of shares $\left(\frac{2{,}00{,}000}{10}\right) = 20{,}000$

12.

Comperative Income Statement of Violet Ltd.
for the years ending 31st March, 2023 and 31st March, 2022

Particulars	31st March, 2023 (₹)	31st March , 2022 (₹)	Absolute Change	% Change
Revenue from Operations	**7,462**	7,098	364	**5.13**
Expenses	8,998	7,931	**1,067**	**13.45**
Net Profit	**(1,536)**	(833)	(703)	**84.39**

Working Note

Absolute Change = Current Year's Figures – Previous Year's Figures

$$\% \text{ Change} = \frac{\text{Absolute Change}}{\text{Previous Year}} \times 100$$

13. (a) Dr **Provision for Tax Account** Cr

Particulars	Amt (₹)	Particulars	Amt (₹)
To Bank A/c (Paid) (Balancing Figure)	45,000	By Balance b/d	50,000
To Balance c/d	80,000	By Statement of Profit and Loss (Made)	75,000
	1,25,000		1,25,000

Tax paid by the company = ₹ 45,000

(b) The opening value and closing value of plant and machinery is same despite the purchase of machinery due to 'depreciation' provided on the fixed asset.

(c) Cash Inflow from Issue of 7% Debentures = Face Value of Debentures − Discount on Debentures
= 5,00,000 − 25,000 = ₹ 4,75,000

(d) Cash Outflow for Dividend Paid = Dividend of Previous Year − Unclaimed Dividend
= 30,000 − 6,000 = ₹ 24,000

(e) The value of land appreciates over time. So, decrease in the value of land is 'sale of land' and will be shown under investing activities.

Or

Cash Flow Statement

Particulars		Amt (₹)
A. **Cash Flow from Operating Activities**		
Net Profit after Appropriation and Tax	1,26,000	
(+) Provision for Tax	50,000	
Net Profit before Appropriation and Tax		1,76,000
Adjustments for		
(+) Interest on Debentures	75,000	
Depreciation	1,00,000	
Loss on Sale of Plant and Machinery	70,000	2,45,000
Operating Profit before Working Capital Changes		4,21,000
(−) Increase in Current Assets and Decrease in Current Liabilities		
Current Investments	(2,46,000)	(2,46,000)
Cash Generated from Operations		1,75,000
(−) Tax Paid During the Year		(70,000)
Cash Flow from Operating Activities		1,05,000
B. **Cash Flow from Investing Activities**		
Sale of Plant and Machinery	50,000	
Cash Flow from Investing Activities		50,000
C. **Cash Flow from Financing Activities**		
Issue of Share Capital		50,000
Issue of 15% Debentures		2,00,000
Interest on Debentures		(75,000)
Cash flow from Financing Activities		1,75,000
Net Increase in Cash and Cash Equivalents (A + B + C)		3,30,000
(+) Cash and Cash Equivalents in the Beginning of the Year		1,40,000
Cash and Cash Equivalents in the End of the Year		4,70,000

Working Notes

1. Interest on Debentures

$$= \left[\left(4{,}00{,}000 \times \frac{15}{100} \times \frac{6}{12}\right) + \left(6{,}00{,}000 \times \frac{15}{100} \times \frac{6}{12}\right)\right] = 30{,}000 + 45{,}000 = ₹\ 75{,}000$$

2. Dr **Plant and Machinery Account** Cr

Particulars	Amt (₹)	Particulars	Amt (₹)
To Balance b/d	9,00,000	By Accumulated Depreciation A/c	38,000
		By Bank A/c	50,000
		By Statement of Profit and Loss	70,000
		By Balance c/d	7,42,000
	9,00,000		9,00,000

3. Dr **Accumulated Depreciation Account** Cr

Particulars	Amt (₹)	Particulars	Amt (₹)
To Plant and Machinery A/c	38,000	By Balance b/d	2,00,000
To Balance c/d	2,62,000	By Depreciation A/c	1,00,000
	3,00,000		3,00,000

14. (i) Net Profit after Tax but before Preference Dividend = Net Profit before Tax–Tax

$$= 20,00,000 - (30\% \times 20,00,000)$$
$$= 20,00,000 - 6,00,000$$
$$= ₹\ 14,00,000$$

$$\text{Earning Per Share} = \frac{\text{Net Profit after Tax and Preference Dividend}}{\text{Number of Equity shares}}$$

Net Profit after Tax and Preference Dividend = EPS × Number of Equity Shares

$$= 2.75 \times 4,00,000$$
$$= ₹\ 11,00,000$$

Now, Preference Dividend = 14,00,000 – 11,00,000 = ₹ 3,00,000

(ii) **Total Current Assets**

	Amt (₹)
Current Assets (Other than inventory of consumables, finished goods and WIP)	3,229.23
(+) Closing Inventory of Consumables (Raw Materials)	389.85
Closing Inventory of Finished Goods and working-in-progress	197.24
Total Current Assets	3,816.32

$$\text{Current Ratio} = \frac{\text{Current Assets}}{\text{Current Liabilities}} = \frac{3,816.32}{936.52} = 4.08:1$$

(iii) (a) $\text{Return on Investment} = \frac{\text{Net Profit before Interest and Tax}}{\text{Capital Employed}} \times 100$

(b) $20\% = \frac{\text{Net Profit before Interest and Tax}}{50,00,000}$

$$\text{Net Profit before Interest and Tax} = 50,00,000 \times \frac{20}{100} = ₹\ 10,00,000$$

(iv) Working Capital = Current Assets* – Current Liabilities** = 15,00,000 – 5,00,000 = ₹ 10,00,000

*Current Assets = 10,00,000 + 3,00,000 + 2,00,000 = ₹ 15,00,000

**Current Liabilities = ₹ 5,00,000

$$\text{Working Capital Turnover Ratio} = \frac{\text{Revenue from Operations}^{***}}{\text{Working Capital}} = \frac{15,00,000}{10,00,000} = 1.5 \text{ times}$$

***Revenue from Operations = Cost of Revenue from Operations + Gross Profit#

$$= 12,00,000 + 3,00,000 = ₹\ 15,00,000$$

$$^{\#}\text{Gross Profit} = 12,00,000 \times \frac{25}{100} = ₹\ 3,00,000$$

ISC

Examination Paper 2025

Time : 3 hrs
Marks : 80

Accounts XII

General Instructions

1. Candidates are allowed additional 15 minutes for only reading the paper. They must not start writing during this time.
2. Section-A is compulsory for all candidates.
3. Candidates have to attempt all questions from either Section-B or Section-C*.
4. There are internal choices provided in each section.
5. The intended marks for questions or parts of questions are given in the brackets [ ].
6. All calculations should be shown clearly.
7. All working, including rough work, should be done on the same page as and adjacent to, the rest of the answer.

* Section-C has not been covered.

Section A (60 Marks)

(Answer all questions)

1. In subparts (i) to (v) choose the correct options and in subparts (vi) to (x) answer the questions as instructed.

(i) Shiv, Ravi and Roshan are partners in a firm following the fixed capital method. During the year 2023-24, Shiv withdrew ₹ 15,000 in the middle of each half year; Ravi withdrew ₹ 20,000 to pay for premium of his life insurance policy; Roshan withdrew ₹ 12,000 from his capital.

What is the interest on drawings charged from the partners at the end of the year, if the rate of interest on drawings mentioned in the partnership deed is 6% per annum? **[1]**

(a) Shiv - ₹ 900; Ravi - Nil; Roshan - ₹ 360
(b) Shiv - ₹ 900; Ravi - ₹ 600; Roshan - Nil
(c) Shiv - ₹ 1,800; Ravi - ₹ 1,200; Roshan - ₹ 720
(d) Shiv - ₹ 900; Ravi - ₹ 1,200; Roshan - ₹ 360

(ii) To value the goodwill of a partnership firm at the time of its reconstitution, which one of the following items is added back to the previous year's profit to find the normal profit? **[1]**

(a) Gain from sale of shares
(b) Insurance premium paid
(c) Undervaluation of closing stock
(d) Overvaluation of closing stock

(iii) Read the following news item regarding issue of shares by TVS Supply Chain and answer the question that follows. **[1]**

TVS Supply Chain IPO subscribed 2.8 times

Source *The Hindu, Business Line, 15th August, 2023*

Which of the following options can TVS Supply Chain avail to deal with its over-subscribed shares?

P Reject all the over-subscribed shares and refund the excess application money.
Q Allot all shares applied for on a pro-rata basis.
R Allot all shares applied for.
S Allot in full to some applicants, allot shares on a pro-rata basis to a few applicants and refund the application money to some applicants.

(a) P, Q and R (b) Q, R and S
(c) P, R and S (d) P, Q and S

(iv) Premium on Redemption of Debentures is debited to
(a) Debentures A/c **[1]**
(b) Loss on Issue of Debentures A/c
(c) Debenture Holders' A/c
(d) Debenture Application and Allotment A/c

(v) **Assertion** (A) A partnership firm is said to maintain its accounts by the fixed capital account method when it has a separate capital account and current account for every partner.
Reason (R) A fixed capital account method is maintained to ensure that the balance in the current account of any partner is not overdrawn at any point of time.
Which one of the following is correct? **[1]**
(a) Both Assertion (A) and Reason (R) are true and Reason (R) is the correct explanation for Assertion (A).
(b) Both Assertion (A) and Reason (R) are true but Reason (R) is not the correct explanation for Assertion (A).
(c) Assertion (A) is true and Reason (R) is false.
(d) Both Assertion (A) and Reason (R) are false.

(vi) What does a new partner acquire by contributing his share to the self-generated goodwill of the firm? **[1]**

(vii) At the time of dissolution of a partnership firm on 31st March, 2024, its bills payable of ₹42,000 due to be paid on 31st July, 2024, was settled at a rebate of ₹ 350.
Calculate the per annum percentage of rebate at which the bills payable was settled. **[1]**

(viii) At the time of the dissolution of the partnership firm of Sanjay and Mitali, its Balance Sheet showed deferred revenue expenditure of ₹30,000.
Give the journal entry to treat this item. **[1]**

(ix) Read the following news item and answer the questions which follow. **[1]**
In a strong display of innovation, IIT Kanpur filed a total of 122 Intellectual Property Rights (IPR) applications in 2023. To date, it has 1,039 successful IPRs. The patents for inventions are from varied domains such as MedTech and Nano Technology.
Source *(edited) Financial Express. 11th January, 2024*
(a) Mention the sub-head under which patents would be shown in the Balance Sheet of a company prepared as per Schedule III of the Companies Act, 2013.
(b) Give any one other item under the same sub-head.

(x) Why is it advisable for an unlisted manufacturing company to start transferring its profits to Debenture Redemption Reserve from the year of the issue of its non-convertible debentures? **[1]**

2. Ajay and Bijoy are two partners sharing profits and losses in the ratio of 2:1.

Balance Sheet of Ajay and Bijoy (extract)
As at 31st March, 2024

Liabilities	Amt (₹)	Assets	Amt (₹)
Workmen Compensation Reserve	1,200		

Additional Information
(a) On 1st April, 2024, they admitted Sujay as a partner with $\frac{1}{4}$ share in the profits.
(b) The workmen compensation reserve to be reduced to ₹ 900 in the reconstituted firm.
You are required to give the accounting treatment of workmen compensation reserve on the date of Sujay's admission. **[3]**

Or

Gita and Mita are partners in a firm sharing profits and losses in the ratio of 3:2. An extract of their Balance Sheet as at 31st March, 2024, is as follow

Balance Sheet of Gita and Mita (extract)
As at 31st March, 2024

Liabilities	Amt (₹)	Assets		Amt (₹)
Creditors	15,000	Plant and Machinery		1,20,000
		Sundry Debtors	1,50,000	
		Provision for Doubtful Debts	(15,000)	1,35,000

On the admission of Rita as a third partner for $\frac{1}{4}$ share in the profits, the assets and liabilities of the firm were revalued as under
(i) Creditors include an amount of ₹ 5,000 received as commission from Ajay. The necessary adjustment to be made.
(ii) Creditors include ₹ 1,000 due to Nikhil paid by partner Gita privately for which she is not to be reimbursed.
(iii) The value of machinery, overvalued by ₹ 20,000 in the Balance Sheet, to be revised.
(iv) Out of the total insurance premium paid, ₹ 6,000 to be treated as prepaid insurance. The amount was earlier debited to Profit and Loss A/c.
(v) ₹ 20,000 for damages claimed by a customer had been disputed by the firm. It was agreed at 70% by a compromise between the customer and the firm.
(vi) The provision for doubtful debts to be increased to ₹ 20,000.

You are required to prepare the revaluation account.

3. On 1st April, 2023, Vishesh Co. Ltd, made an issue, which was fully subscribed, of 8,000, 5% debentures of ₹ 100 each at a premium of 10% repayable at par at the end of 10 years. The debentures were allotted on 31st August, 2023, subscriptions being payable.

10% with Applicatio

50% (along with premium) on Allotment

20% with First Call

Balance on the Second and Final Call

One debenture holder holding 200 debentures paid the First Call with Allotment.

You are required to prepare the cash book for the year 2023-24 to record the above issue of debentures. (Ignore interest on debentures). **[3]**

Or

Mint Ltd. issued 5,000, 6% debentures of ₹ 100 each to be redeemed at par after five years. The issue price was payable as follows

₹ 25 on Application payable on 1st May, 2023

₹ 25 on Allotment payable on 1st July, 2023

₹ 20 on First Call payable on 1st October, 2023

Balance on second and final call payable on 1st February, 2024.

All these debentures were subscribed and amounts due on them duly received.

One debenture holder holding 1,000 debentures, paid the amount of both the calls with allotment.

According to the Articles of Association of the company, interest @ 12% per annum is payable on calls-in-advance. The interest on calls-in-advance was paid by the company to the debenture holder on 1st February, 2024.

The company follows the financial year and closes its books accordingly.

You are required to prepare the following for the year 2023-24

(i) Interest on calls-in-advance account **[1]**

(ii) Second and final call account **[2]**

4. Shyla Ltd., an unlisted manufacturing company, had 30,000, 6% Debentures of ₹ 100 each due for redemption at par on 31st March, 2024. On this date, the company had the required amount in its Debenture Redemption Reserve.

Investment, as required by the law, made on 1st April, 2023, earning interest @ 5% per annum, was realised at 97% on the date of redemption and the debentures were redeemed on the due date.

Tax @ 10% on the interest was deducted at the source of the investment.

You are required to prepare the following for the year 2023-24

(i) Debenture Redemption Investment Account **[1½]**

(ii) Interest on Debenture Redemption Investment Account **[1½]**

5. Anu, Benu and Sara are partners in a firm sharing profits and losses in the ratio of $\frac{4}{9}:\frac{2}{9}:\frac{1}{3}$. Anu retires from the firm on 1st April, 2024. She gives half of her share to Benu and the remaining half to Sara.

On Anu's retirement, it is decided that goodwill of the firm be valued at two years' purchase of the average profits of the preceding four years which were as follows

Year	Profit
2020-21	₹ 40,000 (including gain from speculation ₹ 4,000)
2021-22	₹ 80,000 (excluding repairs of machinery ₹ 6,000)
2022-23	₹ 1,10,000
2023-24	₹ 40,000 (loss)

You are required to calculate

(i) The new profit-sharing ratio of the remaining partners in the reconstituted firm. **[1]**

(ii) The firm's goodwill on the date of Anu's retirement. (Show the workings clearly with the formula) **[2]**

6. Hoody Ltd. made the following borrowings in the year 2023-24. **[6]**

On 1st April, 2023 Ten year, 10% Bank Loan from AZ Bank secured by a primary security and 20,000, 6% Debentures of ₹ 100 each as collateral security, the issue of which was recorded in the books.	₹ 25,00,000
On 1st October, 2023 5,000, 8% Debentures of ₹ 100 each, redeemable at par in five equal annual instalments.	₹ 5,00,000

The terms of the borrowings were

- The redemption of 8% Debentures to begin from 30th September, 2024.
- Interest on Bank Loan and Debentures to be paid annually.

Additional Information

In the year 2023-24, the company defaulted on the payment of the interest on bank loan.

You are required to show the above items in Notes to Accounts accompanying the Balance Sheet of Hoody Ltd. prepared as per Schedule III of the Companies Act, 2013, as at 31st March, 2024.

7. Uma and Aman were partners in a firm sharing profits and losses in the ratio of 2:1. They closed their books on 31st March every year. Uma died on 31st July, 2024, when the Balance Sheet of the firm was as follows

Balance Sheet of Uma and Aman
As at 31 July, 2024

Liabilities		Amt (₹)	Assets	Amt (₹)
Sundry Creditors		30,000	Cash at Bank	84,000
Loan from Uma		10,000	Fixed Assets	78,000
General Reserve		24,000	Goodwill	24,000
Profit for four months (before any interest and appropriations)		62,000		
Capital Accounts				
Uma	36,000			
Aman	24,000	60,000		
		1,86,000		1,86,000

According to the terms of their partnership deed

(a) Interest on capital to be allowed to the partners @ 4% per annum.

(b) Uma to be allowed a salary of ₹ 250 per month.

The firm's non-purchased goodwill on the date of Uma's death was valued at ₹ 12,000.

The amounts due to Uma were transferred to her representative's loan account.

You are required to prepare

(i) Uma's capital account **[5]**

(ii) Uma's loan account **[1]**

Or

Ravi Ali and Siya are partners in a firm sharing profits and losses in the ratio of 4:3:2. Ali retired from the firm on 31st March, 2024, when the capitals of the partners before the following necessary adjustments stood at

Ravi	₹ 23,000
Ali	₹ 12,000
Siya	₹ 9,000

Adjustments

(a) The firm's goodwill to be valued at ₹ 21,600.

(b) Loss on revaluation of assets and liabilities to be ₹ 2,700.

On the date of Ali's retirement, the firm had General Reserve of ₹ 6,300

Cash and Bank Balance of ₹ 18,600

It was decided that Ali be paid through cash brought in by Ravi and Siya in such a manner so as to make their capitals proportionate to their new profit-sharing ratio and a minimum Cash and Bank Balance of ₹ 10,000 to be maintained in the reconstituted firm.

You are required to pass journal entries to record the above transactions. **[6]**

8. Mihir and Farhan were partners in a firm sharing profits and losses equally. They dissolved their partnership firm on 31st March, 2024.

On this date, the Balance Sheet of their firm, apart from the realisable assets and outside liabilities, showed the following

Particulars	Amt (₹)
Mihir's Capital	60,000 (Cr)
Farhan's Capital	20,000 (Dr)
Workmen Compensation Reserve	12,000
Profit and Loss Account	6,000 (Cr)
Bank Account	'?'

On the date of dissolution

(a) The firm, upon realisation of assets and settlement of liabilities, suffered a loss of ₹ 10,000.

(b) The amount paid to settle the liabilities exceeded the amount realised from the sale of the assets by ₹ 8,000.

(c) Stock worth ₹ 3,000 was taken over by Farhan.

(d) Mihir discharged the Bills Payable, recorded in the books at ₹ 5,000, at a rebate of ₹ 100.

(e) There was a workmen compensation claim of ₹ 4,000.

You are required to prepare on the date of dissolution of the firm **[6]**

(i) The partners' capital accounts.

(ii) The bank account to determine its balance at bank as shown in the Balance Sheet as at 31st March, 2024, represented by '?'.

9. Tim and Leena started a partnership business on 1st July, 2023, with fixed capital contributions of ₹ 3,00,000 and ₹ 2,50,000 respectively.

On 1st January, 2024, they decided that

The total fixed capital of the firm to be ₹ 6,00,000 contributed by the partners in the profit-sharing ratio. Accordingly on 1st January, 2024, Tim and Leena introduced or withdrew capital.

Their partnership deed chained the following clauses

(a) Interest on capital to be allowed @ 10% per Annum to both the partners.

(b) Rent @ ₹ 2,000 per month to Tim for the use of his premises for business purposes

(c) 10% of of the Trading Profit to be transferred to General Reserve.

(d) The profit-sharing ratio of the partners to be 3:2.

The trading profit of the firm for the first year the partnership after considering all charges against profits was 1,50,000.

You are required to pass journal entries for the year 2023-24. **[10]**

Or (A) Nida and Pia, each doing business as sole proprietors, started a partnership on 1st April, 2023, with capital contributions of ₹ 5,00,000 and ₹ 4,00,000.

Their partnership deed contained the following clauses

(a) Interest on capital to be allowed @ 10% per annum to both the partners.

(b) Annual commission of ₹ 30,000 to be allowed to Nida.

(c) Interest on drawings to be charged @ 4% per annum.

(d) The profit-sharing ratio to be 3:2.

Nida withdrew ₹ 10,000 during the year 2023-24.

The trading profit of the firm for the year ending 31st March, 2024, was ₹ 70,640 before considering accrued interest on investments of ₹ 1,600.

Although the accountant had recorded the drawings made by the partners, he distributed the profits before charging interest on drawings from Nida but after considering the following

- Accrued interest on investments of ₹ 1,600.
- Allowing the appropriations of interest on capital and commission.

You are required to prepare the following for the year 2023-24

(i) Profit and Loss Appropriation Account as prepared by the accountant of the firm. **[5½]**

(ii) Nida's Drawings Account **[2]**

(B) At the beginning of the next financial year, the accountant realised his error of not having charged interest on drawings from Nida. He rectified the error by passing a single adjustment entry.

You are required to give the rectified adjustment entry passed by the accountant.

(Show your workings clearly) **[2½]**

10. Cosmic Ltd. issued 40,000 Equity shares of ₹ 10 each at a premium of ₹ 1 per share payable.

On application	₹ 3
On allotment	₹ 4 (including premium)
On first and final call	Balance

The public applied for 60,000 shares. Pro-rata allotment was made to the applicants of 50,000 shares. Where no allotment was made, money was to be refunded in full.

One shareholder who had applied for 500 shares did not pay the allotment money and his shares were forfeited after the allotment stage. The company was able to immediately reissue all the forfeited shares at ₹ 5 per share.

Three months later, the First and Final Call was made to all the shareholders.

You are required to

(i) Pass journal entries to record the above transactions in the books of the company. **[8½]**

(ii) Prepare the Calls-in-Arrears Account. **[1½]**

Or

NM Co. Ltd. issued a prospectus inviting applications for 12,000 shares of ₹ 10 each at a premium of ₹1 per share.

The public applied for 30,000 shares. The company made pro-rata allotment on 24,000 shares. A shareholder who had applied for 2,000 shares, was allotted 1,000 shares. After having paid ₹ 4 per share on application he did not pay the allotment money of ₹ 5 per share (including premium).

On his subsequent failure to pay the first call of ₹ 1 per share, his shares were forfeited.

These shares were reissued at the rate of ₹ 7 per share ₹ 9 paid up.

The company incurred ₹ 5,000 as share issue expenses.

Based on the information given above and the ledger accounts given below, answer the questions that follow.

Dr **Share Issue Expenses A/c** Cr

Particulars	Amt (₹)	Particulars	Amt (₹)
To '?'	'?'	By '?'	'?'

Dr **Calls-in-Arrears A/c** Cr

Particulars	Amt (₹)	Particulars	Amt (₹)
To Share Allotment A/c	'?'	By Share Capital A/c	'?'
To Share First Call A/c	'?'	By Securities Premium A/c	'?'

You are required to

(i) Draw the ledger accounts given above filling up the missing information represented by '?'. **[3]**

(ii) What is the balance left in the Securities Premium A/c after all the transactions relating to the shares have been completed by NM Co. Ltd? **[1]**

(iii) Give the journal entries for **[6]**

(a) The amount due on allotment.

(b) The amount received on allotment.

(c) Transferring the net gain made on reissue of shares to Capital Reserve Account.

Section B

(Answer all questions) **(20 Marks)**

11. In subparts (i) and (ii) choose the correct options and in subparts (iii) to (v) answer the questions as instructed.

(i) Red Health, an ambulance aggregator has paid its employees only half their January salaries. The company has gone in for funding. In response to queries from Mint, Red Health's founder and CEO said, "Our funding round is closed and we are waiting money to be wired by this week. On the basis of that, and to manage our working capital, we had given a choice to our old employees to hold their salaries back."

Sources *(edited): Mint, 14th February, 2024*

The original Current Ratio and Quick Ratio of Red Health are more than one.

Which one of the following will be correct for the month of January 2024 if the company had held back the salaries of its employees for the same month? **[1]**

(a) Both Current Ratio and Quick Ratio will decrease.
(b) Both Current Ratio and Quick Ratio will increase.
(c) No change in the Quick Ratio but the Current Ratio will increase.
(d) No change in the Current Ratio but the Quick Ratio will increase.

(ii) On 1st April, 2023, Tarzan Ltd. purchased 7,000, 7% Debentures of ₹ 100 each of Tintin Ltd. It received interest of ₹ 7,000 on these debentures on 31st March, 2024. How will this information be presented in the Cash Flow Statement of Tarzan Ltd. for the year 2023-24? **[1]**

P ₹ 70,000 as cash outflow in investing activity
Q ₹ 70,000 as cash outflow in financing activity
R ₹ 7,000 as cash inflow in investing activity
S ₹ 7,000 as cash outflow in operating activity

(a) Only P and R (b) Only P and S
(c) Only P and Q (d) Only R and S

(iii) According to the ratings agency, Crisil, the food and grocery players will cap their debt raising in FY 25 in order to ensure that one of the key debt protection metrics, the interest cover, remains healthy in line with the previous fiscal's level of 13 times.

Source *(edited): Financial Express, 23rd December, 2023*

You are required to give the formula to calculate the interest cover. **[1]**

(iv) While preparing the Cash Flow Statement, the accountant of Red Hill Co. Ltd. was undecided about the impact of amortisation of discount on issue of debentures of ₹ 10,000 on the company's Net Operating Profit before working capital changes. What should the accountant do to resolve this issue? Give a reason for your answer. **[1]**

(v) Read the news item given below and answer the questions that follow. **[1]**

Online news aggregator, Inshorts, saw its loss widen by over a third during the year ended March, 2023, to ₹ 309.7 crore, from ₹ 231.8 crore in fiscal 2022, as expense rose faster than revenue. Advertisement income the company gets most of its ads on its app-increased 4.3% to ₹ 147 crore. The remainder of its income came from support services.

Source *Economic Times, 26th November, 2023*

(a) Mention whether Advertising income is an operating income or a non-operating income for InShorts.
(b) What is the percentage increase in loss of InShorts in the Fiscal Year 2022-23 as compared to 2021-22?

12. Following are the particulars of Richmond Ltd.

Particulars	31st March, 2024 (₹)	31st March, 2023 (₹)
Revenue form Operations	5,00,000	4,00,000
Purchases of stock-in-trade	3,00,000	3,60,000
Opening inventory of stock-in-trade	1,40,000	1,00,000
Adjusted purchases of stock-in trade	4,10,000	3,20,000

You are required to calculate the absolute change and percentage change of the following items at the end of the year 2023-24 vis-a-vis the closing amounts of the year 2022-23. **[3]**

(i) Revenue from operations
(ii) Purchases of stock in trade
(iii) Closing inventory of stock-in-trade

13. Answer any three of the following questions

(i) Calculate the gross profit of Saturn Ltd. from the particulars given below. **[2]**

Particulars	Amt (₹)
Average Inventory	8,000
Inventory Turnover Ratio	6 times
Selling Price	25% above cost

(ii) Calculate the trade receivables turnover ratio of Planet Ltd. from the particulars given below. **[2]**

Particulars	Amt (₹)
Revenue from Operations	3,60,000
Cash Revenue from Operations	90,000
Net Closing Trade Receivables	45,000
Provision for Doubtful Debts	10,000

(iii) Bajaj Hindustan Sugar, one of the largest sugar and ethanol producers, in order to revive the company, has offered to invest ₹ 2,500 crore as fresh equity of which ₹ 1,000 crore has already been infused.
Source *(edited): Economic Times, Mumbal Edition 8th, August, 2023*
What will be the effect of this decision of Bajaj Hindustan Sugar on its following ratios? **[2]**
(a) Proprietary ratio
(b) Debt to total assets ratio

(iv) Calculate the earning per share of Hemisphere Ltd. from the particulars given below. **[2]**

Particulars	Amt (₹)
10% Debentures	5,00,000
8% Bank Loan	3,00,000
5% Preference Share Capital	2,00,000
Profit before Interest and Tax	2,44,000
Provision for Tax	20,000
Tax paid	18,000
Equity Share Capital (@ ₹10 each)	8,00,000

14. From the following information of Realty Ltd., you are required to calculate the company's cash and cash equivalent as on 31st March, 2024, by preparing a Cash Flow Statement (as per AS 3). **[6]**

Information pertaining to the year 2023-24

(i) Net profit before tax was ₹ 14,00,000.
(ii) Tax of ₹ 5,00,000 was paid.
(iii) The opening inventory was higher than the closing inventory by ₹ 50,000.
(iv) The Trade Creditors showed a decrease of ₹ 20,000 on 31st March, 2024, when compared to the amount of Trade Creditors on 31st March, 2023.
(v) Plant and Machinery on 31st March, 2023, and 31st March, 2024, amounted to ₹ 20,00,000 and ₹ 26,00,000 respectively.
(vi) New machinery was purchased for ₹ 9,00,000; the purchase consideration being 4% Debentures of the face value of ₹ 100 each issued at a discount of 10%.
(vii) The 4% Debentures on 31st March, 2023, and 31st March, 2024, amounted to ₹ 5,00,000 and ₹ 20,00,000 respectively.
(viii) ₹ 60,000 was paid by the company for interest on debentures against the amount due of ₹ 80,000.
(ix) Investments of ₹ 5,00,000 were purchased on 30th November, 2023, on which interest of ₹ 40,000 was earned and received.
(x) The cash and cash equivalent as on 31st March, 2023, was ₹ 3,15,000.

Or

Read the following information of Celestial Ltd., and answer the questions that follow.

Statement of Profit and Loss for the year ended 31st March, 2024

Particulars	Note No.	Amt (₹)
Revenue from operations		10,00,000
Other Income	1	40,000
Total Revenue Expenses		**10,40,000**
Employee Benefit Expenses		1,60,000
Depreciation and Amortisation Expenses	2	60,000
Finance Cost	3	50,000
Other Expenses		2,20,000
Total Expenses		**4,90,000**
Profit before Tax		5,50,000
(–) Provision for Tax		(2,00,000)
Profit after Tax		3,50,000

Notes to Accounts

Particulars	Amt (₹)
1. **Other Income**	
Interest on Short-term Loans and Advances (including interest accrued ₹ 10,000)	1,00,000
2. **Depreciation and Amortisation Expenses**	
Depreciation on Plant and Machinery	60,000
3. **Finance Cost**	
Interest on Debentures (including outstanding interest ₹ 20,000)	50,000

Additional Information

1. During the year 2023-24, the company paid tax of ₹ 2,50,000.
2. An extract of the Balance Sheets of the company as at 31st March, 2023, and as at 31st March, 2024 is as follows

Particulars	31st March, 2024 (₹)	31st March, 2023 (₹)
Plant and Machinery (At Gross Value)	19,00,000	16,00,000
Accumulated Depreciation	4,00,000	5,00,000
Short-term Loans and Advances	5,00,000	6,50,000

(i) State the reason for a part of the accumulated depreciation being written off by the company. **[1]**
(ii) What is the cash flow of interest on debentures? **[1]**
(iii) Calculate Cash from Investing Activities. **[1½]**
(iv) Calculate Cash from Operating Activities. **[2½]**

Answers

1. (i) (b) Shiv – ₹ 800 ; Ravi – ₹ 600 ; Roshan – Nil

Interest on Drawings

$$\text{Shiv} = 30{,}000 \times \frac{6}{100} \times \frac{6}{12} = ₹\, 900$$

$$\text{Ravi} = 20{,}000 \times \frac{6}{100} \times \frac{6}{12} = ₹\, 600$$

Roshan = Nil

(ii) (c) Undervaluation of closing stock

(iii) (d) P, Q, and S

(iv) (b) Loss on Issue of Debentures A/c

(v) (c) Fixed Capital account method is maintained to keep the initial capital contributions of partner separate from other appropriation like interest on capital, etc.

(vi) New partner brings his share of goodwill in order to have share in future profits of the firm.

(vii) $$\text{Rebate} = \text{Bills Payable} \times \frac{\text{Rate}}{100} \times \frac{\text{No. of Months}}{12}$$

$$350 = 42{,}000 \times \frac{\text{Rate}}{100} \times \frac{4}{12}$$

$$\text{Rate} = \frac{350 \times 100 \times 12}{42{,}000 \times 4} = 2.5\%$$

(viii)

Particulars		Amt (Dr)	Amt (Cr)
Sanjay's Capital A/c	Dr	15,000	
Mitali's Capital A/c	Dr	15,000	
To Deferred Revenue Expenditure A/c			30,000
(Being deferred revenue expenditure transferred to partners' capital account on dissolution of partnership firm)			

(ix) (a) Intangible asset (b) Goodwill

(x) It will be easy to the company to compliance with the requirement of preparation of Debenture Redemption Reserve (DRR) according to the Companies Act, 2013. Thus, the burden will be less in the year of redemption of debentures.

2.

Particulars		Amt (Dr)	Amt (Cr)
(i) Workmen Compensation Reserve A/c	Dr	300	
To Ajay's Capital A/c			200
To Bijoy's Capital A/c			100
(Being workmen compensation reserve transferred to old partners' capital account)			

Particulars		Amt (Dr)	Amt (Cr)
(ii) Sujay's Current A/c	Dr	225	
To Ajay's Capital A/c			150
To Bijay's Capital A/c			75
(Being balance reserve retained in the firm)			

Or

Dr **Revaluation Account** Cr

Particulars	Amt (₹)	Particulars		Amt (₹)
To Plant and Machinery	20,000	By Creditors A/c (5,000 + 1,000)		6,000
To Outstanding claim for damages	14,000	By Prepaid insurance		6,000
To Provision for doubtful debts	5,000	By Revaluation Loss		27,000
		Gita	16,200	
		Mita	10,800	
	39,000			39,000

3.

Dr **Cash Book** Cr

Particulars	Amt (₹)	Particulars	Amt (₹)
To Debenture Application A/c	80,000		
To Debenture Allotment A/c	4,80,000		
To Calls-in-Advance (200 × 20)	4,000		
To Debenture First Call A/c (7,800 × 20)	1,56,000		
To Debenture Second Call A/c	1,60,000	By Balance c/d	8,80,000
	8,80,000		8,80,000

Or

(i) **Interest on Calls-in-Advance**

$$\text{On first call} = (1{,}000 \times 20) \times \frac{12}{100} \times \frac{3}{12} = ₹\, 600$$

$$\text{On second and final call} = (1{,}000 \times 30) \times \frac{12}{100} \times \frac{7}{12} = ₹\, 2{,}100$$

Total interest = ₹ 2,700 (600 + 2,100)

Dr **Interest on Calls-in-Advance Account** Cr

Date	Particulars	Amt (₹)	Date	Particulars	Amt (₹)
2024 Feb 1	To Debenture holder A/c	2,700	2024 Mar 31	By Statement of Profit and Loss	2,700
		2,700			2,700

(ii) Dr **Second and Final Call Account** Cr

Date	Particulars	Amt (₹)	Date	Particulars	Amt (₹)
2024			2024		
Feb 1	To 6% Debentures A/c	1,50,000	Feb 1	By Bank A/c	1,20,000
			Feb 1	By Calls-in-advance A/c	30,000
		1,50,000			1,50,000

4. (i) Dr **Debenture Redemption Investment Account** Cr

Date	Particulars	Amt (₹)	Date	Particulars	Amt (₹)
2023			2024		
Apr 1	To Bank A/c	4,50,000	Mar 31	By Bank A/c $\left(\frac{4,50,000 \times 97}{100}\right)$	4,36,500
			Mar 31	By Statement of Profit and Loss	13,500
		4,50,000			4,50,000

(ii) Dr **Interest on Debenture Redemption Investment Account** Cr

Date	Particulars	Amt (₹)	Date	Particulars	Amt (₹)
2024			2024		
Mar 31	To Statement of Profit and Loss	22,500	Mar 31	By Bank A/c	20,250
			Mar 31	By T.D.S Deposited A/c	2,250
		22,500			22,500

5. (i) **Gaining Ratio**

$$\text{Benu} = \frac{4}{9} \times \frac{1}{2} = \frac{4}{18}; \ \text{Sara} = \frac{4}{9} \times \frac{1}{2} = \frac{4}{18}$$

New Ratio

$$\text{Benu} = \frac{2}{9} + \frac{4}{18} = \frac{4+4}{18} = \frac{8}{18}$$

$$\text{Sara} = \frac{1}{3} + \frac{4}{18} = \frac{6+4}{18} = \frac{10}{18}$$

$\therefore$ New profit-sharing ratio $= 8:10 = 4:5$

(ii)

Year	Profits
2020-21	40,000 – 4,000 = 36,000
2021-22	80,000 – 6,000 = 74,000
2022-23	1,10,000
2023-24	(40,000)

Average Profit

$$= \frac{36,000 + 74,000 + 1,10,000 - 40,000}{4} = \frac{1,80,000}{4}$$

$= ₹\, 45,000$

$\therefore$ Goodwill $= 2 \times 45,000 = ₹\, 90,000$

6. **Balance Sheet**
as at 31st March, 2020

Particulars	Note No.	Amt (₹)
I. **Equity and Liabilities**		
1. **Non-Current Liabilities**		
(a) Long-term Borrowings	1	29,00,000
2. **Current Liabilities**		
(a) Short-term Borrowings	2	1,00,000
(b) Other-current Liabilities	3	2,70,000

Notes to Accounts

Particulars		Amt (₹)
1. **Long-term Borrowings**		
(i) Loan from AZ Bank		25,00,000
(ii) 20,000, 6% Debentures of ₹ 100 each	20,00,000	
(–) Debenture Suspense A/c	(20,00,000)	—
(iii) 4,000, 8% Debentures of ₹ 100 each		4,00,000
		29,00,000
2. **Short-term Borrowings**		
Current Maturities to Long-term Debt		1,00,000
3. **Other Current Liabilities**		
Interest Accrued and due on Bank Loan		2,50,000
Interest Accrued but not due on 8% Debentures		20,000
		2,70,000

7. (i) Dr **Uma's Capital Account** Cr

Particulars	Amt (₹)	Particulars	Amt (₹)
To Goodwill A/c	16,000	By Balance b/d	36,000
To Uma's Executor's Loan A/c	85,613	By General Reserve A/c	16,000
		By Interest on Capital A/c $\left(36{,}000 \times \frac{4}{100} \times \frac{4}{12}\right)$	480
		By Partner's Salary A/c (250×4)	1,000
		By Aman's Capital A/c	8,000
		By Profit and Loss Appropriation A/c (W.N.1)	40,133
	1,01,613		1,01,613

Working Note

1. Dr **Profit and Loss Appropriation Account** Cr

Particulars		Amt (₹)	Particulars	Amt (₹)
To Interest on Capital			By Profit	62,000
Uma's Capital A/c	480			
Aman's Capital A/c	320	800		
To Uma's Salary		1,000		
To Divisible Profits				
Uma's Capital A/c	40,133			
Aman's Capital A/c	20,067	60,200		
		62,000		62,000

(ii) Dr **Uma's Loan Account** Cr

Particulars	Amt (₹)	Particulars	Amt (₹)
To Uma's Executor's loan A/c	10,200	By Balance b/d	10,000
		By Interest on Loan A/c $\left(10{,}000 \times \frac{6}{100} \times \frac{4}{12}\right)$	200
	10,200		10,200

Or

JOURNAL

S. No.	Particulars		LF	Amt (Dr)	Amt (Cr)
(i)	Ravi's Capital A/c	Dr		1,200	
	Ali's Capital A/c	Dr		900	
	Siya's Capital A/c	Dr		600	
	To Revaluation A/c				2,700
	(Being revaluation loss distributed)				
(ii)	Ravi's Capital A/c	Dr		4,800	
	Siya's Capital A/c	Dr		2,400	
	To Ali's Capital A/c				7,200
	(Being goodwill distributed)				
(iii)	General Reserve A/c	Dr		6,300	
	To Ravi's Capital A/c				2,800
	To Ali's Capital A/c				2,100
	To Siya's Capital A/c				1,400
	(Being general reserve distributed)				
(iv)	Cash A/c	Dr		11,800	
	To Ravi's Capital A/c				6,200
	To Siya's Capital A/c				5,600
	(Being cash brought in by remaining partner)				
(v)	Ali's Capital A/c	Dr		20,400	
	To Cash A/c				20,400
	(Being cash paid to retiring partner)				

Working Notes

1. **Partner's Capital after all the Adjustments**

   Ravi = 23,000 – 1,200 + 2,800 – 4,800 = 19,800; Ali = 12,000 – 900 + 2,100 + 7,200 = 20,400

   Siya = 9,000 – 600 + 1,400 – 2,400 = 7,400

2. **Adjustment of Capital**

   (i) Total capital of the new firm = 19,800 + (20,400 – 8,600) + 7,400 = 39,000

   (ii) New profit-sharing ratio = 4 : 2 or 2 : 1 ; Ravi's Capital = $39,000 \times \frac{2}{3} = 26,000$

   Siya's Capital = $39,000 \times \frac{1}{3} = 13,000$

   (iii) Surplus/Deficiency

   Ravi = 26,000 – 19,800 = 6,200 Deficiency; Siya = 13,000 – 7,400 = 5,600 Deficiency

8. (i) Dr **Partner's Capital Account** Cr

Particulars	Mihir (₹)	Farhan (₹)	Particulars	Mihir (₹)	Farhan (₹)
To Balance b/d		20,000	By Balance b/d	60,000	
To Realisation Loss	5,000	5,000	By Workmen Compensation Reserve	4,000	4,000
To Realisation A/c		3,000	By Profit and Loss A/c	3,000	3,000
To Bank A/c	66,900		By Realisation A/c	4,900	
			By Bank A/c		21,000
	71,900	28,000		71,900	28,000

(ii) Dr **Bank Account** Cr

Particulars	Amt (₹)	Particulars	Amt (₹)
To Balance b/d (B/F)	57,900	By Realisation A/c	8,000
To Farhan's Capital A/c	21,000	By Mihir's Capital A/c	66,900
		By Workmen Compensation Claim A/c	4,000
	78,900		78,900

9. **JOURNAL**

Date	Particulars		LF	Amt (Dr)	Amt (Cr)
2024					
Jan 1	Cash A/c	Dr		60,000	
	To Tim's Capital A/c				60,000
	(Being capital brought in by Tim)				
Jan 1	Leena's Capital A/c	Dr		10,000	
	To Cash A/c				10,000
	(Being capital withdrawn by Leena)				
Mar 31	Interest on Capital A/c [W.N.I]	Dr		42,500	
	To Tim's Current A/c				24,000
	To Leena's Current A/c				18,500
	(Being interest on capital provided to the partners)				
Mar 31	Profit and Loss Appropriation A/c	Dr		42,500	
	To Interest on Capital A/c				42,500
	(Being interest on capital transferred to profit and loss appropriation account)				
Mar 31	Rent to Partner	Dr		18,000	
	To Tim's Current A/c				18,000
	(Being rent paid to Tim for 9 months)				
Mar 31	Profit and Loss Appropriation A/c	Dr		18,000	
	To Rent to Partner A/c				18,000
	(Being rent to partner transferred to profit and loss appropriation account)				

Date	Particulars		LF	Amt (Dr)	Amt (Cr)
Mar 31	Profit and Loss Appropriation A/c	Dr		15,000	
	To General Reserve A/c				15,000
	(Being 10% of the trading profit transferred to reserve)				
Mar 31	Profit and Loss Appropriation A/c [W.N.2]	Dr		92,500	
	To Tim's Current A/c				55,500
	To Leena's Current A/c				37,000
	(Being divisible profit transferred to partners' current account)				

Working Notes

1. Interest on Capital

$$\text{Tim} = \left[\left(3,00,000 \times \frac{10}{100} \times \frac{6}{12}\right) + \left(3,60,000 \times \frac{10}{100} \times \frac{3}{12}\right)\right] = 15,000 + 9,000 = 24,000$$

$$\text{Leena} = \left[\left(2,50,000 \times \frac{10}{100} \times \frac{6}{12}\right) + \left(2,40,000 \times \frac{10}{100} \times \frac{3}{12}\right)\right] = 12,500 + 6,000 = 18,500$$

2. Divisible Profit = 1,50,000 – 42,500 – 15,000 = ₹ 92,500

Or

A. (i) **Profit and Loss Appropriation Account**
(As presented by the accountant)

Dr | Cr

Particulars		Amt (₹)	Particulars	Amt (₹)
To Interest on Capital			By Net Profit (70,640 + 1,600)	72,240
Nida	50,000			
Pia	40,000	90,000		
To Nida's Commission		30,000		

Since, the appropriations are more than the available profits, profit will be distributed in following ratio

Nida = 50,000 + 30,000 = 80,000

Pia = 40,000

∴ Ratio = 8 : 4 or 2 : 1

So, Nida's Profit $= 72,240 \times \frac{2}{3} = 48,160$; Pia's Profit $= 72,240 \times \frac{1}{3} = 24,080$

(ii) **Nida's Drawings Account**

Dr | Cr

Particulars	Amt (₹)	Particulars	Amt (₹)
To Cash A/c	10,000	By Nida's Capital A/c	10,000
	10,000		10,000

B. **Statement Showing Adjustment**

Particulars	Nida		Pia		Firm	
	Dr (₹)	Cr (₹)	Dr (₹)	Cr (₹)	Dr (₹)	Cr (₹)
Interest on Drawings	200					200
Profit		120		80	200	
	200	120	0	80	200	200
	80 Dr		80 Cr			

Nida's Capital A/c	Dr	80	
To Pia's Capital A/c			80
(Being adjustment entry passed)			

10. (i)

JOURNAL

Date	Particulars		LF	Amt (Dr)	Amt (Cr)
	Bank A/c	Dr		1,80,000	
	To Share Application A/c				1,80,000
	(Being amount received on application)				
	Share Application A/c	Dr		1,80,000	
	To Share Capital A/c				1,50,000
	To Share Allotment A/c [W.N.1]				30,000
	To Bank A/c [W.N.1]				30,000
	(Being application money adjusted)				
	Share Allotment A/c	Dr		1,60,000	
	To Share Capital A/c				1,20,000
	To Securities Premium A/c				40,000
	(Being allotment money, including premium due on 40,000 shares at ₹ 4 per share)				
	Bank A/c (W.N.5)	Dr		1,28,700	
	Calls-in-arrears A/c [W.N.4]	Dr		1,300	
	To Share Allotment A/c				1,30,000
	(Being amount received on allotment except on 400 shares)				
	Share Capital A/c	Dr		2,400	
	Securities Premium A/c	Dr		400	
	To Calls-in-arrears A/c [W.N.4]				1,300
	To Share Forfeiture A/c [W.N.3]				1,500
	(Being forfeiture of 400 shares)				
	Bank A/c (400 × 5)	Dr		2,000	
	Share Forfeiture A/c (400 × 1)	Dr		400	
	To Share Capital A/c (400 ×6)				2,400
	(Being reissue of 400 forfeited shares)				
	Share Forfeiture A/c	Dr		1,100	
	To Capital Reserve A/c				1,100
	(Being balance of share forfeiture account transferred to capital reserve account)				
	Share First and Final Call A/c	Dr		1,58,400	
	To Share Capital A/c				1,58,400
	(Being first and final call due on 39,600 shares at ₹ 4 per share)				
	Bank A/c	Dr		1,58,400	
	To Share First and Final Call A/c				1,58,400
	(Being first call received on 39,600 shares @ ₹ 4 per share)				

Working Notes

1.

Applied Shares	50,000	10,000
Alloted Shares	40,000	0
Excess Shares	10,000	10,000
Application share	3	3
Excess Amount	30,000	30,000
Allotment	30,000	—
Refund	—	30,000

2. **Alloted Shares of Defaulter**

Applied : Alloted

5 : 4

500 : x

$$x = \frac{500 \times 4}{5} = 400$$

3. **Excess on Application**

500× 3 = 1,500 [Share forfeiture A/c]

(−) 400× 3 = (1,200)

300

4. **Allotment not Paid**

400× 4 = 1,600

(−) Excess on application = (300)

1,300 [Calls-in-arrears]

5. **Total Allotment Received**

40,000 × 4 = 1,60,000

(−) Adjusted from Application = (30,000)

(−) Allotment not paid = (1,300)

1,28,700

(ii) Dr **Calls-in-Arrears Account** Cr

Particulars	Amt (₹)	Particulars	Amt (₹)
To Share Allotment A/c	1,300	By Share Capital A/c	900
		By Securities Pre. A/c	400
	1,300		1,300

Or

(i) Dr **Share Issue Expenses Account** Cr

Particulars	Amt (₹)	Particulars	Amt (₹)
To Bank A/c	5,000	By Statement of Profit and Loss	5,000

Dr **Calls-in-Arrears Account** Cr

Particulars	Amt (₹)	Particulars	Amt (₹)
To Share Allotment A/c [W.N.2]	1,000	By Share Capital A/c	1,000
To Share First Call A/c [W.N.3]	1,000	By Securities Premium A/c	1,000

Working Notes

1. **Excess on Application**

2,000× 4 = 8,000

(−) 1,000× 4 = (4,000)

4,000

2. **Allotment not Paid**

1000× 5 = 5,000

(−) Excess on Application = (4,000)

1,000 (Calls-in-arrears)

3. **Calls-in-Arrears on First Call**

First call (1,000× 1) = 1,000

4.

Share Capital A/c	Dr	9,000	
Securities Premium A/c	Dr	1,000	
To Share Forfeiture A/c			8,000
To Calls-in-Arrears A/c			2,000

(ii) Amount of premium to be received = 12,000× 1 = 12,000

(−) Premium not received = (1,000)

(+) Premium received on reissue of shares (1,000× 2) = 2,000

Balance left in Securities Premium A/c = 13,000

(iii) **JOURNAL**

	Particulars		LF	Amt (Dr)	Amt (Cr)
(a)	Share Allotment A/c	Dr		60,000	
	To Share Capital A/c				48,000
	To Securities Premium A/c				12,000
	(Being allotment due)				
(b)	Bank A/c	Dr		34,000	
	Calls-in-Arrears A/c	Dr		2,000	
	To Share Allotment A/c				36,000
	(Being allotment money received except on 1,000 shares)				
(c)	Share Forfeiture A/c	Dr		8,000	
	To Capital Reserve A/c				8,000
	(Being profit on forfeiture transferred to capital reserve)				

11. (i) (a) Both current ratio and quick ratio will decrease because current liabilities will increase.

(ii) (a) Only P and R

(iii) $\text{Interest Coverage Ratio} = \dfrac{\text{Earnings before Interest and Tax}}{\text{Interest Charges}}$

(iv) If loss on issue of debentures is written off using securities premium, it will not be shown in operating activity. If loss on issue of debentures is written off using statement of profit and loss, it will be added in operating activity under 'items to be added'.

(v) (a) Advertising income is one of the main sources of income for online apps like InShorts. Therefore, it is an operating income.

(b) $\% \text{ increase in losses} = \dfrac{(309.7-231.8)}{231.8} \times 100 = \dfrac{77.9}{231.8} \times 100 = 33.61\%$

12. Adjusted Purchase = Opening Inventories + Purchase of Stock – Closing Inventories

Closing Inventories of 2023 = 1,00,000 + 3,60,000 – 3,20,000 = 1,40,000

Closing Inventories of 2024 = 1,40,000 + 3,00,000 – 4,10,000 = 30,000

Comparative Statement of Profit and Loss

Particulars	2023 (₹)	2024 (₹)	Absolute change (₹)	% Change
(i) Revenue from operations	4,00,000	5,00,000	1,00,000	25%
(ii) Purchase of stock-in-trade	3,60,000	3,00,000	(60,000)	(16.67%)
(iii) Closing inventory of stock-in-trade	1,40,000	30,000	(1,10,000)	(78.57%)

13. (i) $\text{Inventory Turnover Ratio} = \dfrac{\text{Cost of Revenue from Operations}}{\text{Average Inventory}} \Rightarrow 6 = \dfrac{\text{Cost of Revenue from Operations}}{8,000}$

Cost of Revenue from Operations = 8,000 × 6 = ₹ 48,000; Gross Profit = $48,000 \times \dfrac{25}{100}$ = ₹ 12,000

(ii) $\text{Trade Receivables Turnover Ratio} = \dfrac{\text{Credit Sale*}}{\text{Average Trade Receivables}} = \dfrac{2,70,000}{45,000} = 6 \text{ Times}$

Revenue from Operations = Cash Sale + Credit Sale ⇒ 3,60,000 = 90,000 + Credit Sale

∴ *Credit Sale = ₹ 2,70,000

(iii) (a) Proprietary ratio will increase as equity and assets both will increase.

(b) Debt to total assets ratio will decrease as debt will not change.

(iv) $\text{Earning per Share} = \dfrac{\text{Net Profit After Tax and Preference Dividend *}}{\text{Number of Equity Shares}} = \dfrac{1,42,000}{80,000}$ = ₹ 1.78

Profit before Tax = Profit before Interest and Tax – Interest = 2,44,000 – 50,000 – 24,000 = ₹ 1,70,000

Profit after Tax = Profit before Tax – Tax = 1,70,000 – 18,000 = ₹ 1,52,000

*Net Profit after Tax and Preference Dividend = Profit after Tax – Preference Dividend = 1,52,000 – 10,000 = ₹ 1,42,000

14. Cash Flow Statement

Particulars		Amt (₹)
I. Cast Flow from Operating Activities		
Net profit before tax		14,00,000
(+) Items to be added		
Discount on issue of debentures	1,00,000	
Depreciation (WN 1)	3,00,000	
Interest on debentures	80,000	4,80,000
(–) Items to be deducted		
Interest received	(40,000)	(40,000)
Operating profit before working capital changes		18,40,000
(+) Decrease in current assets and increase in current liabilities Inventory		50,000
(–) Increase in current assets and decrease in current liabilities		
Trade creditors		(20,000)
Cash generated from operations		18,70,000
(–) Tax paid		(5,00,000)
Cash flow from operating activities		13,70,000
II. Cash Flow from Investing Activities		
Purchase of investments	(5,00,000)	
Interest received on investment	40,000	
Cash used in investing activities		(4,60,000)
III. Cash Flow from Financing Activities		
Issue of debentures (WN 2)	5,00,000	
Interest on debentures	(60,000)	
Cash flow from financing activities		4,40,000
IV. Net Increase in Cash and Cash Equivalents		13,50,000
(+) Opening cash and cash equivalent		3,15,000
Cash and cash equivalent at the end		16,85,000

Working Notes

1. Dr Plant and Machinery Account Dr

Particulars	Amt (₹)	Particulars	Amt (₹)
To Balance b/d	20,00,000	By Depreciation A/c (B/F)	3,00,000
To Vendor A/c	9,00,000	By Balance c/d	26,00,000
	29,00,000		29,00,000

2. No. of debentures issued to purchase plant and machinery $= \frac{9,00,000}{90} = 10,000$

Face value of debentures issued $= 10,000 \times 100 = 10,00,000$

Total debentures issued $= 20,00,000 - 5,00,000 = 15,00,000$

Debentures issued for cash $= 15,00,000 - 10,00,000 = 5,00,000$

Or (i) The accumulated depreciation of ₹ 1,60,000 (W.N. 1) is written off by the company because the machinery is fully depreciated with no book value and scrap value.

(ii) Cash flow of interest on debentures = 50,000 – 20,000 = ₹ 30,000 (outflow)

(iii) Cash flow from Investing Activities

Particulars	Amt (₹)
Purchase of plant and machinery	(4,80,000)
Decrease short-term loans and advances	1,50,000
Cash used in investing activities	(3,10,000)

(iv) **Cash Flow from Operating Activities**

Particulars		Amt (₹)
Net profit before tax		5,50,000
(+) **Items to be added**		
Depreciation	60,000	
Interest on debentures	50,000	1,10,000
(–) Interest on short-term loans and advances		(1,00,000)
Cash generated from operations		5,60,000
(–) Tax paid		(2,50,000)
Cash flow from operating activities		3,10,000

Working Note

1. Dr **Plant and Machinery Account** Cr

Particulars	Amt (₹)	Particulars	Amt (₹)
To Balance b/d	16,00,000	By Accumulated Depreciation A/c	1,60,000
To Bank A/c (Purchase)	4,60,000	By Balance c/d	19,00,000
	20,60,000		20,60,000

Dr **Accumulated Depreciation Account** Cr

Particulars	Amt (₹)	Particulars	Amt (₹)
To Plant and Machinery A/c	1,60,000	By Balance b/d	5,00,000
To Balance c/d	4,00,000	By Depreciation A/c	60,000
	5,60,000		5,60,000

ISC

SAMPLE PAPER 01

Time : 3 hrs
Marks : 80

Accounts XII

General Instructions

1. Candidates are allowed additional 15 minutes for only reading the paper. They must not start writing during this time.
2. Section A and B are compulsory.
3. There are internal choices provided in each section.
4. The intended marks for questions or parts of questions are given in the brackets [ ].
5. All calculations should be shown clearly.
6. All working, including rough work, should be done on the same page as, and adjacent to, the rest of the answer.

Section A (60 Marks)

(Answer all questions)

1. In subpart (i) to (v) choose the correct options and in subparts (vi) to (x) answer the questions as instructed.

(i) With context to debit side of partners' current account, pick the odd one out. [1]

(a) Interest on drawings (b) Rent to partner
(c) Interest on loan (d) Both (b) and (c)

(ii) What journal entry will be passed if goodwill is appearing in the balance sheet of the firm? [1]

(a) Debit Goodwill A/c and Credit Partners' Capital A/c
(b) Debit Premium for Goodwill and Credit Partners' Capital A/c
(c) Debit Partners' Capital A/c and Credit Goodwill A/c
(d) None of the above

(iii) Read the following news items regarding issue of shares by Hindustan Aeronautics

Hindustan Aeronautics ltd. IPO The public offer of the state-run defence-PSU Hindustan Aeronautics Ltd (HAL) remain undersubscribed on the last day of subscription despite an overbidding by institutional investors.

Source *Financialexpress.com*

Which of the following statements are correct? [1]

I. HAL cannot issue shares since the issue was undersubscribed.
II. HAL can issue shares if its memorandum of association allows.
III. HAL can issue shares only if the receive minimum subscription even if the issue is undersubscribed.
IV. HAL can issue shares if SEBI gives permission.

Options

(a) II and III
(b) Only I
(c) Only III
(d) II and IV

(iv) **Assertion** (A) Dissolution of the firm will certainly dissolve the partnership.

Reason (R) Dissolution of partnership would not necessarily involve dissolution of firm. [1]

Alternatives

(a) Both Assertion (A) and Reason (R) are true and Reason (R) is the correct explanation for Assertion (A)

(b) Both Assertion (A) and Reason (R) are true, but Reason (R) is not the correct explanation for Assertion (A)

(c) Assertion (A) is true, but Reason (R) is false

(d) Assertion (A) is false, but Reason (R) is true

(v) Neil and Nitin are partners in a firm sharing profits in the ratio of 3:2. They admitted Mukesh into the partnership. Mukesh acquires his share 2/10th from Neil and 1/10th from Nitin.

What is the profit share of Mukesh? **[1]**

(a) 2/10 (b) 1/10 (c) 3/10 (d) 4/25

(vi) "An intangible asset is an identifiable non-monetary asset, without physical substance, held for use in the production or supply of goods or services, for rental to others, or for administrative purposes."

Based on this statement, explain the nature of goodwill. **[1]**

(vii) P, Q and R are partners in a firm sharing profits in the ratio of 3:2:1. On 1st April, 2025 R decided to retire. Show how goodwill will be recorded in the books of accounts in case of retirement of a partner. **[1]**

(viii) A, B and C were partners in firm sharing profits in the ratio of 4:2:1. Cash received from sale of assets ₹ 5,00,000 and outside liabilities to be paid amounted to ₹ 3,00,000. Loans provided by A (an active partner) and C (a sleeping partner) to the firm was ₹ 3,00,000 and ₹ 1,00,000. What amount of loan will be repaid to C? **[1]**

(ix) Under what head, the calls-in-advance is shown in the balance sheet of the company? **[1]**

(x) Main market-bound HI Mobility Bhd has received 4,010 applications for 75.74 million issue shares amounting to RM92.4 million, resulting in an overall oversubscription rate of 6.57 times.

Source *Business today*

What are the various options does the company have? **[1]**

2. A, B and C are partners in a trading firm. The firm has a fixed total capital of ₹ 60,000 held equally by all the partners. Under the partnership deed the partners were entitled to

(i) A and B to a salary of ₹ 1,800 and ₹ 1,600 per month respectively.

(ii) In the event of the death of a partner, goodwill was to be valued at 2 years' purchase of the average profits of the last 3 years.

(iii) Profit upto the date of the death based on the profit of the previous year.

(iv) Partners were to be charged interest on drawings @ 5% per annum and allowed interest on capital @ 6% per annum.

B died on 1st January, 2021. His drawings to the date of death were ₹ 2,000 and the interest thereon was ₹ 60. The profit of the three years ending 31st March, 2018, 2019 and 2020 were ₹ 21,200, ₹ 3,200 (Dr) and ₹ 9,000 respectively.

(i) Prepare B's capital account, to calculate the amount to be paid to his executors. **[2]**

(ii) Calculate the value of goodwill of the firm. **[1]**

Or Arjun, Bheem and Nakul are partners sharing profits and losses in the ratio of 14 : 5 : 6 respectively. Bheem retires and surrenders his 5/25th share in favour of Arjun.

The goodwill of the firm is valued at 2 years' purchase of super profits based on average profits of last 3 years.

The profits of the last three years are ₹ 50,000, ₹ 55,000 and ₹ 60,000 respectively. The normal profits of the similar firms are ₹ 30,000. Goodwill already was appears in the books of the firm at ₹ 75,000. The profit for the first year after the Bheem's retirement was ₹ 1,00,000.

(i) Calculate new profit-sharing ration. **[1]**

(ii) Give necessary journal entries. **[2]**

3. Mohit Ltd took over assets of ₹ 8,40,000 and liabilities of ₹ 80,000 of Ram Ltd at an agreed value of ₹ 7,20,000. Mohit Ltd paid to Ram Ltd by issue of 9% debentures of ₹ 100 each at a premium of 20%. Pass necessary journal entries to record the above transactions in the books of Mohit Ltd. **[3]**

4. PMR Ltd a listed company, issued 1,00,000, 8% debentures of ₹ 10 each on 1st April, 2021 redeemable at par on 30th June, 2023.

The company received applications for 1,10,000 debentures and the allotment was made to the applicants on pro-rata. The debentures were redeemed on due date. Investment was made on 1st April of the financial year in which redemption is due.

Pass journal entries for issue and redemption of debentures, ignoring interest on debentures. **[3]**

Or West Coast Paper Ltd., an unlisted, Non-NBFC/HFC company, had 15,000, 12% debentures of ₹100 each outstanding as on 31st March, 2022, which are due for redemption on 31st January, 2023. It was decided to transfer amount to DRR on 31st March, 2022.
Pass the necessary journal entries for redemption of debentures.

5. R, S and T are partners in a firm sharing profits and losses in the ratio of 4 : 3 : 1. As per the terms of partnership deed on the death of any partner, his share of goodwill was to be valued at 50% of the net profits credit to that partner's capital account during the last three completed years before his death. R died on 28th February, 2023. The profits for the last five years were 2018 ₹ 18,000; 2019 ₹ 29,100; 2020 ₹ 31,500; 2021 ₹ 9,000 and 2022 ₹ 25,200.

On the date of R's death, building was found undervalued by ₹ 24,000, which was to be considered.

(i) Calculate R's share of goodwill in the firm and gaining ratio, if S and T decided to share future profits equally. **[1.5]**

(ii) Record the adjustment journal entries of goodwill and revaluation of building. **[1.5]**

6. Under what heads and sub-heads, will the following items appear in the balance sheet of a company as per Schedule III of the Companies Act, 2013

(i) Subsidy reserve (ii) Mining rights

(iii) Interest accrued on investment

(iv) Preliminary expenses

(v) Loose tools (vi) Prepaid insurance **[6]**

7. Ram, Rahim and Rehman were partners in a firm sharing profits in the ratio 4 : 1 : 5. On 28th February, 2020 the firm was dissolved. On the date of dissolution, the balance sheet of the firm was as follows

Balance Sheet
as at 28th February, 2020

Liabilities		Amt (₹)	Assets		Amt (₹)
Bank Loan		4,34,000	Bank		48,000
Creditors		3,80,000	Debtors	2,74,000	
General Reserve		1,40,000	(–) Provision for Doubtful Debts	(8,000)	2,66,000
Capital A/cs			Stock		1,08,000
Ram	14,00,000		Furniture		1,32,000
Rahim	6,00,000		Machinery		4,00,000
Rehman	10,00,000	30,00,000	Building		30,00,000
		39,54,000			39,54,000

Assets realised as follows

Debtors ₹ 2,70,000, stock at 15% less, furniture was taken over by Ram for ₹ 79,000, building was sold for ₹ 29,00,000, Rehman took over 50% of the machinery at 5% less than the book value. Bank loan was paid with interest ₹ 9,500, creditors allowed a discount of 5%, expenses on dissolution ₹ 7,000 were paid by Rehman, remaining machinery was sold at 50% profit.

Prepare realisation account and partners' capital account. **[6]**

8. On 31st March, 2020 the balance sheet of W and R who shared profits in 3 : 2 ratio was as follows

Balance Sheet
as at 31st March, 2020

Liabilities		Amt (₹)	Assets		Amt (₹)
Creditors		20,000	Cash		5,000
Profit and Loss A/c		15,000	Sundry Debtors	20,000	
Capital A/cs			(–) Provision for Doubtful Debts	(700)	19,300
W	40,000				
R	30,000	70,000	Stock		25,000
			Plant and Machinery		35,000
			Patents		20,700
		1,05,000			1,05,000

On this date, B was admitted as partner on the following conditions

(i) B will get 4/15th share of profits.

(ii) B had to bring ₹ 30,000 as his capital to which amount other partners' capital shall have to be adjusted.

(iii) He would pay cash for his share of goodwill which would be based on 2.5 years' purchase of average profits of past 4 years.

(iv) The assets would be revalued as under

Sundry debtors at book value less 5% provision for doubtful debts, stock at ₹ 20,000, plant and machinery at ₹ 40,000.

(v) The profits of the firm for the year's ending on 31st March, 2017, 2018 and 2019 were ₹ 20,000, ₹ 14,000 and ₹ 17,000 respectively.

Prepare revaluation account and partners' capital account. **[6]**

Or X and Y are partners sharing profits and losses in the ratio of 3: 2. On 31st March, 2023, their Balance Sheet was as follows

Liabilities		Amt (₹)	Assets	Amt (₹)
Bank Loan		5,00,000	Cash	50,000
Bills Payable		2,00,000	Bank	11,50,000
Workmen Compensation Reserve		3,00,000	Debtors	1,00,000
Capital A/cs			Stock	6,00,000
X	16,00,000		Building	10,00,000
Y	8,00,000	24,00,000	Machinery	4,00,000
			Goodwill	1,00,000
		34,00,000		34,00,000

They admit Z as a partner with effect from 1st April, 2023 for 1/3rd share on the following terms

(i) Z will bring in ₹ 10,00,000 as capital and ₹ 4,00,000 as his share of goodwill but he actually contributed only ₹ 2,40,000 towards goodwill.

(ii) Building and machinery to be depreciated by 5%.

(iii) Stock to be revalued at ₹ 8,00,000.

(iv) There is an unrecorded delivery van worth ₹ 2,40,000.

(v) One month salary of ₹ 60,000 is outstanding.

You are require to

(a) Prepare revaluation account and capital accounts of partners. **[5]**

(b) Calculate new profit-sharing ratio of the partners. **[1]**

9. P, Q and R are partners sharing profits in the ratio of 3:2:1. However, R is guaranteed ₹ 20,000 as his share of profits every year. Deficiency if any would be borne by the other partners. R has given loan of ₹ 45,000 to the firm on 30th September, 2018. The net profits for the two years ending 31st March, 2018 and 31st March, 2019 had been ₹ 75,000 and ₹ 80,000 respectively.

(i) Calculate the interest on loan to be paid to R. **[1]**

(ii) Pass journal entry for loan provided by R to the firm. **[3]**

(iii) Show the profit and loss appropriation account for the two years. **[6]**

Or The capitals of P, M and S as on 31st March, 2023 amounted to ₹ 4,50,000, ₹ 16,50,000 and ₹ 33,00,000 respectively. Divisible profit amounting to ₹ 9,00,000 for the year ended 31st March, 2023 was distributed in the ratio of 4 : 1 : 1 after allowing interest on capital @ 10% p.a. During the year, each partner withdrew ₹ 1,50,000 per month in the beginning of each month. The partnership deed was silent as to profit sharing ratio and interest on drawings but provided for interest on capital @ 12% p.a.

(i) What amount of interest is charged on drawings at the end of the year? **[1.5]**

(ii) Pass necessary adjustment entry to rectify the above. **[8.5]**

10. (A) ABC Ltd. invited application for 1,00,000 equity shares of ₹ 10 each at a premium of ₹ 2.50 each payable on application (1st January, 2022), ₹ 5 on allotment (21st February, 2022 with premium) and balance on call (31st March, 2022). The issue was oversubscribed received applications and allotted shares are summarised as below

Categories	A	B	C
No. of Applicants	80	40	2
No. of Shares Applied by each Applicant	1,000	10,000	40,000
No. of Shares Allotted to each Applicant	500	1,000	10,000

It was decided that amounts overpaid on application by respective applicants to be adjusted on allotment. All surplus amounts after adjusting towards allotment was refunded on 25th January, 2022. Manish, who has paid ₹ 5,000 on 1,000 shares applied (category A) was unable to pay the call due on 31st March, 2022. The directors forfeited his shares on 21st April, 2022. All other shareholders paid the sums on due dates. The forfeited shares were reissued to Himani on 10th May, 2022 for ₹ 5,500.

(i) Pass journal entries in the books of company related to forfeiture reissue and capital reserve. **[5.5]**

(ii) Prepare the calls-in-arrears account. **[2]**

(B) MBA Ltd. forfeited ₹500 equity shares of ₹ 100 each for the non-payment of first call of ₹ 30 per share. The final call of ₹ 10 per share was not yet made. Company reissued all the forfeited shares at ₹ 80 per share ₹ 90 paid up. Pass necessary journal entry of forfeiture, reissue and capital reserve. **[2.5]**

Or BBG Ltd. had issued 1,00,000 equity shares of ₹ 10 each at a premium of ₹ 3 per share payable with application money. You are required to complete the missing information given below **[10]**

JOURNAL

Date	Particulars		LF	Amt (Dr)	Amt (Cr)
2015					
Jul 5	....	Dr		...	
	To				...
	(Being application money received for 1,40,000 shares @ ₹ 6 per share including premium)				
Jul 17	Equity Share Application A/c	Dr		...	
	To				...
	To				...
	To				...
	To				...
	(Being application money transferred to share capital account, securities premium account, refunded for 20,000 shares for rejected applications and balance adjusted towards money due on allotment)				

Date	Particulars	LF	Amt (Dr)	Amt (Cr)
Jul 17	.... Dr		...	
	To			...
	(Being allotment money due @ ₹ 4 per share)			
Aug 20	.... Dr		...	
	To			...
	(Being balance allotment amount received)			
Oct 1	.... Dr		...	
	To			...
	(Being first and final call money due)			
Oct 20	.... Dr		...	
	Calls-in-arrears A/c Dr		3,000	
	To			...
	(Being first and final call money received)			

Date	Particulars	LF	Amt (Dr)	Amt (Cr)
Nov 20	.... Dr		...	
	To			...
	To			...
	(Being the shares forfeited on which first and final call was not received)			
Dec 15	.... Dr		...	
	.... Dr		3,000	
	To			...
	(Being forfeited shares re-issued)			
......	.... Dr		...	
	To			...
	(..)			

Section B

(20 Marks)

(Answer all questions)

11. In subparts (i) and (ii) choose the correct options and in subparts (iii) to (v) answer the questions as instructed.

(i) Which of the following is a non-operating income? **[1]**

(a) Revenue from sale in a trading concern

(b) Profit on the sale of used plant in manufacturing company

(c) Dividend received by an investment company

(d) Premium received by an insurance company

(ii) Reliance industries limited said, "we have a very clear roadmap to becoming a zero net-debt company within the next 18 months."

Assuming that the company's debt to equity ratio is 0.5 before the above decision, what will be the impact of this decision on the debt-equity ratio of the company if company is issuing fresh shares to become a zero net-debt company? **[1]**

(a) Debt-equity ratio will improve
(b) Debt-equity ratio will reduce
(c) No change to the debt-equity ratio
(d) Either (a) or (b)

(iii) Under which type of activity will you classify 'proceeds from sale of investment' while preparing cash flow statement? **[1]**

(iv) What is meant by a common size statement? **[1]**

(v) Net profit of PSD Ltd. after interest and tax is ₹ 3,00,000. Tax rate is 40%. The company has issued 5% debentures of ₹ 20,00,000 @ ₹100 each. Calculate the net profit before interest and tax. **[1]**

12. From the following information, prepare a comparative income statement for the years 2019 and 2020.

Particulars	2020 (₹)	2019 (₹)
Sales	9,00,000	6,00,000
Materials Consumed	4,80,000	3,00,000
Manufacturing and Office Expenses	2,80,000	2,00,000
Other Incomes	30,000	30,000

Other Information

Manufacturing expenses are 50% of the total of the category. **[3]**

13. Read the following, balance sheet of Ronak Ltd and answer the questions that follow

Particulars	Note No.	31st March, 2022 (₹)	31st March, 2021 (₹)
I. EQUITY AND LIABILITIES			
1. Shareholders' Funds			
(a) Equity Share Capital		3,50,000	2,50,000
(b) Reserves and Surplus	1	5,000	40,000
2. Non-current Liabilities			
Long-term Borrowings (12% Debentures)		1,00,000	60,000
3. Current Liabilities			
Trade Payables		1,25,000	1,50,000
Total		5,80,000	5,00,000
II. ASSETS			
1. Non-current Assets			
(a) Property, Plant and Equipment and Tangible Assets		2,80,000	2,00,000
(b) Non-current Investments		1,00,000	1,00,000
2. Current Assets			
(a) Trade Receivables		1,60,000	1,50,000
(b) Cash and Cash Equivalents		40,000	30,000
(c) Other Current Assets (Discount on issue of debentures)		—	20,000
Total		5,80,000	5,00,000

Notes to Accounts

Particulars	31st March, 2022 (₹)	31st March, 2021 (₹)
1. **Reserves and Surplus**		
Statement of Profit and Loss	(20,000)	40,000
Securities Premium Reserve	25,000	—
	5,000	40,000

Additional Information

(a) Debentures were issued on 1st April, 2021.

(b) During the year a machine included in fixed assets costing ₹ 1,20,000 was purchased and another machine of the book value of ₹ 30,000 was sold at a loss of ₹ 2,000.

(i) What is the amount of interest charged on debentures? **[1]**

(ii) What is the amount of depreciation charged by the company? **[1]**

(iii) What is the cash from operating and investing activities of the company? **[2.5]**

(iv) What is the cash from financing activities of the company? **[1.5]**

Or Following are the balance sheet of Hydra Ltd. as at 31st March, 2023 and 2022

Hydra Ltd
Balance Sheet

Particulars	Note No.	31st March 2023 (₹)	31st March 2022 (₹)
I. **EQUITY AND LIABILITIES**			
1. Shareholders' Funds			
(a) Share Capital		12,00,000	11,00,000
(b) Reserves and Surplus	1	3,00,000	2,00,000
2. Non-current Liabilities			
Long-term Borrowing		2,40,000	1,70,000
3. Current Liabilities			
(a) Trade Payables		1,79,000	2,04,000
(b) Short-term Provisions		50,000	77,000
Total		19,69,000	17,51,000
II. **ASSETS**			
1. Non-Current Assets			
Property, Plant and Equipment and Intangible Assets			
(i) Property, Plant and Equipment	2	10,70,000	8,50,000
(ii) Intangible Assets	3	40,000	1,12,000
2. Current Assets			
(a) Current Investments		2,40,000	1,50,000
(b) Inventories		1,29,000	1,21,000
(c) Trade Receivables		1,70,000	1,43,000
(d) Cash and Cash Equivalents		3,20,000	3,75,000
Total		19,69,000	17,51,000

Notes to Accounts

Particulars	31st March, 2023 (₹)	31st March, 2022 (₹)
1. Reserves and Surplus		
Surplus, i.e, Balance in Statement of Profit and Loss	3,00,000	2,00,000
2. Property, Plant and Equipment		
Machinery	12,70,000	10,00,000
(–) Accumulated Depreciation	(2,00,000)	(1,50,000)
	10,70,000	8,50,000
3. Intangible Assets		
Goodwill	40,000	1,12,000

Additional Information

During the year, a piece of machinery costing ₹ 24,000 on which accumulated depreciation was ₹ 16,000 was sold for ₹ 6,000.

Prepare cash flow statement. **[6]**

14. Following are the statement of trading and profit and loss for the year ended 31st March, 2021 and the balance sheet as at that date

Statement of Profit and Loss
for the year ended 31st March, 2021

Particulars	Amt (₹)
I. **Revenue from Operations** (Sales)	1,00,000
II. **Expenses**	
Purchase of Stock-in-trade	50,000
Changes in Inventories of Stock-in-trade	(5,000)
Employees Benefit Expenses	5,000
Finance Cost (Interest)	3,000
Other Expenses	27,000
Total Expenses	80,000
III. **Profit for the Period** (I – II)	20,000

Balance Sheet
as at 31st March, 2021

Particulars	Amt (₹)
I. **EQUITY AND LIABILITIES**	
1. Shareholders' Funds	
(a) Share Capital	1,00,000
(b) Reserves and Surplus	20,000
2. Current Liabilities	
Trade Payables	40,000
Total	1,60,000
II. **ASSETS**	
1. Non-current Assets	
Property, Plant and Equipment	1,00,000
2. Current Assets	
(a) Inventories	15,000
(b) Trade Receivables (Debtors)	27,500
(c) Cash and Cash Equivalents	17,500
Total	1,60,000

Notes

- Employees benefit expenses are towards wages paid.
- Other expenses comprise of

	Amt (₹)
Administrative expenses	15,000
Selling expenses	12,000
	27,000

From the above, calculate

(a) Gross profit ratio **[2]**

(b) Current ratio **[2]**

(c) Stock turnover ratio **[2]**

Answers

1. (i) (d) Both (b) and (c) (ii) (c) Debit Partners' Capital A/c and Credit Goodwill A/c
(iii) (c) Only III
(iv) (b) Both Assertion (A) and Reason (R) are true, but Reason (R) is not the correct explanation for Assertion (A)
(v) (c) 3/10
(viii) ₹ 50,000

2. (i) Balance in B's Executor Accounts = ₹ 41,490; (ii) Goodwill = ₹ 18,000

Or (i) New Profit Sharing Ratio = 19 : 6; Firm's Goodwill = ₹ 50,000

3. Number of Debentures Issued = 6,000

5. R's Share is Goodwill= ₹ 16,425; Gaining ratio = 1 : 3

7. Loss on Realisation Account = ₹ 72,700

8. Net Loss Transferred to Capital Accounts = ₹ 5,400
Loss on Revaluation = ₹ 300
Balance in Partner's Capital Accounts

W	R	B
49,500	33,000	30,000

Or (a) Revaluation Profit = ₹ 3,10,000
Capital Balance X = ₹ 21,46,000, Y = ₹ 11,64,000, Z = ₹ 10,00,000
(b) New Profit Sharing Ratio = 6 : 4 : 5

9. (i) ₹ 1,350
(iii) Profit transferred to
2018 P = ₹ 33,000 ; Q = ₹ 22,000 ; R = ₹ 20,000
2019 P = ₹ 36,000 ; Q = ₹ 24,000 ; R = ₹ 20,000

Or (ii) Debit P's Capital A/c ₹ 3,30,000, Credit M's Capital A/c ₹ 1,50,000 and S's Capital A/c ₹ 1,80,000

10. (B) Capital Reserve = ₹ 25,000

11. (i) (b) Profit on the sale of used plant in manufacturing company (ii) (b) Debt-equity ratio will reduce
(v) ₹ 6,00,000

13. (i) ₹ 12,000 (ii) ₹ 10,000 (iii) ₹ (51,000); ₹ (92,000) (iv) ₹ 1,53,000

Or Cash Flow from Operating Activities = ₹ 1,53,000
Cash Used in Investing Activities = ₹ 2,88,000
Cash Flow from Financing Activities = ₹ 1,70,000
Net Increase in Cash and Cash Equivalents = ₹ 35,000

14. (a) Gross Profit Ratio = 50% (b) Current Ratio = 1.5 : 1 (c) Stock Turnover Ratio = 4 times

ISC

SAMPLE PAPER 02

Time : 3 hrs
Marks : 80

Accounts XII

General Instructions

1. Candidates are allowed additional 15 minutes for only reading the paper. They must not start writing during this time.
2. Section A and B are compulsory.
3. There are internal choices provided in each section.
4. The intended marks for questions or parts of questions are given in the brackets [ ].
5. All calculations should be shown clearly.
6. All working, including rough work, should be done on the same page as, and adjacent to, the rest of the answer.

Section A

(60 Marks)

(Answer all questions)

1. In subpart (i) to (v) choose the correct options and in subparts (vi) to (x) answer the questions as instructed.

(i) B, S and P are partners in a firm sharing profits in the ratio of 3:2:1. B died on 30th June, 2022. Share of profit or loss of B from the beginning of the year up to the date of his death will be calculated on the basis of last year's profit. What will be the journal entry for B's share of profit or loss up to the date of his death? **[1]**

(a) Debit Profit and Loss Suspense A/c and Credit B's Capital A/c
(b) Debit S and P's Capital A/c and Credit B's Capital A/c
(c) Debit B's Capital A/c and Credit Profit & Loss Suspense A/c
(d) Debit B's Capital A/c and Credit S and P's Capital A/c

(ii) Daksh Mohan Ltd. called first call money of ₹ 3 per share on its 70,000 shares. A shareholder holding 2,000 shares failed to pay the amount. How much amount will be due on first call? **[1]**

(a) ₹ 2,00,000 (b) ₹ 2,10,000
(c) ₹ 2,04,000 (d) ₹ 6,000

(iii) Adani enterprises' ₹ 400 crore public issue of debentures, which opened on Wednesday, was oversubscribed by around 221% on day two, driven by heavy participation from retail investors.

Source *Economictimes.indiatimes.com*

What are the options does Adani enterprises have? **[1]**

I. Adani enterprises can reject all the excess debentures applied.
II. Adani enterprises can issue debentures on proportionate bases.
III. Adani enterprises can reject some applications and issue all the debentures to remaining applicants on pro-rata basis.
IV. Adani enterprises can wait for the instructions of SEBI.

Options

(a) I, II and IV (b) II, III and IV
(c) I, III and IV (d) I, II and III

(iv) The debentures which can be transferred only by executing a regular transfer deed are called **[1]**
(a) Registered debentures
(b) Irredeemable debentures
(c) Convertible debentures
(d) Bearer debentures

(v) **Assertion** (A) If a creditor accepts an asset in full and final settlement of his account, journal entry needs to be recorded.

Reason (R) If a creditor accepts an asset only as a part payment of his/her dues, the entry will be made for cash payment only.

Alternatives **[1]**
(a) Both Assertion (A) and Reason (R) are true and Reason (R) is the correct explanation for Assertion (A)
(b) Both Assertion (A) and Reason (R) are true, but Reason (R) is not the correct explanation for Assertion (A)
(c) Assertion (A) is false, but Reason (R) is true
(d) Both Assertion (A) and Reason (R) are false

(vi) A and B are partners sharing profits in the ratio of 10 : 2. C is admitted and the new profit sharing ratio is now 5:3:2.

At the date of admission, general reserve appears in the books. Pass journal entry to distribute general reserve. **[1]**

(vii) "According to Section 39 of the Indian Partnership Act, 1932, dissolution of the firm means dissolution of partnership among all the partners in the firm." Based on the statement, name two modes of dissolution. **[1]**

(viii) On D's retirement, his final amount after all the adjustments of revaluation, goodwill, accumulated reserves, profits and losses turns out to be ₹ 2,85,000. This amount was transferred to D's loan account. At what rate interest will be paid on D's loan account in the absence of partnership deed? **[1]**

(ix) K, L and M are partners with capitals ₹ 10,00,000, ₹ 7,50,000 and ₹ 5,00,000 respectively. On M's retirement, his share is acquired by K and L in ratio of 5:3. Calculate gaining ratio. **[1]**

(x) Name two characteristics of financial statements of a company. **[1]**

2. The balance sheet of Radha, Sohan and Madan, who were sharing profits in the ratio of 4 : 3 : 1 respectively, as on 31st March, 2022 was as follows

Balance Sheet
as at 31st March, 2022

Liabilities		Amt (₹)	Assets	Amt (₹)
General Reserve		65,000	Cash	39,000
Bills Payable		25,000	Stock	88,000
Loan		29,000	Debtors	61,000
Capital A/cs			Machinery	2,23,000
Radha	1,50,000		Madan's Loan	33,000
Sohan	1,00,000			
Madan	75,000	3,25,000		
		4,44,000		4,44,000

Madan died on 1st September, 2022. The partnership deed provided for the following on the death of a partner

(i) Goodwill of the firm to be valued at two years' purchase of average profits for the last three years which were ₹ 64,000.
(ii) Madan's share of profit till the date of his death was to be calculated on the basis of sales. Sales for the year ended 31st March, 2022 amounted to ₹ 1,50,000 and that from 1st April to 1st September, 2022 ₹ 90,000. The profit for the year ended 31st March, 2022 was ₹ 50,000.
(iii) Interest on capital was to be provided @ 10% per annum.

Prepare Madan's capital account to be rendered to his executor. **[3]**

Or Naresh, David and Aslam are partners sharing profits in the ratio of 5 : 3 : 7. On 1st April, 2022, Naresh gave a notice to retire from the firm. David and Aslam decided to share future profits in the ratio of 2 : 3. The adjusted capital accounts of David and Aslam showed a balance of ₹ 33,000 and ₹ 70,500 respectively. The total amount to be paid to Naresh is ₹ 90,500. This amount is to be paid by David and Aslam in such a way that their capitals become proportionate to their new profit sharing ratio.

(i) Calculate their gaining ratio. **[1]**
(ii) Pass necessary journal entries for the above transactions in the books of the firm. Show your working clearly. **[2]**

3. Arihant Ltd. issued 20,000; 9% debentures of ₹100 each at a discount of 4% on 1st April, 2018, payable ₹ 30 on application and the balance on allotment. The debentures are redeemable after 5 years.

(i) Give the necessary journal entries. Ignore interest. **[1.5]**
(ii) Prepare 9% debentures account. **[1.5]**

4. Mukesh Ltd. had 15,000, 8% debentures of ₹100 each due for redemption on 31st March, 2023. Assuming that the debentures were redeemed 100% out of profits, pass necessary journal entries for the redemption of debentures. There was a credit balance of ₹ 15,00,000 in the profit and loss account. **[3]**

Or

On 1st April, 2018 Blue Star Ltd. a listed company issued 10,000, 11% debentures of ₹ 100 each at a discount of 4%, redeemable at a premium of 5% after 5 years. This issue was fully subscribed. Debentures were redeemed on due date.

Pass necessary entries for issue and redemption of debentures, assuming that the loss on issue was written-off at the end of first year.

5. M, R and F are partners, sharing profits in the ratio of 4 : 3 : 1. It is provided in the partnership deed that, on the death of any partner, deceased partners' share of goodwill be valued at half of the profits credited to his account during the previous four completed years. R died on 1st April, 2023. The firm's profits/losses for the last four years ended 31st March are 2020 ₹ 24,000; 2021 ₹ 12,000; 2022 ₹ 4,000 (loss); 2023 ₹ 16,000.

(i) Determine the amount that is to be credited to R's capital account as his share of goodwill. **[1]**

(ii) Pass journal entry for adjustment of goodwill if profit sharing ratio between M and F in future will be 3: 2. **[2]**

6. The following balance have been extracted from the books of Ronak Ltd. as at 31st March, 2022

Equity Share Capital	4,00,000
(Fully paid shares of ₹ 100 each)	
Property, Plant and Equipment and Intangible Assets (at Cost)	6,60,000
Inventories	40,000
Cash and Bank Balance	50,000
Creditors	30,000
Bills Receivable	20,000
Accumulated Depreciation	30,000
Provision for Taxation	25,000
Reserves and Surplus	1,00,000
5% Debentures (Secured against land)	2,00,000
Unsecured Loan from Subsidiaries	50,000
Underwriting Commission	5,000
Investments	70,000
Interest Accrued and Due	10,000

You are required to prepare a balance sheet. **[6]**

7. Prachi, Ritika and Ishita were partners in a firm sharing profits and losses in the ratio of 5 : 3 : 2. Inspite of repeated reminders by the authorities, they kept dumping hazardous material into a nearby river. The court ordered for the dissolution of their partnership firm on 31st March, 2022. Prachi was deputed to realise the assets and pay the liabilities. She was paid ₹ 1,000 as commission for her services. The financial position of the firm was as follows

Balance Sheet
as at 31st March, 2022

Liabilities		Amt (₹)	Assets	Amt (₹)
Creditors		10,000	Furniture	37,000
Investment Fluctuation Fund		4,500	Stock	5,500
Capital A/cs			Investments	15,000
Prachi	40,000		Cash	9,000
Ritika	30,000	70,000	Ishita's Capital	18,000
		84,500		84,500

Following was agreed upon

Prachi took over investments for ₹ 12,500. Stock and furniture realised ₹ 41,500. There was old furniture which has been written-off completely from the books. Ritika agreed to take away the same at the price of ₹ 3,000. Compensation paid to the employees amounted to ₹ 8,000. This liability was not provided in the above balance sheet. Realisation expenses amounted to ₹ 1,000. Prepare realisation account, partners' capital accounts and cash account to close the books of the firm. **[6]**

8. Sahaj and Nimish are partners in a firm. They share profits and losses in the ratio of 2 :1. Since, both of them are specially abled, sometimes they find it difficult to run the business on their own. Gauri, a common friend decides to help them. Therefore, they admit her into partnership for a 1/3rd share. She brought her share of goodwill in cash and proportionate capital. At the time of Gauri's admission, the balance sheet of Sahaj and Nimish was as under

Balance Sheet
as at ...

Liabilities		Amt (₹)	Assets	Amt (₹)
Capital A/cs			Machinery	1,20,000
Sahaj	1,20,000		Furniture	80,000
Nimish	80,000	2,00,000	Stock	50,000
General Reserve		30,000	Sundry Debtors	30,000
Creditors		30,000	Cash	20,000
Employees' Provident Fund		40,000		
		3,00,000		3,00,000

It was decided to

(i) Reduce the value of stock by ₹ 5,000.

(ii) Depreciate furniture by 10% and appreciate machinery by 5%.

(iii) ₹ 3,000 of the debtors proved bad. A provision of 5% was to be created on sundry debtors for doubtful debts.

(iv) Goodwill of the firm was valued at ₹ 45,000.

You are required to

(a) Prepare revaluation account and partners' capital account. **[5]**

(b) Calculate the new profit-sharing ratio. **[1]**

Or P and Q share profits of a business in the ratio of 5 : 3. They admit R into the firm for one-fourth share in the profits to be contributed equally by P and Q. On the date of admission the balance sheet of P and Q was as follows

Liabilities	Amt (₹)	Assets	Amt (₹)
Capital A/cs		Land and Building	52,000
P	60,000	Machinery	36,000
Q	40,000	Stock	20,000
Reserve Fund	8,000	Debtors	16,000
Bank Loan	24,000	Cash	12,000
Bills Payable	4,000		
	68,000		68,000

The terms of N's admission were as follow

(i) R will bring ₹ 50,000 as his capital.

(ii) Goodwill of the firm is to be valued at 4 years' purchase of the average super profits of the last three years. Average profits of the last three years are ₹ 40,000. While the normal profits that can be earned on the capital employed are ₹ 24,000.

(iii) Machinery is to be revalued at ₹ 45,000 and the value of stock to be reduced by 20%.

Prepare revaluation account, partners' capital account and the balance sheet of the firm after admission of R.

9. Ankur, Bhavna and Disha are partners in a firm. On 1st April, 2021 the balance in their capital accounts stood at ₹ 14,00,000, ₹ 6,00,000 and ₹ 4,00,000 respectively. They shared profits in the proportion of 7 : 3 : 2 respectively. Partners are entitled to interest on capital @ 6% per annum and salary to Bhavna @ ₹ 50,000 per annum and a commission of ₹ 3,000 per month to Disha as per the provisions of the partnership deed. Drawings of Ankur and Disha during the year amounted to ₹ 14,000 and ₹ 22,000.

Bhavna's share of profit (excluding interest on capital) is guaranteed at not less than ₹ 1,70,000 per annum. Disha's share of profit (including interest on capital but excluding salary) is guaranteed at not less than ₹ 1,50,000 per annum. Any deficiency arising on that account shall be met by Ankur. The profits of the firm for the year ended 31st March, 2022 amounted to ₹ 9,50,000.

(a) At what rate, interest on drawings will be provided to the partners? **[1]**

(b) Pass necessary journal entries for drawings of the partners. **[3]**

(c) Prepare 'profit and loss appropriation account' for the year ended 31st March, 2022. **[6]**

Or A, K and V are partners in a firm. Their capital accounts on 1st April, 2023 stood at ₹ 30,000, ₹ 15,000 and ₹ 15,000 respectively.

V advanced a sum of ₹ 5,000 to firm on 1st October, 2021 in the form of a loan. The partners withdrew ₹ 1,000 each during the year.

The partnership deed provides the following

(i) Interest on capital be allowed @ 10% p.a.

(ii) Interest on drawings to be charged @ 5% p.a.

(iii) K to be allowed an annual salary of ₹ 1,250.

(iv) Profit sharing ratio is 5 : 3 : 2.

Ignoring all the terms of the deed, the net profit of ₹ 22,500 for the year ended 31st March, 2023 was divided equally among the partners.

(a) How much interest will be allowed on V's loan? **[1.5]**

(b) Pass a single journal entry to rectify the error. **[8.5]**

10. (A) Starplus Company issued for public subscription 1,50,000 shares of the value of ₹ 90 each payable per share as follows
₹ 20 on application, ₹ 30 on allotment and ₹ 40 on call.

The company received applications for 3,00,000 shares. The allotment was done as under

(i) Applicants of 30,000 shares were allotted 10,000 shares.

(ii) Applicants of 1,40,000 shares were allotted 80,000 shares.

(iii) Remaining applicants were allotted 60,000 shares.

After adjusting excess money on allotment, the money was returned. Harit, a shareholder who had applied for 7,000 shares of group (ii), failed to pay allotment and call money.

Roshan, another shareholder who was allotted 6,000 shares, paid the call money alongwith the allotment. Roshan also belonged to group (ii).

(i) Pass necessary journal entries to record the above transactions in the books of the company. **[5.5]**

(ii) Prepare the cash book to record the above issue of shares. **[2.5]**

(B) GLA Ltd. purchased machinery costing ₹ 1,00,000 from FDL Ltd. The company paid the price by issue of equity shares of ₹ 10 each at a premium of 25%. Pass necessary journal entries for the above transactions in the books of GLA Ltd. **[2]**

Or SME Ltd. had issued 4,00,000 equity shares of ₹ 10 each at a premium of ₹ 3 per share payable with application money. While passing journal entries related to the issue, some blanks are left, you are required to complete these blanks **[10]**

JOURNAL

Date	Particulars		LF	Amt (Dr)	Amt (Cr)
2022 Jan 5	...	Dr		...	
	To ...				...
	(Being application money received for 5,60,000 shares @ ₹ 6 per share including premium)				
Jan 17	Equity Share Application A/c	Dr		...	
	To				...
	To				...
	To				...
	To				...
	(Being application money transferred to share capital account, securities premium account, refunded for 80,000 shares for rejected applications and balance adjusted towards money due on allotment as shares were alloted on pro-rata basis)				
Jan 17	....	Dr		...	
	To				...
	(Being allotment money due @ ₹ 4 per share)				
Feb 20	....	Dr		...	
	To				...
	(Being balance allotment amount received)				
Apr 1	....	Dr		...	
	To				...
	(Being first and final call money due)				
Apr 20	....	Dr		...	
	Calls-in-Arrears A/c	Dr		12,000	
	To				...
	(Being first and final call money received)				
May 20	....	Dr		...	
	To				...
	To				...
	(Being the shares forfeited on which first and final call was not received)				
Jun 15	....	Dr		...	
	....	Dr		12,000	
	To				...
	(Being forfeited shares re-issued)				

Section B

(20 Marks)

(Answer all questions)

11. In subparts (i) and (ii) choose the correct options and in subparts (iii) to (v) answer the questions as instructed.

(i) .... ratios are calculated for measuring the efficiency of operations of business based on effective utilisation of resources. **[1]**

(a) Liquidity ratios
(b) Solvency ratios
(c) Activity ratios
(d) None of the above

(ii) "Cash equivalents are short-term, highly liquid investments that are readily convertible into known amounts of cash and which are subject to an insignificant risk of changes in value." **[1]**

Based on the statement, which of the following is not a cash equivalent?

(a) Cash at bank
(b) Cheque in hand
(c) Bank overdraft
(d) Short-term investments

(iii) State how qualitative aspects are ignored in financial statement analysis. **[1]**

(iv) Gross profit of a firm is ₹ 8,00,000 and revenue from operations ₹ 32,00,000. What will be the gross profit ratio? **[1]**

(v) Under which type of activity will you classify 'increase in the value of goodwill'? **[1]**

12. Following is the income statement of Raj Ltd. for the year ended 31st March, 2021.

Particulars	Amt (₹)
I. **Revenue from Operations** (Sales)	2,00,000
II. **Other Incomes**	15,000
III. **Total Revenue** (I + II)	2,15,000
IV. **Expenses**	
Cost of Goods Sold	1,10,000
Operating Expenses	5,000
Total Expenses	1,15,000
V. **Profit before Tax** (III – IV)	1,00,000
(–) Income Tax	40,000
VI. **Profit after Tax**	60,000

Prepare a common size income statement of Raj Ltd. for the year ended 31st March, 2021. **[3]**

13. Following are the balance sheets of Krishtec Ltd. for the year ended 31st March, 2021 and 2022.

Particulars	2021-22 (₹)	2020-21 (₹)
I. **EQUITY AND LIABILITIES**		
1. **Shareholders' Funds**		
(a) Share Capital	12,00,000	8,00,000
(b) Reserves and Surplus (Statement of profit and loss balance)	3,50,000	4,00,000
2. **Non-current Liabilities**		
Long-term Borrowings	4,40,000	3,50,000
3. **Current Liabilities**		
Trade Payables	60,000	50,000
Total	20,50,000	16,00,000
II. **ASSETS**		
1. **Non-current Assets**		
(a) Property, Plant and Equipment and Intangible Assets		
(i) Property, Plant and Equipment	12,00,000	9,00,000
2. **Current Assets**		
(a) Inventories	2,00,000	1,00,000
(b) Trade Receivables	3,10,000	2,30,000
(c) Cash and Cash Equivalents	3,40,000	3,70,000
Total	20,50,000	16,00,000

Prepare a cash flow statement after taking into account the following adjustments

(i) The company paid interest ₹ 36,000 on its long-term borrowings.

(ii) Depreciation charged on tangible fixed assets was ₹ 1,20,000. **[6]**

Or Following extracts are taken from the balance sheets of M/s Karan Ltd., on 31st March and the additional information provided as follows

Particulars	2023 (₹)	2022 (₹)
I. **EQUITY AND LIABILITIES**		
Equity Share Capital	6,00,000	4,00,000
10% Preference Share Capital	20,000	40,000
Securities Premium Reserve Account	19,000	—
Profit and Loss Balance	1,60,000	80,000
10% Debentures	2,00,000	2,00,000

Additional Information

(a) Fresh equity shares were issued on 31st March, 2023 at a premium of 10%.

(b) Interim dividend was paid on equity shares @ 8%.

(c) Preference shares were redeemed on 31st March, 2023 at premium of 5%. Premium on redemption was charged against premium received on issue of fresh equity shares.

You are required to calculate

(i) Cash flows from operating and financing activities. **[2.5]**

(ii) Make a statement showing the calculation of securities premium. **[1.5]**

(iii) Make a statement showing the computation of amount of net profit before tax. **[1]**

(iv) What is the amount of interim dividend paid by the company? **[1]**

14. Following is the statement of profit and loss of Hindustan Products Ltd. for the year ended 31st March, 2022 and the balance sheet of the company as at that data

Statement of Profit and Loss
for the year ended 31st March, 2022

Particulars	Amt (₹)
I. **Revenue from Operations**	8,00,000
II. **Expenses**	
Purchase of Stock-in-trade	5,45,000
Changes in Inventories of Stock-in-trade [Opening inventory (₹ 99,000) Closing inventory (₹ 1,99,000)]	(1,00,000)
Other Expenses	2,95,000
Total Expenses	7,40,000
III. **Profit for the Period** (I – II)	60,000

Note Other expenses include direct expenses of ₹ 15,000.

Balance Sheet
as at 31st March, 2022

Particulars	Amt (₹)
I. **EQUITY AND LIABILITIES**	
1. **Shareholders' Funds**	
(a) Share Capital	2,90,000
(b) Reserves and Surplus	60,000
2. **Current Liabilities**	
(a) Trade Payables (Creditors)	1,15,000
(b) Other Current Liabilities (Outstanding expenses)	15,000
Total	4,80,000

Particulars	Amt (₹)
II. **ASSETS**	
1. **Non-current Assets**	
(a) Property, Plant and Equipment and Intangible Assets	
(i) Property, Plant and Equipment	2,30,000
2. **Current Assets**	
(a) Inventories	1,99,000
(b) Trade Receivables (Debtors)	21,000
(c) Cash and Cash Equivalents	30,000
Total	4,80,000

Calculate any three of the following ratios
(i) Quick ratio [2]
(ii) Stock turnover ratio [2]
(iii) Current ratio [2]
(iv) Proprietary ratio [2]

Answers

1. (i) (a) Debit Profit and Loss Suspense A/c and Credit B's Capital A/c
(ii) (b) ₹ 2,10,000
(iii) (d) I, II and III
(iv) (a) Registered debentures
(v) (c) Assertion (A) is false, but Reason (R) is true
(ix) 5 : 3

2. To Madan's Executor = ₹ 73,000 Or (i) Gaining ratio = 3 : 2

5. (i) ₹ 9,000

6. Balance Sheet Total = ₹ 8,10,000

7. Loss on Realisation Prachi = ₹ 2,500, Ritika = ₹ 1,500, Ishita = ₹ 1,000
Capital Accounts Total Prachi = ₹ 41,000
Ritika = ₹ 30,000, Ishita = ₹ 19,000
Cash Account Total = ₹ 69,500

8. (i) Loss on Revaluation Sahaj = ₹ 7,567, Nimish = ₹ 3,783
Balance of Capital Accounts Sahaj = ₹ 1,42,433
Nimish = ₹ 91,217 ; Gauri = ₹ 1,16,825

Or Profit on Revaluation P = ₹ 5,000, Q = ₹ 3,000
Balance of Capital Accounts P = ₹ 78,000
Q = ₹ 54,000, R = ₹ 50,000
Total of Balance Sheet = ₹ 2,10,000

9. (c) Profit transferred to Ankur = ₹ 4,14,000
Bhavna = ₹ 1,80,000, Disha = ₹ 1,26,000

10. (B) Number of Shares = 8,000

11. (i) (c) Activity ratios (ii) (c) Bank overdraft
(iv) 25%

13. Cash Flow from Operating Activities = ₹ (64,000)
Cash Flow from Investing Activities = ₹ (4,20,000)
Cash Flow from Financing Activities = ₹ 4,54,000

Or (i) Cash Flow from Operating Activities = ₹ 1,36,000
Cash Flow from Financing Activities = ₹ 1,43,000
(iv) Interim Dividend = ₹ 32,000

14. (i) 0.39 : 1 (ii) 3.09 times
(iii) 1.92 : 1 (iv) 0.73 : 1

ISC

SAMPLE PAPER 03

Time : 3 hrs
Marks : 80

Accounts XII

General Instructions

1. Candidates are allowed additional 15 minutes for only reading the paper. They must not start writing during this time.
2. Section A and B are compulsory.
3. There are internal choices provided in each section.
4. The intended marks for questions or parts of questions are given in the brackets [ ].
5. All calculations should be shown clearly.
6. All working, including rough work, should be done on the same page as, and adjacent to, the rest of the answer.

Section A

(60 Marks)

(Answer all questions)

1. In subparts (i) to (v) choose the correct options and in subparts (vi) to (x) answer the questions as instructed.

(i) D and M are partners in a firm sharing profits and losses in the ratio of 3:2. Their capitals were ₹ 3,20,000 and ₹ 2,00,000 respectively. N was admitted for 1/5th share in the profits of the firm. He brought ₹ 2,40,000 as his capital, the goodwill of the firm will be [1]

(a) ₹ 4,40,000 (b) ₹ 1,50,000
(c) ₹ 6,30,000 (d) ₹ 2,42,000

(ii) At the time of dissolution of partnership firm, journal entry for the settlement of loan advanced by the firm to a partner would be [1]

(a) Debit Partner's Capital A/c and Credit Loan to Partner A/c
(b) Debit Loan to Partner A/c and Credit Bank A/c
(c) Debit Realisation A/c and Credit Loan to Partner A/c
(d) None of the above

(iii) The following statement is provided to you

"Debentures can be a financing option for entrepreneurs who don't want to give up share value or for fast-growing firms that don't have a lot of assets".

Source *bank for Canadian entrepreneurs*

Which of the following statements are true for debentures? [1]

I. Debentures are written acknowledgement of debt.
II. Debenture holders have voting rights if MOA allows.
III. A debenture cannot have maturity period exceeding 10 years.
IV. Funds raised by issue of debentures are generally short-term in nature.

Options

(a) I and IV (b) II, III and IV
(c) I, III and IV (d) I and III

(iv) At the time of forfeiture of shares, share capital account will be debited with [1]

(a) Nominal value of the share
(b) Called-up value of the share
(c) Paid-up value of the share
(d) Market value of the share

(v) **Assertion** (A) Debentures cannot be issued for consideration other than cash or as a collateral security.

Reason (R) Debentures can be issued at par, at a premium or at a discount. **[1]**

Alternatives

(a) Both Assertion (A) and Reason (R) are true and Reason (R) is the correct explanation for Assertion (A)

(b) Both Assertion (A) and Reason (R) are true, but Reason (R) is not the correct explanation for Assertion (A)

(c) Assertion (A) is true, but Reason (R) is false

(d) Assertion (A) is false, but Reason (R) is true

(vi) What is coupon rate? Explain zero coupon bond. **[1]**

(vii) Seeze Ltd is an unlisted non-NBFC having 1,000 outstanding 9% debentures of ₹ 100 each which were issued at a premium of 10%.

Find the amount of debenture redemption investment to be created by them. **[1]**

(viii) Name any two items that are listed under the head short-term provisions. **[1]**

(ix) "Admission of a partner is the reconstitution of the firm because with the admission of a partner, existing agreement ends and a new agreement among all the partners comes into existence."

Based on the statement, name two modes through which a partner can be admitted into the firm. **[1]**

(x) How does the factor 'efficient management' affects the value of the goodwill of the firm? **[1]**

2. P, Q and R were partners in a firm sharing profits in the ratio of 5 : 4 : 1. Their capitals were P ₹ 4,00,000, Q ₹ 3,00,000 and R ₹ 50,000. The firm closes its books on 31st March every year. On 31st March, 2021, Q died.

According to the partnership deed, the executor of a deceased partner was entitled to

(i) Interest on capital from the first day on the accounting year till the date of his death @ 10% per annum.

(ii) His share of goodwill – The goodwill of the firm on Q's death was valued at ₹ 6,00,000.

(iii) His share of profit – The profit of the firm for the year ended 31st March, 2021 was ₹ 3,00,000.

Q's executor was paid the sum due in two annual installments.

Pass necessary journal entries at the time of his death on 31st March, 2021. **[3]**

Or The balance sheet of A, B and C who were sharing profits and losses in the ratio of 1/2, 1/3 and 1/6 respectively, was as follows on 1st April, 2021

Balance Sheet
as at 1st April, 2021

Liabilities		Amt (₹)	Assets	Amt (₹)
Bills Payable		6,400	Cash	25,650
Sundry Creditors		12,500	Bills Receivable	5,400
Capital A/cs			Debtors	17,800
A	40,000		Stock	22,300
B	25,000		Furniture	3,500
C	20,000	85,000	Plant and Machinery	9,750
Profit and Loss A/c		4,500	Building	24,000
		1,08,400		1,08,400

A retired from the business on 1st April, 2021 and his share in the firm was to be ascertained on the revaluation of the assets as follows

Stock ₹ 20,000, furniture ₹ 3,000, plant and machinery ₹ 9,000, building ₹ 20,000, ₹ 850 was to be provided for doubtful debts. The goodwill of the firm was valued at ₹ 6,000.

A was to paid ₹ 11,500 in cash on retirement and the balance to be transferred to his loan account.

Yor are required to

(i) Prepare revaluation account, on the date of A's retirement. **[1.5]**

(ii) Calculate the amount of A's loan account. **[1.5]**

3. Nav Lakshmi Ltd. invited applications for issuing 3,000, 12% debentures of ₹ 100 each at a premium of ₹ 50 per debenture. The full amount was payable on application. Applications were received for 4,000 debentures. Applications for 1,000 debentures were rejected and application money was refunded. Debentures were allotted to the remaining applicants.

(i) Pass necessary journal entries for the above transactions in the books of Nav Lakshmi Ltd. **[2]**

(ii) Calculate the interest payable on debentures. **[1]**

4. Mukesh Ltd. has 30,000, 9% debentures of ₹100 each due for redemption on 31st March, 2023. Assuming that debentures are to be redeemed out of profits fully and debenture redemption reserve has a balance ₹ 10,80,000 on that date record necessary journal entries at time of redemption of debentures. **[3]**

Or Punjab National Bank issued 4,000, 12% debentures of ₹ 50 each at a premium of 8% on 30th June, 2013 redeemable on 30th June, 2023. The issue was fully subscribed. Record necessary entries for issue and redemption of debentures.

5. B, N, D are partners in a firm sharing profits and losses in the ratio of 3: 2: 1. D dies on 1st April, 2023. On the date of her death, it was decided to value goodwill on the basis of two years' purchase of weighted average profits of the firm for the last three years.

The profits of the last three years and weights assigned were

Year	Profit (₹)	Weights assigned
2020-21	12,000 (including gain from speculation ₹ 4,000)	1
2021-22	32,000	2
2022-23	40,000	3

(i) Calculate the firm's goodwill on the date of D's death (show working formula). **[1]**

(ii) Pass the necessary journal entry to credit D's capital account with his share of goodwill. **[2]**

6. Jio Telemart Ltd. issued 28,000 equity shares of ₹ 10 each at a premium of ₹ 5 per share, payable as ₹ 7 (including premium) on application, ₹ 5 on allotment and the balance after two months of allotment.

A shareholder to whom 280 shares were allotted failed to pay the allotment and call money and his shares were forfeited. 224 of the forfeited shares were reissued for ₹1,600.

Prepare the balance sheet of the company. **[6]**

7. M, N and C are partners in a firm sharing profits in the ratio of 2 : 1 : 1. Their balance sheet as at 31st March, 2023 was as follows

Liabilities		Amt (₹)	Assets	Amt (₹)
Creditors		1,00,000	Goodwill	60,000
Capital A/cs			Land and Building	1,60,000
M	1,60,000		Plant and Machinery	1,12,000
N	1,60,000		Furniture	1,08,000
C	1,20,000	4,40,000	Trade Receivables	96,000
			Cash	4,000
		5,40,000		5,40,000

The firm was dissolved and the assets realised goodwill ₹ 40,000, land and building ₹ 2,00,000, plant and machinery ₹ 1,00,000, furniture ₹ 56,000 and trade receivables 50% of the book value.

Realisation expenses were ₹ 4,000. Prepare realisation account. **[6]**

8. On 31st March, 2019, the balance sheet of Ram and Shyam who were sharing profits in the ratio of 3 : 1 was as follows

Balance Sheet
as at 31st March, 2019

Liabilities		Amt (₹)	Assets		Amt (₹)
Creditors		2,800	Cash at Bank		2,000
Employees Provident Fund		1,200	Debtors	6,500	
General Reserve		2,000	(–) Provision for Doubtful Debts	(500)	6,000
Capital A/cs			Stock		3,000
Ram	6,000		Investments		5,000
Shyam	4,000	10,000			
		16,000			16,000

They decided to admit Mohan on 1st April, 2019 for 1/5th share on the following terms

(i) Mohan shall bring ₹ 6,000 as his share of premium.

(ii) That unaccounted accrued income of ₹ 100 be provided for.

(iii) The market value of investments was ₹ 4,500.

(iv) A debtor whose dues of ₹ 500 was written-off as bad debts paid ₹ 400 in full settlement.

(v) Mohan to bring in capital to the extent of 1/5th of the total capital of the new firm.

You are required to

(a) Calculate the new profit-sharing ratio after Mohan's admission. **[1]**

(b) Prepare revaluation account and partners' capital account. **[5]**

Or Amit and Sumit are carrying on business in partnership and sharing profits and losses in the ratio of 3 : 2. Their balance sheet as at 31st March, 2023 stood as

Liabilities		Amt (₹)	Assets	Amt (₹)
Creditors		23,600	Cash	3,000
General Reserve		40,000	Stock	56,000
Amit's Capital	1,02,900		Debtors	39,000
Sumit's Capital	73,500	1,76,400	Furniture	5,000
			Machinery	97,000
			Goodwill	40,000
		2,40,000		2,40,000

They admit Mukesh into partnership on 1st April, 2022 and give him 1/8th share in future profits on the following terms

(i) Goodwill of the firm be valued at four times the average of the last three years' profits which amounted to ₹ 21,000, ₹ 24,000 and ₹ 25,560.

(ii) Mukesh is to bring cash for the amount of his share of goodwill.

(iii) Mukesh is to bring cash ₹ 15,000 as his capital.

Pass journal entries recording these transactions.

9. Jai and Bhanu entered into partnership on 1st April, 2022, contributing ₹ 5,00,000 and ₹ 2,00,000 respectively. Bhanu also introduced ₹ 1,00,000 as additional capital on 1st July, 2022. They agreed to share profits and losses in the ratio of 3 : 2. Following information is provided regarding the partnership

(i) Jai and Bhanu, each are allowed a salary of ₹ 5,000 per quarter.

(ii) Interest is to be allowed on capitals @ 8% p.a. and charged on drawings at 10% p.a.

Drawings of Jai and Bhanu during the year were ₹ 12,000 and ₹ 10,000 respectively. Profit as at 31st March, 2023 before the above mentioned adjustments was ₹ 1,96,000.

(a) Pass journal entry for additional capital introduced by Bhanu. **[1]**

(b) Pass journal entry for drawings of the partner and interest on drawings. **[3]**

(c) Profit and loss appropriation account, and partner's capital accounts. **[6]**

Or

P and Q are partners sharing profits and losses in the ratio of 7 : 3. Their capital accounts as at 1st April, 2022 stood at P ₹ 2,50,000, Q ₹ 2,00,000. Partners are allowed interest on capital @ 5% p.a. Drawings of the partners during the year ended 31st March, 2023 were ₹ 36,000 and ₹ 25,000 respectively.

Profit for the year before allowing interest on capital and salary to Q @ 2,500 per month was ₹ 4,00,000. 10% of the net profit is to be set aside as general reserve.

(i) Prepare profit and loss appropriation account for the year ended 31st March, 2023. **[5.5]**

(ii) Prepare capital and current accounts of the partners. **[2.5]**

(iii) What amount will be transferred to general reserve? **[2]**

10. (A) Prabhas Ltd. had issued 25,000 equity shares at a premium of ₹ 3 per share having face value of ₹10 each, payable with application money.

Below given are following entries related to issue. But, these entries are incomplete, so you are required to complete these entries **[8.5]**

JOURNAL

Date	Particulars	LF	Amt (Dr)	Amt (Cr)
(i)	.... Dr		...	
	To			...
	(Being application money received for 35,000 shares @ ₹ 6 per share including premium)			
(ii)	Equity Share Application A/c Dr		...	
	To			...
	To			...
	To			...
	To			...
	(Being application money transferred, excess amount refunded for 5,000 shares being rejected and balance adjusted towards money due on allotment)			
(iii)	.... Dr		...	
	To			...
	(Being allotment money due @ ₹ 4 per share)			
(iv)	.... Dr		...	
	To			...
	(Being balance allotment amount received)			
(v)	.... Dr		...	
	To			...
	(Being first and final call money due)			
(vi)	.... Dr		...	
	Calls-in-Arrears A/c Dr		750	
	To			...
	(Being first and final call money received)			
(vii)	.... Dr		...	
	To			...
	To			...
	(Being the shares forfeited on which first and final call was not received)			

Date	Particulars		LF	Amt (Dr)	Amt (Cr)
(viii)	....	Dr		...	
	....	Dr		750	
	To				...
	(Being forfeited shares reissued)				
......	....	Dr		...	
	To				...
	(.................................. ....)				

(B) Gagan Ltd. forfeited 1,500 equity shares of ₹ 10 each for the non-payment of first call of ₹ 2 per share. The final call of ₹ 1 per share was not yet made. The forfeited shares were reissued for ₹ 21,000 fully paid-up.

Pass necessary journal entries in the books of the company for forfeiture and reissue of the shares. **[1.5]**

Or PNG Ltd. invited applications for issuing 25,000 equity shares of ₹ 20 each. The amount was payable as

On application – ₹ 6 per share

On allotment – ₹ 8 per share

On first and final call – ₹ 6 per share

Applications were received for 37,500 shares and pro-rata allotment was made as

Applicants for 20,000 shares were allotted 15,000 shares on pro-rata basis.

Applicants for 17,500 shares were allotted 10,000 shares on pro-rata basis.

Ramu, to whom 600 shares were allotted out of the group applying for 20,000 shares, failed to pay the allotment money.

His shares were forfeited immediately after allotment. Shamu, who had applied for 350 shares out of the group applying for 17,500 shares, failed to pay the first and final call. His shares were also forfeited. Out of the forfeited shares, 500 shares were reissued @ ₹ 16 per share as fully paid-up.

The reissued shares included all the forfeited shares of Shamu. Pass necessary journal entries to record the above transactions. **[10]**

Section B

(20 Marks)

(Answer all questions)

11. In subparts (i) and (ii) choose the correct options and in subparts (iii) to (v) answer the questions as instructed.

(i) Auto major Tata Motors, which hopes to deliver positive cash flows further, is targeting a net zero debt by FY25.

Source *Economic Times*

Assuming that the company's total assets to debt ratio is 3:1 before the above decision, what will be the impact of this decision on the total assets to debt ratio of the company if the company is paying the debt in order to become a zero net debt company? **[1]**

(a) Total assets to debt ratio will improve
(b) Total assets to debt ratio will reduce
(c) No impact on total assets to debt ratio
(d) Either (a) or (b)

(ii) Proposed dividend is ...... to the net profit in operating activities. **[1]**

(a) Added (b) Subtracted
(c) Either (a) or (b) depending upon the year
(d) None of the above

(iii) Why is a comparative income statement prepared? **[1]**

(iv) Give the formula for debtors turnover ratio. **[1]**

(v) State whether increase in prepaid insurance by ₹ 2,000 with increase, decrease or have no effect on cash flow statement. **[1]**

12. From the following income statement, prepare a common size income statement. **[3]**

Statement of Jayant Ltd.
for the year ended 31st March, 2021

Particulars	Amt (₹)
I. **Revenue from Operations** (Sales)	25,38,000
II. Other Income	38,000
III. Total Incomes (I + II)	25,76,000
IV. **Expenses**	
Cost of Goods Sold	14,00,000
Operating Expenses	5,00,000
Total Expenses	19,00,000

Particulars	Amt (₹)
V. **Profit before Tax** (III – IV)	6,76,000
VI. (–) Income Tax	3,38,000
VII. Profit after Tax	3,38,000

13. Following are the balance sheets of Sewak Ltd. as on 31st March, 2018 and 2019.

Particulars	Note No.	31st March, 2019 (₹)	31st March, 2018 (₹)
I. **EQUITY AND LIABILITIES**			
1. **Shareholders' Funds**			
Share Capital		7,00,000	4,00,000
Reserve and Surplus (Statement of profit and loss)		(3,20,000)	(50,000)
2. **Non-current Liabilities**			
Long-term Borrowings (9% debentures)		4,00,000	2,00,000
3. **Current Liabilities**			
Payables (Creditors)		1,50,000	1,10,000
Current Liabilities (Expenses)		20,000	10,000
Total		9,50,000	6,70,000
II. **ASSETS**			
1. **Non-current Assets**			
Property, Plant and Equipment and Intangible Assets		5,00,000	3,00,000
Non-current Investments		1,40,000	2,00,000
2. **Current Assets**			
Inventories (Stock)		1,00,000	50,000
Trade Receivables (Debtors)		1,70,000	1,00,000
Cash and Cash Equivalents		40,000	20,000
Total		9,50,000	6,70,000

Additional Information

In property, plant and equipment, a piece of machinery costing ₹ 70,000 on which depreciation charged @ ₹ 40,000 was included and it was sold for ₹ 30,000. During the year ₹ 1,40,000 as depreciation was charged on property, plant and equipment.

Prepare

(i) Cash flow from operating activities. **[2.5]**

(ii) Cash flow from investing and financing activities. **[2.5]**

(iii) Prepare machinery account. **[1]**

Or Following are the balance sheets of Black Box Ltd. as on 31st March, 2023 and 2022.

Particulars	Note No.	2023 (₹)	2022 (₹)
I. **EQUITY AND LIABILITIES**			
1. **Shareholders' Funds**			
(a) Share Capital		3,50,000	3,00,000
(b) Reserves and Surplus (Profit and Loss Balance)		1,00,000	55,000
2. **Non-current Liabilities**			
Long-term Borrowing		1,50,000	1,00,000
3. **Current Liabilities**			
Trade Payables		15,000	12,500
Total		6,15000	4,67,500
II. **ASSETS**			
1. **Non-current Assets**			
(a) Property, Plant and Equipment		5,50,000	4,00,000
2. **Current Assets**			
(a) Inventories		35,000	30,000
(b) Trade Receivables		16,000	20,000
(c) Cash and Cash Equivalents		14,000	17,500
Total		6,15,000	4,67,500

Adjustments

During the year a piece of machinery of the book value of ₹ 40,000 was sold for ₹ 32,500.

Depreciation provided on tangible assets during the year amounted to ₹ 1,00,000

Prepare a cash flow statement. **[6]**

14. Balance sheet of XYZ Ltd. as at 31st March, 2021 and 2022 are as follow

Particulars	2022 (₹)	2021 (₹)
I. **EQUITY AND LIABILITIES**		
1. **Shareholders' Funds**		
(a) Share Capital	1,00,000	1,00,000
(b) Reserve and Surplus	28,700	13,000
2. **Current Liabilities**		
(a) Short-term Borrowings	26,000	25,000
(b) Trade Payables	31,000	36,000
Total	1,85,700	1,74,000
II. **ASSETS**		
1. **Non-current Assets**		
Property, Plant and Equipment	1,12,000	1,08,000
2. **Current Assets**		
(a) Inventories	27,000	25,000
(b) Trade Receivables	45,000	40,000
(c) Cash and Cash Equivalents	1,000	450
(d) Other Current Assets	700	550
Total	1,85,700	1,74,000

Additional Information

Sales (Revenue from operations) amounted to ₹ 4,00,000 in 2021 and ₹ 5,00,000 in 2022.

You are required to calculate the following ratios

(i) Working capital turnover ratio **[2]**

(ii) Current ratio **[2]**

(iii) Quick ratio **[2]**

Answers

1. (i) (a) ₹ 4,40,000

(ii) (a) Debit Partner's Capital A/c and Credit Loan to Partner A/c

(iii) (d) I and III

(iv) (b) Called-up value of the share

(v) (d) Assertion (A) is false, but Reason (R) is true

(vii) ₹ 15,000

2. *Or* (i) Loss on Revaluation = ₹ 8,400

(ii) A's Loan A/c = ₹ 29,550

5. D's Goodwill = ₹10,667

7. Realisation Loss = ₹ 96,000

8. (a) 3 : 1 : 1

(b) Balance in Partner's Capital Account
Ram = ₹ 12,000, Shyam = ₹ 6,000,
Mohan = ₹ 4,500

9. (c) Profit transferred to Capital Accounts
Jai = ₹ 57,060, Bhanu = ₹ 38,040
Balance of Capital Accounts
Jai = ₹ 6,04,450, Bhanu = ₹ 3,69,540

Or (i) Divisible Profit = ₹ 3,07,500

10. (B) Capital Reserve = ₹ 10,500

Or Capital Reserve = ₹ 3,200

11. (i) (a) Total assets to debt ratio will improve

(ii) (a) added

13. (i) Cash Used in Operating Activities = ₹ (1,82,000)

(ii) Cash Used in Investing Activities = ₹ (2,80,000)
Cash flow from Financing Activities = ₹ 4,82,000

Or Operating Activity = ₹ 1,54,000
Investing Activity = ₹ (2,57,500)
Financing Activity = ₹ 1,00,000

14. (i) 2021 = 80 times; 2022 = 29.9 times

(ii) 2021 = 1.08 : 1; 2022 = 1.29 : 1

(iii) 2021 = 0.66 : 1; 2022 = 0.80 : 1

ISC

Latest ISC Specimen Paper

Time : 3 hrs
Marks : 80

Accounts XII

General Instructions

1. Candidates are allowed additional 15 minutes for only reading the paper. They must not start writing during this time.
2. Section-A is compulsory for all candidates.
3. Candidates have to attempt all questions from either Section-B or Section-C*.
4. There are internal choices provided in each section.
5. The intended marks for questions or parts of questions are given in the brackets [ ].
6. All calculations should be shown clearly.
7. All working, including rough work, should be done on the same page as and adjacent to, the rest of the answer.

* Section-C has not been covered.

Section A (60 Marks)

(Answer all questions)

1. In subparts (i) to (iv) choose the correct options and in subparts (v) to (x) answer the questions as instructed.

(i) The commission due to a partner is closed by **(Understanding) [1]**

(a) debiting it to partner's capital account
(b) crediting it to partner's capital account
(c) debiting it to profit and loss appropriation account
(d) crediting it to profit and loss appropriation account

(ii) On the admission of Adil as a partner, the capitals of Rohan and Pavan, after all adjustments were ₹ 50,000 and ₹ 40,000. Their capitals before Adil's admission were ₹ 45,000 and ₹ 48,000. The capital account of the partner having surplus capital was adjusted through his current account by passing the journal entry. **(Application) [1]**

(a) Debit Rohan's Capital A/c ₹ 5,000; Credit Rohan's Current A/c ₹ 5,000
(b) Debit Pavan's Capital A/c ₹ 8,000; Credit Pavan's Current A/c ₹ 8,000
(c) Debit Rohan's Current A/c ₹ 5,000; Credit Rohan's Capital A/c ₹ 5,000
(d) Debit Pavan's Current A/c ₹ 8,000; Credit Pavan's Capital A/c ₹ 8,000

(iii) Choose the components required to calculate goodwill of a firm by capitalisation of average profits method. **(Recall) [1]**

P – The normal profits of a similar firm in the industry.
Q – The average profits of the firm.
R – The number of years' purchase.
S – The actual capital employed in the business.

Codes

(a) P, Q, R (b) Q, R, S
(c) P, Q, S (d) P, R, S

(iv) Given below is a fictitious scenario. Read the information and answer the question that follows.
Bhim International Ltd. in order to raise additional funds for expansion purpose, took a loan of ₹ 10,00,000 at a rate of 12% per annum from NZ Bank on 1st July, 2023, against which it offered ₹ 15,00,000, 8% debentures of ₹ 100 each as a collateral security.
Calculate the finance cost to the company for the year 2023-24. **(Application) [1]**
(a) ₹ 1,20,000 (b) ₹ 2,40,000
(c) ₹ 90,000 (d) ₹ 1,80,000

(v) Ira (a partner in a firm) was allowed to retain the whole of the stock as her remuneration for services rendered by her in the course of dissolution of the firm. The value of stock was ₹ 10,000 which had been transferred to the realisation account. Complying with the accounting principle of full disclosure, record the above transaction in the books of the partnership firm at the time of its dissolution. **(Application) [1]**

(vi) Aman and Vinod are partners in a firm. Their balance sheet showed
Gross debtors ₹ 1,52,000
Provision for doubtful debts ₹ 1,000
On Milin's admission as a new partner, the assets and liabilities are to be revalued as
(a) Unaccounted accrued income of ₹ 10,000 to be provided for.
(b) Bills payable of ₹ 10,000 which were recorded, to be discharged at a rebate of 10%.
(c) Debtors of ₹ 2,000 to be irrecoverable.
(d) Provision for doubtful debts to be provided @ 2% of the debtors.
What is the net effect of revaluation of assets and liabilities? **(Application) [1]**

(vii) **Assertion** (A) A company can reissue a forfeited share at an amount which is less than the amount not received on it.
Reason (R) A company can write-off the net loss made on the reissue of a forfeited share from its capital reserve. **(Evaluate) [1]**
Alternatives
(a) Both Assertion (A) and Reason (R) are true and Reason (R) is the correct explanation of Assertion (A)
(b) Both Assertion (A) and Reason (R) are true, but Reason (R) is not the correct explanation of Assertion (A)
(c) Assertion (A) is false, but Reason (R) is true
(d) Both Assertion (A) and Reason (R) are false

(viii) Mention the liability of a partnership firm which is not shown in its balance sheet, but is paid-off at the time of the dissolution of the firm. **(Understanding) [1]**

(ix) The Adani family has raised their stake in Ambuja Cements by the conversion of 21.20 crore warrants into shares in a transaction that will see them infusing nearly ₹ 6,661 crore.
Source *The Telegraph, Kolkata, 29th March, 2024*
(a) What is a share warrant?
(b) Mention the head under which money received against share warrants is shown in the balance sheet of a company prepared as per Schedule III of the Companies Act, 2013. **(Recall) [1]**

(x) On 1st April, 2023, Zara Ltd. issued ₹ 10,000, 6% debentures of ₹ 100 each at a discount of 5%. On 31st March, 2024, the company had ₹ 40,000 in its capital reserve account and ₹ 30,000 as balance of securities premium.
Give the journal entry to write-off the discount on issue of debentures on 31st March, 2024. **(Application) [1]**

2. Mita, Sita and Rita are partners in a firm. Rita retires from the firm on 31st March, 2024.
Her claim, including her capital and her share of goodwill, is determined at ₹ 2,50,000.
On this date the firm's books showed
(i) An unrecorded investment valued at ₹ 60,000 which was given to an unrecorded creditor of ₹ 1,16,000 in settlement of his claim of ₹ 70,000.
(ii) An unrecorded vehicle which was given to Rita at the market value of ₹ 46,000 in part settlement of her claim. The balance of Rita's claim was discharged by cheque.
You are required to pass journal entries to record the above transactions in the books of the firm on 31st March, 2024. **(Application) [3]**

Or Akshat, Javed and Gaurav are partners in a firm sharing profits in the ratio of 5 : 3 : 7. Akshat died on 31st March, 2024.
Javed and Gaurav decided to share the profits in reconstituted firm in the ratio 2 : 3. The capital accounts of the partners on 31st March, 2024, before considering the firm's goodwill were
Akshat ₹ 1,66,000 Javed ₹ 66,000
Gaurav ₹ 1,41,000
After considering the adjustment for goodwill, Akshat's share was determined to be ₹ 1,81,000.

It was decided that this amount would be paid to Akshat's executor immediately by the firm through a cheque, the amount being contributed by Javed and Gaurav in such a manner that their capitals would become proportionate to their new profit sharing ratio.

You are required to pass journal entries to record

(i) The adjustment for self-generated goodwill of the firm.

(ii) Cash brought in by Javed and Gaurav to pay-off Akshat's executor.

(iii) Payment made to Akshat's executor. **(Application)**

3. On 1st April, 2023, Ruth Ltd. purchased plant and machinery for ₹ 11,00,000 from Pablo Ltd. payable as to ₹ 1,00,000 by accepting a promissory note and the balance by an issue of 11% debentures of ₹ 100 each at a premium of 10% to be redeemed at a premium of 2% after six years.

You are required to pass journal entries in the books of Ruth Ltd. only to record the payment made to Pablo Ltd. **(Application) [3]**

Or A limited company made an issue, which was fully subscribed of 2,000, 5% debentures of ₹ 100 each at ₹ 96, to be redeemed at par after five years. The debentures were allotted on 31st May, 2023, subscriptions being payable

15% on application

30% on allotment

30% on 30th June, 2023

Balance on 30th September, 2023

One debentureholder holding 100 debentures paid the allotment with the first call along with interest on calls-in-arrears @ 10% per annum.

You are required to

(i) Give the amounts in rupees payable with

(a) Allotment

(b) Second and final call **[2]**

(ii) Prepare the interest on calls-in-arrears account **(Application) [1]**

4. Ronny Ltd. (an unlisted construction company) redeems its 7,000, 10% debentures of ₹ 100 each at a premium of 5% in instalments, as follows

Date of Redemption	Debentures to be Redeemed
31st March, 2022	2,000
31st March, 2023	3,000
31st March, 2024	2,000

You are required to prepare for the year 2023-24

(i) General reserve account

(ii) Debentureholders' account (Ignore interest on debentures) **(Application) [3]**

5. Kriti and Atif are partners sharing profits and losses equally. On 31st March, 2024, they admitted David as a third partner for 1/5 share in the profits.

It is decided that on David's admission

- Atif would retain his original share.
- Goodwill would be valued by the super profit method on the basis of the following information

(i) **Balance Sheet of Kriti and Atif** (An extract) as at 31st March, 2024

Liabilities		Amt (₹)	Assets	Amt (₹)
General Reserve		25,000	Current A/c	
Capital A/cs			Atif	10,000
Kriti	2,50,000			
Atif	1,75,000	4,25,000		
Current A/c				
Kriti		40,000		

(ii) The normal rate of return is 12% per annum.

(iii) Average profits of the firm for last four years are ₹ 74,000.

You are required to calculate

(a) The sacrificing ratio of the partners.

(b) The value of goodwill of the firm at four years' purchase of the super profit. **(Application) [3]**

6. The following balances have been extracted from the books of Nirvana Ltd. as at 31st March, 2024

Particulars	Amt (₹)	Particulars	Amt (₹)
Security Deposit for Electricity for Ten Years	30,000	Uncalled Amount on Partly Paid-up Shares	8,00,000
Underwriting Commission	20,000	10% Debentures	5,00,000
General Reserve	70,000	Statement of Profit and Loss (Dr)	10,000
Fixed Deposits	2,00,000	Calls-in-arrears @ ₹ 1 per Share	40,000
Premium on Redemption of Debentures	20,000	Securities Premium	2,00,000
Equity Share Capital (1,00,000 shares of ₹ 10 each)	10,00,000		

You are required to show the above items in notes to accounts accompanying the balance sheet of Nirvana Ltd. prepared as per Schedule III of the Companies Act, 2013 as at 31st March, 2024. **(Application) [6]**

7. **Anita and Anil are partners in a firm. On 1st April, 2024, they admitted Jia as a third partner. The capital accounts of the partners after considering the following adjustments on Jia's admission are given below**

(i) Loss on revaluation due to depreciation on machinery @ 20% per annum.

(ii) The general reserve maintained in the old firm was not to be disturbed in the reconstituted firm.

Partners' Capital Account

Dr | | | | | | | | Cr

Particulars	Anita (₹)	Anil (₹)	Jia (₹)	Particulars	Anita (₹)	Anil (₹)	Jia (₹)
To Goodwill A/c	10,000	10,000	—	By Balance b/d	90,000	80,000	—
To Profit and Loss A/c	5,000	5,000	—	By Bank A/c	—	—	75,000
To Revaluation A/c	7,500	7,500	—	By Premium for Goodwill A/c	25,000	25,000	—
To Balance c/d	1,17,500	1,07,500	75,000	By Jia's Current A/c	25,000	25,000	—
	1,40,000	1,30,000	75,000		1,40,000	1,30,000	75,000

Additional Information

On 31st March, 2024, the firm of Anita and Anil, apart from plant and machinery and a bank balance of ₹ 15,000, had no other asset.

You are required to prepare the balance sheet of the reconstituted firm on the date of Jia's admission after considering the information given above. (Show your workings clearly) **(Application) [6]**

Or **Alfa and Beta are partners in a firm. Their balance sheet as at 31st March, 2024, is given below**

Balance Sheet of Alfa and Beta
as at 31st March, 2024

Liabilities		Amt (₹)	Assets	Amt (₹)
Sundry Creditors		1,16,000	Cash at Bank	93,600
Workmen's Compensation Reserve		24,000	Sundry Debtors	76,400
Capital A/cs			Stock	1,10,000
Alfa	1,00,000		Investment	20,000
Beta	80,000	1,80,000	Goodwill	20,000
		3,20,000		3,20,000

On 1st April, 2024, they admit Beta's son Gama, as a partner on the following terms

(i) Gama to have 1/4 share of profits, half of which is to be gifted to him by his father and the remaining half to be purchased from Alfa.

(ii) Gama to bring in ₹ 60,000 as his capital but would be unable to bring in cash his share of goodwill.

(iii) Goodwill of the firm to be valued at ₹ 40,000.

(iv) 50% of the investment to be taken over by Alfa and Beta in their profit sharing ratio.

(v) The liability on account of workmen's compensation claim to be ₹ 30,000.

You are required to

(a) Calculate the new profit sharing ratio of all the partners. **[1]**

(b) Prepare the partners' capital account. **(Application) [5]**

8. **Atul and Peter were partners in a firm sharing profits and losses in the ratio of 3 : 5. They dissolved their firm on 31st March, 2024, when their balance sheet showed the following balances.**

Particulars	Amt (₹)
Atul's Capital	40,000
Peter's Capital	35,000
Atul's Current Account	3,000 (Dr)
General Reserve	22,000
Loan from Atul	12,000

On the date of dissolution of the firm

(i) Peter paid the realisation expenses of ₹ 2,000 on behalf of the firm.

(ii) Atul discharged his wife's loan of ₹ 5,000 which she had given to the firm.

(iii) The dissolution resulted in a profit of ₹ 24,000 from the realisation of assets and settlement of liabilities.

You are required to pass journal entries to close the books of the firm (including the entries to show the final settlement of the amount due from the partners/ due to the partners by the firm). **(Application) [6]**

9. (i) Deb, Riza and Ved entered into a partnership on 1st July, 2023, without any agreement as to profit sharing, except that Deb guaranteed that Ved's share of profit, after considering interest into account, would not be less than ₹ 8,500 per annum.

The initial capital provided by the partners was as follows

Deb ₹ 60,000

Riza ₹ 20,000

Ved ₹ 12,000 (increased on the following 1st January, 2024, to ₹ 16,000)

In addition to the above capital, Deb and Riza gave temporary loans to the partnership firm as follows

- Deb advanced ₹ 18,000 on 1st October, 2023 and was repaid on 1st April following.
- Riza advanced ₹ 40,000 on 1st September, 2023 and was repaid along with interest, on 1st December, 2023.

The profit of the firm for the year ended 31st March, 2024, before providing for any interest was ₹ 21,000.

You are required to prepare for the year 2023-24

(a) Profit and loss appropriation account **[4½]**

(b) Riza's loan account **[1½]**

(c) Ved's capital account **(Application) [2]**

(ii) Krish and Tarun are partners in a firm with capitals of ₹ 40,000 and ₹ 60,000. As per their partnership deed

(a) Interest on capital is to be allowed to them @ 5% per annum.

(b) Profits are to be shared in the ratio of 3 : 2.

The trading profits for the year 2023-24 was ₹ 3,600.

You are required to calculate the interest on capital allowed to the partners in the year 2023-24. **(Application) [2]**

Or Deepa, Ridhi and Adit are partners in a firm. Following are the particulars of their capital and drawings accounts for the year 2023-24

Particulars	Deepa (₹)	Ridhi (₹)	Adit (₹)
Capital as on 1st April, 2023	1,00,000	80,000	20,000 (Dr)
Drawings (in two instalments of ₹ 7,500 each made at the end of every half year)	—	15,000	—
Interest free Loan from the Firm	—	—	5,000

According to their partnership deed

- Profits were to be shared in the ratio of 2 : 2 : 1.
- Interest on capital to be allowed @ 5% per annum.
- Interest on drawings to be charged @ 8% per annum.

The trading profits of the firm for the financial year 2023-24 were ₹ 50,000, before considering the discrepancy of having recorded the inventory at ₹ 10,000 when its realisable value was ₹ 4,000.

(i) You are required to give

(a) The adjusting entry and closing entry for drawings made by Ridhi. **(Recall) [2]**

(b) The adjusting entry and closing entry for interest on drawings. **(Application) [2]**

(c) The adjusting entry and closing entry for interest on capital. **(Application) [2]**

(d) The entry to close the Adit's loan account. **(Application) [2]**

(ii) The accountant of the firm distributed the divisible profit among the partners in the ratio 2:1:2 instead of in the ratio mentioned in the deed.

You are required to rectify the lapse in accounting by passing a single adjusting entry. **(Application) [2]**

10. Hero Ltd. was registered with a capital of ₹ 5,00,000 divided into 20,000 shares of ₹ 25 each, payable as

On Application	₹ 5 per share
On Allotment	₹ 10 per share
On Call	₹ The balance

The company offered to the public for subscription 10,000 shares. It received applications for 11,100 shares.

From amongst the applicants

(i) Vimal, who had applied for 1,200 shares, paid ₹ 6,000 on application, but was allotted only 600 shares.

(ii) Mohan applied for 1,000 shares, paid the full amount of ₹ 25,000 with his application but was allotted only 500 shares.

(iii) Vineet, who had applied for 1,500 shares, paid his application and allotment money in order but did not pay the call money.

(iv) The remaining applicants paid as and when due.

The surplus money paid by both Vimal and Mohan was used towards allotment and call and any surplus beyond the call was refunded. The company forfeited Vineet's shares and later re-issued 500 of the forfeited shares @ ₹ 20 per share fully paid-up.

You are required to pass journal entries in the books of Hero Ltd. **(Application) [10]**

Or Stem Ltd. came up with an IPO inviting the public to subscribe to its equity shares of ₹ 10 each. The issue was oversubscribed. The company allotted 80,000 shares to all the applicants making a pro-rata allotment in the ratio of 3 : 2.

The face value of the share was payable in three installments.

Based on the information given above and the following extract of ledger accounts and cash book (bank column), answer the questions that follow

Dr **Cash Book** (Bank column) (Extract) Cr

Particulars	Amt (₹)	Particulars	Amt (₹)
To Share Application A/c	4,80,000	By Balance c/d	......
To Share Allotment A/c	......		

Dr **Share Capital Account** (Extract) Cr

Particulars	Amt (₹)	Particulars	Amt (₹)
To Share Forfeiture A/c		By Share Allotment A/c	......
To Calls-in-arrears A/c	......	By Share Allotment A/c	4,00,000
		By Share Final Call A/c	......

Dr **Calls-in-Arrears Account** (Extract) Cr

Particulars	Amt (₹)	Particulars	Amt (₹)
To Share Allotment A/c	6,000		

(i) What are the number of shares applied for by the public? **[1]**

(ii) What is the amount payable per share with application? **[1]**

(iii) What is the amount payable per share with first and final call? **[1]**

(iv) Stem Ltd. did not receive the allotment money and call money due from the shareholder Rehan, who had applied for 3,000 shares.

What is the amount received by Stem Ltd. with allotment? **[2]**

(v) Stem Ltd. forfeited Rehan's shares after the final call. It re-issued 1,500 forfeited shares fully called-up @ ₹ 13 per share.

Give the journal entries passed by the company for

(a) Forfeiture of these shares. **[2]**

(b) Re-issue of the forfeited shares.

(Application) [3]

Section B **(20 Marks)**

11. In subparts (i) and (ii) choose the correct options and in subparts (iii) to (v) answer the questions as instructed.

(i) According to the ratings agency Chrisil, healthy demand for grocery items and expansion into tier II and III cities will help organised brick-and-mortar Food and Grocery (F&G) retailers log a revenue of 14-15% in FY25. The agency further said the debt raising will be capped to ensure healthy key debt protection metrics.

Source *(Edited) Financial Express, 23rd December, 2023*

From the following ratios

- Choose the formula of the ratio to be used by the F&G retailers as a debt protection metrics. **(Analysis)**

(a) $\dfrac{\text{Revenue Operations}}{\text{Working Capital}}$

(b) $\dfrac{\text{Cost of Revenue from Operations + Operating Expenses}}{\text{Revenue from Operations}} \times 100$

(c) $\dfrac{\text{Net Profit before Interest and Taxes}}{\text{Fixed Interest Charges}}$

(d) $\dfrac{\text{Net Profit after Tax and Preference Dividend}}{\text{Number of Equity Shares}}$

- Mention the name of the ratio so chosen. **(Recall) [1]**

(ii) Read the following news item of ITC Ltd. and answer the question that follows

The company's board declared an interim dividend of ₹ 6.25 per share for the financial year ending March, 2024.

The dividend will be paid between 26-28th February, 2024, to the eligible shareholders.

Source *The Hindu, Financial Express, 30th January, 2024*

Which of the following are the attributes of interim dividend? **(Understanding) [1]**

P – It is a charge against profits.

Q – It is an appropriation of profits.

R – Its declaration and payment will decrease the company's current ratio.

S – Its declaration and payment will increase the company's debt equity ratio.

Codes

(a) Only P

(b) Only Q

(c) P, R and S

(d) Q, R and S

(iii) Bajaj Hindustan Sugar, one of the largest sugar and ethanol producers, in order to revive the company, has offered to invest ₹ 2,500 crore as fresh equity of which ₹ 1,000 crore has already been infused.

Source *(Edited) Economic Times, Mumbai Edition 8th August, 2023*

What will be the effect of this decision of Bajaj Hindustan Sugar on its debt equity ratio? **(Analysis) [1]**

(iv) Jubilant Food Works Ltd. the company that operates Domino's restaurants in India, reported a net profit of ₹ 65.7 crore for the three months ending, 31st December, 2023, against ₹ 80 crore for the three months ending, 31st December, 2022.

Source *(Edited) Mint, 1st February, 2024*

You are required to give, for the three months ending, 31st December, 2023, as compared to the same period ending, 31st December, 2022

(a) The formula to calculate the percentage change in net profit of the company.

(b) The percentage change in the net profit of Jubilant Food Works Ltd. of the three months ending 31st December, 2023 *vis-a-vis* the three months ending, 31st December, 2022, mentioning the increase/decrease. **(Analysis) [1]**

(v) Read the news item given below and answer the questions which follow

Tata Consultancy Services ₹ 17,000 crore share buy-back programme will open on 1st December and close on 7th December, India's largest software exporter said on Tuesday.

"The company believes that the buy-back is not likely to cause any material impact on the profitability or earnings of the company except to the extent of reduction in the amount available for investment, which the company could have otherwise deployed towards generating investment income", TCS said in a regulatory filing.

Source *Economic Times, 29th December, 2023*

How would the cash flow from investing activities of TCS be affected, if instead of buying-back its shares, the company had proceeded with its investing programme? **(Application) [1]**

12. From the following information, you are required to prepare a common size balance sheet of Super Ltd. as at 31st March, 2024. **(Application) [3]**

Particulars	Amt
Non-current Liabilities	₹ 2,00,000
Shareholders' Funds	2.5 times more than the non-current liabilities
Current Liabilities	₹ 1,00,000
Current Assets	₹ 3,00,000
Non-current Assets	70% of the equity and liabilities

13. Anand Ltd. reported a loss of ₹ 80,000 for the year ended 31st March, 2024, after considering the depreciation charged on plant and machinery represented by '??' and the following items.

S. No.	Particulars	Amt (₹)
(a)	Tax Provided During the Year	84,000
(b)	Loss on Sale of Plant and Machinery	15,000
(c)	Interest on Short-term Loans and Advances	2,000
(d)	Depreciation on Plant and Machinery	??

Additional Information

1. During the year 2023-24

   A machine having a book value ₹ 40,000, was disposed-off for ₹ 25,000 and a machine costing ₹ 2,20,000 was purchased.

   Credit sales were ₹ 1,00,000.

2. An extract of the balance sheet of the company as at 31st March, 2023, and as at 31st March, 2024

Particulars	31st March, 2024 (₹)	31st March, 2023 (₹)
Trade Receivables	20,000	15,000
Cash at Bank	8,000	10,000
Short-term Loans and Advances	49,000	11,000
Trade Payables	5,000	2,000
Plant and Machinery (At net value)	6,00,000	4,90,000
Provision for Depreciation	1,50,000	1,10,000

(i) You are required to calculate for the year 2023-24. (Show the workings clearly)

(a) The net operating profit of the company before working capital changes. [2]

(b) Cash from investing activity. [2]

(ii) Taking the information of credit sales into consideration, state with reason, whether the increase in trade receivables in the year 2023-24 over the year 2022-23 will cause the cash from operating activities before tax paid to be more or less then the net operating profit of the company before its working capital changes. **(Evaluate) [2]**

Or From the following balance sheets of Ronald Ltd. You are required to prepare a cash flow statement (as per AS-3) for the year 2023-24.

Balance Sheets of Ronald Ltd.
as at 31st March, 2024 and 31st March, 2023

Particulars	Note No.	31st March, 20024 (₹)	31st March, 2023 (₹)
I. EQUITY AND LIABILITIES			
1. **Shareholders' Funds**			
(i) Share Capital		6,00,000	6,00,000
(ii) Reserves and Surplus (Statement of profit and loss)		80,000	(60,000)
2. **Non-current Liabilities**			
Long-term Borrowings		1,00,000	1,50,000
3. **Current Liabilities**			
(i) Short-term Borrowings (Bank overdraft)		1,75,000	22,000
(ii) Short-term Provisions (Provision for tax)		15,000	28,000
Total		9,70,000	7,40,000
II. ASSETS			
1. **Non-current Assets**			
Property, Plant and Equipment and Intangible Assets			
(i) Property, Plant and Equipment (Plant and machinery)		5,50,000	6,40,000
(ii) Non-current Investments (7% debentures of Violet Ltd.)		1,40,000	50,000
2. **Current Assets**			
Cash and Bank Balance (Bank)		2,80,000	50,000
Total		9,70,000	7,40,000

Additional Information

(i) The debentures of Violet Ltd. were purchased on 31st March, 2024.

(ii) During the year 2023-24

(a) Tax of ₹ 20,000 was paid. (b) Interest on all borrowings due and paid was ₹ 25,000. **(Application) [6]**

14. Answer any three of the following questions. **(Application) [6]**

(i) Calculate interest coverage ratio of Criss Cross Ltd. (upto two decimal places) from the following information.

Particulars	Amt (₹)
Net Profit after Interest and Tax	80,000
Tax Rate	50 %
12% Debentures	3,00,000
9% Bank Loan	1,00,000

(ii) Calculate the operating ratio of Zen Ltd. (upto two decimal places) from the following information.

Revenue from Operations – ₹ 9,00,000; Gross Profit – 20 % of cost

Operating Expenses – ₹ 60,000

(iii) A company had current assets of ₹ 3,00,000 and current liabilities of ₹ 1,50,000, having a current ratio of 2 : 1. What will be its revised current ratio after it endorses a bills receivable of ₹ 40,000 to one of its creditors?

(iv) From the following particulars of NB Ltd., calculate its cost of revenue from operations for the year 2023-24.

Current Assets – ₹ 6,80,000 ; Current Liabilities – ₹ 3,40,000

Quick Ratio – 1·5 : 1; Inventory Turnover Ratio – 4 times

Answers

1. (i) (c) debiting it to profit and loss appropriation account

(ii) (b) Debit Pavan's Capital A/c account ₹ 8,000; Credit Pavan's Current A/c ₹ 8,000

(iii) (c) P, Q, S

(iv) (c) $10,00,000 \times 12\% \times 9/12 =$ ₹ 90,000

(v)

Ira's Capital A/c	Dr	10,000	
To Realisation A/c			10,000
Realisation A/c	Dr	10,000	
To Ira's Capital A/c			10,000

(vi) Net gain of ₹ 7,000

Working Note

Dr **Revaluation Account** Cr

Particulars	Amt (₹)	Particulars	Amt (₹)
To Provision of Doubtful Debts	4,000	By Unrecorded Income	10,000
To Gain on Revaluation	7,000	By Discount on Bills Payable	1,000
	11,000		11,000

(vii) (d) Both Assertion (A) and Reason (R) are false

(viii) Unrecorded liability *or* contingent liability which becomes a definite liability

(ix) (a) A share warrant is a financial instrument which gives the holder the right to acquire equity shares specified therein at a specified date at a pre-determined price.

(b) Shareholder's funds.

(x)

Securities Premium A/c	Dr	30,000	
Statement of profit and loss	Dr	20,000	
To Discount on Issue of Debentures A/c			50,000

2. **JOURNAL**

Date	Particulars		LF	Amt (Dr)	Amt (Cr)
	Revaluation A/c	Dr		46,000	
	To Creditors A/c				46,000
	(Being creditors revalued and settled)				
	Vehicle A/c	Dr		46,000	
	To Revaluation A/c				46,000
	(Being vehicle revalued)				
	Rita's Capital A/c	Dr		2,50,000	
	To Vehicle A/c				46,000
	To Bank A/c				2,04,000
	(Being Rita's claim settled)				

Or

JOURNAL

Date	Particulars		LF	Amt (Dr)	Amt (Cr)
	Javed's Capital A/c	Dr		9,000	
	Gaurav's Capital A/c	Dr		6,000	
	To Akshat's Capital A/c				15,000
	(Being Akshat compensated for his share of goodwill)				
	Bank A/c	Dr		1,81,000	
	To Javed's Capital A/c	Dr			89,200
	To Gaurav's Capital A/c	Dr			91,800
	(Being cash brought in by Javad and Gaurav to pay-off Akshat's executor)				

Date	Particulars		LF	Amt (Dr)	Amt (Cr)
	Akshat's Executor's A/c	Dr		1,81,000	
	To Bank A/c				1,81,000
	(Being Akshat's executor paid-off)				

3. **In the Books of Ruth Ltd.**

JOURNAL

Date	Particulars		LF	Amt (Dr)	Amt (Cr)
	Pablo Ltd. A/c	Dr		1,00,000	
	To Bills Payable A/c				1,00,000
	(Being part payment made by accepting a bill of exchange)				
	Pablo Ltd. A/c	Dr		10,00,000	
	Loss on Issue of Debentures A/c	Dr		18,180	
	To 11% Debentures A/c				9,09,000
	To Securities Premium A/c				90,900
	To Premium on Redemption of Debentures A/c				18,180
	To Bank A/c				100
	(Being 9,090, 11% debentures issued at a premium of 10%)				

Working Notes

Number of Debentures $= \frac{10,00,000}{110} = 9,090$ Debentures

Or (i) (a) ₹ 30

(b) ₹ 21 (100 − 4 − 15 − 30 − 30)

(ii) Dr **Interest on Calls-in-arrears Account** Cr

Date	Particulars	Amt (₹)	Date	Particulars	Amt (₹)
2024 Mar 31	To Statement of Profit and Loss	25	2023 Jun 31	By Debentureholders' A/c	25
		25			25

Working Note

Amount to be paid by holder of 100 debentures on allotment (100 × 30) = 3,000

Interest on calls-in-arrears $= 3,000 \times \frac{10}{100} \times \frac{1}{12} =$ ₹ 25

4. Dr **General Reserve Account** Cr

Date	Particulars	Amt (₹)	Date	Particulars	Amt (₹)
2024 Mar 31	To Balance c/d	70,000	2024 Apr 1	By Balance b/d	50,000
			2024 Mar 31	By DRR	20,000
		70,000			70,000

Dr **Debentureholders' Account** Cr

Date	Particulars	Amt (₹)	Date	Particulars	Amt (₹)
2024 Mar 31	To Bank A/c	2,20,000	2024 Mar 31	By 10% Debentures A/c	2,00,000
				To Premium on Redemption of Debentures A/c	20,000
		2,20,000			2,20,000

5. (a) Sacrificing Ratio = $\frac{1}{5}$: 0

(b) Normal Profit = Capital Employed × $\frac{\text{Normal Rate of Return}}{100}$ = 4,80,000* × $\frac{12}{100}$ = ₹ 57,600

*Capital employed = ₹ 4,80,000

Now, Super Profit = Average Profit – Normal Profit

= 74,000 – 57,600 = ₹ 16,400

Goodwill = 16,400 × 4 = ₹ 65,600

6. **Notes to Accounts**

	Particulars		Amt (₹)
1.	**Share Capital**		
	Authorised Capital		
	.... Equity Shares @ ₹ 10 each		(—)
	Issued Capital		
	.... Equity Shares @ ₹ 10 each		(—)
	Subscribed Capital		
	Subscribed and Fully Paid		
	60,000 Equity Shares @₹10 each		6,00,000
	Subscribed, but not Fully Paid		
	40,000 Equity Shares @₹10 each	4,00,000	
	(–) Calls-in-Arrears	(40,000)	3,60,000
			9,60,000
2.	**Reserves and Surplus**		
	Securities Premium	2,00,000	
	(–) Underwriting Commission	(20,000)	
	General Reserve	70,000	
	Statement fo Profit and Loss (Dr)	(10,000)	2,40,000
3.	**Long-term Borrowings**		
	10% Debentures	5,00,000	
	Premium on Redemption of Debentures	20,000	
	Fixed Deposits	2,00,000	7,20,000
4.	**Long-term Loans and Advances**		
	Security Deposit for Electricity for Ten Years		30,000
5.	**Contingent Liabilities and Capital Commitments**		
	Capital Commitments		
	Uncalled Amount on Partly Paid-up Shares		8,00,000

7. **Balance Sheet of Anita, Anil and Jia**
as at 1st April, 2024

Liabilities		Amt (₹)	Assets	Amt (₹)
Capital A/cs			Cash at Bank	3,40,000
Anita	1,17,500		Plant and Machinery	60,000
Anil	1,07,500		Jia's Current A/c	50,000
Jia	75,000	3,00,000		
General Reserve		1,50,000		
		4,50,000		4,50,000

Working Notes

Value of Machinery = $15{,}000 \times \frac{100}{20}$ = ₹ 75,000

Amount of General Reserve = 50,000 × 3 = ₹1,50,000

Or (a) New Ratio = 7 : 7 : 2

Working Note

Gifted by Beta $= \frac{1}{2}$ of $\frac{1}{4} = \frac{1}{8}$ Purchased from Alfa $= \frac{1}{8}$

New Ratio Alfa $= 1 - \frac{1}{8} = \frac{7}{8}$; Beta $= 1 - \frac{1}{8} = \frac{7}{8}$; Gama $= \frac{1}{4}$

New Ratio = 7 : 7 : 2

(b) Dr **Partners' Capital Account** Cr

Particulars	Alpha (₹)	Beta (₹)	Gama (₹)	Particulars	Alpha (₹)	Beta (₹)	Gama (₹)
To Goodwill	10,000	10,000		By Balance b/d	1,00,000	80,000	
To Investment	5,000	5,000		By Cash/Bank	—	—	60,000
To Revaluation	3,000	3,000		By Gama's Current A/c	5,000	—	—
To Balance c/d	87,000	62,000	60,000				
	1,05,000	80,000	60,000		1,05,000	80,000	60,000

Working Note

Sacrificing Ratio $= 0 : \frac{1}{8}$

Gama's Share of Goodwill $= \frac{1}{8}$ of 40,000 = ₹ 5,000

8. **JOURNAL**

Date	Particulars		LF	Amt (Dr)	Amt (Cr)
	Atul's Capital A/c	Dr		3,000	
	To Atul's Current A/c				3,000
	(Being Atul's current account closed)				
	Atul's Loan A/c	Dr		12,000	
	To Bank A/c				12,000
	(Being workmen compensation claim met out of the reserve)				
	General Reserve A/c	Dr		22,000	
	To Atul's Capital A/c				8,250
	To Peter's Capital A/c				13,750
	(Being balance of general reserve transferred to partners' capital account)				
	Realisation A/c	Dr		2,000	
	To Peter's Capital A/c				2,000
	(Being realisation expenses paid by Peter)				
	Realisation A/c	Dr		5,000	
	To Atul's Capital A/c				5,000
	(Being Atul's wife's loan discharged by Atul)				
	Realisation A/c	Dr		24,000	
	To Atul's Capital A/c				9,000
	To Peter's Capital A/c				15,000
	(Being profit on realisation transferred to partners' capital account)				
	Atul's Capital A/c	Dr		59,250	
	Peter's Capital A/c	Dr		65,750	
	To Bank A/c				1,25,000
	(Being partner's capital account settled)				

9. (i) (a)

Profit and Loss Appropriation Account
for ending 31st March, 2024

Dr | | | | | | Cr

Particulars		Amt (₹)	Particulars		Amt (₹)
To Deb's Capital A/c	6,620		By Profit and Loss A/c		21,000
	(1,880)	4,740	(–) Interest on Loan		
To Riza's Capital A/c		6,620	Deb	540	
To Ved's Capital A/c	6,620		Riza	600	(1,140)
	1,880	8,500			
		19,860			19,860

Working Notes

Interest on Loan

$\text{Deb} = 18{,}000 \times \frac{6}{100} \times \frac{6}{12} = ₹\ 540$ $\qquad$ $\text{Riza} = 40{,}000 \times \frac{6}{100} \times \frac{3}{12} = ₹\ 600$

(b)

Riza's Loan Account

Dr | | | | | Cr

Date	Particulars	Amt (₹)	Date	Particulars	Amt (₹)
2023			2023		
Dec 1	To Bank	40,600	Sep 1	By Bank A/c	40,000
			Dec 1	By Interest on Loan	600
		40,600			40,600

(c)

Ved's Capital Account

Dr | | | | | Cr

Date	Particulars	Amt (₹)	Date	Particulars	Amt (₹)
2023			2023		
Mar 31	To Balance c/d	24,500	Jul 1	By Bank A/c	12,000
			Apr 1	By Bank A/c	4,000
			Mar 31	By Profit and Loss Appropriation A/c	6,620
				By Deb's Capital	1,880
		24,500			24,500

(ii) Interest on Capital

$\text{Krish} = 40{,}000 \times 5\% = ₹\ 2{,}000$ $\qquad$ $\text{Tarun} = 60{,}000 \times 5\% = ₹\ 3{,}000$

Since, total profit is less than interest on capital, therefore profit will be distributed in the ratio of interest on capital.

∴ Interest on Capital (Available profit only)

$\text{Krish} = 3{,}600 \times \frac{2}{5} = ₹\ 1{,}440;$ $\qquad$ $\text{Tarun} = 3{,}600 \times \frac{3}{5} = ₹\ 2{,}160$

Or (i) (a)

JOURNAL

Date	Particulars		LF	Amt (Dr)	Amt (Cr)
2023					
Sep 30	Ridhi's Capital A/c	Dr		7,500	
	To Cash/ Bank A/c				7,500
	(Being drawings made by Ridhi)				
2024					
Mar 31	Ridhi's Capital A/c	Dr		7,500	
	To Cash/ Bank A/c				7,500
	(Being drawings made by Ridhi)				
2024					
Mar 31	Ridhi's Capital A/c	Dr		15,000	
	To Ridhi's Drawing A/c				15,000
	(Being drawings account closed by transferring to capital account)				

(b) **JOURNAL**

Date	Particulars	LF	Amt (Dr)	Amt (Cr)
2024 Mar 31	Ridhi' Capital A/c Dr		300	
	To Interest on Drawings A/c			300
	(Being interest on drawings charged)			
2024 Mar 31	Interest on Drawings A/c Dr		300	
	To Profit and Loss Appropriation A/c			300
	(Being interest on drawings account closed)			

(c) **JOURNAL**

Date	Particulars	LF	Amt (Dr)	Amt (Cr)
2024 Mar 31	Interest on Capital A/c Dr		9,000	
	To Deepa's Capital A/c			5,000
	To Rishi's Capital A/c			4,000
	(Being interest on capital allowed)			
2024 Mar 31	Profit and Loss Appropriation A/c Dr		9,000	
	To Interest on Capital A/c			9,000
	(Being interest on capital account closed)			

(d) **JOURNAL**

Date	Particulars	LF	Amt (Dr)	Amt (Cr)
2024 Mar 31	Adit's Capital A/c Dr		5,000	
	To Loan to Adit A/c			5,000
	(Being Adit's loan account closed)			

(ii) **Adjusting Journal Entry**

Date	Particulars	LF	Amt (Dr)	Amt (Cr)
2024 Mar 31	Adit's Capital A/c Dr		7,060	
	To Ridhi's Capital A/c			7,060
	(Being error of profits distributed in incorrect ratio rectified)			

Working Notes

Table Showing Adjustments

Partners	Amount which has been credited in the ratio 2 :1 : 2 44,000 + 300 – 9,000 = 35,300	Amount which should have been credited in the ratio 2: 2 :1 44,000 + 300 – 9,000 = 35,300	Difference (Dr or Cr)
Deepa	14,120	14,120	—
Ridhi	7,060	14,120	7,060 (Cr)
Adit	14,120	7,060	7,060 (Dr)

10. **In the Books of Hero Ltd.**

JOURNAL

Date	Particulars	LF	Amt (Dr)	Amt (Cr)
	Bank A/c Dr		75, 500	
	To Share Application A/c			75, 500
	(Being share application received)			

Date	Particulars		LF	Amt (Dr)	Amt (Cr)
	Share Application A/c	Dr		75,500	
	To Share Capital A/c				50,000
	To Share Allotment A/c				8,000
	To Calls-in-advance A/c				5,000
	To Bank A/c				12,500
	(Being share application transferred to share capital and subsequent installments)				
	Share Allotment A/c	Dr		1,00,000	
	To Share Capital A/c				1,00,000
	(Being share allotment due)				
	Bank A/c	Dr		92,000	
	To Share Allotment A/c				92,000
	(Being share allotment received)				
	Share First and Final Call A/c	Dr		1,00,000	
	To Share Capital A/c				1,00,000
	(Being share capital due)				
	Bank A/c	Dr		80,000	
	Calls-in-advance A/c	Dr		5,000	
	Calls-in-arrear A/c	Dr		15,000	
	To Share First and Final Call A/c				1,00,000
	(Being share final call received)				
	Share Capital A/c	Dr		37,500	
	To Share Forfeiture A/c				22,500
	To Calls-in-arrear A/c				15,000
	(Being 1,500 shares forfeited)				
	Bank A/c	Dr		10,000	
	Shares Forfeiture A/c	Dr		2,500	
	To Share Capital A/c				12,500
	(Being 1,500 shares reissued)				
	Share Forfeiture A/c	Dr		5,000	
	To Capital Reserve A/c				5,000
	(Bing net gain on reissued shares trnansferred to capital reserve)				

Or (i) Share applied $= 80{,}000 \times \frac{3}{2} = 1{,}20{,}000$ shares

(ii) ₹ 4

Working Note

$$\text{Amount Payable per Share with Application} = \frac{\text{Total Amount paid on Application}}{\text{Number of Shares Applied}} = \frac{4{,}80{,}000}{1{,}20{,}000} = ₹\,4$$

(iii) ₹ 1 (10 − 4 − 5)

(iv) ₹ 2,34,000

Working Note		**Amt (₹)**
Amount to be received on Allotment	=	4,00,000
(−) Amount to received on Application adjusted in Allotment (40,000 × 4)	=	(1,60,000)
(−) Amount not received from Rehan a shareholder of $3{,}000 \times \frac{2}{3} = 2{,}000$ shares [(2,000 × 5) − (1,000 × 4)]	=	6,000
	=	2,34,000

(v) (a) **JOURNAL**

Date	Particulars		LF	Amt (Dr)	Amt (Cr)
	Share Capital A/c	Dr		20,000	
	To Share Forfeiture A/c				12,000
	To Calls-in-arrears A/c				8,000
	(Being 2,000 shares forfeited)				

(b) **JOURNAL**

Date	Particulars		LF	Amt (Dr)	Amt (Cr)
	Bank A/c	Dr		19,500	
	To Share Capital A/c				15,000
	To Securities Premium				4,500
	(Being 1,500 shares reissued)				
	Share Forfeiture A/c	Dr		9,000	
	To Capital Reserve A/c				9,000
	(Being net gain on reissued shares transferred to capital reserve)				

11. (i) • (*c*) $\dfrac{\text{Net Profit before Interest and Taxes}}{\text{Fixed Interest Charges}}$ • Interest coverage ratio

(ii) (*d*) Q, R and S

(iii) The ratio will reduced/decline

(iv) (a) $\dfrac{\text{Absolute Change in Net Profit}}{\text{Base Year (Previous Year) Profit}} \times 100$ (b) Decrease of 21.77 %

(v) Outflow of cash to the extent of investment made.

Inflow of cash- Interest income from the investments.

12.

Common Size Balance Sheet of Super Ltd.

as at 31st March, 2024

Particulars	Note. No.	31st March, 2024 (₹)	% to Balance Sheet Total
I. **EQUITY AND LIABILITIES**			
1. Shareholders' Fund		7,00,000	70
2. Non-current Liabilities		2,00,000	20
3. Current Liabilities		1,00,000	10
Total		10,00,000	100
II. **ASSETS**			
1. Non-current Assets		7,00,000	70
2. Current Assets		3,00,000	30
Total		10,00,000	100

13. (i) (a)

Particulars	Amt (₹)
Net Profit for the Year	(80,000)
Provision for Tax	84,000
Net Profit before Tax	4,000
(+) Depreciation on Plant and Machinery (W.N.1)	70,000
(+) Loss on Sale of Machine (W.N.2)	15,000
(–) Interest on Short-term Loans and Advances	(2,000)
Net Operating Profit before Working Capital changes	87,000

Working Notes

1. Dr **Provision for Depreciation Account** Cr

Particulars	Amt (₹)	Particulars	Amt (₹)
To Plant and Machinery A/c	30,000	By Balance b/d	1,10,000
To Balance c/d	1,50,000	By Depreciation A/c	70,000
	1,80,000		1,80,000

2. Dr **Plant and Machinery Account** Cr

Particulars	Amt (₹)	Particulars	Amt (₹)
To Balance b/d	6,00,000	By Provision for Depreciation A/c	30,000
To Bank A/c	2,20,000	By Bank A/c	25,000
		By Loss on Sale A/c	15,000
		By Balance c/d	7,50,000
	8,20,000		8,20,000

(b)

Particulars	Amt (₹)
Purchase of Plant and Machinery	(2,20,000)
Sale of Plant and Machinery	25,000
Short-term Loans and Advances	(38,000)
Interest on Short-term Loans and Advances	2,000
Cash used in Investing Activities	(2,31,000)

(ii) **Less** Although the operating profit increased by ₹ 1,000,000 because of the credit sales, the increase in cash was only ₹ 95,000 (1,00,000 + 15,000– 20,000).

Or

Cash Flow Statement of Rohald Ltd.
for the year ending 31st March, 2024

Particulars		Amt (₹)
I. **Cash Flow from Operating Activities**		
Net Profit before Tax (WN 3)	1,47,000	
(+) Non operating/Non-cash Expenses		
Depreciation on Plant and Machinery	90,000	
Interest on Borrowings	25,000	
(–) Interest on Investment Received	(3,500)	
Net Operating Profit before Working Capital Changes /Cash from Operating Activities before Tax Paid	2,58,500	
(–) Tax Paid	(20,000)	
Cash Flow from Operating Activities		2,38,500
II. **Cash Flow from Investing Activities**		
Purchase of Investments	(90,000)	
Interest on Investments Received	3,500	
Cash used in Investing Activities		(86,500)
III. **Cash Flow from Financing Activities**		
Repayment of Long-term Borrowings	(50,000)	
Interest on Borrwings Paid	(25,000)	
Bank Overdraft taken	1,53,000	
Cash Flow from Financing Activities		78,000
Net Increase in Cash as per I, II and III		2,30,000
(+) Opening Cash and Cash Equivalents		
Bank		50,000
Closing Cash and Cash Equivalents		
Bank		
		2,80,000

Working Notes

1. Dr **Provision for Tax Account** Cr

Particulars	Amt (₹)	Particulars	Amt (₹)
To Bank A/c	20,000	By Balance b/d	28,000
To Balance c/d	15,000	By Statement of Profit and Loss	7,000
	35,000		35,000

2.

Particulars	Amt (₹)
Statement of Profit and Loss	1,40,000
Provision for Tax	7,000
Net Profit before Tax	1,47,000

14. (i) Interest Coverage Ratio $= \dfrac{\text{Net Profit before Interest and Taxes}}{\text{Fixed Interest Charges}} = \dfrac{2,05,000}{45,000} = 4.56$ times

(ii) Operating Ratio $= \dfrac{\text{Cost of Revenue from Operations} + \text{Operating Expenses}}{\text{Revenue from Operations}} \times 100$

Or $= \dfrac{\text{Cost of Revenue from Operations} + \text{Operating Expenses} - \text{Operating Income}}{\text{Revenue from Operations}} \times 100 = \dfrac{8,10,000}{9,00,000} \times 100 = 90\%$

(iii) Current Ratio $= \dfrac{\text{Current Assets}}{\text{Current Liabilities}} = \dfrac{2,60,000}{1,10,000} = 2.36:1$

(iv) Quick Ratio $= \dfrac{\text{All Current Assets} - \text{Inventories (Excluding Loose Tools and Spare Parts)} - \text{Prepaid Expenses}}{\text{Current Liabilities}}$

$$\frac{1.5}{1} = \frac{6,80,000 - \text{Inventory}}{3,4,000}$$

$\therefore$ Inventory = ₹ 1,70,000

Now, Inventory Turnover Ratio $= \dfrac{\text{Cost of Revenue from Operations}}{\text{Average Inventory}}$

$$4 = \frac{\text{Cost of Revenue Operations}}{1,70,000}$$

$\therefore$ Cost of Revenue from Operations = ₹ 6,80,000